KARL MARX
the story of his life

KARL
MARX

The Story of His Life

by Franz Mehring

Translated by Edward Fitzgerald
New Introduction by Max Shachtman

Ann Arbor Paperbacks
For the Study of Communism and Marxism

The University of Michigan Press

TO CLARA ZETKIN

INTRODUCTION

INTEREST in economics and politics, indeed, in the trend and problems of social development in general, cannot be enlightened without an understanding—regardless of the conclusions drawn from it—of the ideas of Karl Marx. Ignorance of Marxism, or even indifference to it, is as inexcusable in the fields of social science and politics as ignorance of Newton and Darwin would be (to use a loose but adequate comparison) in the fields of physics and biology. The belief that Marxism has been outlived, or that it is irrelevant to events and problems of our day, or that it has failed in this or that or in all respects, is nowhere so widely held as in the United States. It would be more appropriate to hold that this belief itself, and in all its forms, has been outlived and is irrelevant to the need to know Marx's ideas.

Marx is unique among all the social thinkers of his time. If "his time" is extravagantly broadened to include the centuries that have marked the passage from the feudal world to the modern, his distinction is only enhanced. To the name of Marx, as to that of no one else in his field, are attached enduring interest, passion, controversy, and great political movements in almost every part of the world. This alone invites thoughtful consideration. But there is more.

The governments of some one-third of the world proclaim Marxism as their official doctrine and guide. The relations between these governments and the rest of the world form the principal axis of world politics today; and the kind of relations that are established largely determine the direction in which the axis revolves. To seek such relations without understanding the doctrine nominally avowed by the forces these governments represent is at best parochialism. The legitimacy of the communist governments' claim to Marxism is debatable. The claim of Marxism to be studied is not.

In the countries of the West outside the communist world, the political life and destiny of the most important countries—the United States appears to be the outstanding exception—are decisively influenced by socialist movements which enjoy the allegiance of millions. Unlike the communist movement, the socialist movement today is not Marxist in name. Despite its substantially Marxist origins, contemporary European socialism has either disavowed Marxism or has significantly revised many of its ideas. The importance of this disavowal and revision cannot be disregarded. It does not follow that Marxism can be disregarded.

What Marxism means has been interpreted to the satisfaction of literally hundreds of writers on the subject, by supporters as well as opponents, by those who have studied it, and by those who regard a study of it as an unnecessary impediment. Whatever Marxism may mean to others, Marx himself took pains to set forth what he considered his own central thought. He made it clear in 1852 in a famous letter to a party friend, Georg Weydemeyer, a former Prussian artillery officer who was later active in the American Civil War as a Northern regimental colonel:

" . . . as for myself, no credit is due me for discovering the existence of classes in modern society nor yet the struggle between them. Long before me bourgeois historians had described the historical development of this class struggle and bourgeois economists the economic anatomy of the classes. What I did that was new was to prove: (1) that the *existence of classes* is only bound up with *particular, historic phases in the development of production;* (2) that the class struggle necessarily leads to the *dictatorship of the proletariat;* (3) that this dictatorship itself only constitutes the transition to the *abolition of all classes* and to a *classless society.*"

The old term "dictatorship of the proletariat" has long ago been discarded by all socialists, understandably and wisely. It had acquired abhorrent connotations with the rise of the Stalinist regime, which was nothing but a dictatorship *over* the proletariat and against it. Ambiguity and misconception have been reduced to a minimum by using the terms "labor" or "socialist" government. In any case, by that harsh Latinic phrase, Marx had in mind, as he put it in his classical statement of the *Communist Manifesto*, "the first step in the workers' revolution [which] is to make the proletariat the ruling class, to establish democracy."

The value of knowing Marxism is difficult to reject. The validity of Marxism is not so difficult to reject. It is indeed far more widely rejected than accepted. And where, as in the Communist world, it is honored in the word it is outraged in the deed. It is hardly necessary to go much further than to compare the reality of the so-called communist societies of today with what was explicitly set forth as the view of the early communists of Marx's time. Only a few weeks before Marx wrote his *Manifesto* in 1847, the first English journal published in London by the German communist society which sponsored the *Manifesto* declared:

"We are not among those communists who are out to destroy personal liberty, who wish to turn the world into one huge barrack or into a gigantic workhouse. There certainly are some communists who, with an easy conscience, refuse to countenance personal liberty and would like to shuffle it out of the world because they consider that it is a hindrance to complete harmony. But we have no desire to exchange freedom for equality . . .''

The present Communist regimes may draw their inspiration from "some communists" of a century ago, but not from Marx. They are no more a confirmation of Marxism than they are its realization—except perhaps in the sense in which Marx wrote that where the struggle of the classes does not end in a "revolutionary change in the whole structure of society," it ends "in the common ruin of the contending classes."

It is said that whatever may be the merit of explaining the "failure of Marxism" in backward countries like tsarist Russia or China, its failure in the capitalistically developed Western countries cannot be explained away. This is undoubtedly true. The incontestable fact that the class struggle has not—in any case, has not yet—led to the rule of the working class that was to be transitional to a classless society (the perspective that Marx himself held to be his unique contribution) is a challenge to all Marxists, most of whom have been too occupied with committing blunders in Marx's name to leave time for reflecting on this difficult and complex problem.

To meet this challenge, however, other facts also deserve consideration, and by critics of Marxism as well. Outstanding is the fact that even those continuing socialist parties of Europe that have abjured or extensively modified Marxism, and even officially renounced the class struggle, do not seem able to make a fundamental change in their own class character. Their appeals to middle-class elements, entirely proper within limits, have not eliminated the essential fact that they remain the organized working class in politics. Their program and aims may be formulated ever so moderately and modestly, but so long as they continue to strive for political power in the hands of an organized working-class force, they remain a confirmation of the basic historical and social movement that Marx foresaw.

In this respect, even the United States may prove before too long that its exceptional position is less reality than form and appearance. Marxism, as a theoretical system, has never found great popularity in this country. Class struggle, even the existence of classes, is almost universally denied. It is repeatedly repudiated not only by spokesmen of government, but by leaders of labor and capital. Class harmony, identity, or at least mutuality of interests—that is the American way of life. Yet the most conservative labor leader does not propose to abandon the strictly working-class character of the unions; the most liberal capitalist has a correspondingly rigid attitude with regard to the unions of capital and commerce. Neither side has yet vigorously proposed the merger of the two types of class organizations into one as a living testimonial to the identity of interests they espouse so ceremoniously. Moreover, the class organizations of both sides have been increasingly and antagonistically active in politics in recent years. Each seeks to increase its power and influence in government, each seeks to reduce not only the political influence but the political activity of the others. Thoughtful, or at least instinctive, capitalist judgment more or less grasps the objective implications of labor's organized, class intervention into political life, even if it is still not as advanced, open-faced, and assertive as it is in other countries. This is not the confirmation of Marxism, to be sure. Neither is it the refutation. But it, too, is a challenging development, certainly not to supporters of Marxism alone. Once again, a knowledge of what Marx thought and wrote and did is a valuable aid to understanding.

Franz Mehring once recalled that the philosopher Fichte scolded the German reader for his refusal to read a book because he first wanted to read a book about the book. We Americans deserve the same or a stronger scolding, because we first want to read an authoritative review of a book about the book. That being the case, and reform of habits being a long way off, Mehring's biography of Marx is to be recommended—as it always has been by serious scholars and students—as the best introduction to the works, to the life, and struggle of the most eminent figure in world socialism.

1962   MAX SHACHTMAN

TRANSLATOR'S PREFACE

THE author of this biography was born in 1846 in Pomerania of a well-to-do middle-class family. He studied at the universities of Berlin and Leipzig, taking the degree of Doctor of Philosophy at the latter. From the beginning his leanings were democratic and liberal, and when the time came for him to submit himself to the stupidities of the Prussian drill sergeant he left Prussia and went to live in Leipzig, which in those days was " foreign territory ". This deliberate revolt caused the breaking off of relations between him and his family. Whilst still a young man he began to take an active part in public life and in the political struggles of the day. At the age of 25 he was a member of the small band of democrats led by Guido Weiss and Johann Jacoby which had sufficient courage to protest openly against the annexation of Alsace-Lorraine by Bismarck after the Franco-Prussian War.

Mehring's chief activities were journalistic and literary, and for many years he was a contributor to prominent liberal and democratic newspapers, and later on an editor. All his life he had a keen sense of justice, and the feeling that injustice was being done was always sufficient to bring him on the scene. He defended Platen against Heine, Lassalle and Bakunin against Marx and Engels, Schweitzer against Bebel, and Bernstein against Liebknecht, and together with Rosa Luxemburg he fought a brilliant polemic against Kautsky and Riazanov. That he was not always on the side of the angels the reader of this book will discover for himself, but wherever he was to be found it was not because he had first considered the consequences to himself, but because his own sense of justice had compelled him with imperative logic.

At about the age of 30 he became a socialist of the Lassallean school, appearing in the arena with a pamphlet against the historian Treitschke. It is to this period of socialism strongly tinged with nationalism that his attacks on Social Democracy and on Marx belong. Like many another well-meaning and liberal-minded man from the ranks of the possessing classes, he approached the working-class movement equipped with democratic and liberal principles and a desire to assist the workers, and he suffered the failure and disappointment which such an approach inevitably brings with it. However, unlike many others, he did not then withdraw to nurse his wounded dignity and bemoan the proletarian lack of gratitude, but, spurred on by his initial failure, he came to grips with the problem and emerged as a Marxist.

It was in 1890 that the final breach with his own class took place. He was then the chief editor of the democratic *Berliner Volkszeitung* and in its columns he resolutely opposed Bismarck's policy and defended the social democrats, who were still being persecuted under the Anti-Socialist Law. His attacks on Bismarck were extremely effective, and the latter answered with a threat of suppression unless the shareholders dismissed the uncomfortable critic. True to those traditions of pusillanimity which caused both Marx and Engels to despair of the German bourgeoisie the shareholders swallowed their democratic principles to defend their economic interests, and Franz Mehring was sacrificed. At the age of 44 he now took the final and logical step and joined the Social Democratic Party.

The period of his greatest literary activity then opened up. The *Neue Zeit*, at that time under the editorship of Karl Kautsky, published many brilliant articles from his pen, including the famous series which appeared in book form in 1893 as *The Lessing Legend*, the classic Prussian history of the Frederician age, and caused Friedrich Engels to write to Kautsky from London declaring that the articles made him look forward with impatience to every new number of the publication. Throughout the years which followed up to the time of his death Mehring's pen produced innumerable articles on philosophic, historical, military, literary and political subjects, and won him a foremost position in the international socialist movement. The chief scene of his activities was the writing-desk, but for all that he was no arm-chair strategist, but a fighter all the time with the sharpest weapons at his disposal, and he used them with all his energy against a powerful enemy.

From the closing years of the last century onwards when the revisionist efforts of Bernstein and his friends undermined revolutionary Marxism in the social-democratic organization and provided the yearnings of its leaders for respectability with a theoretical cloak, Mehring was in the front ranks of those who fought strenuously against a policy which led logically to the collapse of the German working-class movement in 1914. Throughout the war years he remained true to the principles of socialist internationalism and despite his advanced years he spent many months in prison. Together with Clara Zetkin and Rosa Luxemburg, " the only real men in the social-democratic movement " as he was fond of calling them, he raised aloft the banner of proletarian internationalism in the heroic Spartakist League. He lived to see the first post-war class struggles and the defeat of the revolutionary workers, and he died in January 1919 shortly before his seventy-third birthday, his death undoubtedly being hastened by the terrible tidings which reached him a day or two before that his two friends Rosa Luxemburg and Karl Liebknecht had been slaughtered by white mercenaries. With his death German literature lost a brilliant author and trenchant critic, and the German working class lost a great historian and socialist theoretician and the greatest literary man the socialist movement has yet produced.

Artistic or other talent may not in itself be a suitable subject for historical research, but historical conditions render it fit matter for such investigation, and, apart from his historical writings, Mehring's greatest service to the working-class movement was his practical application of the Marxist historical materialist method to cultural and literary problems. In this respect he was a pioneer, for both Marx and Engels very rarely ventured into this field, their time being almost wholly taken up with the more direct economic, philosophical and political phases of the revolutionary movement. How long and how often will socialists continue to regret that Marx finally never did carry out his intention of writing a monograph on Balzac and his *Comédie Humaine*? The significance of Franz Mehring on this field is nowhere better described than in a letter of congratulation written to him on his seventieth birthday by Rosa Luxemburg:

" . . . For decades now you have occupied a special post in our movement, and no one else could have filled it. You are the representative of real culture in all its brilliance. If the German proletariat is the historic heir of classic German philosophy, as Marx and Engels declared, then you are the executor of that testament. You have saved everything of value which still remained of the once splendid culture of the bourgeoisie and brought it to us, into the camp of the socially disinherited. Thanks to your books and articles the German proletariat has been brought into close touch not only with classic German philosophy, but also with classic German literature, not only with Kant and Hegel, but with Lessing, Schiller and Goethe. Every line from your brilliant pen has taught our workers that socialism is not a bread-and-butter problem, but a cultural movement, a great and proud world-ideology. When the spirit of socialism once again enters the ranks of the German proletariat the latter's first act will be to reach for your books, to enjoy the fruits of your life's work. . . . To-day when intellectuals of bourgeois origin are betraying us in droves to return to the flesh-pots of the ruling classes we·can laugh contemptuously and let them go : we have won the best and last the bourgeoisie still possessed of spirit, talent and character—Franz Mehring."

The biography of Karl Marx which is now presented to the English-speaking reader was the culmination of Mehring's work.

It was first published in Germany in 1918, after long and irritating delays owing to the military censorship, which wished to prevent its publication altogether or permit it only in a mutilated form. Despite the troublous times its success was immediate, and half a dozen editions and many thousands of copies were sold. In 1933, on the fiftieth anniversary of the death of Marx, a new edition was published, and it is a translation of this edition which is now before the reader. Franz Mehring dedicated the first edition to : " Clara Zetkin—heiress to the Marxist Spirit " and this first English edition therefore respects his wishes, although since then she too has joined her old friends Franz Mehring and Rosa Luxemburg in the ranks of those who will be " enshrined for ever in the great heart of the working class ".

After Mehring's death a new era in Marxist research was opened up with its centre in the Marx-Engels Institute in Moscow, and many facts unknown to him were brought to light. The fiftieth anniversary edition was therefore brought up to date by means of an appendix prepared under the direction of Eduard Fuchs, an old friend of Mehring and his literary executor. This appendix, which the reader will find at the end of this volume, deals with all points of importance brought to light concerning Marx and Marxism, and in particular concerning the Lassalle-Bakunin polemics, since Mehring's death.

The footnotes to the present edition were added by me in order to assist the English-speaking reader to a better understanding of references which might otherwise have been obscure, but I have kept them as few as possible. The bibliography at the end of this volume makes no claim to completeness, but it is hoped that it will prove of service to those who would like to study Marxism more thoroughly. Some of Marx's works are still untranslated, but these are becoming fewer and fewer, and before long nothing of any importance will be beyond the reach of the English-speaking reader.

The honour of introducing Mehring to the English-speaking public has fallen to me, and I hope that I may be found to have done it not unworthily. However, I feel that a word of apology is necessary for my rendering of the various items of poetry quoted, but here I can claim to be in company with Marx and Engels, for the Muses omitted to place the gift of verse in my cradle too. In conclusion I wish to express my thanks to Elisabeth Kühnen, Eduard Fuchs, Dr. Hans Glaubauff and Frank Budgen for friendly assistance in various ways.

EDWARD FITZGERALD.

AMSTERDAM,
July 4th, 1935.

AUTHOR'S INTRODUCTION

THIS book has a little history of its own. When a proposal was made to publish the correspondence which had passed between Marx and Engels, Marx's daughter, Madame Laura Lafargue, made it a condition of her agreement that I should take part in the editorial work as her representative. In a letter from Draveil dated the 10th of November 1910 she authorized me to make what notes, explanations or deletions I might consider necessary.

As a matter of fact I made no practical use of this authorization because no important differences of opinion arose between the editors, or rather the editor, Bernstein—Bebel did no more than give his name to the work—and myself, and I had no occasion, no right and naturally no inclination to interfere with his work in the interests of Madame Lafargue without cogent and urgent reasons.

However, during the long work I did in connection with the publication of the correspondence the knowledge which I had gained of Karl Marx during many years of study was rounded off, and involuntarily I felt the wish to give it a biographical frame, particularly as I knew that Madame Lafargue would be delighted at the idea. I won her friendship and her confidence not because she thought me the most learned or the most sagacious amongst the followers of her father, but because she felt that I had obtained the deepest insight into his character and would be able to portray it most clearly. Both in conversation and in her letters she often assured me that many half-forgotten memories of her home life had become fresh and vivid again from the descriptions in my history of the German Social Democracy and in particular in the posthumous edition which I issued,[1] and that many names often heard from her parents developed from a shadowy existence into a tangible reality thanks to my writings.

Unfortunately this noble woman died long before the correspondence between her father and Engels could be published. A few hours before she voluntarily took leave of life she sent me a last, warm message of friendship. She inherited the great qualities of her father, and I thank her beyond the grave for having entrusted me with the publication of many treasures from his literary remains without having made even the slightest attempt to influence my critical judgment in any way. For instance, she gave me the letters of Lassalle to her father, although she knew from my history of the German Social Democracy how energetically and how often I had defended Lassalle against him.

When I finally began to carry out my intention of writing a

---

[1] The famous *Nachlassausgabe*. See Bibliography.—TR.

biography of Marx, two of the stalwart defenders of Zion in the Marxist ranks failed to show even a trace of the generosity of this great-hearted woman. They sounded the horn of moral indignation with all their might because I had made one or two observations in *Die Neue Zeit* [1] concerning the relations of Marx to Lassalle and to Bakunin without first having made the traditional kow-tow to the official party legend.

First of all, Karl Kautsky accused me of " anti-Marxism " in general, and of " a breach of confidence " towards Madame Lafargue in particular, and when I nevertheless insisted on carrying out my intention of writing a biography of Marx he even sacrificed sixty odd pages of *Die Neue Zeit*, whose space was notoriously precious, to an attack on me by D. Riazanov, in which the latter did his best to prove me guilty of the basest betrayal of Marx, and accompanied his efforts with a flood of accusations whose lack of conscience was equalled only by their lack of sense. I have permitted these people to have the last word out of a feeling which for politeness' sake I will not call by its real name, but I owe it to myself to point out to my readers that I have not given way one hair's-breadth to their intellectual terrorism and that in the following pages I have dealt with the relations of Marx to Lassalle and to Bakunin strictly in accordance with the exigencies of historical truth whilst completely ignoring the official party legend. Naturally, in doing so I have again avoided any sort of polemic.

My admiration and my criticism—and both these things must have an equal place in any good biography—have been centred on a great man who never said anything about himself more often or with greater pleasure than " nothing human is foreign to me ". The task which I set myself when I undertook this work was to present him in all his powerful and rugged greatness.

My end determined the means which I took to attain it. All historical writing is at the same time both art and science, and this applies in particular to biographical writing. I cannot remember at the moment what droll fellow first gave vent to the extraordinary idea that aesthetic considerations have no place in the halls of historical science, and I must frankly confess, perhaps to my own shame, that I do not loathe bourgeois society quite so thoroughly as I loathe those stern thinkers who, in order to have a smack at the worthy Voltaire, declare that a boring and tiresome style is the only permissible one. In this connection Marx himself is more than suspect with me. With the old Greeks he

[1] *Die Neue Zeit* (*The New Age*), Stuttgart, 1883 to 1923. Under Kautsky's editorship until 1917. Official theoretical organ of the German Social Democratic Party.—Tr.

loved so well he counted Clio one of the nine Muses. The truth is that only those scorn the Muses who have been scorned by them.

If I may assume the agreement of the reader with the form I have chosen for my work I must nevertheless ask him for some forbearance with its content. From the beginning I was faced with one inexorable necessity, that of preventing the book growing too large and at the same time keeping it within the reach and comprehension of at least the more advanced workers. In any case, it has already grown to half as long again as the length I originally planned. How often have I been compelled to content myself with a word when I would rather have written a line, with a line when I would rather have written a page, with a page when I would rather have written a chapter ! My analysis of the scientific writings of Marx has suffered in particular from this outward compulsion, and in order to forestall any doubt about the matter I have refrained from giving my book the second part of the traditional sub-title of any biography of a great writer : " The Story of His Life and Works."

There is no doubt that the incomparable stature of Marx is due not a little to the fact that in him the man of ideas was indissolubly bound up with the man of action, and that the two mutually complemented and supported each other. But there is also no doubt that the fighter in him always took precedence over the thinker. The great pioneers of socialism were all in agreement in this respect ; as Lassalle once put it, how gladly would he leave unwritten all he knew if only the time for action would come ! And in our own days we have observed with horror how right they were. Lifelong followers of Marx, men who had brooded for three and even four decades over every comma in his writings, failed utterly at an historical moment when for once they might and should have acted like Marx and when instead they swung this way and that like quivering weather vanes in a blustering wind.

Nevertheless, I have no wish to pretend that I feel myself called before all others to mark down the boundaries of that tremendous field of knowledge which was Marx's domain. For instance, in order to give the reader a clear and adequate picture of the second and third volumes of Marx's *Capital* I appealed to my friend Rosa Luxemburg for assistance, and he will thank her as I do for readily agreeing to assist me. Chapter XII No. 3 " The Second and Third Volumes " was written by her.

I am happy to be able to embody a treasure from her pen in my book, and I am no less happy that our joint friend Clara Zetkin has given me permission to launch my little ship and send it out on to the high seas under her flag.   The friendship of these two women has been an incalculable consolation to me at a time when boisterous storms have swept away so many " manly and steadfast pioneers of socialism " like dry leaves in the autumn winds.

FRANZ MEHRING.

BERLIN-STEGLITZ,
   March 1918.

CONTENTS

LIST OF ILLUSTRATIONS

IN THE TEXT

CHRONOLOGICAL TABLE

1818 5th May   Karl Marx born in Trier (Trèves).

1835   College Finals in Trier (Trèves).

1835–6   Student of Jurisprudence at Bonn University. Engagement to Jenny von Westphalen.

1836–41   Student of Jurisprudence, History and Philosophy at Berlin University. Beginning of his Hegelian studies. Joins Young Hegelian circle : Bruno Bauer, Rutenberg, Ed. Meyen and Köppen. First literary attempts (Poems, etc.).

1838   Death of Marx's Father.

1841   Graduation at Jena University.

1842–3   Contributor to and later editor of the *Rheinische Zeitung* in Cologne. Collaboration with Arnold Ruge.

1843   Marriage to Jenny von Westphalen.

1843–5   Stay in Paris.

1844   Issues *Deutsch-Französische Jahrbücher* together with Ruge. Contributor to the Paris *Vorwärts* (H. Börnstein and Bernays). Studies French socialism and communism. Association with Heinrich Heine, Proudhon and others. First meeting with Friedrich Engels. Economic and philosophical studies.

1845   Expulsion from Paris by Guizot at the instance of the Prussian government.

1845–8   Stay in Brussels. Collaboration with Engels : *The Holy Family* and the *German Ideology* (Polemic with the Hegelians, Feuerbach, Stirner and the " True Socialists "). Contributions to the *Gesellschafts-spiegel*, the *Westphälisches Dampfboot* and the *Deutsche Brüsseler Zeitung*.

1847   Meeting and Discussion with Weitling. Polemic with Proudhon : *The Poverty of Philosophy*. Joins the Communist League. Lectures on Protection, Free Trade, Wage-Labour and Capital. Visits London for conference of the Communist League. Instructed with Engels to draft communist manifesto.

1848   Publication of *The Communist Manifesto*. Expulsion from Brussels. Reorganization of the Communist League (Engels, Schapper, Wolff, Stephan Born and others).

1848–9   In Cologne as the editor of the *Neue Rheinische Zeitung*. Meeting with Lassalle and Freiligrath. Visits Vienna : Lectures to the Vienna Workers Association.

1849   Marx acquitted by a jury in Cologne charged with

KARL MARX

the story of his life

CHAPTER ONE: EARLY YEARS

1. Home and School

KARL HEINRICH MARX was born on the 5th May 1818 in Trier (Trèves). Owing to the confusion and destruction caused amongst the official registers in the Rhineland during the troubled times which prevailed at the end of the eighteenth and the beginning of the nineteenth centuries little is known with certainty about his antecedents. For instance, even the year in which Heinrich Heine was born is still the subject of dispute.

With regard to Karl Marx, however, the situation is not quite so bad as this, for he was born in more peaceable times, but when a sister of his father died about fifty years ago leaving an invalid will, not all the legal investigations begun to ascertain the lawful heirs were able to discover the birth and death dates of her parents, that is to say, of the grandparents of Karl Marx. His grandfather was Marx Levi, but later on the Levi was dropped. This man was a Rabbi in Trier and is believed to have died in 1798. In any case, he was no longer alive in 1810, but his wife Eva Marx, *née* Moses, was, and she is believed to have died in 1825.

This pair had numerous children, and two of them, Samuel and Hirschel, devoted themselves to scholarly professions. Samuel, who was born in 1781 and died in 1829, became the successor of his father as Rabbi in Trier. Hirschel, the father of Karl Marx, was born in 1782. He studied jurisprudence and became an advocate in Trier. Later he became a *Justizrat*,[1] and in 1824 he adopted Christianity, taking the name Heinrich Marx. He died in 1838.

Heinrich Marx married a Dutch Jewess named Henrietta Pressburg, whose genealogical tree showed, according to the statement of her granddaughter Eleanor Marx, a century-long line of Rabbis. Henrietta Pressburg died in 1863. Heinrich Marx and his wife Henrietta left a large family, but at the time of the testamentary investigations which provided us with these genealogical notes only four of the children were still alive: Karl Marx, Sophie the widow of an advocate named Schmalhausen in Mastricht, Emilie the wife of an engineer named

[1] Approximately the German equivalent of taking silk.—Tr.

1

Conrady in Trier, and Luise the wife of a merchant named Juta in Cape Town.

Thanks to his parents, whose marriage was an extremely happy one, and to his sister Sophie, the eldest child, Karl Marx enjoyed a cheerful and care-free youth. His " splendid natural gifts " awakened in his father the hope that they would one day be used in the service of humanity, whilst his mother declared him to be a child of fortune in whose hands everything would go well. However, Karl Marx was neither the son of his mother like Goethe nor the son of his father like Lessing and Schiller. With all her affectionate care for her husband and her children, Marx's mother was completely absorbed in her domestic affairs. All her life she spoke broken German and took no part in the intellectual struggles of her son, beyond perhaps wondering with a mother's regret what might have become of him had he taken the right path. In later years Karl Marx appears to have been on intimate terms with his maternal relatives in Holland, and in particular with his " uncle " Philips. He repeatedly refers in terms of great friendship to this " fine old boy ", who proved helpful to him later on in the material troubles of his life.

Although Karl Marx's father died a few days after his son's twentieth birthday, he too seems to have observed with secret apprehension " the demon " in his favourite son. It was not the petty and fidgety anxiety of a parent for his son's career which troubled him, but rather the vague feeling that there was something as hard as granite in his son's character, something entirely foreign to his own yielding nature. As a Jew, a Rhinelander and a lawyer, he should have been thrice armed against the wiles of the East Elbian Junkers, but in fact Heinrich Marx was a Prussian patriot, though not in the humdrum sense the term has to-day, but a Prussian patriot of the Waldeck and Ziegler type, saturated with bourgeois culture and having an honest belief in the " Old Fritzian " [1] enlightenment, an " idéologue " of the type hated by Napoleon with good reason. Although the conqueror had given the Rhenish Jews equality of civil rights, and the Rhineland itself the Code Napoléon, a jealously guarded treasure ceaselessly attacked by the Old-Prussian reaction, Marx's father hated Napoleon.

His belief in the " genius " of the Prussian monarchy was not even shaken by the fact that the Prussian government would have compelled him to change his religion in order to save his bourgeois position. It has often been said, even by otherwise well-informed persons, that this was the case, apparently in

[1] " Old Fritz ", an affectionate nickname for Frederick the Great of Prussia.—Tr.

order to justify or at least to excuse an action which requires neither justification nor excuse. Even considered from a purely religious standpoint, a man who acknowledged " a pure belief in God " with Locke, Leibniz and Lessing no longer had any place in the synagogue and belonged rather in the fold of the Prussian State Church in which at that time a tolerant rationalism prevailed, a so-called religion of reason which had left its mark even on the Prussian Censorship Edict of 1819.

At that time the renunciation of Judaism was not merely an act of religious emancipation, but also, and even more so, an act of social emancipation. The Jewish community as such had taken no part whatever in the great intellectual labours of the German thinkers and poets. The modest light of Moses Mendelssohn had vainly attempted to guide his " nation " into the intellectual life of Germany, and just at the time when Heinrich Marx decided to adopt Christianity a circle of young Jews in Berlin revived Mendelssohn's efforts only to meet with the same failure, although such men as Eduard Gans and Heinrich Heine were in their ranks. Gans, who was the helmsman of the venture, was the first to strike his flag and go over to Christianity. Heinrich Heine hurled a robust curse after him— " *Gestern noch ein Held gewesen, ist man heute schon ein Schurke* " [1]— but it was not long before Heine himself was compelled to follow this example and take out " an entrance card into the community of European culture ". Both Gans and Heine contributed their historic share to the intellectual labours of the century in Germany, whilst the names of their companions who remained loyal to the cultural development of Judaism have long since been forgotten.

Thus for many a decade the adoption of Christianity was an act of civilized progress for the freer spirits of Judaism, and the change of religion made by Heinrich Marx for himself and his family in 1824 must be understood in this sense and no other. It is possible that external circumstances determined the moment at which the change was made, but they were certainly not the cause. The breaking up of estates and farms by Jewish usurers took place on a growing scale during the agricultural crisis in the 'twenties, and as a result it produced a violent wave of anti-Semitism in the Rhineland. In this situation it was not the duty of a man of irreproachable honesty like Marx's father to bear any share of this hatred, and having regard to his children he would have had no right to do so. Perhaps the death of his mother, which occurred at about this time, freed him from considerations of filial piety, feelings which would have been in

[1] "A hero but yesterday, a villain to-day."

harmony with his whole character, or perhaps the fact that the eldest son came of school age the year the father changed his religion may have played a part in the final decision.

But whether this was the case or not, there can be no doubt that Heinrich Marx had attained that humanistic culture which freed him entirely from all Jewish prejudices, and he handed on this freedom to his son Karl as a valuable heritage. There is nothing in the numerous letters Heinrich Marx wrote to his student son which betrays a trace of any specifically Jewish traits, either good or bad. His letters are written in an old-fashioned fatherly, sentimental and circumstantial way and in the style prevailing in eighteenth-century correspondence when a true German gushed in love and blustered in anger. Without any trace of petty-bourgeois narrow-mindedness the letters deal willingly with the intellectual interests of the son whilst showing a decisive and thoroughly justifiable objection to the latter's hankerings after fame as a " common poetaster ". But with all his delight in the thoughts of his son's future, the old man, with " his hair blanched and his spirit a little subdued ", cannot quite rid himself of the idea that perhaps his son's heart is not as great as his brain and that perhaps it will not find room enough for those mundane but milder feelings which are so very consoling in this human vale of tears.

In this sense his doubts were probably justified. The real love which he bore for his son " in the depths of his heart " did not make him blind, but rather prophetic. But as no man can ever foresee the final consequences of his actions, so Heinrich Marx did not think and could not have·thought that the rich store of bourgeois culture which he handed on to his son Karl as a valuable heritage for life would only help to deliver the " Demon " he feared, not knowing whether it was " heavenly " or " Faustian ". Whilst still in the house of his parents Karl Marx surmounted with the greatest ease things which cost Heine and Lassalle the first great struggles of their lives and left them with wounds from which neither of them ever fully recovered.

It is not so easy to see what school life contributed to the development of the growing lad. Karl Marx never spoke of any of his school companions and none of them has left any information about him. He soon completed the curriculum of his college in Trier, and his leaving certificate is dated the 25th August 1835. It accompanies the hopeful youth in the usual fashion with an expression of good wishes for his further progress and stereotyped observations concerning his attainments in the various subjects. However, it stresses in particular the fact that Karl Marx was often able to render and interpret the most difficult passages in the classics, and in particular such passages where the difficulty lay less in the peculiarities of the language than in the subject matter and the relation of ideas. His Latin themes, it declares, show richness of thought and a deep acquaintance with their subject, but are often overweighted with unsuitable matter.

In the actual finals religion presented some difficulties and history also, but in his German composition the examining masters found an " interesting " idea, an idea in fact which we shall find of much greater interest. The subject set was " The Reflections of a Youth before choosing a Profession ", and the verdict on Marx's attempt was that it recommended itself by a richness of ideas and good systematic construction, but that otherwise its author fell into his usual error of exaggerated searchings after unusual and picturesque expressions. And then the following passage is quoted literally : " We cannot always take up the profession for which we feel ourselves suited ; our relations in society have begun to crystallize more or less before we are in a position to determine them." Thus the first flash of an idea shows itself like summer lightning in the mind of the lad, an idea whose development and completion was to be the immortal service of the man.

2. Jenny von Westphalen

In the autumn of 1835 Karl Marx entered the University of Bonn and remained a student there for a year, though it is to be feared that his studies of jurisprudence were neither very wide nor deep.

No direct information is available concerning this period, but to judge from the letters of his father it would appear that a certain amount of wild oats was sown in it. At first we find his father complaining only of " Bills à la Karl, without relation and without result " (and it is true of Marx throughout his life that as far as accounts were concerned the classic theoretician of money could never quite make his own tally), but later on we find his father in a very bitter mood and complaining of " wild frolics ".

Coming on top of the merry year he had just spent in Bonn it had all the appearance of a typical student escapade when at the mature age of eighteen Karl Marx became engaged to a playmate of his childhood, a close friend of his elder sister Sophie, who helped to smooth the path to the union of the two young hearts. In reality, however, it was the first and most joyous victory of this born master of men, a victory which appeared " absolutely incomprehensible " to his father until he discovered that the girl too had " something of genius " about her and was capable of making sacrifices which would have been impossible for an ordinary girl.

Indeed, Jenny von Westphalen was a girl not only of unusual beauty, but of unusual spirit and character. She was four years older than Karl Marx, but still only in the early twenties. Her youthful beauty was in its first glorious bloom and she was greatly admired and much courted, and as the daughter of a highly-placed official she might have made a brilliant match. Jenny von Westphalen sacrificed all her brilliant prospects for " a dangerous and uncertain future ", as Marx's father put it, and occasionally he believed that he could observe in her also the anxious presentiments which disturbed him, but by that time he was so certain of the " angelic girl ", the " enchantress ", that he swore to his son that not even a prince should rob him of her.

The future turned out to be more dangerous and more uncertain than Heinrich Marx had feared even in his worst forebodings, but Jenny von Westphalen, whose youthful portrait radiates childlike grace and charm, held to the man of her choice with the steadfast courage of a heroine in defiance of terrible sufferings and affliction. It was not in the humdrum sense of the word perhaps that she lightened the heavy burden of his life, for she was one of the favoured children of fortune and not always capable of dealing with the minor misfortunes of life as a woman of the people more inured to hardship might have done, but in the high sense in which she understood his life's work she became his worthy partner.

In all her letters which are still extant there is a breath of real womanliness. Hers was a nature such as Goethe has described, ringing equally true in every mood, whether it was reflected in the delightful chatter of happy days or in the tragic anguish of a Niobe robbed of a child by poverty and privation and unable to give it even a modest grave. Her beauty was always the pride of her husband and after their fates had been linked together for twenty years we find him writing in 1863 from Trier where he had gone to attend the funeral of his mother : " Everyday I made a pilgrimage to the old Westphalen house (in the Römerstrasse) and it interests me more than all the Roman remains because it reminds me of the happy days of my youth and because it once sheltered my treasure. Everyday I am asked left and right about the quondam ' most beautiful girl in Trier ', the ' Queen of the ball '. It is damned agreeable for a man to find that his wife lives on in the memory of a whole town as ' an enchanted princess '." And the dying Marx, free as he was of all sentimentality, spoke in a sorrowful and deeply-moving tone of the most beautiful period of his life embodied in Jenny von Westphalen.

The young people became engaged without first asking the permission of the girl's parents, a circumstance which caused the conscientious father of Karl Marx no little misgiving, but it was not long before their consent was obtained. Despite his name and title, Privy Councillor Ludwig von Westphalen belonged neither to the East Elbian Junkers nor to the old Prussian bureaucracy. His father was Philip Westphalen, one of the most remarkable figures in military history. He was civil secretary to Duke Ferdinand of Brunswick who, at the head of a miscellaneous army in English pay, successfully defended Western Germany during the Seven Years War against the invasive proclivities of Louis XV and his Pompadour. Philip Westphalen became the real Chief-of-Staff of the Duke in the face of all the English and German generals with the army. His services were recognized in such measure that the King of England proposed to make him Adjutant-General of the army, an honour which Philip Westphalen refused. He was, however, compelled to tame his independent spirit to the extent of " accepting " a title, and his reasons for so doing were similar to those which caused Herder and Schiller to submit to the same indignity : in order to marry the daughter of a Scottish baronial family who had come to the camp of Duke Ferdinand to visit a sister married to the General commanding the English auxiliary troops.

One of the sons of this pair was Ludwig von Westphalen. From his father he had inherited an historic name and on his mother's side his ancestors recalled great historical memories : one of her forefathers in the direct line of descent had gone to the stake during the struggle for the Reformation in Scotland and another, Earl Archibald of Argyle, was executed in the market-place at Edinburgh as a rebel against James II. With such family traditions Ludwig von Westphalen was far above the reeking and musty narrow-mindedness of the beggar-proud Junkers and of the obscurantist bureaucracy. Originally in Brunswick service, he had not hesitated to continue this career when Napoleon amalgamated the little Dukedom with the Kingdom of Westphalia, for he was obviously less interested in the hereditary Guelphs than in the reforms with which the French conquerors remedied the decaying conditions in his own little Fatherland. However, his objection to foreign dominance was none the less strong on that account, and in 1813 he felt the stern hand of the French Marshal Davoust.

His daughter Jenny was born in Salzwedel on the 12th February 1814 where he was Landrat,[1] and two years later he was transferred to Trier as adviser to the government. In his preliminary zeal the Prussian Prime Minister Hardenberg had sufficient acumen to realize that he must send the most capable men and those least affected by the common idiosyncrasies of Junkerdom into the newly-won Rhineland, which in its heart still leaned towards France.

To the end of his life Karl Marx spoke with the greatest devotion and gratitude of Ludwig von Westphalen, and when he addressed him as his " dear fatherly friend " and assured him of his " filial love " it was more than the perfunctory flourish of a son-in-law. Westphalen could recite whole passages from the poems of Homer and he knew most of the dramas of Shakespeare by heart both in English and in German. In the " old Westphalen house " Karl Marx obtained much stimulation which his own home was unable to offer him and his school still less. From his earliest years he was one of Westphalen's favourites, and it is not unlikely that Westphalen gave his consent to the engagement in view of the happy marriage of his own parents, for in the eyes of the world the daughter of an aristocratic baronial family had also made a bad match when she married a commoner who was poor and no more than a civil servant.

The spirit of the father did not live on in the eldest son, who developed into a bureaucratic careerist and worse than that : during the period of reaction in the 'fifties he was the Prussian Minister of the Interior and he defended the feudal claims of the most obdurate and obscurantist Junkers even against the Prime Minister Manteuffel, who was at least a shrewd bureaucrat. There were never any particularly close relations between this son, Ferdinand von Westphalen, and his sister, in fact she was only his step-sister, for he was fifteen years older than Jenny and the son of his father by an earlier marriage.

Jenny's real brother was Edgar von Westphalen, who developed as far to the left of his father's path as his step-brother did to the right. Occasionally Edgar even appended his signature to the communist manifestos of his brother-in-law Karl Marx, but he never became a very reliable supporter. He went overseas and experienced changing fortunes, returned and turned up here and there, a thoroughly wild character whenever he was heard of, but he always kept a warm corner in his heart for Jenny and Karl Marx and they named their first son after him.

[1] Approximately the German equivalent of Sheriff of the County.—Tr.

CHAPTER TWO: A PUPIL
OF HEGEL

1. The First Year in Berlin

EVEN before Karl Marx had become engaged to Jenny von Westphalen his father had decided that his studies should be continued in Berlin and a document dated the 1st of July 1836 is still extant in which Heinrich Marx not only gives his permission but declares it his wish that his son Karl shall enter the University of Berlin to continue studies in jurisprudence and political economy begun at Bonn.

The engagement itself probably strengthened this decision, for in view of the remote nature of their prospects the cautious character of Marx's father caused him to feel that for the moment at least a separation of the lovers was desirable. His Prussian patriotism may have influenced him in his choice of Berlin, and also perhaps the fact that the Berlin University did not foster the " glorious college days " tradition which, in the opinion of his prudent parent, Karl Marx had supported quite enough at Bonn. " Other universities are positively Bacchanalian compared with this workhouse," declared Ludwig Feuerbach, referring to Berlin.

The young student certainly did not choose Berlin himself. Karl Marx loved the sunny Rhineland, and the Prussian capital remained obnoxious to him all his life. The philosophy of Hegel cannot have exercised any attraction because he knew nothing at all about it, although it ruled still more absolutely at the University of Berlin since the death of its founder than it had done even during his life. And then there was the accompanying separation from his sweetheart. It is true that he had promised to content himself with her agreement to marry him in the future and to renounce all present signs of affection, but such lovers' oaths are notoriously writ in water. In later years Marx told his children that his love for their mother had turned him into a raving Roland in those days, and in fact his young and ardent heart did not rest until he had obtained at least permission to write to Jenny.

However, the first letter he received from her arrived only

9

after he had been in Berlin a year. Thanks to a letter he wrote to his parents on the 10th of November 1837 to give them " some idea of the past year here ", we are perhaps better informed about this year than about any other in his life either earlier or later. This interesting document reveals the whole man even in the youngster, the man striving after truth even to the point of moral and physical exhaustion, his insatiable thirst for knowledge, his inexhaustible capacity for work, his merciless self-criticism, and that fierce fighting spirit which might over-rule the heart, but only when it seemed to be in error.

Karl Marx matriculated on the 22nd October 1836. He did not bother much about the academic lectures and in nine half-yearly terms he put his name down for only twelve, including for the most part the obligatory lectures on jurisprudence, and even of these twelve he probably heard very few. Eduard Gans was the only one of the official University lectures who exercised any influence on his mental development. Marx attended the lectures of Gans on criminal law and the Prussian civil code, and Gans himself has testified to the " excellent diligence " which Marx displayed at both these courses. How-ever, the merciless polemic which Marx wages in his earliest writings against the historical school of law is of far greater value than any such testimony (which always tends to be influenced by personal considerations), for it was the philosophically trained jurist Gans who had raised his eloquent voice so strongly against its narrowness and mustiness and its deleterious influence on legislation and the development of law.

According to his own account Marx studied jurisprudence merely as a subordinate discipline together with history and philosophy. As far as these last-mentioned subjects were con-cerned, he did not bother about the lectures at all and did no more than put down his name for the usual obligatory lectures on logic by Gabler, the official successor of Hegel but the most mediocre amongst Hegel's mediocre followers. Karl Marx was essentially a thinker and even at the university he worked independently, so that in a year he obtained a wealth of know-ledge which ten years of the usual slow spoon-fed academic lectures could hardly have given him.

On his arrival in Berlin " the new world of love " clamoured for attention. " Full of yearning and empty of hope " his feelings poured themselves into three exercise books full of poems all dedicated " To my dear and ever-beloved Jenny von West-phalen ". They were in Jenny's hands in December 1836, welcomed with " tears of joy and sadness ", as Marx's sister Sophie reported to Berlin. A year later in his long letter to his parents the poet himself passes a very disrespectful verdict on these children of his Muse : " Feeling stamped flat and formless ; nothing natural about them ; everything up in the air ; utter contradiction between what is and what should be ; rhetorical reflections instead of poetical ideas ". At the end of this list of sins the young poet is prepared to grant " perhaps a certain warmth of feeling and a striving after poetic fire " as an extenuating circumstance, but even this was true only in the same way and to the same extent as it is true of the Laura Lieder of Schiller.

In general these youthful poems breathe a spirit of trivial romanticism, and very seldom does any true note ring through. In addition the technique of their verse is more clumsy and helpless than it had a right to be after Heine and Platen had both sung. Thus the artistic talent which Marx possessed in great measure and which later expressed itself in his scientific works began to develop along peculiar by-paths. In the figurative power of his language Marx rose to the level of the greatest masters of German literature and he attached great value to the æsthetic harmony of his writing, unlike those poor spirits who regard a dry-as-dust style as the first condition of scholarly achievement ; but still, the gift of verse was not amongst the talents placed in his cradle by the Muses.

As he wrote to his parents, poetry must be for him no more than an agreeable subordinate interest. He would study jurisprudence thoroughly and felt above all a desire to wrestle with philosophy. He went through Heineccius, Thibaut and the authorities, translated the first two books of the Pandects [1] into German, and sought to found a philosophy of law. This " unfortunate opus " he declares got almost as far as 300 Bogen, [2] but this may very well have been a slip of the pen. In the end he saw " the falsity of the whole thing " and then flung himself into the arms of philosophy to draft a new metaphysical system, only to realize once again the folly of his efforts. During his studies he adopted the habit of making summaries of the books he read, for instance, Lessing's *Laocoon*, Solger's *Ervin*, Winckelmann's *History of Art*, Luden's *German History*, etc., and at the same time jotting down his own reflections. He also translated the *Germania* of Tacitus and the Elegies of Ovid, and began learning English and Italian on his own, that is to say, from grammars, but he made little progress. He read Klein's *Criminal Law* and the *Annals*, and also all the new literary productions, but this was only by the way and in his spare time.

---

[1] The *corpus juris civilis* of Justinian. Presumably the Institutions and Digests.—Tr.
[2] A " Bogen " or printer's sheet is sixteen printed pages.—Tr.

The end of the term was then again devoted to the " Dance of the Muses and Music of the Satyrs," when suddenly the domain of real poetry opened up before his eyes like a far-off fairy palace and all his own creations fell to nothing.

According to all this, therefore, the result of the first term was " many nights of wakefulness, many battles fought, and much internal and external stimulation received ", but nevertheless little gained, nature, art and the world neglected and friends lost. In addition his health suffered from over-exertion, and acting on medical advice he moved to Stralau, which at that time was still a peaceful little fishing village. In Stralau he recuperated rapidly and took up his spiritual wrestling once again.

In the second term he also mastered a mass of the most varied knowledge, but gradually it became more and more evident that the one firm pole in the ceaseless flow of things was the philosophy of Hegel. Marx's first acquaintance with it was rather fragmentary and its " grotesque and rough-hewn melody " did not please him at all, but during a second bout of illness he studied it from beginning to end and soon after fell in with a club of young Hegelians where, in the conflict of opinions, he became more and more attached to " the present world philosophy ", but certainly not without silencing everything sonorous in him and causing " a downright rage of irony at so much negation ".

Karl Marx explains all this to his parents and concludes by asking permission to come home at once instead of at Easter in the following year as his father had already promised. He declared that he wanted to discuss with his father " the many vicissitudes " to which his character had been subjected in process of formation, and that only in the " dear presence " of his parents would he be able to lay " the restless ghosts ". This letter is of great value to us to-day because it is a mirror in which we can see the young Marx clearly, but it was not favourably received by his parents. His father, already ailing, again caught sight of the " Demon " which he had always feared and which he now doubly feared since his son had fallen in love with " a certain person " whom the old man loved as his own child and since an honourable family had been persuaded to approve of a relationship which apparently and according to the usual way of the world would be full of danger and gloomy prospects for its beloved child. Marx's father was not egoist enough to dictate a course of life to his son if other courses would also permit the fulfilment of " sacred obligations ", but what the old man now saw ahead was a storm-troubled sea with no prospect of any safe anchorage.

Therefore, despite his "weakness", which he realized better than anyone else, he decided "to be hard for once", and in his reply he was hard after his own fashion, and reckless exaggeration alternated with woeful sighs. He asks his son how the latter has fulfilled his tasks and answers the question for him : "God help us ! ! ! Lack of order, a brooding prowling around in all the fields of science, a stuffy brooding under a dismal oil lamp. Going to seed in a scholastic dressing-gown with unkempt hair as a change from going to seed with beer glass in hand. Repellent unsociability and the consignment of everything decent, even including consideration for your own father, to a secondary position. The limitation of the social art to a dirty room where in woeful disorder the love letters of a Jenny and the well-meaning exhortations of a father, written with tears perhaps, are used as pipe-lighters, which, by the way, is better than that they should fall into the hands of third persons as a result of still more irresponsible disorder."

And then he is overcome by melancholy, and in order to remain merciless he fortifies himself with the pills the doctor has prescribed for him. Karl's poor management is taken to task severely : "My worthy son spends 700 thaler in a year as though we were made of money. In defiance of all advice and against all usages and although the richest need no more than 500 thaler." Naturally, he admits, Karl is neither a spendthrift nor a waster, and how can a man who invents new systems every week and scraps them the next be expected to bother his head about such trivial matters ? Everyone had his hand in Karl's pocket and everyone swindled him right and left.

The letter proceeds in this style for some time and finally the father sternly refuses his son permission to return home : "To come home now would be foolish. I am very well aware that you do not bother much about the lectures—probably paid for—but at least I insist on decorum being observed. I am no slave to the opinions of other people, but I don't like chatter at my expense." Karl could come home at Easter, as arranged, or even ten days earlier if he cared, for his father was not pedantic.

Throughout all these complaints we can detect the reproach that the son has no heart, and as this reproach has been levelled against Karl Marx repeatedly it is as well to say here, when it is raised for the first time and probably with greater justification, what there is to say about it. Naturally, we have no use for the popular phrase " the right to enjoy life to the full " which was invented by a pampered civilization to cloak its cowardly egoism, and not much use for the older phrase " the right of genius " to

permit itself more than the ordinary human being. The ceaseless striving for the greatest truth which always characterized
Marx sprang from the depths of his heart. As he once said
bluntly, his hide was not thick enough to let him turn his back
on " the sufferings of humanity ", or, as Hutten has expressed
the same idea, God had burdened him with a heart which caused
the common sorrows of humanity to touch him more acutely
than the others. No man has ever done so much as Karl Marx
to destroy the root causes of " the sufferings of humanity ".
His ship ploughed its way across the high seas of life through
storm and stress and under constant fire from his enemies. His
flag was always at the mast-head, but the life on board was not
a comfortable one either for the captain or the crew.

Marx was certainly not devoid of feelings towards those
nearest to him. His fighting spirit could overrule the feelings
of his heart where necessary, but it never completely stifled
them, and the man in his maturity often complained bitterly
that those who were nearest to him suffered more under the
inexorable lot of his life than he did himself. The young student
too quickly showed that he was not impervious to the distress
of his father. He abandoned his wish to go home immediately
and even his Easter visit, much to the disappointment of his
mother but to the great satisfaction of his father, whose anger
quickly began to subside. He held fast to his complaints, but
he abandoned his exaggerations : in the art of abstract reasoning
he was certainly no match for his son, he wrote. And he was
already too old to study the necessary terminology before plunging
into the holy of holies, but on one point nothing transcendental
offered much assistance and just on this point his son wisely
maintained a dignified silence, namely on the paltry question
of money, whose value to the father of a family the son still
apparently failed to recognize. However, he declared, weariness
compelled him to lay down his arms.

Unfortunately this last sentence had a more serious meaning
than was suggested by the sly humour which again began to
show in the letter. It was dated the 10th February 1838 and
Heinrich Marx had just risen from a sick bed to which he had
been confined for five weeks. The improvement in his health
which had permitted him to rise was not maintained and the
trouble, apparently a liver disease, returned and grew worse,
until just three months later on the 10th of May 1838 he died.
Death came just in time to spare him the disappointments which
would have broken his heart little by little.

Karl Marx always realized with gratitude what his father
had been to him, and as his father had borne him in the depths

of his heart, so the son bore a picture of his father next to his heart until the day when he took it into the grave with him.

2. The Young Hegelians

From the spring of 1838 when he lost his father Karl Marx spent three years in Berlin, and the intellectual life in the circle of Young Hegelians opened up the secrets of the Hegelian philosophy to him.

At that time Hegelian philosophy was regarded as the Prussian State philosophy and the Minister of Culture Altenstein and his Privy Councillor Johannes Schulze had taken it under their special care. Hegel glorified the State as the reality of the moral idea, as the absolute reason and the absolute aim in itself, and therefore as the highest right as against the individual, whose paramount duty it was to be a member of the State. This teaching concerning the State was naturally very welcome to the Prussian bureaucracy, for it transfigured even the sins of the Demagogue Hunt.[1]

Hegel's philosophy was not hypocritical and his political development explains why he regarded the monarchical form embracing the best efforts of all the servants of the State as the most ideal State form. At the utmost he considered it necessary that the dominant classes should enjoy a certain indirect share in the government, but even that share must be limited in a corporative fashion. He was no more prepared to consider a general representation of the people in the modern constitutional sense than was the Prussian King or his oracle Metternich.

However, the system which Hegel had worked out for himself was in irreconcilable antagonism to the dialectical method which he adopted as a philosopher. With the conception of being, the conception of non-being is given, and from the antagonism of the two the higher conception of becoming results. Everything is and is not at one and the same time, for everything is in a state of flux, in a state of permanent change, in permanent development and decline. According to this, therefore, history is a process of development rising from the lower to the higher in uninterrupted transformation, and Hegel with

---

[1] " Demagogue " was the name given to the Radicals and Liberals of the Metternich era on the Continent, and as all forms of democratic agitation were prohibited by the Carlsbad Decisions in 1819 the Demagogues were outlaws. The " Demagogue Hunt " was the name given to the fierce campaign of persecution conducted against them.—Tr.

his universal knowledge set out to prove this in the most varied branches of historical science, though only in that form which accorded with his own idealist conception of the absolute idea expressing itself in all historical happenings. This absolute idea Hegel declared to be the vitalizing spirit of the whole world, without, however, giving any further information about it.

The alliance between the philosophy of Hegel and the State of the Frederick-Williams could therefore be no more than a marriage of convenience lasting as long as each partner was prepared to minister to the convenience of the other. This worked excellently in the days of the Carlsbad Decisions and the demagogue hunt, but the July revolution of 1830 gave European development such a strong impetus that Hegel's method was seen to be incomparably more reliable than his system. When the effects of the July Revolution, weak enough in any case as far as Germany was concerned, had been stifled and the peace of the graveyard had again descended on the land of thinkers and poets, Prussian Junkerdom hastened to dig out the old dilapidated lumber of mediæval romanticism for use against modern philosophy. This was made easier for it by the fact that Hegel's admiration was directed less to the cause of Junkerdom than to the cause of the tolerably enlightened bureaucracy, and by the fact that with all his glorification of the bureaucratic State Hegel had done nothing to maintain religion amongst the people, an endeavour which is the alpha and omega of all feudal traditions and, in the last resort, of all exploiting classes.

The first collision took place therefore on the religious field. Hegel declared that the biblical stories should be regarded in the same way as one would regard profane stories, for belief had nothing to do with the knowledge of common and real matters, and then along came David Strauss, a young Swabian, and took the master at his word in deadly earnest. He demanded that biblical history should be subjected to normal historical criticism, and he carried out this demand in his *Life of Jesus*, which appeared in 1835 and created a tremendous sensation. In this book Strauss picked up the threads of the bourgeois enlightenment movement of the eighteenth century, whereas Hegel had spoken of its " pseudo-enlightenment " all too contemptuously. Strauss's capacity for dialectical thought permitted him to go far more thoroughly into the question than old Reimarus had done before him. Strauss did not regard the Christian religion as a fraud or the Apostles as a pack of rogues, but explained the mythical components of the Gospel story from the unconscious creations of the early Christian communities. Much of the

New Testament he regarded as a historical report concerning the life of Jesus, and Jesus himself as a historical personage, whilst he assumed an historical basis for all the more important incidents mentioned in the Bible.

Politically considered Strauss was completely harmless and he remained so all his days, but the political note was sounded rather more sharply and clearly in the *Hallische Jahrbücher*,[1] which was founded in 1838 by Arnold Ruge and Theodor Echtermeyer as the organ of the Young Hegelians. This publication also dealt with literature and philosophy, and at first it was intended to be no more than a counterblast to the *Berliner Jahrbücher*, the stick-in-the-mud organ of the Old Hegelians. Ruge, who had played a part in the *Burschenschaft* movement[2] and suffered six years' imprisonment in Köpenick and Kolberg as a victim of the insane Demagogue Hunt, quickly took the lead in the partnership with Echtermeyer, who died young. Ruge had not taken his earlier fate tragically, and later on a fortunate marriage gave him a lectureship at the University of Halle. He led a comfortable life and, despite his earlier misfortunes, this permitted him to declare the Prussian State system free and just. Indeed, he would have liked to justify in his person the malicious saying of the old Prussian mandarins that no one made a career for himself more quickly than a converted Demagogue, but this was just the trouble.

Ruge was not an independent thinker and still less a revolutionary spirit, but he had sufficient education, industry and fighting spirit to make a good editor of a scientific magazine, and on one occasion he called himself, not without a certain amount of truth, a wholesale merchant of intellectual wares. Under his leadership the *Hallische Jahrbücher* developed into a rendezvous of all the unruly spirits, men who possess the advantage—unfortunate from the governmental point of view—of bringing more life into the press than anyone else. For instance, David Strauss as a contributor did more to hold the attention of readers than all the orthodox theologians, fighting tooth and nail for the infallibility of the Bible, put together could have done. Ruge, it is true, made a point of assuring the authorities

---

[1] *Hallische Jahrbücher : Halle Annuals.* The custom, widely prevalent in Germany at the time, of issuing so-called " Annuals," which were in fact collections of articles, was due to a desire to circumvent the censorship which, although it applied strictly to shorter publications, excepted those of more than 20 " Bogen " or 320 pages.—Tr.

[2] The " Burschenschaft " movement was founded in Jena in 1815 as a bourgeois-democratic students' organization opposed to the traditional aristocratic students' " Corps." It was imbued with a libertarian and militant spirit, and in consequence it was suppressed by the decisions of the Carlsbad Congress in 1819. The " Burschenschaften " still exist, but their original significance has naturally long ago been lost.—Tr.

that his publication propagated " Hegelian Christianity and Hegelian Prussia ", but the Minister of Culture Altenstein, who was already being hard pressed by the romanticist reaction, did not trust this assurance and refused to be moved by Ruge's urgent pleadings for a State appointment as a recognition of his services. The result was that the *Hallische Jahrbücher* began to realize that something ought to be done to break the fetters which imprisoned Prussian freedom and justice.

The Berlin Young Hegelians, in whose midst Karl Marx spent three years of his life, were almost all contributors to Ruge's *Hallische Jahrbücher*. The club membership was composed chiefly of university lecturers, teachers and writers. Rutenberg, who is described in one of Marx's earlier letters to his father as " the most intimate " of his Berlin friends, had been a teacher of geography to the Berlin Corps of Cadets, but had been dismissed, allegedly for having been found one morning drunk in the gutter, but in reality because he had come under suspicion of writing " malicious articles " in Hamburg and Leipzig newspapers. Eduard Meyen was connected with a short-lived journal which published two of Marx's poems, fortunately the only two that ever saw the light of day. Max Stirner was teaching at a girls' school in Berlin, but it has not been possible to discover whether he was a member of the club at the same time as Marx and there is no evidence that the two ever knew each other personally. In any case, the matter is not of much interest because no intellectual connection existed between them. On the other hand, the two most prominent members of the club, Bruno Bauer, a lecturer at the University of Berlin, and Karl Friedrich Köppen, a teacher at the Dorotheen Municipal Secondary School for Modern Subjects, had a great influence on Marx.

Karl Marx was hardly twenty years old when he joined the club of Young Hegelians, but, as so often happened in later years when he entered a new circle, he soon became its centre. Both Bauer and Köppen, who were about ten years older than Marx, quickly recognized his superior intellect and asked for no better comrade than this youngster who was still in a position to learn much from them and did so. The impetuous polemic which Köppen published in 1840 on the centenary of the birth[1] of Frederick the Great of Prussia was dedicated " To my Friend Karl Marx of Trier ".

Köppen possessed historical talent in very great measure and his contributions to the *Hallische Jahrbücher* still vouch for this fact. It is to Köppen that we owe the first really historical

---

[1] Should read "accession to the throne."

treatment of the reign of terror during the Great French Revolution. He subjected the representatives of contemporary historical writing, Leo, Ranke, Raumer and Schlosser, to the liveliest and most trenchant criticism and himself made sallies into various fields of historical research: from a literary introduction to Nordic mythology, which is worthy of a place beside the works of Jakob Grimm and Ludwig Uhland, to a long work on Buddha, which earned even the recognition of Schopenhauer who was otherwise not well disposed towards the old Hegelian. The fact that a man like Köppen yearned for " the spiritual resurrection " of the worst despot in Prussian history in order " to exterminate with fire and sword all those who deny us entrance into the land of promise " is sufficient to give us some idea of the peculiar environment in which these Berlin Young Hegelians lived.

However, two factors must certainly not be overlooked : first of all the romanticist reaction and everything connected with it did its utmost to blacken the memory of " Old Fritz ". Köppen himself described these efforts as " a horrible caterwauling : Old and New Testament trumpets, moral Jew's harps, edifying and historical bagpipes, and other horrible instruments, and in the middle of it all hymns of freedom boomed out in a beery Teutonic bass ". And secondly, there had as yet been no critical and scientific examination which did more or less justice to the life and actions of the Prussian King, and there could not have been any such examination because the decisive sources necessary for such a work had not yet been opened up. Frederick the Great enjoyed a reputation for " enlightenment " and that was sufficient to make him hated by the one and admired by the other.

Köppen's book also aimed at picking up the threads of the eighteenth-century bourgeois enlightenment movement, and, in fact, Ruge once declared of Bauer, Köppen and Marx that their chief joint characteristic was that they all proceeded from this movement ; they represented a philosophic Mountain Party and wrote a Mene-Mene-Tekel-Upharsin on the storm-swept horizon of Germany. Köppen refuted the " superficial declamations " against the philosophy of the eighteenth century. Despite their tendency to bore, much was owing to the German pioneers of the bourgeois enlightenment movement. Their one deficiency had been that they were not enlightened enough. Here Köppen was tilting chiefly at the thoughtless imitators of Hegel, " the lonely penitents of the idea ", " the old Brahmins of logic " sitting with crossed legs, eternally and monotonously gabbling the Holy Three Vedas again and again, pausing only now and then to throw a lustful glance into the world of the dancing Bayadere.

The shaft went home, for Varnhagen promptly condemned the book in the organ of the Old Hegelians as "disgusting" and "repulsive", probably feeling himself particularly wounded by the plain speaking of Köppen about "the toads of the marsh", those reptiles without religion, without a Fatherland, without convictions, without conscience, without heart ; feeling neither cold nor heat, nor joy nor sorrow, nor love nor hatred ; without God and without the devil, miserable creatures who squatted around the gates of hell and were too vile to be granted admittance.

Köppen honoured "the great King" only as "a great philosopher", but he went further in his advocacy than was permissible even according to the standards of Frederician knowledge then prevailing. "Unlike Kant," he declared, "Frederick the Great did not subscribe to two forms of reason : a theoretical one bringing forward its doubts, objections and negations fairly honestly and audaciously, and a practical one, under guardianship and in the public pay, to make good what the other did ill and to whitewash its student pranks. Only the most elementary immaturity can contend that as compared with the royal and practical reasoning his philosophical theoretical reasoning appears particularly transcendental, and that often Old Fritz dismissed the hermit of Sans Souci from his mind. On the contrary, the King never lagged behind the philosopher in the man."

Anyone who dared to repeat Köppen's contentions to-day would certainly lay himself open to the reproach of most elementary immaturity even from the Prussian historical school ; and even for the year 1840 it was going rather too far to place the lifelong enlightenment work of a philosopher like Kant in the same category as the pseudo-enlightenment jokes played by the Borussian despot on the French brilliants who were content to act as his court jesters.

Köppen suffered under the peculiar poverty and emptiness of Berlin life which was fatal to all the Young Hegelians living there, and although he should have been able to guard himself against it more easily than the others, it affected him still more than it did them and it expressed itself even in a polemic which had certainly been written with all his heart. Berlin lacked the powerful backbone which industry in the Rhineland, already highly-developed, gave to bourgeois consciousness there. The result was that when the questions of the day took on a practical form the Prussian capital dropped behind Cologne, and even behind Leipzig and Königsberg. Writing of the Berliners of the day the East Prussian Walesrode declared : "They think themselves tremendously free and daring when they make fun of Cerf and Hagen, of the King and the events of the day, sitting safely in their cafés and joking in their familiar corner-boy style." Berlin was in fact nothing more than a military garrison and residence town, and the petty-bourgeois populace compensated itself with malicious and paltry back-biting for the cowardly subservience it showed to every court equipage. A regular rendezvous for this sort of opposition was the salon for scandal maintained by Varnhagen, the same man who crossed himself in pious horror at the idea of even Frederician enlightenment as Köppen understood it.

There is no reason to doubt that the young Marx shared the opinions expressed in the book which brought his name before the general public for the first time. He was closely acquainted with Köppen and adopted the latter's style to a considerable extent. Although their paths soon branched off in different directions, the two always remained good friends, and when Marx returned to Berlin twenty years later on a visit he found Köppen "just the same as ever" and they celebrated a joyful reunion and spent many happy hours in each other's company. Not very long afterwards, in 1863, Köppen died.

3. The Philosophy of Self-Consciousness

The real leader of the Young Hegelians in Berlin was not Köppen, however, but Bruno Bauer, who was officially recognized as an orthodox pupil of the master, particularly as he had shown great speculative arrogance in an attack on Strauss' *Life of Jesus*, a proceeding which earned him an energetic drubbing from Strauss. Bauer enjoyed the protection of the Minister of Culture, Altenstein, who regarded him as a very promising and talented young man.

However, Bruno Bauer was not a careerist and Strauss turned out to be a poor prophet when he declared that Bauer would end his days in the " petrified scholasticism " of the orthodox chieftain Hengstenberg. On the contrary, in the summer of 1839 Bauer came to grips with Hengstenberg who wanted to present the God of the Old Testament, the God of anger and vengeance, as the God of Christianity. The literary exchanges which resulted remained well within the limits of an academic polemic, but they were sufficiently sharp to cause the decrepit and very much alarmed Altenstein to remove his protégé from the suspicious glare of the orthodox, who were as vengeful as they were simon pure. In the autumn of 1839 he sent Bauer to the University of Bonn as a lecturer with the intention of appointing him to a professorship before the end of the year.

But Bruno Bauer, as his letters to Marx indicate, was already in a period of intellectual development which was to take him far beyond Strauss. He began a criticism of the Gospels which finally demolished the last ruins which Strauss had left still standing. He contended that there was not an atom of historical truth in the Gospel story, that everything in it was the product of fantasy, and that Christianity was not forced as a world religion on the classic Græco-Roman world, but that it was the natural product of that world. With this development he took the one path which offered a possibility of scientifically investigating the origin of Christianity, and it is not without good reason that our contemporary fashionable, court and salon theologian Harnack, who is at the moment engaged in furbishing up the Gospels in the interests of the ruling classes, roundly abuses any attempt to proceed along the path opened up by Bruno Bauer.

Whilst these ideas were beginning to mature in Bruno Bauer's head Karl Marx was his inseparable companion and Bauer recognized his nine year younger friend as a most capable brother in arms. He had hardly settled down in Bonn when he began his attempts to persuade Marx to follow him. A club of professors in Bonn was " simple Philistinism " compared with the Hegelian club in Berlin, he declared. The latter had at least always been a centre of intellectual interests. There was also plenty of amusement in Bonn, what they called amusement there, but he had never laughed so much in Bonn as he had in Berlin when he had no more than crossed the street with Marx. Marx should polish off his " trivial examination " finally (after all only Aristotle, Spinoza and Leibniz were necessary), and stop taking such farcical nonsense seriously. He would find the Bonn philosophers easy game. And, above all, a radical publication was necessary, one they could issue jointly, for the Berlin chit-chat of the *Hallische Jahrbücher* was no longer tolerable. He felt sorry for Ruge, but why on earth didn't the fellow drive the vermin out of his paper ?

Bauer's letters sound revolutionary enough at times, but it is always a philosophical revolution he has in mind and he was far more inclined to count on the support of the State than on its hostility. He had hardly written to Marx in December 1839 that Prussia seemed destined to make progress only on account of its Jenas, though naturally such battles need not always be fought over a hecatomb of corpses, when a few months later— following on the almost simultaneous decease of his protector Altenstein and the old king—he pledged himself to " the highest idea of our State life ", the family spirit of the princely House of Hohenzollern which had devoted four centuries of high-minded effort to the settlement of the relations of Church and State. At the same time Bauer promised that science would not falter in its defence of the State idea against the usurpation of the church. The State might err, it might become suspicious of science and use the weapon of intimidation, but reason belonged too innately to the State for it to err long. The new King answered this homage by appointing the orthodox reactionary Eichhorn as Altenstein's successor, and Eichhorn immediately proceeded to sacrifice the freedom of science, as far as it was connected with the State idea, that is to say, the freedom of academic teaching, to the usurpation of the church.

Politically considered, Bauer was far less reliable than Köppen, who might have made a mistake concerning one Hohenzollern who surprisingly rose above the general family level, but was not likely to make any mistake concerning " the family spirit " of that princely house. Köppen was by no means so thoroughly at home with the Hegelian ideology as was Bauer, but it must not be overlooked that the latter's political short-sightedness was only the reverse side of his philosophical acumen. He discovered in the gospels the intellectual deposit of the time in which they had originated, and he was of the opinion—and considered from a purely ideological standpoint it was not illogical—that if even the Christian religion with its turbid ferment of Græco-Roman philosophy had succeeded in overcoming the culture of the classic world, then the clear and free criticism of modern dialectics would succeed still more easily in shaking off the incubus of Christian-Germanic culture.

It was the philosophy of self-consciousness which gave him such inspiring confidence. The Greek philosophic schools which developed from the national disintegration of Greek life and did most to fructify the Christian religion, the Sceptics, the Epicureans and the Stoics, had united under this name. They could not be compared with Plato in speculative depth nor with Aristotle in universal knowledge, and they had been somewhat contemptuously treated by Hegel. Their joint aim was to make the individual, separated by a terrible cataclysm from everything which up to them had stayed and fortified him, independent of everything outside himself and to lead him back into his inner life to seek his real happiness in the peace of the spirit, a peace which might remain unshaken whilst the whole world was collapsing around his ears.

However, declared Bauer, on the ruins of a vanished world the emaciated ego feared itself as the only power. It estranged and alienated its own consciousness by representing its own general power as an alien power outside itself. In the Lord and Master of the Gospel story, who overcame the laws of nature with one breath of his mouth, subjugated his enemies and announced himself, even on earth, as the Lord of the world and the Judge of all things, it created a hostile brother, but still a brother, to the world ruler in Rome holding sway over all rights and carrying the power over life and death on its lips. Under the slavery of the Christian religion, however, humanity was trained so that it might prepare itself all the more thoroughly for freedom and encompass it all the more completely when it should finally be won. The eternal consciousness of self, realizing itself, understanding itself and comprehending its essence, had power over the creations of its own alienation.

If we brush aside the typical phraseology current in the philosophic language of the day we can express in simpler and more understandable terms what it was that attracted Bauer, Köppen and Marx to the Greek philosophy of self-consciousness. Here too they were in reality again picking up the threads of the bourgeois enlightenment movement. The old Greek philosophic schools of self-consciousness produced no one comparable to the geniuses of the old natural philosophy Democritus and Heraclitus, or of the later abstract philosophy Plato and Aristotle, but nevertheless they played a great historic rôle. They opened up new and wider horizons to the human intellect and they broke down both the national limitations of Hellenism and the social limitations of slavery, limitations which neither Plato nor Aristotle had dreamed of overstepping. They greatly fructified primitive Christianity, which was the religion of the oppressed and the suffering, and only later, after it had become the religion of an oppressing and exploiting power, did it go over to Plato and Aristotle. Although generally speaking Hegel treated the philosophy of self-consciousness in a very off-hand fashion, even he expressly pointed out the great significance of the inner freedom of the individual amidst the utter calamity of the Roman world empire which effaced all the nobility and beauty of spiritual individuality with a brutal hand. The bourgeois enlightenment movement of the eighteenth century revived the Greek philosophies of self-consciousness : the doubts of the Sceptics, the hatred the Epicureans bore towards religion, and the republican sentiments of the Stoics.

In his work on Frederick the Great, whom he regarded as one of the heroes of the enlightenment movement, Köppen sounded the same note when he declared : " Epicureanism, Stoicism and Scepticism represent the nerves and internal system of the antique organism whose direct and natural unity determined the beauty and morality of classical antiquity and which collapsed when the latter died out. Frederick the Great adopted all three and wielded them with wonderful power. They became the chief factors in his world outlook, in his character and in his whole life." Marx was prepared to grant at least that what Köppen said here concerning the relation of the three philosophies to Greek life possessed " a deeper significance ".

The problem which occupied his older friends occupied Marx no less, but he dealt with it in a different fashion. He sought " human self-consciousness as the supreme Godhead ", tolerating no other Gods before it, neither in the distorting mirror of religion nor in the philosophic dilettantism of a despot, but by going back to the historical origins of this philosophy, whose systems represented for him also the key to the real history of the Greek spirit.

4. The Doctoral Dissertation

When Bruno Bauer urged Marx to polish off his " trivial examination " finally, he had some grounds for impatience, for it was the autumn of 1839 and Marx had already been studying for eight terms, but he certainly did not suppose that Marx was suffering from any examination fever in the usual and disagreeable sense of the term or he would never have credited him with being able to bowl over the professors of philosophy in Bonn at the first encounter.

It was characteristic of Marx, and it remained so until the end of his days, that his insatiable urge to knowledge permitted him to master difficult problems quickly, whilst his merciless self-criticism prevented him from having done with them equally quickly. In accordance with his usual thoroughness Marx must have plunged into the greyest depths of Greek philosophy, and the representation of only the three systems of the philosophy of self-consciousness was no matter which could be settled in a few terms. Bauer, who turned out his own works at a great speed, much too quickly in fact for their permanence, had little understanding for this, much less than Friedrich Engels showed later on, and even Engels sometimes became impatient when Marx could find no limit and no end to his self-criticism.

However, the " trivial examination " presented other difficulties, if not for Bauer then for Marx. Whilst his father was still alive Marx had decided on an academic career without thereby abandoning completely the choice of a practical profession, but with the death of Altenstein the most attractive feature of a professorial career and one which might have made up for its numerous disadvantages began to disappear, namely, the comparative freedom granted to philosophers in their university chairs. Bauer himself never tired of pointing out that the academic gown was good for nothing else.

And, in fact, it was not long before Bauer discovered that even the scientific investigations of a Prussian professor could not be conducted entirely without let or hindrance. After Altenstein's death in May 1840 the Ministry of Culture was taken over for a few months by Privy Councillor Ladenberg who showed sufficient piety towards the memory of his old superior to make him want to fulfil the latter's promise to provide Bauer with a permanent appointment in Bonn. However, immediately Eichhorn was appointed Minister of Culture the Theological Faculty in Bonn rejected the appointment of Bauer as professor on the ground that it would disturb the harmony of the faculty. Under Eichhorn it succeeded in summoning up that rare heroism which German professors display when they are sure of the secret approval of their superiors.

Bauer had spent his autumn holidays in Berlin and was on the point of returning to Bonn when the news reached him. A discussion immediately took place in the circle of his friends as to whether or not an irreparable breach had already occurred between the religious and the scientific schools, and whether a supporter of the latter could reconcile membership of a theological faculty with his scientific conscience. Bauer himself maintained his optimistic attitude towards the Prussian State and rejected a semi-official proposal made to him that he should occupy himself with literary work and receive a grant from the State funds the while. He returned to Bonn full of fighting spirit and in the hope that together with Marx, who was soon to follow him, he would be able to bring the crisis to a head.

Neither of them abandoned the idea of issuing a radical journal together, but Marx's prospects of an academic career at the Rhenish University now appeared decidedly poor. As the friend and assistant of Bauer he had to reckon with a hostile reception at the hands of the professorial clique in Bonn, and nothing was further from his thoughts than to curry favour with Eichhorn or Ladenberg, as Bauer advised him to do in the justifiable hope that then everything in Bonn would be " all right ". In such matters Marx's ideas were always very strict, but even had he felt inclined to trust himself on such a slippery path it was easy to foresee that sooner or later he must lose his balance, for Eichhorn was not long in showing his true colours.

In order to finish off the decrepit mob of fossilized Hegelians at the University of Berlin once and for all he appointed a professor named Schelling as Rector, a man who had come round in his old age to a belief in revelation, and he disciplined the students of Halle University who had drawn up a respectful petition to the King as their Rector begging him to appoint Strauss to a professorship in Halle.

With such prospects Marx as a Young Hegelian decided not to take his examination in Prussia at all. He had no desire to give the zealous satellites of Eichhorn a chance of plaguing him, though he had no intention of evading the struggle. Quite the contrary, in fact, and he decided to take his doctor's degree at one of the smaller universities and then to publish his doctoral dissertation as a proof of his knowledge and capacity, together with a challenging foreword, and after that to settle down in Bonn and publish the proposed magazine with Bauer. In this way Bonn University would not be completely closed to him because, as *Doktor Promotus* of " a foreign university ", he would have only one or two formalities to comply with in order to be given the freedom of the university as an independent lecturer.

This was the plan that Marx actually carried out. On the 15th April he was awarded the degree of Doctor of Philosophy in his absence by the University of Jena on the basis of a written dissertation dealing with the differences between Democritean and Epicurean natural philosophy. This dissertation was an anticipatory part of a larger work in which Marx intended to deal with the whole cycle of the Epicurean, Stoic and Sceptic philosophy in its relation to Greek speculative philosophy as a whole. For the moment he demonstrated this relation on the basis of one example only and in connection with only the older speculative philosophy.

Amongst the older natural philosophers of Greece Democritus was the one who had adhered most closely to materialism. Out of nothing nothing can come. Nothing that is can be destroyed. All change is nothing but the joining and separation of parts. Nothing happens fortuitously and everything that happens happens with reason and necessity. Nothing exists but the atoms and empty space, everything else is opinion. The atoms are endless in number and of an infinite variety in form. Falling eternally through infinite space the larger atoms, which fall more quickly, collide with the smaller atoms, and the material movements and rotations which result are the beginning of the formation of worlds. Innumerable worlds form and pass away, co-existently and successively.

Epicurus took over this conception of nature from Democritus, but he made certain alterations. The most famous of these alterations consisted in the so-called " swerve of the atoms ". Epicurus contended that in their fall the atoms " swerved ", that is to say, that they did not fall vertically, but in a deviation from the straight line. From Cicero and Plutarch to Leibniz and Kant Epicurus has been thoroughly ridiculed for propounding this physical impossibility, and he has been dubbed an imitator of Democritus who merely botched the model which he took from his master. However, parallel with this condemnation of its physical absurdity, there is a tendency which regards the Epicurean philosophy as the most highly-developed materialist system in the classic world, thanks largely to the fact that it has been perpetuated in the didactic poem of Lucretius,[1] whereas only insignificant remnants of the philosophy of Democritus have weathered the storm and stress of the centuries. Kant dismissed the swerve of the atoms as " an insolent invention ", but nevertheless he recognized Epicurus as the most noble philosopher of the senses as against Plato the most noble philosopher of the intellect.

Naturally, Marx did not deny the physical unreasonableness of the Epicurean philosophy and he condemned " the reckless irresponsibility of Epicurus in the explanation of physical phenomena ", but he pointed out that the only test of truth for Epicurus was the evidence of his senses : Epicurus believed the diameter of the sun to be two feet because it looked so to his eyes. However, Marx did not content himself with dismissing these evident absurdities with a phrase or two, but set himself to track down the philosophic reason in the physical unreason. He acted in accordance with the fine words he had used in honour of his master Hegel in a note to his dissertation pointing out that a philosophic school whose master had committed a sin of accommodation should not blame him, but seek to explain the accommodation from the inadequacy of the principle in which it must have its root, thus turning into a progress of science what must appear a progress of conscience.

That which was an end in itself for Democritus was nothing but a means to an end for Epicurus. Epicurus did not aim at an understanding of nature, but at a view of nature which would support his philosophic system. The philosophy of self-consciousness as it was known to the classical world, fell into three schools, and according to Hegel the Epicureans represented the abstract individual consciousness of self, and the Stoics the abstract general consciousness of self, both as one-sided dogmas opposed immediately on account of their one-sidedness by the

[1] *De Rerum Natura.*—Tr.

Sceptics. Or, as a later historian of Greek philosophy expressed the same relation : in Stoicism and Epicureanism the individual and the general aspects of the subjective spirit, the atomistic isolation of the individual and his pantheistic surrender to the whole, faced each other irreconcilably with the same claims, whilst this antagonism was neutralized in Scepticism.

Despite their common aims, the Epicureans and the Stoics were led far away from each other by their different starting-points. Their surrender to the whole made the Stoics philosophically into determinists for whom the necessity of every happening was axiomatic, and politically into convinced republicans, whilst in the religious sphere they were unable to free themselves from a superstitious and restricted mysticism. They looked for support to Heraclitus, in whom the surrender to the whole had taken on the form of the most uncompromising self-consciousness, though they treated him with as little ceremony as the Epicureans treated Democritus. On the other hand, the principle of isolated individuality made the Epicureans philosophically into indeterminists, into proclaimers of the free-will of each individual, and politically into patient sufferers—the biblical exhortation : be subject to the authorities which have power over you, is a heritage of Epicurus—whilst at the same time it freed them from all religious bonds.

Marx then shows in a series of trenchant investigations how " the difference between Democritean and Epicurean natural philosophy " can be explained. Democritus concerned himself exclusively with the material existence of the atom, whereas Epicurus concerned himself further with the atom as a conception, with its form as well as its matter, with its essence as well as its existence. Epicurus regarded the atom as being not only the material basis of the world of phenomena, but also the symbol of the isolated individual, the formal principle of abstract individual self-consciousness. From the vertical fall of the atoms Democritus concluded the necessity of all happenings, whilst Epicurus caused his atoms to swerve from the straight line in their fall, for otherwise where—as Lucretius, the best-known interpreter of Epicurean philosophy, asks in his didactic poem—would be free will, the will of the living human being wrested from the inexorable course of fate ? This contradiction between the atom as a phenomenon and the atom as a conception is evident throughout the whole of the Epicurean philosophy and compels it to adopt that utterly arbitrary explanation of physical phenomena which was subjected to such ridicule even in the classic world. The contradictions of Epicurean natural philosophy are reconciled only in the movements of the heavenly bodies, but at the same time the principle of abstract individual self-consciousness is destroyed in face of their general and eternal existence. Epicurean natural philosophy thus abandons all material mummery and Epicurus fights as " the greatest Greek enlightener ", as Marx calls him, against the tyranny of religion intimidating man with a baleful glance from the heights of heaven.

In this his first work Marx reveals himself as a constructive thinker, even if one contests the details of his interpretation of the Epicurean philosophy. In fact, his independent thought becomes even more clear then, because the only possible objection can be that Marx developed the basic principle of Epicureanism further and drew clearer conclusions from it than Epicurus did himself. Hegel declared that the Epicurean philosophy was thoughtlessness on principle, and it is certainly true that its originator who, as a self-taught man, attached great importance to the language of the common people, did not clothe his thoughts in the speculative phraseology of Hegelian philosophy with which Marx explained it. With this dissertation the pupil of Hegel draws up his own certificate of maturity. He uses the dialectical method in a masterly fashion and his style shows that vigour of expression which always characterized the language of his teacher Hegel, but which was so sadly lacking in the ranks of his camp-followers.

However, in this work Marx is still completely on the idealist basis of the Hegelian philosophy and the most surprising thing about it for the present-day reader is the unfavourable verdict passed on Democritus. Marx declares that all Democritus did was to put forward a hypothesis which represented the result of experience and not its energizing principle, and that therefore this hypothesis was never fulfilled and never materially influenced the practical investigation of natural phenomena. On the other hand he praises Epicurus as the founder of the science of atomism, despite the latter's arbitrariness in the explanation of physical phenomena and despite the abstract individual self-consciousness he preaches, although, as Marx admits, this neutralizes all real and authentic science because it is in the nature of things not the individual unit which prevails.

To-day the matter is no longer open for discussion. As far as there is any science of atomism, and as far as the theory of the elementary particles and the development of all phenomena as a result of their movement has become the basis of the modern investigations into natural phenomena, explaining the laws of sound, light and heat and the chemical and physical alterations in material bodies, Democritus was the pioneer and not Epicurus.

However, for the Marx of that period philosophy, or to be more accurate, abstract philosophy, was so completely science that he came to a conclusion which we should hardly be able to understand to-day but for the fact that the very essence of his character was revealed in it.

As far as Marx was concerned, living always meant working and working fighting. What turned him against Democritus therefore was the lack of an " energizing principle " or, as he put it later on, " the chief weakness of all previous materialism ", the appreciation of the thing, the reality, sensualism only in the form of the object or the idea and not subjectively, not in practice, not in human sensual activity. And on the other hand, what drew him to Epicurus was the " energizing principle " which permitted this philosopher to revolt against and defy the crushing weight of religion.

> Weder von Blitzen geschreckt, noch durch das Geraune von Göttern,
> Oder des Himmels murrenden Groll. . . .[1]

The foreword which Marx intended to publish together with the dissertation and which he dedicated to his father-in-law breathes an unquenchable and fierce fighting spirit. " As long as one drop of blood still pulses through the world-conquering and untrammelled heart of philosophy it will always defy its enemies with the words of Epicurus : ' Not he is Godless who scorns the Gods of the multitude, but he who accepts the opinions of the multitude concerning the Gods.' " Philosophy does not reject the avowal of Prometheus :

> Mit schlichtem Wort, den Göttern allen heg' ich Hass.[2]

And to those who complain of the apparent worsening of their state it replies as Prometheus replied to Hermes, the servant of the Gods :

> Für deinen Frondienst gäb'ich mein unselig Los,
> Das sei versichert, nimmermehr zum Tausche dar.[3]

Prometheus is the noblest saint and martyr in the philosophic calendar. This was the closing passage of Marx's defiant foreword, which alarmed even his friend Bauer, but what seemed to the latter to be " unnecessary temerity " was in fact no more than the simple avowal of a man who was destined to be a second Prometheus both in struggle and in suffering.

---

[1] Frightened neither by lightning, nor the threats of the Gods,
Nor the growling thunders of Heaven.
[2] In simple truth, I harbour hate 'gainst all the Gods.
[3] For your vile slavery, be assured,
Never would I change my own unhappy lot.

5. The *Anekdota* and the *Rheinische Zeitung*

Marx had hardly pocketed the diploma of his new-won dignity when all the plans he had built up for his future collapsed as a result of further blows delivered by the romanticist reaction.

In the summer of 1841 Eichhorn mobilized all the theological faculties in a shameful campaign against Bruno Bauer on account of his criticism of the Gospels, and with the exception of Halle and Königsberg all the universities at once betrayed the principle of Protestant academic freedom and Bauer had to give way. With this all hope of Marx obtaining a foothold at the University of Bonn disappeared.

At the same time the plan for the issue of a radical philosophical journal also collapsed. The new King considered himself a supporter of the freedom of the press and at his instance a mitigated censorship order was drawn up. At the end of 1841 this order actually saw the light of day, but it was then seen that the freedom of the press was to be limited to a romanticist whim. The freedom of the press as understood by the King was also demonstrated in the summer of 1841 when an Order in Council was issued calling on Ruge to submit his magazine, which was printed and published by Wigand in Leipzig, to Prussian press censorship or to make up his mind to its prohibition in the Prussian States. This action enlightened Ruge sufficiently concerning his " free and just Prussia " to cause him to move to Dresden, where from the 1st July 1841 he issued his magazine as the *Deutsche Jahrbücher*. At the same time and on his own initiative he adopted that sharper tone which both Bauer and Marx had missed in his previous writings, and this made them decide to contribute to his publication rather than found one of their own.

In the end Marx did not publish his doctoral dissertation. Its immediate aim was no longer a matter of urgency and according to a later indication of its author it was put on one side to await its resurrection as part of a larger work on Epicurean, Stoic and Sceptic philosophy as a whole, but as it turned out, " political and philosophic affairs of quite another kind " did not permit Marx to carry out his original intention.

One of the most important of these affairs was to prove that not only Epicurus but also Hegel were thorough-going atheists. In November 1841 Wigand published an " Ultimatum " entitled *The Last Trump of Judgment against Hegel, the Atheists and the Anti-Christs*. Under the mask of an orthodox believer the anonymous pamphleteer bemoaned Hegel's atheism in the accents of biblical prophecy and proved his point in the most convincing fashion from Hegel's own works. The pamphlet created a great sensation, particularly as in the beginning the orthodox mask actually deceived the public, and even Ruge was taken in by it. In reality the author of *The Last Trump* was Bruno Bauer and he intended to continue the work together with Marx and to prove on the basis of Hegel's æsthetics, his philosophy of law, etc., that the Young Hegelians and not the Old Hegelians had inherited the real spirit of the master.

In the meantime, however, *The Last Trump* was prohibited, and Wigand made difficulties about publishing any more of it. In addition Marx fell ill, as also did his father-in-law, who was bedridden for three months until he died on the 3rd of March 1842. Under the circumstances Marx found it " impossible to do anything worth while ", but he did send in " a minor contribution " on the 10th of February and at the same time promised Ruge that he would place himself at the disposal of the publication to the full extent of his powers. The " minor contribution " referred to was an article on the latest censorship instructions issued at the instance of the King with a view to securing a mitigated application of the censorship, and it represents the beginning of Marx's political career. Point by point his trenchant criticism laid bare the logical absurdities hidden beneath a cloak of hazy romanticism. His attitude was in uncompromising contradiction to the joy of the " pseudo-liberal " Philistines and even of some of the Young Hegelians who thought to descry " the sun already high in the heavens " because of " the royal spirit " which pervaded the instructions.

In his accompanying letter Marx requests that the article be put into print as quickly as possible " unless the censor censors my censure ". His foreboding did not deceive him and on the 25th of February Ruge wrote informing him that the *Deutsche Jahrbücher* was having the greatest difficulties with the censorship and that " your contribution has become impossible ". Ruge also informed Marx that he had chosen " an élite of pungent and excellent things " from amongst the material rejected by the censorship and that he intended to publish them in Switzerland as " Anekdota Philosophica ". On the 5th of March Marx wrote expressing great enthusiasm for the proposal. " Owing to the sudden resurrection " of the censorship in Saxony the publication of his essay on Christian art, which was to have appeared as the second part of *The Last Trump*, was made quite impossible. Marx then went through it again and offered it to Ruge for the *Anekdota*, together with a criticism of Hegelian natural law as far as it referred to the inner constitution. This latter criticism showed a tendency to attack constitutional monarchy as a thoroughly self-contradictory and self-neutralizing hybrid. Ruge accepted both, but apart from the article on the censorship instructions he received nothing.

On the 20th of March Marx announced that he intended to free his essay on Christian art from the style of *The Last Trump* and from the irksome limitations of the Hegelian phraseology, at the same time giving it a freer and more thorough treatment. This he promised to have finished by the middle of April. On the 27th of April it was " almost finished " and Ruge was requested to " excuse him for another few days " and informed that he would receive only 'a summary of the essay on Christian art because during the course of the work it had grown into a book. But by the 9th of July Marx was prepared to abandon all attempts to find an excuse, unless " unpleasant external matters " were sufficient excuse. In the meantime he promised to touch nothing else until his contributions to the *Anekdota* were finished. On the 21st of October Ruge reported that the *Anekdota* was ready and that it would be published by the *Literarisches Kontor* in Zurich. He was still holding a place open for Marx's contributions though up to the moment the latter had been more generous in promise than in performance, still, he, Ruge, knew very well what Marx could do in the way of performance once he settled down to it.

Ruge was sixteen years older than Marx, but like Bruno Bauer and Köppen he had the greatest respect for the capacities of the younger man, though Marx had severely strained his editorial patience. Marx was never an accommodating author either for his collaborators or his publishers, but none of them ever thought of ascribing to neglect or laziness what was caused only by an overbrimming richness of ideas and a self-criticism which was never satisfied.

In this particular case there was another circumstance which excused him even in the eyes of Ruge, for an incomparably more powerful interest than philosophy had begun to occupy his attention. With his article on the censorship instructions he had entered the political arena, and he continued this activity in the columns of the *Rheinische Zeitung* instead of spinning on the philosophical thread in the *Anekdota*.

The *Rheinische Zeitung* was founded in Cologne on the 1st of January 1842 and originally it was not an opposition paper at all, but rather pro-governmental. Since the trouble with the bishops in the 'thirties the *Kölnische Zeitung* with its eight thousand subscribers had become the mouthpiece of the ultramontane party which held undisputed sway in the Rhineland and caused the jack-boot policy of the government much trouble. The attitude of the *Kölnische Zeitung* sprang less from any righteous enthusiasm for the Catholic cause than from purely business considerations, for it was well aware that its readers were far from being enamoured of the blessings of the Berlin dispensation. The monopoly of the *Kölnische Zeitung* was so powerful that its owners invariably succeeded in buying out any competitive newspapers even when the latter enjoyed support from Berlin. In December 1839 the necessary concession for publication had been granted to the *Rheinische Allgemeine Zeitung* in the hope that it would succeed in breaking the monopoly of the *Kölnische Zeitung*, but it was not long before the former was threatened with the fate which had overtaken all its predecessors. At the last moment, however, a group of well-to-do citizens clubbed together to raise new share-capital and place the paper on a new basis. The government favoured the plan and gave provisional permission for the re-organized paper, which was to be known as the *Rheinische Zeitung*, to use the concession which had been granted to its predecessor.

The bourgeoisie of Cologne had no intention of making difficulties for the Prussian régime, although it was hated by the mass of the people in the Rhineland as an alien yoke. Business was proceeding satisfactorily and the bourgeoisie in the Rhineland had therefore abandoned its pro-French sympathies, and after the creation of the *Zollverein* it practically demanded Prussian hegemony throughout Germany. The political demands of the bourgeoisie in the Rhineland were extremely moderate and not so far-reaching as its economic demands, which aimed at furthering the capitalist mode of production in the Rhineland, where it had already made great progress. The demands put forward were : economical administration of the State finances, extension of the railway services, reduction of court fees and stamp duties, a common flag and common consuls for the *Zollverein*, and in short, all those items which invariably appear on a list of bourgeois desiderata.

However, the two young people who were entrusted with the reorganization of the editorial board, Georg Jung, a young barrister, and Dagobert Oppenheim, a young assessor, turned out to be enthusiastic Young Hegelians and very much under the influence of Moses Hess, who was also the son of a Rhenish business man and had not only studied the Hegelian philosophy, but also made himself familiar with French socialism. These two re-cruited the new contributors from amongst their own intellectual circle and above all from amongst the Young Hegelians in Berlin, and, at the recommendation of Marx, Rutenberg even took over the editorship of the regular German article although this recom-mendation was not, as it turned out, one of Marx's happiest notions.

Marx himself must have been closely connected with the venture from the beginning. He had intended to move from Trier to Cologne at the end of March, but he found life in the latter town too noisy for him and instead he provisionally pitched his tent in Bonn, from which Bruno Bauer had in the meantime disappeared, observing, " It would be a pity if no one remained to annoy the orthodox." In Bonn he began those contributions to the *Rheinische Zeitung* which were to carry him far above the heads of all the other contributors.

Although the personal connections of Jung and Oppenheim were the first means of turning the paper into a rendezvous of the Young Hegelians it is difficult to believe that this change in its character could have taken place without the approval or without the knowledge of the actual shareholders. The latter were in all probability acute enough to realize that they could not have found more capable intellects anywhere in Germany. The Young Hegelians were pro-Prussian, even exuberantly so, and whatever else they did which the good bourgeois of Cologne were unable to understand or found suspicious was probably regarded as harmless idiosyncrasies. Whatever the explanation may have been, the shareholders did not in fact interfere, although in the very first weeks of its existence complaints about the " subversive tendency " of the paper began to come in from Berlin and there was even a threat to suppress it altogether at the end of the first quarter. The thing which chiefly shocked the Berlin dispensation was the appointment of Rutenberg, who was regarded as a terrible revolutionary and kept under strict political surveillance. Even in the March days of 1848 Frederick William IV trembled before him believing him to be the real instigator of the revolution. Despite the dissatisfaction felt in Berlin the deadly bolt was not discharged and this was due chiefly to the Minister of Culture Eichhorn who, although he was thoroughly reactionary, felt the necessity for some counter-weight to the ultramontane tendencies of the *Kölnische Zeitung*. Although the tendency of the *Rheinische Zeitung* was " almost more dangerous ", nevertheless it played with ideas which could not possibly have any attraction for the solid and reliable elements of society.

This was certainly not the fault of the contributions which Marx sent in and in fact the practical fashion in which he dealt with the affairs of the day did more to reconcile the shareholders with Young Hegelianism than even the contributions of Bruno Bauer and Max Stirner. Otherwise it would be impossible to understand how it came about that in October 1842, a few months after he had sent in his first article, he was made editor of the paper.

For the first time Marx was now given an opportunity of showing his incomparable ability to take things as they were and to make petrified conditions dance by singing them their own melody.

6. The Rhenish Diet

In the previous year the Diet of the Rhenish province had sat for nine weeks in Düsseldorf, and in a series of five long treatises Marx now proceeded to elucidate its activities. The provincial Diets were impotent, pseudo-representative bodies instituted by the Prussian Crown to cloak the betrayal of its 1815 promise to grant a constitution. They held their sessions behind closed doors and were permitted at the utmost a little say in petty communal affairs. However, since the trouble with the Catholic Church in Cologne and in Posen in 1837 the Diets had not been convened at all. Opposition to the government, if it came at all, was to be expected only from the Rhenish and Posen Diets, but even then only an ultramontane opposition.

These precious bodies were protected very effectively from liberalist aberrations by the provision that the possession of landed property was a necessary condition of membership. The country gentry were to provide one-half of the membership, the urban landowners one-third and the peasant landowners one-sixth. However, this edifying principle could not be put into operation in all its glory everywhere, and in the newly-won Rhineland, for instance, one or two concessions had to be made to the spirit of modernism, but always the country gentry provided over one-third of the membership and in view of the fact that all the decisions of the Diets had to be adopted with a two-thirds majority nothing could be passed without their approval. Urban landowners were subjected to the further limitation that their land must have been in their uninterrupted possession for a period of at least ten years before it conferred the boon of eligibility for election to the Diet. As a further precautionary measure the government reserved the right to veto the election of any urban official.

Although the Diets were the object of general contempt Frederick William IV convened them again in 1841 after his accession to the throne, and he even extended their rights somewhat, but only in order to trick the creditors of the State, who

had been promised by the Crown in 1820 that no new loans
would be floated without the consent and the guarantee of the
future Reich's Corporative Assembly. Johann Jacoby issued a
famous pamphlet calling on the Diets to demand the fulfilment
of the royal promise, but he preached to deaf ears.

Even the Rhenish Diet gave way ignominiously and it did
so precisely on those political questions relating to the church
on account of which the government had most feared it. With
a two-thirds majority it rejected a demand that the illegally
arrested Archbishop of Cologne should either be brought before
the courts or reinstated in his office, although the justice of such
a demand was beyond all discussion both from the liberal and
the ultramontane standpoints. It did not even mention the
question of a constitution and it dealt in the most pusillanimous
fashion with a petition signed by over a thousand citizens of
Cologne demanding the admission of the general public to the
Diet sessions, the publication of a daily and unexpurgated report
of the Diet proceedings, the right to discuss the affairs of the Diet
and all other provincial affairs in the press, and the issue of a
definite press law in place of the censorship. All the Diet did
was to request the King for permission to publish the names
of the speakers in its records, and instead of demanding a press
law it asked for a censorship law designed merely to prevent
arbitrariness in the application of the censorship. The well-
earned consequence of its cowardice was a rebuff at the hands
of the Crown even for these modest requests.

The Diet showed signs of life only when it sprang to defend
the interests of the landowners. The restoration of the old
feudal glories was out of the question (as even the officials sent
into the Rhineland from East Prussia reported back to Berlin)
for any attempt to do so would have aroused fierce opposition
on the part of the Rhinelanders, who were not prepared to put
up with anything of the sort. In particular they were not
prepared to tolerate any interference with the right to partition
landed property at will, whether in the interests of the country
gentry or in the interests of the peasantry, although the unlimited carving up of landed property had already led to
the downright atomization of landholdings, as the government
pointed out with more than a little justification. A government proposal to place certain limits on the partitioning of
landed property " in the interests of maintaining a strong
peasantry " was therefore rejected by the Diet by 49 votes
against 8, for it was in agreement with the province on this
point. But after this the Diet plunged into legislation more
after its own heart and it passed a number of laws put forward

by the government against stick-gathering, trespass and poaching on private lands and in the woods. The landowners in the Diet shamelessly and unscrupulously prostituted their legislative powers to their own private interests.

Marx had drawn up a comprehensive plan for taking the Diet to task. In the first treatise, which was composed of six long articles, he dealt with the debates of the Diet on the freedom of the press and on the publication of the Diet proceedings. Permission to publish a report of the proceedings without publishing the names of the speakers was one of the reforms with which the King had tried to encourage the Diets, but he met with violent opposition from the Diets themselves. The Rhenish Diet did not go so far as the Pomeranian and the Brandenburg Diets, which flatly refused to publish any reports of their proceedings, but that stupid arrogance which would make elected representatives into higher beings secure from the criticism of the electors gave itself airs enough. " The Diet cannot stand the light of day. The privacy of its own circle is better suited to it. If the province has sufficient confidence in a body of individuals to entrust them with the representation of its rights, then it is only natural that these individuals should be condescending enough to accept the honour, but it would really be going too far to demand that they should give a Roland for an Oliver and submit themselves, their modes of living and their characters to the judgment of the province which has just given them such a vote of confidence." With delicious humour Marx derides the first appearance of that phenomenon which he was later to dub " parliamentary cretinism ", a thing he hated all his life.

And for the freedom of the press his rapier play has never been equalled in brilliance and trenchancy. Without envy Ruge admitted : " It would be impossible to say anything more deep or more thorough in favour of the freedom of the press. We may congratulate ourselves that this maturity, genius and sovereign mastery over the vulgar confusion of ideas have made their début in our press." In one passage Marx refers to the free and happy climate of his homeland, and in these articles there is, even to-day, still something of the brightness and warmth of the summer sun playing on the vineyards along the banks of the Rhine. Hegel once spoke of " the miserable subjectivity of a bad press which would liquidate everything ", but Marx reached back to the bourgeois enlightenment movement, and in the *Rheinische Zeitung* he recognized Kantism as the German theory of the French Revolution. However, he reached back to it with all the breadth of political and social horizon which the historical dialectics of Hegel had opened up to him. One has only to compare the articles of Marx in the *Rheinische Zeitung* with Jacoby's " Four Questions " in order to realize what an advance the former were. Jacoby appealed again and again to the royal promise of a constitution as the alpha and omega of the whole question, whilst Marx did not consider it worthy of even a casual mention.

With all his praise of a free press as the watchful eye of the people as against a censored press with its fundamental vice of hypocrisy, a vice which gave rise to all its other imperfections including the evil of passivity, revolting even from an æsthetic standpoint, Marx did not overlook the dangers which threatened the former. One of the representatives of the urban property owners had demanded the freedom of the press as part and parcel of the freedom of trade whereupon Marx demanded : " Is a press which degrades itself to a trade free ? A writer must certainly earn money in order to exist and write, but he should not exist and write in order to earn money. . . . The first freedom of the press must consist in its emancipation from commerce. The writer who degrades the press to a material means deserves as a punishment for this inner slavery that outer slavery which is the censorship, or perhaps his very existence is his punishment." All his life Marx lived up to these principles and to that standard which he demanded from others : a man's writings must always be an end in themselves. They must be so little a means for himself and others that if necessary he must sacrifice his own existence to his writings.

The second treatise on the proceedings of the Rhenish Diet dealt with " The Archbishop Affair " as Marx wrote to Jung. This treatise was blue-pencilled by the censor and it was never published, although Ruge offered to include it in his *Anekdota*. Writing to the latter on the 9th of July 1842 Marx declared : " Don't think we are living in a political Dorado here in the Rhineland. It needs the most determined persistence to conduct a newspaper like the *Rheinische Zeitung*. My second article on the Diet dealing with the church troubles has been rejected by the censor. I pointed out in it that the defenders of the State had taken up a religious attitude and the defenders of the church a political attitude. The rejection of my article is all the more disagreeable because the foolish Catholics of Cologne would have fallen into the trap and the defence of the Archbishop would have attracted new subscribers. You can hardly imagine, by the way, how disgustingly and at the same time how stupidly the despots have treated the orthodox blockhead. But success has crowned the affair. Prussia has kissed the

Pope's toe before the eyes of the whole world but our governmental automatons still appear in public without blushing." The last passage refers to the fact that in accordance with his romanticist leanings Frederick William IV had ventured into negotiations with the Papal Curia whereupon the latter had shown its gratitude by overreaching him right and left in the best traditions of the Vatican.

What Marx writes in this letter to Ruge about his article must not be taken to mean that Marx really undertook the defence of the Archbishop in order to lead the unwary Catholics of Cologne into a trap. On the contrary, he remained absolutely true to his principles and completely logical when he declared that with the illegal arrest of the Archbishop for having performed his religious functions, and with the demand of the Catholics that the illegally arrested man should be given a legal trial, the defenders of the State had taken up a religious attitude and the defenders of the church a political attitude. It was certainly a decisive question for the *Rheinische Zeitung* that it should adopt a correct attitude in a topsy-turvy world, precisely for the reasons which Marx gives later on in the same letter to Ruge, namely, because the ultramontane party, which the paper energetically opposed, was the most dangerous force in the Rhineland and because the opposition had grown far too accustomed to conducting its struggle exclusively within the church.

The third treatise, which was composed of five long articles, dealt with the proceedings of the Diet concerning a law against the pilfering of sticks in the forests. At this point Marx was compelled to " come down to earth " or, as he expressed the same idea in another connection, he was embarrassed by having to speak of material interests for which Hegel had made no provision in his ideological system, and in fact he did not master the problem presented by this law with the incisiveness which he would have shown in later years. The point at issue was a fight between the developing capitalist era and the last remnants of common ownership of the land, a brutal struggle to expropriate the masses of the people. Out of 207,478 penal proceedings begun in Prussia in 1836 no less than 150,000, or almost three-quarters, referred to the pilfering of sticks in the forests, poaching offences, trespassing, etc.

During the discussion which took place in the Diet the exploiting interests of the private landowners shamelessly forced through their claims, going even beyond the provisions of the government draft, and Marx now entered the field with caustic criticism on behalf of " the propertyless masses without political and social rights ". However, his reasoning is still based on considerations of justice and not yet of economics. He demanded that the customary rights of the poor people should not be violated, and he found the basis of these rights in a somewhat vague form of property whose character was neither definitely private property nor definitely common property, but a mixture of both such as evidences itself in all the institutions of the Middle Ages. These hybrid and vague forms of property had been abolished by applying the categories of abstract civil law taken from Roman law, but an instinctive sense of justice was embodied in the customary rights of the poorer classes and their roots were positive and legitimate.

Although the historical perception of this article bears " a certain vacillating character " it nevertheless, or rather precisely on that account, shows us what in the last resort roused this great defender of " the poorer classes ". His description of the villainies committed by the landowners and of the way in which they trampled under foot logic and reason, law and justice, and in the last resort the interests of the State, in order to satisfy their own private interests at the expense of the poor and the dispossessed reveals the fierce anger against injustice which moved him. " In order to destroy the poacher and the pilferer the Diet has not only broken the limbs of the law, but it has pierced it to the very heart." On the basis of this one example Marx wished to show what might be expected of a class assembly of private interests when once it seriously set about the task of legislating.

At the same time he still adhered to the Hegelian philosophy of law and the State, though he did not do so after the fashion of the orthodox disciples of Hegel who praised the Prussian State as ideal. On the contrary, he compared the Prussian State with the ideal State resulting from the philosophical hypotheses of Hegel. Marx regarded the State as the great organism within which legal, moral and political freedom must find its fulfilment, whilst the individual citizen obeyed the laws of the State only as the natural laws of his own reason, of human reason. From this standpoint Marx succeeded in dealing satisfactorily with the debates of the Diet on the law against wood pilfering, and he would probably have dealt equally satisfactorily with the fourth treatise discussing a law against poaching and trespassing, but not with the fifth which was intended to crown the whole work and discuss " the mundane question in life size ", the question of partitioning the land.

Together with the bourgeois Rhineland, Marx was in favour of complete freedom to partition landed property. His attitude was that to refuse the peasant the right to divide up his property as he wished would be to add legal impoverishment to physical impoverishment. However, this legal consideration was not wide enough to provide a solution of the problem. The French socialists had already pointed out that unlimited freedom to partition landed property created a helpless proletariat and placed it on a level with the atomistic isolation of the artisan. If Marx wanted to deal with this problem therefore he must first try conclusions with socialism.

It is certain that Marx recognized this necessity and it is equally certain that he would not have evaded it had he concluded the series. However, he did not get as far as that, and by the time his third treatise was published in the *Rheinische Zeitung* he was already its editor and found himself faced with the socialist riddle before he was in a position to solve it.

7. Five Months of Struggle

During the course of the summer months the *Rheinische Zeitung* made one or two minor excursions into the social field. In all probability Moses Hess was responsible for them. On one occasion it reprinted an article on housing conditions in Berlin taken from one of Weitling's publications and entitled it " A Contribution to an Important Contemporary Question ". And on another occasion it published a report on a congress of savants in Strassburg which had also touched on the socialist question, and added a harmless remark to the effect that if the non-possessing classes were now casting their eyes on the riches of the middle classes this might be compared to the struggle of the middle classes against the feudal aristocracy in 1789 with the difference that this time the problem would meet with a peaceable solution.

Small though the inducement was, it proved sufficient to cause the *Allgemeine Zeitung* in Augsburg to accuse the *Rheinische Zeitung* of flirting with communism. As a matter of fact the conscience of the *Allgemeine Zeitung* was not quite clear in this respect, for it had published much sharper articles from the pen of Heinrich Heine on French socialism and communism, but it was the only German newspaper of any national and even international importance and it felt its position threatened by the *Rheinische Zeitung*. Although the violent attack launched by the *Allgemeine Zeitung* had thus no very edifying motive, it was not without a certain malicious dexterity. Together with various allusions to the sons of well-to-do merchants who in their innocent simplicity played with socialist ideas without the least intention of sharing their possessions with the dockers or with the men at work on Cologne Cathedral, it played a trump card by declaring it childish to threaten the middle classes in an economically backward country like Germany with the fate of the feudal aristocracy in France in 1789, particularly in view of the fact that the German middle classes were hardly granted room to breathe freely themselves.

It was Marx's first editorial task to parry this biting attack and he found it uncomfortable enough. He was unwilling to defend things which he himself thought to be amateurish, but he was also not in a position to say quite what he thought of communism. Therefore he did his best to carry the war into Egypt by accusing the enemy of communist leanings, but at the same time he admitted that the *Rheinische Zeitung* had no right to dispose with a phrase or two of a problem at whose solution two great peoples were working. The *Rheinische Zeitung* would subject the ideas of communism to thorough criticism " after protracted and deep study ", for writings like those of Leroux and Considérant, and above all the sagacious writings of Proudhon, could not be disposed of by the superficial and chance ideas of the moment. However, in their present form the *Rheinische Zeitung* was not prepared to grant these ideas even theoretical reality, much less wish for their realization or think such realization possible.

Later on Marx declared that this polemic had spoiled his enthusiasm for the work on the *Rheinische Zeitung* and that he had therefore " eagerly " seized the opportunity of withdrawing into his study. However, as so often happens when one thinks back to past events, cause and effect were brought too close together. For the moment Marx was heart and soul in his work for the *Rheinische Zeitung* and it even appeared important enough to him to risk a breach with his old companions in Berlin for its sake. There was very little to be done with them, for the issue of the mitigated censorship instructions had turned the Hegelian Club, which had " at least always been a centre of intellectual interests ", into a society of so-called " Freemen " which embraced almost all the pre-March literary lights in the Prussian capital. They now met to play at being political and social revolutionaries like unhinged Philistines. Even during the summer months Marx had been disquieted by this development, declaring that it was one thing to proclaim one's emancipation, that was conscientiousness, but quite another to indulge in advance in self-adulation and self-advertisement. However, he went on, Bruno Bauer was in Berlin and he would see to it that at least no " imbecilities " were committed.

Unfortunately Marx was wrong in this assumption. According to reliable information Köppen kept himself aloof from the antics of the " Freemen ", but Bruno Bauer certainly did not, and in fact he even played the rôle of standard-bearer in their buffooneries. The ragging processions through the streets, the scandalous scenes in brothels and taverns, and the deplorable guying of a defenceless clergyman at Stirner's wedding when Bauer removed the brass rings from a knitted purse he was carrying and handed them to the officiating clergyman with the remark that they were quite good enough to serve as wedding rings, made them the object half of admiration and half of horror for all tame Philistines, but they hopelessly compromised the cause which they were supposed to represent.

Naturally, these guttersnipe antics had a devastating effect on the intellectual production of the " Freemen ", and Marx had great difficulties with their contributions to the *Rheinische Zeitung*. Many of their contributions were blue-pencilled by the censor, but as Marx declared in a letter to Ruge : " I permitted myself to dispose of at least as many. Meyen and his satellites sent us piles of world-uprooting scribblings, empty of ideas and written in a slovenly style, the whole tinged with a little atheism and communism (which the gentlemen have never bothered to study). Owing to Rutenberg's complete lack of any critical faculty, independence or capacity, they had grown used to regarding the *Rheinische Zeitung* as their complaisant tool, but I had no intention of letting that sort of thing go on." This was the first reason why " the Berlin horizon became over-clouded ", as Marx put it.

The breach came in November 1842 when Herwegh and Ruge paid a visit to Berlin. At that time Herwegh was on his triumphant career through Germany, and in Cologne he had quickly made friends with Marx. In Dresden he met Ruge and went on with him to Berlin where they were naturally unable to find any virtue in the antics of the " Freemen ". Ruge came to grips with his collaborator Bruno Bauer, because, as he pointed out, the latter wanted him to agree to " the most absurd things ", for instance that the State, private property and the family must be dissolved as conceptions without bothering about the practical side of the question at all. Herwegh disapproved equally strongly of the " Freemen " and they revenged themselves for his disdain by slating him in their usual fashion in connection with his audience with the King and his engagement to a rich girl.

Both parties appealed to the *Rheinische Zeitung*. In agreement with Ruge, Herwegh asked for the publication of a statement to the effect that although the "Freemen" were quite excellent as individuals, their political romanticism, their megalomania and their itch for self-advertisement compromised the cause and the party of freedom, as both Herwegh and Ruge had told them frankly. Marx published this statement and was then bombarded with impolite letters from Meyen who had made himself the mouthpiece of the "Freemen".

In the beginning Marx answered these letters coolly and objectively in an endeavour to secure fruitful co-operation with the "Freemen": "I demanded less vague complainings, fewer fine-sounding phrases, less self-adulation and rather more concreteness, a more detailed treatment of actual conditions and a display of greater practical knowledge of the subjects dealt with. I told them that in my opinion it was not right, that it was even immoral, to smuggle communist and socialist dogmas, i.e. an entirely new way of looking at the world, into casual dramatic criticisms, etc., and that if communism were to be discussed at all then it must be done in quite a different fashion and thoroughly. I also asked them to criticize religion by criticizing political conditions rather than the other way about, as this would be more in accordance with the character of a newspaper and the necessity for educating our public, because religion, quite empty in itself, lives from earth and not from heaven and will disappear on its own once the inverted reality whose theory it represents is dissolved. And finally I told them that if they wanted to deal with philosophy they should flirt less with the idea of atheism (which is reminiscent of those children who loudly inform anyone who cares to listen that they are not afraid of the bogyman) and do more to acquaint the people with its meaning." These remarks afford us an instructive glance at the principles according to which Marx edited the *Rheinische Zeitung*.

However, before this advice reached those for whom it was intended, Marx received "an insolent letter" from Meyen in which the latter demanded no more and no less than that the paper should stop "temporizing" and "go the limit", in other words, that it should challenge suppression for the sake of the "Freemen". At this Marx became impatient and wrote to Ruge: "All this shows a terrible degree of vanity. They are quite unable to realize that in order to save a political organ we should be quite prepared to abandon some of the Berlin gasbaggery which deals with nothing but its own clique concerns. . . . Day after day we have to put up with the chicanery of the censorship, ministerial letters, complaints from the provincial governor, wails from the Diet, protests from the shareholders, etc., etc., and as I am sticking to my post only because I feel it my duty to foil the intentions of the despots as far as possible, you can imagine that I was rather irritated by this letter and I have sent Meyen a pretty sharp reply."

In fact, this represented the final breach between Marx and the " Freemen ", almost all of whom came to a more or less woeful political end, from Bruno Bauer who later worked on the *Kreuz-Zeitung* and the *Post*, to Eduard Meyen who ended his days as the editor of the *Danziger Zeitung* and characterized his wasted life with the dismal joke that he was now permitted to ridicule only the Protestant orthod-" oxen " because the liberal owner of his paper had forbidden him to criticize the Papal syllabus out of consideration for his Catholic readers. Others of the circle found a shelter in the semi-official and even the official press. Rutenberg, for instance, died a few decades later as editor of the *Preussischer Staats-Anzeiger*.

However, at that time, in the autumn of 1842, Rutenberg was a much-feared man and the government demanded his removal from the *Rheinische Zeitung*. Throughout the summer the government had done its best to make life a nuisance for the paper, but it had spared it in the hope that it would die of its own accord. On the 8th of August the governor of the Rhineland, von Schaper, reported to Berlin that the paper had only 885 subscribers, but on the 15th of October Marx took over the editorship and on the 10th of November von Schaper was compelled to report that the number of subscribers was steadily increasing, it having risen from 885 to 1,820, and that the tendency of the paper was becoming more and more insolent and hostile. To make matters worse the *Rheinische Zeitung* obtained a copy of a marriage Bill of an extremely reactionary nature and published its contents before the authorities were ready for it. This greatly embittered the King because the Bill aimed at making divorce more difficult and was thus certain of strenuous opposition amongst the masses of the people, and he therefore demanded that the paper should be threatened with immediate suppression unless it revealed the name of the person who had provided it with the draft. However, the King's Ministers were unwilling to place the crown of martyrdom on the brow of the *Rheinische Zeitung*, for they knew very well that such a degrading proposal would be rejected immediately it was made, and they therefore contented themselves with demanding the removal of Rutenberg and the appointment of a responsible editor to sign for the paper in place of the publisher Renard. At the same time an assessor named Wiethaus was appointed censor in place of Dolleschall, whose utter stupidity had brought him into bad odour.

On the 30th of November Marx reported to Ruge : " Owing to the colossal stupidity of our State dispensation Rutenberg, who had already been deprived of the German article (his work on it consisted chiefly in correcting the punctuation) and was given the French article only at my intervention, is regarded as dangerous, although he is dangerous to nothing and no one apart from the *Rheinische Zeitung* and himself. Still, his removal was demanded categorically. The Prussian dispensation, this *despotisme prussien, le plus hypocrite, le plus fourbe*, has spared the guarantor (Renard) an unpleasant experience, and the new martyr, who is already an adept in the physiognomy, carriage and language of his new role, is exploiting the occasion to the full. He is writing everywhere, including Berlin, declaring that he represents the exiled principle of the *Rheinische Zeitung* and that the latter is now about to revise its attitude towards the government." Marx mentions the incident because it aggravated his quarrel with the Berlin " Freemen ", but it would appear almost as though he went a little too far in his mockery of the poor devil, the " martyr " Rutenberg.

Marx's observation that the government had " categorically " demanded the removal of Rutenberg and that the guarantor Renard had thereby been spared an unpleasant experience can only mean that the *Rheinische Zeitung* gave way to the pressure exerted by the government and that it made no attempt to keep Rutenberg. In any case, such an attempt would have been hopeless and in addition there was every reason to spare the publisher " an unpleasant experience ", i.e. an examination by the police and the drawing up of a protocol, an ordeal which the absolutely unpolitical man was quite unsuited to stand. However, he signed a written protest against the threat to suppress the paper, but the handwriting of the document (which is now in the town archives of Cologne) shows that it was drawn up by Marx.

It announces that, " giving way to force ", the *Rheinische Zeitung* agrees to the temporary removal of Rutenberg and to the appointment of a responsible editor. It also assures the authorities that the *Rheinische Zeitung* will gladly do everything reconcilable with the character of an independent newspaper to save itself from suppression, and that it is prepared to moderate the form of its articles in so far as the subject matter may permit. This document is drawn up with a diplomatic caution of which the life of its author offers no second example, but it would be unfair to weigh scrupulously every word of it and equally unfair to say that the young Marx did any noticeable violence to his convictions at the time even when he referred to the pro-Prussian attitude of the paper. Apart from its polemical articles against the anti-Prussian tendencies of the *Allgemeine Zeitung* in Augsburg, and its agitation in favour of the extension of the *Zollverein* to North-Western Germany, its Prussian sympathies had expressed themselves chiefly in repeated references to North German science as against the superficiality of French and South German theories. Marx also points out in this document that the *Rheinische Zeitung* was the first " Rhenish and South German newspaper " to introduce the North German spirit into the South, thus contributing to the intellectual unification of the separated branches of the German people.

The answer of the governor of the Rhineland, von Schaper, to this address was somewhat ungracious : even if Rutenberg were dismissed immediately and a thoroughly suitable editor named it would still depend on the future conduct of the paper whether it would be granted a definite concession or not. However, the paper was granted until the 12th of December to appoint a responsible editor, though things did not progress as far as that, for in the middle of December a new cause for dissension arose. Two articles from a correspondent in Berncastel concerning the impoverished situation of the Mosel peasants caused von Schaper to send in two corrections which were as empty of content as they were formally ill-mannered in style. For the moment the *Rheinische Zeitung* again made the best of a bad job and praised the " calm dignity " of von Schaper's corrections, declaring that they put the agents of the secret police to shame and were calculated " as much to dissolve mistrust as to restore confidence ", but when it had collected sufficient material it published five articles, beginning in the middle of January, containing a mass of documentary evidence showing that the government had stifled the complaints of the Mosel peasants with brutal severity. The highest government official in the Rhineland was thus exposed to general ridicule, but he had the agreeable consolation of know ing that on the 21st of January 1843 the Cabinet had decided, in the presence of the King, that the paper should be suppressed.

Towards the close of the previous year a number of happenings had angered the King : a sentimentally defiant letter which Herwegh had addressed to him from Königsberg and which the *Allgemeine Zeitung* in Leipzig had published without the knowledge of the author ; the acquittal of Johann Jacoby by the Supreme Court on charges of high treason and lèse-majesté ; and finally the New Year's proclamation of the *Deutsche Jahrbücher* in favour of " Democracy with all its practical problems ". The

Deutsche Jahrbücher was immediately suppressed and the *Allgemeine Zeitung* also as far as Prussian territory was concerned, and the " sister harlot on the Rhine " was to be suppressed in the general clear up, particularly as it had still further irritated the authorities by publishing an indignant protest against the suppression of the other two publications.

The formal pretext for the suppression of the *Rheinische Zeitung* was the alleged lack of an official concession—" As though it could have appeared in Prussia for a single day without official permission when not even a dog can exist without a government licence ", as Marx exclaimed. The supplementary and " objective " reason was the usual babble about its nefarious tendency—" The old stuff and nonsense about its ill-will, its empty theorizing, diddledumdey, etc.," as Marx declared contemptuously. Out of consideration for its shareholders the paper was permitted to appear until the end of the quarter. Writing to Ruge, Marx declared : " During our gallows respite we are under double censorship. Our real censor, a very decent fellow, is himself under the censorship of the Provincial President von Gerlach, a passive and obedient blockhead. When it is ready for print the paper must be thrust under the noses of the police and if they think they can smell anything un-Christian or un-Prussian then the paper may not appear."

Assessor Wiethaus showed spirit and decency enough to give up his post as censor and for this action he was honoured with a serenade by the Cologne Choral Society. Ministerial Secretary Saint-Paul was then sent from Berlin to take his place and this man did the garrotting so thoroughly that the double censorship was withdrawn on the 18th of February.

The suppression of the paper was felt as a personal insult by the whole population of the Rhineland and the number of subscribers jumped to 3,200 whilst petitions with thousands of signatures were sent to Berlin in an attempt to ward off the final blow. A deputation from the shareholders went to Berlin in order to see the King, but they were not permitted an audience, the petitions from the populace wandered into the waste-paper baskets of government offices and those officials who had signed them were severely reprimanded. However, much worse was the fact that the shareholders were inclined to demand that the policy of the paper should be toned down in the hope that this would prove successful where their appeals had failed, and it was chiefly this circumstance which caused Marx to resign his post as editor on the 17th of March, though naturally, this did not prevent him giving the censorship as much trouble as possible up to the last moment.

The new censor, Saint-Paul, was a youthful Bohemian. In Berlin he had caroused with the " Freemen " and in Cologne he was soon mixed up in affrays with night watchmen outside the brothels. However, he was a cunning fellow and he soon discovered the " doctrinaire centre " of the *Rheinische Zeitung* and " the living source " of its theories. In his reports to Berlin he speaks with involuntary respect of Marx, whose character and intellect obviously made a deep impression on him despite " the great speculative errors " which he thought he discovered in Marx's views. On the 2nd of March he was able to report to Berlin that " under the existing circumstances " Marx had decided to sever his connection with the *Rheinische Zeitung* and to leave Prussia. This report caused the Berlin wiseacres to make a note in their records to the effect that it would be no loss if Marx emigrated because his " ultra-democratic opinions are in utter contradiction to the principles of the Prussian State ", a statement which it would be difficult to dispute. On the 18th of March the worthy Saint-Paul then sent a triumphant report to Berlin : " The *spiritus rector* of the whole undertaking, Dr. Marx, definitely retired yesterday, and Oppenheim, on the whole a really moderate though insignificant man, took over the editorship. . . . I am very pleased at this and to-day I had to spend hardly a quarter of the usual time on the censorship." The censor then paid the departing Marx the flattering compliment of suggestion to Berlin that in view of Marx's retirement the *Rheinische Zeitung* might now be permitted to continue publication. However, his masters displayed even greater cowardice than he did, for they instructed him to bribe the editor of the *Kölnische Zeitung*, a certain Hermes, and to intimidate its publishers, who had been made to realize by the *Rheinische Zeitung* that dangerous competition was possible, and the underhand trick was successful.

As early as the 25th of January, the day on which the decision to suppress the *Rheinische Zeitung* had become known in Cologne, Marx wrote to Ruge : " I was not surprised. You know what I thought about the censorship instructions from the beginning. What has now happened I consider nothing but a logical consequence. I regard the suppression of the *Rheinische Zeitung* as an indication of the progress of political consciousness and I am therefore resigning. In any case, the atmosphere was becoming too oppressive for me. It is a bad thing to work in servitude and to fight with pinpricks instead of with the sword even in the cause of freedom. I am tired of the hypocrisy, the stupidity and the brutality of the authorities and of our submissiveness, pliancy, evasiveness and hair-splitting, and now the government

has given me back my freedom. . . . There is nothing more
I can do in Germany. One debases oneself here."

8. Ludwig Feuerbach

In the same letter Marx acknowledges the receipt of the
collection to which he had given his political first-born. This
collection appeared in two volumes under the title, *Anekdota zur
neuesten deutschen Philosophie und Publizistik*, and it was published
in Zürich at the beginning of March 1843 by the Literarisches
Kontor which Julius Fröbel had made into an asylum for those
authors who had been compelled to flee the German censorship.

In this collection the Old Guard of the Young Hegelians took
the field once again, but its ranks were already wavering. In
the van was Ludwig Feuerbach, the daring thinker who had
already thrown the whole philosophy of Hegel on to the scrapheap, who had declared the " absolute idea " to be nothing
more than the deceased spirit of theology and thus a belief in
pure phantoms, who found all the secrets of philosophy resolved
in the contemplation of humanity and nature. The " Preliminary Theses on the Reform of Philosophy " which he
published in the *Anekdota* were a revelation for Marx also.

In later years Engels dated the great influence which Feuerbach exercised on Marx's intellectual development from *The
Essence of Christianity*, Feuerbach's most famous work, which was
published in 1841. Referring to " the liberating effect " of this
book Engels declared that one must have read it in order to
realize its effect : " The enthusiasm was general and we were
all followers of Feuerbach immediately ". However, Marx's
writings for the *Rheinische Zeitung* reveal no trace of Feuerbach's
influence, and although Marx did, in fact, " enthusiastically
welcome " the new ideas, whilst making one or two critical
reservations, this was not until February 1844, when the *Deutsch-
Französische Jahrbücher* appeared and indicated even in its title
a certain relation to Feuerbach's ideas.

The ideas of the " Preliminary Theses " are already contained
in germ in *The Essence of Christianity* and therefore the trick
which Engels' memory played him would seem to be of very
little importance, but it is in reality not quite so unimportant
because it tends to misrepresent the intellectual relations between
Feuerbach and Marx. Feuerbach was only at ease in rural
seclusion, but he was no less a fighter on that account. With

Galileo he regarded the town as a prison for speculative minds, whilst in the freedom of rural life the book of nature was open to the eyes of anyone with sufficient intelligence to read it. This was always Feuerbach's defence against all the reproaches directed against him on account of the secluded life he led in Bruckberg. He loved rural seclusion, not in the sense of the old minatory maxim that he is fortunate who lives in obscurity, but because in seclusion he found the strength necessary to carry on the fight. It was the need of the thinker to compose his thoughts in peace away from the noise and bustle of the town which might have distracted him from the contemplation of nature which he regarded as the great source of all life and of all its secrets.

Despite the rural seclusion in which he lived, Feuerbach was in the forefront of the great struggles of his day. His contributions had given Ruge's publications their point and trenchancy. In his *Essence of Christianity* he pointed out that man makes religion and not religion man, and that the higher being which man's fantasy creates is nothing but the fantastic reflection of his own being. However, just at the time when this book was published Marx had turned his attention to the political struggle and it led him right into the hurly-burly of public life, as far as it was possible to speak of such a thing in Germany, and the weapons which Feuerbach had forged in his writings were not suited to such surroundings. The Hegelian philosophy had already proved itself incapable of solving the material problems which had arisen during Marx's work on the *Rheinische Zeitung*, when the " Preliminary Theses on the Reform of Philosophy " appeared and gave Hegelian philosophy the *coup de grâce* as the last refuge and the last rational prop of theology. The work, therefore, deeply impressed Marx, although he immediately made critical reservations.

Writing to Ruge on the 13th of March he declared : " Feuerbach's aphorisms are not to my liking in one point only, namely, that they concern themselves too much with nature and too little with politics, although an alliance with politics is the only way in which contemporary philosophy can become truth, but I suppose it will be the same as in the sixteenth century when the nature enthusiasts were faced with another set of State enthusiasts." Marx's objection was reasonable enough, for in his " Preliminary Theses " Feuerbach mentioned politics only once, and even then his attitude represented rather a retrogression from Hegel than an advance on him. The upshot was that Marx determined to examine Hegel's philosophy of law and the State as thoroughly as Feuerbach had examined his philosophy of nature and religion.

Another passage in this letter to Ruge reveals how strongly Marx was under Feuerbach's influence at the time. As soon as he had realized that he could not write under Prussian censorship and that the air of Prussia was altogether too oppressive, Marx had decided to leave Germany, but not without his future wife. On the 25th of January he had written to Ruge inquiring whether it would be possible for him to find something to do on the *Deutscher Bote* which Herwegh intended to publish in Zürich. However, owing to his own expulsion from Zürich Herwegh had been unable to carry out his plan. Ruge had then made other proposals, including the joint editorship of the re-named *Jahrbücher*, suggesting that when his " editorial purgatory " in Cologne was at an end Marx should come to Leipzig to discuss " the place of our resurrection ".

In his letter of the 13th of March Marx agreed in principle, but expressed his " provisional opinion on our plan " as follows : " After the fall of Paris some proposed that the son of Napoleon should be made Regent, whilst others suggested Bernadotte as the ruler of France, whilst still others were in favour of Louis Philippe. But Talleyrand answered : either Louis XVIII or Napoleon. That would be a matter of principle, anything else would be intrigue. And I should call everything with the exception of Strassburg (and perhaps Switzerland) an intrigue and not a matter of principle. Voluminous books are not for the people and the best we can do is to issue a monthly. Even if the *Deutsche Jahrbücher* was permitted to appear again the utmost we could manage would be a feeble imitation of the late lamented and that is not enough to-day. The *Deutsch-Französische Jahrbücher*, on the other hand, that would be a matter of principle, an event of consequence, an undertaking to inspire enthusiasm."

In this letter one can hear the echo of Feuerbach's " Preliminary Theses " in which he declares that a real philosophy in harmony with life and humanity must be of Gallo-Germanic origin. The heart must be French and the head German. The head must reform and the heart revolutionize. Only where there was movement, emotion, passion, blood and feeling could there be any spirit. Only the spirit of Leibniz with his sanguinary materialist-idealist principle had rescued the Germans from their pedantry and scholasticism.

Replying to Marx's letter on the 19th of March Ruge declared himself in complete agreement with the " Gallo-Germanic principle ", but the settlement of the business side of the arrangements took up a few further months.

9. Marriage and Banishment

During the lively years of his first public struggles Marx also had to contend with a number of domestic difficulties. He always referred to them unwillingly and only when unpleasant necessity compelled him to. In direct contrast with the pitiful lot of the Philistine who can forget God and the world in his own petty troubles, it had been given to Marx to raise himself above his bitterest troubles in " the great affairs of mankind ". Unfortunately his life offered him all too frequent opportunity for exercising this power.

We find his attitude to such matters expressed in a very characteristic fashion in the first utterance concerning his " paltry private affairs " which has come down to us. Writing to Ruge on the 9th of July 1842 to excuse himself for not having sent in the contributions he had promised for the *Anekdota* he mentions a number of difficulties and then declares : " The remaining time was wasted and upset by the most unpleasant family controversies. Although quite well off, my family has put difficulties in my way which have temporarily placed me in most embarrassing circumstances. I cannot possibly bother you with a description of these paltry private affairs and it is really fortunate that the state of our public affairs makes it impossible for any man of character to let his private troubles irritate him." This is one of the many indications of that unusual strength of character which has always enraged the Philistines with their " irritability in matters private " against the " heartless " Marx.

No details have become known about these " most unpleasant family controversies ", and Marx referred to them again only on one occasion and even then only very generally when the *Deutsch-Französische Jahrbücher* was about to be launched. Writing to Ruge he declared that as soon as their plans had taken on a more definite form he would go to Kreuznach, where the mother of his future wife had gone to live after the death of her husband, get married there and spend some time in the house of his mother-in-law " because we must have a certain amount of material ready before we start work. . . . I can assure you without any romanticism that I am head over heels and in all seriousness in love. We have been engaged now for over seven years and my future wife has had to fight hard struggles on my behalf partly against her pious aristocratic relatives who regard their ' Father in Heaven ' and the government in Berlin as equal objects of veneration, and partly against my own family in which a number of parsonical individuals and other enemies of mine have got a hold, and these struggles have almost undermined her health.

For years, therefore, my future wife and I have been compelled to engage in unnecessary and exhausting conflicts, more so in fact than many people three times our age who are always talking about their ' experience of life '." Apart from these rather vague indications we know nothing of the difficulties of the engagement period.

Not without trouble, but comparatively quickly, the arrangements for the issue of the new publication were made without Marx having to go to Leipzig. After Ruge, who was well-to-do, had declared himself ready to put up 6,000 thaler [1] as a shareholder in the *Literarisches Kontor*, Fröbel agreed to undertake the publishing. Marx was promised a salary of 500 thaler as editor and with these prospects he married his Jenny on the 19th of June 1843.

It still remained to decide where the *Deutsch-Französische Jahrbücher* should be published, and the choice was between Brussels, Paris and Strassburg. The young pair would have preferred the Alsatian capital, but finally the decision was taken in favour of Paris after both Ruge and Fröbel had visited Paris and Brussels and made various inquiries. In Brussels the press had more elbow room than in Paris with its provision for the deposit of securities and its September laws, but the French capital was in closer touch with German life, and Ruge wrote encouragingly that with 3,000 francs or perhaps a little more Marx would be able to live quite comfortably there.

In accordance with his plans Marx spent the first few months of his married life in the house of his mother-in-law, and in November he moved his young household to Paris. The last documentary evidence of his early life in Germany is a letter written to Feuerbach on the 23rd of October 1843 asking him for a contribution to the first issue of the new *Jahrbücher*, preferably a criticism of Schelling : " I feel myself almost justified in assuming from your introduction to the second edition of *The Essence of Christianity* that you have something in store for this windbag. That would be a fine début, don't you think ? How cleverly Herr Schelling has succeeded in deceiving the French : first the feeble and eclectic Cousin, and later on even the brilliant Leroux. Pierre Leroux and his associates still regard Schelling as the man who put reasonable realism in the place of transcendental idealism, ideas of flesh and blood in the place of abstract ideas, world philosophy in the place of formal philosophy. . . . You would therefore render our publication a great service and the cause of truth a still greater one if you gave us a characterization of Schelling for our first issue. You are just the man for the

---

[1] Thaler : a three-mark piece.—Tr.

job because you are the exact opposite of Schelling. As far as Schelling is concerned the honest ideas of his youth—we are entitled to believe the best of our opponents—for whose realization he had no other means but imagination, no other energy but vanity, no other motive force but opium, no other organ but the irritability of an effeminate receptive capacity, have never been anything more than a fantastic youthful dream, but in you they have become truth, reality and manly gravity. . . . I regard you therefore as the necessary and natural opponent of Schelling, appointed by the twin powers of nature and history." How amiable is the tone of this letter and at the same time how delighted is its author at the prospect of a great struggle !

But Feuerbach hesitated. He had already praised the venture to Ruge and then refused to assist it. Even an appeal to his " Gallo-Germanic principle " had not moved him. It had been his writings which had chiefly aroused the ire of the authorities and caused them to bludgeon out of existence what still remained of philosophic freedom in Germany, thus compelling the philosophical opposition to leave the country unless it was prepared to capitulate miserably.

Feuerbach himself was not the man to capitulate, but at the same time he was unable to summon up sufficient courage to plunge into the breakers which surged around the dead land of Germany. Feuerbach's reply to the fiery words with which Marx sought to win him was friendly and interested, but it was nevertheless a refusal. It was a black day in his life and from then on his isolation gradually became an intellectual one also.

CHAPTER THREE: EXILE IN PARIS

1. The *Deutsch-Französische Jahrbücher*

THE new publication was not born under a lucky star. A double volume was published at the end of February 1844. It was the first number and also the last.

It proved impossible to realize the " Gallo-Germanic Principle ", or, as Ruge had renamed it, " the intellectual alliance between France and Germany ". The " political principle of France " showed no eagerness to accept Germany's contribution, the " logical acumen " of Hegelian philosophy, which was to serve it as a sure compass in the metaphysical regions in which Ruge saw the French drifting at the mercy of wind and wave.

Ruge intended to approach first Lamartine, Lamennais, Louis Blanc, Leroux and Proudhon, but even this preliminary list was mixed enough in all conscience. Only Leroux and Proudhon had any idea of German philosophy, and of these two one lived in the provinces whilst the other had temporarily abandoned writing in order to rack his brains over the invention of a linotype machine. The others, including even Louis Blanc, who regarded anarchism in politics as a development from atheism in philosophy, all refused to co-operate, advancing this or that religious objection.

On the other hand, however, the new publication collected an imposing array of German contributors : apart from the editors themselves there were Heine, Herwegh and Johann Jacoby, all names of the first magnitude, whilst in the second rank, Moses Hess and a young lawyer from the Palatinate named F. C. Bernays were men of consequence, not to mention the youngest contributor of all, Friedrich Engels, who, after various excursions into the field of authorship, now appeared in the arena for the first time in full armour and with raised visor. But even this German band was mixed. Some of them understood little of Hegelian philosophy and still less of its " logical acumen ", and, above all, disagreement between the two editors themselves soon arose and rendered further co-operation impossible. The double number, which was to prove its one and only issue, opened with " Correspondence " between Marx,

Ruge, Feuerbach and Bakunin, a young Russian who had attached himself to Ruge in Dresden and written a much-discussed contribution to the *Deutsche Jahrbücher*. This " Correspondence " consists of eight letters, each signed with the initials of its author, and showing us that three each were written by Marx and Ruge, and one each by Bakunin and Feuerbach. At a later date Ruge declared that the " Correspondence " was his work, though he had " used extracts from real letters here and there ". It is included in his collected works, but it is interesting to note that serious mutilations have been made and that the final letter, which is signed with the initials of Marx and contains the real point of the whole correspondence, has been suppressed. The contents of the letters leave no doubt that they are really the work of the authors whose initials they bear, and as far as they represent a uniform composition Marx plays the first fiddle in the concert, but it is not necessary to deny that Ruge may have tinkered with his own letters and those of Bakunin and Feuerbach.

Marx opened and closed the correspondence. His introduction is like a short and spirited fanfare. The romanticist reaction was leading to revolution. The State was much too serious a matter to be degraded to the level of a harlequinade. A shipload of fools might drift before the wind for quite a time before anything happened, but it would finally meet its doom just because the fools refused to believe it. Whereupon Ruge answered with a long jeremiad on the inexhaustible and sheeplike patience of the German Philistine. His contribution was " plaintive and hopeless " as he afterwards declared himself, or, as Marx replied immediately and more politely : " Your letter is a good elegy, a breath-robbing dirge, but it is not in the least political." If the world was the property of the Philistines then it was worth while studying these Lords of the World, although the Philistine was the Lord of the World only because, like the worms in a corpse, he filled the world with his society. So long as the Philistine was the material basis of the monarchy, the monarch himself could never be more than King of the Philistines. More wideawake and alive than his father, the new King of Prussia had attempted to dissolve the Philistine State on its own ground, but so long as the Philistines remained Philistines he would be able to make neither himself nor his subjects really free men. Thus the old petrified servile and slave State had returned, but even in this desperate situation there was new hope. Marx then pointed to the incompetence of the masters and the inertia of their servants and subjects, who let everything come and go as God pleased, and both things together were sufficient to bring about a catastrophe. He pointed to the enemies of Philistinism, all thinking and suffering men, who had come to an understanding. He pointed even to the perpetuation of the old servile system, which recruited new fighters every day in the cause of a newer humanity ; whilst the system of profits and trading, of property and the exploitation of humanity, was leading even more rapidly to a split within society, a split which the old system would be unable to repair because it did not heal and create, but only exist and enjoy. The task was therefore to drag the old world into the full light of day, and to develop the new world in a positive fashion.

Both Bakunin and Feuerbach wrote to Ruge encouragingly, each in his own way, whereupon the latter declared that he had been converted by " the new Anarchasis and the new philosophers ". Feuerbach compared the end of the *Deutsche Jahrbücher* with the end of Poland, declaring that the efforts of a few men must prove ineffective in the general quagmire of a rotten society, and Ruge then wrote to Marx : " As the Catholic faith and aristocratic freedom failed to save Poland, so theological philosophy and respectable science failed to save us. We can continue our career only by making a decisive breach with them. The *Jahrbücher* are dead and Hegelian philosophy belongs to the past. Let us strive for an organ in Paris in which we can criticize ourselves and Germany as a whole with complete freedom and relentless honesty."

Marx had the first word and he also had the last : Clearly, a new rallying-point must be created for thinking and independent brains. Although there was no doubt about the past, there was confusion enough about the future. " General anarchy has broken out amongst the reformers, and all of them would be compelled to admit that they have no exact ideas about the future. However, it is just the great advantage of the new movement that we do not seek to anticipate the new world dogmatically, but rather to discover it in the criticism of the old. Up to now the philosophers have always had the solution of the riddle lying ready in their writing desks, and all the stupid exoteric world had to do was to close its eyes and open its mouth to receive the ready-baked cake of absolute science. Philosophy has secularized itself, and the most striking proof of this is that the philosophic consciousness itself has been drawn into the heat of the fray not only superficially, but thoroughly. It is certainly not our task to build up the future in advance and to settle all problems for all time, but it is just as certainly our task to criticize the existing world ruthlessly. I mean ruthlessly in the sense that we must not be afraid of our own conclusions and equally unafraid of coming into conflict with the prevailing powers."

Marx had no desire to unfurl any dogmatic standard, and communism as preached by Cabet, Dézamy and Weitling he regarded as a dogmatic abstraction. Whether one liked it or not, the chief interest of contemporary Germany was in religion and only secondarily in politics. It was no use presenting them with a ready-made system such as was contained in *The Journey to Icaria*,[1] one must begin with them just as they were.

Marx condemned the attitude of the " crass socialists " who felt that political questions were beneath their dignity. Social truth could be arrived at everywhere from the contradiction in the political State, from the conflict between its ideal mission and its practical hypothesis. " There is therefore nothing to prevent us beginning our criticism with a criticism of politics, taking part in politics, that is to say, in real struggles. In this way we should avoid presenting ourselves to the world in a doctrinaire fashion and with a new principle, declaring : here is truth, bow down and worship it. We should develop new principles for the world out of its old principles. We must not say to the world : stop your quarrels, they are foolish, and listen to us, for we possess the real truth. Instead we must show the world why it struggles, and this consciousness is a thing it must acquire whether it likes it or not." Marx sums up the programme of the new organ as follows : to assist the age to come to a realization (critical philosophy) of its struggles and its wishes.

Marx came to this realization, but not Ruge. Even the " correspondence " shows that Marx was the driver and Ruge the driven. A supplementary factor was that after his arrival in Paris Ruge fell ill and was able to take very little part in the editorial work. He was thus unable to exercise his chief capacity to the full and Marx seemed to him to be " too circumstantial " for the purpose. He was unable to give the organ the form and the attitude which he considered the most suitable and he was even unable to publish a contribution of his own in it. However, he was not altogether displeased with the first issue, and he found " some quite remarkable things in it which will create a sensation in Germany ", although he complained that " a number of unpolished things " had been served up in a hurry and that he would have improved them. The undertaking would probably have continued to appear, but for the fact that a number of outside hindrances prevented it.

First of all, the funds of the *Literarisches Kontor* soon became exhausted and Fröbel declared that he could not carry on without more money ; and, secondly, the Prussian government took

[1] Etienne Cabet's Utopia.—Tr.

action immediately after the first announcement of the publication of the *Deutsch-Französische Jahrbücher*. It met with no particular sympathy from Metternich and still less from Guizot, and it had to content itself for the moment with informing the governors of all Prussian provinces that the *Jahrbücher* represented high treason and lèse-majesté, and this it did on the 18th April 1844. At the same time the governors were instructed to cause their police to arrest Ruge, Marx, Heine and Bernays with as little stir as possible and to confiscate their papers should they set foot on Prussian soil. As a hare must be caught before it can be jugged, this action was comparatively harmless, but the uneasy conscience of the King of Prussia became more dangerous when it caused him to instruct his subordinates to increase their vigilance at the frontiers. They succeeded in confiscating 100 copies of the *Deutsch-Französische Jahrbücher* on a Rhine steamer, and well over 200 copies on the French-Palatinate frontier near Bergzabern. In view of the very small circulation with which the publishers were entitled to reckon these were very grievous blows.

Where internal differences already exist they are readily embittered and accentuated by external difficulties. According to Ruge these circumstances accelerated his breach with Marx or even caused it, and there may be something in this because, whilst Marx always displayed a sovereign indifference in money matters, Ruge did just the contrary, displaying the suspicious avarice of a grocer. He did not hesitate to apply the truck system when paying out the salary agreed upon to Marx, presenting him with copies of the *Jahrbücher* in lieu of money, but he became really indignant at an alleged suggestion that he should risk his money in an attempt to proceed with the publication, pointing out that he had no knowledge of the book trade. In a similar situation Marx certainly risked his own money, but it is very unlikely that he proposed that Ruge should. Perhaps he advised Ruge not to throw down his arms at the first failure, and it is possible that Ruge, who had already been " angered " by a proposal that he should put up a few more francs to secure the publication of Weitling's works, suspected this advice to be a dangerous attack on his pocket-book.

Further, Ruge himself indicates the real reason for the breach when he admits that the immediate occasion was a quarrel about Herwegh, whom he had called " a rogue ", though " perhaps with rather too much emphasis ", whilst Marx had stressed Herwegh's " great future ". As a matter of fact, as far as Herwegh was concerned, Ruge was right ; the man had no " great future ", and the mode of life he was leading in Paris at the time would really seem to have been open to objection.

Even Heine condemned him sharply, whilst Ruge himself admits that Marx also was none too pleased with the man. In any case, the generous error of the " bitter " and " malignant " Marx did him more honour than the uncanny instinct of the " honest and irreproachable " Ruge did the latter, for Marx was concerned with the revolutionary poet whilst Ruge was thinking of petty-bourgeois morality.

This was the deeper significance of the insignificant incident which separated the two men for ever. The breach with Ruge did not possess the political significance of the later polemics with Bruno Bauer and Proudhon. As a revolutionary Marx had probably been annoyed with Ruge for a long time before the quarrel about Herwegh caused his bile to rise, even assuming that it all took place exactly as Ruge describes.

If one wishes to know Ruge from his best side one must read the memoirs which he published about twenty years later. The four volumes deal with his life up to the time when the *Deutsche Jahrbücher* ceased publication, that is to say, throughout a period when Ruge was an irreproachable example of that literary advance-guard of schoolmasters and students who spoke on behalf of a bourgeoisie which lived on small business and great illusions. They contain a wealth of charming *genre* pictures from Ruge's childhood spent on the lowlands of Rügen and Pomerania, and they give a description unique in German literature of the stirring times of the *Burschenschaften* and the Demagogue Hunt. Ruge's misfortune was that his memoirs appeared at a time when the German bourgeoisie was beginning to abandon its great illusions in favour of big business, and so his memoirs went almost without notice, whilst Reuter's *Festungstid*, a book incomparably inferior both historically and as literature, was received with storms of applause. Ruge had really been an active member of the *Burschenschaften* whereas Reuter had fallen in with them as a happy-go-lucky fellow who might just as easily have been anywhere else. However, the German bourgeoisie was already flirting with Prussian bayonets, and it much preferred Reuter's " golden humour " and the jocular manner in which he treated the infamous mockery of justice committed in the days of the Demagogue Hunt, to the " audacious humour ", to quote Freiligrath's appropriate words, with which Ruge described how his gaolers had failed to break his spirit and how he won inner-liberty during his imprisonment.

But even in the graphic descriptions of Ruge one feels keenly that pre-March liberalism was in the last resort nothing but Philistinism despite all its fine words, and that its spokesmen were Philistines and must remain so to the last. Ruge was the most high-spirited of them all and within his ideological limits he fought bravely enough, but the same temperament made his defection all the easier when in Paris he came face to face with the great contradictions of modern life.

He had reconciled himself with socialism as the hobby of philosophic philanthropists, but the communism of the Paris artisans filled him with panic-stricken horror and Philistine fear, not so much for his personal safety as for his pocket-book. In the *Deutsch-Französische Jahrbücher* he had signed the death-warrant of Hegelian philosophy with a flourish, but before the year was out he had welcomed its most grotesque successor, the philosophy of Stirner, as a champion against communism, which he regarded as the most stupid of all stupidities, as the new Christianity preached by the simple, as a system whose realization would mean the degeneration of human society into a farmyard.

The breach between Ruge and Marx became irreparable.

2. A Philosophic Perspective

The *Deutsch-Französische Jahrbücher* was therefore a still-born child. Once it became clear that its editors could not work together permanently, then it mattered little when and how they separated ; in fact, an early breach was preferable to a later one. It was enough that Marx himself should have taken a great step forward along the path to a clear view of things.

He published two contributions in the *Deutsch-Französische Jahrbücher* : an " Introduction to a Critique of the Hegelian Philosophy of Law ", and a notice of two books which Bruno Bauer had published on the Jewish question. Despite the different matter with which these two contributions deal, they are very closely connected in ideological content. Later Marx summed up his criticism of the Hegelian philosophy of law in the declaration that the key to an understanding of historical development must be sought in society, which Hegel disdained, and not in the State, which he praised. In the second contribution he deals with this viewpoint in still greater detail than in the first.

From another angle the two contributions are related to each other as means and end. The first gives a philosophic outline of the proletarian class struggle, whilst the second gives a philosophic outline of socialist society. However, neither the one nor the other appeared like a bolt from the blue, and both indicate the intellectual development of their author in a strictly logical order. The first contribution proceeded directly from Feuerbach, who had completed the criticism of religion, the hypothesis of all criticism, in its essentials : man makes religion, religion does not make man.

But, begins Marx, man is not an abstract being existing outside the world. Man is the world of men, the State, society, a world which has produced religion as an inverted world consciousness because it is an inverted world. The struggle against religion is therefore indirectly the struggle against that world whose spiritual aroma is religion. Thus it becomes the task of history to establish the truth of contemporary reality after the supernality of truth has disappeared. The criticism of heaven thus turns into a criticism of earth, the criticism of religion into a criticism of law, the criticism of theology into a criticism of politics.

For Germany, however, this historical task can be performed only by philosophy. If one negatives the conditions in Germany in 1843 one finds oneself, according to French historical computation, hardly in the year 1789, still less in the focus of contemporary problems. If modern politico-social reality is to be subjected to criticism then criticism finds itself outside of German reality or it would fail to reach its real object. As an example of the fact that up to then German history had, like a clumsy recruit, only the task of performing the same old wearisome drill, Marx mentions " one of the chief problems of modern times ", the relation of industry, the relation of the world of wealth in general, to the political world.

This problem occupies the Germans in the form of protective tariffs, prohibitory duties, the system of national economy. The Germans are thus beginning where the English and the French are ending. The old and rotten conditions against which these latter countries are theoretically in rebellion and which they tolerate only as one tolerates chains, are being welcomed in Germany as the rising sun of a rosy future. Whilst in France and England the problem is " political economy or the dominance of society over wealth ", in Germany it is " national economy or the dominance of private property over nationality ". In the one case it is a question of resolving the knot, and in the other one of first tying it.

Although they are not historical contemporaries of other nations, the Germans are philosophic contemporaries. The criticism of the German philosophy of law and the State, which has received its most logical form in the hands of Hegel, leads directly into the centre of these burning questions of the day.

Marx then clearly defines his attitude both to the two tendencies which had existed side by side in the *Rheinische Zeitung* and to Feuerbach. Feuerbach had thrown philosophy on to the scrapheap, but if one wished to deal with really vital matters one must not forget, points out Marx, that up to the present the really vital life of the German people had flourished in its skull only. To " the cotton barons and iron magnates " he declares : you are quite right to demand the liquidation of philosophy, but you cannot liquidate it without first having realized it. And to his old friend Bruno Bauer and the latter's followers he declares on the contrary : you are quite right to demand the realization of philosophy, but you cannot realize it without first having liquidated it.

The criticism of the philosophy of law resolves itself into tasks for which there is only one means of solution—practice. How can Germany raise itself to a practical level *à la hauteur de principes*, that is to say, to a revolution which will not only raise it to the level of the modern peoples, but to that human level which will be the immediate future of these peoples ? How can it jump with a *salto mortale* not only over its own limitations, but at the same time over the limitations of the modern peoples, limitations which it must in reality feel to be an emancipation from its own limitations, and which it must itself seek to attain ?

The weapon of criticism can certainly not supplant the criticism of weapons. Material force must be overthrown by material force, but theory itself becomes a material force when it takes hold of the masses, and it does so immediately it becomes radical. However, a radical revolution needs a passive element, a material basis. Theory is realized in a people only in so far as it is the realization of its needs. It is not enough that the idea should press forward to realization, reality must urge itself to the idea. However, this would seem to be lacking in Germany where the various spheres of society are related not dramatically, but epically, where even the moral confidence of the middle class is based solely on the consciousness that it is the general representative of the Philistine mediocrity of all other classes, where each sphere of burgeois society suffers its defeat before it has celebrated its victory, and shows its narrow-mindedness before it has had a chance of showing its broad-mindedness, so that each class is involved in a struggle with the class below it before it can engage in a struggle with the class above it.

However, this does not prove that the radical revolution, general human emancipation, is impossible in Germany, but only that the merely political revolution, the revolution which would leave the pillars of the house standing, is impossible.

The preliminary conditions for such a political revolution are lacking in Germany : on the one hand a class which undertakes the general emancipation of society from its own particular situation, but only on condition that the whole of society finds itself in the same situation as this class, i.e. that it possesses, for instance, money or education, or can obtain them at its pleasure. And on the other hand a class in which all the defects of society are concentrated, a particular social sphere which is held responsible for the notorious crime of the whole of society, so that emancipation from this class appears as the general self-emancipation of society. The negative-general significance of the French aristocracy and the French clergy conditioned the positive-general significance of the immediately contiguous and opposing class, the bourgeoisie.

From the impossibility of a half-revolution Marx concludes the possibility of a radical revolution. Asking where this possibility exists, he answers : " In the formation of a class with radical chains ; a class of bourgeois society which is not a class of bourgeois society ; a class which is the dissolution of all classes ; a sphere of society which has a universal character as a result of its universal suffering ; a sphere which demands no particular right, because no particular wrong has been done to it, but wrong as such ; a sphere which can no longer appeal to a historical title, but to a human title only ; a sphere which does not stand in a one-sided contradiction to the consequences, but in a general and all-round contradiction to the very hypo- theses of the German State ; and finally, a sphere which cannot emancipate itself without at the same time emancipating itself from all other spheres of society and thus emancipating all other spheres of society also ; a class which, in a word, represents the complete loss of humanity and can therefore win itself only through the complete re-winning of humanity. This dissolu- tion of society is the proletariat." This class began to develop in Germany as a result of the industrial movement which swept over the country, for it was formed not by poverty of natural origin, but poverty artificially produced, not by the mass of human beings mechanically oppressed by the weight of society, but by the mass of human beings resulting from the acute dis- solution of society, and chiefly from the dissolution of the middle classes, although gradually and as a matter of course natural poverty and Christian-Germanic serfdom entered its ranks.

As philosophy finds its material weapons in the proletariat, so the proletariat finds its intellectual weapons in philosophy, and as soon as the lightning of thought has struck deep into the mass of the common people, the emancipation of the Germans into human beings will take place. The emancipation of the German is the emancipation of man. Philosophy cannot be realized without the liquidation of the proletariat; the proletariat cannot liquidate itself without realizing philosophy. When all the inner conditions have been fulfilled the day of German resurrection will be announced by the crowing of the Gallic chanticleer.

Judged both by its form and its content, this article is in the front rank of all those youthful writings of Marx which have been preserved. A short sketch of the basic ideas contained in it cannot give even an approximate idea of the overflowing richness of thought which Marx disciplines in such an epigrammatic and concise form, and those German professors who found its style grotesque and its manner in appalling taste have thereby borne inglorious testimony against themselves. However, even Ruge found its " epigrams " " too artificial ". He criticized its " formlessness and super-form ", but discovered in it " a critical talent developing into dialectic, but occasionally degenerating into arrogance ". This is not unfair criticism, for the youthful Marx sometimes exulted in the mere swish of his sword through the air, though in action it proved sharp and heavy enough. Arrogance is the dowry of all talented youth.

However, the philosophic perspective into the future which this article opens up is still a far-off one. No one has proved more conclusively than the later Marx that no nation can spring with a *salto mortale* over the necessary stages of its historical development, but the shadowy perspectives he sketched in this article were not incorrect. In detail many things have come about differently, but on the whole they have come about as he prophesied. Both the history of the German bourgeoisie and that of the German proletariat are his vindication.

3. *On the Jewish Question*

The second contribution which Marx published in the *Deutsch-Französische Jahrbücher* is not so arresting in its form, but in the power of critical analysis it displays it is almost superior. In this second contribution he examines the difference between human emancipation and political emancipation on the basis of two treatises on the Jewish question written by Bruno Bauer.

At that time the question had not sunk so deeply into the morass of anti-semitic and philo-semitic badgering. A class of society which was increasing its power as one of the most prominent representatives of mercantile and loan capital was deprived of all civil rights on account of its religion, with the exception of those special privileges it enjoyed as a result of its usurious practices. The most famous representative of " enlightened absolutism ", the philosopher of Sans Souci, Frederick the Great, gave the world an edifying object-lesson by granting " the liberty of Christian bankers " to those moneyed Jews who assisted him in his coining forgeries and other doubtful financial operations, whilst tolerating the presence of the philosopher Moses Mendelssohn within his territory not because the latter was a philosopher and strove to guide his " nation " into the intellectual life of Germany, but because he occupied the post of book-keeper to one of the privileged and moneyed Jews. His dismissal by his master would have deprived him of all rights.

With one or two exceptions, even the pioneers of the bourgeois enlightenment movement displayed no particular objection to the proscription of a whole section of the population merely on account of its religion. The Israelitic religion was repugnant to them because it was the prototype of religious intolerance from which Christianity had first learnt its " human censoriousness ", whilst on the other hand the Jews showed no interest whatever in the bourgeois enlightenment movement. The Jews were delighted when enlightened criticism took the Christian religion to task, for they had themselves always cursed it, but when the same criticism turned its attention to the Jewish religion they howled aloud as though humanity were being betrayed. The Jews demanded political emancipation for Judaism, but not in the sense of equal rights for all and with the intention of abandoning their own special position, but rather with the intention of consolidating that special position ; and all the time they were prepared to abandon liberal principles the moment they came into conflict with any specifically Jewish interest.

The criticism of religion conducted by the Young Hegelians naturally extended to the Jewish religion, which they regarded as a preliminary stage of Christianity. Feuerbach had analysed Judaism as the religion of egoism : " The Jews have maintained their special peculiarities down to the present day. Their principle, their God, is the practical principle of the world— egoism in the form of religion. Egoism centres and concentrates man upon himself, but at the same time it limits his theoretical outlook because he is indifferent to everything which is not directly related to his own welfare." Bruno Bauer said much the same thing, declaring that the Jews had crawled into the nooks and crannies of bourgeois society to exploit its uncertain elements like the Gods of Epicurus who lived in the interstices of the world where they were freed from certain labour. The religion of the Jews was animal cunning and trickery, and with it they satisfied their sensual needs. They had always opposed historical progress and in their hatred of all other peoples they had cut themselves off from the world and lived the most overweening and circumscribed life.

Feuerbach explained the character of the Jewish religion from the character of the Jew, whilst despite the thoroughness, daring and trenchancy of his treatises on the Jewish question, which earned high praise from Marx, Bauer saw the question exclusively through theological spectacles. Like the Christians, he declared, the Jews could win through to freedom only by overcoming their religion. Owing to its own religious character the Christian State was unable to emancipate the Jews, whilst at the same time the Jews could not be emancipated owing to their own religious character. Christians and Jews must cease to be Christians and Jews if they wished to be free. However, as Judaism as a religion had been superseded by Christianity, the Jew had a longer and more difficult path to traverse than the Christian before he could win freedom. In Bauer's opinion the Jew must first take a course in Christianity and Hegelian philosophy before he could hope to emancipate himself.

At this point Marx intervened, declaring that it was not enough to ask who was to emancipate and who was to be emancipated. Criticism must go further and ask what kind of emancipation was in question, political emancipation or human emancipation. In certain States both Christians and Jews were completely emancipated politically without thereby being humanly emancipated. There must therefore be some difference between political emancipation and human emancipation.

The essence of political emancipation was the highly developed modern State and this State was also the fully developed Christian State, for the Christian-Germanic State, the State of privileges, was only the incomplete, the still theological State as yet undeveloped in all its political clarity. However, the political State in the highest stages of its development did not demand the abandonment of Judaism by the Jews or the abandonment of religion in general by humanity as a whole. It had emancipated the Jews and its very character had compelled it to do so. Even where the State Constitution expressly declared the exercise of political rights to be completely independent of religious beliefs, the citizens of that State nevertheless refused to believe that a man without religion could be a decent man and a good citizen. Thus the existence of religion was not in any way in contradiction to the full development of the State. The political emancipation of the Jew, of the Christian, of the religious man in general, was the emancipation of the State from Judaism, Christianity and religion in general. The State could free itself from a hindrance without the human being in the State really being free of that hindrance, and here lay the limit of political emancipation.

Marx then develops this idea still further. The State as a State negatived private property. The human being liquidated private property in a political fashion immediately he abolished the property qualification for active and passive franchise, as had been done in many of the North American States. The State liquidated differences in birth, social standing, education and occupation in its own way when it declared differences of birth, social standing, education and occupation to be unpolitical differences, and when, regardless of such differences, it declared every member of the body politic to be an equal participant in the sovereignty of the people. Nevertheless, the State permitted private property, education and occupation to operate in their own fashion and to make their own particular character felt, that is to say, as private property, education and occupation. Far from abolishing these actual differences, the existence of the State rather presupposed their existence. It regarded itself purely as a political State and made its universality felt in contradiction to these its constituent elements.

The fully developed political State was essentially the social life of humanity as opposed to its material life. All the hypotheses of this egoistic life remained in existence outside the State sphere in bourgeois society and as attributes of bourgeois society. The relation of the political State to its own hypotheses, whether they are material elements such as private property, or ideological elements such as religion, was the antagonism between public interests and private interests. The conflict in which the human being as the adherent of a particular religion found himself with his State citizenship and with other men as members of the community, reduced itself to the cleavage between the political State and bourgeois society.

Bourgeois society is the basis of the modern State as classical slavery was the basis of the classical State. The modern State recognized its origins with the proclamation of the general rights of man, whose enjoyment is as much open to the Jews as the exercise of political rights. The general rights of man recognize the egoistic bourgeois individual and the untrammelled movement of the intellectual and material elements which make up the content of his life and the content of contemporary bourgeois life. They do not free man from religion, but give him religious freedom. They do not free him from property, but give him the freedom of property. They do not free him from the indignity of trading, but give him freedom to trade. The political revolution created bourgeois society by destroying the patchwork system of feudalism and all the corporations, guilds and associations which were so many expressions of the separation of the people from the commonwealth. It created the political State as the concern of all, as a real State.

Marx then sums up : " Political emancipation is the reduction of man to a member of bourgeois society, the egoistic independent individual, on the one hand, and to a citizen of the State, a moral being, on the other. Only when the real, individual man takes back the abstract citizen of the State into himself and becomes a social being as an individual man in his empirical life, in his individual work and in his individual conditions, only when man recognizes and organizes his *forces propres* as social forces and, therefore, no longer separates the social force from himself in the form of political force, only then will the emancipation of humanity be completed."

The contention that the Christian as such was more capable of emancipation than the Jew, a contention which Bauer sought to prove from the Jewish religion, still remained to be examined. Marx proceeded from Feuerbach, who had explained the Jewish religion from the Jew and not the Jew from the Jewish religion, but he went beyond Feuerbach by revealing the special social element which reflects itself in the Jewish religion. What was the secular basis of Judaism ? Practical necessity, self-interest. What was the secular cult of the Jew ? Buying and selling. What was his secular God ? Money. " Very well then : emancipation from buying and selling and from money, that is to say, from practical, real Judaism, would be the self-emancipation of our time. An organization of society which abolished the necessary conditions for buying and selling, that is to say, the possibility of buying and selling, would make the Jew impossible. His religious consciousness would dissolve like stale fumes in the clear and vital atmosphere of society. On the other hand, when the Jew recognizes this, his practical character, as futile, and works for its abolition, then he is working from the basis of his own previous development for the emancipation of humanity itself and turns against the highest practical expression of human self-alienation." Marx regards Judaism as a general, contemporary, anti-social element driven to its present height by historical development and the zealous co-operation of the

Jews themselves, a height at which it must necessarily dissolve itself.

What Marx achieved with this treatise was a twofold gain. He went to the root basis of the connection between society and the State. The State was not, as Hegel imagined, the reality of the moral idea, absolute reason and the absolute aim in itself, and it had to content itself with the incomparably more modest task of presiding over the anarchy of bourgeois society which had enrolled it as watchman ; the anarchy of the general struggle of man against man, and individual against individual ; the war of all individuals, separated from each other only by their individuality, against all ; the general and unhindered movement of all the elementary forces released from their feudal fetters ; actual slavery although the individual was apparently free and independent, mistaking the unhindered movement of his alienated elements such as property, industry and religion for his own freedom, whereas in reality it represented his complete enslavement and alienation from humanity.

And then Marx recognized that the religious questions of the day had no more than a social significance. He showed the development of Judaism not in religious theory, but in industrial and commercial practice, which found a fantastic reflection in the Jewish religion. Practical Judaism is nothing but the fully developed Christian world. As bourgeois society is of a completely commercial Jewish character the Jew necessarily belongs to it and can claim political emancipation just as he can claim the general rights of man. However, the emancipation of humanity is a new organization of the social forces which will make man the master of those sources which give him life. Thus in shadowy contours we observe an outline of socialist society beginning to form.

In the *Deutsch-Französische Jahrbücher* Marx is still ploughing the philosophic field, but in the furrows turned over by his critical ploughshare the first shoots of the materialist conception of history began to sprout, and under the warm sun of French civilization they soon began to flower.

4. French Civilization

Judging by the way in which Marx usually worked it is very probable that he had already drafted the two contributions to the *Deutsch-Französische Jahrbücher*, at least in their fundamentals, which he was still in Germany, very likely during the first few months of his happy marriage. As the ideas contained in them turned on the Great French Revolution, nothing was more natural than that he should plunge into the study of the history of this revolution as soon as his presence in Paris gave him an opportunity of exploring its sources, and also the sources of its predecessor, French materialism, and of its successor, French socialism.

Paris at that time could justly claim that it was in the van of bourgeois civilization. After a series of illusions and catastrophes, the French bourgeoisie had finally secured in the July revolution of 1830 what it had begun in the Great Revolution of 1789. Its forces were now relaxing comfortably, although the resistance of the old powers had by no means been completely broken, and new powers were beginning to make themselves felt. The result was that a ceaseless battle of intellects raged—rolling now here, now there—such as could be found nowhere else in Europe and certainly not in Germany, which lay motionless in the silence of intellectual death.

Marx now plunged into this rejuvenating flood. In 1844 Ruge wrote to Feuerbach informing him that Marx was reading a tremendous amount and working with unusual intensity. However, he finished nothing, broke off his work constantly and plunged again and again into an endless sea of books. He was irritable and violent, particularly when he had worked himself sick and had not been to bed for three or four nights in succession. He had put his criticism of Hegelian philosophy on the shelf in order to utilize his stay in Paris to write a history of the Convention, having already collected the necessary material and adopted a number of very fruitful viewpoints. The evidence of this letter is all the more valuable because it was written in no commendatory sense.

Marx did not write a history of the Convention, but this fact does not disprove the information of Ruge. On the contrary, it makes it, if anything, rather more credible. The deeper Marx penetrated into the historical significance of the revolution of 1789 the easier it became for him to dispense with a criticism of the Hegelian philosophy as a means of arriving at a clear view of the struggles and demands of the age. However, the history of the Convention alone could not satisfy him because although it represented a maximum of political energy, political power and political understanding, it had proved itself impotent in the face of social anarchy.

Apart from the meagre indications of Ruge there is unfortunately no evidence to assist us to follow in any detail the course of study Marx pursued in the spring and summer of 1844. However, the general way in which his studies developed can be seen. The study of the French Revolution led him on to the historical literature of the " Third Estate ", a literature which originated under the Bourbon restoration and was developed by men of great historical talent who followed the historical existence of their class back into the eleventh century and presented French history as an uninterrupted series of class struggles. Marx owed his knowledge of the historical nature of classes and their struggles to these historians—he mentions in particular Guizot and Thierry —and he then proceeded to study the economic anatomy of the classes from the bourgeois economists, mentioning Ricardo in particular. Marx always denied having originated the theory of the class struggle. What he claimed as his contribution was having supplied proof that the existence of classes was linked up with definite historical struggles in the development of production, that the class struggle necessarily led to the dictatorship of the proletariat, and that this dictatorship was only a transitional period leading to the complete abolition of classes and the establishment of a classless society. This series of ideas developed during his stay in Paris.

The most brilliant and most trenchant weapon used by the " Third Estate " in its struggle against the ruling classes in the eighteenth century was the philosophy of materialism. During his exile in Paris Marx zealously studied this philosophy, paying less attention to the branch represented by Descartes, which developed into natural science, than to the branch which originated with Locke and developed into social science. Other stars which illuminated the Paris studies of the young Marx were Helvetius and Holbach, who carried materialism into social life and made the natural equality of human intellects, the essential unity between the progress of reason and the progress of industry, the natural goodness of humanity, and the omnipotent power of education the chief points in their system. He called their teachings " real humanism " as he had called Feuerbach's philosophy, the difference being that the materialism of Helvetius and Holbach had become " the social basis of communism ".

Paris now offered him all the opportunities he needed for studying communism and socialism as he had promised in the *Rheinische Zeitung*. The intellectual world which he had entered in Paris was dazzling, almost confusing, in its richness of ideas and forms. The intellectual atmosphere of Paris was pregnant with the germs of socialism, and even the *Journal des Débats*, the traditional organ of the ruling finance oligarchy, which was in receipt of a considerable government subsidy annually, was unable to hold itself completely aloof from the spirit of the day, though it did no more than publish Eugène Sue's socialist thrillers in its feuilleton columns. The opposing camp contained such brilliant thinkers as Leroux, men who were now being produced by the proletariat. Between the hostile camps were the remnants of the Saint-Simonists and the active Fourierist sect led by Considérant, whose organ was the *Démocratie Pacifique*, Christian socialists like the Catholic priest Lamennais and the former Carbonari Buchez, petty-bourgeois socialists like Sismondi, Buret, Pecquer and Vidal, whilst in literature the magnificent songs of Béranger and the novels of George Sand brilliantly reflected socialist ideas and problems.

The common characteristic of all these socialist systems was that they all reckoned on the good-will and the reasonableness of the possessing classes, whom they hoped to convince by peaceful propaganda of the necessity of social reforms or revolution. They were all born out of the disappointments of the Great Revolution, and they disdained the political path which had resulted in these disappointments. They desired to assist the suffering masses because the latter were unable to assist themselves. The insurrections of the workers in the 'thirties had failed, and even their most determined leaders, men like Barbès and Blanqui, knew nothing of any socialist theory or of any definite practical means for achieving a social revolution.

But the working-class movement grew all the more rapidly on account of this, and with the prophetic eye of the poet Heinrich Heine sketched the problem which arose in the following words : "The communists represent the only party in France deserving of respect. I should feel the same way about the remnants of the Saint-Simonists perhaps, who still exist under strange banners, or about the Fourierists, who are still alive and active, but these good fellows are moved by the word only, by the social problem as a question of traditional conceptions and not by any demoniacal necessity. They are not the slaves predestined by the supreme world spirit to fulfil its tremendous decisions. Sooner or later the scattered army of Saint-Simon and the whole general staff of the Fourierists will go over to the growing army of communism, there to play the rôle of the Fathers of the Church, lending brutal necessity the creative word." Thus Heine on the 15th of June 1843, and within the year the man arrived in Paris who was to play the rôle Heine thought the Saint-Simonists and the Fourierists might play : he lent brutal necessity the creative word.

In all probability whilst he was still in Germany, and in any case whilst his standpoint was still predominantly philosophical, Marx had declared himself against cut-and-dried systems for the future, against any attempt to settle all problems for all time, against the unfurling of any dogmatic standard, and against the idea of the " crass socialists " that political questions were beneath their dignity. And when he declaried it not enough that the idea should press forward to reality, but that reality must become the idea, this condition fulfilled itself before his eyes. Since the last insurrection of the workers in 1839 the working-class movement and socialism had begun to approach each other in three ways.

First of all there was the Democratic Socialist Party. Its socialism was not of any very great import because it was composed of lower middle-class and proletarian elements together, and the slogans which it inscribed on its banners, the organization of labour and the right to work, were nothing but lower middle-class utopias impossible of fulfilment in capitalist society. The latter organizes labour as it must be organized, namely, as wage-labour, and this presupposes the existence of capital and can be abolished only with capital, whilst the situation with regard to the right to work is no different. Such a right can be fulfilled only in the joint ownership of the means of production, that is to say, by the abolition of bourgeois society, but the leaders of this party, Louis Blanc, Ledru-Rollin and Ferdinand Flocon, solemnly refused to lay the axe to the roots of bourgeois society, declaring that they were neither communists nor socialists.

However, although the social aims of this party were completely utopian, it nevertheless represented a great step forward because it chose the political path for their realization. It declared that no social reform was possible without political reform, and that the conquest of political power was the only means by which the suffering masses could save themselves, and therefore it demanded the universal franchise. This demand met with a lively echo in the ranks of the proletariat, which was tired of putsches and conspiracies, and sought more effective weapons for the prosecution of the class struggle.

Still greater masses of the workers rallied to the banner of proletarian communism unfurled by Cabet, who had originally been a Jacobin and was later converted to communism by his reading and in particular by the *Utopia* of Sir Thomas More. Cabet professed communism as openly as the Democratic Socialist Party rejected it, but he agreed with the latter that political democracy was a necessary transitional stage. Thus *The Journey to Icaria*, in which Cabet attempted to describe the society of the future, became an incomparably more popular work than the brilliant fantasies of Fourier, although the narrow limits of Cabet's work made it immeasurably inferior to the genius of the former.

And finally, voices began to sound loud and clear within the ranks of the proletariat itself, indicating beyond a doubt that it was preparing to cast off its leading strings. Marx was acquainted from the days of the *Rheinische Zeitung*, with Leroux and Proudhon, both of whom were printers and members of the working class, and he had already promised to study their works thoroughly. Their works appealed to him because both men sought to harness the results of German philosophy to their own aims, although both of them fell victims to serious misunderstandings. Marx himself has informed us that he spent many hours, often throughout the night, trying to explain Hegelian philosophy to Proudhon. The two men came together for a while only to part soon afterwards, but writing after Proudhon's death Marx readily bore witness to the great impetus which Proudhon's first appearance gave to the working-class movement, an impetus, in fact, which undoubtedly affected him also. Marx regarded Proudhon's first work (in which the latter abandoned all utopianism and subjected private property to a thorough and ruthless criticism as the cause of all social evil), as the first scientific manifesto of the modern proletariat.

All these tendencies helped to prepare the way for a unification between the working-class movement and socialism, but they were all in contradiction with each other, and after the first few steps they involved themselves in new contradictions. Marx had studied socialism and he now began to study the proletariat. In July 1844 Ruge wrote to a friend in Germany : " Marx has plunged into German communism here—socially, I mean, for he can hardly consider the dismal affair of any political import-ance. Germany can stand the minor damage the artisans (particularly the baker's dozen converts here) are likely to do without much doctoring." Ruge was soon to discover why Marx took " the baker's dozen " artisans and their doings seriously.

5. The *Vorwärts* and the Expulsion of Marx

We have no very detailed record of Marx's personal life during his exile in Paris. His wife presented him with their first child, a daughter, and then returned proudly to Germany to show it to their relatives. Marx remained on the best of terms with his friends in Cologne and a gift of a thousand thaler helped consider-ably towards making the year in Paris such a fruitful one.

He was in close touch with Heinrich Heine and he did much to make the year 1844 a memorable one in the life of the poet, assisting at the birth of the *Winter Fables*, the *Song of the Weavers* and the immortal satires on the German despots. They were not long together, but Marx remained loyal to Heine even when the howling of the Philistines against him became still more furious than it had been against Herwegh, and he generously remained silent when the bedridden Heine cited him untruthfully as a witness that the annual grant the poet received from the Guizot Ministry was irreproachable. As we know, in his youth Marx himself had vainly yearned for poetic laurels and all his life he retained a lively sympathy for poets, invariably showing great toleration towards their little weaknesses. He felt that poets were peculiar people who should be permitted to go their own way and must not be measured by the standards of ordinary or even extraordinary mortals. If they were to sing they must be flattered ; it was no use belabouring them with severe criticism.

But he regarded Heine as something more than a poet, as a fighter also, and in the dispute between Börne and Heine, which served at the time as a sort of dividing line between the sheep and the goats, he steadfastly supported Heine, declaring that the doltish treatment accorded to Heine's work on Börne by the Christian-Germanic donkeys was unique in any period of German literature, which had never at any time lacked its full complement of dolts. He was never misled by the shout about Heine's alleged treachery, which even affected Engels and Lassalle, though both had the excuse of extreme youth. " We need very few signs to understand each other," wrote Heine on one occasion to excuse his " confused scribble ", and the sentence had a deeper significance than the immediate one which prompted it.

Marx was still a student when in 1834 Heine declared : " The spirit of freedom breathed by our classical literature is less active amongst our scholars, poets and literary men than amongst the great mass of our artisans and workers." And ten years later, when Marx was living in Paris, Heine declared : " In their struggle against the existing state of affairs the proletarians can claim the progressive spirits, the great philosophers, as their leaders ". The freedom and accuracy of this judgment become still clearer when one realizes that at the same time Heine was pouring scorn on the pot-house politics of the little conventicles of exiles in which Börne played the rôle of giant-killer. Heine realized that there was a great difference between Marx occupying himself with " a baker's dozen artisans " and Börne doing so.

Heine and Marx were bound together by the spirit of German philosophy and French socialism, and by a common and deep-rooted dislike for that Christian-Germanic sloth, that false Teutonism, which sought to modernize the ancient garb of

German folly with radical phrases. The Massmanns and Venedys who live in Heine's satires trudged along in Börne's footsteps, though Börne may have been far above them in intellect and wit. Börne had no feeling either for art or philosophy, as was revealed in his declaration that Goethe was a rhymed and Hegel an unrhymed slave, and when he broke with the great traditions of German history he established no new intellectual relation to the new powers of Western European culture. Heine, on the other hand, could not abandon Goethe and Hegel without abandoning himself, and he therefore plunged with fierce avidity into French socialism as a new source of intellectual life. His works live on and arouse the anger of the grandchildren as they aroused the anger of their grandfathers, whilst the writings of Börne are forgotten, less on account of their " jog-trot " style than on account of their content.

Referring to the back-biting gossip which Börne had set going against Heine even whilst the two were standing shoulder to shoulder, and which Börne's literary executors were unwise enough to publish later on, Marx declared that he had never imagined the man to be so absurd, superficial and petty. However, he would never have called the personal honesty of the gossiper into question on that account had he actually carried out his intention of writing about the dispute. It is always difficult to find worse Jesuits in public life than those narrow-minded and orthodox radicals who wrap themselves up in the threadbare cloak of their own virtue and stop at nothing in their insinuations against the finer and freer spirits to whom it is given to recognize the deeper relations of history. Marx was always on the side of the latter and never of the former, particularly as he had made the acquaintance of the virtuous ones himself.

In later years Marx referred to " Russian aristocrats " who had carried him shoulder high during his exile in Paris, adding that this was of little importance : the Russian aristocracy was educated at German universities and spent its youth in Paris. Its members invariably snatched at the extremest things the West had to offer, but this did not prevent them becoming thorough blackguards immediately they entered the service of the State. Marx appears to have been referring to a certain Count Tolstoi, a secret agent of the Russian government, or to others of a like kidney. He was certainly not referring to that Russian aristocrat on whose intellectual development he exercised a great influence in those days, namely, Michael Bakunin. Even after the paths of the two men had widely separated Bakunin bore witness to this influence, and in the dispute between Marx and Ruge he took Marx's side, although up to then Ruge had been his protector.

This dispute flared up again in the summer of 1844 and this time publicly. A paper entitled the *Vorwärts* had been appearing twice a week in Paris since the New Year of 1844. Its origin was by no means irreproachable. It was founded by a certain Heinrich Börnstein who ran a theatrical and general advertisement business and sought to further his interests thereby. The necessary funds had been provided by Meyerbeer, who preferred living in Paris. We know from Heine that this Royal Prussian conductor was very keen on obtaining the greatest possible amount of advertisement, and he probably needed it. As a cunning business man Börnstein gave his paper a patriotic cloak and appointed, as its editor, Adalbert von Bornstedt, a former Prussian officer and a thoroughly venal character who was the " confidant " of Metternich and at the same time in the pay of the Berlin government. When the *Deutsch-Französische Jahrbücher* appeared it was greeted with a salvo of abuse by the *Vorwärts*, and it would be difficult to say whether the abuse was characterized more by its foolishness or its vulgarity.

However, the affairs of the paper did not prosper. Börnstein had organized a regular translation factory in order to sell the latest pieces played in Paris with the greatest possible speed to German stage managers, and he sought to cut out the young German dramatists and win the German Philistines, who were becoming restive, by mouthing a few phrases about " moderate progress " and condemning " ultra-ism " both on the left and on the right. His editor Bornstedt was in the same boat because he had to lull the suspicions of the emigrants if he was to associate with them freely, a proceeding which was absolutely necessary if he was to earn his blood-money. However, the Prussian government was blind even to its own interest of self-preservation, and it prohibited the sale of the *Vorwärts* on its territory, an example which was followed by the other German governments.

Bornstedt threw in his hand at the beginning of May, regarding the game as hopeless, but not so Börnstein, who wanted to do business and was not at all particular about the way in which he did it. With the cold-blooded calculation of a cunning speculator he said to himself that if the *Vorwärts* was to be prohibited in Prussia in any case, it might just as well don the crown of martyrdom and take advantage of the interest aroused by a prohibited paper, for the German Philistines would consider it worth while to obtain such a paper secretly. It suited his book extremely well therefore when the youthful firebrand Bernays offered him a fiery article for the *Vorwärts*, and after a certain amount of preliminary skirmishing Bernays was made editor in place of Bornstedt. Owing to the lack of any other medium, the German exiles in Paris now began to contribute to the *Vorwärts*, each on his own responsibility and without being attached to the editorial board.

One of the first to do so was Ruge, who came forward under his own name and even defended Marx's contributions to the *Deutsch-Französische Jahrbücher* as though he were in agreement with them. A few months later, however, he published two anonymous articles in the *Vorwärts* : a few short observations concerning Prussian policy and a long article containing nothing but gossip about the Prussian dynasty, interlarded with remarks about " the drinking King " and " the limping Queen " and their " purely spiritual marriage ", etc. The articles were signed "A Prussian", and under the circumstances it appeared as though Marx was the author, for Ruge was a member of the Dresden Town Council and registered at the Saxon Embassy in Paris, Bernays was a Bavarian from Rhineland-Westphalia, whilst Börnstein was a Hamburger, and although he had lived for a long time in Austria he had never lived for any length of time in Prussia.

It is impossible to discover now what Ruge had in mind when he adopted such a misleading pen-name, but, as his letters to his friends and relatives show, he had worked himself up into a furious rage against Marx, to whom he referred as " a thoroughly vile fellow " and " an insolent Jew ", and it is undeniable that two years later in a penitent petition to the Prussian Minister of the Interior he betrayed the comrades of his exile in Paris, and against his better knowledge loaded on the shoulders of these " nameless young men " the sins he had himself committed in the *Vorwärts*. It is of course quite possible that he signed his articles " A Prussian " in order to give them greater weight as they dealt with Prussian affairs, but if this were the case he acted with irresponsible thoughtlessness, and it is quite understandable that Marx hastened to parry the trick of the alleged " Prussian ",

Marx's answer was couched in a dignified tone : he dealt solely with the one or two, so to speak, objective observations which Ruge had made on Prussian policy and dismissed the whole gossip about the Prussian dynasty in a short footnote : " Special reasons cause me to point out that the above contribution is the first I have made to the *Vorwärts*." As a matter of fact, it was also the last.

The point at issue was the revolt of the Silesian weavers in 1844, which Ruge treated as an unimportant affair, declaring that it had no political soul and that without a political soul no social revolution was possible. The essence of Marx's reply had already been dealt with in his treatise " On the Jewish Question ". Political force can heal no social evils because the

State cannot abolish the conditions whose product it is. He sharply attacked utopianism, declaring that socialism was not possible without a revolution, but he attacked Blanqui and his followers just as sharply, declaring that political understanding was deceiving the social instinct when it sought to make progress by means of small, useless putsches. He defined the character of the revolution with epigrammatic trenchancy : " Every revolution dissolves the old society and in so far as it does this it is social. Every revolution overthrows the old power and in so far as it does this it is political." A social revolution with a political soul, as demanded by Ruge, was senseless, but a political revolution with a social soul was reasonable. The revolution in general—the overthrow of the existing power and the dissolution of the old relations—was a political act. In so far as socialism first needed destruction and dissolution it needed this political act, but when its organizational activity began, when its innate aim, its soul, appeared, socialism flung off the political cloak.

These ideas were developed from Marx's own treatise " On the Jewish Question ", and the revolt of the Silesian weavers quickly confirmed what he had written about the feebleness of the class struggle in Germany. His friend Jung wrote from Cologne that there was now more communism to be found in the columns of the *Kölnische Zeitung* than formerly in the columns of the *Rheinische Zeitung*, and that the former had opened up a subscription list for the families of the fallen and imprisoned weavers. At a farewell dinner-party for the retiring district governor a hundred thaler had been collected for the list amongst the highest officials and richest merchants of Cologne, and sympathy was being shown everywhere to the dangerous rebels. " What a few months ago would have been a daring and completely new attitude for them, has now become a matter of course."

Marx made use of the general sympathy shown towards the weavers against Ruge's underestimation of their revolt, but he was not deceived for one moment by the " lack of resistance shown by the bourgeoisie towards new social tendencies and ideas ". He realized that immediately the working-class movement gained any real power the effect would be to stifle the political antipathies and antagonisms within the camp of the ruling classes and to cause the latter to direct their whole hostility against the workers. He showed the deep difference between bourgeois and proletarian emancipation when he pointed out that the one sprang from social well-being and the other from social misery. The bourgeois revolution was caused by isolation from the political commonwealth and the State, whilst the proletarian revolution was caused by isolation from humanity and the real commonwealth of humanity. The isolation from the latter was incomparably more thorough, more intolerable, more terrible and more innately contradictory than isolation from the political commonwealth, and therefore the liquidation of this isolation, even as a partial phenomenon represented by the revolt of the Silesian weavers, was a much more tremendous affair, just as the human being was more than the citizen, and human life more than political life.

Marx's views on the revolt of the Silesian weavers were thus fundamentally different from those of Ruge : " Consider only the song of the weavers ; the striking, trenchant, ruthless and powerful way in which the proletariat hurls the slogan of its antagonism against the society of private property. The Silesian revolt began where the French and English insurrections ended, with the consciousness of the proletariat as a class. The whole action was of this character. Not only did it destroy machinery, the rival of the workers, but also the merchants' records, their property titles. In the beginning at least, all other movements were directed exclusively against the industrialists, against the visible enemy, but this movement was also directed against the banker, the invisible enemy. And finally, no English insurrection was carried out with the same courage, deliberation and persistence."

In this connection Marx also refers to the brilliant writings of Weitling, who often excelled Proudhon in his theories, although he remained behind him in practice : " Can the bourgeoisie—its philosophers and scribes included—show us a work on its own emancipation, political emancipation, comparable to Weitling's *Guarantees of Harmony and Liberty* ? When one compares the sober and subdued mediocrity of German political literature with this incomparably brilliant début of the German worker, and when one compares the undersized and down-at-heel political shoes of the German bourgeoisie with the giant boots of the youthful proletariat, one is entitled to prophesy the frame of an athlete for this neglected son of Germany." Marx declared that the German proletariat was the theoretician amongst the European proletariats, as the English proletariat was the economist and the French proletariat the politician.

Marx's verdict on Weitling's writings has been confirmed by the judgment of posterity. For their time they were brilliant achievements, and their brilliance was enhanced by the fact that the German journeyman tailor prepared the way for an understanding between the working-class movement and socialism before Louis Blanc, Cabet and Proudhon, and more effectively.

However, Marx's historical estimation of the revolt of the Silesian weavers seems extraordinary to us to-day. He read tendencies into it which were certainly not present, and Ruge seems to have estimated the revolt more correctly when he declared it to be no more than a hunger revolt without any deeper significance. However, as was the case with regard to their earlier dispute about Herwegh, so here we see also that to be formally in the right against genius is the whole error of the Philistine, and that in the last resort a great heart always triumphs over a narrow understanding.

The " baker's dozen artisans " referred to so contemptuously by Ruge, but zealously studied by Marx, were organized in the " League of the Just " which had developed in the 'thirties from the French secret societies and out of their final defeat in 1839. This defeat had been a good thing for the organization because its dispersed elements reassembled not only in their old centre Paris, but also in England and Switzerland, where the freedom of meeting and association offered them more room for development, so that these branches from the old trunk began to develop more powerfully than the mother-tree. The Paris organization was led by Hermann Ewerbeck of Danzig, who was entangled in Cabet's moralizing utopianism and had translated Cabet's utopia into German. Weitling, who led the agitation in Switzerland, proved himself the intellectual superior of Ewerbeck, whilst the London leaders of the League, the watchmaker Joseph Moll, the shoemaker Heinrich Bauer, and Karl Schapper, a a former student of forestry who earned his living sometimes as a compositor and sometimes as a teacher of languages, also proved themselves superior to Ewerbeck at least in revolutionary determination.

Marx probably first heard about these " three real men " from Engels, who, when he visited Marx in September 1844 whilst passing through Paris, spoke of the " deep impression " they had made on him. During the ten days Engels stayed in Paris much of his time was spent in the company of Marx, and they had an opportunity of confirming the far-reaching agreement in their ideas which had already revealed itself in their contributions to the *Deutsch-Französische Jahrbücher*. In the meantime their old friend Bruno Bauer had turned against these ideas and published a criticism in a literary publication he had founded. The two learned of this attack whilst they were together and immediately decided to answer it. Engels sat down at once and put all he had to say about the matter on paper, but in accordance with his character Marx went much more deeply into the matter than they had originally planned and in several months of hard work he produced a book of over 300 pages. With the conclusion of this work in January 1845 his stay in Paris also came to an end.

After taking over the editorship of the *Vorwärts* Bernays had energetically continued his attacks on " the Christian-Germanic simpletons in Berlin," and there was no lack of *lèse-majesté* in the paper, whilst Heine shot one barbed arrow after the other against " the new Alexander " in the Palace of Berlin. It was not long before the legitimate monarchy in Germany petitioned the illegitimate bourgeois monarchy in France for the use of the police cudgel against the *Vorwärts*, but Guizot proved hard of hearing. Despite his reactionary opinions he was a man of some culture, and in addition he had no desire to play the myrmidon to Prussian despotism and thus court the scorn and contempt of the opposition at home, but he became more complaisant when the *Vorwärts* published " a nefarious article " on the attempt made by Mayor Tschech on the life of Frederick William IV.[1] After a discussion in the Cabinet Guizot agreed to take action against the *Vorwärts* on two counts : the prosecution of the responsible editor for not having deposited a sufficient sum with the authorities and his indictment on a charge of incitement to regicide.

The Berlin government agreed to the first proposal, but when it was carried into execution it proved ineffective. Bernays was sentenced to two months' imprisonment and fined 200 francs for his failure to comply with the deposit provisions, but the *Vorwärts* immediately announced that in the future it would appear as a monthly, and in this way it completely circumvented the deposit law. The Berlin government would not hear of the second proposal, in all probability in the well-founded fear that the jurymen of Paris would show little inclination to strain their consciences on behalf of the King of Prussia, but it continued to lodge complaints, and finally it demanded the expulsion of the editors and contributors of the paper from France. After long negotiations Guizot agreed.

It was assumed at the time, and Engels repeated the charge in his speech at the grave of Frau Marx, that Guizot was won over by the inglorious mediation of Alexander von Humboldt, who was related to the Prussian Minister for Foreign Affairs by marriage. Lately attempts have been made to clear Humboldt's memory of this charge on the ground that the Prussian archives contain no reference to any such mediation, but that is hardly

---

[1] Heinrich Ludwig Tschech, Mayor of Storckow in Prussia, democrat and philanthropist, made an unsuccessful attempt on the life of Frederick William IV in July 1844 and was executed the same year.—Tr.

enough to clear him because, first of all, the archives are known to be incomplete and, secondly, it is not usual for such matters to be committed to writing. All that the archives prove is that one of the decisive acts in the affair took place behind the scenes.

The Berlin government had been irritated chiefly by Heine, who had published eleven of his sharpest satires on the situation in Prussia and in particular on the King in the *Vorwärts*, but for Guizot Heine represented the most ticklish point in the whole disagreeable business. He was a poet with a European reputation, and the French people regarded him almost as a national poet. Naturally, Guizot could not explain these difficulties direct to Berlin, and therefore a little bird seems to have made some mention of the matter to the Prussian Ambassador in Paris, for on the 4th of October the latter suddenly reported to Berlin that it was very doubtful whether Heine, who had published only two of his poems in the *Vorwärts*, was a member of the editorial staff of the paper, and at last the authorities in Berlin understood.

Heine himself was therefore not molested, but on the 11th of January 1845 a number of other German fugitives who had contributed to the *Vorwärts* or who were suspected of having done so, received orders of expulsions, including Marx, Ruge, Bakunin, Börnstein and Bernays. Some of them saved themselves: Börnstein by giving an undertaking to cease publishing the *Vorwärts*, and Ruge by running from the Saxon Ambassador to various French deputies and back again in order to assure everyone what a loyal citizen he really was. Naturally, Marx was not to be had for anything of that sort and he therefore prepared to move to Brussels.

His exile in Paris had lasted a little over a year, but it was perhaps the most important one in all his years of wandering and apprenticeship. It was rich in experience and stimulation, and it was made still richer by the winning of a comrade-in-arms who served him magnificently and to the very end.

CHAPTER FOUR: FRIEDRICH ENGELS

1. Office and Barracks

FRIEDRICH ENGELS was born on the 28th of November 1830 in Barmen. Like Marx, he did not acquire his revolutionary opinions in the home of his parents and he was not driven into revolutionary paths by personal indigence, but by high intelligence. His father was a well-to-do manufacturer of conservative and orthodox views, and religiously Engels had more to overcome than Marx.

He attended college in Elberfeld up to a year before his finals when he left to enter business life. Like Freiligrath, he became a very capable business man without his heart ever having been in " this damned business ", as he called it. We make his acquaintance for the first time in the letters written by the then 18-year-old apprentice in the office of Consul Leupold in Bremen to the brothers Gräber, two of his school-friends who were then studying theology. There is not much about business in these letters, except remarks like the following which is found in one of them : " Given from our office stool when for once we were not feeling seedy ". The youthful Engels, like the later Engels, was a convivial drinker, and although he never gave himself up to reverie like Hauff or sang like Heine, he tells us with robust humour of the drinking bouts at which he was present within the time-honoured walls of the *Ratskeller* in Bremen.

Like Marx he first tried his hand at poetry, but he realized as quickly as Marx had done that there were no laurels growing for him in the garden of verse. In a letter dated the 17th of September 1838, that is to say, before he had completed his 18th year, he declares that Goethe's advice " For Young Poets " has cured him of all belief in any poetic mission. He is referring to the two short essays in which the master of German poetry pointed out that the German language had reached such a high level of development that it was not difficult for anyone to express himself felicitously in rhythm and rhyme, a faculty therefore about which no one was entitled to compliment himself very highly. Goethe concludes his advice with the rhyme :

Jungling, merke dir in Zeiten,
Wo sich Geist und Sinn erhöht,
Dass die Muse zu begleiten
Doch zu leiten nicht versteht.[1]

The youthful Engels found himself aptly described in Goethe's advice, and he realized that his rhyming was not likely to produce anything worth while in the cause of poetry ; still, he would retain it as " an agreeable supplement ", as Goethe said, and also submit a poem for publication, " because other fellows who are just as big or even bigger donkeys than I am have done it, and because I shall neither raise nor lower the level of German literature thereby ". The jocular tone which Engels always adopted concealed nothing frivolous in his character even in youth, and in the same letter we find him asking his friends to send him popular classics from Cologne : Siegfried, Eulenspiegel, Helena, Octavian, Schildbürger, Heymonskinder and Doktor Faust, and announcing that he is studying Jakob Böhme. " His is an overcast, but deep soul. Most of what he writes must be thoroughly studied if one wants to understand any of it."

It was not long therefore before Engels plunged into the depths and lost all taste for the superficial literature of " Young Germany ". [2] In a letter written a little later, on the 10th of January 1839, we find him attacking " this fine company " chiefly because it sent things out into the world which did not exist in reality. " This fellow Theodor Mundt is scribbling a fine lot of rubbish about Demoiselle Taglione, who gives dance interpretations of Goethe's poetry, decorating himself with fine feathers borrowed from Goethe, Heine, Rahel and Stieglitz, and writing precious nonsense about Bettina, but all of it is so modern, so modern that it must be a pleasure for any snapper up of trifles or for any vain and lascivious young lady to read it. . . . And Heinrich Laube ! The fellow churns out one non-existent character after the other, travel stories which are no travel stories, nonsense on top of nonsense. It is awful."

Engels found that " the new spirit " in literature dated from the " thunderclap " of the July revolution, which he declared was " the finest expression of the will of the people since the wars for independence ", and that the most prominent representatives of this new spirit were Beck, Grün, Lenau, Immermann,

---

[1] " Youthful scribe, take heed, in moments
When both heart and soul exult,
That the muse may well go with you,
But your guide can never be."
[2] " Das Junge Deutschland " : A group of young authors under the influence of Börne and Heine formed itself under this name after the French July Revolution in 1830.—Tr.

Platen, Börne, Heine and Gutzkov, placing the latter with certain judgment above the other lights of Young Germany. According to a letter of the 1st of May, Engels contributed an article to the *Telegraph*, a publication issued by "this quite capital and excellent fellow",[1] but he requested the strictest discretion from the editor as otherwise he feared he might get into "a hellish scrape".

The tirades about freedom delivered by Young Germany did not deceive Engels concerning the æsthetic inferiority of its literary products, but he was not inclined to be more tolerant on that account to the orthodox and reactionary attacks on it. He joined forces unconditionally with the party of the persecuted and probably signed himself "Young German", and in a letter we find him threatening his friend : "And I can tell you one thing, Fritz, if you should ever become a pastor you can be as orthodox as you like, but if you become a pietist then you will have me to deal with." His particular preference for Börne was probably due to similar reflections, and in the opinion of the young Engels Börne's attack on the informer Menzel was stylistically the finest production in Germany, whilst Heine had to be content with an occasional reference such as "smutty fellow". Feelings ran high against Heine in those days and even the young Lassalle wrote in his diary : "And this man has abandoned the cause of freedom ! This man has torn the Jacobin cap of liberty from his head and pressed a galooned hat upon his noble locks ! "

However, neither Börne nor Heine nor any other poet guided Engels into the path his life finally took, and his fate alone moulded him into the man he became. He was born in Barmen, one of the strongholds of German pietism, and lived in Bremen, the other. His liberation from these bonds marked the beginning of that great struggle for emancipation which filled his whole life. We find him, when still struggling with the beliefs of his childhood, speaking with unusual gentleness : "I pray every day, indeed almost all day, for truth, and I have done so ever since I began to doubt, but still I cannot go back to your belief. . . . The tears are welling up as I write. I am deeply moved, but I feel that I am not lost, that I shall find my way to God, for whom I long with my whole heart. And that is also a manifestation of the Holy Ghost, my life on that, and if the Bible says the contrary ten thousand times."

In these mental struggles Engels developed from Hengstenberg and Krummacher, the leaders of contemporary orthodoxy, to David Strauss, putting up on the way for a while with Schleier-

[1] Karl Gutzkov.—Tr.

macher, but seeking temporary support from him rather than a permanent basis. And then he confessed to his theological friends that there could be no going back for him. A right-wing rationalist might be able to abandon his natural explanation of miracles and his shallow moralizing in order to crawl back into the strait-jacket of orthodoxy, but philosophic speculation could never descend from " snow-capped peaks flooded with the glory of the morning sun " into " the misty valleys " of orthodoxy. " I am on the point of becoming a Hegelian. Whether I shall or not I certainly don't yet know, but Strauss has thrown light on Hegel for me and it all appears very plausible. The fellow's philosophy of history is in any case thoroughly after my own heart."

Engels' breach with the church then led him direct to political heresy. A parsonical speech in praise of the King of Prussia, the man responsible for the Demagogue Hunt, caused this Percy Hotspur to exclaim : " I expect something good only of that prince whose head is sore from the buffetings of his people and whose palace windows are crashing in under the stones of the revolution."

With such ideas of course Engels was already far beyond Gutzkov's *Telegraph* and rather in the orbit of the *Deutsche Jahrbücher* and the *Rheinische Zeitung*. Whilst he was in Berlin serving his year in the Brigade of Artillery from October 1841 to October 1842 he was quartered in the Kupfergraben Barracks, not far from the house in which Hegel lived and died, and he contributed occasionally to both these publications. Probably out of consideration for the feelings of his conservative and orthodox family he had adopted the pen-name of Friedrich Oswald, and whilst he was wearing " the King's uniform " he was compelled to retain it for still more cogent reasons. On the 6th of December 1842 Gutzkov wrote a consoling letter to a writer whom Engels had sharply criticized in the *Deutsche Jahrbücher* : " The poor service of having introduced F. Oswald into literature is unfortunately mine. Years ago a young business man named Engels sent me letters from Bremen about the situation in Wuppertal. I corrected his matter, struck out the personalities when they were too glaring, and printed it. After that he sent me further stuff, but I always had to re-write it, and then suddenly he forbade me to make correction in his work, began to study Hegel and went off to other journals. Only a little while before his criticism of you appeared I had sent him 15 thaler to Berlin. That is always the way with these young fellows : they owe us thanks for having taught them to think and write, and then their first independent act is intellectual parricide. Naturally, this evil would not flourish so greatly if the *Rheinische Zeitung* and Ruge's paper did not cater for it." This is certainly not the groaning of the old Moor in the hunger tower, but rather the horrified cackle of an old hen when she sees the duckling she has hatched out swim cheerfully away from her.

Engels had been a capable servant of commerce in his office and in the barracks he became a capable soldier. From his service days until the end of his life military science was one of his favourite studies. Close and constant contact with practical daily life made up for what his philosophic consciousness lacked in speculative depth. During his year of military service in Berlin he caroused lustily with the " Freemen " and contributed one or two papers to their disputes, though this was at a time when their doings had not yet degenerated. In April 1842 a fifty-five page pamphlet written by Engels was published anonymously in Leipzig. It was entitled *Schelling and Revelation* and criticized " the latest reactionary attacks on free philosophy ", or the attempt of Schelling to drive Hegelian philosophy from the field at the University of Berlin with his own belief in revelation. Ruge, who thought that Bakunin was the author, welcomed the work flatteringly with the remark : " This promising young man is outstripping all the old donkeys in Berlin ". The work, in fact, represented philosophic Young Hegelianism in its extremist consequences, but other critics were not being unreasonable when they declared that it was characterized less by trenchant criticism than by poetic-philosophic exuberance.

At about the same time and under the fresh impression of Bruno Bauer's dismissal, Engels published *A Christian Epic* in four cantos, satirizing the " triumph of belief " over the " Arch-Satan " to the great horror and dismay of the latter. It was published in Neumünster near Zürich, and in it Engels made full use of the privilege of youth to despise carping criticism. The verses in which he describes himself and Marx, with whom he had not yet come into personal contact, give us some idea of his manner :

> Doch der am weitsten links mit langen Beinen toset,
> Ist Oswald, grau berockt und pfefferhaft behoset,
> Auch innen pfefferhaft, Oswald der Montagnard,
> Der wurzelhafteste mit Haut und auch mit Haar.
> Er spielt ein Instrument, das ist die Guillotine,
> Auf ihr begleitet er stets eine Cavatine ;
> Stets tönt das Höllenlied, stets brüllt er den Refrain :
> Formez vos bataillons ! Aux armes, citoyens !

Wer jaget hinterdrein mit wildem Ungestüm?
Ein schwarzer Kerl aus Trier, ein markhaft Ungetüm.
Er gehet, hüpfet nicht, er springet auf den Hacken
Und raset voller Wut und gleich als wollt' er packen
Das weite Himmelszelt und zu der Erde ziehn,
Streckt er die Arme sein weit in die Lüfte hin.
Geballt die böse Faust, so tobt er sonder Rasten,
Als wenn ihn bei dem Schopf zenhtausend Teufel fassten.[1]

When his year of military service was at an end in September 1842 Engels returned home and two months later left for England to become a clerk in the office of the big spinning firm of Ermen & Engels in which his father was a partner. On his way to England he passed through Cologne and made the acquaintance of Marx in the editorial offices of the *Rheinische Zeitung*. However, this first meeting was cool, for Marx was about to break off relations with the " Freemen ", and he regarded Engels as one of their supporters, whilst Engels was prejudiced against him by letters from the brothers Bauer.

2.   English Civilization

The twenty-one months Engels then spent in England had the same significance for him as the year spent in Paris had for Marx. Both of them had gone through the German philosophic school and whilst abroad they came to the same conclusions, but while Marx arrived at an understanding of the struggles and the demands of the age on the basis of the French Revolution, Engels did so on the basis of English industry.

England had also gone through its bourgeois revolution, a century before France in fact, but just on that account the

---

[1] " But he who dances long of leg and farthest left,
Is Oswald, with coat of grey and pepper-coloured breeches ;
Pepper without and pepper within, Oswald the Montagnard.
Most radical of all from pate to toe,
He thumps an instrument, it is the Guillotine
And on its keys he plays a Cavatine.
Ever sounds the hellish song, howling the refrain :
Formez vos bataillons ! Aux armes citoyens !

.   .   .   .   .   .

Who charges on his tracks with reckless rage ?
A dark-browed limb from Trier, a thorough rip,
Who neither walks nor hops, but springs upon his heels
And stretches high his arms into the air
As though his wrath would seize at once
The mighty tent of Heaven and tear it to the earth.
With clenched and threatening fist he rages without rest,
As though ten thousand devils were dancing on his chest."

English bourgeois revolution had taken place under far less developed conditions, finally resolving itself into a compromise between the aristocracy and the bourgeoisie which resulted in the setting up of a joint monarchy. The English " middle class " was not compelled to wage such a long and bitter struggle with the monarchy and the aristocracy as fell to the lot of the " Third Estate " in France, but whereas French historians came to the conclusion that the struggle of the " Third Estate " was a class struggle only on subsequent consideration, the idea of the class struggle in England sprang up, so to speak from a fresh source, when the proletariat took up the struggle against the ruling classes at the time of the Reform Bill in 1832.

This difference is explained by the fact that in England large-scale industry had ploughed up the country far more deeply than was the case in France. In an almost visible process of development English industry had destroyed old classes and created new ones. The internal structure of modern bourgeois society was much more clearly visible in England than in France. Studying the history and character of English industry Engels learned that economic facts, although they had played no rôle in historical research, or at the utmost a very minor one, represented a decisive historical force, at least in the modern world, and that they formed the basis for the development of existing class antagonisms, whilst where the latter were completely formed thanks to the development of large-scale industry they represented the basis for the development of political parties and political struggles, and thus the basis of the whole of political history.

The fact that Engels directed his attention primarily to the economic field was largely the result of his profession. His contribution to the *Deutsch-Französische Jahrbücher* was a criticism of national economy whilst Marx's contribution was a criticism of the philosophy of law. Engels' contribution is written with all the avidity of youth, but it reveals an unusual maturity of judgment. It remained the privilege of the German professorial Philistines to dub it " an utterly confused piece of work, whilst Marx declared it to be " a brilliant sketch ". It was, in fact, no more than a sketch because what Engels had to say about Ricardo and Adam Smith was by no means exhaustive and not always correct, whilst the objections he brought forward had perhaps already been made by the English and French socialists. However, his attempt to explain all the contradictions of bourgeois economics from their real source, private property as such, was brilliant, and it carried Engels far beyond Proudhon, who never got any further than fighting private property on its own ground. The observations of Engels concerning the inhuman effects of capitalist competition, the population theory of Malthus, the ever-increasing momentum of capitalist production, the commercial crises, the law of wages, the progress of science, which he declared had degenerated under the rule of private property into a means for consolidating the slavery of humanity instead of being a means for the emancipation of humanity, etc., contained the fruitful seeds of scientific communism on the economic field, and it was Engels in fact who was the pioneer on this field.

He was much too modest about his own contributions. On one occasion he declared that Marx had given his economic writings " their final shape and form ", on another occasion that " Marx was greater, saw further, saw more and saw more quickly than all of us ", and on a third occasion that Marx would have discovered what he, Engels, had discovered in any case. However, the fact remains that in the beginning it was Engels who gave and Marx who received on that field on which in the last resort the decisive struggle must be fought out and is being fought out.

There is no doubt that Marx was philosophically the greater of the two and that his brain was more highly trained, but if one cares to seek amusement in a childish game of ifs and whens with no relation to serious historical research, then one may let one's imagination loose on the question of whether Engels could have solved alone the problem which both men solved, whether he could have solved it in its more complicated French form in the way that Marx did. However, a fact which has been unjustly overlooked is that Engels solved the problem in its simpler English form none the less happily. If one regards his criticism of political economy exclusively from the economic standpoint, then it is open to certain objections, but what gives it its essential character and makes it a fundamental advance in economic knowledge is the treatment its author owes to the dialectical school of Hegelian philosophy.

The philosophic starting-point can be seen still more clearly in Engels' second contribution to the *Deutsch-Französische Jahrbücher* in which he describes the situation in England on the basis of one of Carlyle's books, declaring it to be the only book worth reading out of the literary harvest of a whole year, a literary poverty in characteristic contrast to the literary riches of France. He adds a note with reference to what he describes as the intellectual exhaustion of the English aristocracy and bourgeoisie. The educated Englishman, who was regarded on the Continent as the measure of the English national character, was, he declared, the most contemptible slave under the sun, and stifled by prejudices, particularly of a religious nature : " The only decent section of English society is that one unknown to the Continent, the workers, the pariahs of England, the poor— despite their coarseness and demoralization. England's hope for salvation lies in them. They are uneducated, but they have no prejudices and they represent good material for education. They have still sufficient vitality for a great national movement. They still have a future." Engels then pointed out, using the expression of Marx, that philosophy was beginning to sink deep into " the naïve mass of the people ". No respectable English translator had dared to do Strauss' *Life of Jesus* into English and no reputable publisher had dared to publish it, but a socialist lecturer had translated it and it was now being sold amongst the workers in London, Birmingham and Manchester in a penny pamphlet.

Engels translated the " most beautiful, often wonderfully beautiful ", passages of Carlyle in which the latter described the situation in England in the blackest colours. However, he quoted Bruno Bauer and Feuerbach against Carlyle's remedial proposals, a new religion, a pantheistic hero cult, and the rest of it, pointing out that all the possibilities of religion had been exhausted, including pantheism, which Feuerbach's theses in the *Anekdota* had disposed of for ever. " Up to the present the question raised has always been, what is God ? And German philosophy has given us the answer : God is man. Man has but to realize himself, to measure all the conditions of life against himself, to judge them according to his own character, to create the world in a thoroughly human fashion in accordance with the demands of his own nature, and he has solved the riddle of our age." Marx immediately interpreted Feuerbach's " man " as the character of man, the State, society, whilst Engels interpreted the character of man as his history, " our one and all " which must be held higher " by us " than by any other former philosophic school, higher even than by Hegel, who in the last resort had regarded it as no more than a test of his own logical conclusions.

It is extremely interesting to study in detail in the contributions which Marx and Engels made to the *Deutsch-Französische Jahrbücher*, how the same ideas developed, coloured in the one case by the French Revolution and in the other case by English industry, the two great historical transformations from which the history of modern bourgeois society dates, but essentially the same. Marx arrived at a realization of the anarchic character of bourgeois society from the Rights of Man, whilst Engels declared that competition was "the chief category of the economist, his favourite daughter" : "What are we to think of a law which can come into operation only as a result of the periodical revolutions of commercial crises? It is simply a natural law based on the unconsciousness of the parties concerned." Marx came to the conclusion that the emancipation of humanity would be achieved only when man had become a social being through the organization of his *forces propres* as social forces, whilst Engels declared : produce consciously as men and not as atomized individuals without social consciousness, and you will have overcome all artificial and untenable contradictions.

One observes that the agreement between the conclusions of Marx and Engels extends almost to the letter.

3. *The Holy Family*

The first work jointly undertaken by Marx and Engels was the overhauling of their philosophic consciences, and it took the form of a polemic against the *Allgemeine Literatur-Zeitung*, published in December 1843 in Berlin-Charlottenburg by Bruno Bauer and his brothers Edgar and Egbert.

In the columns of this organ the Berlin " Freemen " attempted to justify their world outlook, or what they referred to as such. Bruno Bauer had been invited by Fröbel to contribute to the *Deutsch-Französische Jahrbücher*, but after some hesitation he had not done so. His personal vanity had been deeply wounded by Ruge and Marx, although this was not the real reason why he clung to his old philosophy of self-consciousness. For all their bitterness his acid remarks about " the late-lamented *Rheinische Zeitung* ", the " Radicals " and the " clever sticks of anno domini 1842 " had a basis in fact. The thoroughness and despatch with which the romanticist reaction had crushed the *Deutsche Jahrbücher* and the *Rheinische Zeitung* as soon as they had turned from philosophy to politics, and the complete indifference of " the masses " to this " intellectual massacre " had convinced him that no progress could be made along such lines. For him salvation could be found solely in a return to pure philosophy, pure theory and pure criticism, and, naturally, once the retirement to the ideological clouds had been accomplished, it was not a matter of any great difficulty to create an omnipotent ruler of the world from these materials.

The programme of the *Allgemeine Literatur-Zeitung*, as far as it is possible to speak of anything so tangible, was summed up by Bruno Bauer as follows : " Up to the present all the great movements of history have been misguided and doomed to failure from the beginning because the masses interested themselves in them or were enthusiastically in favour of them ; or they came to a miserable end because the idea around which they centred was one requiring no more than a superficial understanding, and reckoning therefore with the applause of the masses." This antagonism between "intellect" and "the masses" was the *Leitmotiv* running through the whole of the *Allgemeine Literatur-Zeitung,* which declared that intellect at last knew where it must seek its only opponent, namely in the self-deception and spinelessness of the masses.

Accordingly, therefore, Bauer's organ treated all "mass" movements with the contempt they deserved : Christianity and Judaism, Pauperism and Socialism, the French Revolution and English industry. Engels was almost too polite about it when he wrote : " Its decayed and shrivelled Hegelian philosophy is like an old hag whose body has withered to a revolting caricature of its former self, but who still decorates and bedizens herself and leers around in the hope of finding a suitor ", for in the *Allgemeine Literatur-Zeitung* Hegelian philosophy was reduced to an absurdity. When Hegel declared that the absolute idea as the creative world spirit came to consciousness only subsequently in the philosopher, he meant only that the absolute idea apparently made history in the imagination, and he expressly forestalled the misunderstanding that the philosophic individual himself was the absolute idea. However, the Bauers and their disciples regarded themselves as the personal incarnation of criticism and of the absolute idea consciously living in them as the world spirit as against the rest of humanity. Such vapourings were bound to disperse rapidly even in the philosophic atmosphere of Germany, and in fact the *Allgemeine Literatur-Zeitung* met with a very tepid welcome even amongst the " Freemen ". Neither Köppen, who maintained a reserved attitude, nor Stirner co-operated and in fact Stirner was secretly preparing an attack on it. Meyen and Rutenberg also held themselves aloof, and with the one exception of Faucher, the Bauers had to content themselves with the third-raters amongst the " Freemen " : a certain Jungnitz and a pseudonymous Szeliga, a Prussian lieutenant named von Zychlinski, who lived to a ripe old age and died in 1900 as a General of Infantry. Within a year the whole hubbub had subsided completely, and by the time Marx and Engels took the field against it the *Allgemeine Literatur-Zeitung* was not only dead but forgotten.

This fact was not propitious for their first joint work, *A Criticism of Critical Criticism* as they called it themselves, or *The Holy Family* as it was called at the suggestion of their publisher. Their opponents immediately derided them for beating dead donkeys, and when Engel received the first copy of the printed book he declared that although it was a fine piece of work, the sovereign contempt with which it treated critical criticism was in sorry contradiction to its bulk, which was well over 300 pages. Most of it would be lost on the general public, he thought, and it would not meet with general interest. That verdict is much more applicable to-day than it was even then, but, on the other hand, it has now an added attraction which it did not have then, or at least, not in the same way. After condemning its hair-splitting, its quibbling and the monstrous straining of ideas, a later critic declared that it contained some of the most brilliant revelations of its authors' genius, and that in the mastery of its form and the iron compactness of its language it ranked among the finest things Marx had ever written.

In the passages to which the critic is referring, Marx shows himself a master of that constructive criticism which defeats ideological fantasies with positive facts, which creates whilst it destroys, and builds up whilst it is pulling down. He answers the critical observations of Bruno Bauer on French materialism and the French Revolution with brilliant sketches of these historical phenomena. Dismissing Bauer's talk about the contradiction between " intellect " and the " masses ", between the " idea " and " interest ", Marx answers coolly : " The idea always came to grief in so far as it was distinct from interest." Every mass interest which found historical expression and entered the world arena as an idea invariably proceeded far beyond its real limits and identified itself with the interests of humanity as a whole. It was the illusion which Fourier called the tone of every epoch in history. " Far from being ' misguided ', the interests of the bourgeoisie gained everything in the Revolution of 1789 and met with ' real success ', although the ' pathos ' disappeared and the ' enthusiastic ' garlands with which it had decorated its cradle faded. These interests were so powerful, in fact, that they successfully vanquished the pen of a Marat, the guillotine of the terrorists, the sword of Napoleon, the crucifix of the church and the blue blood of the Bourbons." The bourgeoisie had consummated its wishes of 1789 in 1830, with the difference that by that time its political enlightenment was at an end. It no longer aimed at achieving the ideal State and working for the good of the world and for the general interests of humanity in its constitutional representative State, but recognized it as the official expression of its exclusive power and as the political expression of its particular interests. The revolution was a failure only in so far as the masses were concerned, for their political idea did not correspond with their real interests, their vital principle was thereore not identical with the vital principle of the revolution, and the real conditions for their emancipation were essentially different from those under which the bourgeoisie could emancipate itself and society.

Replying to Bauer's contention that the State holds together the atoms of bourgeois society, Marx declared that they were held together by the fact that they were atoms only in the imagination, in the heaven of their fantasy, whilst in reality they were vastly different from atoms, namely, not divine egoists, but egoistic human beings. " To-day only crass political ignorance can imagine that bourgeois life must be held together by the State. The truth is that the State is held together by bourgeois life." And Bauer's scorn of the significance of industry and nature for historical knowledge Marx answers by asking whether critical criticism can be said to have arrived even at the beginning of historical knowledge so long as it continues to exclude the theoretical and practical attitude of man to nature, natural science and industry from the historical movement : " As it separates thinking from feeling and the soul from the body, so also does it separate history from natural science and industry, and regards the birthplace of history as being in the hazy cloud formations of heaven rather than in the raw, material production on earth."

Just as Marx defended the French Revolution against critical criticism, so Engels defended English history. His particular opponent was young Faucher, who paid rather more attention to earthly reality than any other contributor to the *Allgemeine Literatur-Zeitung*. It is diverting to observe how accurately Engels expounds the capitalist law of wages which twenty years later when Lassalle adopted it he was to consign to the depths of hell as " a rotten Ricardian law ". Engels proved Faucher guilty of many blatant errors—the man did not know in 1844 that the English anti-combination laws had been repealed in 1824—but his own arguments were often dangerously near to hair-splitting and in one important point he was wrong, though in a different way from Faucher. Faucher scorned the Ten Hour Bill of Lord Ashley as " a superficial slipshod measure " which would not lay the axe to the root of the matter, whilst Engels declared that " with the whole thoroughness of England " it was the expression, though the mildest possible, of a completely radical principle because it would not only lay the axe to the roots of foreign trade and thus of the factory system, but bite deep into them. At the time Engels, and Marx also, regarded Lord Ashley's Bill as an attempt to place reactionary fetters on large-scale industry, although they felt that the conditions of capitalist society would shatter such fetters again and again.

In *The Holy Family* neither Marx nor Engels has completely overcome their philosophical past. At the very beginning of the introduction they quote the " real humanism ' of Feuerbach against the speculative idealism of Bruno Bauer. They recognize unconditionally the brilliant advance of Feuerbach and his great services in having provided the great and masterly fundamentals for a criticism of all metaphysics, and in having set the human being in place of the old lumber and in place of the old eternal philosophic self-consciousness, but they advance again and again beyond the humanism of Feuerbach towards socialism—from the abstract to the historic human being—and in the chaotic and confused world of socialism they find their way about with remarkable acumen. They reveal the secret of that socialist dilettantism on which the satiated bourgeoisie prides itself. Human misery, the utter degradation which must accept alms to live, serves the aristocracy of wealth and education as an amusement, as a means to satisfy its vanity, as a means to gratify its arrogance. And all the numerous welfare associations in Germany, the charitable organizations in France and the various Quixotic doings in England, the philanthropic concerts, balls and performances, the charity spreads for the poor, and even the public subscriptions for the victims of labour and industry, have no deeper significance than this.

Fourier was the one amongst all the great utopians who contributed most to the ideological content of *The Holy Family*, but Engels distinguished between Fourier and Fourierism, declaring that the emasculated Fourierism preached by the *Démocratie Pacifique* [1] was nothing more than the social teachings of a section of the philanthropic bourgeoisie. Like Marx he stresses again and again the importance of historical development and the independent movement of the working class, things which even the greatest of the utopians failed to understand. Replying to Edgar Bauer Engels declares : " Critical criticism creates nothing, whilst the worker creates everything, so much so, in fact, that his intellectual creations put the whole of criticism to shame. The English and French workers can give evidence of this."

Marx disposes of the alleged mutually exclusive contradiction

[1] The organ edited by Victor Considérant in Paris.—Tr.

between " intellect " and the " masses " by pointing out that the communist criticism exercised by the utopians was, in fact, in accordance with the movement of the great masses. In order to gain some idea of the nobility of this movement one must make the acquaintance of the insatiable thirst for knowledge, the moral energy and the indefatigable urge forward of the French and English workers. It is not difficult to understand the great vigour with which Marx attacked Edgar Bauer on account of his poor translation of Proudhon and his absurd comments on Proudhon in the *Allgemeine Literatur-Zeitung.* To object that Marx glorified Proudhon in *The Holy Family* only to attack him fiercely a few years later, is a facile academic trick. In *The Holy Family* Marx is defending Proudhon's real achievements from being obscured and misrepresented by the empty phrases of Edgar Bauer. Marx recognized Proudhon's work as being just as much a pioneer achievement on the economic field as Bruno Bauer's own work was on the theological field, but just as Marx attacked Bauer's theological limitations so he attacked Proudhon's economic limitations.

Proudhon deals with property on the basis of the bourgeois economic system as an internal contradiction, but Marx declares : " Private property as such, as wealth, is compelled at the same time to maintain in being itself and its opposite, the proletariat. It is the positive side of the contradiction, private property sufficient in itself. The proletariat as such, on the other hand, is compelled to abolish itself and at the same time its conditional antithesis, that which makes it the proletariat. It is the negative side of the contradiction, its disintegrating side, dissolved and dissolving private property. Within the antithesis, therefore, the property owner is the conservative and the proletarian the destructive party. From the one proceeds the action to maintain the contradiction, and from the other the action to destroy it. In its economic movement private property advances to its own dissolution, but by means of a development independent of itself, unconsciously and against its will, a development conditioned by the nature of the problem, in that it produces the proletariat as the proletariat, as intellectual and physical misery conscious of its misery, inhumanity conscious of its inhumanity and therefore liquidating itself. The proletariat carries out the verdict which private property pronounces on itself by the creation of the proletariat, just as it carries out the verdict which wage-labour pronounces on itself by the production of riches for others and misery for itself. When the proletariat is victorious it will not thereby become the absolute side of society because it can be victorious only by dissolving both itself and its antithesis. With this not only the proletariat, but also its conditional antithesis, private property, will disappear."

Marx points out expressly that he is not turning the proletarians into Gods when he credits them with this historic rôle : " The contrary is true : because the abstraction of all humanity, even the appearance of humanity, is practically complete in the fully developed proletariat, because the living conditions of the proletariat represent the focal point of all inhuman conditions in contemporary society, because the human being is lost in the proletariat, but has won a theoretical consciousness of loss and is compelled by unavoidable and absolutely compulsory need— the practical expression of necessity—to revolt against this inhumanity, the proletariat can and must emancipate itself. However, it cannot emancipate itself without abolishing the conditions which give it life, and it cannot abolish these conditions without abolishing all those inhuman conditions of social life which are summed up in its own situation.

" It does not go through the hard but hardening school of labour fruitlessly. It is not a question of what this or that proletarian, or even the proletariat as a whole, may imagine for the moment to be the aim. It is a question of what the proletariat actually is and what it will be compelled to do historically as the result of this being. The aim and the historical action of the proletariat are laid down in advance, irrevocably and obviously, in its own situation in life and in the whole organization of contemporary bourgeois society." Again and again Marx lays stress on the fact that large sections of the French and English proletariat are already conscious of the historic task of the proletariat and are striving ceaselessly to develop this consciousness to complete clarity.

The cooling streams which bear fresh water through the fields pass through wide stretches of arid land, and two chapters in *The Holy Family* in particular, which deal with the incredible wisdom of the worthy Szeliga, put the patience of the reader to a severe test. Most justice is done to the work if it is regarded as an improvization, as apparently it was. Just at the time when Marx and Engels were getting to know each other personally, the eighth number of the *Allgemeine Literatur-Zeitung* arrived in Paris and contained an attack by Bruno Bauer in a veiled but none the less acid form on the conclusions the two had arrived at in the *Deutsch-Französische Jahrbücher*, and it is possible that the idea occurred to them of answering their old friend in a jovial, mocking fashion and as quickly as possible, in a short pamphlet. In any case, Engels immediately sat down and wrote his contribution, which amounted to a little over sixteen pages, and was very much astonished when he heard that Marx had extended the answer to over 300 pages. He also felt it to be "curious" and "peculiar" that in view of the minor part he had played in the production of the book his name should appear on the title page together with and even before that of Marx.

Marx probably began the work in his usual thorough fashion and then discovered, in accordance with the old all too true proverb, that he had no time to be brief, or perhaps he stretched the matter out in order to take advantage of the provision which exempted books of over 320 pages from the censorship.

The authors of the polemic announced that it was only the preliminary to the publication of independent works in which they would discuss—each for himself—their attitude to the newest philosophic and social doctrines. That they were deadly serious in their intentions can be seen from the fact that when Engels received the first printed copy of *The Holy Family* he had already completed the manuscript of the first of these independent writings.

4. A Fundamental Socialist Work

The manuscript which Engels had completed was *The Condition of the Working Class in England in 1844*, and it was published in the summer of 1845 in Leipzig by Wigand, who had been the publisher of the *Deutsche Jahrbücher* and had published Stirner's *Ego and His Own* a few months before. As the last offshoot of Hegelian philosophy Stirner slid into the shallow wisdom of capitalist competition, whilst Engels in his book laid the basis for those German theorists who had developed to communism and socialism as a result of Feuerbach's dissolution of Hegelian speculative philosophy, and who represented the majority. He described the conditions of the English working class in all their ghastly reality, a reality typical of the rule of the bourgeoisie.

When Engels reissued his book almost twenty years later he called it a phase in the embryonic development of modern international socialism and added : "Just as in the earlier stages of its development the human embryo still shows the gill formations of our forefathers the fish, so this book betrays everywhere the signs of the origin of modern socialism from one of its forefathers, German classic philosophy." This is true, but with the modification that these signs are much weaker than they were in Engels' contributions to the *Deutsch-Französische Jahrbücher*. This time neither Bruno Bauer nor Feuerbach are mentioned, and " friend Stirner " only occasionally, and then in order to make game of him a little. The influence of German philosophy on this book must be considered as definitely progressive and no longer retrograde.

The real value of the book lies not so much in the descriptions it gives of the proletarian misery which developed in England as a result of the capitalist mode of production, for in this respect Engels had numerous predecessors, Buret, Gaskell and others, from whom he quoted freely. And it is not even the burning indignation against a social system which subjected the working masses to such terrible sufferings, or the moving and graphic descriptions of those sufferings and the deep and heartfelt sympathy with the victims, which give the book its special character. The most admirable and at the same time the most noteworthy historical feature of the book is the thoroughness with which the twenty-four-year-old author understands the spirit of the capitalist mode of production and succeeds in explaining from it not only the rise, but also the decline of the bourgeoisie, not only the misery of the proletariat, but also its salvation. The aim of the book was to show how large-scale industry created the modern working class as a dehumanized, physically shattered race, degraded intellectually and morally to the point of bestiality, and how, thanks to a process of historical dialectics, whose laws he reveals in detail, it develops, and must inevitably develop, to the point of overthrowing its creator. The rule of the proletariat in England, it declared, would come about as the result of the amalgamation of the working-class movement with socialism.

Such an achievement as this book represented could only have been the work of one who had mastered Hegelian dialectics until they had become second nature and who had placed them squarely on their feet instead of leaving them upside down. The book therefore became one of the foundation stones of socialism, as its author had intended. However, the great interest which it aroused on its publication was not due to this, but rather to the matter with which it dealt. One of the academic bigwigs observed with comic vanity that the book made socialism " fit for the university ", but this was true only in the sense that this or that professor broke a rusty lance against it. Above all, the learned critics swelled with pride when the revolution which Engels observed on the threshold of England did not materialize, but fifty years later he declared imperturbably that the astonishing thing was not that this or that prophecy " made in youthful ardour " did not come to pass, but that so much had come about although at the time he had seen it " in the much-too-near future ".

To-day " the youthful ardour " which saw many things " in the much-too-near future " is not the least attraction of this pioneering book. Without its shadows its light would be unthinkable. The eye of genius which descries the shape of the future from the present sees the coming things more clearly and therefore nearer than the eye of common-sense, which has difficulty in getting used to the idea that it is not quite inevitable that just at dinner time the steaming soup must necessarily appear on the table. However, there were other people in England besides Engels who saw the revolution approaching, including even *The Times*, the chief mouthpiece of the English bourgeoisie, but in this case an uneasy conscience saw only devastation and slaughter in the revolution, whilst the social eye of Engels saw new life springing from the ashes.

Engels' " youthful ardour " found expression apart from this book. During the winter of 1844-5, whilst it was still on the anvil, he had other irons in the fire. Apart from the continuation of the book, which was to be only the first section of a larger work on the social history of England, he proposed to issue a socialist monthly together with Moses Hess, a library of foreign socialist authors, a critique of List, and other things as well. His plans often coincided with those of Marx and he tirelessly urged on the latter : " Finish off your economic work finally, even if you are not completely satisfied with it. It doesn't matter. Men's minds are ripe now and we must strike the iron while it's hot. . . . Time is pressing and therefore see to it that you are finished by April. Do as I do : set yourself a date by which you must positively be finished and then see to it that it appears in print as quickly as possible. If you can't have it printed there then try Mannheim or Darmstadt or somewhere else, but the great thing is that it must appear quickly." Engels even consoled himself over the " astonishing " length of *The Holy Family* with the idea that it wasn't a bad thing after all : " In that way a lot has already seen the light of day which might otherwise have lain in your desk heaven knows how long." How often was he to raise his voice in similar exhortations during the coming years !

He was impatient when he urged Marx to complete his work, but he was the most patient helper when genius, engaged in a hard struggle with itself, was at the same time hard pressed by the petty miseries of practical life. Immediately news came to Barmen that Marx had been expelled from Paris Engels opened up a subscription, " to divide communistically amongst us all the extra expenses which you have been caused." Reporting the " good progress of the subscriptions " he adds : " I don't know whether you will find the sum sufficient to set yourself up in Brussels, but I should like to point out that as a matter of course the honorarium which I hope to receive soon, at least in part, for my first English thing is at your disposal with the greatest pleasure. In any case I don't need it myself for the moment because the old gentleman must lend me anything I need if necessary. The *canaille* shall at least not have the pleasure of causing you pecuniary embarrassment as a result of their infamy." And for a generation Engels was tireless in his efforts to rob the *canaille* of this pleasure.

Light-hearted as Engels appears from his youthful letters, he was very far from being frivolous. The " first English thing ", to which he refers in such an offhand fashion, has since proved its sterling worth for over seventy years. It was an epoch-making work, the first great document of scientific socialism. When he wrote it Engels was twenty-four years old, and this in itself was sufficient to raise the dust in clouds from the academic bigwigs, but his was not a precocious talent rapidly developed in the clammy heat of a hot-house to wither away as rapidly in the open air. His " youthful ardour " developed from the inexhaustible fire of a great idea which warmed his declining years as it had inspired his youth.

And in the meantime he led " a quiet and peaceful life in all godliness and respectability " in the house of his parents, a life which must have satisfied the most punctilious Philistine. But he soon grew tired of it and only the " doleful faces " of his parents caused him to give commerce another trial. In the spring he planned to leave home and go first of all to Brussels. His " family troubles " were greatly intensified by communist propaganda in Elberfeld-Barmen in which he took a lively part. In a letter to Marx he reports that three communist meetings had been held with 40 people at the first, 130 at the second and 200 at the third : " The thing is a great attraction. People are talking of nothing but communism and we are winning new supporters every day. Communism is a *vérité* in Wuppertal ; indeed, it is a power already." This power afterwards capitulated before a simple police order and the situation was peculiar enough in all conscience. Engels himself reports that only the proletariat remained aloof from this communist movement, whilst the stupidest, laziest and most Philistine people, who normally interested themselves in nothing but their own private affairs, were beginning to be almost enthusiastic about it.

CHAPTER FIVE: EXILE IN BRUSSELS

1. The *German Ideology*

DRIVEN out of France Marx went with his family to Brussels. Engels feared that in the end the authorities would make trouble for him in Belgium also, and in fact the trouble came immediately.

In a letter to Heine Marx writes that immediately after his arrival in Brussels he was summoned to the *Administration de la Sûreté Publique* to sign an undertaking not to print anything concerning current Belgian politics. He agreed to this with an easy conscience, for he had neither the intention nor the possibility of doing anything of the kind, but as the Prussian government continued to importune the Belgian authorities with demands for his expulsion Marx formally abandoned Prussian citizenship in the same year, on the 1st of December 1845.

Neither at that time nor at any subsequent period did he seek citizenship in any other country, although in the spring of 1848 the provisional government of the French Republic offered him French citizenship in a fashion which did him all honour. Like Heine, Marx was unable to make up his mind to such a course, though Freiligrath, who was so often played off against them as a German to the core and the brilliant antithesis of the two " vagabonds without a Fatherland ", saw no objection at all to taking out naturalization papers during his exile in England.

In the spring of 1845 Engels arrived in Brussels and the two friends then went together to England for the purposes of study and stayed there for six weeks. Whilst he was in Paris Marx had begun to occupy himself with MacCulloch and Ricardo, and during this visit to England he was able to take a deeper look into the economic literature of the island kingdom, although for the moment he saw " only those books obtainable in Manchester " and the extracts and writings in Engels' possession. During his first stay in England Engels had contributed to *The New Moral World*, the organ of Owen, and to *The Northern Star*, the organ of the Chartists, and he now renewed old friendships and together the two friends established many new contacts with the Chartists and socialists.

When they returned from this journey they began a new joint work. "We decided", as Marx observed laconically later, "to work out our own standpoint together as against the opinions and the ideology of German philosophy, in fact, to settle accounts with our former philosophic conscience. We did this in the form of a criticism of post-Hegelian philosophy. The manuscript, two big octavo volumes, was already in the hands of a Westphalian publisher when we were informed that altered circumstances rendered publication impossible, whereupon we abandoned our manuscript to the gnawing criticism of the mice. We did so with little regret because our main object had been achieved—we had come to an understanding with ourselves." As a matter of fact, the mice really did get at the manuscript, but its remnants are sufficient to explain to us why its authors were not all too depressed at the misfortune.

Their thorough, even all too thorough, settlement of accounts with Bruno Bauer proved a hard nut for their readers to crack, and the two big volumes, comprising together about 800 pages, would have been a still harder one. The title of the work was *The German Ideology, a Criticism of Recent German Philosophy and its Representatives Feuerbach, Bruno Bauer and Stirner, and a Criticism of German Socialism and its Various Prophets*. Speaking from memory Engels declared later that the criticism of Stirner was no less voluminous than Stirner's own book, and the examples which have since been published indicate that Engels' memory was thoroughly reliable. The work is a still more discursive superpolemic than *The Holy Family* even in its most arid chapters, and the oases in the desert are still more rare, though they are by no means entirely absent, whilst even when dialectical trenchancy does show itself it soon degenerates into hair-splitting and quibbling, some of it of a rather puerile character.

It is true that our taste in these matters is more fastidious to-day, but that alone is not sufficient explanation, particularly as both Marx and Engels had shown before and have shown since, and showed even at the same time, that they were capable of epigrammatically trenchant criticism and that their style suffered little from prolixity. The decisive factor was that these intellectual struggles took place in a very small circle and most of the combatants were very young. It was the same phenomenon that literary history has observed in Shakespeare and his dramatic contemporaries: a tendency to ride a turn of speech to the death, to give the statements of their opponents as foolish a meaning as possible by literal interpretation or misrepresentation, a tendency to exaggeration and recklessness of expression—all that was not meant for the general public but for the esoteric understanding of the fellow-expert. Much that is indigestible or even ununderstandable in Shakespeare's humour to-day can be explained by the fact that, consciously or unconsciously, he was influenced in his work by considerations of what Greene and Marlowe, Ben Jonson, Beaumont and Fletcher would think about it.

Something of the sort is probably the explanation of the tone which Marx and Engels consciously or unconsciously adopted when dealing with Bauer and Stirner and others of their old companions in the art of purely intellectual gymnastics. What they had to say about Feuerbach would have been much more interesting because it would have been something more than purely negative criticism, but unfortunately this part of the work was never completed. Fairly clear indications of their attitude are given in one or two aphorisms about Feuerbach jotted down by Marx in 1845 and published a few decades later by Engels. Marx complained chiefly that Feuerbach's materialism lacked an " energizing principle ", just as he had complained in the same way in his student days about Democritus. This, he declared, was " the chief weakness of all previous materialism ", the appreciation of the thing, the reality, the sensuality, only in the form of the object or the idea, and not subjectively, not in practice, not in human sensual activity. In consequence the active side had been developed by idealism as against materialism, but abstractly only, for naturally idealism knew no real sensual activity. In other words, when Feuerbach abandoned the whole of Hegel he had abandoned too much whilst, in fact, it was necessary to transfer Hegel's revolutionizing dialectics from the realm of thought to the realm of reality.

Whilst still in Barmen Engels had written audaciously to Feuerbach in order to win him for communism and the latter had answered in a friendly tone, but, for the moment at least, in the negative. Feuerbach expected to go to the Rhineland in the summer and Engels was planning " to drum it in to him " that he must go on to Brussels, and in the meantime he sent Hermann Kriege, a pupil of Feuerbach, to Marx, describing him as " a splendid agitator ".

However, Feuerbach did not go to the Rhineland, and his subsequent works showed that it was too late for him to discard his " old shell ". His pupil Kriege also failed to come up to the mark. He did carry communist propaganda over the Atlantic, but he caused irreparable mischief in New York and it reacted ruinously on the communist colony which Marx had begun to gather around him in Brussels.

2. " True Socialism "

The second part of the work which Marx and Engels had planned was to deal with German socialism and its various prophets and to dissolve critically " the whole flat and stale literature of German socialism ".

This attack was launched against men like Moses Hess, Karl Grün, Otto Lüning, Hermann Püttmann and others, who had created quite a respectable literature particularly in magazines. There was the *Gesellschaftsspiegel* which appeared monthly from the summer of 1845 to the summer of 1846, the *Rheinische Jahrbücher* and the *Deutsches Bürgerbuch*, which both appeared in 1845 and 1846, the *Westfälisches Dampfboot*, a monthly which first appeared in 1845 and which lasted into the German revolution, and finally one or two dailies such as the *Triersche Zeitung*.

The extraordinary phenomenon which Karl Grün once termed " True Socialism ", an expression which Marx and Engels adopted ironically, had a short life. By 1848 practically nothing was left of it and what remained disappeared immediately the first shot of the revolution was fired. It exercised no effect whatever on the intellectual development of Marx, who was its masterful critic from the beginning, but the harsh verdict he passes on it in *The Communist Manifesto* does not sum up his whole attitude towards it, and for a time he regarded it as a mixture which for all its absurdities might produce something worth while, and Engels was even more firmly of this opinion.

Engels co-operated with Moses Hess in the publication of the *Gesellschaftsspiegel* and even Marx made one contribution to it. Both Marx and Engels co-operated with Hess on numerous occasions during the Brussels period, and at one time it appeared as though Hess had completely adopted their ideas. Marx repeatedly tried to persuade Heine to contribute to the *Rheinische Jahrbücher*, whilst this publication and the *Deutsches Bürgerbuch*, both of which were issued by Püttmann, printed contributions from Engels. Both Marx and Engels contributed to the *Westfälisches Dampfboot*, and this organ published the only part of the second section of *The German Ideology* which has yet seen the light of day.[1] It was a thorough and sharp criticism of a book which Karl Grün had published on the social movement in France and Belgium.

The fact that " True Socialism " also developed out of the dissolution of Hegelian philosophy has led to the contention that in the beginning Marx and Engels were its adherents and that for this reason they criticized it all the more sharply later, but

[1] No longer true. See Bibliography.—Tr.

this was not true. The difference between Marx and Engels and the supporters of " True Socialism " was that although both sides had arrived at socialism from Hegel and Feuerbach, Marx and Engels had studied the character of socialism from the French Revolution and from English industry, whilst the supporters of " True Socialism " had contented themselves with translating socialist formulas and slogans into " corrupt Hegelian German ". Marx and Engels did their best to raise " True Socialism " above this level and at the same time they were fair enough to recognize the whole tendency as a product of German history. It was flattering enough for Grün and his friends when their interpretation of socialism as an idle speculation on the realization of the human character was compared with the fact that Kant understood the expression of the will of the Great French Revolution only as the law of the really human will.

In their pedagogic efforts to improve " True Socialism " Marx and Engels spared neither patience nor severity. Co-operating with Hess on the *Gesellschaftsspiegel* Engels let many of Hess' things pass, though it must have gone against the grain, but in the *Deutsches Bürgerbuch* in 1846 he proceeded to make things hot for the " True Socialists ". " A little humanity, as they have begun to call the thing, a little ' realization ' of this humanity, or rather monstrosity, a little about property— at third or fourth hand—a minor proletarian jeremiad, the organization of labour, the formation of pitiful associations for uplifting the lower classes, plus an all-embracing ignorance of economics and the real nature of society—that is the whole business, and even then it loses the last drop of blood and the last vestige of energy and vitality thanks to theoretical im-partiality and ' the absolute calm of thought '. And with this tiresome stuff they want to revolutionize Germany, to set the proletariat in movement, to make the masses think and act ! " It was consideration for the proletariat and the masses which chiefly determined the attitude which Marx and Engels took up towards " True Socialism ". They attacked Karl Grün more violently than any other of its representatives not only because he in fact offered them the most opportunity, but because, living in Paris, he was causing hopeless confusion amongst the workers there and had won a disastrous influence over Proudhon. And when they dissociated themselves so sharply from " True Socialism " in *The Communist Manifesto*, even clearly indicating their former friend Moses Hess, they did so because thereby they were opening up the path for practical agitation on the part of the international proletariat.

In the same way they were perhaps prepared to forgive " True Socialism " the " pedantic naïveté " with which it took " its clumsy elementary exercises so seriously and solemnly, and trumpeted them out into the world in such a blatant fashion ", but certainly not its alleged preparedness to support the government. The struggle of the bourgeoisie against pre-March absolutism and feudalism allegedly offered it " the desired opportunity " for attacking the liberal opposition in the rear. " It served the German absolutist governments, with their camp following of parsons, schoolmasters, clod-hopping squires and bureaucrats, as a welcome scarecrow against the threatening advance of the bourgeoisie. It formed the sweetened supplement to the bitter scourge and the volleys of bullets with which the same governments belaboured the insurrection of the German workers." This was greatly exaggerated in point of fact and quite unjust as far as the persons were concerned.

In the *Deutsch-Französische Jahrbücher* Marx himself had pointed out that the peculiarity of conditions in Germany made it impossible for the bourgeoisie to rise against the government without itself being attacked in the rear by the proletariat, declaring that the task of socialism was thus to support liberalism where it was still revolutionary and to oppose it where it was already reactionary. In detail, however, this task was not easy to perform. Even Marx and Engels had occasionally defended liberalism as still revolutionary when it was in fact already reactionary, whilst the " True Socialists " sinned in the other direction and condemned liberalism whole and entire, a proceeding which was naturally agreeable to the German governments. The biggest sinner in this respect was Karl Grün, but Moses Hess was not without fault, whilst Otto Lüning, who edited the *Westfälisches Dampfboot*, was perhaps least guilty. In any case, their errors in this respect were committed from foolishness and lack of judgment and not from any desire to support the governments. In the revolution which passed sentence of death on all their illusions they were all without exception on the left wing of the bourgeoisie, not to mention Moses Hess, who fought in the ranks of the German Social Democracy. Not one single man amongst the " True Socialists " went over to the enemy, and of all the shades of bourgeois socialism in their day and since, the " True Socialists " have the best record in this respect.

In addition they harboured great respect for Marx and Engels and placed their publications willingly at the disposal of the two friends even when " True Socialism " came in for a drubbing thereby. It was obviously not secret malice, but a lack of understanding which prevented them slipping their old skin. Unfortunately they subscribed whole-heartedly to the old Philistine idea that things must always go smoothly and without uproar. They felt that a young party could not afford to be particular, and that when discussions became inevitable they should be conducted with all decorum and in the best of taste. In particular they felt that reputations like those of Bauer, Ruge and Stirner must be treated with respect. Naturally they caught a Tartar in Marx and on one occasion he declared : " It is characteristic of these old women that they are always striving to gloss over and whitewash all real party disputes ". However, the robust ideas of Marx on this subject met with understanding here and there even in the ranks of the " True Socialists ". For instance, Josef Weydemeyer, who was related to Lüning by marriage and who collaborated in the editorship of the *Westfälisches Dampfboot*, became one of the loyalest supporters of Marx and Engels.

Weydemeyer had been a lieutenant in the Prussian artillery but had abandoned a military career on account of his political convictions. As sub-editor of the *Triersche Zeitung*, which was under the influence of Karl Grün, he had fallen in with the " True Socialists ". In the spring of 1846 he went to Brussels. Whether he did so with the express intention of meeting Marx and Engels we do not know, but in any case he quickly became friendly with them and stoutly opposed the chorus of protest which arose in the ranks of the " True Socialists " at the ruthlessness of the criticism exercised by Marx and Engels, although even his brother-in-law Lüning joined in the protest. Born in Westphalia, Weydemeyer had something of the quiet and even slow, but loyal and tenacious character attributed to his countrymen. He never became a writer of any outstanding talent, and when he returned to Germany he obtained work as a surveyor in connection with the building of the Cologne-Minden railway, collaborating in the editorship of the *Westfälisches Dampfboot* only in his spare time. In his own practical way he now sought to be of assistance to Marx and Engels in a difficulty which was becoming more and more serious the longer it made itself felt, namely, the difficulty of obtaining a publisher.

Owing to the spite of Ruge the *Literarisches Kontor* in Zürich was closed to them. Ruge knew very well that whatever Marx might write it would hardly be of poor quality, but he practically presented a pistol at the head of his partner, Fröbel, in order to prevent him having any business relations with Marx, whilst Wigand in Leipzig, the chief publisher of the Young Hegelians, had already refused to publish a criticism of Bauer, Feuerbach and Stirner. Weydemeyer therefore opened up a welcome prospect when he persuaded two rich communists in Westphalia, Julius Meyer and Rempel, to agree to put up the necessary money to found a publishing house which was to begin its activities with no less than three productions : *The German Ideology*, a library of socialist authors, and a quarterly magazine edited by Marx, Engels and Hess.

However, when it came to the point and the promised money fell due the two capitalists went back on their word, although they had in the meantime confirmed it to Moses Hess. " Business difficulties " cropped up just at the right moment to. paralyse their spirit of communist self-sacrifice. The result was a bitter disappointment for Marx and Engels, and it was aggravated by the fact that Weydemeyer was unsuccessful in his efforts to place the manuscript of *The German Ideology* elsewhere, and the latter was now abandoned for good and all to the gnawing criticism of the mice.

3.   Weitling and Proudhon

The discussions which now took place between Marx and the two brilliant proletarian theorists who had exercised such an important influence on his early development were incomparably more moving from a human point of view and incomparably more significant politically than his criticisms of the Post-Hegelian philosophers and of the " True Socialists ".

Weitling and Proudhon were both born in the ranks of the proletariat. Both were blessed with healthy and vigorous characters, both were generously talented and both were so favoured by outward circumstances that it would probably have been possible for them to be amongst those rare exceptions which flatter that Philistine axiom which declares that the ascent into the ranks of the possessing classes is open to anyone of real talent in the ranks of the working class. Both men scorned to take this path, and instead they remained voluntarily in poverty and devoted themselves to fighting for their class and for their fellow-sufferers.

They were both well-built men, strong and vigorous, and made to enjoy the good things of life, but instead they gladly suffered the severest privations in order to pursue their aims. " A modest bed, often with three persons in the same room, a piece of board as a writing desk, and now and then a cup of black coffee ".

That was the life Weitling was living at a time when his name was already a sound of fear in the ears of the great ones of the earth, and Proudhon was living similarly in a Paris attic, " clothed in a knitted woollen jacket with his feet in clattering wooden clogs ", at a time when he already enjoyed a European reputation.

Both French and German culture went to the making of both men. Weitling was the son of a French officer, and when he grew old enough he hurried to Paris to study French socialism at the source. Proudhon came from the old free county of Burgundy, which had been annexed to France under Louis XIV. His associates always declared that he had a German head—and occasionally a German thick head. But, one way or the other, when he awakened to intellectual activity Proudhon felt drawn to German philosophy, whose representatives Weitling regarded as nothing but hazy " confusionists ", whilst on the other hand Proudhon condemned with extreme severity the great utopians who had meant so much to Weitling.

The two men shared the same fame and the same fate. They were the first members of the modern proletariat to provide historical proof of the intellect and vigour of the proletariat, proof that it could free itself, and they were the first to break down the vicious circle in which the working-class movement and socialism revolved. To this extent therefore they opened up a new epoch, and their work and their activity were exemplary and exercised a fruitful influence on the development of scientific socialism. No one has praised the beginnings of Weitling and Proudhon more generously than Marx. That which the critical dissolution of Hegelian philosophy had given him as the result of speculative thought he now saw confirmed in real life chiefly by Weitling and Proudhon.

Despite all their discernment and far-sightedness, however, Weitling never developed beyond the German artisan or Proudhon beyond the French petty-bourgeois, and thus they parted from the man who completed magnificently what they had so brilliantly begun. It was the result neither of personal vanity nor obstinate dogmatism, though perhaps both played some rôle the more the two felt themselves being stranded by the flow of historical development. Their discussions with Marx show that they simply did not grasp what he was driving at. They were the victims of a limited class consciousness which was all the more effective because it influenced both of them unconsciously.

Weitling arrived in Brussels in the beginning of 1846. After his agitation in Switzerland had come to an end, partly owing to internal dissension and partly owing to the exercise of brute force by the authorities, he had left for London, where however he was unable to get along with the members of the League of the Just. His efforts to save himself from a cruel fate by seeking refuge in prophetic arrogance made matters worse instead of better. Although the waves of Chartist agitation were rising high in England at the time he did not plunge into the English working-class movement, but turned his attention to drawing up a system of thought and speech with a view to founding a world language, and from that time on this became increasingly his favourite fad. He plunged recklessly into tasks for which his capacities and knowledge in no way fitted him and as a result he fell into an intellectual isolation which separated him more and more from the real source of his strength, the life of his class.

His journey to Brussels was certainly the best thing he could do, for if anyone could save him intellectually it was Marx. The latter received him hospitably, and this fact is vouched for not only by Engels but also by Weitling himself. However, any intellectual agreement between them proved impossible, and at a meeting of communists which took place in Brussels on the 30th of March 1846 the two came to grips violently. Weitling had irritated Marx extremely, as can be seen from a letter written by the former to Moses Hess. Negotiations were proceeding in connection with a new publishing house and Weitling insinuated that Marx and his friends were trying to cut him off from the " financial sources " in order to do well themselves with " well-paid translations ", but even after this Marx did what he could for Weitling. Writing to Marx on the basis of a report from Weitling, Moses Hess declared in a letter from Verviers on the 6th of May : " It was to be expected from you that your hostility towards him would not go so far as to close your purse hermetically so long as there was still something in it." There was, in fact, desperately little in it.

A few days later Weitling forced matters to the point of an irreparable breach. The propaganda conducted by Kriege in America had not justified the hopes both Marx and Engels had placed in it. The *Volkstribun*, a weekly newspaper which Kriege issued in New York, carried on fantastic and gushingly sentimental propaganda in a fashion both childish and pompous. This propaganda had nothing to do with any communist principles, and it tended to demoralize the workers utterly. Even worse than this, however, was the fact that Kriege began to send out grotesque letters to rich Americans begging them for financial support for the paper. As he presented himself in America as the literary representative of German communism its real representatives had every reason to protest against the compromising association.

On the 16th of May Marx and Engels and their supporters

decided to make a detailed protest in a circular to be sent to Kriege's paper for publication and to all their sympathizers. Weitling was the only one who refused to associate himself with the protest and he sought to justify his attitude with various empty pretexts : the *Volkstribun* was after all a communist organ and it was suited to American conditions ; the communists had enough powerful enemies in Europe without looking for trouble in America, particularly with their own comrades, etc. However, he was not satisfied with his refusal alone, but wrote a letter to Kriege warning him against those who had signed the protest as " cunning intriguers ". " The League, which is rolling in money, and consists of perhaps a dozen or a score of individuals, has nothing better to do than fight against me, the reactionary. I am to be polished off first, then the others and finally their friends, whilst in the end of course they will cut their own throats. . . . And tremendous sums of money are now coming in for this sort of thing, whilst I cannot even find a publisher. Hess and I are quite alone on this side, but Hess is boycotted also." After that Hess also abandoned the deluded man.

Kriege published the protest of the Brussels communists and it was also published by Weydemeyer in the *Westfälisches Dampfboot*. However, Kriege published Weitling's letter, or at least its worst passages, as a sort of antidote, and persuaded the Social Reform Association, a German workers organization in America which had chosen Kriege's weekly as its organ, to appoint Weitling as editor and to send him the money for the journey. Weitling accepted and disappeared from Europe.

In the same month, May, the breach between Marx and Proudhon came nearer. In order to make up for the lack of an organ of their own Marx and his friends issued printed or lithographed circulars, as in the Kriege affair, and at the same time sought to establish permanent correspondence connections between the various big towns in which there were communist groups. Such Corresponding Bureaux, as they were called, existed in Brussels and London, and one was to be set up in Paris, and Marx therefore wrote to Proudhon asking him to co-operate. On the 17th of May 1846 Proudhon sent a letter from Lyon agreeing, but pointing out that he would be able to write neither often nor much. At the same time he utilized the occasion to deliver a moral lecture to Marx which revealed to the latter how wide was the gulf which had opened up between them.

Proudhon now professed " an almost absolute anti-dogmatism " in economic matters and advised Marx not to fall into the error of his countryman Luther, who, after the overthrow of

Catholic theology, had immediately begun to found a Protestant theology to the accompaniment of a great wealth of anathema and excommunications. "We should not give mankind new work by creating new confusion. Let us rather give the world an example of wise and far-seeing toleration. We should not play the rôle of apostles of a new religion even if that religion is the religion of logic and reason." In other words, like the "True Socialists", he wished to maintain that pleasant confusion whose abolition Marx considered the preliminary condition for any real communist propaganda.

Proudhon also abandoned the revolution in which he had believed so long : "I prefer to burn property in a slow fire rather than give it new force in a St. Bartholomew's Night of property owners." He announced that he had given a detailed explanation of how this problem was to be solved in a work which was already half printed, and promised to submit it to the scourge of Marx's criticism gladly in the expectation of his revenge. "In passing I may remark that in my opinion the situation is : our proletarians in France have such a great thirst for knowledge that we should get a bad reception if we offered them nothing to drink but blood." Proudhon then defended Karl Grün against whose misunderstood Hegelianism Marx had warned him. Owing to his ignorance of German Proudhon was dependent on Grün and Ewerbeck in his studies of Hegel and Feuerbach and Marx and Engels. He informed Marx that Grün intended to translate his, Proudhon's, latest work into German, and asked whether Marx would assist in the distribution, adding that this would be honorable for everyone concerned.

The conclusion of Proudhon's letter sounds almost like mockery, though it was probably not intended to, but in any case Marx can hardly have found it edifying to be described as bloodthirsty in the bombastic gibberish of Proudhon, and in consequence the doings of Grün gave rise to even stronger suspicion. This was one of the reasons why in August 1846 Engels decided to go to Paris for a while and take over the reporting there, for Paris was still the most important centre of communist propaganda. It was necessary to inform the Paris communists at first hand about the breach with Weitling, the Westphalian publishing fiasco and about those various other matters which had stirred up the dust, particularly as Ewerbeck was not altogether reliable, and Bernays still less so.

In the beginning the reports sent by Engels from Paris, some to the Brussels Corresponding Bureau and others to Marx personally, were quite hopeful, but gradually he came to the conclusion that Grün had thoroughly "mucked up" the whole situation.

The work mentioned by Proudhon in his letter appeared in the autumn of the same year and turned out in fact to lead into the morass as his letter had already indicated. Marx then proceeded to wield the scourge of criticism thoroughly as Proudhon had invited, but all the revenge that the latter took, consisted in a certain amount of round abuse.

4. Historical Materialism

Proudhon entitled his book *The System of Economic Contradictions*, with the sub-title " The Philosophy of Poverty ",[1] and Marx therefore entitled his reply *The Poverty of Philosophy* and he wrote it in French in order to hit his opponent still more certainly. As a matter of fact, Marx did not succeed, for Proudhon's influence on the French working class and on the proletariat of the neo-Latin countries in general rose rather than fell, and for many decades Marx had still to contend with Proudhonism.

However, neither the immediate value of his reply nor its historical significance was diminished thereby. It represented a milestone both in the life of its author and in the history of social science. In this book the decisive factors of historical materialism were scientifically developed for the first time. In his earlier writings these ideas flash up like isolated comets, and in later writings he collected them in epigrammatic form, but in his reply to Proudhon he developed them systematically with all the convincing clarity of a triumphant polemic. The greatest scientific service rendered by Marx was his development of historical materialism, and it did for the historical sciences what Darwin's theories did for the natural sciences.

Engels had a share in this, and it was a larger share than his modesty was prepared to admit, but the classic formulation of the basic idea he ascribes, and probably with justice, exclusively to his friend. He describes how when he went to Brussels in the spring of 1845 Marx placed the basic idea of historical materialism before him in its finally developed form, namely that economic production in each historical period, and the social structure necessarily following from it, formed the basis for the political and intellectual history of the period, that in consequence the whole of history had been a history of class struggles, struggles between the exploited and the exploiters and between the ruled and the ruling classes at various stages of social development,

[1] *Système des Contradictions économiques ou Philosophie de la Misère*, Paris, 1846.

and that these struggles had now reached a stage at which the exploited and oppressed class, the proletariat, could no longer free itself from the exploiting and oppressing class, the bourgeoisie, without at the same time freeing the whole of society from exploitation and oppression for ever.

This is the basic idea presented in the reply to Proudhon, the focal point from which a multitude of rays irradiate. The style of the reply is magnificently clear and incisive, in strong contrast to the discursiveness which sometimes tires the reader in the polemics against Bruno Bauer and Max Stirner. This time the vessel is not being pushed and dragged along through a marsh, but speeds along over the open sea with a fresh breeze in its sails.

The book is in two parts. In the first part, to quote Lassalle, Marx shows himself as a Ricardo turned socialist, and in the second part as a Hegel turned economist. Ricardo had proved that the exchange of commodities in capitalist society took place upon the basis of the labour time contained in them. Proudhon demanded that this " value " of commodities should be " constituted " so that the product of one producer should exchange with the product of another containing the same amount of labour time. Society was to be reformed by turning all its members into workers exchanging similar quantities of labour. English socialists had already drawn this " egalitarian " conclusion from Ricardo's theory and had attempted to put it into practice, but their " exchange banks " had soon gone into liquidation.

Marx now pointed out that " the revolutionary theory " which Proudhon thought he had discovered to emancipate the proletariat was, in fact, nothing but the formula of modern working-class slavery. On the basis of his law of value Ricardo logically developed his law of wages : the value of the commodity labour-power is determined by the amount of time necessary to obtain the products which the worker needs in order to live himself and perpetuate his kind. It is a bourgeois illusion to imagine individual exchange without class contradictions, and to suppose in bourgeois society the possibility of a state of harmony and eternal justice permitting no one to enrich himself at the cost of others.

Marx describes the real development of things in the words : " With the beginning of civilization production begins to build itself up on the antithesis of occupation, social position and class, and finally on the antithesis of accumulated and direct labour. Without antithesis there can be no progress : civilization has acknowledged this law down to the present day. Up to the present the productive forces have been developed on the basis of this dominance of class contradiction." With his theory of " constituted value " Proudhon thought to secure for the worker the ever-increasing product of everyday labour resulting from the progress of social labour, but Marx pointed out that the development of the productive forces which permitted the English workers to produce twenty-seven times more in 1840 than in 1770 depended on historical conditions based on class contradictions : the accumulation of private capital, the modern division of labour, anarchic competition and the wage system. For the production of surplus labour there must be a class which profited and a class which lost.

Proudhon put forward gold and silver as the first examples of his " constituted value ", declaring that they had become money from their sovereign consecration at the hands of sovereigns. Nothing of the sort, answered Marx. Money was not a thing in itself but a social relation and, like individual exchange, it reflected a certain definite mode of production. " Indeed, an utter ignorance of history is necessary in order not to know that at all times sovereign rulers have had to submit to economic conditions and have never been able to dictate laws to them. Both political and civil legislation do no more than recognize and protocol the will of economic conditions. . . . Law is nothing but the recognition of fact." The sovereign seal on money gave it its weight and not its value. Gold and silver fitted to " constituted value " about as comfortably as a blister. Precisely in their function as tokens of value they were of all commodities the only ones not determined by their costs of production, and could be replaced in circulation by paper money, as Ricardo had long since made clear.

Marx hinted at the final aim of communism by pointing out that " the correct balance between supply and demand " for which Proudhon was looking had been possible only in times when the means of production were limited, when exchange took place within very narrow boundaries, when demand governed supply and consumption governed production. With the development of large-scale industry this had become impossible because the latter was compelled by its tools alone to produce in steadily increasing quantities without waiting for demand, and must therefore experience with inevitable necessity and in constant succession the phases of prosperity and depression, crises and stagnation, new prosperity and so on. " In present-day society, in industry which is based on individual exchange, productive anarchy which is the source of so much evil is at the same time the cause of all progress. Therefore the alternatives are : one must strive to obtain the correct proportions of former centuries with the means of production of our own day, in which case one is both reactionary and utopian, or one must strive for progress without anarchy, in which case one must abandon individual exchange in order to maintain the productive forces."

The second chapter of Marx's reply to Proudhon is even more important than the first. In the first chapter he deals with Ricardo without as yet having won through to complete scientific objectivity towards him, for instance, he still accepts Ricardo's law of wages without reservation, but in the second chapter he deals with Hegel and then he is in his element. Proudhon had grossly misunderstood Hegel's dialectical method. He held fast to those aspects which had already become reactionary, for instance, that the world of reality is derived from the world of ideas, whilst he rejected its revolutionary aspect : the auto-activity of the idea which formulates both thesis and antithesis in order to develop in the conflict that higher unity which maintains the real content of both aspects by resolving its contradictory form. He differentiated a good and a bad side in each economic category and then sought for a synthesis, for a scientific formula which would embody the good side and destroy the bad. The good side he observed stressed by the bourgeois economists and the bad side condemned by the socialists. With his formulas and syntheses he thought to have raised himself above both the bourgeois economists and the socialists.

Marx answered this claim in the words : " Monsieur Proudhon flatters himself that he has criticized both economics and communism, but in reality he has remained far below either of them : below the economist because as a philosopher with a magic formula in his pocket he imagines himself spared the necessity of going into economic details, and below the socialist because he has neither sufficient insight nor sufficient courage to raise himself, even speculatively, above the bourgeois horizon. He aspires to be the synthesis and he is in fact nothing but a composite error. He desires to hover above both bourgeois and proletarian as a man of science, but in fact he is nothing but a petty-bourgeois thrown hither and thither between capital and labour, between economics and socialism." However, one must not confuse the petty-bourgeois here with the Philistine, for Marx always regarded Proudhon as a capable man unfortunately unable to go beyond the limits of petty-bourgeois society.

It was not difficult for Marx to reveal the defectiveness of the methods adopted by Proudhon : if one split up the dialectical process into a good and a bad side and offered the one category as an antidote against the other, then all life fled from the idea ; it could no longer function, no longer formulate the thesis and the antithesis. As an authentic student of Hegel Marx was well aware that the bad side which Proudhon was so anxious to abolish everywhere was just the side which made history by producing the struggle. Had one tried to maintain the better aspects of feudalism, the patriarchal life in the towns, the prosperity of rural domestic industry and the development of urban handicraft, whilst at the same time seeking to exterminate everything which cast a shadow over the picture, serfdom, privilege and anarchy, then everything which produced the struggle would have been wiped out and the bourgeoisie would have been strangled at birth. One would thereby have taken on the grotesque task of emasculating history.

The correct formulation of the problem was given by Marx in the following words : " If one wishes to estimate feudal production correctly one must regard it as a mode of production based on contradiction. One must show how riches were produced within this contradiction, how the productive forces developed simultaneously with the struggle of the classes, and how one of these classes, the bad side, the social evil, grew ceaselessly until the material conditions for its emancipation had ripened." And he then showed the same historical process of development in connection with the bourgeoisie. The productive relations in which it moves have not a simple and uniform character, but a double one : misery is produced under the same conditions as riches ; as the bourgeoisie develops so the proletariat develops to the same degree, and, as a result, the struggle between the two classes. The economists are the theoreticians of the bourgeoisie whilst the communists and socialists are the theoreticians of the proletariat. The latter are utopians who draw up systems and seek for a healing science to meet the needs of the oppressed classes so long as the proletariat is not sufficiently developed to constitute itself as a class and so long as the productive forces of bourgeois society are not developed sufficiently to reveal the material conditions necessary for the emancipation of the proletariat and the building up of a new society. " But to the extent to which history advances, and with it the struggle of the proletariat, it is no longer necessary for them to seek science in their heads. All they need do is give themselves an account of what is going on before their eyes and make themselves its instruments. So long as they are still seeking science in their heads and drawing up systems, so long as they are at the beginning of their struggle only, they see only misery in misery, and fail to realize the revolutionary side of misery which will overthrow the old society. From this moment on science becomes the conscious product of the historical movement ; it has ceased to be doctrinaire and has become revolutionary."

Marx regards economic categories as nothing but the theoretical expression, the abstraction of social relations. " Social relations are closely connected with the productive forces. With the attainment of new productive forces mankind alters its mode of production ; with the way in which it obtains its living mankind alters all its social relations. . . . But the same men who form their social relations in accordance with their material mode of production, form also their principles, their ideas and their categories in accordance with their social relations." Marx compares the bourgeois economists who speak of " the eternal and natural institutions " of bourgeois society with those orthodox theologians who consider their own religion a revelation from God and all other religions as the inventions of man.

Marx revealed the defectiveness of Proudhon's methods on the basis of a number of economic categories : the division of labour and machinery, competition and monopoly, landownership and rent, strikes and workers' organizations, on which he had tried his methods. The division of labour was not, as Proudhon assumed, an economic category, but an historical category, which had taken on various forms in various periods of history. According to bourgeois economics the factory is the condition for its existence, but the factory did not originate, as Proudhon assumed, as the result of friendly agreement amongst the workers and not even in the lap of the old Guilds. The merchant became the head of the modern workshop and not the old Guild master.

Competition and monopoly are thus not natural, but social categories. Competition is not industrial, but commercial zeal. It is not concerned with the product, but with profit. It is not a necessity of the human soul, as Proudhon assumed, but the result of historical necessity originating in the eighteenth century, and it could disappear in the nineteenth century for historical reasons.

Proudhon's idea that landed property had no historical origin, that it was based on psychological and moral considerations having only a very distant connection with the production of wealth, that ground-rent should bind man closer to nature, was just as erroneous : " In every period property developed differently and under quite different social relations. To explain bourgeois property therefore means nothing more than to explain all the social relations of bourgeois production. To explain property as an independent relation is nothing but an illusion of metaphysics or jurisprudence." Ground-rent—the surplus of the price of agricultural produce above the cost of production, including the prevailing rate of profit on capital and the interest on capital—originated under definite social relations and could have originated only under those definite social relations. It is landownership in its bourgeois form, feudal property subjected to the conditions of bourgeois production.

And finally Marx explains the historic significance of strikes and unions, both of which Proudhon rejected. Although both bourgeois economists and socialists may warn the workers, though perhaps for opposite reasons, against the use of such weapons, strikes and unions will develop parallel with the development of large-scale industry. Divided in their interests by competition the workers have nevertheless a common interest in maintaining their wages. The idea of resistance, common to them all, united them in unions which contain all the elements of a coming struggle, just as the bourgeoisie began with sectional combinations against the feudal lords and then constituted itself as a class and, as a constituted class, transformed feudal society into bourgeois society.

The antagonism between proletariat and bourgeoisie is a struggle of class against class, a struggle which, brought to its highest expression, means a complete revolution. The social movement does not exclude the political movement because there is no political movement which is not at the same time a social movement. Only in a society without classes will social evolution cease to be political revolution, but until then the last word of social science on the eve of all general social transformations will always be : " Victory or death ! Bloody war or nothing ! This is the pitiless formulation of the question." Marx used this quotation from George Sand to conclude his reply to Proudhon.

In this book Marx developed historical materialism from a series of its most important angles and at the same time he finally settled accounts with German philosophy. He went beyond Feuerbach by going back to Hegel. The official Hegelian school had certainly gone bankrupt. It had degenerated the dialectical methods of its master to a mere formula which it applied to everything and everybody, often with the greatest clumsiness. One could say of these Hegelians, and it was said of them, that they understood nothing and wrote about everything.

Their hour had struck when Feuerbach challenged the speculative conception ; the positive content of science once again outweighed its formal side. But the materialism of Feuerbach lacked an " energizing principle ". It remained pure natural science and excluded the historical process. This was not enough for Marx, and how right he was was seen later when the peripatetic preachers of this materialism, Büchner and Vogt, appeared on the scene. Their narrow-minded Philistine methods of thought caused even Feuerbach to exclaim that though he might agree with such materialism from behind yet never would he from the front. Or to quote a comparison once used by Engels : " The stiff-kneed cart-horse of bourgeois common sense naturally shies at the ditch which separates essence from appearance and cause from effect, but if one wants to hunt over the rough country of abstract thought one must not ride a cart-horse."

However, the Hegelians were not Hegel. They might display their ignorance, but Hegel himself was amongst the best brains of all time. Far more than all other philosophers, his method of thought had an historic significance which permitted him a magnificent conception of history, although this conception was a purely ideological one which saw things, so to speak, in a concave mirror and conceived world history as no more than a practical example of the development of thought. Feuerbach had not succeeded in coping with this real content of the Hegelian philosophy and the orthodox Hegelians had abandoned it.

Marx took it up anew, but he reversed it in that he no longer proceeded from " pure thought ", but from the pitiless facts of reality, thus giving materialism the historical dialectical method and an " energizing principle " which sought not merely to explain society, but to transform it.

5. The *Deutsche Brüsseler Zeitung*

Marx found publishers both in Brussels and in Paris for his answer to Proudhon, but although it was not very long he had to pay for the costs of the printing himself. When the book appeared in midsummer 1847 he also had a press organ in the *Deutsche Brüsseler Zeitung* which offered him the possibility of placing·his views before the public.

The paper had been issued twice a week since the beginning of the year by Adalbert von Bornstedt, who had formerly edited Börnstein's *Vorwärts* in Paris and who had been in the pay of both the Austrian and Prussian governments, a fact which has since been irrefutably established from the documents in the Berlin and Vienna archives, and the only point which is not quite clear is whether Bornstedt was continuing his spying in Brussels. There was a certain amount of suspicion against him, but this was dispelled by the fact that the Prussian Ambassador in Brussels roundly denounced his paper to the Belgian authorities.

Naturally, these denunciations may very well have.been made in order to throw dust into the eyes of the revolutionary elements which had collected in Brussels, and to accredit Bornstedt in their ranks, for the defenders of Throne and Altar have never been squeamish in their choice of means to further their lofty aims.

Marx in any case did not believe that Bornstedt was a Judas. Despite its many weaknesses, the *Deutsche Brüsseler Zeitung* was doing good work, he declared, and those who thought it not good enough should work to make it better and not shield themselves behind the facile pretext that suspicion clung to Bornstedt's name. On the 8th of August we find Marx writing bitterly to Herwegh : " Either the man's no good, or it may be the woman, or it's the tendency, or the style, or the size, or the distribution involves a certain amount of danger. . . . Our Germans have always a thousand words of wisdom up their sleeves to prove why they should once again let an opportunity slip by unutilized. An opportunity for doing something is nothing but a source of embarrassment for them." He then sighs that his manuscripts are suffering the same fate as the *Deutsche Brüsseler Zeitung* and ends up with a robust curse at the donkeys who reproached him because he preferred to write in French rather than not write at all.

Even if we assume from this that Marx treated the suspicion against Bornstedt somewhat lightly in order not to " let an opportunity slip by unutilized ", it would hardly be possible to reproach him for it because the opportunity was a favourable one, and it would have been foolish to let it slip by merely on account of suspicion. In the spring of 1847 pressing financial need had compelled the King of Prussia to call together the United Diet, a gathering of the former Provincial Diets, that is to say, a feudal body along corporative lines similar to the one called by Louis XVI in the spring of 1789 under similar outward compulsion. Matters had certainly not developed so rapidly in Prussia as they had previously in France, but still the United Diet kept its purse-strings tightly drawn and brusquely informed the government that it would refuse to vote any moneys until its rights had been extended and in particular until a guarantee had been given that it would be convened regularly. With this things had begun to move, for the financial straits of the government were really pressing. Sooner or later the dance would have to begin anew, and the sooner the music struck up the better.

This was the idea which pervaded the contributions of Marx and Engels to the *Deutsche Brüsseler Zeitung*. An article which was published anonymously, but which, to judge from style and content, came from the pen of Engels, dealt with the debates in the United Diet on free trade and protective tariffs. At the time Engels was thoroughly convinced that the German bourgeoisie needed protective tariffs in order to prevent itself being driven to the wall by foreign industry, and to give itself an opportunity of generating sufficient strength to overcome feudalism and absolutism. For this reason, and for this reason only, Engels advised the proletariat to support the agitation for protective tariffs. In his opinion, List, the authority of the protectionists, had produced the best bourgeois German economic literature, although he declared that List's best work had been written by the Frenchman Ferrier, the theorist of the Continental system. He also warned the workers against being fooled by phrases about " the welfare of the labouring classes " which were being used by both protectionists and free-traders as an ostentatious shield for their own self-serving agitation, and declared that the wages of the workers would remain the same under protectionism as under free trade. He defended protectionism purely and simply as " a progressive bourgeois measure ", and this was Marx's standpoint also.

A longer contribution which appeared in the *Deutsche Brüsseler Zeitung* repulsing an attack on the part of Christian-feudal socialism was the joint work of Marx and Engels. The attack had been launched in the *Rheinischer Beobachter*, an organ which the government had recently founded in Cologne in order to play off the workers of the Rhineland against the bourgeoisie. It was in the columns of this paper that young Hermann Wagener won his spurs, as he afterwards placed on record in his memoirs. Marx and Engels maintained close connections with Cologne and they were obviously aware of Wagener's activities, for mocking references to " neat ecclesiastical commissioners " formed a sort of refrain to their observations and at the time Wagener was an ecclesiastical assessor in Magdeburg.

The *Rheinischer Beobachter* now used the failure of the government to obtain what it wanted from the United Diet for an attempt to mislead the workers, declaring that by refusing to vote the necessary moneys the bourgeoisie had shown that all it cared about was seizing power in the State in its own interests. It cared nothing for the welfare of the people, but merely pushed forward the masses in order to intimidate the government. The masses were being treated as nothing but cannon-fodder in an attack on the government. Marx and Engels replied in a fashion which is obvious to us to-day : the proletariat had no more illusions about the bourgeoisie than it had about the government, and its only consideration was which served its purpose better, the rule of the bourgeoisie or the rule of the government. The answer to the question could be obtained by a simple comparison between the situation of the German workers and that of the English and French workers.

"Happy people!" declared the *Rheinischer Beobachter.* "You have won the battle of fundamental principles, and if you don't know what that is, ask your representatives to explain it to you, and perhaps during their long speeches you will forget your hunger." These demagogic phrases were answered by Marx and Engels with caustic mockery : from the fact that such incitement went unpunished it was easy to see that the press in Germany was really free. And they declared that in fact the German proletariat had thoroughly understood the fundamental principles at stake, so much so that it reproached the United Diet not with having won them, but with having lost them. Had the United Diet not contented itself with demanding merely the extension of its own rights, but instead have demanded trial by jury, equality before the law, the abolition of forced labour, the freedom of the press, the right of free association and the convening of a really representative body, then it would have received the wholehearted support of the proletariat.

The pious mumblings of the *Rheinischer Beobachter* about the social principles of Christianity which made communism unnecessary were thoroughly disposed of : " The social principles of Christianity have had eighteen hundred years in which to develop and they need no further development at the hands of Prussian ecclesiastical commissioners. The social principles of Christianity justified slavery in the classic world and they glorified mediæval serfdom, and if necessary they are quite willing to defend the oppression of the proletariat even if they should wear a somewhat crestfallen appearance the while. The social principles of Christianity preach the necessity of a ruling and an oppressed class, and all they have to offer to the latter is the pious wish that the former may be charitable. The social principles of Christianity transfer the reparation of all infamies to the realms of heaven and thus they justify the perpetuation of these infamies on earth. The social principles of Christianity declare that all the villanies of the oppressors against the oppressed are either the just punishment for original or other sin, or tribulations which God in his own inscrutable wisdom causes the elect to suffer. The social principles of Christianity preach cowardice, self-abasement, resignation, submission and humility—in short, all the characteristics of the *canaille* ; but the proletariat is not prepared to let itself be treated as *canaille*, and it needs its courage, confidence, pride and independence even more than it needs its daily bread. The social principles of Christianity are sneaking and hypocritical whilst the proletariat is revolutionary."

It was this revolutionary proletariat which Marx and Engels led into the field against the juggleries of monarchist social reform. A people prepared to thank its rulers with tears in its eyes for a kick accompanied by a penny existed only in the imagination of a king. The real people, the proletariat, was, in the words of Hobbes, a robust and dangerous youth, and its way of dealing with kings who tried to worst it could be seen graphically in the fate of Charles I of England and Louis XVI of France.

This answer broke over the feudal-socialist crop like a storm of hail, but some of the stones fell wide of the mark. Marx and Engels were right when they defended the action of the United Diet in refusing to grant moneys to a reactionary and negligent government, but they did the Diet too much honour when they adopted the same attitude towards its rejection of a government income-tax proposal. The proposal was, in fact, a trap set for the bourgeoisie by the government. The demand that the milling and slaughtering taxes, which weighed most heavily on the workers in the big towns, should be abolished and the resultant financial deficit made up by means of an income tax on the propertied classes, had first been raised by the Rhenish bourgeoisie, which was moved by considerations similar to those which moved the English bourgeoisie in its struggle for the repeal of the Corn Laws. The government itself was strongly opposed to this proposal because it cut into the flesh of the rich landowners, who could not expect any fall in the wages of the workers employed by them as a result of the abolition of the taxes, which were imposed in the big cities only. However, it nevertheless brought in the necessary Bill because it felt sure that a feudal corporative body like the United Diet would never agree to a tax reform which benefited the working classes even only temporarily at the expense of the possessing classes, and it hoped therefore to make itself popular and the Diet unpopular. How right the government was in its calculation was seen when the Bill came before the Diet and almost all the princes, almost all the junkers and almost all the officials voted against it. In addition, the government had the good fortune that even a section of the bourgeoisie turned tail hurriedly when it came to the point.

The rejection of the income-tax proposal was then thoroughly exploited by all the official pens as a striking proof of the hypocritical and deceitful game being played by the bourgeoisie, and the *Rheinischer Beobachter* in particular rode the poor nag to death.

When Marx and Engels answered their " ecclesiastical com-missioner " by informing him that he was " the biggest and most shameless ignoramus in economic matters " for asserting that the introduction of an income tax would alter the existing social misery by one hair's-breadth, they were quite right, but they were not right when they defended the rejection of the bill by the bourgeoisie as a justifiable blow against the government. The action of the bourgeoisie was, in fact, not a blow against the government at all, and the rejection of the Bill rather strengthened the government's financial position than otherwise, for it retained its efficient milling and slaughtering taxes instead of experi-menting with a new income tax, whose imposition would certainly have met with innumerable difficulties, as the history of all such taxes has shown. In this case, therefore, Marx and Engels regarded the bourgeoisie as still revolutionary when, in fact, it was already reactionary.

On the other hand, the " True Socialists " made the opposite mistake often enough, and it is understandable that at a time when the bourgeoisie was girding its loins for the fray Marx and Engels delivered another attack on them. The attack was delivered in a number of belletristic contributions which Marx published in the *Deutsche Brüsseler Zeitung* " Against German Socialism in Prose and Verse ", and in an unpublished contribu-tion which is in Engels' handwriting but was probably a joint work. " True Socialism " was attacked this time chiefly from its æsthetic-literary aspect, which was its weakest, or, according to taste, its strongest side. In their attack on this literary per-version Marx and Engels did not always sufficiently respect the rights of literature and art; for instance, in the handwritten contribution referred to above, Freiligrath's splendid " *Ça ira* " is treated with unconscionable severity, whilst Karl Beck's " Songs of the Poor " were also harshly treated by Marx in the *Deutsche Brüsseler Zeitung* on account of their " petty-bourgeois illusions ", but at the same time Marx prophesied the sorry fate of that pretentious naturalism which was to develop fifty years later when he wrote : " Beck belauds this cowardly petty-bourgeois misery. His hero is the ' poor man ', the *pauvre honteux* with his pious, petty and inconsequent longings, instead of the proud, menacing and revolutionary proletarian." The unfortunate Grün then came in for a thorough castigation on account of a long-since forgotten book in which he had maltreated Goethe " from a human standpoint " by painstakingly piecing together a picture of what he alleged was " the real man " out of all the petty, boring and Philistine traits of the great poet.

More important than this skirmishing was a longer work in

which Marx dealt as severely with the usual radical phraseology of the bourgeoisie as he did with the pseudo-socialist phraseology of the government. In a polemic against Engels Karl Heinzen had sought to explain injustice in the distribution of property as the result of State power, declaring everyone a coward and a fool who attacked the bourgeoisie for its accumulation of money whilst leaving the king with his accumulation of power in peace. Heinzen himself was a very mediocre phrasemonger and unworthy of any particular attention, but his arguments were very much after the heart of the " enlightened " Philistine : the monarchy owed its existence to the fact that for centuries humanity had been without common sense and without human dignity, and now that humanity was once again in possession of these valuable attributes all social problems paled into insignificance before the great question : monarchy or republic. This brilliant argument was a suitable complement to the argument of the princes that revolutions were caused purely by the wickedness of demagogues.

Marx demonstrated, chiefly on the basis of German history, that history made the princes, not vice-versa. He laid bare the economic causes of the absolute monarchy, pointing out that it developed in a transitional period when the old feudal classes were in decline and the new class of modern bourgeois still in process of formation. The fact that the absolute monarchy had developed later in Germany and was lasting longer was due to the crippled development of the German bourgeoisie. The violently reactionary rôle being played by the princes was thus due to economic reasons. Where the absolute monarchy formerly encouraged trade and industry and the simultaneous rise of the bourgeoisie as necessary conditions of national power and of its own magnificence, it now sought to hamper them everywhere as increasingly dangerous weapons in the hands of a bourgeoisie already grown too powerful. It was now turning its dull and anxious glance away from the town, the origin of its own rise to power, to the countryside, whose fields were manured with the corpses of its old and valiant feudal opponents.

This work contains many fruitful ideas, but the " common sense " of the worthy Philistine was proof against it. The same theory which Marx took up on Engels' behalf against Heinzen had to be taken up again a full generation later by Engels on Marx's behalf against Dühring.

6. The Communist League

During the year 1847 the communist colony in Brussels had grown to quite considerable proportions, although there was no one in the group who could measure himself with Marx or Engels. Occasionally it seemed as though either Moses Hess or Wilhelm Wolff, both of whom contributed to the *Deutsche Brüsseler Zeitung*, might play the third in the alliance, but in the end neither of them did. Hess was never quite able to brush away his earlier philosophic cobwebs and finally the painfully severe fashion with which *The Communist Manifesto* dealt with his writings led to a complete breach between him and Marx and Engels.

The friendship of Marx and Engels with Wilhelm Wolff was of a later date, Wolff having come to Brussels only in the spring of 1846, but it proved to be a staunch one and ended only with the death of Wolff, which unfortunately occurred very early. He was not an independent thinker, but as a writer he had " the popular manner ". He came from the ranks of the hereditarily subject Silesian peasantry, and under tremendous difficulties he had worked his way up to the university where he fanned a white-hot hatred against the oppressors of his class with the works of the great thinkers and poets of classic antiquity. As a Demagogue he had been dragged from one Silesian fortress to the other for a few years, and after that he had earned his living as a private teacher whilst at the same time conducting ceaseless guerilla warfare against the bureaucracy and the censorship until the filing of new proceedings against him caused him to go abroad in preference to rotting in a Prussian prison.

From his stay in Breslau he was friendly with Lassalle, and the latter and Marx and Engels have laid imperishable laurels on his grave. Wolff was one of those noble natures who, in the words of the poet, pay their way in life with what they are themselves. His steadfast character, his incorruptible loyalty, his scrupulous conscientiousness, his invariable unselfishness and his never-failing modesty made him an exemplary revolutionary fighter and won him the respect of both friends and foes, irrespective of whether they supported or hated his political opinions.

Another member of the circle around Marx and Engels, though not quite so intimate with them, was Ferdinand Wolff. Ernst Dronke, who had written an excellent book about pre-March Berlin and had been sentenced to two years imprisonment in a fortress for alleged *lèse-majesté*, arrived in the circle at the last moment, having made his escape from the fortress of Wesel. Another member of the inner circle was Georg Weerth, who was acquainted with Engels from the latter's Manchester days and who had lived in Bradford as an employee of another German firm. Weerth was a real poet, and in consequence he was free from all the affectations of the poetaster. He too unfortunately died young, and as yet no reverent hand has gathered together the verses which he sang in the spirit of the fighting proletariat and carelessly scattered. The circle of intellectuals was strengthened by a number of capable artisans, men like Karl Wallau and Stephan Born, the two compositors of the *Deutsche Brüsseler Zeitung*.

Brussels, as the capital of a State which boasted that it was an exemplary bourgeois monarchy, was the best place to establish international connections as long as Paris, which was still regarded as the centre of the revolution, was stifled by the notorious September Laws. Marx and Engels had established good relations with the participants in the revolution of 1830 in Belgium. In Germany, and particularly in Cologne, they had old and new friends, above all Georg Jung and the two doctors d'Ester and Daniels. In Paris Engels had established connections with the Democratic Socialist Party and in particular with its literary representatives Louis Blanc and Ferdinand Flocon, who edited *Reforme*, the organ of the party. Still closer relations existed with the revolutionary wing of the Chartists, with Julian Harney, the editor of *The Northern Star*, and Ernest Jones, who had been educated in Germany. The Fraternal Democrats, an international organization in which the League of the Just was represented by Karl Schapper, Josef Moll and others, was strongly under the intellectual influence of these Chartist leaders.

In January 1847 the league took a very important step. As the " Communist Corresponding Committee " in London it maintained relations with the " Corresponding Committee " in Brussels, but these relations were mutually somewhat frigid. On the one side there was mistrust of the " intellectuals ", who could not possibly know just where the shoe pinched the workers, and on the other side there was mistrust of the " Straubingers ", that is to say, of the artisan-guild narrow-mindedness which was still strong amongst the German workers at that time. Engels had his hands full with the job of keeping the " Straubingers " in Paris away from the influence of Proudhon and Weitling, but he felt that the " Straubingers " in London were made of better stuff, although he characterized an address which the League of the Just had issued in the autumn of 1846 in connection with the Sleswig-Holstein question as " sheer rubbish ", declaring that the " Straubingers " in England had learned nothing from the English apart from their folly of ignoring all existing concrete conditions and their failure to grasp the process of historical development.

CREDENTIALS OF CITIZEN JOSEPH MOLL

A good decade later Marx referred to his attitude towards the League of the Just at the time in the words : " We issued a series of pamphlets, some of them printed, others lithographed, mercilessly criticizing the mixture of Anglo-French socialism or communism and German philosophy which represented the secret teachings of the League, and putting forward instead a scientific insight into the economic structure of bourgeois society as the only tenable basis, explaining this in a popular form and pointing out that the task was not to work out a utopian system but to participate consciously in the historic process of social transformation taking place before our eyes." In January 1847 the League sent a member of its Central Committee, the watch-maker Josef Moll, to Brussels to request Marx and Engels to join the organization as it intended to adopt their views, and Marx attributed this step to the efficacy of the pamphlets.

Unfortunately, none of the pamphlets referred to by Marx has been preserved, with the exception of the circular against Kriege who is ridiculed in it as, amongst other things, the emissary and prophet of an Essene association, the " League of Justice ". He is also accused of mystifying the real historical development of communism throughout the world by ascribing its origin and progress to the fabulous and romantic intrigues, wholly figmentary, of this association about whose secret power he spread the most ridiculous and fantastic accounts.

The fact that this circular had such an effect on the members of the League of the Just proves that they were something more than " Straubingers " and that they had learned more from English history than Engels supposed. Although their organization was referred to as an " Essene association " and came in for one or two very unfriendly remarks, they took it in much better part than Weitling, who was not mentioned at all, but who nevertheless went over to Kriege. As a matter of fact the League of the Just in London had remained much fresher and more vital in the invigorating and cosmopolitan atmosphere of London than its counterparts in Zürich and even in Paris. Intended in the first place for propaganda amongst the German workers, it had adopted an international character in London. It maintained close relations with political fugitives from all manner of countries, and, with the example of the Chartist movement before it, which was rapidly growing in power and activity, its leaders broadened their horizon and progressed far beyond their old handicraft conceptions. Apart from the older leaders Schapper, Bauer and Moll, younger men, such as the miniature painter Karl Pfänder of Heilbronn and the tailor Georg Eccarius of Thuringia, distinguished themselves by their theoretical ability.

The authorization which Moll presented to Marx in Brussels and afterwards to Engels in Paris was dated the 20th of January 1847 and written by Schapper. It was drafted with a certain amount of caution and authorized the bearer to report on the situation of the League and to give detailed information on all important points, but in conversation Moll was much less reserved. He requested Marx to join the League and dispelled his original objections by informing him that a League congress was to be called in London with a view to accepting the critical opinions expressed by Marx and Engels, and incorporating them in a public manifesto as the principles of the League. However, he declared, Marx and Engels must join the League and assist it to overcome the old-fashioned and reluctant elements.

Marx and Engels allowed themselves to be persuaded and they both joined the League. However, for the moment the result of the League congress which took place in the summer of 1847 was no more than a democratic reorganization to suit the needs of a propagandist body compelled to work in secret, but eschewing all conspiratorial airs. The League was organized in communes of not less than three and not more than ten members, circles, leading circles, the central authority and the congress. Its aims were declared to be the overthrow of the bourgeoisie, the establishment of the rule of the proletariat, the abolition of the old society based on class contradictions, and the building up of a new society without classes and without private property.

In accordance with the democratic character of the League, which now called itself the Communist League, the new statutes were first of all placed before the individual communes for discussion, the final decision being left to a second congress which was to be convened before the end of the year and which would also discuss the new programme of the League. Marx was not present at the first congress, but Engels was there as the representative of the Paris communists and Wilhelm Wolff as the representative of the Brussels circle.

7. Propaganda in Brussels

The League began first of all to found educational associations of German workers which would give it an opportunity of conducting open propaganda and at the same time form a reservoir from which it could draw in order to extend and strengthen its own ranks.

The procedure of these associations was the same everywhere : one day in the week was marked down for discussion and another for social intercourse (singing, recitation, etc.) ; libraries were founded everywhere in connection with the associations and where possible classes were organized to instruct the workers in the elementary principles of communism.

This was the plan according to which the German Workers Association (*Deutscher Arbeiterverein*) was founded in Brussels at the end of August. The two chairmen of the association were Moses Hess and Wallau, and its secretary was Wilhelm Wolff. The members of the association, who soon numbered over a hundred, met every Wednesday and Saturday evening. On Wednesdays important questions of interest to the proletariat were discussed, whilst on Saturdays Wolf gave a political review of the week, a task at which he very quickly became highly proficient, and after that the gathering became a social one and women were also present.

On the 27th of September this association held an international banquet to demonstrate the fraternal feelings harboured by the workers of each country for the workers of other countries. At the time it was customary to choose banquets as a framework for political propaganda in order to avoid the police interference inevitable at public meetings. However, there was a special purpose behind this particular banquet, which had been arranged by Bornstedt and other dissatisfied elements in the German colony " in order ", as Engels, who happened to be in Brussels at the time, wrote to Marx, who happened to be absent, " to push us into a secondary rôle as against the Belgian Democrats and to form a much more magnificent and universal organization than our miserable little workers association ". Engels succeeded in foiling this intrigue in good time, and despite his reluctance on account of the fact that he " looked so frightfully young ", he was elected one of the two Vice-Presidents, together with the Frenchman Imbert, whilst General Mellinet was elected Honorary President and the advocate Jottrand, both active fighters in the Belgian Revolution of 1830, Acting President.

One hundred and twenty guests were present at the banquet, including Belgians, Germans, Swiss, Frenchmen, Poles, Italians and one Russian. After a number of speeches it was decided to found an Association of the Friends of Reform in Belgium along the lines of the Fraternal Democrats. Engels was elected into the preparatory commission, but as he was soon afterwards compelled to leave Brussels he wrote to Jottrand recommending that Marx should be accepted in his stead, pointing out that had Marx been present at the meeting of the 27th of September he would

undoubtedly have been elected : " It would therefore not be as though M. Marx were taking my place in the commission, on the contrary, it was I who represented him at the meeting." In fact, when the Democratic Association for the Unification of all Countries finally constituted itself on the 7th and 15th of November, Imbert and Marx were elected Vice-Presidents whilst Mellinet was confirmed as Honorary President and Jottrand as Acting President. The statutes of the association were signed by Belgian, German, French and Polish democrats, about sixty names in all. Amongst the Germans who signed were Marx, Moses Hess, Georg Weerth, the two Wolffs, Stephan Born and Bornstedt.

The first big meeting organized by the new association was on the 29th of November to celebrate the anniversary of the Polish Revolution. Stephan Born spoke on behalf of the Germans and his remarks were received with great applause. Marx himself was not present, being in London as the official representative of the Democratic Association at a meeting held by the Fraternal Democrats in London on the same day and for the same purpose. The speech he delivered at this latter meeting was couched in a thoroughly proletarian and revolutionary tone : " Old Poland has disappeared and we should be the last to wish its resurgence. However, not only old Poland, but old Germany, old France and old England, in fact, the whole of old society is lost. However, the loss of the old society is no loss for those who have nothing to lose in it, and to-day this is the situation for the great majority of the people in all countries." In the eyes of Marx the victory of the proletariat over the bourgeoisie would see the delivery of all oppressed nations, and the victory of the English proletariat over the English bourgeoisie the victory of all the oppressed over all the oppressors. Poland would be freed not in Poland, but in England. If the Chartists defeated their enemies at home they would have defeated the whole of society.

Answering the address which Marx had handed to them on behalf of the Democratic Association, the Fraternal Democrats adopted the same tone : " Your representative, our friend and brother Marx, will tell you with what enthusiasm we welcomed his appearance and the reading of your address. All eyes shone with joy, all voices shouted a welcome and all hands stretched out fraternally to your representative. . . . We accept with the liveliest feelings of satisfaction the alliance you have offered us. Our association has existed now for over two years with the motto : all men are brothers. At our last anniversary commemoration we recommended the formation of a democratic congress of all nations, and we are happy to hear that you have publicly made the same proposal. The conspiracy of kings must be answered with a conspiracy of the peoples. . . . We are convinced that we must address ourselves to the real people, to the proletarians, to the men who drip sweat and blood daily under the pressure of the existing social system, if we are to achieve general fraternity. . . . We shall soon see, in fact we can already see, the bearers of fraternity, the chosen knights of humanity, approaching along the same avenue from the cottage, the garret, the plough, the anvil and the factory." The Fraternal Democrats then proposed the holding of a general democratic congress in Brussels in September 1848 as a sort of counterblast to the Free Trade Congress which had taken place there in September 1847.

However, Marx had gone to London for other reasons apart from delivering an address to the meeting of the Fraternal Democrats. Immediately after the meeting of the latter to celebrate the anniversary of the Polish Revolution, and in the same rooms, the headquarters of the Communist Workers Educational League (*Kommunistischer Arbeiterbildungsverein*) founded in 1840 by Schapper, Bauer and Moll, the second congress of the Communist League took place to adopt its new statutes definitely and to discuss its new programme. Engels was also present at this congress. He had left Paris on the 27th of November and met Marx in Ostende in order to go with him to England. After a discussion which lasted about ten days Marx and Engels were given the task of drawing up the fundamental principles of communism in a public manifesto.

In the middle of December Marx returned to Brussels and Engels to Paris via Brussels. Neither of them seems to have been in any hurry to carry out the task with which they had been entrusted, and on the 24th of January 1848 the Central Committee of the Communist League sent an energetic warning to the district committee in Brussels threatening measures against citizen Marx unless the Manifesto of the Communist Party which he had agreed to draw up was in the hands of the Central Committee by the 1st of February. It is hardly possible to discover now what caused the delay, perhaps it was the thorough fashion in which Marx was accustomed to carry out everything he undertook, perhaps it was the separation from Engels, or perhaps the Londoners grew impatient when they heard that Marx was zealously continuing his propaganda in Brussels.

On the 9th of January 1848 Marx delivered a speech on free trade to the Democratic Association. He had intended to deliver this speech to the Free Trade Congress in Brussels, but he had been unable to obtain the floor. He thoroughly exposed the swindle of the Free Traders who pretended that " the welfare of the workmen " was the prime motive of their agitation, but although free trade favoured the capitalists at the expense of the workers he recognized that it was in accordance with the fundamental principles of bourgeois political economy. Free trade, he declared, was the freedom of capital, which was engaged in pulling down the national limitations which still hampered it in order to release its full energies. Free trade disintegrated the nations and aggravated the contradiction between the bourgeoisie and the proletariat, thus it accelerated the social revolution, and in this revolutionary sense Marx was in favour of free trade.

At the same time he defended himself against the suspicion that he harboured protective tendencies, and his plea for free trade involved him in no contradiction with his support of protectionist measures in Germany as " progressive bourgeois measures ". Like Engels, Marx regarded the whole free trade versus protection question purely from a revolutionary standpoint. The German bourgeoisie needed protective tariffs as a weapon against feudalism and absolutism, as a means to concentrate its forces, to establish free trade on the home market and to develop large-scale industry, which would then sooner or later become dependent on the world market, that is to say, on free trade. His speech was received with lively applause by the members of the Democratic Association, which decided to have it printed and distributed in French and Flemish at its own cost.

However, far more important than this speech were the lectures he delivered to the German Workers Association on wage-labour and capital. He proceeded from the assumption that wages were not a share of the worker in the commodity produced by him, but that share of the already existing commodities with which the capitalist purchased a certain amount of productive labour-power. The price of labour-power, he declared, was determined, like the price of any other commodity, by its costs of production. The costs of production of simple labour-power were the costs of providing the worker with the means enabling him to exist and perpetuate his kind. The price of these costs represented wages, and, like the prices of all other commodities, this price was sometimes above and sometimes below the costs of production, according to the vacillations of competition, but within the limits of these vacillations it approximated to a wage minimum.

He then examined capital. In reply to the assertion of the bourgeois economists that capital is accumulated labour, he asked : " What is a Negro slave ? A human being of the coloured race. One explanation is as good as the other. A Negro is a Negro, but under certain circumstances he may become a slave. A cotton-spinning machine is a machine for spinning cotton, and only under certain circumstances does it become capital. Without these circumstances it is no more capital than gold is money, or sugar the price of sugar." Capital is a social productive relation, a productive relation of bourgeois society. A sum of commodities, of exchange values, becomes capital when it appears as an independent social power, that is to say, as the power of a section of society, and increases itself by exchange with direct living labour-power. " The existence of a class possessing nothing but its capacity to labour is a necessary condition for the existence of capital. The power of accumulated, past, externalized labour over direct living labour-power first makes accumulated labour into capital. Capital does not consist in the fact that accumulated labour serves living labour-power as a means for further production. It consists in the fact that living labour-power serves accumulated labour as a means of maintaining and increasing its exchange value." Capital and labour-power mutually condition each other ; they produce each other mutually.

When the bourgeois economists conclude from this that the interests of the capitalists and the interests of the workers are identical it is true only in the sense that the worker must starve unless the capitalist employs him, and that capital must perish unless it exploits the worker. The more rapidly productive capital increases, that is to say, the more flourishing industry becomes, then the more workers the capitalist needs and the dearer the worker can sell his labour-power. The indispensable condition for a tolerable situation of the working class is therefore the speediest possible growth of productive capital.

Marx points out that in this case any considerable increase in wages presupposes a still more rapid increase in productive capital. When capital grows then wages may increase also, but all the more rapidly do the profits of capital increase. The material situation of the workers has improved therefore, but at the expense of his social situation ; the social chasm between him and the capitalist has grown wider. Therefore, to say that the most favourable condition for wage-labour is the speediest possible growth of capital means only that the more rapidly the working class strengthens the hostile power, the alien riches which dominate it, the more favourable will be the conditions under which it is permitted to work anew to increase the power of capital, satisfied with forging the golden chains which drag it along at the heels of the bourgeoisie.

However, continues Marx, the growth of capital and the increase of wages are by no means so indissolubly connected as the bourgeois economists contend. It is not true to say that the fatter capital waxes the better will its slave be fed. The growth of productive capital embraces the accumulation and concentration of capital. Its centralization involves a still greater division of labour and a still greater use of machinery. The increased division of labour destroys the special skill of the worker, and when it replaces this special skill with a form of labour which anyone can perform it increases competition amongst the workers.

This competition also becomes stronger the more the division of labour permits one worker to do the work formerly done by three. Machinery produces this result to a still greater degree. The growth of productive capital compels the industrial capitalists to work with increasingly growing means, thereby ruining the smaller industrialists and throwing them into the ranks of the proletariat. Further, as the rate of interest falls in accordance with the accumulation of capital, the smaller shareholders can no longer live on their interest and are compelled to turn to industry for employment, thus increasing the ranks of the proletariat.

And finally, the more productive capital grows the more it is compelled to work for a market whose needs it does not know. Production forges ahead of demand, supply strives to compel demand, and the result is seen in the crises : those industrial earthquakes in which the world of commerce manages to maintain itself only by sacrificing a section of its riches, a section of its products, and even a section of the productive forces themselves, to the dark gods of the underworld, and these crises become more frequent and more violent. Capital not only lives from labour, but like a noble and barbarian chieftain it drags the corpses of its slaves into the tomb with it: whole hecatombs of workers who perish in its crises. Marx then sums up : If capital grows rapidly, the competition amongst the workers grows still more rapidly, that is to say, the more, comparatively, are the means of occupation and the means of life of the workers reduced, but nevertheless, the speedy growth of capital is the most favourable condition for wage-labour.

Unfortunately, this fragment is all that remains of the lectures delivered by Marx to the German workers in Brussels, but it is sufficient to show us with what seriousness and what thoroughness he carried on his propaganda. Bakunin was of another opinion. He arrived in Brussels at about this time after having been expelled from France owing to a speech he had delivered on the anniversary of the Polish Revolution. On the 28th of December 1847 we find him writing to a Russian friend : " Marx is still carrying on the same old vain activities, spoiling the workers by making logic-choppers out of them. It's the same old insane theorizing and dissatisfied self-satisfaction." And in a letter to Herwegh about Marx and Engels he was still more savage : " In a word, lies and stupidity, stupidity and lies. It is impossible to breathe freely in their company. I keep away from them and I have told them very definitely that I will not join their communist artisans group and that I refuse to have anything to do with it."

These remarks of Bakunin are noteworthy not so much on account of the personal irritation they betray, for Bakunin had judged Marx quite differently on former occasions and was to do so again, but because they reveal an antagonism which was to lead to violent struggles between the two revolutionaries.

8. *The Communist Manifesto*

In the meantime the manuscript of what was afterwards to be known as *The Communist Manifesto* had been sent off to London.

There had been plenty of preparatory work immediately after the first congress, which had left the discussion of the programme to the second congress. Naturally, it was the theorists of the movement who occupied themselves with the task, and drafts were drawn up by Marx, Engels and Moses Hess.

However, the only one of these preliminary drafts which still exists is the one which Engels refers to in a letter to Marx dated the 24th of November 1847, that is to say, shortly before the second congress : " Think over the confession of faith a bit. I think it would be better to drop the catechism form and call the thing a communist manifesto. As a certain amount of history will have to be brought in I think the present form is unsuitable. I am bringing along what I have done here. It is in simple narrative form, but miserably edited and done in a terrible hurry." Engels then adds that he had not yet submitted his draft to the Paris branches but that, apart from one or two minor details perhaps, he hoped to get it through.

This draft is completely in catechism form and this would rather have enhanced the general understanding of it than otherwise and it would have been better suited to the purpose of immediate agitation than the subsequent manifesto with whose ideological content it was in complete harmony. Engels immediately sacrificed his twenty-five questions and answers in favour of the historical method of presentation, and in doing this he gave proof of his conscientiousness, for he realized that the manifesto in which communism presented itself to the world must be, in the words of the Greek historian, a work of lasting importance and not a polemic for the casual reader.

It was, in fact, the classical form which won a lasting place in world literature for *The Communist Manifesto*, although this statement is not intended as the least concession to the droll fellows who are so anxious to prove by tearing out this or that passage from its context that its authors have plagiarized Carlyle or Gibbon or Sismondi or someone or the other. That is sheer nonsense, and in fact the manifesto is as independent and original as any writing ever was. However, it contained no idea which Marx and Engels had not already dealt with in their previous writings. It was therefore not a revelation, but a presentation, of the world outlook of its authors in a mirror whose glass could not have been clearer or its frame smaller. As far as the style permits us to judge it would appear that Marx had the greater hand in shaping its final form, but, as his own draft shows, Engels was not behind Marx in his understanding of the problems at issue and he ranks side by side with Marx as the author of it.

Two-thirds of a century have passed since the manifesto was first published and the six or seven decades which have unrolled have been full of tremendous economic and political changes which have not left it untouched. In certain respects historical development has proceeded differently, and above all it has proceeded less quickly than the authors of the manifesto antici-pated. The further their glance penetrated into the future the nearer it appeared to them. One can say that without this shadow the light would not have been possible. It was a psycho-logical phenomenon which Lessing had already noticed in those human beings " who cast accurate glances into the future " : " That for which nature requires thousands of years, must ripen in the moment of their existence ". Marx and Engels were certainly not thousands of years out, but they were in error to the tune of decades. When they drew up *The Communist Manifesto* they regarded capitalism as having reached a level which it has hardly reached in our own day. In his draft Engels says it even more clearly than the final form of the mani-festo when he declares that in all civilized countries almost all branches of production are conducted in factories, and that handicraft and manufacture have been squeezed out by large-scale industry in almost all branches of production.

The comparatively sketchy beginnings of the working-class parties provided in the manifesto are in peculiar contrast to this. Even the most important working-class movement of the day, Chartism, was strongly influenced by petty-bourgeois elements, not to speak of the Democratic Socialist Party of

France. The Radicals in Switzerland and those Polish revolutionaries who regarded the emancipation of the peasants as the preliminary condition for national freedom were no more than shadows on the wall. Later on the authors of the manifesto themselves pointed out how narrow had been the field occupied by the proletarian movement of that day, and in particular they stressed the absence of Russia and of the United States : " It was the period when Russia represented the last great reserve of European reaction and when emigration to the United States absorbed the surplus forces of the European proletariat. Both countries provided Europe with raw materials and both served at the same time as markets for the industrial production of Europe. Both therefore were in the one way or the other bulwarks of the European social order." How much had the situation changed a generation later ! And how much has it changed in our own day !

Is it really a refutation of the manifesto when we admit that the " highly revolutionary rôle " which it ascribed to the capitalist mode of production has taken longer to make itself felt than the authors of the manifesto thought ? The magnificent and powerful description of the class struggle between the bourgeoisie and the proletariat contained in its first section remains fundamentally unchanged to-day, although the course of the class struggle is dealt with somewhat too summarily. To-day one cannot generalize in quite the same fashion and declare that the modern worker—as distinct from the members of former oppressed classes who, at least, were sure of conditions in which they could continue their slavish existence—falls deeper and deeper below the conditions of his own class instead of raising himself with the progress of industry. It is true that the capitalist mode of production has definitely this general tendency, but nevertheless broad sections of the working class have succeeded in securing for themselves on the basis of capitalist society an existence which raises them even above the level of existence of some petty-bourgeois strata.

Naturally, one must take care not to fall into the error of the bourgeois critics of the manifesto who conclude from this that the " theory of increasing misery " allegedly put forward in it was wrong. This theory, the contention that the capitalist mode of production impoverishes the masses wherever it prevails, was put forward long before *The Communist Manifesto* was published, even before either Marx or Engels put pen to paper. It was put forward by socialist thinkers and radical politicians, in fact, first of all by bourgeois economists. The *Essay on Population* written by Malthus was an attempt to refine this

" theory of increasing misery " and turn it into an eternal natural law. It represented a state of affairs over which the legislation of the ruling classes constantly stumbled. Poor Laws were passed and bastilles erected for the paupers, pauperization was regarded as the fault of the paupers and punished accordingly. Far from inventing this " theory of increasing misery " both Marx and Engels opposed it from the beginning ; not in the sense that they attempted to deny the indisputable and generally recognized fact of mass misery, but in that they proved that it was not an eternal law of nature, but an historical phenomenon which could and would be abolished by the effects of the same mode of production which had caused it.

If there is to be any attack on *The Communist Manifesto* from this angle then it can only be that its authors had not yet thoroughly freed themselves from the influence of this bourgeois " theory of increasing misery ". It adopted the wage theory which Ricardo had developed on the basis of the Malthusian theory of population, and as a result it underestimated the importance of wage struggles and of the trade union organizations of the workers, which it regarded primarily as training schools to prepare them for the political class struggle. At that time Marx and Engels did not regard the English Ten Hour Bill as " the victory of a principle ", but, within capitalist conditions, as a reactionary fetter on large-scale industry. The manifesto did not recognize the Factory Laws and trade-union organizations as stages in the proletarian struggle for emancipation, a struggle which must transform capitalist society into socialist society and be fought out to the bitter end unless the first hard-won successes were to be lost again.

The manifesto therefore regarded the reaction of the proletariat to the impoverishing tendencies of the capitalist mode of production too one-sidedly in the light of a political revolution. It based its conclusions on the English and French Revolutions, and expected several decades of civil war and national wars in whose hectic atmosphere the proletariat would quickly ripen into political maturity. The opinions of its authors can be seen clearly in those passages of the manifesto which deal with the tasks of the Communist Party in Germany. It favours co-operation between the proletariat and the bourgeoisie when the latter acts in a revolutionary fashion against the absolutist monarchy, against feudal large-scale landownership and against petty-bourgeoisdom, but it points out expressly that the communists must not fail to make the workers understand thoroughly the fundamental antagonism between the bourgeoisie and the proletariat, and it then declares :

" The main attention of the communists is directed towards Germany because Germany is on the eve of a bourgeois revolution and because it will experience this revolution under far more highly developed conditions of European civilization and with a far more developed proletariat than was the case in England in the seventeenth and France in the eighteenth century, and therefore a German bourgeois revolution can be only the immediate prelude to a proletarian revolution." The bourgeois revolution referred to in the manifesto soon took place, but the conditions under which it took place had exactly the opposite effect : they caused the bourgeois revolution to pause hesitantly with its task only half fulfilled until a few months later the Paris June fighting cured the bourgeoisie in general and the German bourgeoisie in particular of all revolutionary hankerings.

Thus we observe that, magnificently chiselled as the manifesto is, nevertheless the passage of time has not left it unscathed. In 1872 in a preface to a new edition, the authors themselves pointed out that it had grown out of date here and there, but with equal truth they were able to add that on the whole the principles laid down in it had proved correct, and that is a statement which will remain valid until the world historic struggle between the bourgeoisie and the proletariat has been fought to a finish. The first section of the manifesto sketches the fundamental principles of this struggle with incomparable mastery, whilst the second section deals equally effectively with the main ideas of modern scientific communism. Although the third section which criticizes socialist and communist literature goes only to the year 1847 it does its work so thoroughly that since then no socialist or communist tendency which has arisen which has not already been criticized in advance in this section. Even the prophecy contained in the fourth and last section of the manifesto on the development of Germany has come true though in another sense than the one intended by its authors : the German revolution, pausing hesitantly with its tasks only half completed, has become no more than the prelude to the powerful development of the proletarian class struggle.

Irrefutable in its fundamental truths and instructive even in its errors, *The Communist Manifesto* has become a historic document of world-wide significance and the battle-cry with which it closes still re-echoes throughout history : " Workers of the World Unite ! "

CHAPTER SIX: REVOLUTION AND COUNTER-REVOLUTION

1. February and March Days

On the 24th of February 1848 the bourgeois monarchy in France was overthrown by a revolution. This movement was not without its repercussions in Brussels, but King Leopold, a wily old Coburger fox, succeeded in extricating himself from the situation more cleverly than his father-in-law in Paris. He announced to his Liberal Ministers, the Deputies and the Mayors that if the nation demanded it he would abdicate at once, and this generous gesture so touched the hearts of the sentimental bourgeois statesmen that they immediately suppressed all their rebellious feelings.

But after that the King caused his soldiers to disperse all public meetings and set his police to hunt down foreign fugitives. Marx was treated with particular brutality. Not only did the police arrest him, but they also arrested his wife, who was held for one night in the company of common prostitutes. The police official responsible for this piece of infamy was later removed from his post and the order of arrest had to be withdrawn immediately, but not so the order of expulsion, although it was a thoroughly unnecessary piece of chicanery, for Marx was in any case about to leave Brussels for Paris.

Immediately after the outbreak of the revolution the central authorities of the Communist League in London transferred executive authority to the district representatives in Brussels, but in view of the situation in Brussels, which was practically under martial law, the latter handed on this authority to Marx together with instructions to form a new central leadership in Paris, to which he had been recalled by a letter signed by Flocon on behalf of the provisional government, an incident which greatly honoured him.

On the 6th of March he once again had an opportunity of putting his superior understanding of the political situation to good account when at a big meeting of German fugitives living in Paris he energetically opposed an adventurous plan to invade Germany by armed force in order to revolutionize the country.

This plan had been hatched out by the dubious Bornstedt, who had unfortunately succeeded in winning Herwegh for it. Bakunin was also in favour of the plan, though he later regretted having given it his support. The provisional government was also prepared to support the plan, but less from any real revolutionary enthusiasm than with the *arrière pensée* that in view of the prevailing unemployment it would be an excellent thing to get rid of many foreign-born workers. It placed barracks at the disposal of the revolutionaries and made them a daily grant of 50 centimes per man for the march to the frontier. Herwegh had no illusions about the reasons which prompted the provisional government to support the venture and he himself referred to " the egoistic motive ", the desire " to get rid of many thousands of foreign-born artisans who were competing with the French ", but his lack of political vision caused him to pursue the adventure to its pitiful end near Niederdossenbach.

Whilst Marx energetically opposed this revolutionary foolery, which had lost any justification it might have had with the victory of the revolution in Vienna on the 13th of March and in Berlin on the 18th of March, he was busily engaged in forging the weapons to further the German revolution effectively, a task on which the communists had concentrated their main attention. In accordance with his instructions he formed a new central leadership in Paris, consisting of himself, Engels and Wolff from Brussels, and Bauer, Moll and Schapper from London. This new body then issued an appeal containing seventeen demands " in the interests of the German proletariat, the petty-bourgeoisie and the peasantry ", including a demand that Germany should be proclaimed a republic, one and indivisible, and further demands for the arming of the people, the nationalization of the princely and other feudal estates, of the mines and of the transport system, the establishment of national workshops, and the introduction of a general system of compulsory education at State cost, etc. Naturally, these demands were intended only as laying down the general lines of communist propaganda, for no one knew better than Marx that they could not be carried out from one day to the next, but only as the result of a long process of revolutionary development.

The Communist League was much too weak to act alone in the work of accelerating the revolutionary movement, and it was soon seen that its reorganization on the Continent was only in its infancy. However, this was no longer so important because the working class had now won the means and the possibility of conducting its propaganda openly and therefore the chief reason for the existence of the League was removed.

Under these circumstances Marx and Engels founded a German communist club in Paris and strongly advised its members to keep away from Herwegh's guerilla bands and instead to make their way singly into Germany in order to further the revolutionary movement there. They succeeded in sending several hundred workers back to Germany, and thanks to the mediation of Flocon they obtained the same support for them as the provisional government had granted to Herwegh and his volunteers.

As the result of these efforts the majority of the members of the Communist League succeeded in getting back into Germany and their activities there demonstrated that the League had been an excellent training school for the revolution. Wherever the revolutionary movement in Germany showed any signs of vigorous development the members of the League were seen to be the driving force behind it : Schapper in Nassau, Wolff in Breslau, Stephan Born in Berlin and other members elsewhere. Born hit the nail on the head when he wrote to Marx : " The League has ceased to exist and yet it exists everywhere." As an organization it had ceased to exist, but its propaganda was visible everywhere the conditions for the proletarian struggle for freedom existed, although this was true of a comparatively small area of Germany only.

Marx and his nearest friends went to the Rhineland, which was the most progressive part of Germany and where the *Code Napoléon* afforded greater freedom of movement than the Prussian Civil Code in Berlin, and there they succeeded in securing the lead in preparations which were being made in Cologne by democratic and in part communist elements to found a newspaper. However, things were not by any means all plain sailing, and Engels in particular suffered the disappointment of discovering that his communism in Wuppertal was not even a reality, much less a power in the land and that since the revolution had begun to show real signs of life Wuppertal communism was nothing but a faint shadow of the past. Writing to Marx, who was in Cologne, he declared in a letter of the 25th of April from Barmen : " It is damned little use reckoning on any shares here. . . . They all avoid any discussion of social questions like the plague ; they call it incitement. . . . There is nothing whatever to be got out of my old gentleman. He regards the *Kölnische Zeitung* as the last word in incitement and he would sooner send us a thousand bullets to finish us off than a thousand thaler to help us along." However, Engels succeeded in floating fourteen shares, and on the 1st of June 1848 the first number of the *Neue Rheinische Zeitung* appeared. It was signed by Marx as chief editor whilst Engels, Dronke, Weerth and the two Wolffs were members of the editorial staff.

2. June Days

The *Neue Rheinische Zeitung* described itself as " an Organ of Democracy ", but it did not mean left-wing parliamentary democracy. It harboured no such ambitions, and it considered it urgently necessary to watch the official Democrats closely. Its ideal, it declared, was by no means the black, red and gold republic, and in fact its real oppositional work would begin only after the republic had been established.

Completely in the spirit of *The Communist Manifesto* it sought to further the revolutionary movement on the basis of existing conditions. This task was made all the more urgent by the fact that the revolutionary ground which had been won in March was half lost again by June. In Vienna, where the class antagonisms were still undeveloped, a happy-go-lucky anarchy prevailed, whilst in Berlin the bourgeosie had the book of words in its hands, but it was only too anxious to slip it back at first opportunity into the hands of the vanquished pre-March powers. In the little German States and Statelets Liberal Ministers were giving themselves airs, but they did not distinguish themselves from their feudal predecessors by the display of any manly pride before the throne of kings, but rather by the possession of still more pliable spines. And to crown it all, the first meeting of the Frankfort National Assembly on the 18th of May, which was to create German unity by virtue of its own sovereign authority, proved itself to be no more than a hopeless talking shop.

In its very first number the *Neue Rheinische Zeitung* dealt with this shadowy unreality so energetically that half of its not very numerous shareholders immediately beat a retreat. Not that the paper placed any exaggerated demands on the political vision and courage of the parliamentary heroes. It criticized the federal republicanism of the left-wing of the Frankfort parliament and declared that a federation of constitutional monarchies, little principalities and republics with a republican government at their head could not be accepted as the final constitution for a united Germany, but it immediately added :

" We do not put forward any utopian demand for the immediate establishment of a German Republic, one and indivisible, but we do demand that the so-called Radical Democratic Party should not confuse the first stage of the struggle and of the revolutionary movement with their final aim. German unity and a German constitution can be achieved only as the result of a movement which will be forced to seek a decision both as a result of inner conflicts and of a war against the East. The definitive constitution cannot be decreed and it will come about as a result of the movement we have yet to experience. It is therefore not a question of fulfilling this or that political idea or of holding this or that opinion, but of grasping the general trend of development. The National Assembly has only to take the immediately possible practical steps."

However, the National Assembly did something which according to all the laws of logic should have been practically out of the question : it elected the Austrian Archduke Johann as Reich's Regent, thus playing the movement into the hands of the princes.

Events in Berlin were more important than those in Frankfort. The Prussian State was the most dangerous enemy of the revolution inside Germany. On the 18th of March the revolution overthrew the Prussian government, but in the given historical situation the fruits of victory fell first into the lap of the bourgeoisie, and the latter hurried to betray the revolution. In order to ensure " the continuity of legal relations ", or, in other words, to deny its own revolutionary origin, the bourgeois Camphausen-Hansemann Ministry called a meeting of the United Diet in order to entrust this feudal-corporative body with the drawing up of a bourgeois constitution. On the 6th and 8th of April two laws were passed establishing various bourgeois rights as the basis of the new constitution and providing for the introduction of a general, secret and indirect franchise to elect a new assembly whose task it would be to draw up the constitution in agreement with the Crown.

With the establishment of this brilliant principle of " agreement with the Crown " the victory which the proletariat of Berlin had won on the 18th of March against the Prussian Guards was rendered ineffective, for if the decisions of the proposed new assembly required the agreement of the Crown then obviously the latter was once again in a strong position. It could again dictate its will unless it was brought to heel by a second revolution, a possibility which the Camphausen-Hansemann Ministry did its utmost to prevent. It subjected the assembly, which met on the 22nd of May to the pettiest chicanery, placed itself as " a shield " before the dynasty and gave the leaderless counter-revolution a head by recalling the Prince of Prussia from England

whither the thoroughly reactionary heir to the throne had fled
to escape the anger of the masses on the 18th of March.

The Berlin Assembly was certainly not a very spirited revolutionary body, but at least it was not able to keep its head so
consistently in the clouds as its Frankfort companion. It gave
way on the question of " agreement with the Crown ", a principle
which sucked the marrow from its bones, but after the Berlin
masses had again spoken a menacing word by storming the
Zeughaus [1] on the 14th of June it rallied again and took up a
more or less determined attitude towards the Crown, and as a
result Camphausen resigned, though Hansemann clung to office.
The difference between the two was that whilst Camphausen
was still troubled by remnants of progressive bourgeois ideology,
Hansemann dedicated himself utterly, without shame or scruples,
to the naked profit interests of the bourgeoisie, and thought to
further them most effectively by kow-towing more zealously
than ever to the King and the Junkers, by corrupting the assembly
and by oppressing the masses to a greater extent than ever before.
For the moment and for reasons of its own the counter-revolution
willingly let him have his head.

The *Neue Rheinische Zeitung* did its utmost to stem this fatal
development. It pointed out that Camphausen was sowing the
seeds of reaction in the interests of the bourgeoisie, but that the
crop would be reaped in the interests of the feudal party. It
did its utmost to stiffen the resistance of the Berlin Assembly and
in particular its left-wing, and it fought against the indignation
aroused by the fact that a number of old flags and weapons had
been destroyed in the storm on the Zeughaus, declaring that the
people had shown unerring instinct not only in attacking its
oppressors, but in destroying the brilliant illusions of its own
past. And, above all, it warned the left wing against contenting
itself with the deceptive appearance of parliamentary victories,
pointing out that the reaction would gladly grant it such illusions
providing the really commanding positions still remained in the
hands of the old powers.

It prophesied a miserable end for the Hansemann Ministry,
which sought to create a basis for bourgeois dominance by
compromising with the old feudal and police State. " In this
ambiguous and contradictory task it sees itself and its aim, the
founding of bourgeois dominance, outwitted at every turn by the
reaction in the absolutist and feudal interests—and it will be the
loser. The bourgeoisie cannot establish its own dominance without winning the whole people as its temporary ally and without

---

[1] A military building on the Unter den Linden now used exclusively as a museum
of military relics.—Tr.

taking up a more or less democratic attitude." Caustic scorn was poured on the attempts of the bourgeoisie to turn the emancipation of the peasantry, the legitimate task of the bourgeois revolution, into a piece of legerdemain : " The German bourgeoisie of 1848 is betraying the peasantry, without decency and without shame, although the peasantry represents its natural ally, flesh of its flesh and blood of its blood, and although it is helpless against the aristocracy without the support of the peasantry." The German Revolution of 1848 was nothing but a parody of the French Revolution of 1789, it declared.

It was a parody in another sense also, for the German Revolution had not gained the victory as a result of its own strength but as the result of a French revolution which had already given the proletariat a share in the government. This neither justifies nor excuses the treachery of the German bourgeoisie to the revolution, but at least it explains it. Whilst the Hansemann Ministry was beginning its grave-digging services the spectre it feared was almost banned. In a terrible street battle which lasted four days the proletariat of Paris was defeated thanks to the joint services rendered to capital by all bourgeois classes and parties.

In Germany the banner of " the victorious vanquished " was raised from the dust by the *Neue Rheinische Zeitung*, and in a striking article Marx pointed out which side democracy must take in the class struggle between the bourgeoisie and the proletariat : " They will ask us whether we have no tears, no sighs and no words of regret for the victims in the ranks of the National Guard, the Mobile Guard, the Republican Guard and the Regiments of the Line who fell before the anger of the people. The State will look after their widows and orphans, pompous decrees will glorify them and solemn processions will bear their remains to the grave. The official press will declare them immortal and the European reaction from East to West will sing their praises. On the other hand, it is the privilege and right of the democratic press to place the laurel wreaths on the lowering brows of the plebeians tortured with the pangs of hunger, despised by the official press, abandoned by the doctors, abused as thieves, vandals and galley-slaves by all respectable citizens, their wives and children plunged into still greater misery, and the best of their survivors deported overseas."

This magnificent article, which breathes the fires of revolutionary passion even to-day, cost the *Neue Rheinische Zeitung* the greater number of those shareholders who still remained.

3.   The War against Russia

In foreign politics the war against Russia was the pivot around which the *Neue Rheinische Zeitung* moved. It regarded Russia as the one really dangerous enemy of the revolution and one which would inevitably enter the struggle as soon as the revolutionary movement took on a European character.

It was quite right in this respect, for whilst it was calling for a revolutionary war against Russia the Tsar was offering the Prince of Prussia the use of the Russian army to re-establish despotism in Prussia by armed force. The *Neue Rheinische Zeitung* was not aware of this, but it has since been proved by documentary evidence, and a year later the Russian bear saved Austrian despotism by crushing the Hungarian Revolution in its clumsy embrace. The German Revolution could not be finally victorious without destroying both the Prussian and Austrian absolutist States, declared the *Neue Rheinische Zeitung*, and this would remain impossible so long as the power of the Tsar was unbroken.

As the result of such a war against Russia the *Neue Rheinische Zeitung* hoped for a tremendous release of revolutionary forces such as had taken place in France in 1789 as a result of the war against feudal Germany. In the words of Weerth, it treated the German nation *en canaille*, and this was true in that it bitterly scourged the lackey services which the Germans had rendered for seventy years against the freedom and independence of other nations in America and France, in Italy and Poland, in Holland and Greece, and still other countries : " Now that the Germans are beginning to cast off their own yoke they must alter their whole policy towards other countries, otherwise they will find that the chains they have forged for others will entangle their own young and only half-descried freedom. Germany will win its own freedom to the extent that it leaves other countries in freedom." The paper denounced the Machiavellian policy which, although it was being shaken to the roots in Germany itself, deliberately fomented a narrow-minded hatred of things foreign in defiance of the cosmopolitan character of the Germans and in order to paralyse democratic energies, turn the molten lava of the revolution from its course, and forge a weapon of internal oppression.

" Despite the patriotic howling and drumming of almost the whole of the German press ", the *Neue Rheinische Zeitung* came out from the beginning on the side of the Poles in Posen, the Italians in Italy and the Hungarians in Hungary, and mocked at " the profundity of the combination " and " the historical paradox " which sought to lead the Germans into a crusade against the liberty of Poland, Hungary and Italy at a time when the same Germans were fighting against the very governments which proposed to lead them. " Only a war against Russia would be a revolutionary war for Germany. In such a war it could wash away the sins of the past, vindicate its own manliness, defeat its own despots, advance the cause of civilization by sacrificing its own sons in a manner worthy of a people which has flung off the chains of long-suffered and dull slavery, and win freedom at home by freeing itself externally."

As a result of this attitude the *Neue Rheinische Zeitung* supported the cause of Polish freedom more passionately than that of any other oppressed nation. The movement in Poland in 1848 was limited to the' Prussian province of Posen because Russian Poland was still exhausted from the revolution of 1830 and Austrian Poland from the insurrection of 1846. It was modest enough in its attitude and demanded hardly more than had been promised by the treaties of 1815 but never granted : the replacement of the army of occupation by native troops and the occupation of all positions by natives. In the first spasm of fear occasioned by the events of the 18th of March the Berlin government promised " a national reorganization ", though naturally, it had no intention of ever carrying it out. The Poles were trustful enough to believe in its good-will, but it deliberately incited the German and Jewish population of the province of Posen and systematically provoked a civil war whose atrocities were almost completely the guilt of the Prussians and the responsibility for them entirely so. Deliberately provoked to armed resistance, the Poles fought gallantly and more than once they routed forces superior to their own in numbers and equipment, for instance, on the 30th of April near Miloslav, but in the long run the fight of the Polish scythes against Prussian shrapnel was hopeless.

In the Polish question also the German bourgeoisie played its usual rôle of treachery and panic. Before the March Revolution it had realized clearly enough how closely the cause of Poland was connected with the cause of Germany, and even after the 18th of March its spokesmen had declared at the so-called preliminary parliament in Frankfort that to work for the re-establishment of national unity in Poland was the solemn duty of the German nation, but this did not prevent Camphausen from playing the lackey to the Prussian Junkers in this question also. He carried out the promise of " national reorganization " in a shameful fashion by wresting one piece after the other from the province of Posen, in all over two-thirds, and causing the United Diet to incorporate it in the German League. This piece of infamy was the last gasp of that body, which ended its life miserably amidst the general contempt of the German people. The National Assembly in Frankfort was now faced with the question of whether it should recognize those deputies who had been elected in the annexed parts of Posen as its members or not. After a debate which lasted three days it decided as might have been expected of it, and this degenerate offspring of the revolution gave its blessing to the infamy of the counter-revolution.

The importance attached by the *Neue Rheinische Zeitung* to this question can be seen from the fact that it dealt with the debate in Frankfort in great detail and published eight or nine articles, some of them very long, on the subject, in striking contrast to the contemptuous brevity with which it usually dismissed the parliamentary phrasemongering of this assembly. This series of articles represent the longest work ever published in the paper and both content and style suggest that Marx and Engels were joint authors. In any case, Engels had a large share in the work, which bears unmistakable signs of his style and manner.

The first thing which strikes one in these articles, and it is a feature which does the paper all honour, is the refreshing frankness with which they expose the contemptible game which was being played with Poland. However, the moral indignation of which both Marx and Engels were capable—far more capable than the worthy Philistine could even imagine—had nothing in common with the sentimental sympathy which, for instance, Robert Blum in France showed the maltreated Poles. Their judgment on the efforts of the respected leader of the left wing in this direction read : " Empty tub-thumping, but as we are gladly prepared to admit, tub-thumping on the grand scale and in a good cause," and their judgment was well founded, for Blum failed to realize that the betrayal of Poland was at the same time the betrayal of the German Revolution, which thereby lost an indispensable weapon against its deadly enemy Tsarism.

Marx and Engels passed the same disrespectful judgment on the demand for " the general fraternization of the peoples ", that vague aspiration towards fraternity irrespective of the historical situation and the social development of the peoples involved. For them such phrases as " Justice ", " Humanitarianism ", " Liberty ", " Equality ", " Fraternity " and " Independence " were no more than moral phrases which sounded fine but played no rôle in historical and political questions. What they termed " modern mythology " was always abhorrent to them and in the hectic days of the revolution they admitted only one test : " For or against ? "

The Polish articles of the *Neue Rheinische Zeitung* breathe a spirit of real revolutionary passion which raises them high above the usual pro-Polish phrases indulged in by the common run of democrats, and even to-day they stand as an eloquent proof of the keen and penetrating political insight of their authors. However, they are not completely free of errors with regard to Polish history. It was certainly of great importance to point out that the struggle for Polish independence could be successful only if it were at the same time a victory of agrarian democracy over patriarchal-feudal absolutism, but they were wrong in assuming that since the Constitution of 1791 the Poles themselves had realized this. It was also incorrect to say that the old Poland of aristocratic democracy was dead and buried, but had left behind a vigorous son, the Poland of peasant democracy. The Polish Junkers who had fought with incomparable bravery on the Western European barricades to free their people from the stifling embrace of the Eastern powers were regarded by Marx and Engels as the representatives of the Polish aristocracy, whereas in fact the Leléwels and the Mieroslavskis had been steeled and purified in the flames of the struggle and had raised themselves above their class as Hutten and Sickingen had once raised themselves above the German feudal class, or, in the less distant past, Clausewitz and Gneisenau above Prussian Junkerdom.

Marx and Engels soon abandoned this error, but Engels always clung to the disdainful judgment passed by the *Neue Rheinische Zeitung* on the struggle of the Southern Slav nations and groups for national freedom. In 1882 he still maintained the attitude he had taken up in 1849 in his polemic with Bakunin. In July 1848 Bakunin came under suspicion of being an agent of the Russian government, and a report to that effect was published in the *Neue Rheinische Zeitung* from its Paris correspondent Ewerbeck, whilst a simultaneous and similar report was published by the Havas Bureau. However, this suspicion was revealed almost immediately as baseless, and the *Neue Rheinische Zeitung* published a handsome apology. At the end of August and the beginning of September Marx travelled to Berlin and Vienna, and in Berlin he resumed his old friendly relations with Bakunin, and when Bakunin was expelled from Prussia in October Marx came out with a strong condemnation of the authorities. When Engels published his polemic against Bakunin in connection with an appeal the latter had issued to the Slavs, he began with the assurance that Bakunin was " our friend ", and only then proceeded to attack Bakunin's Pan-Slav tendencies, though he did so with considerable severity.

In the Slav question also the interests of the revolution were paramount in determining the attitude of Marx and Engels. The Austrian Slavs—with the exception of the Poles—had sided with the reaction in the struggle of the Vienna government against the revolutionary Germans and against Hungary. They had taken revolutionary Vienna by storm and handed it over to the merciless vengeance of the "Royal and Imperial" authorities. At the time when Engels was conducting his polemic against Bakunin they were again in action against insurrectionary Hungary, whose revolutionary war was reported by Engels with great expert knowledge in the columns of the *Neue Rheinische Zeitung*, but at the same time with such passionate partizanship that he overestimated the level of the historical development of the Magyars as he had previously overestimated that of the Poles. Answering Bakunin's demand that the Austrian Slavs should be guaranteed their independence he declared : " Not on your life ! Our answer to the sentimental phrases about fraternity which are now offered to us on behalf of the most counter-revolutionary nations in Europe is : hatred of Russia was the first revolutionary passion of the Germans and it still is. Since the revolution this hatred of Russia has been enhanced by hatred of the Czechs and the Croats, and we can secure the victory of the revolution, together with the Poles and the Magyars, only by energetic terrorism against these Slav peoples. We know now where the enemies of the revolution are concentrated : in Russia and in the Austrian Slav countries, and no amount of phrases and appeals to a vague democratic future for these countries will prevent us treating our enemies as our enemies." And therefore Engels proclaims a merciless struggle to the death against " counter-revolutionary Slavdom ".

These lines were not due solely to a fierce wave of anger and indignation at the slavish services rendered by the Austrian Slavs to the European reaction. With the exception of the Poles, the Russians and perhaps the Slavs in Turkey, Engels denied the Slav peoples any historical future, "for the simple reason that all other Slavs have not the first historical, geographical, political and industrial conditions for independence and national life ". Their struggle for national independence made them into the willing tools of Tsarism, and not all the well-meaning self-deceptions of the democratic Pan-Slavs could alter this fact in the least. The historic right of the great cultural peoples to pursue their revolutionary development was more important than the struggle of these small, crippled and impotent nations and groups for independence, even if here and there some delicate national bud should be broken off at the stem. As a result of the greater struggle these little nations and groups would be privileged to take part in a process of historical development which would remain completely foreign to them if they were left to themselves. And in 1882 he again said very much the same thing : if the struggle of the Balkan Slavs for their independence ran counter to the interests of the proletariat of Western Europe then these lackeys of Tsardom could go to the devil as far as he was concerned ; poetic sympathies had no place in the political struggle.

Engels was wrong when he denied any historical future to the smaller Slav nations, but the fundamental idea which governed his attitude was undoubtedly correct and the *Neue Rheinische Zeitung* held fast to this idea even in a case when it coincided with the " poetic sympathies " of the Philistines.

4. September Days

This case was the war begun by the Prussian government after the 18th of March against Denmark at the instructions of the German League in the Sleswig-Holstein question.

Holstein was a German district and belonged to the German League. Sleswig was not a member of the League and its Northern section at least was preponderatingly Danish. Both Duchies were connected with Denmark by a joint ruling house, although in Sleswig-Holstein the principle of exclusively male succession prevailed whilst in Denmark, which was very little larger and very little more populated than the two Duchies, both male and female succession were permissible. Sleswig and Holstein had a joint administration and enjoyed State independence together.

That at least was the formal relation of Denmark to the two Duchies according to international treaties, but in fact up to the verge of the nineteenth century the German spirit was dominant in Copenhagen and the German language was the official language of the kingdom whilst the nobles of Sleswig-Holstein exercised decisive influence in Danish governmental circles. During the Napoleonic wars national antagonisms began to develop. In the Vienna Treaties Denmark had to pay for its loyalty to the heir of the Great French Revolution with the loss of Norway, and in the struggle for existence it was compelled to annex Sleswig-Holstein because the gradual expiration of the male line of its ruling house imminently threatened the complete separation of the two Duchies from Denmark because in such circumstances they would fall into the possession of a collateral line.   Denmark began to emancipate itself as far as possible from German influence, and as it was too small to develop a really national spirit it began to foster a sort of artificial Scandinavianism with a view to uniting itself with Norway and Sweden in a joint cultural community.

The attempts of the Danish government to obtain complete control over the two Elbian Duchies met with obstinate resistance within the latter and the conflict soon developed into a national question for Germany.   Particularly after the formation of the *Zollverein* Germany began to recognize the importance of the Sleswig-Holstein isthmus for its flourishing trading and maritime relations, and it welcomed the resistance to Danish propaganda in Sleswig-Holstein with increasing approval.   From 1844 onwards the song *Schleswig-Holstein meerumschlungen* became a sort of national anthem.[1]   The movement certainly did not go much beyond the usual sleepy and boring tempo of pre-March agitation, but the German governments were not able to free themselves completely from its influence.   In 1847 King Christian VIII of Denmark made a decisive move in the game by issuing a Royal Letter declaring the Duchy of Sleswig, and even a part of the Duchy of Holstein, to be integral parts of the Kingdom of Denmark, and then even the Germanic Diet pulled itself together sufficiently to lodge a lame protest instead of declaring itself non-competent as was its custom whenever it was necessary to defend the interests of the German people against princely violence.

The *Neue Rheinische Zeitung* naturally felt not the least sympathy with the sea-surrounded pot-thumping enthusiasms of the bourgeoisie, which it regarded as the reverse side of Scandinavianism, "enthusiasm for a brutal, grubby, piratical Old-Nordic nationality which is unable to express its deep-seated aspirations in words, but certainly can in deeds, namely, in brutality towards women, chronic drunkenness, and alternate tear-sodden sentimentality and Berserker fury".   The situation shifted in the most extraordinary fashion because it was the bourgeois opposition in Denmark which fought under the banner of Scandinavianism, the party of the so-called Eider-Danes, which wanted to make the Duchy of Sleswig Danish, to extend Denmark's economic activities and to consolidate the Danish State by giving it a modern constitution, whilst on the

[1] " Sleswig-Holstein sea-surrounded."

other hand the fight of the two Duchies for their old-established rights developed more and more into a struggle for feudal traditions and dynastic privileges.

In January 1848 Frederick VII came to the throne of Denmark as the last of the male line, and in accordance with the death-bed advice of his father he immediately began to prepare a liberal constitution for Denmark and for the two Duchies. A month later the February revolution in Copenhagen awakened a vigorous people's movement which brought the Eider-Danes into power, and the latter immediately began to put their programme into execution with relentless energy, aiming at the annexation of the Duchy of Sleswig up to the River Eider. The two Duchies then declared themselves independent of the Danish Royal House, formed a provisional government in Kiel and raised an army of 7,000 men. The aristocracy had the upper hand in the provisional government and instead of mobilizing the resources of the two Duchies, which were quite in a position to pit themselves against Denmark, the government appealed to the Germanic Diet and to the Prussian government for assistance, for it had no cause to fear that either of these bodies would attempt to interfere with the feudal privileges of the aristocracy.

It found willing support from these two bodies which gladly seized on " the defence of the German cause " as a convenient opportunity of recovering from the heavy blows dealt by the revolution. After the signal defeat of his Guards Regiments at the hands of the Berlin barricade fighters on the 18th of March the Prussian King was anxious to re-establish their prestige by a military walk-over, and Denmark, which was militarily weak, seemed to offer the desired opportunity. The King hated the Eider-Danish Party as one of the fruits of the revolution, but at the same time he regarded the Sleswig-Holsteiners as rebels against a God-given authority, and he therefore instructed his generals to perform their " lackey service for the revolution " in as dilatory fashion as possible. At the same time he sent a secret envoy to Copenhagen in the person of Major von Wildenbruch to inform the Danish government that he wished above all that Sleswig-Holstein should retain its ducal rulers and that he was intervening merely in order to forestall the radical and republican elements.

However, Denmark was not deceived by this message and it appealed to the Great Powers for assistance, and both Great Britain and Russia proved very willing to grant it. Their help permitted little Denmark to pummel big Germany like a schoolboy. The Danish men-of-war struck crippling blows at

Germany's maritime trade, but the German Federal Army under the command of the Prussian general Wrangel invaded the two Duchies and despite miserable generalship pressed back the weak Danish forces only to find its military successes rendered nugatory by the diplomatic intervention of the Great Powers. At the end of May Wrangel received orders from Berlin to withdraw his troops from Jutland, whereupon, on the 9th of June, the National Assembly announced that the cause of the two Duchies was the cause of the German nation and therefore came within the province of the Assembly, which would undertake to defend Germany's honour.

The war was, in fact, being conducted in the name of the German League, and its leadership should have been in the hands of the National Assembly and the Habsburg prince it had elected Reich's Regent; but the Prussian government ignored these facts, and on the 28th of August, under English and Russian pressure, it concluded the seven months' truce of Malmoe, at the same time treating with contempt the conditions put forward by the Reich's Regent and utterly ignoring his representative. The terms of the truce were ignominious for Germany : the provisional government of Sleswig-Holstein was dissolved and supreme control for the period of the truce placed in the hands of a Danish supporter, the decrees of the provisional government were cancelled and the Sleswig and Holstein troops separated from each other. Germany also suffered a distinct military disadvantage from the truce which embraced the whole of the winter season, during which the Danish fleet would have been helpless and unable to blockade the German coasts whilst the German troops would have been able to take advantage of the ice to cross the Little Belt and conquer Fyen, thus reducing Denmark to the island of Zealand.

The news of the signing of the armistice arrived in the first days of September and burst like a bomb-shell in the Frankfort National Assembly, whose deputies were endlessly discussing " with the washerwoman loquacity of mediæval scholastics " the " fundamental rights " of the future Reich's Constitution. In their first consternation the deputies actually decided on the 5th of September to inhibit the armistice, and this caused the resignation of the Reich's Ministry.

This decision was welcomed with lively satisfaction, but without any illusions by the *Neue Rheinische Zeitung*, which demanded the prosecution of the war against Denmark as a result of historical development quite apart from any treaty rights : " The Danes are a people unconditionally dependent on Germany commercially, industrially, politically and in literature. It is a well-known fact that Hamburg is the capital of Denmark and not Copenhagen, and that Denmark derives its literary imports from Germany in the same way as it does its material imports. With the sole exception of Holberg, Danish literature is nothing but a feeble copy of German literature. . . . Germany must take Sleswig with the same justification that France took Flanders, Alsace and Lorraine, and sooner or later will take Belgium. It is the right of civilization against barbarism, of progress against stagnation. . . . The war which we are carrying on in Sleswig-Holstein is a real national war. Who has taken the side of Denmark from the beginning ? The three most counter-revolutionary powers in Europe : Russia, England and the Prussian government. As long as it possibly could the Prussian government waged the war only in appearances. Remember von Wildenbruch's Note, the willingness with which Prussia evacuated Jutland at the request of England and Russia, and now the conclusion of this armistice. Prussia, England and Russia are the three powers which have most to fear from the German revolution and its firstfruit, German unity : Prussia because it would thereby cease to exist, England because the German market would be lost to its exploitation, and Russia because democracy would advance thereby not only to the Vistula, but to the Dvina and the Dnieper. Prussia, England and Russia have conspired together against Sleswig-Holstein, against Germany and against the revolution. The war which may come about as a result of the Frankfort decisions would be a war of Germany against Prussia, England and Russia. The German revolutionary movement needs such a war to rouse it from its lethargy, a war against the three great powers of the counter-revolution, a war which would finally make Prussia an integral part of Germany, which would make an alliance with Poland an urgent and unavoidable necessity, which would immediately give Italy its freedom and be waged directly against the old counter-revolutionary allies of Germany from 1792 to 1815, a war which would ' endanger the Fatherland ' and save it just because the victory of Germany would depend on the victory of democracy."

These clear and sharp passages from the *Neue Rheinische Zeitung* reflected what the revolutionary masses instinctively felt. Thousands of men streamed into Frankfort from a radius of fifty miles around, ready and eager for new revolutionary struggles, but, as the *Neue Rheinische Zeitung* pointed out, such a struggle would abolish the National Assembly itself, and the latter preferred suicide by cowardice to suicide by heroism. On the 16th of September it gave its approval to the Truce of Malmoe, whilst, with one or two exceptions, the representatives of its left wing· rejected a demand that it should constitute itself as a revolutionary Convention. The only fighting which took place was a minor barricade engagement in Frankfort itself, and even this was deliberately permitted to grow by the worthy Reich's Regent in order to give him a pretext for bringing in an overwhelming force of troops from the neighbouring federal garrison of Mayence and overawing the sovereign parliament with its bayonets.

At the same time the Hansemann Ministry in Berlin was overtaken by the miserable fate which the *Neue Rheinische Zeitung* had prophesied for it. It had strengthened the " State power " against " the forces of anarchy ", thus assisting the old Prussian military, police and bureaucratic State to rise to its feet again after the buffeting it had received on the 18th of March, but it had not even succeeded in furthering the naked profit interests of the bourgeoisie for which it had betrayed the revolution. And above all, as a member of the Berlin Assembly sighed dolefully, " Despite the breach in the March days the old military system is with us in its entirety again ". This was true, and since the Paris June days it had resumed its menacing sabre-rattling almost automatically. It was an open secret that one of the reasons why the Prussian government had agreed so readily to the truce with Denmark was its desire to recall Wrangel and his troops to the neighbourhood of Berlin in order to prepare a counter-revolutionary coup. On the 7th of September therefore the Berlin Assembly plucked up sufficient courage to demand from the Minister for War that he should issue an order warning all army officers against reactionary activities and calling upon all those officers whose political convictions ran counter to the existing constitutional situation to resign their commissions as a matter of honour.

This demand was really of no very great importance, particularly as similar appeals had in fact already been issued to the members of the bureaucracy without producing any result whatever, but it was more than militarism was prepared to stand from a bourgeois Ministry. The Hansemann Ministry fell and a purely bureaucratic Ministry was formed under General Pfuel, who then calmly issued the order in question to the officers corps as proof to the world that militarism no longer feared the bourgeoisie and was now in a position to mock at it.

In this way the " petulant, super-clever and impotent " Assembly experienced the fulfilment of the prophecy of the *Neue Rheinische Zeitung* that .one fine morning its left-wing would wake up to find that its parliamentary victory had coincided with its material defeat. Replying to the hubbub raised by the counter-revolutionary press, which declared that the victory of the left wing had been won under the pressure of the Berlin masses, the *Neue Rheinische Zeitung* spurned the lame denials of the liberal newspapers and declared frankly : " The right of the democratic masses of the people to exercise a moral influence on the actions of constitutional assemblies by their presence is an old revolutionary right and no period since the English and French revolutions has seen its abandonment. History has to thank this right for almost all the energetic steps taken by such assemblies." This hint was directed as much to the " parliamentary cretinism " of the Frankfort Assembly in those September days of 1848 as to the Berlin Assembly.

5. The Cologne Democracy

The September crises in Berlin and Frankfort had strong repercussions in Cologne. The Rhineland represented the biggest anxiety of the counter-revolution and it was flooded with troops recruited from the Eastern provinces. Almost one-third of the Prussian army was quartered in the Rhineland and in Westphalia, and under the circumstances minor insurrections were quite useless. The need of the moment was the carrying out of a thorough and disciplined organization of democracy for the day when it would be possible to turn the half-hearted revolution into a whole one.

A congress of 88 democratic associations had taken place in Frankfort in June, and it had been decided to found a democratic organization. However, it was only in Cologne that this body took on any firm and solid form, whilst in the rest of Germany it remained a very loose affair. The Cologne democracy was organized in three big associations, each of which had several thousand members : the Democratic Association led by Marx and the advocate Schneider, the Workers Association led by Moll and Schapper, and the Association of Employers and Employees led by the young barrister Hermann Becker. When the Frankfort congress decided on Cologne as the centre for the Rhineland and for Westphalia these associations formed a joint central committee which then convened a congress of all the democratic associations in the Rhineland and in Westphalia to take place in the middle of August in Cologne. Forty delegates representing 17 associations came to the congress, and they con-

firmed the joint central committee of the three Cologne democratic associations as the district committee for the Rhineland
and Westphalia.

Marx was the intellectual leader of this organization as he
was of the *Neue Rheinische Zeitung*. He had the gift of leadership
to a high degree, and the banal democrats were unwilling to forgive him this. Karl Schurz, who was then a nineteen-year-old
student, saw him for the first time at the Cologne congress and
afterwards described him from memory : " Marx was thirty
years old at the time and already the acknowledged leader of
a socialist school of thought. The thick-set man with his broad
forehead and dark flashing eyes, his jet-black hair and full
beard immediately attracted general attention. He had the
reputation of being a very considerable scholar in his own field
and, in fact, what he said was weighty, logical and clear, but
never in my life have I met a man whose attitude was so hurt-
fully and intolerably arrogant." Schurz, who afterwards
became one of the heroes of the bourgeoisie, always particularly
remembered the cutting scorn and the contemptuous tone with
which Marx invariably used the term " bourgeois "—as though
he were spitting something disagreeable from his tongue.

It was the same tune sung a couple of years later by Lieutenant
Techov, who wrote after a conversation with Marx : " Marx
impressed me not only by his unusual superiority, but also by
his very considerable personality. If his heart were as big as
his brain and his love as great as his hate I would go through
fire for him, despite the fact that he indicated his low opinion
of me on several occasions and finally expressed it quite frankly.
He is the first and only one amongst us to whom I would ascribe
the quality of leadership, the capacity to master a big situation
without losing himself in insignificant details." And after that
followed the usual litany that the dangerous personal ambition
of Marx had eaten away everything else.

In the summer of 1848 Albert Brisbane, the American apostle
of Fourier, was in Cologne as the correspondent of *The New
York Tribune* together with its publisher Charles Dana, and his
judgment of Marx was different : " I saw Karl Marx the leader
of the people's movement. At that time his star was just in
the ascendant. He was a man in the 'thirties with a squat
powerful body, a fine face and thick black hair. His features
indicated great energy and behind his moderation and reserve
one could detect the passionate fire of a daring spirit." That
was true—in those days Marx was leading the Cologne democracy
with cool but daring courage.

Although the September crises had caused great excitement

in its ranks, the Frankfort Assembly was unable to summon up sufficient courage to organize a revolution, whilst on the other hand the Pfuel Ministry was not ready to organize a counter-revolution. A local insurrection would have had no chance of success whatever and therefore the authorities were anxious to provoke one in order to drown it in blood with ease. Legal proceedings were begun and police measures taken against the members of the democratic district committee and the editors of the *Neue Rheinische Zeitung*. The pretexts put forward were so flimsy that they were soon abandoned even by the authorities. Marx raised a warning voice against the treacherous cunning of the authorities : at the moment no great question was exercising the people as a whole and urging it into a struggle, and therefore any attempt at a putsch must fail. An insurrection at the moment would be worse than useless because great events might take place in the near future and it behoved the democrats not to let themselves be disarmed before the day of battle arrived. If the Crown dared to organize a counter-revolution then the hour would strike for a new revolution on the part of the people.

However, minor disturbances did occur when on the 25th of September Becker, Moll, Schapper and Wilhelm Wolff were to be arrested. The news that troops were advancing to break up a public meeting even caused the erection of barricades, but in fact the military made no move and only after complete calm had descended again did the military commandant summon up sufficient courage to proclaim martial law in Cologne. Under martial law the *Neue Rheinische Zeitung* was suppressed and on the 27th of September it ceased to appear. This was probably the only aim of the senseless military coup and a few days afterwards the Pfuel Ministry raised the state of siege. The *Neue Rheinische Zeitung* was, in fact, very heavily hit, and it was the 12th of October before it appeared again.

The editorial board was broken up owing to the fact that most of its members were compelled to go over the frontier to avoid arrest : Dronke and Engels went to Belgium, and Wilhelm Wolff to the Palatinate, and it was some time before they returned. At the beginning of January 1849 Engels was still in Berne, where he had gone through France, mostly on foot. Above all, the finances of the paper were in a sad state. After the shareholders had turned their backs on it the paper managed to exist for a while on its increased circulation, but after the latest blow it was saved from final disappearance only by the fact that Marx took it over as his " personal property ", that is to say, by the fact that he sacrificed that little he had inherited from his father, or that little he was able to obtain in advance on his future inheritance. Marx himself never said a word about the affair, but from the letters of his wife and the utterances of his friends it would appear that he sacrificed about 7,000 thaler to further the agitation and keep the paper alive, though naturally the exact sum is unimportant, the main thing being that he sacrificed all he had in order to keep the flag flying.

Marx's position was very insecure in another respect also. After the outbreak of the revolution the Federal Council had decided on the 30th of March that the German fugitives should be given both the active and passive franchise in the elections for the German National Assembly provided they returned to Germany and gave notice of their desire to renew their former civil rights. This decision was expressly recognized by the Prussian government and Marx, who fulfilled all the conditions guaranteeing him national civil rights, was therefore all the more entitled to demand that he should be given back his Prussian civil rights. In fact, when he applied in April 1848 the Cologne Town Council immediately granted his application and when he pointed out to the Police President of Cologne, Müller, that he could not very well bring his family from Trier to Cologne so long as the affair was uncertain, Müller replied that the district authorities, who according to an old Prussian law had to confirm the decision of the Town Council, would certainly give their permission for his re-naturalization. However, in the meantime the *Neue Rheinische Zeitung* began to appear, and on the 3rd of August Marx received an official intimation from the commissarial Police President Geiger to the effect that under the circumstances the Royal Government had decided to make no use "for the moment" in his case of its right to grant Prussian civil rights to a foreigner, and that therefore he must continue to regard himself as an alien. On the 22nd of August he appealed indignantly to the Minister of the Interior, but his appeal was rejected.

Devoted husband and father as he was, Marx had in the meantime brought his family to Cologne despite the uncertainty. In the meantime its numbers had increased : the first daughter, who was called Jenny after her mother and was born in May 1844, was followed by a second daughter Laura, who was born in September 1845 and was followed, presumably not long afterwards, by a son, Edgar. Edgar is the only one of Marx's children whose exact birth date is not known. Since its Paris days the family had been accompanied by Helene Demuth, a loyal and devoted servant and friend.

Marx was not one of those men who greet every new acquaintance as a friend and a brother immediately, but his loyalty to his friends was beyond reproach and his friendship firm. At the same congress at which his intolerable arrogance is alleged to have repulsed men who would gladly have approached him, he won lifelong friends in the lawyer Schily of Trier and the teacher Imandt of Krefeld, and although the stern oneness of purpose which guided him throughout his life made him appear sinister to semi-revolutionaries like Schurz and Techov, at the same time it irresistibly drew real revolutionaries like Freiligrath and Lassalle into his intellectual and personal orbit.

6. Freiligrath and Lassalle

Ferdinand Freiligrath was eight years older than Marx and in his youth he had been liberally suckled with the pure milk of orthodoxy. On one occasion he had felt the lash of the old *Rheinische Zeitung* for having published a mocking poem on the unsuccessful tour of Herwegh after the latter's expulsion from Prussia. However, it had not been long before the pre-March re-action had turned Saul into Paul, and during the period of exile in Brussels he had made the acquaintance of Marx. Their acquaint-ance in the beginning was slight but friendly. "A nice fellow, interesting and modest in his attitude," he declared of Marx, and he was no bad judge of character. Freiligrath himself was utterly free of all personal vanity and perhaps just for this reason he had a fine feeling for anything which suggested arrogance in others.

The acquaintance of the two men ripened into a firm friend-ship in the summer and autumn of 1848, and the thing which drew them together was the respect which each felt for the courageous and uncompromising fashion in which the other represented their joint revolutionary principles in the Rhenish movement. Referring to Freiligrath Marx declared in a letter to Weydemeyer : "He is a real revolutionary and a thoroughly honest man, and that is praise I would give to very few." At the same time Marx advised Weydemeyer to flatter the poet a little, declaring that all poets needed a little flattering encourage-ment if they were to give of their best. Marx was not a man who wore his heart on his sleeve, but in a moment of tension he wrote to Freiligrath : "I tell you frankly that I am not prepared to lose one of the few men I regard as my friends in the best sense of the word merely on account of unimportant misunderstandings." Apart from Engels, Marx had no better friend than Freiligrath in the times of his worst troubles.

Because this friendship was so simple and so real it has always been a source of annoyance to the Philistines. Sometimes they declared that the passionate fantasy of the poet had played him a scurvy trick by leading him into bad company, and at other times they declared that a demoniacal demagogue had breathed poisonously on a harmless poet and shrivelled up his song. It would not be worth while to waste a word on this nonsense, but for the fact that a wrong antidote has been offered against it. An attempt has been made to turn Freiligrath into a modern social democrat and this puts him in a wrong light. Freiligrath was a revolutionary from passionate instinct and poetic feelings, and not out of any scientific considerations. He regarded Marx as a pioneer of the revolution and the Communist League as the revolutionary advance-guard, but the historical arguments of *The Communist Manifesto* always remained more or less foreign to him, and above all, his glowing fantasy could make nothing of the often miserable and sober petty details of the everyday agitational work.

Ferdinand Lassalle, who joined Marx's circle at about the same time, was a totally different type. He was seven years younger than Marx, and up to that time his reputation was based exclusively on his zealous struggle on behalf of the Countess Hatzfeldt, who had been ill-treated by her husband and betrayed by her caste. In February 1848 he had been arrested on a charge of instigating the theft of a deed-box,[1] but on the 11th of August he was acquitted by a Cologne jury, after putting up a brilliant defence, and he was then able to devote himself to the revolutionary struggles. With his "unfailing sympathy for all real strength" he naturally could not fail to be deeply impressed with the leader of the revolutionary struggle, Marx.

Lassalle had also gone through the Hegelian school and had thoroughly mastered its methods without up to that time harbouring any doubts as to their infallibility and without being affected by the decadence of Hegel's successors. During a visit to Paris he had made the acquaintance of French socialism and received the accolade of a great future from Heine's prophetic vision. However, the great expectations which the young man had aroused were hampered in their development to a certain extent by an ambiguity of character which he had been unable to master completely in his struggle against the impeding heritage of an oppressed race. The stale atmosphere of Polish Judaism had

[1] A deed-box containing or alleged to contain documents of value as evidence in the Hatzfeldt process.—Tr.

prevailed absolutely in the home of his parents. In his·champion-
ship of Countess Hatzfeldt even unprejudiced spirits were not
always able to appreciate the truth of his contention, justifiable from his own point of view, that in this individual case he
was fighting against the social misery of a whole period now
labouring its way towards the grave. Even Freiligrath, who was
never particularly fond·of him, spoke contemptuously of the
" wretched domestic trivialities " around which world-history
seemed to revolve for him.

Seven years later Marx expressed himself in much the same
fashion : Lassalle considered himself a world-conqueror because
he had been ruthless in a private intrigue, as though a man of
any real character would be prepared to sacrifice ten years of
his life on such a bagatelle. And several decades later Engels
declared that Marx had harboured an antipathy towards Lassalle
from the very beginning and that the *Neue Rheinische Zeitung* had
deliberately published as little as possible about the Hatzfeldt
case in order to avoid any impression that it had anything in
common with Lassalle in the matter. However, in this respect
Engels' memory was deceiving him, for in fact, up to the day of
its suppression on the 27th of September, the *Neue Rheinische
Zeitung* published very detailed reports of the trial of Lassalle in
connection with his alleged instigation of the theft of the deed-box,
although of course its reports did not conceal the fact that the
whole affair had less agreeable sides. And further, Marx himself,
as he informed Freiligrath in a letter, assisted Countess Hatzfeldt
financially in her dire straits from his own modest means, and
when after his Cologne period he got into serious difficulties
himself he chose Lassalle, together with Freiligrath, as his confidant
in a town in which he had many old friends.

But Engels was certainly right when he said that Marx
harboured an antipathy to Lassalle, and he and Freiligrath did
also. It was an antipathy which had little to do with reason,
and there is sufficient evidence available to show that Marx did
not let it blind him to the deeper significance of the Hatzfeldt
affair, not to speak of the fiery enthusiasm which Lassalle showed
for the cause of the revolution, his outstanding talents and finally
the devoted friendship which the younger comrade-in-arms
showed towards him.

It is necessary to examine carefully the development of the
relations between the two men from the beginning, not on
Lassalle's account, for his historical claims have long ago been
vindicated, but in order to shield Marx himself from misunderstandings, for his attitude to Lassalle represents the most difficult
psychological problem of his life.

7. October and November Days

On the 12th of October the *Neue Rheinische Zeitung* began to appear again and announced that Freiligrath had joined its staff. It was fortunate enough to be able to welcome a new revolution immediately, for on the 6th of October the proletariat of Vienna had brought down its fist resoundingly and upset the treacherous plans of the Habsburg counter-revolution, which after Radetzky's victories in Italy intended, with the help of the Slav peoples, to crush first the rebellious Hungarians and then the rebellious Germans.

Marx himself had been in Vienna from the 28th of August to the 7th of September in order to enlighten the masses there, but to judge from occasional newspaper references he had not been particularly successful, and that is not surprising, for the workers of Vienna were still at a comparatively low level of development. The revolutionary instinct with which they had opposed the departure of the regiments ordered to Hungary to suppress the revolution there was therefore all the more praiseworthy. Their action drew the first fire of the counter-revolution upon themselves, a noble sacrifice of which the Hungarian aristocracy proved unworthy. It was anxious to wage its struggle for Hungarian independence on the basis of its historical rights, and the Hungarian army made only one half-hearted drive which increased rather than diminished the difficulties of the Vienna insurrectionaries.

The attitude of the German democracy was no better. It certainly recognized how much depended for itself on the success of the Vienna insurrection, for if the counter-revolution gained the upper hand in the Austrian capital then it would inevitably deal the decisive blow in the Prussian capital also, where it had been awaiting its opportunity long enough. However, the German democracy contented itself with sentimental dirges, fruitless expressions of sympathy and vain appeals for aid to the impotent Reich's Regent. At the end of October the democratic congress met in Berlin for the second time and it issued an appeal on behalf of besieged Vienna drawn up by Ruge, but the *Neue Rheinische Zeitung* pointed out aptly that it tried to make up for its lack of revolutionary energy by a sermonizing and tearful pathos, and that the whole appeal contained not a vestige of revolutionary passion or ideas. However, the passionate appeals of Marx in powerful prose and of Freiligrath in magnificent verse to afford the besieged Viennese the only effective assistance possible by overthrowing the counter-revolution at home re-echoed like voices in the desert.

Thus the fate of the Vienna revolution was sealed. Betrayed by the bourgeoisie and by the peasants and supported only by the students and a section of the petty-bourgeoisie, the workers of Vienna fought heroically, but on the evening of the 31st of October the besieging troops succeeded in effecting an entry into the town and on the 1st of November the great black and yellow flag of the counter-revolution waved from the steeple of St. Stephen's Cathedral.

The moving tragedy in Vienna was quickly followed by a grotesque tragi-comedy in Berlin. The Pfuel Ministry resigned to make way for the Brandenburg Ministry, which immediately ordered the Assembly to retire to the provincial town of Brandenburg and caused General Wrangel to march into Berlin with the Guards Regiments to support this order by force of arms. Brandenburg, an illegitimate Hohenzoller, compared himself somewhat too flatteringly with an elephant which would trample the revolution under foot, but the *Neue Rheinische Zeitung* declared more truthfully that Brandenburg and his accomplice Wrangel were " two men without heads, without hearts and without principles, nothing more than imposing whiskers ", but as such just the right opponents for the pusillanimous Assembly.

And in fact Wrangel's martial whiskers proved sufficient to intimidate the Assembly. It is true that it refused to vacate its constitutional seat, Berlin, but when one blow followed the other and one act of violence the other : the dissolution of the citizens guard, the proclamation of martial law, etc., it declared the Ministers traitors and denounced them—to the Public Prosecutor. It ignored the demand of the Berlin workers that the rights of the people should be defended by force of arms and proclaimed " passive resistance " instead, or in other words, the noble decision to suffer the blows of the enemy without answering back. It was then driven out of one hall after the other by Wrangel's troops, and in a sudden burst of temperament caused by a new appearance of Wrangel's bayonets it solemnly declared that the Brandenburg Ministry had no right to dispose of State moneys or collect taxes so long as the Assembly was not permitted to hold its sessions in Berlin without let or hindrance. However, hardly had the Assembly been broken up than its President, von Unruh, fearing for the safety of his precious skin, called together the bureau of the Assembly in order to place on record in the Minutes that the decision against the Ministry was invalid on account of a technical formality, although he let the decision be made public without hindrance.

It was left to the *Neue Rheinische Zeitung* to oppose the brutal coup of the government in a worthy fashion. It declared that the moment had arrived to oppose the counter-revolution with a second revolution, and it called on the masses to oppose the violence of the authorities with every possible form of counter-violence. Passive resistance must have active resistance as its basis, it declared, otherwise it was nothing but the ineffective struggles of the sheep against the slaughterman. At the same time it ruthlessly demolished the legal quibbling about the theory of agreement with the Crown, behind which the cowardice of the bourgeoisie sought to hide itself : " The Prussian Crown is absolutely within its rights when it acts as an absolutist power towards the Assembly, and the Assembly is in the wrong because it does not act towards the Crown as a sovereign Assembly. . . . The old bureaucracy is unwilling to become the servant of the bourgeoisie, whose despotic schoolmaster it has been up to the present. The feudal party is not willing to sacrifice its privileges and its interests on the altar of the bourgeoisie. And finally, the Crown sees its real and native social basis in the elements of the old feudal society, whose highest expression is found in the Crown, whilst it regards the bourgeoisie as a foreign and artificial basis which will bear it only on condition that it withers away. The rousing ' By the Grace of God ' becomes a sober legal title for the bourgeoisie, the right of blood becomes the right of paper, and the Royal Sun a bourgeois farthing dip. The Crown therefore refused to let itself be persuaded by the phrases of the bourgeoisie, but answered the half-revolution of the latter with a whole counter-revolution. It flung back the bourgeoisie into the arms of the revolution, into the arms of the people, when it shouted, ' Brandenburg in the Assembly and the Assembly in Brandenburg ! ' "

The *Neue Rheinische Zeitung* aptly parodied this slogan as, " The guard-room in the Assembly, and the Assembly in the guard-room ! " expressing the hope that the people would be victorious under this slogan and turn it into the epitaph on the grave of the House of Brandenburg.

After the decision of the Berlin Assembly to deprive the government of the right to collect taxes, the democratic district committee in Cologne issued an appeal on the 18th of November signed by Marx, Schapper and Schneider demanding that the democratic associations in the Rhineland should immediately take steps to put the following measures into effect : any attempt made by the authorities to collect taxes by force should be resisted by every possible means ; citizens guards to be organized everywhere immediately to offer resistance to the enemy ; arms and munitions to be supplied to the poor at municipal cost and by voluntary contributions ; should the government refuse to recognize and respect the decisions of the Assembly then committees of public safety should be elected everywhere, if possible in agreement with the municipalities, those municipalities resisting the Assembly to be re-elected by popular vote. Thus the Democratic Association did what the Berlin Assembly should have done and must have done had it taken its decision to refuse the payment of taxes seriously. However, the heroes of the Berlin Assembly trembled at their own courage and hurried off to their constituencies in order to prevent the carrying out of their decision, and after that they slunk off to Brandenburg to continue their sessions. With this the last vestige of dignity and influence had been abandoned so that on the 5th of December it was an easy matter for the government to dismiss the Assembly altogether and to impose a new constitution and a new franchise.

The treachery of the Berlin Assembly paralysed the district committee in the Rhineland, which was flooded with troops. On the 22nd of November Lassalle, who had enthusiastically welcomed the appeal, was arrested in Düsseldorf, whilst in Cologne the Public Prosecutor took action against those who had signed it, although he did not dare to arrest them. On the 8th of February the signatories to the appeal appeared before a jury in Cologne on a charge of having incited the people to armed resistance against the authorities and against the military forces of the Crown.

The attempt of the Public Prosecutor to use the laws of the 6th and 8th of April, the same laws which the government had trodden underfoot with its coup, against the Assembly and against the accused was demolished by Marx in a powerful speech : those who had carried out a successful revolution might logically hang their opponents, but not sit in judgment upon them ; they might get rid of their defeated enemies, but not try them as criminals. It was cowardly hypocrisy to use the laws which a successful revolution or counter-revolution had just overthrown against those who had upheld them. The question of whether the Assembly was in the right or the Crown was an historical one and could be determined only by history and not by a jury.

But Marx went still further, he refused to recognize the laws of the 6th and 8th of April at all, declaring them to have been manufactured by the United Diet in order to save the Crown from having to admit its defeat in the March struggles. An assembly representing modern bourgeois society could not be judged according to the laws of a feudal body. The principle that society was based on law was a legal fiction. On the contrary, in reality law was based on society : " In my hand is the *Code Napoléon*. It did not produce bourgeois society. On the

contrary, it was produced by bourgeois society, which, arising
in the eighteenth century and continuing its development in the
nineteenth, found no more than its legal expression in the Code.
The moment the Code failed to reflect social relations faithfully,
it would be no more than a scrap of paper. You cannot make the
old laws the basis of the new society any more than the old laws
made the old society."

The Berlin Assembly had failed to understand the historic
rôle which had developed for it out of the March Revolution.
The reproach of the Public Prosecutor that the Assembly had
refused all mediation was baseless because the misfortune and the
mistake of the Assembly lay precisely in the fact that it had
degraded itself from a revolutionary convention into an ambiguous
association of conciliants : " What we have witnessed was not a
political conflict between two fractions on the basis of one society,
but a conflict between two societies, a social conflict in a political
form. It was the struggle of the old feudal-bureaucratic society
against modern bourgeois society, the struggle between the society
of free competition and the society of the guilds and corporations,
between the society of landownership and the society of industry,
between the society of authoritarian belief and the society of
knowledge." There could be no peace between these two
societies, but only a struggle in which one of them must go under.
The refusal to pay taxes did not shake the foundations of society,
as the Public Prosecutor had amusingly contended. It was an
act of self-defence on the part of society against a government
which threatened the foundations of society.

The Assembly had not acted illegally with regard to its refusal
to pay taxes, but not legally with its announcement of passive
resistance : " If the collection of taxes is declared illegal it is my
duty to oppose, by force if necessary, any attempt to carry out
an illegal act." Although those who had proclaimed the refusal
to pay taxes had refused to take the revolutionary path for fear
of their own skins, the masses of the people were nevertheless
compelled to do so when carrying out this proclamation. The
attitude of the Assembly was not decisive for the people : " The
Assembly has no rights of its own ; the people has merely transferred to the Assembly the task of defending its rights. When the
Assembly fails to perform this task its rights expire, and the people
then appears in the arena in person to act in its own right.
When the Crown organizes a counter-revolution the people justly
answers with a new revolution." Marx concluded his speech
with the statement that only the first act in the drama had been
played out. The final dénouement would be the complete victory
of the counter-revolution or a new and victorious revolution,

though perhaps the latter would be possible only after the completed victory of the counter-revolution.

After this proud revolutionary speech the jury acquitted all the accused and the foremen of the jury thanked Marx for his instructive explanation.

8. An Act of Perfidy

With the victory of the counter-revolution in Vienna and in Berlin the decisive word had been spoken in Germany. All that was left of the achievements of the revolution was the Frankfort Assembly, which had long ago lost all its political credit and which frittered away its energies in endless torrents of discussion about a paper constitution. In reality the only question still outstanding was whether the Assembly would be dismissed at the point of Prussian or Austrian bayonets.

In December the *Neue Rheinische Zeitung* described the development of the Prussian revolution and counter-revolution in a series of brilliant articles, and then turned a hopeful eye to the rise of the French working class, from which it expected a world war. "The country which has turned whole nations into its proletarians, which holds the whole world in its gigantic tentacles, which has already paid the expenses of a European restoration once, and in whose own lap the class contradictions have developed in their clearest and most shameless form—England, appears to be the rock against which the waves of revolution will break. England will starve the new society before it is born. England dominates the world market, and a transformation of economic relations in every country of Europe, on the whole Continent, would be a storm in a tea-cup without England. The relations of industry and commerce within each country are determined by their relations with other countries, by their relations with the world market. But England dominates the world market and England is dominated by the bourgeoisie."

Thus any social upheaval in France would be crushed by the English bourgeoisie, by the industrial and commercial world power of Great Britain. Any partial social reform in France or anywhere else on the European Continent would remain, in so far as it was intended to be definitive, a pious and empty wish. Old England could be overthrown only by a world war, which alone could offer the Chartists, the organized party of the English proletariat, the conditions necessary for a successful insurrection against its powerful oppressors. Only when the Chartists were at the head of the English government would the social revolution advance from the world of utopia into the world of reality.

The preliminary conditions for this future hope did not materialize. The French working class, still bleeding from a thousand wounds received in the June days, was not capable of any new rising. Since the counter-revolution had begun its tour of Europe in Paris in the June days, going on to Frankfort, Vienna and Berlin, to end for the moment on the 10th of December with the election of the false Bonaparte as President of the French Republic, the revolution was still alive only in Hungary, and it found an eloquent and expert advocate in Engels, who had in the meantime returned to Cologne. For the rest the *Neue Rheinische Zeitung* was compelled to limit its activities to a guerilla war against the advancing counter-revolution, but it waged this struggle as daringly and as determinedly as it had waged the greater struggles of the previous year. A bundle of press writs loaded on it by the Reich's government as the worst paper in a bad press, was greeted with the mocking remark that the Reich's power was the most comic of all comic powers, and the boastful display of " Prussianism " which the East Elbian Junkers had adopted since the Berlin coup was answered with deserved sarcasm : " We Rhinelanders have had the good fortune to win a Grand-Duke of the Lower Rhineland from the great reshuffle in Vienna, a man who has not fulfilled the conditions under which he became ' Grand-Duke . A King of Prussia exists for us only since the Berlin Assembly, and as there is no Assembly for our ' Grand-Duke of the Lower Rhineland ', thus no King of Prussia exists for us. We fell into the hands of the ' Grand-Duke of the Lower Rhineland ' as a result of jugglery with the fate of the peoples, and as soon as we are in a position to reject this jugglery we shall ask the ' Grand-Duke ' for his credentials." These lines were written during the wildest orgies of the counter-revolution.

One thing is missing at first glance in the columns of the *Neue Rheinische Zeitung*, something which one would expect to find there above all, namely, a detailed account of the activities of the German workers at the time. This movement was by no means insignificant, and it extended even into the districts of the East Elbian Junkers themselves. It had its congresses, its organizations and its newspapers, and a capable leader in Stephan Born, who was friendly with Marx and Engels from the Paris and Brussels period and who still contributed to the *Neue Rheinische Zeitung* from Berlin and from Leipzig. Born understood *The Communist Manifesto* very well, but he was less successful in applying its principles to the undeveloped class-consciousness of the proletariat of the greater part of Germany. Later on Engels condemned Born's activities with unjust severity, but it is quite possible that Born is right when he declares in his memoirs that during the years of revolution neither Marx nor Engels ever expressed a word of dissatisfaction with his activities, though this naturally does not exclude the possibility that they may have been dissatisfied with this or that detail. In any case, in the spring of 1849 Marx and Engels made the first move towards the working-class movement, which had developed in the meantime independent of their influence.

The fact that in the beginning the *Neue Rheinische Zeitung* paid very little attention to this movement can be explained in part by the fact that the Cologne Workers Association had its own special organ, which appeared twice a week under the editorship of Moll and Schapper, and in part, in greater part in fact, by the circumstance that the *Neue Rheinische Zeitung* was above all " an organ of democracy ", that is to say that it aimed at representing the joint interests of the bourgeoisie and of the proletariat against absolutism and feudalism. At that time this task was most important because it helped to create the basis on which the proletariat could begin its own discussion with the bourgeoisie. However, the bourgeois section of the democracy demoralized rapidly, and at every more or less serious test it collapsed miserably. There were such people as Meyen and Kriege (who had in the meantime returned from America) on the Committee of Five which had been elected in June 1848 by the first Democratic Congress. Under such leadership the organization began to decline rapidly, and this was seen disastrously when it met for the second time on the eve of the Prussian *coup d'état*. A new committee was elected and d'Ester, a personal friend and political supporter of Marx, was a member of it, but this was little more than a bill drawn on the future. The parliamentary left wing of the Berlin Assembly failed in the November crisis, and the left wing of the Frankfort Assembly sank deeper and deeper into the morass of miserable compromises.

In this situation Marx, Wilhelm Wolff, Schapper and Hermann Becker announced their resignation from the democratic district committee on the 15th of April, justifying their action as follows : " In our opinion the present form of organization of the democratic associations embraces too many heterogeneous elements to make possible any useful activity in furtherance of its aim. In our opinion a closer association of workers organizations will be more useful because these organizations are composed of more homogeneous elements." At the same time the Cologne Workers Association resigned from the Association of Rhenish Democratic Organizations and invited all working-class and other organizations upholding the principles of social democracy to send representatives to a provincial congress on the 6th of May. This latter congress was called to decide on an organization of Rhenish-Westphalian workers associations, and whether delegates should be sent to a congress of all working-class organizations called for June in Leipzig by Born's organization, the Leipzig Workers Brotherhood.

On the 20th of March, before these steps were taken, the *Neue Rheinische Zeitung* had begun to publish Wilhelm Wolff's articles on the Silesian milliards, which so aroused the rural proletariat, and on the 5th of April it began to publish the lectures which Marx had delivered to the workers associations in Brussels on wage-labour and capital. After showing on the basis of the tremendous mass struggles of 1848 that every revolutionary insurrection must fail, no matter how removed its aim might appear to be from the class struggle, so long as the working class had not been victorious, the paper turned its attention to the problem of economic relations, on which the existence of the bourgeoisie and the slavery of the workers were both based.

However, this promising development was interrupted by the struggles which now took place around the paper constitution which had finally been botched together by the Frankfort Assembly. In itself the precious constitution was not worth the shedding of a single drop of blood, and the hereditary imperial crown it sought to place on the head of the King of Prussia was for all the world like a fool's cap. The King of Prussia did not accept, but he also did not definitely refuse. He wanted to negotiate with the German princes on the question of the Reich's Constitution in the secret hope that they would agree to Prussian hegemony in return for Prussian military services in destroying what was left of the gains of the revolution in the small States and Statelets.

This was a blatant piece of body-snatching, and it fanned the spark of revolution into a flame again, causing a number of insurrections which received their name if they did not derive their content from the Reich's Constitution. Despite its weaknesses the Constitution represented the sovereignty of the people, and the authorities sought to destroy it in order to establish the sovereignty of the princes once again. Armed insurrections in support of the Reich's Constitution took place in the kingdom of Saxony, in the grand-duchy of Baden and in the Bavarian Palatinate. Everywhere the King of Prussia played the part of hangman, though afterwards the other potentates cheated him of the hangman's wage. Isolated insurrections also took place in the Rhineland, but they were crushed immediately by an overwhelming weight of numbers, thanks to the strong military forces which the government had drafted into the much-feared province.

The authorities then plucked up sufficient courage for an annihilating blow against the *Neue Rheinische Zeitung*. As the signs of a new revolutionary rising made themselves felt everywhere so the flames of revolutionary enthusiasm rose higher and higher in its columns, and in fact the special editions it issued in April and May were nothing but appeals to the people to hold itself in readiness for the coming insurrection. The reactionary *Kreuz-Zeitung* did it the honour of declaring that its insolence was monumental and that the activities of the *Moniteur* of 1793 paled before it. The government was itching to lay its hands on the paper, but did not dare. Thanks to the spirit amongst the jurymen of the Rhineland, two processes against Marx had done nothing but win him new laurels, and a suggestion from Berlin that martial law should again be declared in Cologne was evaded by the nervous commandant of the garrison who instead applied to the police for the expulsion of Marx as " a dangerous individual ".

The request embarrassed the police, who turned the matter over to the provincial governor, who in his turn passed on his share of the unpleasantness to Manteuffel, the Minister of the Interior. On the 10th of March the provincial government reported to Berlin that Marx was still in Cologne, though he had no police permission to stay there and that the newspaper he edited was still pursuing its destructive aims, its incitement against the existing constitution and its demand for the establishment of a social republic, whilst at the same time mocking and ridiculing everything humanity respected and held dear. The paper was becoming more and more dangerous in view of the fact that the temper and insolence with which it was written were steadily increasing the number of its readers. However, the police harboured misgivings with regard to the request of the commandant of the garrison for the expulsion of Marx, and the provincial government was compelled to support the police because an expulsion " without any particular reason other than the tendency and the dangerousness of the newspaper edited by him " might cause a demonstration on the part of the Democratic Party.

After receiving this report Manteuffel approached Eichmann, the President of the Rhine Province, to obtain his opinion. On the 29th of March Eichmann declared that the expulsion of

Marx would be justifiable, but attended with difficulties unless Marx were guilty of further offences. On the 7th of April Manteuffel then informed the provincial government that he had no objection to the expulsion, but that he must leave the time and circumstances to the provincial government, and that he felt it desirable that the order of expulsion should be issued in connection with some particular offence. In the end, however, the order of expulsion was issued solely on account of the " dangerous tendency " of the paper edited by Marx and not on account of any particular offence. This was done on the 11th of May when apparently the government felt itself strong enough to deliver a blow it had been too cowardly to deliver on the 29th of March or the 7th of April.

The Prussian professor who recently unearthed the documentary record of the affair in the State archives did great honour to the poetic and prophetic vision of Freiligrath, who wrote under the immediate impression of the expulsion :

> Kein offner Hieb in offner Schlacht—
> Es fällen die Nücken und Tücken,
> Es fällt mich die schleichende Niedertracht
> Der schmutzigen Westkalmücken.[1]

9. And Another Cowardly Trick

Marx was not in Cologne when the order of expulsion arrived. Although the circulation of the *Neue Rheinische Zeitung* was steadily increasing and it now had about 6,000 subscribers, its financial difficulties were by no means at an end. With the increasing sales the immediate expenses also increased, whereas the revenue increased only later, so that Marx was in Hamm negotiating with Rempel, one of the two capitalists who had declared themselves prepared to put up the money for a communist publishing house in 1846. However, the generous fellow still kept his purse-strings tightly drawn and referred Marx to an ex-lieutenant named Henze who in fact did advance 300 thaler for the paper, a loan for which Marx accepted personal responsibility. Although Henze was later exposed as an *agent-provocateur*, at that time he was also being persecuted by the police, and he

---

[1] " No honest blow in an honest fight—
But the spite of malice and trick,
The skulking infamy lays me low
Of the wretched Western Kalmuck."

accompanied Marx back to Cologne, where the latter found the expulsion order awaiting him.

This sealed the fate of the *Neue Rheinische Zeitung*. Several of the other editors were in the same position as Marx and could be expelled at any moment as "foreigners", whilst the others were all being prosecuted. On the 19th of May the final red number appeared with the famous valediction of Freiligrath and a defiant farewell article by Marx in which the latter belaboured the government fiercely : "Why bother with your foolish lies and your formal phrases ? We are ruthless ourselves and we ask no consideration from you. When our turn arrives we shall make no apologies for our terrorism ; but the royal terrorists, the terrorists by the Grace of God and the right of law, are brutal, contemptible and vile in practice, secretive and double-faced in theory, and without honour in both theory and practice." The *Neue Rheinische Zeitung* warned the workers against any putsch as the military situation rendered any such attempt hopeless, and the editors thanked their readers for their sympathy and support, declaring that their final word always and everywhere would be : "The emancipation of the working class ! "

And at the same time Marx fulfilled the duties which devolved upon him as captain of the sinking ship. The 300 thaler he had received from Henze, 1,500 thaler paid in by subscribers, the presses, etc., which belonged to him, all resources in fact were used to meet the liabilities of the paper to its printers, its paper merchants, its clerks, its correspondents, its editorial staff, etc. Marx kept only the silver of his wife for himself and his family and that had to pay a visit to the pawnbrokers in Frankfort. The few hundred guilders which Marx obtained for this silver was all he and his family had to live on.

From Frankfort he went with Engels to the scene of the insurrection in Baden and the Palatinate, visiting first Karlsruhe and then Kaiserslautern, where they met d'Ester, who was the moving spirit in the provisional government. From d'Ester Marx received a mandate of the Democratic Central Committee to represent the German revolutionary party in Paris towards the *Montagne* of the National Assembly, the social democracy of the day, a mixture of petty-bourgeois and proletarian elements, which was preparing a great blow against the parties of "law and order" and their representative, the false Bonaparte. On their way back they were arrested by Hessian troops on suspicion of having taken part in the insurrection and taken to Darmstadt and from there to Frankfort where they were finally released. Marx then went to Paris whilst Engels went to Kaiserslautern to become the adjutant of a volunteer corps which had been raised by a former Prussian lieutenant named Willich.

Writing from Paris on the 7th of June Marx declared that a royalist reaction was in the saddle and that it was even worse than under Guizot, but that nevertheless a tremendous outbreak of the revolutionary volcano had never been nearer. However, his expectations were disappointed, for the blow which the *Montagne* was planning failed and it failed in a not very edifying fashion. A month later the vengeance of the victors descended on Marx also. On the 19th of July the Prefect of Police conveyed an order of the Minister of the Interior to Marx that he should take up his domicile in the Departement Morbihan. It was a cowardly blow, " the infamy of infamies ", as Freiligrath declared in a letter to Marx after receiving the news. " Daniels declares Morbihan to be the most unhealthy district in France, marshy and fever-racked, the Pontine swamps of the Bretagne." Marx did not submit tamely to this " cloaked attempt at murder ", but succeeded in securing a stay of execution by an appeal to the Minister of the Interior.

By this time Marx was in desperate financial straits and he appealed to Freiligrath and Lassalle for assistance. Both men did their best, but Freiligrath complained of Lassalle's indiscretion in collecting the necessary money, declaring that he had made the affair the talk of the taverns. Marx was greatly embarrassed at this and in a reply on the 30th of July he declared : " The greatest financial difficulties are preferable to public begging and I have written to him saying so. The business has annoyed me terribly." However, Lassalle succeeded in dissipating Marx's annoyance by a letter overflowing with good-will, although his assurances that henceforth he would treat the matter " with the greatest delicacy " left room for doubt.

On the 23rd of August Marx wrote to Engels telling him that he was leaving France, and on the 5th of September he wrote to Freiligrath that his wife would follow him on the 15th though he still did not know where he was to find the money necessary for her journey and for her settling down when she arrived. Black care accompanied him on his third exile and it remained an all too steadfast companion.

CHAPTER SEVEN: EXILE IN LONDON

1. The *Neue Rheinische Revue*

In the last letter which Marx wrote to Engels from Paris he informed him that there was every prospect of founding a German paper in London and that a part of the necessary money was already available. At the same time he asked Engels, who was then living as a political fugitive in Switzerland after the collapse of the insurrection in Baden and the Palatinate, to go to London at once, and Engels did so, making the journey in a sailing ship from Genoa.

It is no longer possible to discover where they obtained the necessary money for the venture. It cannot have been very much, and in any case they did not reckon with any very long life for the paper, and Marx hoped that a world war would come within the next three or four months. The share prospectus of the *Neue Rheinische Zeitung*, politico-economic Review, edited by Karl Marx, is dated the 1st of January 1850 in London and signed by Konrad Schramm as guarantor. The document declares that after having taken part in the revolutionary movements in Southern Germany and in Paris during the previous summer, the editors of the *Neue Rheinische Zeitung* had come together again in London and decided to continue the publication of their paper. In the beginning it would appear as a monthly publication containing about 80 pages, but when finances permitted it would be issued fortnightly in the same format, or perhaps every week as a newspaper along the lines of the big English and American weeklies, whilst as soon as conditions permitted a return to Germany it would appear again as a daily newspaper. And finally the document invites its readers to take up shares to the value of 50 Francs each.

It is unlikely that many shares were floated. The magazine was printed in Hamburg, where a bookseller undertook to produce it on a commission basis and demanded 50 per cent of the 25 silver groschen which represented its quarterly net sale price per copy. The firm did not take much trouble about the publication, particularly as the Prussian army of occupation in Hamburg hampered its activities, but the situation would hardly have been improved even if it had shown real zeal in the matter. Lassalle succeeded in obtaining only 50 subscribers in Düsseldorf, whilst Weydemeyer, who had ordered 100 copies for sale in Frankfort, had taken only 51 guilders after six months of effort : " I put enough pressure on the people, but nevertheless no one is in a hurry to pay." Frau Marx wrote to him with justifiable bitterness that the venture had been utterly ruined by careless management, and that it was impossible to say what or who was most responsible, the dilatoriness of the bookseller, or the manager and friends in Cologne, or the attitude of the democracy.

In any case, a certain amount of responsibility attaches to the insufficient editorial preparation of the first number, and Marx and Engels were chiefly responsible for this. The manuscript for the January number arrived in Hamburg on the 6th of February. However, we have every reason to be satisfied that the plan was carried out at all, for a few months' further delay and it would have been made completely impossible owing to the rapid ebb of the revolutionary wave. As it is, the six numbers of the Review provide us with a valuable example of how Marx raised himself above the petty troubles of life which besieged him " in a revolting form " daily and even hourly, with, to use the words of his wife, " all his energy and all the calm, clear and collected strength of his character ".

In their youth Marx and Engels, the latter even more so than the former, saw the coming things much nearer than they were in reality, and often they hoped to pick the ripe fruit where the first blossoming had hardly begun. How often have they been denounced as false prophets on that account ! And to be regarded as a false prophet does not enhance the reputation of a politician. However, it is necessary to distinguish between false prophecies which spring from clear and acute thought and those which are the result of conceited self-reflection in pious wishes. In the latter case the resulting disappointment is enervating because an illusion disappears utterly, whilst in the former case it is salutary because the thinking man tracks down the cause of his error and thus gains new knowledge.

Probably no one has ever been quite so ruthless in his self-criticism as Marx and Engels were. Both of them were completely free of that wretched dogmatism which still seeks to deceive itself even in the face of the bitterest disappointments, declaring that it would certainly have been right if only this or that had happened a little differently. And they were just as free of cheap defeatism and fruitless pessimism. They learned from their defeats and gained new strength to prepare for the coming victory.

With the defeat of the Paris workers on the 13th of June, the failure of the Reich's Constitution campaign in Germany, and the crushing of the Hungarian revolution by the Tsar, a great stage in the revolutionary movement came to an end, and if there was to be any resuscitation of the revolution then it could take place only in France where, despite all that had happened, the last word had not been spoken. Marx held firmly to the hope of such a resuscitation, but that did not prevent him subjecting the previous development of the French revolution to a ruthless criticism which mocked at all illusions. On the contrary, it impelled him to do so, and in this criticism the chaotic confusion of the revolutionary struggles, which necessarily appeared more or less insoluble to the idealist politician, was examined from the standpoint of the economic antagonisms which collided in these struggles.

This criticism was published in the first three numbers of the Review, and in it Marx often succeeds in unravelling the most complicated questions of the day with a few epigrammatical sentences. How many words had been expended on the right to work by the most prominent representatives of the bourgeoisie and even by the doctrinaire socialists, and how completely Marx summed up the historic sense and nonsense of this slogan in a few sentences ! "The first draft of the constitution drawn up before the June days contained a demand for the right to work. It was the first clumsy formulation of the revolutionary desires of the proletariat. Later it was transformed into the right to public support, and what modern State does not support its paupers in one form or the other ? From the bourgeois point of view the right to work is nonsense, a pitiful and pious wish, but behind the right to work stands the power over capital, and behind the power over capital stands the appropriation of the means of production and their subordination to the associated working class, that is to say, the abolition of wage-labour and capital and of their mutual relations." Marx first recognized the class struggle as the motive power of historical development on the basis of French history, in which the class struggle has shown itself in a particularly clear and classic form from the days of the middle ages, and this explains his particular preference for French history. This dissertation and the later one on the Bonapartist *coup d'état*, and the still later one on the Paris Commune, are the most brilliant gems in the crown of his minor historical works.

The first three numbers of the Review also contained an amusing contrast to this, but it was one not without its own tragic upshot. It was the sketch of a petty-bourgeois revolution which Engels drew in his description of the Reich's Constitution campaign in Germany. The reviews of the month, which were drawn up by Marx and Engels jointly, dealt chiefly with the course of economic events. In the February number they referred to the discovery of the Californian gold mines as a fact of " even greater importance than the February revolution," and one which would have even greater and more far-reaching results than the discovery of America : " A coastal stretch of 30 degrees latitude, one of the most beautiful and fertile areas in the world, and practically unpopulated up to the present, is now turning before our eyes into a rich and civilized country thickly populated with men of all races, from the Yankee to the Chinese, the Negro to the Indian and the Malayan, the Creole and Mestizo to the European. Californian gold is pouring in streams over America and over the Asiatic coasts of the Pacific, sweeping the unwilling barbarian peoples into the orbit of world trade, into the province of civilization. For the second time world trade is receiving a new alignment. . . . Thanks to the gold of California and to the tireless energy of the Yankees both coasts of the Pacific will soon be as thickly populated, as highly industrialized and as open for trade as the coast from Boston to New Orleans is now. The Pacific Ocean will then play the rôle the Atlantic Ocean is playing now and the rôle that the Mediterranean played in the days of classical antiquity and in the middle ages—the rôle of the great water highway of world communications—and the Atlantic Ocean will sink to the level of a great lake such as the Mediterranean is to-day. The one chance which the civilized countries of Europe have to avoid falling into the same industrial, commercial and political dependence as Italy, Spain and Portugal lies in a social revolution whilst there is still time, a revolution which would transform the mode of production and intercourse in accordance with the needs of production arising from the nature of modern productive forces, thus making possible the development of new forces of production which would maintain the superiority of European industry and counteract the disadvantages of geographical situation." All that needed to be added to this magnificent perspective, as its authors were soon to discover, was that the chances of any immediate revolution foundered on the discovery of the Californian gold mines.

Marx and Engels also jointly criticized a number of works in which the intellectual leaders of the pre-March period did their best to unravel the problems of the revolution, including books by the German philosopher Daumer, the French historian Guizot and the English genius Carlyle. Daumer had developed from the Hegelian school, whilst Guizot had exercised considerable influence on Marx, and Carlyle on Engels, but the verdict now passed on all three was : weighed in the balance of the revolution and found wanting. The incredible platitudes with which Daumer preached " the religion of the new world era " were summed up in the " touching picture " : German philosophy is wringing its hands and lamenting at the death-bed of its economic sire German Philistinism. Their criticism of Guizot pointed out that even the most capable brains of the *ancien régime*, even those with considerable historical talent, had been thrown into utter confusion by the fatal February events, so that they had lost all historical understanding, even for their own former actions. Finally, they declared that Guizot's book demonstrated the intellectual decline of the great leaders of the bourgeoisie, whilst a few pamphlets of Carlyle showed the decline of literary genius in face of the acute historic struggles on which it sought to exercise its misunderstood, direct and prophetic inspirations.

Although in these brilliant criticisms Marx and Engels demonstrated the disastrous effects of the revolutionary struggles on the bourgeois literary lights of the pre-March period, they were very far from believing in any mystical power of the revolution, although on various occasions they have been accused of doing so. The revolution had not created the picture which shocked Daumer, Guizot and Carlyle; it had done no more than tear away the curtain which had concealed it. Historical development did not alter its course during revolutions, but merely accelerated its progress, and in this sense Marx once called revolutions " the locomotives of history ". The stupid Philistine belief that " peaceful and legal reform " is superior to all revolutionary outbreaks was naturally never shared by men like Marx and Engels, who regarded force as an economic power, as the midwife of all new societies.

2. The Kinkel Affair

With its fourth number, which appeared in April 1850, the *Neue Rheinische Revue* ceased to appear regularly and a contri butory factor was undoubtedly a short article which appeared in this number. Its authors prophesied that the article in question would cause " general indignation amongst sentimental swindlers and democratic demagogues ". It was a brief but annihilating criticism of the speech delivered in his own defence by Gottfried Kinkel on the 7th of August 1849 as a captured volunteer before a court-martial in Rastatt and published in a Berlin newspaper at the beginning of April 1850.

Objectively considered the criticism was absolutely justified, for Kinkel had abandoned not only the revolution, but also his comrades in arms. Before the court-martial, which had already sent 26 of his comrades to their deaths in the barrack square where they had died gallantly, Kinkel praised the " grape-shot prince " and " the Hohenzollern Kaiserdom ", but for all that he was in prison when Marx and Engels attacked him, and it was generally considered that he had been chosen as the special object of royal vengeance because the sentence of imprisonment in a fortress passed on him by the court-martial had been subsequently changed by an Order in Council to the dishonouring one of hard labour in an ordinary prison. To pillory Kinkel in such a situation caused misgivings in the minds of many people who were certainly neither " sentimental swindlers " nor " democratic demagogues ".

Since then the archives have been opened and the Kinkel case is seen to have been a maze of tragi-comic misunderstandings. Originally Kinkel had been a theologian, and an orthodox one at that, but his fall from grace, accompanied and perhaps furthered by his marriage to a divorced Catholic, had brought the irreconcilable hatred of the orthodox down on his head and given him a reputation as a " hero of freedom " far beyond his real deserts. It was due more to a " misunderstanding " than anything else which caused Kinkel to slide into the same party as Marx and Engels. Politically he never advanced beyond the usual slogans of the common rut of German democracy, but the " damnable eloquence ", to use an expression of Freiligrath, which had remained with him from his theological days occasionally swept him off his feet and sent him careering as far to the left as it did to the right before the court-martial in Rastatt, whilst moderate poetical talent contributed to making him better known than the other democrats of his kidney.

During the Reich's Constitution campaign Kinkel joined the volunteer corps raised by Willich, in which Engels and Moll also served. He fought bravely, and during the last engagement of the corps on the Murg, where Moll fell, he was wounded in the head and taken prisoner. The court-martial which tried him sentenced him to lifelong imprisonment in a fortress, but the " grape-shot prince " or, to use the politer expression adopted by Kinkel in his defence, " His Royal Highness the Heir to our Throne ", was not satisfied with this and the military legal authorities in Berlin therefore requested the King to quash the

the sentence and place Kinkel on trial again, as he should have
been sentenced to death.

However, the military legal authorities met with the united
resistance of the Ministry which, although it was prepared to
admit that a traitor had been punished too leniently, declared
that the sentence should be confirmed by the King " as an act
of mercy " and as a concession to public opinion. At the same
time the Ministry declared that it thought it " advisable " that
Kinkel should serve his sentence in " a civil institution ", because
it might cause " a great sensation " if he were treated as a fortress
prisoner. The King accepted the proposals of his Ministry but
thereby caused just the " great sensation " it had been anxious
to avoid, for " public opinion " considered it a piece of cynical
mockery that " as an act of mercy " the King should send a man
to hard labour in a common prison after a court-martial had
sentenced him to imprisonment in a fortress only.

However, owing to its inability to appreciate the finer points
of the Prussian Criminal Code, public opinion was under a
misapprehension. Kinkel had not been sentenced to arrest in
a fortress, but to penal imprisonment in a fortress, which was
something quite different and in fact much more severe and more
revolting than ordinary hard labour in a common prison.
Prisoners under sentence of penal imprisonment in a fortress
were huddled together ten or twenty in one cell with only a
hard bench to sleep on, whilst their food was poor in quality
and insufficient in quantity. They had to perform all kinds of
menial labour, such as cleaning out the latrines and sweeping
the streets, etc., and at the least offence they were given a taste
of the whip. For fear of " public opinion " the Ministry had
been anxious to spare Kinkel this inhumanity, but when " public
opinion " misunderstood the situation the Ministry did not dare
to admit its own " humanitarian motives " for fear of the " grape-
shot prince ", and it therefore left the King under a suspicion
which was bound to damage his reputation and which in fact
actually did so in the eyes of all well-meaning people.

Under the impression of this unfortunate failure the Ministry
was anxious to avoid any further " sensations " as a result of
Kinkel's prison experiences, but its courage went only as far as
ordering that under no circumstances should Kinkel be subjected
to corporal punishment. It would also have liked to free him
from the necessity of forced labour and it suggested to the governor
of the prison in Naugard, where Kinkel was first sent, that he
should take this action on his own initiative. However, the old
bureaucrat turned a deaf ear to the suggestion and carried out
his instructions to the letter, putting Kinkel to the spooling-

wheel. This again caused a great sensation, and "The Song of the Spinning Wheel" appeared and was declaimed with great gusto all over the country, whilst pictures of the poet at the wheel were sold everywhere. Writing to his wife Kinkel declared : "The factional struggles and the play of fate are approaching madness when the hand which gave the German nation ' *Otto der Schütz* ' now turns the spooling-wheel." However, the old experience that the " moral indignation " of the Philistine usually ends in absurdity was soon confirmed. Alarmed by the general indignation and having more courage than the Ministry, the local authorities in Stettin ordered that Kinkel should henceforth be occupied with literary work only, whereupon Kinkel protested and declared that he would prefer to stay at the spooling-wheel because light physical work permitted him to let his thoughts run freely whilst copying all day long might affect his chest and impair his health.

The widespread opinion that Kinkel was being treated with particular severity in prison at the instructions of the King was therefore incorrect, though naturally he had quite enough to put up with. The governor of the prison, Schnuchel, was a strict bureaucrat, but he was not inhuman. In addressing Kinkel he always used the familiar form " Du ",[1] but he granted him as much time as possible in the open air and showed a sympathetic understanding for the ceaseless efforts of Frau Kinkel to secure the release of her husband. In May 1850 when Kinkel was transferred to the prison of Spandau he was granted the formal " Sie ",[2] but he was compelled to submit to having his hair and beard shaved off, and the governor of the prison, a pious reactionary named Jeserich, plagued him with attempts at conversion and immediately began the most revolting petty disputes. However, even this pious fellow made no very great difficulties when the Ministry called on him to make a report in connection with a request of Frau Kinkel that her husband should be released on condition that he should emigrate to America, give his word of honour not to engage in any further political activities, and not return to Europe. Jeserich even declared that his knowledge of Kinkel convinced him that the best cure for the latter's soul would be found in America. Nevertheless, he should be kept in prison for about a year still in order that the sword of justice should not be unduly blunted and notched, but after that, providing that his health did not suffer from the long imprisonment, and up to the present there

---

[1] Du—Thou ; used as a familiar form of address amongst friends or, formerly, by superiors towards inferiors.—Tr.
[2] Sie—You.—Tr.

had been no signs of it doing so, he might be permitted to emigrate.

This report was submitted to the King who, however, proved even more vengeful than the prison governor and the Ministry, and the " All-Highest " decided that Kinkel should not be released after one year because he had not been sufficiently humiliated and punished.

When one considers the personal cult which was developed in connection with Kinkel at the time it is easy to understand that it must have aroused disgust in men like Marx and Engels, for Philistine side-shows of that sort were always hateful to them. In his articles on the Reich's Constitution campaign Engels had already written bitterly of the fuss made about the " educated " victims of the May insurrections, whilst no one bothered about the hundreds and even thousands of simple workers who had lost their lives in the fighting or were rotting in the underground cells at Rastatt or were compelled to eat the bitter bread of banishment down to the last miserable crust in poverty and privation. However, even apart from this there were many men amongst the " educated victims " who were being treated far worse than Kinkel and who nevertheless bore themselves with far greater manliness without anyone waxing indignant at their fate. There was August Röckel, for instance, who was certainly no meaner intellect than Kinkel. He was brutally maltreated in the prison of Waldheim and even subjected to corporal punishment, but even after twelve years of such martyr-dom his torturers could not force him to beg for mercy by as much as the flicker of an eyelid, so that, helpless in the face of such indomitable and manly pride, they were finally compelled, so to speak, to eject him from prison. Röckel was by no means the only one who showed such steadfast manliness, in fact, of all the prisoners Kinkel was the only one who did public penance when, after a few months of by no means intolerable imprison-ment, he caused his speech for the defence at Rastatt to be published. The bitter and ruthless criticism to which Marx and Engels subjected it was therefore thoroughly justified, all the more so as they could say with truth that far from worsening Kinkel's position their attack had improved it.

The further development of the affair showed that they were right. The hero-worship of Kinkel caused the bourgeoisie to loosen its purse-strings, so much so in fact that it was possible to bribe one of the officials of Spandau prison and in November 1850 Kinkel was rescued by Karl Schurz. That was His Majesty's reward for his vengefulness. Had he permitted Kinkel to emigrate to America and accepted his word of honour not to take any further part in politics Kinkel would soon have been forgotten, as even the prison governor Jeserich had realized, but thanks to his successful escape from prison Kinkel was now a thrice-lauded agitator and the King had not only to pocket the damage, but also to swallow the resultant mockery.

However, the King determined to revenge himself in a royal fashion. The report of Kinkel's escape gave birth to an idea which even he was honest enough to admit was " ignoble ", but he nevertheless instructed Manteuffel to make use of the " valuable personality " Stieber with a view to discovering a conspiracy and punishing its authors. Stieber already enjoyed such general contempt that even the Police President of Berlin, Hinckeldey, whose own conscience was elastic enough in all truth when it was a question of persecuting the political opponents of the State, protested against the man's re-employment in the police service, but all to no purpose and Stieber was given a free hand to show what he could do. The result was the Cologne communist trial with its background of theft and perjury.

This piece of official criminality was a dozen times worse than the Kinkel affair and far more infamous, but it is not on record that the worthy petty-bourgeois citizens of Germany gave vent to any particular indignation at it. Perhaps these pleasant characters were anxious to prove how thoroughly Marx and Engels had seen through their hypocrisy from the beginning.

3. The Split in the Communist League

On the whole the significance of the Kinkel affair was more symptomatic than real. The essence of the dispute which developed at about this time between Marx and Engels on the one hand and the London fugitives on the other, can be seen most clearly in connection with the Kinkel affair, although the latter was not its most important factor and certainly not its cause.

The two chief activities of Marx and Engels in 1850, apart from the issue of the *Neue Rheinische Revue*, show us what drew the two friends towards the other emigrants and what tended to separate them. On the one hand there was the Fugitives Aid Committee, which they founded together with Bauer, Pfänder and Willich to assist political fugitives, who were flooding to London all the more freely owing to the fact that the authorities in Switzerland had begun to treat them with scant consideration, and on the other hand there was the re-establishment of the Communist League, a task which became more and more necessary as the victorious counter-revolution ruthlessly deprived the working class to an increasing extent of the freedom of the press and the freedom of assembly, in fact of all the means of open propaganda. One may sum up the situation by saying that Marx and Engels declared themselves in solidarity with the fugitives personally, but not politically, that they shared the sufferings of the fugitives, but not their illusions, that they sacrificed their last penny to assist the fugitives, but not the smallest fraction of their political convictions.

The German, and still more so the international emigration, represented a confused mixture of the most diverse elements. However, they all hoped for a resuscitation of the revolution which would permit them to return home, and they all worked for this aim so that there appeared to be a basis for joint action, but in practice every concrete effort invariably failed. The utmost that was achieved was the adoption of paper resolutions, and the more pompous they sounded the less they really signified. Immediately any practical action was taken the most unedifying quarrels began. These quarrels were not caused by the persons engaged in them, and at the utmost they were only sharpened by the disagreeable situation in which the participants found themselves. Their real basis was the class struggle, which had determined the course of the revolution and which continued in the emigration despite all the well-meaning attempts which were made to exorcise it. Marx and Engels realized the fruitlessness of all such attempts from the beginning and took no part in them, a circumstance which united all the fractions and groups on at least one point, namely that Marx and Engels were the real and incorrigible trouble-makers.

On their part they continued the policy of proletarian class struggle which they had begun even before the revolution. Since the autumn of 1849 the old membership of the Communist League had re-assembled in London almost in its entirety, with the exception of Moll, who had fallen in the engagement on the Murg, Schapper, who arrived only in the summer of 1850, and Wilhelm Wolff, who came to London from Switzerland only a year later. In addition new members had been won. There was August Willich, a former Prussian officer who had been won over by his adjutant Engels and had shown himself a capable leader of his volunteer corps during the campaign in Baden and the Palatinate. He was a very useful man, but theoretically unclear. Then there were many younger men : the merchant Konrad Schramm, the teacher Wilhelm Pieper, and above all

Wilhelm Liebknecht, who had studied at various German universities but had taken his finals in the insurrection in Baden and in exile in Switzerland. In the following years all these men were closely connected with Marx, most devotedly probably Liebknecht. Marx did not always speak so highly of the other two, who caused him a certain amount of trouble, but one must not take every word uttered in annoyance at its face value. Konrad Schramm died young of consumption, and Marx declared that he had been the " Percy Hotspur " of the party, and referring to Pieper he declared that, " all in all he was a *bon garçon* ". Thanks to Pieper the Göttingen advocate Johannes Miquel came into correspondence with Marx and then joined the Communist League, and Marx obviously regarded him as a man of some intelligence. Miquel remained loyal to the flag for a number of years, but in the end, like his friend Pieper, he turned tail and went back to the camp of the liberals.

In March 1850 the Central Committee of the Communist League issued a circular drawn up by Marx and Engels, and it was taken to Germany by Heinrich Bauer as an emissary of the League entrusted with its reorganization in Germany. It was based on the belief that a new revolution was approaching, " perhaps as a result of an independent rising of the French proletariat, or as a result of an invasion of the revolutionary Babel by the forces of the Holy Alliance ". Just as the March Revolution had carried the bourgeoisie to victory, so the coming revolution would carry the petty-bourgeoisie to victory and the latter would then again betray the proletariat.

The attitude of the revolutionary workers party to the petty-bourgeois democrats was summed up as follows : " The revolutionary workers party will co-operate with the petty-bourgeois democrats against the fraction whose overthrow they both desire, but it will oppose them in all points where its own interests arise." The petty-bourgeoisie would utilize a successful revolution in order to reform capitalist society so as to make life easier and more comfortable for itself and to a certain extent for the workers. However, the proletariat could not be content with this. After its own limited demands had been achieved the democratic petty-bourgeoisie would seek to have done with the revolution as quickly as possible, whilst on the other hand it would be the task of the workers to make the revolution permanent " until all the more or less possessing classes have been forced from power and State power has been taken over by the proletariat, and the association of the workers, not only in one country, but in all the most important countries throughout the world, is so far progressed that competition between the workers of these countries has ceased and at least the most important tools of production are in their hands."

The circular therefore warned the workers not to let themselves be deceived by the conciliatory preachings of the petty-bourgeois democrats, or to let themselves be degraded to the rôle of camp-followers of bourgeois democracy. On the contrary, they should organize themselves as strongly and as thoroughly as possible in order, after the victory of the revolution, which would be won as usual by their strength and courage, to dictate such conditions to the petty-bourgeoisie that the rule of the bourgeois democrats would bear within it the seeds of its own decay, thus greatly facilitating its replacement later by the rule of the proletariat.

" During the struggle and immediately afterwards the workers must oppose above all and as far as possible all bourgeois attempts at pacification and compel the Democrats to carry their terrorist phrases into execution. . . . Far from opposing so-called excesses, the vengeance of the people on hated individuals or attacks of the masses on buildings which arouse hateful memories, we must not only tolerate, but even take the lead in them." During the elections for the National Assembly the workers should put forward their own candidates everywhere, even when there was no chance of getting them elected, and ignore all democratic phrases. At the beginning of the movement the workers would naturally not be able to bring forward any definitely communist proposals, but they could compel the Democrats to interfere to the greatest possible extent and in every possible way with the structure of the previous social order, to interfere with its orderly working and thereby compromise themselves, and to place as many of the means of production as possible, transport, factories, railways, etc., in the hands of the State.

Above all, when the revolution abolished feudalism the workers should not tolerate the carving up of the big feudal estates and the distribution of the pieces amongst the peasants as private property, as had been done after the Great French Revolution, for this would perpetuate the rural proletariat and create a petty-bourgeois class of peasant landholders experiencing the same circle of impoverishment and indebtedness as the French peasants. On the contrary, the workers should demand that the confiscated feudal estates remain the property of the State to be turned into workers colonies and run by the associated land proletariat on large-scale agricultural lines. In this way the principle of common ownership would be given a firm basis in the very centre of tottering bourgeois property relations.

Armed with this circular Bauer met with great success on his

mission to Germany. He re-established connections which had
been broken off and established new ones, and above all he
succeeded in winning considerable influence on the remnants
of the workers, peasants, day-labourers and sport associations
which had continued to exist despite the terrorism of the counter-
revolution. The most influential members of the Workers
Brotherhood founded by Stephan Born also joined the Communist League, and Karl Schurz, who was on a tour through
Germany on behalf of a fugitives association in Switzerland,
reported to Zürich that the League was winning " all the most
useful elements ". In a document issued in June 1850 the
Central Committee was able to report that the League had won
a firm footing in a number of German towns and that leading
committees had been formed in Hamburg for Sleswig-Holstein,
in Schwerin for Mecklenburg, in Breslau for Silesia, in Leipzig
for Saxony and Berlin, in Nuremberg for Bavaria, and in Cologne
for the Rhineland and Westphalia.

The same document also declared that London was the
strongest district of the League, that it provided the funds of the
League almost exclusively, directed the work of the German
Workers Educational League (*Deutscher Arbeiterbildungsverein*) and
of the most important emigrant groups, and that the League
maintained close relations with the English, French and Hungarian revolutionary parties. However, judged from another
angle the London district of the League was also its weakest
point because through it the League became involved more and
more in the fierce and hopeless struggles of the emigrants.

During the summer of 1850 the hope that the revolution
would soon revive rapidly disappeared. In France the general
franchise was destroyed without producing any rising on the
part of the workers, and the decision now lay between the Pre-
tender Louis Bonaparte and the monarchist reactionary National
Assembly. In Germany the democratic petty-bourgeoisie retired
from the political arena whilst the liberal bourgeoisie joined in
the body-snatching activities which Prussia immediately began
at the expense of the revolution. However, Prussia was cheated
by the other German States, which all danced to the tune of
Austria, whilst the Tsar flourished the knout threateningly over
the whole of Germany. The more obvious the revolutionary
ebb became, the more the emigration intensified its efforts to
create an artificial revolution. It deliberately ignored all the
warning signs and placed its hope in miracles, which it thought
to perform by strength of will and determination alone. At the
same time and to the same extent it became distrustful of any
self-criticism within its ranks, and as a result Marx and Engels,

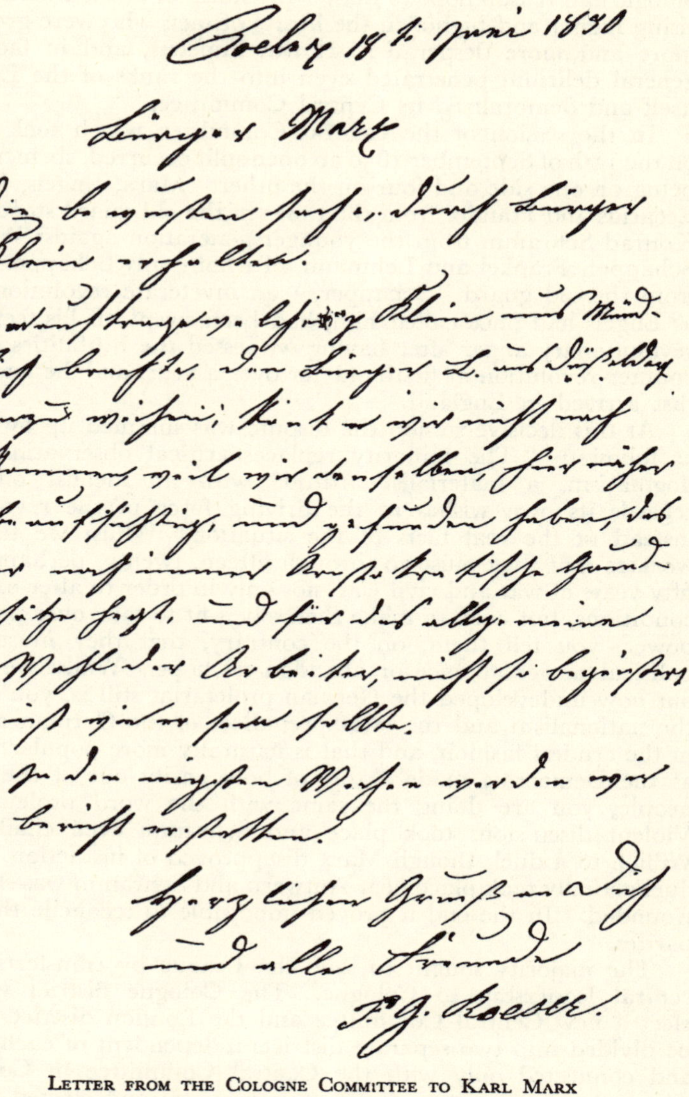
Coeln 18t. Juni 1850

Bürger Marx

Die bewußten Sachen durch Bürger Klein erhalten.

Der Aufforderung gemäß welche Klein uns mündlich brachte, den Bürger L. aus Düsseldorf einzuweihen, konnten wir nicht nachkommen weil wir denselben hier näher beaufsichtigt, und gefunden haben, daß er noch immer kleinbürgerliche Standpunkte hegt, und für das allgemeine Macht der Arbeiter, nicht so begeistert ist wie er sein sollte.

In den nächsten Wochen werden wir Bericht erstatten.

Herzlichen Gruß an Dich und alle Freunde

P. G. Roeser.

LETTER FROM THE COLOGNE COMMITTEE TO KARL MARX

who clearly realized the real situation, came into deeper and deeper conflict with the other emigrants. How could the voice of logic and reason hope to master the storm of passion which was rising higher and higher in the hearts of men who were growing more and more desperate? It was hopeless, and in fact the general delirium penetrated even into the ranks of the League itself and demoralized its Central Committee.

In the session of the Central Committee which took place on the 15th of September 1850 an open split occurred, six members being on one side and four on the other. Marx, Engels, Bauer, Eccarius and Pfänder from the ranks of the old guard stood with Konrad Schramm from the younger generation against Willich, Schapper, Fränkel and Lehmann, of whom only Schapper came from the old guard. Schapper, " an inveterate revolutionary " as Engels had once called him, had been swept off his feet with revolutionary anger after having witnessed the brutalities of the counter-revolution at firsthand for over a year, and he had only just arrived in England.

At this decisive session the dispute was summed up by Marx as follows : " The minority replaces critical observation with dogmatism, a materialist attitude with an idealist one. It regards its own wishes as the driving force of the revolution instead of the real facts of the situation. Whilst we tell the workers that they must go through fifteen, twenty, perhaps even fifty years of war and civil war, not only in order to alter existing conditions, but even to make themselves fit to take over political power, you tell them, on the contrary, that they must seize political power at once or abandon all hope. Whilst we point out how undeveloped the German proletariat still is, you flatter the nationalism and the craft prejudices of the German artisan in the crudest fashion, and that is naturally more popular. Just as the Democrats made a sort of holy entity out of the word people, you are doing the same with the word proletariat." Violent discussions took place and Schramm even challenged Willich to a duel, though Marx disapproved of his action. The duel actually took place near Antwerp and Schramm was slightly wounded. In the end it proved impossible to reconcile the two parties.

The majority sought to save the League by transferring its central leadership to Cologne. The Cologne district was to elect a new Central Committee and the London district would be divided into two separate districts independent of each other and connected only with the Central Committee in Cologne. The Cologne district agreed to this proposal and elected a new Central Committee, but the minority then refused to recognize it. The minority had the upper hand in the London district, and particularly in the German Workers Educational League, from which Marx and his nearest associates then resigned. Willich and Schapper proceeded to form an organization of their own, but it soon degenerated utterly into adventurism and sham revolutionism.

Marx and Engels explained their point of view in the fifth and sixth numbers of the *Neue Rheinische Revue*, which appeared together as a double number in November 1850 and concluded the life of the paper altogether. Their position was given in even greater detail than in the session at which the split took place. The double number also contained a long article by Engels on the peasant war of 1525 from the historical materialist standpoint, and an article by Eccarius on the tailoring trade in London. This latter article was greeted enthusiastically by Marx who declared : " Before the proletariat fights out its battles on the barricades it announces the coming of its rule with a series of intellectual victories."

Eccarius was himself working in one of London's tailoring workshops and he had realized that the replacement of handicraft by large-scale industry was a historical step forwards, and at the same time he observed that the results and achievements of large-scale industry created the conditions for the proletarian revolution and renewed them daily. He adopted a purely materialist standpoint and opposed bourgeois society and its forces without the usual sentimentality. For this reason his article was praised by Marx as a great step forward beyond the sentimental, moral and psychological criticism of existing conditions as practised by Weitling and other working-class writers. It also represented one of the fruits of Marx's own tireless enlightenment work, and it was a very welcome fruit.

However, the most important contribution to this final number was the politico-economic review of the period from May to October. Marx and Engels dealt with the economic causes of the political revolution and counter-revolution in an exhaustive analysis, pointing out that the former had arisen out of the economic crisis whilst the latter had its roots in a new advance of production. The conclusion they came to was : " In view of the general prosperity which now prevails and permits the productive forces of bourgeois society to develop as rapidly as is at all possible within the framework of bourgeois society, there can be no question of any real revolution. Such a revolution is possible only in a period when two factors collide ; when the modern productive forces collide with the bourgeois mode of production. The various squabbles in which the representatives of the individual fractions of the Continental order are now indulging and compromising themselves will not lead to any new revolution. On the contrary, they are only possible because at the moment the basis of prevailing relations is so secure and, a point on which the reaction is ignorant, so bourgeois. All the attempts of the reaction to prevent bourgeois development will break down as helplessly as the moral indignation and the enthusiastic proclamations of the Democrats. A new revolution will be made possible only as the result of a new crisis, but it is just as certain as is the coming of the crisis itself."

This clear and convincing description of the existing situation was then compared with an appeal issued by a European Central Committee and signed by Mazzini, Ledru-Rollin, Darasz and Ruge, which represented a collection of all the illusions of the political emigration in as small a space as possible, explaining the failure of the revolution as the result of the ambitious jealousy of individual leaders and of the contradictory teachings of the various representatives of the people, and concluding with a confession of faith in liberty, equality and fraternity, the family, the community, the State and the Fatherland, in short, in a social system with God and His eternal laws at the apex and the people at the base.

This politico-economic review is dated the 1st of November 1850 and with it the direct and immediate co-operation of its authors ceased for two decades, for Engels went to Manchester to work once again for Ermen & Engels whilst Marx remained in London to devote all his energies to scientific study.

4. Life in Exile

The days of November 1850 fall almost exactly in the middle of Marx's life and they represent, not only externally, an important turning point in his life's work. Marx himself was keenly aware of this and Engels perhaps even more so.

Writing to Marx in February 1851 Engels declares : " One can see more and more that exile is an institution in which everyone must necessarily become a fool, a donkey and a scurvy knave unless he withdraws from it completely and contents himself with being an independent writer who doesn't bother his head in the least even about the so-called revolutionary party." And Marx answered : " I very much like the public isolation in which we two now find ourselves. It is quite in accordance with our attitude and our principles. The system of mutual concessions, of half-measures tolerated for the sake of appearances, and the necessity of taking one's share of the responsibility in the eyes of the general public together with all those donkeys, is now at an end." And Engels again : " We have now once more an opportunity, for the first time for a very long time, of showing that we need no popularity and no support from any party in any country, that our position is completely independent of such trivialities. From now on we are responsible to ourselves alone. . . . By the way, we can hardly complain about the fact that the *petits grands hommes* avoid us. For years we acted as though Krethi and Plethi[1] were our party, although we had no party and the people whom we considered as belonging to our party, at least officially, did not understand even the elementary principles of our cause."

It would be wrong to take the expressions " fools ", " donkeys " and " knaves " all too seriously, and a certain amount may be deducted from these spirited remarks, but what then remains shows us that Marx and Engels rightly regarded their decision to cut themselves loose from the fruitless squabbles of the exiles as their salvation. They withdrew, as Engels said, into " a certain isolation " in order to continue their scientific studies until such time as men should better understand their cause.

However, the cut was not made so thoroughly, so quickly and so deeply as would appear to the retrospective observer. In the letters which the two exchanged in the following years we find that the internal struggles amongst the exiles play a very considerable rôle, and this was due to the ceaseless friction which occurred between the two fractions into which the Communist League had split, if to no other reason. And further, although Marx and Engels had decided to take no part in the noisy squabbles of the emigration period, this certainly did not mean the abandonment of all part in the political struggles of the day. They continued to contribute to the Chartist newspapers, and they did not accept the disappearance of the *Neue Rheinische Revue* as final.

A publisher named Schabelitz in Basel offered to undertake the continuation of the Review, but in the end nothing came of it, and Marx then opened up negotiations with Hermann Becker, who had succeeded in maintaining his position in Cologne as editor of the *Westdeutsche Zeitung* for some time and when that was finally suppressed had taken over a small publishing house. Marx wanted to have his works published in a collected edition and to issue a quarterly magazine from Liège. However, this

---

[1] Krethi and Plethi = university-student expression for Tom, Dick, and Harry.

plan was spoiled by the arrest of Becker in May 1851, though one brochure of the *Collected Works* did actually appear. Two volumes were to have been published, each containing 400 pages, and whoever subscribed to the venture before the 15th of May was to receive the volumes in ten brochures at eight silver groschen each, and after that the sale price was to be one thaler and 15 silver groschen for each volume. The first brochure was quickly sold out, but Weydemeyer's statement that 15,000 copies were sold is probably an error, for even one-tenth of that figure would have been quite a fair success for those days.

When drawing up these plans Marx was under " the urgent necessity of making a living ". He and his family were living in great poverty. In November 1849 the fourth child, a son named Guido, was born, and its mother wrote : " The poor little angel suckled so many cares and worries that it was always ill and in violent pains day and night. Since it came into the world it has not slept a single night properly, and never more than two or three hours at a time." This child died about a year after its birth.

The family was evicted in the most brutal and ruthless fashion from its first home in Chelsea because although the rent had been paid to the tenant the latter had not paid it to the landlord. After many difficulties they succeeded in finding a temporary shelter in a German hotel in Leicester Street near Leicester Square, and shortly afterwards they moved into 28, Dean Street, Soho Square. For the next six years the two rooms in Dean Street offered the family a permanent shelter. However, this did not settle their financial troubles, which steadily increased. Towards the end of October 1850 Marx wrote to Weydemeyer in Frankfort-on-Main asking him to take the family silver out of pawn and sell it at the best price he could get for it, saving only a small case of spoons, etc., belonging to little Jenny. " At the moment my situation is that I must get hold of money under all circumstances in order to be able to go on working." At about the same time Engels departed for Manchester to devote himself to " damned business " and certainly in order to be able to assist his friend financially.

Apart from Engels, friends proved to be rare in need, and in 1850 Frau Marx wrote to Weydemeyer : " The thing that hits me hardest of all and makes my heart bleed is that my husband is worried by so many petty troubles. He could be assisted with so little, but he who always helped others so readily is left helpless himself. Please don't think, Herr Weydemeyer, that we are asking anyone for anything, but at the very least my husband could justly ask those who turned to him for so many ideas and for support, to show a little more business energy and interest in his Review. They owe him that little, and I am not ashamed to say so—after all, no one was defrauded in the matter. It hurts me, but my husband thinks differently. He has never lost his confidence in the future, not even in the worst moments, and he has always kept up his good spirits and was happy if he saw me in a good humour and our dear children making a fuss of me." And as she looked after him when friends were silent, so he looked after her when enemies were all too vociferous in their attacks.

In August 1851 Marx again wrote to Weydemeyer : "You can imagine that my situation is gloomy. My wife will go under if it lasts much longer. The continual troubles and the petty day-to-day struggle to make ends meet are wearing her out. And on top of all this there is the infamy of my opponents, who do not even attempt to attack me objectively, but revenge themselves for their impotence by casting suspicion on me and spreading the most indescribable infamies about me. . . . As far as I am concerned, I should laugh at the whole business and I am not letting it interfere with my work in the least, but you can imagine that it is no relief to my wife, who is ill, whose nervous system is run down and who is forced to struggle with miserable poverty from morning to night, when foolish go-betweens bring her the latest exhalations from the democratic sewers. The tactlessness of some people in this respect is often colossal."

A few months previously (in March) Frau Marx had given birth to a daughter, Franziska, and despite an easy confinement she had been very ill, " more for psychological than for physical reasons ". There was not a penny in the house, "and at the same time we exploited the workers and worked for a dictatorship ", as Marx wrote in a bitter mood to Engels.

Marx's scientific studies were a never-failing source of consolation to him. He sat from nine o'clock in the morning to seven o'clock in the evening in the British Museum, and referring to the empty bombast of Kinkel and Willich he once declared : " Naturally, the democratic simpletons whose inspiration comes ' from above ' have no need to do anything of that sort. Why should the innocents bother their heads about economics and history ? As the worthy Willich used to say to me, everything is so simple. Everything is so simple ! In their confused heads perhaps, for they are really great simpletons." At that time Marx hoped to have his *Critique of Political Economy* completed within a few weeks, and he began to look for a publisher, a search which once again caused him one disappointment after the other.

In May 1851 a loyal friend on whom Marx could rely absolutely, Ferdinand Freiligrath, came to London, and during the next few years the two remained in close touch, but bad news followed quickly on his heels. On the 10th of May the tailor Nothjung was arrested in Leipzig whilst on a tour of agitation as a representative of the Communist League. Papers which he carried betrayed the existence of the League to the police, and soon afterwards the members of the Central Committee in Cologne were arrested. Freiligrath himself had escaped by the skin of his teeth and without even knowing the danger he was in. When he arrived in London the various fractions amongst the German exiles immediately fought each other tooth and nail for the privilege of the famous poet's allegiance, but he put a stop to this by informing them that he stood with Marx and his circle, and he refused to attend a meeting which took place on the 14th of July 1851 in order to make another attempt to compose the differences which existed amongst the exiles. The attempt failed as all previous attempts had failed and it produced only new differences. On the 20th of July the " Agitation Club " was founded under the intellectual leadership of Ruge, and on the 27th of July this was followed by the formation of the " Emigration Club " under the intellectual leadership of Kinkel, and these two associations were soon fighting each other vigorously, particularly in the columns of the German-American press.

Naturally, Marx had nothing but contempt for this " war of the frogs and mice ", and the intellectual attitudes of its leaders were all more or less abhorrent to him. Ruge's attempts to " edit the reason of events " in 1848 had already been dealt with in the *Neue Rheinische Zeitung* in a lighter vein, but heavier artillery had also been brought into action against " Arnold Winkelried Ruge ", the " Pomeranian thinker ", whose writings were " the gully " in which " all the waste phraseology and contradictions of German democracy flowed off ". However, for all his political confusion, Ruge was of a different calibre from Kinkel, who had been engaged in a ceaseless attempt to play the rôle of interesting social lion in London since his flight from prison in Spandau, " now in the 'pub, and now in the club ", as Freiligrath had mocked. In addition, Marx was more interested in Kinkel at the time because Willich had become his ally in order to organize a big swindle, a sort of revolution on a limited liability basis. On the 14th of September 1851 Kinkel landed in New York on a mission to win respected fugitives as guarantors for a German National Loan " in the sum of two million dollars to further the coming republican revolution ", and to collect a preliminary fund of 20,000 thaler. Kossuth had first conceived the brilliant idea of sailing over the herring pond with a collecting box, but on a smaller scale Kinkel carried on the business no less zealously and recklessly, and in the course of their activities both master and pupil preached against slavery in the Northern States and in favour of it in the Southern.

Whilst this farce was proceeding Marx established serious relations with the New World. In his growing financial embarrassment—" It is almost impossible to go on like this," he wrote to Engels on the 31st of July—he proposed to issue a lithographed correspondence for American newspapers, and a few days afterwards he received an offer from *The New York Tribune*, the most widely-read newspaper in the Northern States, to become a regular contributor. The offer was made by Dana, the publisher of the paper, whom Marx knew from his stay in Cologne. At the time Marx did not have the necessary fluent command of the English language so Engels deputized for him and wrote a series of articles on revolution and counter-revolution in Germany, and shortly afterwards Marx was able to secure the publication of one of his books in the United States in German.

5. *The Eighteenth Brumaire*

Throughout the revolutionary years Marx's old friend from Brussels, Josef Weydemeyer, fought courageously as the editor of a democratic newspaper in Frankfort-on-Main. When the counter-revolution became more insolent this paper was also suppressed, and after the discovery of the Communist League, of which Weydemeyer was an active member, the police spies soon got on to his track also.

At first he took refuge " in a quiet little inn in Sachsenhausen ", hoping that the storm would roll by and occupying himself in the meantime with a popular book on political economy. However, instead the atmosphere became more and more oppressive until finally Weydemeyer burst out with " the devil take this endless hanging around in hiding ". He was a husband and the father of two small children, and as he saw no likelihood of being able to earn a living in Switzerland or in London he decided to emigrate to America.

Marx and Engels were both very unwilling to lose such a loyal friend, and Marx racked his brains to find some way of finding him employment as an engineer, railway surveyor or something of the sort, but in vain. " Once you are over there, what guarantee is there that you won't lose yourself somewhere in the Far West ? We have so very few really good men and we must be economical with our forces." However, when Weydemeyer's departure proved unavoidable they found it was not a bad thing to have a capable representative of the communist cause in the New World. " We need a reliable fellow like Weydemeyer in New York," declared Engels. " After all, New York is not out of the world, and we know that if we need him Weydemeyer can be relied on." In the end therefore the two gave him their blessing, and he sailed from Havre on the 29th of September and after a stormy voyage which lasted almost forty days he arrived safely in New York.

On the 31st of October Marx sent a letter after him advising him to set himself up as a bookseller and publisher in New York, and to take the best things out of the *Neue Rheinische Zeitung* and the *Neue Rheinische Revue* and issue them separately. He was therefore delighted when he received a letter from Weydemeyer informing him, to the accompaniment of a certain amount of abuse directed against the shopkeeper mentality, which Weydemeyer declared was nowhere more naked and disgusting than in the New World, that he hoped to be able to issue a weekly under the title of *Die Revolution* at the beginning of January and asking for contributions to be sent over as quickly as possible. Marx immediately enthusiastically mobilized all the communist pens and above all that of Engels. He also secured Freiligrath, from whom Weydemeyer wanted a poem, Eccarius, Weerth and the two Wolffs. In his reply to Weydemeyer he complained that the latter had omitted to mention Wilhelm Wolff when announcing the contributors to the paper and declared : " None of us has his popular manner, but he is very modest and therefore it is all the more our duty to avoid any appearance of considering his co-operation superfluous." For his own share Marx announced that apart from a long discussion of a new work by Proudhon, he intended to write on *The Eighteenth Brumaire of Louis Bonaparte*, or the Bonapartist *coup d'état* of the 2nd of December, which was the most important event of the day in European politics and gave rise to much discussion.

Two of the works written on the subject by others became famous and their authors were richly rewarded. At a later date Marx described the difference between these two works and his own as follows : " Victor Hugo's *Napoleon le Petit* confines itself to bitter and brilliant invective against the responsible author of the *coup d'état*. The coup itself appears to him to have come like a bolt from the blue and to be nothing but the result of the violence of an individual, but he fails to observe that thereby he makes this individual great instead of small by crediting him with a personal power of initiative which would be unexampled in world history. On the other hand, Proudhon's *Coup d'état* attempts to show the coup as the result of a train of previous historical development, but in his hands the historical construction of the coup develops into a historical apologia for the hero of the coup. Thus he falls into the error of our so-called objective historians. In my treatment of the subject, however, I show how the class struggle in France created conditions and circumstances which made it possible for a mediocre and grotesque individual to play the rôle of a hero." Marx's book appeared like a literary Cinderella beside its more fortunate sisters, but whilst the latter have long since become dust and ashes his work still shines in immortal brilliance to-day.

In a work sparkling with wit and humour Marx succeeded, thanks to the materialist conception of history, in analysing a contemporary historical event to the very core The form of the work is as brilliant as its content. From the magnificent comparison contained in its first chapter : " Bourgeois revolutions, like those of the eighteenth century, storm forward more rapidly from success to success, their dramatic effects outdo each other, men and things seem set in fiery brilliance, ecstasy is the prevailing spirit of every day, but they are short-lived, they soon attain their zenith, and then a long period of depression falls on society before it learns to assimilate the results of its storm and stress period soberly. Proletarian revolutions, like those of the nineteenth century, on the other hand, criticize themselves ceaselessly, interrupt themselves constantly in their own course, return to what has apparently already been accomplished in order to begin it again, deride with ruthless thoroughness the half-heartedness, weakness and wretchedness of their first attempts, appear to throw their adversary to the ground only in order that he should draw renewed strength from the earth and rise again still more powerfully before them, recoil again and again from the uncertain and tremendous nature of their own aims until a situation is created which makes retreat impossible and the circumstances themselves cry out : " *Hic Rhodus, hic salta !* "—to the confident words of the prophetic conclusion : " If the imperial mantle finally falls on to the shoulders of Louis Bonaparte the bronze statue of Napoleon will crash down from the Vendôme column."

And under what circumstances was this brilliant work written ! Least important was the fact that after the first number Weydemeyer was compelled to cease publication of his weekly for lack of funds : " The unparalleled unemployment which has prevailed here since the beginning of the autumn makes it very difficult to start any new venture. And then the workers have been exploited in various ways recently, first Kinkel and then Kossuth. Unfortunately, the majority of them would rather give a dollar for propaganda hostile to them than a cent to defend their own interests. American conditions have an extraordinarily corrupting effect and at the same time they inculcate the arrogant idea that Americans are better than their comrades in the Old World." However, Weydemeyer did not give up hope of restoring his paper to life, this time as a monthly, and he wanted no more than a miserable 200 dollars.

Much more important than these troubles was the fact that early in January Marx fell ill and was able to work at all only with great difficulty : " For years nothing has pulled me down as much as this cursed hæmorrhoidal trouble, not even the worst French failure." And above all he was continually troubled by "filthy lucre", or rather the lack of it, which left him no peace, and on the 27th of February he wrote : " My affairs have now reached the agreeable point at which I can no longer leave the house because my clothes are in pawn and can no longer eat meat because my credit is exhausted." But finally, on the 25th of March, he was able to send the last bundle of manuscript to Weydemeyer together with congratulations on the birth of another little revolutionary, of which Weydemeyer had informed him : " It would be impossible to choose a better time to come into the world than at this moment. By the time it is possible to go from London to Calcutta in seven days we shall both have had our heads chopped off or they will be shaky with age. Australia, California and the Pacific ! The new-world citizens will be unable to realize how small our world was." Even in the worst of his personal troubles Marx never lost his optimism with regard to the tremendous prospects of human development, but sad days were immediately before him.

In a letter of the 30th of March Weydemeyer must have robbed him of all hope that his work would be printed. This letter has not been preserved, but an echo it produced has, in the shape of a violent letter written by Wilhelm Wolff on the 16th of April, the day on which one of Marx's children was buried, declaring : " Almost all our friends are afflicted with general misfortune and under horrible pressure." The letter was full of bitter reproaches of Weydemeyer, whose own life was not a bed of roses and who always did his best.

It was a terrible Easter for Marx and his family. The child which had died was their youngest daughter, born a year before, and the following moving description is taken from the diary of Frau Marx : " At Easter 1852 our poor little Franziska fell ill with severe bronchitis. For three days the poor child struggled against death and suffered much. Her small lifeless body rested in our little back room whilst we all went together into the front room and when night came we made up beds on the floor. The three surviving children lay with us and we cried for the poor little angel who now rested so cold and lifeless in the next room. The poor child's death took place in a period of bitterest poverty. I went to a French fugitive who lives near us and who had visited us shortly before. He received me with friendliness and sympathy and gave me two pounds and with that money the coffin in which my child could rest peacefully was paid for. It had no cradle when it was born and even the last little shell was denied it long enough. It was terrible for us when the little coffin was carried out to go to its last resting place." On this black day Weydemeyer's letter with its bad news arrived and Marx was sorely troubled about his wife who had witnessed everything fail to which he had set his hand during the previous two years.

However, during those unhappy hours a new letter was already on its way over the water. It was dated the 9th of April and read : " Unexpected assistance finally cleared away the difficulties which prevented publication of the pamphlet. After I had sent off my last letter I met one of our workers from Frankfort, a tailor who also came over here in the summer, and he immediately placed all his savings, forty dollars, at my disposal." But for this worker *The Eighteenth Brumaire* would not have been published—and Weydemeyer does not even mention his name ! But what does it matter what the man's name was ? The power which moved him was the class-consciousness of the proletariat, which never tires of making noble sacrifices for its emancipation.

The Eighteenth Brumaire formed the first number of the monthly *Revolution* which Weydemeyer now began to issue. The second and final number contained two poetical contributions by Freiligrath in the form of letters to Weydemeyer scourging with brilliant wit and humour the mendicant peregrinations of Kinkel in America. And that was the end of the venture. A number of contributions sent in by Engels were lost on the way.

Weydemeyer printed a thousand copies of *The Eighteenth*

Brumaire and about one-third of this number went to Europe, but not into the hands of the booksellers. They were distributed by friends and sympathizers in England and in the Rhineland, for even " radical " booksellers could not be persuaded to handle such an " untimely " effort, and an English translation drafted by Pieper and polished by Engels was unable to find a publisher.

If it was at all possible to increase the difficulties of Marx in finding a publisher this was done by the circumstance that the Bonapartist *coup d'état* in France was followed by the Cologne communist trial in Germany.

6. The Communist Trial in Cologne

Since the arrests which had taken place in May 1851 Marx had closely followed the course of the preliminary investigations, but as they were repeatedly held up owing to the lack of any " objective basis for an indictment ", as even the official prosecutor was compelled to admit, there was not much to be done. All that could be proved against the arrested men was that they were members of a secret propaganda organization, and for this the *Code Pénal* provided no punishment.

However, the King insisted that his nominee Stieber should be given a chance to show his mettle and provide the Prussian public with the much-desired consummation of a discovered conspiracy and punished conspirators, and Stieber himself was too good a patriot not to execute the will of his hereditary ruler and king. He began his task in a fitting fashion by instigating an act of robbery. One of his tools broke open and rifled the writing desk of a man named Oswald Dietz, who had been minute secretary to Willich's organization. As an astute agent-provocateur Stieber realized that the recklessness of this organization opened up prospects of success for his own edifying task such as " The Marx party " would never have offered.

With the assistance of stolen documents and with the aid rendered to him on the eve of the Bonapartist *coup d'état* by the French authorities Stieber manufactured the so-called " Franco-German Plot " in Paris, and in February 1852 this led to the conviction of a number of unfortunate German workers by the Paris courts, which sentenced them to various terms of imprisonment. However, what Stieber did not succeed in doing was establishing any connection between his Paris plot and the accused in Cologne. For all his cunning the " Franco-German

Plot " did not offer him even the shadow of a proof which could be used in Cologne.

In the meantime the differences between the " Marx Party " and the " Willich-Schapper Party " became still sharper. Willich still made common cause with Kinkel and the latter's return from America caused all the squabbles amongst the exiles to flare up anew so that in the spring and summer of 1852 the tension between the two organizations was acute. Kinkel had not secured the 200,000 thaler which was to have been the backbone of the national revolutionary loan, but he had obtained about half of it, and now the question of what was to be done with the money developed into one over which the democratic fugitives not only racked their brains but also began to break each other's heads. In the end a thousand pounds sterling was deposited with the Westminster Bank as an earnest for the first provisional government, the remainder of the sum collected having been expended on the journey and for administration costs. The deposited sum never served its intended purpose, but fifteen years later the foolishness came to a fairly satisfactory end when it assisted the press of the German social democracy over its initial difficulties.

Whilst the tumult and the shouting surged around this Nibelungen treasure Marx and Engels made sketches of the heroes of the battle, but unfortunately the manuscripts have not been preserved. They were persuaded to do so by a Hungarian colonel named Banya, who presented himself to them with a holograph authorization from Kossuth appointing him Police President of the Hungarian emigration, although in reality the man was a common spy and always at the service of the highest bidder. He was exposed by Marx and Engels because instead of handing the manuscript to the Berlin publishers for whom it was intended Banya gave it to the Prussian police. Marx nailed down the rogue's knavery instantly in a signed declaration which was published in the New York *Kriminal Zeitung*, but he was unable to obtain the return of his manuscript, which has never turned up since. If the Prussian government had hoped to use it as material in the Cologne process it must have been disappointed.

In its desperation at the lack of proofs against the accused the government caused the postponement of the public trial from one assize to the next, thereby increasing the suspense of an eager public to concert pitch until in October 1852 it simply had to raise the curtain and let the performance begin. Not all the determined perjuries of the police agents were sufficient to establish any connection between the accused and the " Franco-German Plot ", i.e. with a plot which was fabricated by the police whilst the accused were in prison and in an organization of which they were not only not members, but even opponents. In the end therefore Stieber in his desperation produced " the original Minute Book of the Marx Party " containing a chronological series of minutes describing meetings at which Marx and his comrades were alleged to have discussed their nefarious plans for world revolution. This " Minute Book " was an infamous forgery botched together by the agents-provocateurs Charles Fleury and Wilhelm Hirsch under the direction of a police officer named Greif. At first glance the precious document bore all the marks of forgery and its contents were simply idiotic, but Stieber counted on the stupidity of his carefully sifted bourgeois jurymen and kept a close watch on the post in order to prevent explanations and enlightenment coming from London.

However, Stieber's wretched plan failed owing to the energy and circumspection with which Marx countered it, although he was ill-prepared for a long and gruelling struggle. On the 8th of September he wrote to Engels : " My wife is ill. Little Jenny is ill. Lenchen has a sort of nervous fever, and I can't call in the doctor because I have no money to pay him. For about eight or ten days we have all been living on bread and potatoes, and it is now doubtful whether we shall be able to get even that. . . . I have written nothing for Dana because I have not had the money to buy newspapers. The best thing that could possibly happen now would be for the landlady to throw us out, for in that case I should have the weight of twenty-two pounds back rent off my mind, but I doubt whether she will be so considerate. And then we are indebted to the baker, the milkman, the grocer, the greengrocer and the butcher. How on earth am I to get out of this devilish mess ? During the past week or so I have borrowed a few shillings and even pence from workers. It was terrible, but it was absolutely necessary or we should have starved." This was the desperate situation in which Marx was compelled to take up the struggle with powerful enemies, but in it both he and his wife forgot their domestic troubles.

Victory was still in the balance when Frau Marx wrote to an American friend : " All the proofs of the forgery have had to be provided from here and my husband has had to work all day and even far into the night. And then we have had to copy everything six or seven times and send it to Germany by various ways, over Frankfort, Paris, etc., because all letters to my husband and all his letters to Germany are opened and confiscated. The whole affair has now been reduced to a struggle between the police on the one hand and my husband on the other, and my husband is being made responsible for everything, even the conduct of the trial. You must excuse my confusion, but I have also had some part in the intrigue, and I have copied and copied until my fingers ached. Whole lists of business addresses and pseudo-business letters have just arrived from Weerth and Engels as a cloak for the safe sending of the documents, etc. Our house has been turned into a regular office. Two or three are writing, others are running messages, and the remainder are engaged in scraping pennies together in order that we can all continue to exist and provide proof of the most shameful scandal the official world has ever perpetrated. And all the time my three lively children are singing and whistling, occasionally earning a severe rebuke from their father. What a life ! "

Marx won the victory and Stieber's forgery was exposed even before the trial, so that the Public Prosecutor was compelled to abandon " the wretched book ". However, the public victory sealed the fate of the accused. The five weeks' proceedings revealed such a mass of infamies committed in part by the highest authorities in the Prussian State that the acquittal of the accused would have meant the conviction of the State in the eyes of the whole world. To spare the State this humiliation the jurymen were prepared to besmirch their honour and violate their consciences, and they therefore found seven of the eleven accused guilty of attempted high treason. The cigar-maker Röser, the author Bürgers, and the journeyman tailor Nothjung were sentenced to six years' imprisonment in a fortress each, the worker Reiff, the chemist Otto and the former barrister Becker were sentenced to five years' imprisonment in a fortress each, whilst the journeyman tailor Lessner received three years. The clerk Ehrhardt and the three doctors Daniels, Jacoby and Klein were all acquitted. However, Daniels died a few years later of consumption contracted during the eighteen months he had been imprisoned awaiting trial. In a moving letter his wife sent his last greetings to Marx, who mourned his death deeply.

The other victims of this shameful process survived Daniels by many years, and some of them even worked their way back into the bourgeois world, for instance, Bürgers, who was elected to the Reichstag as a progressive, and Becker, who later became Lord Mayor of Cologne and a member of the Prussian Upper House and whose highly patriotic attitude on all occasions won him the good graces of the government and the court. Amongst the convicted men who remained loyal to the proletarian flag were Nothjung and Röser, both of whom played an active part in the beginnings of the renewed working-class movement, and

Lessner, who survived both Marx and Engels and became one of their most devoted comrades in exile.

After the Cologne communist trial, the Communist League dissolved and its example was soon followed by Willich's organization. Willich himself emigrated to America and during the civil war he won well-earned fame as a general in the Northern Army, whilst Schapper returned penitently to his old comrades. However, Marx was unwilling to permit the Prussian government to enjoy the miserable victory it had won at the Cologne assizes, and he determined to pillory it in the eyes of the world. To this end he prepared the revelations at the trial for publication in Switzerland and, if possible, also in America. Writing on the 7th of December to friends in America he declared : "You will appreciate the humour of the pamphlet more I think when I tell you that its author is practically an internee owing to the lack of adequate covering for his feet and his behind, and that in addition his family was and still is threatened with really horrible misery. This too is in part a result of the proceedings because for five weeks I was compelled to devote all my energies to defending the party against the machinations of the government, instead of earning a living. Not only that, but the trial has turned the German booksellers against me completely and I had hoped to come to some arrangement with them for the publication of my book on political economy."

However, on the 11th of December the son of Schabelitz, who had taken over his father's business in the meantime, wrote to Marx from Basle informing him that he was already going through the first galleys. "I am convinced that the book will create a tremendous sensation because it is a masterpiece." Schabelitz proposed to print 2,000 copies and fix the price at 10 silver groschen per copy because he reckoned that at least part of the edition would be confiscated. Unfortunately the whole of the edition was confiscated when it was about to be sent into the interior from the little frontier village in Baden where it had been stored for about six weeks.

On the 10th of March the bad news was reported to Engels with the bitter words : "Such misfortunes threaten to rob one of all further encouragement to write. Always to be working *pour le roi de Prusse !* " It proved impossible to discover how the leakage had occurred and the suspicion which Marx had at first harboured against the publisher turned out to be baseless. Schabelitz even offered to distribute the 500 copies he had retained in Switzerland, although little seems to have come of this. The affair had a bitter sequel for Marx when three months later not Schabelitz but his partner Amberger demanded compensation for the printing costs in the sum of 424 francs.

Fortunately, however, the failure in Switzerland was in part compensated by success in America, though naturally the effect of the revelations there concerning the Cologne trial was not so disturbing to the Prussian government as it would have been in Europe. The *Neu-England Zeitung*, which was published in Boston, printed the revelations and Engels had 440 special copies printed at his own expense. With Lassalle's assistance he proposed to distribute them in the Rhine province. Frau Marx corresponded with Lassalle on the point and the latter showed himself zealous enough, but unfortunately the correspondence does not reveal whether the plan was carried out successfully or not.

The revelations found a lively echo in the German-American press and Willich in particular came forward against the work. This caused Marx to write a short reply to him entitled *The Knight of the High-souled Conscience*, but to-day it is hardly worth while to lift the veil of forgetfulness which has long since fallen on it. As is always the case in such controversies, sins were committed by both sides, and, as the victor, Marx gladly refrained from triumphing over the vanquished. Referring to the first years of the emigration period he declared in 1860 that its most brilliant vindication was a comparison between its history and the parallel history of the bourgeois governments and of bourgeois society. With very few exceptions the fugitives could be accused of nothing worse than having harboured illusions which were more or less justified by the conditions of the day, and of having committed follies which necessarily arose out of the unusual circumstances in which the emigrants unexpectedly found themselves.

When he prepared a second edition of the revelations for publication in 1875 he at first hesitated as to whether he should delete the passages dealing with the Willich-Schapper fraction, but finally he let them stand, feeling that any mutilation of the text might appear like tampering with an historic document, but he added : " The violent events of a revolution leave a disturbing heritage in the minds of those who take part in it, and in particular in the minds of those who are hounded into exile away from their homes. This mental disturbance affects even capable men for a longer or shorter period and makes them, so to speak, irresponsible. They fail to understand the meaning of events and they refuse to see that the form of the movement has changed. The result is that they indulge in conspiracies and romantic revolutionism which compromise both them and the cause they have at heart. This is the explanation of the errors of Schapper and Willich. In the American civil war Willich demonstrated that he was something more than a weaver of fantastic projects, whilst Schapper, who was a lifelong pioneer of the working-class movement, recognized and admitted his momentary errors soon after the communist trial in Cologne. Many years later, the day before he died, Schapper referred with caustic irony to the folly of the early emigrant days. On the other hand, the circumstances in which the revelations were originally issued explains the bitterness with which the involuntary helpers of the common enemy were attacked. To lose one's head at a moment of crisis is a crime against the party and it demands public expiation." They were words of wisdom at a time when it was still thought more important to maintain " a good tone " than to establish clarity on matters of principle.

Once the battle was fought and the victory won Marx was the last man to harbour petty rancour. Answering some brusque remarks of Freiligrath in 1850 on " the doubtful and degraded elements " which had found their way into the League, he admitted more than he need have done when he declared : " Storms always raise a certain amount of dirt and dust, and a revolutionary period does not smell of attar of roses. It is clear that occasionally one is bespattered with all sorts of muck. It is impossible to be too particular at such a moment," but he was justified in adding : " However, if one considers the tremendous efforts of the official world against us, the ransacking of the *Code Pénal* against us, the slanderous tongues of ' the Democracy of Stupidity ' (which has never been able to forgive us for displaying greater intelligence and greater strength of character than it did itself) and the history of all other parties, one must come to the conclusion that in this nineteenth century our party is distinguished above all by its cleanness."

When the Communist League ceased to exist the last threads which connected Marx with public life in Germany were broken and from now on exile, " the home of the good ", became his home too.

CHAPTER EIGHT: MARX AND ENGELS

1. Genius and Society

MARX found a second home in England, but the meaning of the word must not be stretched too far. However, he was never interfered with in England on account of his revolutionary agitation, although in the last resort it was naturally directed against the English State also. The government of "greedy and jealous shopkeepers" displayed a greater measure of self-respect and dignity than did those continental governments whose uneasy consciences caused them to hunt down their enemies with every measure of police oppression even when they were guilty of no more than discussion and propaganda.

In another and deeper sense Marx never found a home after his keen eye had penetrated the shams of bourgeois society. A discussion on the fate of genius in bourgeois society would fill a bulky chapter. Various opinions have been expressed on the subject, from the naïve confidence of the Philistine who prophesies the final victory to every man of genius, to the melancholy words of Faust:

> Die Wenigen, die was davon erkannt,
> Die töricht gnug ihr volles Herz nicht wahrten,
> Dem Pöbel ihr Gefühl, ihr Schauen offenbarten,
> Hat man von je gekreuzigt und verbrannt.[1]

The historical method which Marx developed permits us to look more closely into the relation of things in this question also. The Philistine prophesies the final victory to every man of genius because the prophet is a Philistine, and if for once a genius escapes the crucifix and the stake then in the last resort it is because he was modest enough to remain a Philistine. Without the powdered pig-tails hanging down their backs neither Goethe nor Hegel would ever have been acknowledged as geniuses in bourgeois society.

[1] "Those few who saw and understood, and then,
  With folly opened wide their hearts,
  And showed their feelings to the mob,
  Died ever at the stake or on the cross."

225

Bourgeois society, which in this respect is nothing more than the most clearly defined form of all class societies, may have as many other advantages as you please, but it has never been a hospitable host to genius. In fact, it could not be, for the very essence of genius must always consist in releasing the creative impulses of human nature in the face of all traditional obstacles, and in shaking at those barriers without which class society could not exist. Over the entrance to a lonely cemetery on the island of Sylt which affords a last resting-place to the unknown dead washed up by the sea stands the pious inscription : " Here is the Cross of Golgotha, the Home of the Homeless ". Unconsciously, but none the less aptly, this inscription sums up the fate of genius in class society. Homeless in class society, genius finds a resting-place only under the cross on Golgotha.

Unless, however, genius agrees to tolerate class society. When genius placed itself at the service of bourgeois society in order to overthrow feudal society, it apparently won tremendous power, but immediately it attempted to act on its own account that power melted away at once and genius was permitted to end its days on the rocks of St. Helena. Or on the other hand, genius consented to don the sober cutaway of the Philistine, and in that case it was permitted to rise, to become Minister of State to the Grand Duke of Weimar or Royal and Prussian Professor in Berlin. But woe betide that genius which is incorruptible, which holds itself in proud independence of bourgeois society, which prophesies the approaching end of that society from the data supplied by the latter's own internal workings, and which forges the weapons to give bourgeois society the *coup de grâce* ! For such genius bourgeois society has nothing but sufferings and tortures which are still more cruel than the punishments of ancient society or the stake of mediæval society, though outwardly they may appear less brutal.

Amongst the geniuses of the nineteenth century, none suffered more under this lot than the greatest genius of them all, Karl Marx. He was compelled to wrestle with poverty even in the first decade of his public activities, and when he emigrated to London he was loaded with all the burdens of the exile. However, the sufferings which made his lot Promethean befell him only in the prime of his manhood when in his laborious efforts to advance the cause of humanity he was compelled at the same time to struggle day after day with the miserable and trivial worries of life, to struggle depressingly to obtain the bare means of existence for himself and his family within the framework of bourgeois society.

And, in addition, the life he led bore no resemblance to the life the ordinary Philistine regards in his usual ignorance as that of a genius. His tremendous industry matched his tremendous powers, and it was not long before his overworked days and nights began to undermine a constitution originally of iron. He was perfectly serious when he declared that incapacity to work was a death-sentence on any human being not really an animal. On one occasion when he had been ill for several weeks he wrote to Engels : " Although I am quite unable to work I have read Carpenter's *Physiology*, Lord's ditto, Kölliker's *Gewebelehre*, Spurzheim's *Anatomie des Hirns und Nervensystems* and Schwann and Schleiden *Ueber die Zellenschmiere* ".[1] In all his insatiable urge to scientific study he never forgot the words he had once used as a young man : a writer must certainly earn money in order to exist and write, but he should not exist and write in order to earn money, and he always recognized " the categoric necessity of earning a living ".

However, his own efforts in this direction invariably failed in face of the suspicion or hatred or, in the best case, the fear of a hostile world. Even such German publishers who were accustomed to priding themselves on their independence recoiled at the name of the infamous demagogue. All parties in Germany slandered him equally, and where the clear outlines of his giant figure could be distinguished through the artificial cloud around him, the malicious cunning of systematic silence did its infamous work. No nation has ever banished its greatest thinker so utterly and for so long from its national life as Germany did Marx.

The only time he succeeded in providing himself with a half-way secure basis was his work for *The New York Tribune*, which lasted a good decade beginning in 1851. At that time *The New York Tribune* had 200,000 readers and was the most powerful and popular newspaper in the United States, and by its agitation for an American brand of Fourierism it had at least raised itself above the exclusively money-grubbing activities of a purely capitalist undertaking. The formal conditions under which Marx worked for this paper were not unfavourable. He was required to write two articles a week and for each article he was to receive two pounds sterling. That would have meant over 200 pounds a year and would have enabled him to keep his head above water. Freiligrath's commercial activities brought him in no more than that, in the beginning at least, and Freiligrath always boasted that he had never been without " the luscious beef-steak of banishment ".

Naturally, there is no question of whether the amount paid to Marx by the American newspaper was at all in accordance

[1] *Histology, The Anatomy of the Brain and the Nervous System* and *On Cell Matter.*

with the literary and scientific value of his contributions, for a capitalist newspaper concern reckons with market prices and in bourgeois society it is perfectly justified in doing so. Marx never demanded any better treatment than this, but what he was entitled to demand even in bourgeois society was that the agreement should be respected and perhaps that his work should be valued on its own account also. However, the publishers of *The New York Tribune* did neither the one thing nor the other. In theory Dana was a Fourierist, but in practice he was a hard-boiled Yankee business man. In a fit of anger Engels once declared that Dana's socialism resolved itself into the lousiest petty-bourgeois cheating, and in fact, although Dana was well aware of Marx's value as a contributor and did not fail to advertise that value to his readers, he showed Marx every form of ruthlessness which a capitalist exploiter feels himself entitled to show towards exploited labour-power dependent on him for its existence. By no means his worst offence was that he often stole the contributions Marx sent in and published them in a garbled form as editorial articles, a proceeding which caused their real author understandable annoyance.

And further, not only did Dana immediately put Marx on half pay at the first sign of slacking sales, but he paid only for those articles which he actually printed as Marx's work. In fact, he did not hesitate to scrap whole articles and everything in them merely because their general line did not suit his purpose. On occasions it happened that for three weeks, and even six weeks, on end all the contributions which Marx sent over found their way into the waste-paper basket, whilst those German newspapers to which he was able to contribute, for instance, *Die Presse* in Vienna, showed themselves no more decent. It was perfectly true when he declared bitterly that in his newspaper work he was no better off than a penny-a-liner.

In 1853 we find him longing for a few months' peace in which to continue his scientific studies undisturbed : " Apparently I'm not to have it. This constant churning out of stuff for the newspapers bores me. You can be as independent as you like, but in the last resort you are bound to the newspaper and its readers, particularly when you get paid on a cash basis as I do. Purely scientific work is totally different." After he had been working for a few years under Dana's despotic sway his tone became still more bitter : " It is utterly disgusting to have to be grateful when a rag like that kindly consents to take one into its canoe. Grinding bones and making soup out of them like the paupers in the workhouse, that is how much the political work for such a paper amounts to, though I have to do it in full measure." Marx shared the fate of the modern proletariat not only in the scantiness of his means of subsistence, but also in its utter insecurity.

The world always had a general idea of his situation, but in his letters to Engels we find terrible and moving details : on one occasion he was compelled to remain indoors because he had neither coat nor shoes to go out in ; on another occasion he had not enough money to buy either writing paper or news-papers ; and on another occasion we find him dashing around to acquaintances to borrow postage money to send off a manu-script to a publisher. And then there was the constant bickering with the grocer and other small shopkeepers because he was unable to pay promptly even for the barest necessities of life, not to mention the constant trouble with the landlord, who was for ever threatening to put the brokers in, and the eternal visits to the pawnbroker, whose usury swallowed up even that little money which might with difficulty have kept the shadow of starvation from the door.

And often enough the shadow not only fell across the threshold but over the very table itself. Accustomed from earliest childhood to a carefree life, his high-minded wife sometimes staggered under the slings and arrows of a really outrageous fortune, and then she wished herself and her children in the grave. There are indica-tions of domestic scenes in some of Marx's letters, and on one occasion we find him expressing the opinion that people who pursued the general aims of humanity could commit no greater folly than that of marriage because thereby they betrayed them-selves into the toils of the petty cares of private life. However, although his wife's complaints may have made him impatient at times he always excused and justified her, declaring that she had incomparably more to suffer from the indescribable humilia-tions, worries and cares which people in their position had to go through, all the more so because she was denied that respite and refuge in the halls of science which saved him again and again. And to see the innocent pleasures of childhood so brutally shortened for their children weighed equally heavily on both parents.

The lot of his genius was sad enough in all conscience, but it was raised to tragic heights by the fact that he volun-tarily shouldered such torments and sufferings for decades, and steadfastly rejected every temptation to save himself in the peaceful harbour of some bourgeois career, although he might have done so without dishonour. His attitude he explains himself without any bombast and in simple words : " I must follow my goal through thick and thin, and I shall not permit bourgeois society to turn me into a money-making machine." This time it was not the chains of Hæphestus which bound Prometheus, but his own indomitable will, which kept his course pointed unswervingly towards the greatest good for humanity with the certainty of a magnetic compass. His character was like pliant steel. It is extraordinary to experience in one and the same letter how he is apparently crushed down by the weight of petty miseries and then to find him suddenly transformed and discussing the most complicated problems with the calm judiciousness of a scholar whose brow is never furrowed by the material cares of the day.

However, Marx certainly felt the blows which bourgeois society dealt him, and he felt them deeply. It would be foolish stoicism to ask : what do such cares matter to a genius who in any case looks to his justification from the verdict of posterity? That conceited literary ambition which would like to see its name in the papers every day, if possible, is foolish, but for all that creative forces must have elbow-room for their development and they win new strength from the echo their creations arouse. Marx was no virtuous and stilted chatterbox such as can be found in bad plays and novels, but a man like Lessing who liked to enjoy life and the world, and the mood in which the dying Lessing wrote to one of his oldest friends : " I am sure you do not regard me as a man avaricious for praise, but the coldness with which the world is accustomed to indicate to certain people that nothing they do is right, is, if not killing, at least paralysing " was not unknown to Marx. It was the same mood in which he wrote on the eve of his fiftieth birthday : " Half a century on my back and still a pauper ! " On one occasion he wished himself a hundred fathoms under the sea rather than have to go on vegetating, and on another occasion he burst out desperately that he would not wish his worst enemy to go through what he had been going through for eight weeks with his heart suffused with anger because his intellect and working capacities were being broken by trivialities.

But for all that, Marx never became " a damned sorry dog ", an expression he once used mockingly to describe himself, and in this sense Engels was right when he declared that his friend never despaired. Marx has often been credited with a hard character, but the shower of blows he received on the anvil of misfortune made him harder and harder. The blue sky which had hung over his early youth gradually became covered with heavy storm-clouds and his ideas rent them like flashes of lightning. His judgments on his enemies, and often enough on his friends, developed a searing trenchancy which wounded even those who were not unduly sensitive. Those who abuse him as an ice-cold demagogue for this are no more and no less wrong than those worthy subaltern souls who regard a great fighter and a great human being as no more than a stuffed puppet on a parade ground.

2. An Incomparable Alliance

Marx had to thank more than his own tremendous powers for the victory of his life. According to human judgment he must have gone under in the struggle in one way or the other but for the friend he had in Engels, whose self-sacrificing loyalty we are beginning to understand only now that the correspondence between the two friends has been published.

Their friendship is without equal in history, which can show many cases of famous friendships : the friendships of men whose life's work was so closely connected that it can no longer be divided into thine and mine, and German history can show such cases also. But always there has remained some trace of wilfulness or obstinacy, or even no more than a secret objection to abandoning completely the individual personality, something which in the words of the poet is " the highest prize of the children of this earth ". In the last resort Luther regarded Melanchthon as the faint-hearted scholar, whilst Melanchthon regarded Luther as a raw peasant, and one must be the willing victim of obtuseness not to detect the underground note of discordancy between the great Minister of State and the little Councillor in the correspondence which passed between Goethe and Schiller. The friendship which bound Marx and Engels knew nothing of this last remnant of human pettiness. The more their thought and their development became one, the more they each remained a separate entity and a man.

In outward appearance they were very different. Engels the blond German, tall and, as an observer has informed us, with English manners, always carefully dressed and upright as a result of discipline in barracks and office. With six clerks, he declared, he could organize an infinitely more simple and efficient administration than with sixty privy councillors, who could not even write legibly and would muck up the books to such an extent that not a soul would be able to make head or tail out of them afterwards. He was a highly respected member of the Manchester Stock Exchange and prominent both in the business and in the pleasures of the .English bourgeoisie, its fox-hunting and its Christmas parties, but the intellectual leader and fighter had a treasure in a little house far away on the other side of the town, a child of Ireland, and in her arms he recovered his spirits when he had grown all too tired of the bourgeois pack in whose midst he was compelled to live.

Marx, on the other hand, was stocky and powerfully built, with dark, flashing eyes and a lion's mane of jet-black hair which indicated his Semitic origin. He held himself carelessly like the troubled father of a family with no share in the business activities of the metropolis, but he exhausted himself in intellectual labours which hardly left him time to swallow his meals, lasted far into the night and undermined his constitution. He was an indefatigable thinker for whom thought was the highest pleasure and he was a worthy successor of Kant, Fichte and particularly Hegel, whose words he often repeated with pleasure : " Even the criminal thought of a scoundrel is loftier and more magnificent than all the wonders of Heaven," except that Marx's thought strained forward ceaselessly towards fulfilment in action. He was unpractical in small matters, but more than practical in great ones. Much too unpractical to manage a small household, he was incomparable in his genius for raising an army and leading it forward to change the face of the earth.

Style is said to reveal the man and they were different as authors also. Each was a master of language in his own way and each was a brilliant linguist who had mastered many languages and even dialects. In this respect Engels achieved even more than Marx, but when he used his mother tongue, even in his letters, not to speak of his books, he kept a tight hand on the reins and permitted no stumbling either to right or left into foreign pitfalls, whilst at the same time carefully avoiding the pot-holes of the Teutonist purists and language reformers. He wrote easily and with a light touch and his prose is so limpid and clear that at all times one can see through the running stream of his words to the very bottom.

Marx, on the other hand, wrote with less care and greater difficulty. In his early letters, like those of Heine, one can feel the struggle for mastery, and in the letters of his later years, particularly in those he wrote after he went to England, he uses a terrible hodge-podge of German, English and French expressions. His writings also contain more foreign words than was absolutely necessary, and even his German abounds in Anglicisms and Gallicisms, but even so, he was such a master of the German language that his works cannot be translated without grievous loss. After having read a chapter of a French translation of one of Marx's works, Engels declared, despite the fact that Marx himself had polished the translation with great care, that the power, sap and life of the original had gone to the devil. Goethe once wrote to Frau von Stein : " In similes I am running a race with Sancho Panza's proverbs," and in the striking figurativeness of his language Marx could run a race with the greatest masters of language, with Lessing, Goethe or Hegel. He had mastered Lessing's principle that content and form must agree like man and wife in a happy marriage, and for this he was belaboured by the university wiseacres from the veteran Wilhelm Roscher down to the youngest university lecturer, who overwhelmed him with the crushing accusation that he succeeded in making himself understood only vaguely and with " a patchwork of similes ". Marx always dealt with questions in a way which left food for fruitful thought for his reader, and his language was like the play of the waves on the purple depths of the ocean.

Engels always recognized the superior genius in Marx, and he never aspired to play anything but the second fiddle to the other's lead. However, Engels was never merely Marx's interpreter or assistant, but always an independent collaborator, an intellectual force dissimilar to Marx, but his worthy partner. At the beginning of their friendship Engels gave more than he received on a very important field of their activities, and twenty years later Marx wrote to him : " You know that, first of all, I arrive at things slowly, and, secondly, I always follow in your footsteps." Engels wore lighter armour and was able to move more quickly. His eye was keen enough to see the decisive point of any question or any situation immediately, but he did not penetrate into things deeply enough to see all the pros and the cons of the matter at once. For a man of action such a capacity is a great advantage and Marx never made any political decision without first consulting Engels, who invariably hit the nail on the head.

In accordance with this relation between the two men, therefore, the advice which Marx sought and received from Engels in theoretical questions was not as fruitful as that he received in political matters, for in the former Marx was usually ahead of his friend. And there was one piece of advice in particular to which Marx invariably turned a deaf ear. It was when Engels tried to persuade him to finish off his scientific work quickly : " Don't be quite so conscientious with your work. It will be much too good for the general public in any case. The great thing is that you should finish it finally and have it published. The weak points which you may be able to see will never be discovered by the donkeys in any case." This advice was typical of Engels, just as the refusal to follow it was typical of Marx.

From all this we can see clearly that Engels was better able to cope with the daily publicist work than was Marx, who once described his friend as "A positive encylopædia, ready for work at any hour of the day or night, full or sober, quick at writing and as active as the devil". It would appear that after the *Neue Rheinische Revue* ceased publication in the autumn of 1850 the two friends had a new joint project in view in London. At least, Marx wrote to Engels in December 1853 : "If we had started the English correspondence business in London in good time you would not be in Manchester now, plagued with business worries, and I should not be plagued with debts." The fact that Engels preferred to take a job in his father's firm rather than rely on the "correspondence business" was probably due to the dismal situation in which Marx found himself at the time, and in the hope that things would improve, rather than to any intention of devoting himself permanently to "damned commerce". In the spring of 1854 Engels once again considered abandoning business and going to London to take up writing, but this was the last time he did so and at about this time he must have decided to bear the hated yoke permanently in order to assist his friend and at the same time to preserve the greatest intellectual force of the party. Only under such circumstances could Engels have made the sacrifice and Marx have accepted it. Both the offer and its acceptance presuppose the same degree of high-minded selflessness.

In due time Engels rose to be a partner in the firm, but until he did so his own financial situation as a simple employee of the firm was not all too rosy, but nevertheless, from the first days of his stay in Manchester he assisted Marx to the best of his ability and he never grew tired of assisting. Five-pound notes, ten-pound notes, and, later on, even hundred-pound notes, constantly went from Manchester to London. He never grew impatient even when his patience was occasionally subjected to a greater strain than was absolutely necessary by Marx and his wife, whose ideas of how a household should be run would appear to have been none too modest. Even when on one occasion Marx forgot all about his indebtedness on a bill of exchange and was extremely and unpleasantly surprised when it matured, Engels hardly showed any despair at the unpractical nature of his friend. Or when on another occasion he once again placed the family finances on a new footing and Frau Marx, out of false consideration for him, concealed a whole budget of debts in the hope of being able to pay them off herself by saving on the household money, whereas in reality the old privations and difficulties began all over again in consequence. He left it to his friend to enjoy the somewhat pharisaical satisfaction of complaining about " the folly of women " who " obviously needed to be in leading strings all the time ", and contented himself with the good-humoured exhortation : " see to it that it doesn't occur again ".

Not only did Engels drudge for his friend during the day in his office and on the Stock Exchange, but he also sacrificed the greater part of his leisure hours in the evening, often working far into the night. In the beginning he did so in order to draft or translate the letters for *The New York Tribune* because Marx had not a sufficient command of the English language for the purpose, but when this reason was no longer valid he still continued his silent co-operation.

But all this fades into insignificance when compared with the greatest sacrifice of all, his voluntary abandonment of all hope of attaining that measure of scientific achievement which would have been his as the reward of his tremendous capacity for working and of his rich talents. In this case also, it is the correspondence between the two men which first gives us a real idea of the situation, even if we consider only the military and language studies which Engels pursued, partly " from inclination " and partly owing to the practical exigencies of the proletarian struggle for emancipation. Although he hated " auto-didacticism "—" it is always nonsense ", he wrote contemptuously—and although his method of scientific work was thorough, he was no more a mere arm-chair scholar than Marx, and every new piece of knowledge was doubly valuable if it could be put to use immediately in the struggle to break the chains of the proletariat.

For this reason he began to study the Slav languages, declaring that when the time for political action again arrived " at least one of us " must know something about the language, history, literature and social institutions of those nations with which they would immediately come into conflict. In the same way the entanglements in the Far East caused him to study Oriental languages. Arabic with its four thousand roots frightened him off, but Persian he found " mere child's play ", and in three weeks he hoped to have mastered it. And then he turned his attention to the Germanic languages : " I am now up to my eyes in Ulphilas.[1] I ought really to have finished with this damned Gothic long ago, but I am so desultory in my studies. To my astonishment I have discovered that I know far more than I thought. With a good dictionary I ought to be through in about

[1] Goth bishop. Translated the Bible. 311–81.—Tr.

a fortnight, and then I shall go on to Old-Nordic and Old-Saxon, with which I have always had a nodding acquaintance. Up to the moment I have been working without a dictionary, just with the text and Grimm, the old fellow is really marvellous." When the Sleswig-Holstein question became acute in the 'sixties he went in for " a little Frisian-English-Jutish-Scandinavian philology and archæology ", and when the Irish question flared up again he turned his attention to " a little Keltic-Irish ", and so on In later years his magnificent command of many languages stood him in good stead on the General Council of the International. "Engels stutters in twenty languages ", someone once declared, for when he was excited he had a slight tendency to stutter.

Owing to his even more enthusiastic and detailed study of military science he earned the nickname of " General ". In this case also an " old inclination " was encouraged by the practical necessities of revolutionary politics. He reckoned with " the enormous importance which the *partie militaire* must have in the coming movement ". Those officers who had gone over to the side of the people in the years of the revolution had not turned out to be altogether satisfactory. " This mob of military men possesses an incredibly disgusting corps spirit," he declared on one occasion. " They hate each other like poison and envy each other the slightest distinction like schoolboys, but they stand together like one man against the ' civilians '." His aim was to master military science sufficiently to permit him to say a word or two in theoretical military matters without making a fool of himself.

He had hardly settled down in Manchester when he began " to swot up militaria ", beginning with " the most ordinary and humdrum matters such as are demanded in the examinations for cadets and subalterns, things which for that reason are usually taken as read ". He studied military organization in all its technical details : elementary tactics, the fortification system from Vauban to the most modern system of self-contained forts, bridge-building and trench-digging, the use of arms, the various types of gun-carriages and emplacements, the supply system, the hospital system, and numerous other details. And finally he turned his attention to general military history and zealously studied the Englishman Napier, the Frenchman Jomini and the German Clausewitz.

Engels never wasted the time of his readers with platitudinarian enlightenment on the moral irrationalism of war, instead he sought to lay bare the historical reasons for war, and these efforts more than once brought down the hot anger of the democratic demagogues on his head. Byron once poured burning scorn on the leaders of the two armies which fought at Waterloo as the standard-bearers of feudal Europe and delivered the death-blow to the heir of the French Revolution, and a happy chance caused Engels to give a historical sketch of both Wellington and Blücher in one of his letters to Marx. Although the frame is limited the sketch is so clear and concise that even taking the great advance of military science into account it would hardly be necessary to alter as much as a line even to-day.

Engels also worked gladly and arduously on a third field, that of natural science, but here too he was fated never to put the finishing touches to his investigations during the long decades in which he performed task-work to clear the way for the intellectual labours of a still greater man.

It was a tragic fate, but Engels never whined, for sentimentality was as foreign to him as it was to his friend. He always considered it the great good fortune of his life that for forty years he was able to stand shoulder to shoulder with Marx, even at the cost of being overshadowed by the greater figure, and when for a decade and more after the death of his friend he played the leading rôle in the international working-class movement and his authority was undisputed it did not appear to him as a belated satisfaction. On the contrary, he always declared that he was given greater credit than was his due.

Both men gave themselves completely to the common cause, and both of them made, not the same, but an equally great sacrifice in its interests without the faintest trace of discontented grumbling or boasting, and for these reasons their friendship was an incomparable alliance of which history can show no second example.

CHAPTER NINE: THE CRIMEAN WAR AND THE CRISIS

1. European Politics

TOWARDS the end of 1853, just as Marx had concluded his fight against " democratic emigration illusions and amateur revolutionism " with his polemic against Willich, a new period in European politics was opened up by the Crimean War, and it occupied his chief attention in the following few years.

His own views on the subject were given chiefly in his contributions to *The New York Tribune*. Although its editors did their best to force him down to the level of ordinary newspaper correspondence, he could say with truth that " only in exceptional cases " did they succeed. He remained loyal to his principles, and even that work which he was compelled to do in order to earn a living was ennobled in his hands and given a permanent value by being based on laborious studies.

Most of these treasures from his pen are still buried, and it will cost a certain amount of trouble to bring them to the surface again. Owing to the fact that *The New York Tribune* treated his contributions more or less as raw material, flung them into the waste-paper basket at its discretion, published them under its own flag and often, as Marx complained bitterly, published " rubbish " under his name, it will never be possible to reconstruct the whole of his work for the paper, and very careful examination will be necessary to determine its limits with any degree of accuracy.

Indispensable assistance has been offered in this respect only recently with the publication of the Marx-Engels correspondence. For instance, it shows us that the series of articles on revolution and counter-revolution in Germany whose authorship was credited to Marx for many years, was in fact chiefly written by Engels, and that Engels wrote not only the contributions on military questions, a fact that had been known for a long time, but that he co-operated widely in other respects in Marx's work for the paper. Apart from the series of articles on revolution and counter-revolution in Germany, the articles on the Eastern question which appeared in *The New York Tribune* have also been collected, though both with regard to what it contains and what it does not contain, this latter collection is of much more doubtful authenticity than the former which was after all only credited to the wrong author.[1]

But even this critical examination of Marx's work for *The New York Tribune* would represent only a small part of the labours necessary because although Marx certainly succeeded in raising the level of journalist work tremendously, even he could not raise it completely above the circumstances in which it had to be written. The greatest brain in the world cannot make new discoveries or give birth to new ideas twice a week always just in time to catch the regular packet-steamer on Tuesdays and Fridays. As Engels has pointed out, it is impossible under such circumstances to avoid " pure improvization on the spur of the moment and reliance on memory only " altogether. Further, daily work is dependent on daily news and daily moods, and it cannot emancipate itself from them without running the danger of becoming dry and boring. How much, for instance, would the four big volumes of the Marx-Engels correspondence be worth without the hundred and one contradictions out of which the great general line of their ideas and struggles developed?

However, even without the great mass of material which is still awaiting its resurrection in the columns of *The New York Tribune*, the main lines of the European policy which they began to adopt with the Crimean War are quite clear to-day. To a certain extent the adoption of this policy may be said to have marked a turning-point in their activities. The authors of *The Communist Manifesto* and the editors of the *Neue Rheinische Zeitung* concentrated their main attention on Germany. The *Neue Rheinische Zeitung* enthusiastically supported the struggle of the Poles for national independence and then that of the Italians and the Hungarians, and in the upshot it demanded war against Russia as the strongest bulwark of European counter-revolution. But later this demand developed more and more into one for a world war against England because only after the breaking of England's world power would it be possible for the social revolution to emerge from the world of utopia into the world of reality.

This " Anglo-Russian slavery " was the basis on which Marx developed his European policy at the time of the Crimean War. He welcomed the war because it promised to break the European superiority which Tsarism had won as a result of the victory of the counter-revolution in Europe, but he was certainly not in agreement with the fashion in which the Western European

[1] *The Eastern Question*, see Bibliography.—Tr.

powers waged the war. Engels adopted the same attitude, and declared that the whole Crimean War was one colossal comedy of errors whereby it was almost impossible to say from one moment to the next who was the cheater and who the cheated. Despite the million lives and the millions of pounds the war cost, both Marx and Engels regarded it as a pseudo-war as far as France and, in particular, England were concerned.

They were certainly right in so far as neither the false Bonaparte nor Lord Palmerston, the English Foreign Secretary, had any intention of wounding the Russian bear in any vital spot. As soon as they felt convinced that Austria could hold the main forces of the Russian army in check on the Western frontiers they shifted the scene of hostilities to the Crimea, where they battered their heads against the fortress of Sebastopol, succeeding in capturing only half of it after a long-drawn-out campaign. In the end they had to satisfy themselves with this one rather dilapidated laurel wreath of victory and beg " defeated Russia " for permission to evacuate their troops without further interference.

It was easy enough to see why the false Bonaparte was unwilling to challenge the Tsar to a life-and-death struggle, but Palmerston's motives were less clear. The continental governments feared him as a revolutionary " firebrand ", whilst the continental Liberals admired him as a paragon of a constitutional-liberal Minister. Marx solved the riddle by laboriously examining the official Blue books and the Hansard reports for the first half of the century and also a number of diplomatic reports which had been deposited in the British Museum. His efforts were crowned by proof that from the time of Peter the Great down to the opening of the Crimean War there had been secret co-operation between the Cabinets in London and St. Petersburg, and that Palmerston in particular was a venal instrument of Tsarist policy. Marx's contentions did not pass without contradiction, and they are disputed down to this very day, particularly with regard to the rôle of Palmerston. There is no doubt that he judged Palmerston's unscrupulous business policy with its half-measures and its contradictions much more clearly than did either the European governments or the European Liberals, but it does not necessarily result from this that Palmerston had been bought by Russia. However, much more important than the question of whether Marx went too far in his statements or not is the fact that from this time onwards he considered it one of the most indispensable tasks of the working class to probe into the mysteries of international diplomacy in order to counter the diplomatic machinations of the governments or, where this proved impossible, to expose and denounce them.

Above all, he was interested in waging an irreconcilable struggle against the barbarous power which had its seat in St. Petersburg and its hand in every European Cabinet. He regarded Tsarism not merely as the most powerful bulwark of European reaction whose very passive existence was a permanent threat and danger, but also as the chief enemy whose constant intervention in the affairs of Western Europe hampered and disturbed the normal course of development and aimed at winning a geographical position which would give it dominance over Europe and thus make the emancipation of the European proletariat impossible. The great stress which he laid on this standpoint greatly influenced his policy from the Crimean War onwards, even more so than during the years of the revolution.

With this he was merely developing an idea he had first expressed in the *Neue Rheinische Zeitung*, but from now on both for him and for Engels the national struggles of those nations whose cause the paper had championed so enthusiastically began to recede very much into the background. Not that either of them ever ceased to demand the independence of Poland, Hungary and Italy as the right of these countries and in the interests of Germany and Europe in general, but as early as 1851 Engels gave his old favourites marching orders : " The Italians, Poles and Hungarians must be told plainly that when modern questions are under discussion they must hold their tongues." And a few months later he informed the Poles that they were done for as a nation and useful only as a means to an end until Russia itself had been drawn into the vortex of revolution. The Poles had never done anything in history but act with gallant and quarrelsome stupidity. Even against Russia they had never done anything of historical value, whilst Russia was at least progressive towards the East. With all its baseness and Slav filth Russian dominance was a civilizing agency for the lands around the Black Sea and the Caspian Sea, for Central Asia, Bashkiria and Tartary, and Russia had absorbed far more cultural and, in particular, industrial elements than Poland, whose nature was essentially chevaleresque and slothful. These observations are certainly strongly coloured by the passion with which the struggles amongst the exiles were being fought, and in later years Engels' verdict on Poland was much milder, whilst during the last years of his life he declared that Poland had saved European civilization on at least two occasions : by the rising in 1792–3 and by the revolution in 1830–1.

Referring to the belauded hero of the Italian Revolution,

Marx declared : " Mazzini knows only the towns with their liberal aristocracy and their enlightened citizens. The material needs of the Italian agricultural population—as exploited and as systematically emasculated and held in stupidity as the Irish— are naturally too low for the phraseological heaven of his cosmo- politan, neo-Catholic, ideological manifestos. However, it needs courage to inform the bourgeoisie and the aristocracy that the first step towards the independence of Italy is the complete emancipation of the peasants and the transformation of their semi-tenant system into free bourgeois property." And in an open letter of his friend Ernest Jones, the Chartist leader, Marx informed Kossuth, who was playing the lion in London, that the European revolutions were crusades of labour against capital and that they could not be depressed to the intellectual and social level of an obscure and semi-barbarous people like the Magyars, who were still stuck in the semi-civilization of the sixteenth century but actually imagined that they could com- mand the enlightenment of Germany and France and wheedle a cheer from the gullibility of England.

However, Marx developed furthest from the traditions of the *Neue Rheinische Zeitung* in that he not merely no longer concen- trated his chief attention on Germany, but actually put it almost completely out of the sphere of his political interests. It is true that at the time Germany played a very sorry rôle in European politics and could be regarded as little more than a Russian province, but although this more or less explains Marx's attitude, nevertheless both he and Engels were to pay dearly later on for the fact that for a number of years they completely lost touch with developments in Germany. Unfortunately, the contempt which both of them had always felt as Rhinelanders and citizens of an annexed province for the Prussian State was intensified in the days of Manteuffel-Westphalen to such an extent that it fitted ill with their usual keen appreciation of a political situation.

The one exception in those days in which Marx did pay attention to conditions in Prussia offers eloquent proof of this. It was towards the end of 1856, when Prussia came into conflict with Switzerland over the Neufchâtel affair. The incident caused Marx, as he wrote to Engels on the 2nd of December 1856, to supplement his " very insufficient knowledge of Prussian history ", and he summed up the result of his studies by declaring that world history had never produced anything more lousy. The passages which then follow and an article which appeared a few days later in *The People's Paper*, a Chartist organ, dealing with the same matter in still greater detail, reveal him as being very far from his usual high level in historical matters. Indeed, he sinks dangerously near to the low level of the scolding petty-bourgeois democracy, although it is one of his own particular services that he raised historical writing far above this level.

The Prussian State undoubtedly represented a disagreeable morsel for any human being to swallow, but for all that, it was not possible to make it palatable with caustic of mockery of the " Hohenzollerns by the Grace of God ", of the three repeatedly appearing " character masks " : the pietist, the non-commissioned officer and the buffoon, of Prussian history as " an unappetizing family chronicle ", compared with the " diabolical epic " of Austrian history, and similar observations which at the utmost explain the wherefore, but leave the why of the wherefore completely in the dark.

2. David Urquhart, G. J. Harney and Ernest Jones

Whilst he was contributing to *The New York Tribune* Marx also worked in the same way for the Urquhartist and Chartist papers.

David Urquhart was an English diplomat who, thanks to his detailed knowledge of the Russian plans for world dominance and to his ceaseless struggle against them, had rendered valuable services, whose value, however, he diminished by a fanatical hatred of Russia and an equally fanatical enthusiasm for everything Turkish. Marx was often dubbed an Urquhartite, but quite without justification, and in fact it would be truer to say that, like Engels, he was too much irritated by the foolish exaggerations of the man to appreciate fully his real services. The first mention of Urquhart in the Marx-Engels correspondence is in a letter written by the latter in March 1853 : " I am reading Urquhart's book at the moment. He contends that Palmerston is in the pay of Russia. The explanation is very simple, the fellow is a Keltic Scot with a Sassenach-Scottish training, by tendency a romanticist, by education a Free Trader. He went to Greece as a Philo-Hellenist and after skirmishing around with the Turks for three years he went to Turkey and was immediately seized with enthusiasm for the Turks. He is exuberantly Islamitic and declares that if he were not a Calvinist he could be only a Mohammedan." On the whole Engels found Urquhart's book merely highly diverting.

The point of contact between Marx and Urquhart was their common struggle against Palmerston. An article written by

Marx against Palmerston for *The New York Tribune* was reprinted in a Glasgow newspaper, where it attracted the attention of Urquhart. In February 1854 the two met and Urquhart received Marx with the compliment that a Turk might have written the article. However, Urquhart was very disappointed when Marx informed him that he was a "revolutionist", because one of Urquhart's crotchets was that the European revolutionaries were all conscious or unconscious tools of Tsarism used by the latter to embarrass the European governments. "The man is a complete monomaniac," Marx wrote to Engels after this meeting, adding that he agreed with him in nothing except with regard to Palmerston and even then the man had been of no assistance to him.

Naturally, these confidential remarks to Engels must not be taken too seriously. Despite all his critical reservations Marx publicly and repeatedly acknowledged Urquhart's services, and he made no secret of the fact that although he had not been convinced by Urquhart he had nevertheless been stimulated by him, and for this reason he did not hesitate to contribute occasionally to Urquhart's papers and in particular to *The Free Press* in London, and he also gave Urquhart permission to reprint and distribute a number of his articles in *The New York Tribune* in leaflet form. These Palmerston leaflets were distributed in fairly large editions, from fifteen to thirty thousand at a time, and they created a great sensation, but for the rest, Marx gained no greater material advantage from the Scot Urquhart than from the Yankee Dana.

Any really close connection between the two was made quite impossible by the fact that Marx supported Chartism, a movement which Urquhart doubly hated as a Free Trader and as an enemy of Russia, because he thought he could detect the rolling rouble in every revolutionary movement. Chartism never recovered from the heavy defeat it had suffered on the 10th of April 1848, but as long as its remnants struggled for life the movement was gallantly and loyally supported by both Marx and Engels, chiefly in the way of unpaid contributions to the papers published by George Julian Harney and Ernest Jones in the 'fifties. Harney published *The Red Republican*, *The Friend of the People* and *The Democratic Review* in rapid succession, whilst Jones published *The Notes to the People* and *The People's Paper*. *The People's Paper* enjoyed the longest life and was published regularly down to the year 1858.

Harney and Jones belonged to the revolutionary wing of the Chartist movement and amongst all the members of this group they were probably the least insular. They were also regarded as the leading spirits in the international association of the Fraternal Democrats. Harney was the son of a seaman and had grown up in proletarian surroundings. He had obtained his revolutionary knowledge on his own from the revolutionary literature of France, and Marat was his model. He was a year older than Marx, and whilst the latter was editing *The Rheinische Zeitung* he was on the editorial board of *The Northern Star*, the chief organ of the Chartists. Engels visited him in 1843, and Harney described him as " a slim young fellow, so youthful that he seemed almost a boy, but even then he spoke extraordinarily correct English ". In 1847 Harney made the acquaintance of Marx and joined his circle with enthusiasm.

He published an English translation of *The Communist Manifesto* in his *Red Republican*, together with an editorial footnote to the effect that it was the most revolutionary document ever published, and in his *Democratic Review* he published English translations of articles which had appeared in the *Neue Rheinische Zeitung* on the French Revolution, declaring that they represented " the real criticism " of French affairs. In the struggles of the emigration he returned to his old love and came into violent conflict with Ernest Jones and no less so with Marx and Engels. Soon afterwards he went to live on the isle of Jersey, and after a short stay there he left for the United States, where Engels visited him in 1888. Shortly after this visit Harney returned to England, where he died at a ripe old age and perhaps as the last living witness of a great historical period.

Ernest Jones was of Norman descent, but he was born and educated in Germany, where his father was military adviser to the Duke of Cumberland, the man who afterwards became King Ernst August of Hannover. This arch-reactionary rake, who was accused in the English press of every crime in the calendar except suicide, stood godfather to Ernest Jones at the font, but this patronage and the court connections of his parents made no impression on the lad. Even as a boy he showed a vigorous partizanship for the cause of liberty, and as a man he steadfastly resisted all the temptations which were placed in his path and all the attempts which were made to fetter his free spirit with chains of gold. When his family returned to England he was about twenty years old, and he began to study for the bar, to which he was later admitted. He sacrificed all the brilliant prospects which his own high talents and the aristocratic connections of his family opened up to him in order to devote himself to the Chartist cause, which he championed with such fiery zeal that in 1848 he was sentenced to two years' imprisonment. As an added indignity for his treachery to his own class he was treated in prison as a common criminal; but he came out of prison in 1850 as an incorrigible revolutionary, and from the summer of 1850 onwards he maintained close relations with Marx and Engels (he was about midway between their ages) for almost twenty years.

The friendship was certainly not completely cloudless and troubles such as had arisen with Freiligrath, with whom Jones shared poetic talents, and with Lassalle, on whom Marx's verdict was similar but incomparably more severe, occurred. In a letter written in 1855 Marx refers to him in the words : " With all the energy, persistence and activity for which one must give him credit, he spoils everything by his tub-thumping, his tactless snatching after pretexts for agitation and his constant impatience and desire to rush ahead of the times ". Later on there were even more serious differences between them, particularly when the Chartist agitation went more and more to seed and Ernest Jones began to flirt with bourgeois radicalism.

However, basically their friendship remained firm and loyal. During the last years of his life Ernest Jones lived in Manchester, where he died unexpectedly in 1869 whilst still in the prime of life. Engels hurriedly wrote the sad news to London : " Another one of the Old Guard gone home ! " And Marx answered : " The news naturally caused a deep shock to us all, for he was one of our few old friends." A few days later Engels reported that an enormous procession had followed the coffin to the cemetery, where another member of the Old Guard, Wilhelm Wolff, lay buried. He was really a loss, declared Engels. After all, his bourgeois phrases had been nothing but hypocrisy, and he had been the only educated Englishman amongst the politicians who had, at bottom, really been on their side.

3. Family and Friends

During these years Marx remained aloof from all political circles and led practically no social life. He had withdrawn completely into his study and he left it only to be with his family, which had been augmented by the birth of a daughter, Eleanor, in 1855.

Marx, like Engels, was a great lover of children, and when he left his studies for an hour or two it was to play with his children, who idolized him although, or perhaps just because, he never made any attempt to assert any paternal authority. They treated him as a playmate and called him " The Moor ", a nickname given to him on account of his jet-black hair and dark complexion. " Children must educate their parents," he used to say, and his children certainly took him in hand, for they strictly forbade him to do any work on Sundays, on which day he had to belong to them completely, and the Sunday outings into the country, during which the family stopped at wayside inns to drink ginger-beer and eat bread and cheese, were the infrequent rays of sunshine which penetrated through the heavy clouds which invariably hung over the house.

Their favourite outings were to Hampstead Heath, and Liebknecht has given us very charming descriptions of them. Hampstead Heath to-day is not quite the same as it was then, but from Jack Straw's Castle, at whose tables Marx often sat, there is still a magnificent view over the Heath with its picturesque panorama of hills and valleys and on Sundays its crowds of happy people. To the South lies the gigantic town with its vast mass of houses and its familiar landmarks, the dome of St. Paul's and the towers of Westminster, and beyond that in a far-off haze the pleasant uplands of Surrey. To the North the countryside is now covered with houses and to the West is the sister hill of Highgate, where Marx has found his last resting-place.

And then, like a flash of lightning, tragedy struck suddenly into this modest domestic happiness. On Good Friday 1855 Marx's only son, the nine-year-old Edgar, or " Musch " as he was affectionately called, died. The boy, who had already shown great talent, was the family favourite. " Such a sad and terrible loss that I can hardly describe how deeply it has affected me," wrote Freiligrath in a letter to Germany.

The letters in which Marx describes the sickness and death of his child to Engels are heartrending. On the 30th of March he wrote : " My wife had been ill for a week from sheer anxiety, worse than she has ever been before. I am also terribly upset. My heart is heavy and my head is in a whirl, but of course I have to keep up a brave front. Even in his illness the boy is still the same good-natured and independent character." And on the 6th of April he wrote again : " The poor little fellow is gone. He went to sleep (literally) in my arms to-day between five and six o'clock. I shall never forget how your friendship lightened our heavy burden in these terrible days. You can realize my sorrow at the death of my boy." And on the 12th of April he wrote : " The house seems empty and deserted since the boy died. He was its life and soul. It is impossible to describe how much we miss him all the time. I have suffered all sorts of misfortune, but now I know what real misfortune is. . . . In all the terrible anxiety and suffering I have gone through I have been sustained by the thought of you and your friendship, and by the hope that we have still something worth while to do together in the world.

It was a long time before the wound began to close. Answering a letter of sympathy from Lassalle on the 28th of July Marx wrote : " Baco[1] says that really great men have so many interests in nature and the world and so many things which occupy their attention that no loss can mean very much to them. I am afraid that I am not one of those great men. The death of my boy has shaken me deeply and I feel the loss as keenly as though it were still only yesterday, and my poor wife has completely broken down under the blow." On the 6th of October we find Freiligrath writing to Marx : " I am terribly sorry that your great loss still causes you such intense sorrow. Unfortunately there is nothing that a friend can do or advise. I understand and respect your sorrow, but you must try to master it in order to prevent it mastering you. That would be no treachery to the memory of your dear child.'

The death of Marx's son Edgar was the culmination of a series of illnesses which had befallen the family during the preceding few years. In the previous spring Marx himself had also fallen ill and in fact he was never quite well again. His chief complaint was liver trouble, which he believed he had inherited from his father, but there is no doubt that it was aggravated by the miserable housing conditions and the unhealthy neighbourhood in which the family lived. In the summer of 1854 a cholera epidemic was particularly virulent in the district as the result, it was said, of the fact that newly dug drains had been laid through the mass graves of the victims of the Great Plague in 1665. Marx's doctor urged him to leave the neighbourhood of Soho Square, whose atmosphere he had now breathed uninterruptedly for years. A new fatality in the family made it possible for them to do so. In the summer of 1855 Frau Marx went together with her three daughters to Trier to visit her mother who was lying seriously ill. She arrived just in time to close her mother's tired eyes after an illness lasting only eleven days.

The old lady did not leave very much, but a few hundred thaler fell to the share of Frau Marx, and it would appear that at about the same time she inherited a small sum from her Scottish relatives. In any case the money was sufficient to permit the family to move in the autumn of 1856 into a little house at 9, Grafton Terrace, Maitland Park, Haverstock Hill, near Marx's beloved Hampstead Heath. The rent of this house was thirty-six pounds a year. " Compared with the holes we have previously had to live in this is a really princely home," wrote Frau

[1] German student slang for "Bacon"

Marx to a friend, " and although everything we possess cost little more than forty pounds (much of it second-hand rubbish) I felt myself grand in our new parlour in the beginning. All the linen and the other reminders of former glory were rescued from the hands of ' uncle ', and once again I was able to count over my old Scottish damask napkins with delight. However, the idyll did not last very long, for soon one piece after the other found its way back to the ' pop-shop ' (as the children call the house at the sign of the mysterious three brass balls). Still, we were very happy for once in our agreeable bourgeois coziness." Unfortunately it proved to be a very short breathing space.

Death reaped its harvest amongst the friends of the family also. Daniels died in the autumn of 1855, Weerth in January 1856 in Haiti, and Konrad Schramm at the beginning of 1858 on the island of Jersey. Both Marx and Engels did their best to secure the publication of even short obituary notices in the press, but without success. They often complained that the ranks of the Old Guard were being rapidly thinned and that no new blood was forthcoming. Although in the beginning their " public isolation " had pleased them, and although their conviction of final victory was unshakable and sustained hem in their political struggle, a struggle they conducted as confidently as though they represented a European power, they were both too passionately political not to feel in the long run the lack of a party, for their supporters, as Marx himself admitted, did not represent a party, and amongst them there was no one whose ideas rose even approximately to the level of their own, with the one exception of the man towards whom they were never completely able to overcome their mistrust.

Liebknecht was a daily visitor to the Marx household in London, at least as long as it was in Dean Street, but in his own little room under the roof he had to contend vigorously with the material troubles of life, and the same was true of all the old companions of the Communist League days, of Lessner and of the joiner Lochner, of Eccarius and of " the penitent sinner " Schapper. The others were scattered : Dronke was a business man in Liverpool and later in Glasgow, Imandt was a Professor in Dundee, Schily was an advocate in Paris, where Reinhardt, Heine's secretary during the last years of the poet's life, was one of the inner circle.

However, even amongst the faithful political activity began to decline. Wilhelm Wolff, who lived in Manchester, managed to keep his head above water fairly successfully by giving lessons, and he remained " just the same ", as Frau Marx wrote of him, " just the same gallant, capable, plebeian nature ", but with the years he began to develop the crotchets of an old bachelor and his " chief struggles " took place with his landlady about such matters as tea, sugar and coal, and intellectually he ceased to mean very much to his old friends in exile. Freiligrath also remained a loyal friend, and after he had been given the manager-ship of the London agency of a Swiss bank in the summer of 1856 he was able to be of greater assistance to Marx than before, and in particular he was able to prevent any delay in cashing the drafts sent by *The New York Tribune*, which added to its other disadvantages frequent dilatoriness in paying. Freiligrath also remained true to his revolutionary convictions, but he drifted further and further away from the party struggle. Although he declared with conviction that there was no place in the world where a revolutionary could be buried with greater honour than in exile, the poet himself was not happy in exile. The home-sickness of his wife, whom he loved dearly, and the sight of his children lighting the candles of their Christmas tree again and again on foreign soil, caused the stream of his poetry to dry up. He suffered intensely from this, and it was a great consolation to him when his country gradually began to remember its famous poet again.

And then there was the long list of " the living dead ". It happened occasionally that Marx met a number of the com-panions of his early philosophic days : Eduard Meyen, who proved to be the same poisonous old toad, Faucher, who had become Cobden's secretary and thought himself cut out " to make history " in the Free Trade movement, and Edgar Bauer, who played the rôle of communist agitator, but to whom Marx invariably referred as " the clown ". Marx also met his old friend Bruno Bauer on numerous occasions when the latter came to London to visit his brother. As Bruno Bauer proved to be full of enthusiasm for " the primitive strength " of Russia, and regarded the proletariat as nothing but " a mob " to be held in check partly by violence, partly by cunning and partly by conceding it a few pence when unavoidable, there was naturally no basis for any agreement between them. Marx found that he had grown noticeably older, that his brow was larger and that he had developed the manner of a pedantic professor, but his conversations with the " cheerful old gentleman " were reported to Engels in detail.

However, even taking the more immediate past the list of " the living dead " was a long one and it grew longer every year. For instance, there were old friends in the Rhineland : Georg Jung, Heinrich Bürgers, Hermann Becker and others. Some of them, like Becker and later on the worthy Miquel, tried

to justify their attitude " scientifically ", declaring that before
the proletariat could even think of victory the bourgeoisie must
be completely victorious over the feudal Junkers. Becker
declared : " The material interests of the *canaille* will bore
their way through and through the decaying structure of Junkerdom turning it into dust, so that at the first breath of the world
spirit history will simply sweep the whole structure away and
proceed nonchalantly to the next item on the agenda."   It was
a very pretty theory, and no doubt it is still doing good service
to many artful dodgers to-day, but when Becker became Lord
Mayor of Cologne, and Miquel Prussian Minister of Finance,
they found themselves so attached to " the material interests of
the *canaille* " that they fought tooth and nail against any insolence
on the part of the world spirit and against all attempts " to
proceed nonchalantly to the next item on the agenda ".

For all that, however, it was a doubtful substitute for men
like Becker and Miquel when in the spring of 1856 a business
man named Gustav Lewy came from Düsseldorf to London and
offered Marx, so to speak, in apple-pie order and all complete,
an insurrection of the factory workers in Iserlohn, Solingen and
one or two other places.   Marx roundly condemned the dangerous
and useless folly of the venture and told Lewy to inform the
workers he represented, or pretended to represent, that they
should get into touch with him again later and do nothing whatever without first having obtained his agreement.   Unfortunately, Marx did not take up the same attitude to a second mission
with which Lewy declared he had been entrusted by the workers
of Düsseldorf, namely to warn Marx against Lassalle as an
unreliable fellow who after the successful conclusion of the
Hatzfeldt process was living under the shameful yoke of the
Countess as her kept man and intended to go to Berlin with her
to found a salon of intellectuals for her, who flung aside the
workers like worn-out gloves in order to go over to the bourgeoisie, and much more of the same sort.   One may reasonably
doubt that the workers in the Rhineland sent any such message
to Marx, for a few years later the same workers honoured Lassalle
with a solemn address in which they declared enthusiastically
that during the reign of white terror in the 'fifties his house had
been " a steadfast bulwark of fearless and vigorous assistance to
the party ".   It is far more likely that Lewy invented the message
to satisfy his bitterness against Lassalle because the latter had
refused to grant him a loan of 2,000 thaler, being prepared to
advance no more than 500 thaler.

If Marx had known this he would certainly have treated
Lewy with the greatest reserve, but in itself the report was calcu-

lated to awaken the strongest suspicion against Lassalle. Marx had kept up a correspondence with him, though their letters were not very frequent, and he had always found him a reliable friend, both personally and politically, and a loyal party comrade. Marx had even opposed the mistrust which had arisen against Lassalle in the old Communist League days amongst the workers in the Rhineland owing to his share in the Hatzfeldt affair, and hardly a year before, when Lassalle had written him a letter from Paris, he had answered it in a very friendly fashion : " I am naturally surprised to hear that you are so near London and yet are not thinking of coming over even for a few days. I hope you will reconsider the matter and see how short and cheap the journey from Paris to London really is. Unfortunately France is closed to me or I should certainly come over and give you a surprise in Paris."

It is therefore difficult to understand why Marx accepted Lewy's loose talk at its face value and immediately reported it to Engels in a letter dated the 5th of March 1856, adding : " This gives you only the sketchy details of the affair. The whole has made a definite impression on Freiligrath and myself, as much as I was in favour of Lassalle and as much as I dislike workers' gossip." He had told Lewy that it was impossible to come to any definite conclusion on the basis of a report from one side only, but in any case suspicion was useful. Lassalle should be watched, but for the moment any public scandal should be avoided. Engels agreed with this and added a number of observations which occasion less surprise coming from him, for he knew Lassalle less intimately than did Marx. It was a pity, declared Engels, because the fellow undoubtedly had great talent. He had always needed watching like the devil, but now he was going the pace a bit too fast. As a real Jew from the Slav frontier he had always been on the watch for a chance of exploiting anyone for his own private purposes under party pretexts.

Marx then broke off his correspondence with the man who wrote to him truthfully a few years later : " I am the only friend you have in Germany."

4. The Crisis of 1857

When Marx and Engels withdrew from the public squabbles of the exiles in the autumn of 1850 they declared : " A new revolution will be made possible only as the result of a new crisis, but it is just as certain as is the coming of the crisis itself." Since then they had watched carefully for any sign of a new crisis, and as the years passed they became more and more impatient. In his reminiscences Liebknecht tells us that on one or two occasions Marx wrongly prophesied the coming of the crisis and was chaffed by his friends in consequence, and when the crisis finally came in 1857 Marx did in fact tell Wilhelm Wolff through Engels that he would prove that in the normal course of things the crisis should have arrived two years earlier.

The crisis began in the United States, and it made a personal announcement of its arrival to Marx through the instrumentality of *The New York Tribune* which immediately put him on half-pay. This blow was a hard one because the old privations, even worse ones in fact, had since put in an appearance in the new home. In Grafton Terrace Marx was no longer able " to live from hand to mouth as in Dean Street ". He had no prospects, and his family expenditure was steadily increasing. On the 20th of January 1857 he wrote to Engels : " I really don't know what to do next ; in fact my situation is more desperate than it was five years ago." This letter came " like a bolt from the blue " for Engels, who immediately hurried to assist his friend, but complained that he had not been told about the situation earlier. He had, it appeared, just bought himself a horse for which his father had given him the money as a Christmas present : " I find it really too bad that I should be keeping a horse whilst you and your family are in such trouble in London." A few months later Engels was overjoyed when Dana approached Marx with a proposal that he should co-operate in the preparation of an encyclopædia. In particular Dana wanted contributions on military subjects and Engels was " tremendously pleased " because it was " just the very thing " to release Marx from his eternal money troubles. Marx should undertake as many articles as they were prepared to give him and then gradually organize an office.

Nothing came of the suggestion that an office should be organized, chiefly because it proved impossible to obtain sufficient suitable co-operators, and apart from this, the prospects turned out to be far less brilliant than Engels had hoped, because the rate of payment did not amount even to a penny a line and although much of the work was really no more than padding Engels was much too conscientious to churn it out easily. To judge from their correspondence about the work, the derogatory judgment which Engels later passed on the articles, some written by him and some by Marx, was not justified by any means : " Mere pot-boiling and nothing more. It doesn't matter if they are never read again." Gradually this work also came to an end, and it would appear in fact that the regular co-operation of the two friends in the preparation of the encyclopædia never got beyond the letter C.

From the very beginning their work was greatly hampered by the fact that in the summer of 1857 Engels developed glandular trouble and had to live at the seaside for a long time, and Marx's own situation was depressing enough. His liver trouble recurred so violently that he was able to do only the very minimum of the work which was necessary, and even that with tremendous difficulty. In July his wife was delivered of a stillborn child under circumstances which left a terrible impression on Marx and made the memory of the misfortune very painful. " You must have been hard hit when you write like that," the alarmed Engels wrote in reply, but Marx declared that it was better to postpone any discussion until they should meet, for he was unable to write about such things.

However, all personal troubles were forgotten when the crisis came to England in the autumn and then spread rapidly to the Continent. Writing to Engels on the 13th of November Marx declared : " Although I am in serious financial difficulties myself I have not felt so happy since 1849 as I do to-day in face of this eruption." In his reply the next day Engels feared only that things might develop too quickly : " I think it would be better that the ' improvement ' into the chronic crisis should take place before any second and decisive blow follows. Chronic pressure is necessary for a while in order to warm up the people. The proletariat would then fight better and with a better know-ledge of the situation and more unison, just as a cavalry attack has greater élan if the horses must first trot 500 paces before coming within charging distance of the enemy. I shouldn't like anything to happen too soon, before the whole of Europe is com-pletely involved, for then the struggle afterwards would be more severe, more tedious and more fluctuating. May or June would be almost too early. The masses must have become damned lethargic after the long period of prosperity. . . . By the way, I feel just as you do. Once the swindle collapsed in New York I no longer had any peace in Jersey and I now feel in splendid form in this general collapse. The bourgeois mud of the past few years had stuck to me to a certain extent after all, but now it will be washed off and I shall feel a new man. The crisis will do my health as much good as a seaside holiday, I can feel that already. In 1848 we thought our time was coming and in a certain sense it did, but this time it is really coming and every-thing is at stake."

Engels was wrong, of course; everything was by no means at stake. In its own way the crisis did have revolutionary effects, but they were not the ones expected by the two friends, although they certainly did not spend their time spinning utopian and optimistic hopes, but in carefully studying the course of the crisis from day to day, and on the 18th of December Marx wrote : " I am doing a tremendous amount of work, mostly until four in the morning. My work is a double one : (1) the drawing up of the fundamental principles of political economy (it is absolutely necessary for the general public to probe the matter to the bottom, and I must get the incubus off my chest), and (2) the present crisis. Apart from my articles for the *Tribune* I am doing no more than keeping a record, but that takes up a considerable amount of my time. I think that somewhere about next spring you and I should do a pamphlet together on the affair as a sort of reminder to the German public that we are still alive and still the same." Nothing came of this proposal because the crisis did not in fact stir up the masses, but at least this gave Marx sufficient leisure to carry out the theoretical part of his plan.

Ten days previously Frau Marx had written to the dying Konrad Schramm in Jersey : " Although we are feeling the American crisis in our own pockets, because Karl now writes only one article a week instead of two for the *Tribune*, which has got rid of all its European correspondents except Bayard Taylor and Karl, you can imagine how cheerful the Moor is. His working capacity and facility have returned together with a freshness and light-heartedness which he has not known for years, not since our great sorrow when we lost our little boy, a loss which will always make my heart sad. During the day Karl works for our daily bread and at night he works in order to finish his book on political economy. Now that such a book has become so necessary surely we shall be able to find some miserable publisher for it." Thanks to the efforts of Lassalle a publisher was found.

In April 1857 he had again written in the old friendly fashion, but expressing surprise that he had not heard from Marx for such a long time, though naturally, he did not know the reason. Although Engels advised him to do so Marx did not answer this letter. In December of the same year Lassalle wrote again, this time with a definite object in view. His cousin Max Friedländer had asked him to approach Marx to persuade the latter to contribute to *Die Presse* in Vienna, of which Friedländer was an editor. This time Marx did answer, refusing Friedländer's offer and declaring that although he was "anti-French" he was no less "anti-English" and certainly unwilling to write for Palmerston. Lassalle complained that although sentimentality was not one of his vices, he had been hurt by Marx's failure to reply to his April letter. Marx then replied "briefly and coldly" that he had not done so for reasons it was difficult to set down on paper. Although the letter was a short one, he did inform Lassalle that he wanted to publish a work on political economy.

In January 1858 a copy of Lassalle's *Heraclitus* arrived in London together with a few comments on the enthusiastic reception the book had received in educated circles in Berlin. In his December letter Lassalle had announced his intention of sending the book. The postage alone, two shillings, "assured the book a bad reception", but Marx's judgment on the contents was also unfavourable. The "enormous display" of scholarship did not impress him, and he observed that it was easy enough to pile quotation on quotation if one had time and money enough and could have all the necessary books sent into the house from the Bonn University library. Lassalle gave himself airs in all this philosophical tinsel like a fellow wearing an elegant suit for the first time. Marx's judgment was unfair to Lassalle's real scholarship, but his attitude can be explained by the fact that he disliked the book for the same reason that the professorial luminaries liked it, namely the display of so much old-fashioned wisdom in a young man who had the reputation of being a great revolutionary. In any case, the greater part of the book had been written more than ten years before it was published.

Lassalle had still not realized that something serious was wrong from Marx's "brief and cold" reply to his complaining letter and he misunderstood—obviously honestly, though Marx suspected that it was deliberate—the indication that a personal discussion was necessary between them and assumed that Marx had one or two things of no immediate and urgent importance to tell him when opportunity arose. He wrote again in February 1858 without revealing the least embarrassment and describing drastically the gushing ecstasy of the bourgeoisie in Berlin at the marriage of the Crown Prince of Prussia with an English princess. At the same time he offered Marx his services with a view to securing a publisher for the latter's work on political economy. Marx accepted his offer of assistance and by the end of March Lassalle had already drawn up the contract with his own publisher Franz Duncker and had secured even better conditions than Marx had asked. The latter wanted the work to appear in parts and was quite willing to waive any question of payment for the first parts, but Lassalle secured a payment of three Friedrichsdor [1] per printer's sheet [2] although the normal professorial honorarium was only two Friedrichsdor per printer's sheet. However, the publisher reserved the right to discontinue publication should the first parts not sell satisfactorily.

It was a good nine months before Marx was finished with the first bundle of manuscript because recurring attacks of liver trouble and further domestic worries hindered the work. At Christmas 1858 things looked " blacker and more hopeless than ever before " in the Marx household. On the 21st of January 1859 " the unfortunate manuscript " was finished, but there was " not a farthing " in the house to pay for postage and the registration fee. " I don't suppose anyone has ever written about ' money ' and suffered such a lack of it himself. Most of the authors who have written on the subject maintained the best of relations to the object of their investigations ", as Marx wrote to Engels requesting the latter to send him enough money for the postage.

5. The *Critique of Political Economy*

The plan to write an exhaustive work on political economy, one which would delve into the fundamental principles of the capitalist mode of production, was about fifteen years old before Marx actually began to put it into execution. He had considered the idea even before the March Revolution, and his reply to Proudhon was a sort of payment on account. When the struggles of the revolutionary years were past he immediately took up the idea again, and on the 2nd of April 1851 he wrote to Engels : " I am now so far that I have finished with all the drudgery of economics. After that I shall work on my book at home and pitch into some other science in the Museum. It is beginning to bore me. The science of political economy has made no fundamental progress since the days of Adam Smith and David Ricardo, although very much has been done since in the way of individual investigation, some of it super-delicate." Engels was delighted and answered : " I am glad that you are finally through with your political economy. The thing was really lasting too long," but as a man of experience he added : " So long as there is still a book in front of you which you consider important and which you have not read, you don't put pen to

[1] A former Prussian gold coin worth between sixteen and seventeen marks.—Tr.
[2] Sixteen pages.—Tr.

paper ". Engels was always inclined to believe that apart from all other difficulties, " the chief delay " was always to be found in his friend's " own scruples ".

These " scruples " were certainly never superficial and Engels never suggested that they were. Instead of finishing off his work in 1851 Marx started all over again, and in his introduction to the first part he explains why : " The tremendous amount of material stored up in the British Museum suitable for a history of political economy, the favourable vantage point which London in particular offers for an examination of bourgeois society, and finally the new stage of development which appeared to have been opened up for bourgeois society by the discovery of the Australian and Californian gold fields." He also points out that his eight years of work for *The New York Tribune* had caused continual interruptions in his studies, and he might also have added that this work led him back to some extent into the political struggle, which was always of first-class importance for him. And finally, it was the prospect of a resuscitation of the revolutionary working-class movement which caused him to stick to his writing desk and put down in black and white the things which had been occupying his mind ceaselessly for many years.

His correspondence with Engels offers eloquent proof of this, for the discussion of economic problems never ceases and occasionally it develops into regular treatises which one might also describe as " super-delicate ". A few occasional passages show us how the exchange of ideas between the two friends took place. On one occasion Engels writes of his well-known laziness *en fait de théorie*, a laziness against which his better self growled protestingly, but not loudly enough to make him go to the bottom of things, and on another occasion Marx sighs : " If people only knew how little I know about all this business ! " This was called forth by the remark of a manufacturer that Marx must have been a manufacturer himself at some time or the other.

If one deducts the humorous exaggeration what remains indicates that Engels was better acquainted with the inner mechanism of capitalist society than was Marx, whilst the latter with his keen powers of deduction was better able to follow its laws of development. When Marx sketched the plan for the first part of his work to Engels, the latter replied : " Your sketch is really very abstract as I suppose was inevitable in view of its brevity. I had a deal of trouble in finding the dialectical transitions, for all abstract thought has become very unusual for me now." On the other hand, Marx often found it difficult to understand the answers Engels gave him to his questions concerning the way in which manufacturers and merchants reckoned that part of their income which they used for themselves, or concerning the wear and tear of machinery, or the method of reckoning advanced circulating capital. Marx also complained that in the science of political economy matters of practical interest and matters of theoretical necessity were far apart.

Marx really began to give his work its final form only in the years 1857/58, and this can be seen from the fact that the plan changed almost unnoticeably in his hands. In April 1858 he still intended to deal with " capital in general " in the first part, but although this part grew twice and thrice as long as he had originally planned, it contained nothing about capital, but two chapters on commodities and money. The advantage of this would be that criticism would not be able to limit itself to mere tendencious abuse, thought Marx, but he overlooked the fact that he thereby offered it the effective weapon of remaining silent altogether.

In the introduction he sketches the course of his scientific development, and the famous passage in which he sums up the theory of historical materialism is worthy of quotation here : " My examination (of the Hegelian philosophy of law) brought me to the conclusion that neither legal relations nor State forms can be understood in themselves or from the so-called general development of the human intellect, but that they have their roots in the material conditions of life whose totality Hegel, following the example of the English and French scholars of the eighteenth century, summed up in the term ' bourgeois society ', and that the anatomy of bourgeois society must be sought in political economy. . . . The general results which I achieved, and which once achieved formed the guiding line of my subsequent studies, can be summed up as follows : In social production human beings enter into definite and necessary relations to each other quite independent of their will, productive relations which are in accordance with a definite stage of the development of the material productive forces. The totality of these productive relations forms the economic structure of society, the material basis on which the legal and political superstructure rests, and definite forms of social consciousness correspond to it. The mode of production of material life determines the social, political and intellectual process of life in general. It is not the consciousness of human beings which determines their being, but on the contrary, it is their social being which determines their consciousness. At a certain stage of their development the material productive forces of society come into contradiction with the existing productive relations or with the existing property relations, which is only a legal expression for the same thing, within which they have previously moved. These relations then change from forms of development of the productive forces into fetters on these productive forces and an epoch of social revolution begins. With this change in the economic basis of society the whole enormous superstructure also changes more or less rapidly. When observing such changes one must always differentiate between the material changes in the economic conditions of production, which must be registered with scientific accuracy, and the legal, political, religious, artistic and philosophic forms, in short, the ideological forms in which human beings become aware of this comflict and fight it out. Just as one cannot judge the individual by what he thinks of himself, so also one cannot judge such an epoch of change from its own consciousness, but one must rather explain this consciousness from the contradictions of material life, from the existing conflict between the social productive forces and the conditions of production. No form of society declines before it has developed all the forces of production in accordance with its own stage of development, and new and higher productive relations never take the place of the old before the material conditions for their existence have been developed within the shell of the old society itself. Therefore humanity never sets itself tasks but those it is in a position to perform, for if one examines the matter more closely one will invariably find that a task never presents itself for performance unless the material conditions for such performance are already developed or at least in process of development. Speaking generally, the Asiatic, the classic, the feudal and the modern bourgeois modes of production can be termed progressive epochs of the economic social forms. Bourgeois productive relations represent the final antagonistic form of the process of social production, not antagonistic in the sense of individual antagonism, but an antagonism which develops from the social conditions of life of the individuals. However, the productive forces developing within the framework of bourgeois society create at the same time the material conditions for the liquidation of this antagonism. With this form of society therefore the preliminary history of human society ends."

It was in this work, which he entitled *A Critique of Political Economy*, that Marx took a decisive step beyond the limits of bourgeois political economy as it had been developed in particular by Adam Smith and David Ricardo. Bourgeois political economy culminated in the definition of the value of a commodity as the amount of labour-time necessary to produce it, but as it regarded the bourgeois mode of production as the eternal and natural form of social production, it assumed the creation of value to be a natural characteristic of human labour-power as it is given in the individual and concrete labour-power of the individual, and on this assumption it involved itself in a series of contradictions which it was unable to solve. Marx, on the other hand, did not regard the bourgeois mode of production as the eternal and natural form of social production, but merely as a definite historical form of social production succeeding a whole series of previous forms. From this standpoint he subjected the value-producing characteristic of labour-power to a thorough examination. He examined what kind of labour-power produces value and why and how, and why value is nothing but embodied labour-power of this kind.

In this way he arrived at the " vital point " on which the understanding of political economy depends : the double character of labour-power in bourgeois society. Individual concrete labour-power creates use-value, whilst undifferentiated social labour-power creates exchange-value. In so far as labour-power creates use-value it is common to all social forms. As a useful activity for the appropriation of natural resources in one form or the other the use of labour-power is a natural condition of human existence, a condition of the metabolism existing between man and nature quite independent of all social forms. Labour-power requires material on which it can work as the preliminary condition for working, and it is therefore not the only source of that which it produces, namely material wealth. No matter what may be the relation between labour-power and its raw material in the various use-values produced, the use-value always contains a natural substratum.

Exchange-value is different. It contains no natural element, and labour-power is its only source and therefore the only source of all wealth which consists of exchange-values. Considered as an exchange-value one use-value is worth exactly the same as any other, providing that it is present in the correct proportion. " The exchange-value of a palace can be expressed in terms of a certain number of tins of blacking. On the other hand, the London manufacturers of blacking have expressed the exchange-value of multiplied tins of blacking in palaces." Because commodities exchange with each other irrespective of their natural conditions of existence and irrespective of the needs they are intended to satisfy, they represent the same unit ; despite their varied appearance they are the results of uniform, undifferentiated labour-power, " and it is as much a matter of indifference to this labour-power whether it appears in the form of gold, iron, wheat or silk as it is to oxygen whether it is present in iron rust, the atmosphere, the juice of the grape or the blood of a human being ".

The variety of use-values results from the variety of the labour-power producing them, but labour-power producing exchange-values is indifferent to the particular material of the use-value produced and indifferent to the particular form of the labour-power itself. It is uniform, undifferentiated, abstract general labour, and it differs no longer in kind, but merely in quantity, merely in the various amounts which it incorporates in exchange-values of varying volume. The various quantities of abstract general labour find their measure only in time, which itself is measured by the ordinary, conventional periods of hours, days, weeks, etc. Labour-time is the living existence of labour irrespective of its form, its content or its individuality. As exchange-values all commodities are nothing but definite quantities of incorporated labour-time. The labour-time incorporated in use-values is therefore the substance which makes them into exchange-values and commodities, and at the same time the measure of the particular volume of value contained in them.

This double character is a social form of labour which is peculiar to commodity production. Under primitive communism, a social form which can be found on the threshold of the history of all modern peoples, individual labour was directly embodied in the social organism. In the servitude and the deliveries in kind which prevailed in the Middle Ages the particularity of labour and not its generality formed the social bond. In the rural-patriarchal family in which the women spun and the men weaved for the exclusive use of the family, yarn and linen were social products, and spinning and weaving represented social labour within the limits of the family. The family bond with its natural division of labour gave the product of labour-power its special character. Yarn and linen did not exchange as uniformly valid expressions of the same general labour-time. Only under commodity production does individual labour become social labour in that it takes on the form of its immediate antithesis, the form of abstract generality.

Now a commodity is the direct union of use-value and exchange-value, and at the same time it is a commodity only in relation to other commodities. The real relation of commodities to each other is in the process of exchange. In this process, into which individuals independent of each other enter, the commodity represents at the same time both use-value and exchange-value, particular labour which satisfies particular needs and general labour exchangeable against any other equal volume of general labour. The process of commodity exchange must unfold and liquidate the contradiction resulting from the fact that individual labour-power embodied in a particular commodity must have the direct general character.

As exchange-value each separate commodity becomes a measure of the value of all other commodities. On the other hand, each individual commodity, in which all other commodities measure their value, becomes the adequate existence of exchange-value, and thus exchange-value becomes a special and exclusive commodity which directly embodies the general labour-time of money by the transformation of all other commodities into it. Thus, in one commodity the contradiction which a commodity as such contains is resolved : a particular use-value, but also a general equivalent, and therefore use-value in general, general use-value. This one commodity is—money.

The exchange-value of commodities crystallizes itself in money as a particular commodity. This money crystallization is a necessary product of the process of exchange, in which varied products of labour-power are actually made uniform with each other and therefore actually turned into commodities. It developed by instinct and along historical lines. Simple exchange, the primitive form of the exchange process, represented the beginning development of use-values into commodities rather than the development of commodities into money. The more exchange-value develops, the more use-values develop into commodities, the more, that is to say, exchange-value develops an independent form and is no longer bound down to the particular use-value, the greater becomes the necessity for the development of money. At first one particular commodity plays the rôle of money, or perhaps a number of commodities of general use-value such as cattle, grain and slaves. From time to time various more or less unsuitable commodities have performed the functions of money. In the end these functions went over to the precious metals because they possessed the necessary material qualities of the particular commodity in which the money nature of all commodities must crystallize itself, in so far as such qualities proceed directly from the nature of exchange-value itself, namely, the durability of its use-value, its infinite divisibility, the uniform nature of its parts and the uniformity of all examples of such a commodity.

Amongst the precious metals it was gold which became more and more the exclusive money-commodity. It serves as the measure of values and the measure of prices and as the means of circulation for all other commodities. Thanks to this *salto mortale* of the commodity into gold the particular labour-power embodied in it is retained as abstract general, as social labour. Should the commodity fail to accomplish this transubstantiation then it would miss the aim of its existence not only as a commodity, but also as a product, for it is a commodity only because it has no use-value for its owner.

Thus Marx showed how and why the commodity, by virtue of its inner value character, and commodity exchange must necessarily produce the antithesis of commodity and money. In money, which presents itself as a natural thing with particular characteristics, he recognized a social productive relation and he explained the confused explanations of money given by the modern bourgeois economists by pointing out that what they thought to have just nailed down as a thing suddenly appeared to them as a social relation, and what they had hardly nailed down as a social relation suddenly mocked at them as a thing.

In the beginning the flood of light generated by this critical examination dazzled even the friends of the author more than it enlightened them. Liebknecht declared that he had never been so much disappointed by a work before, and Miquel found " very little actually new " in it. Lassalle praised the form in which the work had been cast and placed it without envy above his own *Heraclitus*, but when Marx found that Lassalle's " phrases " gave rise to the suspicion that the latter understood very little of economic matters he was on the right track for once, for it was not long before Lassalle showed that he had not understood the " vital point " of the book, the difference between labour-power producing use-values and labour-power producing exchange-values.

If that was the reception Marx's work had at the hands of those who might have been expected to understand it, what could be expected of others ? In 1885 Engels declared that Marx had put forward the first embracing theory of money and that his theory had been silently adopted, but seven years later the *Handwörterbuch der Staatswissenschaften* (" Encyclopædia of Political Economy "), the standard work on bourgeois political economy, published a fifty-column dissertation on money reviving all the old exploded theories, failing even to mention Marx and concluding by declaring the money riddle insoluble.

Indeed, how should a world which had enthroned money as its God aspire to understand it ?

CHAPTER TEN: DYNASTIC CHANGES

1. The Italian War

THE crisis of 1857 did not develop into a proletarian revolution as Marx and Engels had hoped, but it was certainly not without revolutionary effects even although they took the form of dynastic changes only. The United Kingdom of Italy arose and a little later the United German Empire, whilst the old French Empire disappeared.

This course of events resulted from the double fact that the bourgeoisie never fights its own revolutionary battles and that since the revolution of 1848 it had grown unwilling to let the proletariat fight them for it. The trouble was that in this revolution, and in particular in the June struggles in Paris, the proletariat had abandoned its old custom of letting itself be used merely as cannon-fodder for the bourgeoisie and had demanded a share of the fruits of the victories which were won with its own blood and heroism.

As a result even in the revolutionary years the cunning idea occurred to the bourgeoisie of persuading some power other than the increasingly mistrustful and unreliable proletariat to snatch its chestnuts out of the fire. This was particularly the case in Germany and in Italy, that is to say in those countries where for the moment the chief task presented by historical development was the creation of a national State such as capitalist forces of production require for their fullest development. The obvious solution of the problem was to offer one of the princelings the hegemony over the whole country in return for his promise to grant the bourgeoisie the elbow room it needed for the full development of capitalist exploitation. However, this plan compelled the bourgeoisie to abandon its own political ideals and content itself with the satisfaction of its naked profit interests, for by calling in the aid of the princes it subordinated itself to princely domination.

Even in the revolutionary years therefore, the bourgeoisie began to flirt with the princely States, and with the most reactionary ones at that. In Italy it was the Kingdom of Sardinia,

that " military-Jesuit " Statelet in which, in the bitter words of
the German poet, " both priest and mercenary sucked the people
dry ", and in Germany it was the Kingdom of Prussia, which was
under the thumb of obscurantist East Elbian Junkerdom.   At
first the bourgeoisie was unsuccessful both in Italy and in
Germany.   King Albert of Sardinia did consent to 'make himself
" the sword of Italy ", it is true, but on the battlefield he was
defeated by the Austrian army and died a fugitive on foreign
soil.   And in Prussia Frederick William IV rejected the German
Kaiser Crown offered him by the German bourgeoisie, for he
considered it a purely illusory honour, a crown baked of mud and
clay.   Instead he preferred a little body-snatching at the expense
of the revolution, though he failed woefully in this, but less on
account of the Austrian sword than the Austrian whip in Olmütz.

However, that industrial .prosperity which had sapped the
strength of the revolution in 1848 became a powerful lever for
the furtherance of bourgeois interests in Italy and Germany, and
in both these countries it made national unity more urgent and
necessary than ever.   In 1857 the crisis broke out and reminded
the bourgeoisie of the evanescence of all capitalist glory, but at
last things began to move, first in Italy.   Not that this must be
taken as an indication that capitalist development had proceeded
further in Italy than in Germany.   On the contrary, large-scale
industry did not exist at all in Italy, and therefore the antagonism
between bourgeoisie and proletariat had not yet developed to
the extent of awakening mutual distrust.   No less important was
the fact that Italy's disunity was the result of foreign dominance,
and that it was the common aim of all classes of society to overthrow this dominance.   Austria ruled directly over Lombardy
and the province of Venice and indirectly over Central Italy,
whose little courts took their orders from the Vienna Hofburg.
A struggle against the foreign yoke had been proceeding in Italy
for twenty years without a break, and it had led to brutal measures
of repression on the one hand and desperate reprisals on the other.
The Italy stiletto was the inevitable answer to the Austrian
scourge.

However, all the terrorism, the insurrections and the conspiracies proved useless against the superior power of the
Habsburgs, and even in the revolutionary years the Italian insurrections all failed.   The promise that Italy should win its own
independence (*Italia fara da se*) proved to be a delusion.   Italy
needed outside assistance in order to throw off the Austrian yoke,
and therefore it turned to its sister nation France.   The maintenance of national disunity in Italy and Germany was a traditional
principle of French foreign policy, but the adventurer who sat

on the throne of France was prepared to bargain about the matter. The Second Empire was a farce so long as it was confined within the frontiers drawn for France by the European Powers after the overthrow of the First Empire. France needed territorial conquests, but the false Bonaparte was unable to make them as the real one had done. The false Bonaparte had to content himself with borrowing the so-called " nationality principle " from his alleged uncle and presenting himself in the rôle of the Messiah of the oppressed nations, naturally always on condition that his friendly services were generously rewarded in the way of land and population.

At the same time his whole situation was such that he could not take many risks. He was not in a position to wage a European war, not to speak of a revolutionary war, and the utmost he could do was belabour the scapegoat of Europe with the condescending permission of the other powers. At the beginning of the 'fifties the scapegoat had been Russia, but by the end of them it was Austria. The shameful régime maintained by the Austrian intruders in Italy had developed into a European scandal, whilst at the same time the House of Habsburg had quarrelled with its old partners of the Holy Alliance, with Prussia on account of Olmütz and with Russia on account of the Crimean War. In fact, Bonaparte was quite certain of Russian assistance in case he should attack Austria.

The internal situation of France urgently demanded some foreign political action in order to bolster up Bonapartist prestige. The commercial crisis of 1857 had paralysed French industry, and thanks to the manœuvres with which the government had tried to prevent its outbreak the evil had become chronic, and French trade had lain stagnant for years. As a result both the bourgeoisie and the proletariat were becoming rebellious, whilst even the peasantry, the chief prop of the *coup d'état* régime, were beginning to grumble. The big drop in grain prices which took place from 1857 to 1859 caused the peasants to declare that owing to the low prices they obtained for their produce and the heavy burdens on agriculture the tilling of the soil was rapidly becoming impossible.

In this situation Bonaparte was zealously courted by Cavour, the leading Minister of the Kingdom of Sardinia. This man had taken up the tradition of King Albert, but he pursued his policy with incomparably greater skill, but still, with only the impotent methods of diplomacy at his disposal he made little progress, because the brooding and undecided character of Bonaparte made it difficult for him to take any rapid decision. However, the Italian Party of Action took a hand in the game and as a result

the champion of freedom was compelled to make up his mind
quickly. On the 14th of January 1858 Orsini and his accom-
plices flung their bombs at the imperial carriage, which was hit
by no less than 76 fragments. The occupants of the carriage were
not injured, but as is usually the way with such characters the
false Bonaparte answered the attempt by establishing a reign of
terror. However, the very fury with which he did so indicated
that his régime, which had now lasted seven years, was in reality
based on a very unstable foundation, whilst a letter which he
received from Orsini during the latter's imprisonment gave him
a new shock of fear. " Remember ", declared Orsini, " that the
peace of Europe and your own peace of mind will remain purely
chimerical so long as Italy has not achieved its independence."
Orsini is said to have spoken still more plainly in a second letter.
During the erratic wanderings of his adventurous life Bonaparte
had once fallen in with Italian conspirators and he was well aware
that their vengeance was not a thing to be trifled with.

In the summer of 1858 therefore he invited Cavour to meet
him in Plombières, where the two arranged a little war on Austria.
Sardinia was to receive Lombardy and the province of Venice
and to constitute itself the Kingdom of Upper Italy, and in return
it was to grant Savoy and Nice to France. It was a diplomatic
bargain which fundamentally had little to do with the freedom
and independence of Italy, and no mention was made of Central
and Southern Italy, though no doubt both parties had their own
ideas on the subject. Bonaparte was unwilling to abandon the
traditional French foreign policy and further the unification of
Italy. On the contrary, he wished to maintain the temporal
power of the Papacy and create a League of Italian dynasties
which could be played off against each other, thus securing French
hegemony, and in addition he harboured the idea of creating a
Kingdom of Central Italy for his cousin Jerome. Cavour, on the
other hand, reckoned with the development of a powerful national
movement which would permit him to hold all dynastic and
particularist tendencies in check once Upper Italy had been
forged into a strong State.

On New Year's Day, 1859, Bonaparte received the Austrian
Ambassador in audience and informed him of the French intentions, whilst a few days later the King of Sardinia announced to
the world that he was not deaf to the heart-rending appeals
of the Italian people. These threats were perfectly understood
in Vienna. The outbreak of hostilities approached rapidly,
and the Austrian government was clumsy enough to let
itself be manœuvred into the rôle of attacker. Half-bankrupt,
attacked by France and threatened by Russia, it was in a difficult

position and the lukewarm friendship of the English .Tories was not of very much assistance, so it therefore sought to win the support of the German League. The League was not bound by any agreement to defend the non-German possessions of any of its members, but the Austrian government hoped to inveigle it into doing so with the politico-military slogan that the Rhine must be defended along the Po, or in other words, it tried to persuade the League that the maintenance of Austrian oppression in Italy was a matter of vital national importance for Germany.

Since the outbreak of the crisis in 1857 a national movement had also developed in Germany, but it was different from the national movement in Italy and the difference was not to its credit. The German national movement was not goaded on by the irritation of foreign domination, and in addition, since 1848 the German bourgeoisie had harboured a lively horror of the proletariat although the latter had not really proved so dangerous after all. Nevertheless, the Paris June days represented an awful warning. Up to 1848 France had been the ideal of the German bourgeoisie, but after that it had turned to England for stimulus, a country in which the bourgeoisie and the proletariat seemed to be able to compose their differences peaceably. The marriage of the Prussian Crown Prince to an English princess had caused an ecstasy of delight amongst all good German bourgeois, and when the mentally defective King of Prussia handed over the reins of government to his brother in the autumn of 1858 and the latter appointed a tame liberal Ministry, for reasons which were anything but liberal, " bovine coronation rejoicings ", as Lassalle called them bitterly, burst out. In order not to irritate the Prince Regent the noble bourgeoisie disavowed its own heroes of 1848, and instead of protesting when the new Ministry left things practically as they were before, it adopted the famous slogan, " Gently does it ! " for fear of arousing the displeasure of the new ruler who might then sweep away the " New Era ", which existed only at his whim like a shadow on a wall.

As the clouds of war gathered the national wave began to rise higher in Germany. The way in which Cavour was working for Italian unity was very tempting to the German bourgeoisie, which had long ago chosen Prussia to play the rôle of Sardinia, but the attack of Germany's hereditary enemy France on Germany's ally Austria caused misgivings in the breast of the German bourgeoisie and awakened unpleasant memories. Perhaps the false Bonaparte intended to revive the traditions of the real one ? Perhaps the days of Austerlitz and Jena would return and the chains of foreign domination again rattle in Germany ? The *journaille* in the pay of the Austrian government scribbled for all they were worth to convince the German bourgeoisie of the reality of its fears, and at the same time they drew an idyllic picture of a " Central European Great Power " under the leadership of Austria and embracing the German League, Hungary, the Slav and Roumanian Danubian lands, Alsace-Lorraine, Holland and heaven knows what else. On the other hand, the false Bonaparte naturally let loose his ink-slingers also and they swore by all the Gods that their paymaster harboured no such evil thought as a desire to seize the banks of the Rhine, and that his attack on Austria was prompted solely by the most edifying considerations, to wit, the interests of European civilization.

Naturally, the good German Philistine found it very difficult to form an opinion of his own in this welter of contradictory propaganda, but gradually he began to lend a more willing ear to the voice of the Habsburg charmer to the detriment of the latter's Bonapartist rival. The arguments of the Habsburgers flattered his own pot-valiant patriotism whilst at the same time it was asking rather much of anyone to believe in the civilizing mission of the false Bonaparte. For all that, however, the situation was so complicated that even men used to dealing with political intricacies, and revolutionaries at that, men who agreed absolutely on all fundamental questions, were unable to agree as to the practical policy which Germany should pursue towards the Italian war.

2. The Dispute with Lassalle

In agreement with Marx, Engels entered the arena first with his pamphlet, *Po and Rhine*, and its publication was arranged by Lassalle through Franz Duncker. Engels' aim was to refute the Habsburg argument that the Rhine must be defended on the Po. He pointed out that Germany needed not a hand's-breadth of Italian soil in order to defend itself and declared that if military considerations were to be the decisive factors then France had a much greater claim to the banks of the Rhine than Germany had to the Po. Considered purely from the military point of view Austrian domination in Upper Italy might be indispensable for Germany, but politically it was highly deleterious because the monstrous dragooning of the Italian patriots by the Austrian oppressors engendered fanatical hostility and hatred also against Germany throughout the whole of Italy.

However, he declared, the question of the possession of

Lombardy was a matter between Germany and Italy, and not between Louis Bonaparte and Austria. As far as a third party like Bonaparte was concerned, who was interfering purely in his own interests and anti-German interests at that, Germany's only attitude could be to keep its hold on the province and to yield only under compulsion, to maintain its military position and to evacuate it only when it became untenable. With regard to the Bonapartist threat therefore the Habsburg slogan was quite justified. If Louis Bonaparte made the Po his excuse then the Rhine was certainly his real aim, for only the capture of the Rhine frontier could offer any basis for the consolidation of the *coup d'état* régime in France. It was a classic example of the old proverb in practical application : Bonaparte belaboured the sack but meant the donkey. Italy might be tempted to play the rôle of the sack, but that was no reason whatever why Germany should take the rôle of the donkey. If in the last resort it was merely a question of who should possess the left bank of the Rhine, then Germany could not dream of abandoning the Po and thus one of its strongest, if not its strongest, positions without a fight. On the eve of war just as in warfare itself one occupied every possible position from which one could threaten the enemy or defend oneself, without first of all indulging in moral reflections as to whether such action could be satisfactorily reconciled with eternal justice and the principle of nationality. In a tight corner one defended oneself with any weapons that came to hand.

Marx was completely in agreement with this standpoint, and after he had read the manuscript of the pamphlet he wrote to the author : " Extraordinarily capable : also the political side of the matter, which was damned difficult. The pamphlet will be a great success." Lassalle, on the other hand, declared that he was quite unable to understand Engels' attitude, and almost immediately afterwards he issued a pamphlet of his own on the subject entitled, *The Italian War and Prussia's Task*, which was also published by Duncker. Lassalle proceeded from totally different premises, and in consequence he came to quite different conclusions, " monstrously false " ones according to Marx.

Lassalle declared that the national movement which arose in Germany under the influence of the war threat was " pure hatred of France and nothing else, sheer anti-Gallicism (Napoleon as the pretext, but the real reason a hatred of French revolutionary development) ". In his eyes a Franco-German war in which the two greatest Continental peoples would rend each other for mere nationalist delusions, a really popular war against France not prompted by any vital national interest, but nourished by pathologically irritated nationalism, high-flown patriotism and childish anti-Gallicism, was a tremendous danger to European culture and to all really national and revolutionary interests, and it would represent the most monstrous and incalculable victory of the reactionary principle since March 1848. In his opinion therefore it was the vital task of democracy to oppose such a war with all possible means.

He pointed out in great detail that the Italian war represented no serious threat to Germany, which was deeply interested in a successful culmination of the Italian struggle for national unity. A good cause did not become a bad one merely because a bad man took it up. Bonaparte might hope to win a little popularity through the Italian war, but in that case it was the task of the democracy to see to it that he was unsuccessful, and thus make what he undertook in his own interests useless as a means of furthering those interests. How could one now oppose what one had previously desired just because of Napoleon? On the one side there was a bad man and a good cause, and on the other side there was a bad cause and—" And the man?" Lassalle reminded his readers of Blum's murder, of Olmütz, Holstein and Bronzell, of all the crimes which had been committed against Germany not by Bonapartist, but by Habsburg despotism. The German people, he declared, were not in the least interested in the maintenance of Austria's strength, on the contrary the complete destruction of Austria was the preliminary condition of German unity. On the day Italy and Hungary won their independence the twelve million Austro-Germans would be given back to the German people. Only then would they be able to feel themselves as Germans and only then would German unity be possible.

Lassalle analysed Bonaparte's position and pointed out that this much overrated weakling was not in a position to think seriously of foreign conquests even in Italy, much less then in Germany. And even supposing that the lunatic really harboured fantastic dreams of conquest, was that any reason for such a display of indecent fear on Germany's part? He mocked at the patriotic poltroons who regarded Jena as the normal measure of Germany's national strength and were driven desperate by their own fear. He derided the brave spirits who for fear of a highly improbable attack by France clamoured for an attack by Germany, and pointed out that it was perfectly obvious that if Germany were called upon to repel a French invasion it would be able to muster much greater strength than if it attacked France, a proceeding which would cause the French to rally round Bonaparte and would only strengthen his position.

War against France should be waged only if Bonaparte attempted to keep the booty won from Austria for himself or even if he did no more than attempt to create a Central Italian Kingdom for his cousin Jerome. Should neither of these contingencies arise and if nevertheless the Prussian government showed a tendency to incite the people into a war against France, then democracy must do everything possible to counter such incitement. However, neutrality was not sufficient, the historic task of Prussia in the interests of the German nation was to send its army against Denmark with the announcement : " If Bonaparte insists on altering the map of Europe in the South in the name of the principle of nationality, then we shall do the same thing in the North. If Bonaparte liberates Italy we shall liberate Sleswig-Holstein." Should Prussia continue to do nothing it would prove thereby that the German monarchy was no longer capable of a great national deed.

As a result of this programme Lassalle was extolled as a sort of national prophet who foresaw the later policy of Bismarck, but in reality the dynastic war of conquest which Bismarck waged in 1864 to annex Sleswig-Holstein had nothing in common with the revolutionary national war which Lassalle urged in 1859 for the liberation of Sleswig-Holstein. Lassalle was very well aware that the Prince Regent would not take over the task sketched out for him, and that alone gave him the right to make a proposal which coincided with Germany's national interests even if it immediately turned into a reproach against the government. He was justified in drawing the excited masses away from the wrong path by showing them the right one.

However, apart from the arguments he put forward in his pamphlet, he was moved by " ulterior motives ", as he explained in his letters to Marx and Engels. He knew that the Prince Regent was about to enter the Italian war on the side of the Austria, and he was not greatly perturbed about this because he assumed that the war would be badly led and that it would be possible to make revolutionary capital out of the changing fortunes which would inevitably result, but only on condition that the national movement could be persuaded from the beginning to regard the Prince Regent's war as a dynastic affair without any national justification. In Lassalle's opinion an unpopular war against France would be " an immense piece of luck " for the revolution, whilst a popular war under dynastic leadership might result in all the counter-revolutionary consequences which he had described so eloquently in his pamphlet.

From his point of view therefore, the tactic which Engels proposed in his pamphlet was more or less ununderstandable.

From the military point of view Engels had proved brilliantly that Germany did not need the Po to defend itself, and his subsequent contention that in case of war the Po must neverthe- less be held, that is to say, that the German nation was in duty bound to support Austria against a French attack, seemed highly contestable to Lassalle, for it was perfectly obvious that a successful repulse of Bonaparte's attack on the part of Austria could have only counter-revolutionary consequences. If Austria, supported by the German League, was successful then it was clear that nothing could prevent it maintaining its grip on Upper Italy, just the thing Engels so strongly condemned, and the Habsburg hegemony in Germany would be strengthened and the miserable German League politics galvanized into new life. And even assuming that a victorious Austria would overthrow the French usurper it would do so only in order to replace him by the old Bourbon régime and that would serve neither French nor German national interests, not to mention the interests of the revolution.

In order to understand the point of view which Marx and Engels advanced one must realize that they had their " ulterior motives " no less than Lassalle, and both for the same reason, as Engels indicates in a letter to Marx : " It is absolutely impos- sible to come forward openly in Germany itself, either politically or polemically, in the interests of our party." However, the " ulterior motives " of the two friends in London are not so clear as those of Lassalle because although his letters to them are still extant, their letters to him are not, but still, their motives can be recognized in the main from their general publicist activities at the time. In a second pamphlet, entitled *Savoy, Nice and the Rhine*, which Engels issued about a year later against the annexa- tion of Savoy and Nice by Bonaparte, he clearly describes the standpoint from which his first pamphlet was written.

First of all both Marx and Engels believed that the national movement in Germany was a really genuine one. They believed that it had developed " naturally, instinctively and directly ", and that it promised to sweep the unwilling governments along with it. For the moment both Austrian rule in Upper Italy and the Italian movement for independence were a matter of indif- ference to this national movement. The instinct of the people demanded war against Louis Bonaparte as the representative of the traditions of the First French Empire, and this instinct was right.

Secondly, they assumed that Germany was really seriously threatened by the Franco-Russian alliance. In *The New York Tribune* Marx pointed out that the finances and the internal political situation of the Second Empire had arrived at a critical point and that only a foreign war could lengthen the life of the *coup d'état* régime in France and at the same time the life of the counter-revolution in Europe. He feared that the Bonapartist liberation of Italy was merely a pretext to keep France itself in chains, to subjugate Italy to the *coup d'état* régime, to shift " the natural frontiers " of France farther into Germany, to turn Austria into a tool of Russia, and to jockey the peoples of Europe into a war on behalf of the legitimate and illegitimate counter-revolution. As Engels pointed out in his second pamphlet, he regarded the action of the German League in taking up the cudgels on behalf of Austria as the decisive moment for Russia to appear on the scene in order to win the left bank of the Rhine for France in exchange for a free hand in Turkey.

And finally, Marx and Engels assumed that the German governments, and in particular the wiseacres in Berlin, who had joyfully welcomed the Peace of Basle, which gave France the left bank of the Rhine, and had secretly rubbed their hands in delight when the Austrians were defeated at Ulm and Austerlitz, would leave Austria in the lurch. In their opinion the German governments needed goading on by the national movement, and what they then expected was described by Engels in a passage of a letter to Lassalle which the latter quoted in full in his reply : " Long live a war in which we are attacked simultaneously by the French and the Russians, for in such a desperate situation with disaster immediately threatening, all parties, from those which are now ruling to Zitz and Blum, would exhaust themselves, and the nation would then finally turn to the most energetic party in order to save itself." Lassalle answered that he quite agreed with this and that he was wearing himself out in Berlin in order to prove that if the Prussian government declared war it would be playing into the hands of the revolution, but only on condition that from the very beginning the people regarded the war as a counter-revolutionary scheme of the Holy Alliance. If things turned out as Engels anticipated then the German League system, Austrian domination in Upper Italy and the French *coup d'état* régime would all be destroyed, and only from this point of view did he find it possible to understand Engels tactic completely.

All this shows clearly that there were no fundamental differences of opinion between the disputants, but only, as Marx put it a year later, " opposing judgments on given conditions ". There was no difference of opinion between them either in their national or their revolutionary opinions. For all of them the final aim was the emancipation of the proletariat, and the absolutely necessary condition for the achievement of this aim was the formation of big national States. As Germans they were all primarily interested in securing German national unity, and the absolutely necessary condition for this was the abolition of the multi-dynastic system in Germany. Just because they all had national interests, none of them supported the German governments and all of them wished for their defeat. The brilliant idea that in case of a war between the governments the working class should abandon its own independent policy and place its fate in the hands of the ruling classes did not occur to any of them, for their national spirit was much too authentic and deeply rooted for them to be deceived by dynastic slogans.

However, the situation was complicated by the fact that the heritage of the revolutionary years began to liquidate itself in dynastic changes, and to find the correct attitude in this mixture of revolutionary and reactionary aims was less a question of fundamental principles than a question of facts. Neither standpoint was subjected to the acid test of fulfilment, but the very development which prevented this showed clearly enough that on the whole Lassalle had judged the " given conditions " more accurately than Marx and Engels. The two friends had to pay for having lost touch with conditions in Germany for so long. They had also overestimated, if not the lust of Tsarism for conquest then at least the practical possibilities at its disposal for sating that lust. Lassalle may have exaggerated when he declared that the national movement in Germany was due to nothing but traditional hatred of France, but in any case the movement was certainly not revolutionary, as was later demonstrated by the pitiful outcome of its labours—the miscarriage known as the German *Nationalverein*.

Perhaps Lassalle also underestimated the Russian danger, and in his pamphlet he treated it as an item of secondary importance, but in any case the danger was not an imminent one, as was shown when, exactly as Lassalle had prophesied, the Prince Regent of Prussia mobilized the Prussian Army and called upon the German League to mobilize the troops of the smaller States also. This military demonstration proved sufficient to make both the false Bonaparte and the Tsar very conciliatory. Vigorously encouraged by a Russian general who immediately appeared at the headquarters of the French Army, Bonaparte offered peace to the defeated Emperor of Austria and half abandoned his official programme, agreeing to content himself with Lombardy whilst the province of Venice remained under Austrian sway. He was not in a position to wage a European war on his own, and Russia was held in check by the troubles in Poland, the difficulties it was experiencing in connection with the emancipation of the serfs, and the blows it had received during the Crimean War, from which it had by no means fully recovered.

At the same time the Peace of Villa Franca also settled the dispute on revolutionary tactics in connection with the Italian war, but Lassalle returned to the matter again and again in his letters to Marx and Engels, and insisted that he had been right and that the course of events had demonstrated the correctness of his views. As we are not in possession of their answers and as they did not set out their own views in a manifesto as they had intended it is impossible to weigh the arguments and counter-arguments. Lassalle could point with justification to the actual course of events, the actual development of the movement for Italian unity, the abolition of the Central Italian dynasties by the revolt of their ill-treated " subjects ", the conquest of Sicily and Naples by Garibaldi and his volunteers, and the big spoke that all this had put in Bonaparte's wheel, ruining all his plans, but in the last resort it was the Savoy dynasty which skimmed the cream from the milk.

Unfortunately the dispute was aggravated by the circumstance that Marx was unable to overcome his mistrust of Lassalle although he was honestly anxious to win him over completely, declaring him to be an " energetic fellow " who would not temporize with the bourgeois party. Although his *Heraclitus* was a little crude, it was better than anything the Democrats could boast of. However, although Lassalle approached him with an open heart and an outstretched hand, Marx always felt that diplomacy was necessary in his dealings with him. " Clever management " was necessary, he declared, in order to keep Lassalle up to the scratch, and the least incident was sufficient to awaken all his old suspicions.

For instance, Friedländer renewed his offer that Marx should contribute to *Die Presse* in Vienna. The offer was again made through Lassalle and this time without any conditions, but finally Friedländer let the matter drop, whereupon Marx immediately suspected Lassalle of having deliberately spoiled his prospects. And again, when the printing of Marx's work on political economy was delayed from the beginning of February to the end of May, he was quite sure that it was one of Lassalle's " tricks " and promised that he would not forget it. As a matter of fact the delay was caused solely by the dilatory publisher, and even then the latter had a fairly good excuse, pointing out that he had postponed the printing in order to get out the pamphlets of Engels and Lassalle, which were of greater urgency as they dealt with topical matters.

3. New Struggles in Exile

The ambiguous character of the Italian war renewed old antagonisms and brought new confusion into the ranks of the exiles.

Whilst the Italian and French fugitives opposed the mixing up of the Italian movement for independence with the *coup d'état* régime in France, many of the German fugitives were anxious to repeat the folly which had already cost them ten years of banishment. However, they were very far removed from Lassalle's standpoint and even effusively in favour of the " New Era " which they believed to have opened up in Germany by the grace of the Prince Regent and in which they hoped to share. As Freiligrath declared contemptuously, they were bubbling over with a desire to be pardoned and were eager to perform any patriotic action if only " His Royal Highness " would fulfil Kinkel's prophecy before the court-martial in Rastatt and draw the sword to establish German unity.

Kinkel once again sprang into the breach and made himself the mouthpiece of this tendency, and on the 1st of January 1859 he issued a weekly publication, *Der Hermann*,[1] whose antediluvian title immediately betrayed the ideas it preached. To quote Freiligrath again, it immediately became the favourite organ of all those " home-sick heroes " who were trembling with impatience to receive permission to plunge into " the barrack-square liberalism " which now prevailed in Germany, but just for this reason it became very popular, so much so, in fact, that it killed *Die Neue Zeit*, a little working-class paper issued by Edgar Bauer on behalf of the Workers Educational League. *Die Neue Zeit* lived chiefly on the credit granted to it by its printer, and it was naturally lost when Kinkel offered the latter the far more profitable and reliable order for the printing of *Der Hermann*. However, Kinkel's shabby trick did not meet with unanimous approval even amongst the bourgeois fugitives, and even the Free Trader Faucher formed a finance committee in order to save *Die Neue Zeit*, and these efforts were successful. *Die Neue Zeit* lived on under the new title of *Das Volk*, and Elard Biskamp became its editor. Biskamp was a fugitive from the Electorate of Hesse, and he had contributed to *Die Neue Zeit* from the provinces, but now he gave up his post as a teacher to devote his whole time to the paper.

Shortly afterwards, accompanied by Liebknecht, he visited Marx in an attempt to persuade him to contribute to the paper. Since the

---

[1] *The Warrior*, Hermann der Cherusker, name given to Arminius, who defeated the Romans under Varus in the Teutoburger Forest in the ninth century.—Tr.

dispute in 1850 Marx had maintained no relations with the Workers Educational League and he had even expressed disapproval when Liebknecht had afterwards resumed his connections with the League, though Liebknecht's contention that a workers party without workers was a contradiction in terms had much in its favour. However, it is not difficult to understand that Marx did not succeed in overcoming his unpleasant memories immediately, and he " startled " a deputation from the League by informing them that he and Engels had received their mandate as representatives of the proletarian party from no one but themselves and that it had been confirmed by the general and exclusive hatred which all the parties of the old world bore towards them.

At first Marx was none too sympathetic towards the request that he should contribute to *Das Volk*, but he realized that Kinkel could not be permitted to have things all his own way, and therefore he agreed that Liebknecht should assist Biskamp in the editorial work, although he refused to contribute to a small paper himself or in fact to any exclusively party paper which was not edited by Engels and himself. However, he promised to assist in the distribution of the paper, to place printed articles from *The New York Tribune* at its disposal and to assist the editors with written and oral notes and hints. Writing to Engels he declared that he regarded *Das Volk* as a " boulevard sheet " like the Paris *Vorwärts* and the *Deutsche Brüsseler Zeitung*, but still, a time might come when it would be useful to have a London newspaper at their disposal and Biskamp deserved support, because after all he was working for nothing.

When the " boulevard sheet " began to make itself a nuisance to Kinkel Marx was far too much of a fighter not to throw his weight wholeheartedly into the scales on its behalf. He gave a great deal of time and energy in order to keep its head above water, not so much by contributions, for according to his own account they consisted of no more than a few short notes, as by his efforts to provide the means for at least a hand-to-mouth existence for the paper, which appeared in a four-page edition and a fairly big format. Those few amongst the party members and sympathizers who were able to spare a little money were mobilized, and in particular Engels, who also supported the paper industriously with his pen, writing military technical articles on the Italian war and a valuable criticism of the recently published scientific work of his friend, although the third and fourth articles of this review were never published, because by the end of August the paper was unable to appear any longer. A most disagreeable practical result of Marx' efforts to keep the paper alive was that the printer, a certain Fidelio Hollinger, made him responsible for the outstanding printing bill. It was an unjust demand, but "in view of the fact that the whole Kinkel gang is only waiting for an opportunity to create a public scandal, and because many of the people connected with the paper are not suitable for facing the publicity of the courts" Marx compounded the debt with a payment of five pounds.

Another heritage which *Das Volk* left him cost him incomparably greater sacrifices and trouble. On the 1st of April 1859 Karl Vogt, who was living in Geneva, sent a political programme for the German democracy towards the Italian war to various German fugitives in London, including Freiligrath, at the same time appealing to them to co-operate in the publication of a new weekly in Switzerland in the spirit of the programme. Vogt was a nephew of the brothers Follen, who had played a prominent part in the *Burschenschaft* movement, and he had been one of the leaders of the left wing in the Frankfort Assembly together with Robert Blum ; in fact, one of the last acts of the dying parliament had been to appoint him one of the five Reich's Regents. When he sent out his political programme he was a Professor of Geology and, together with Fazy, who was the leader of the Geneva Radicals, he represented Geneva in the Swiss Diet. Vogt kept his memory alive in Germany by zealous agitation for materialism on the basis of natural science, a very limited form of materialism which went hopelessly wrong immediately it ventured into the historical field. He propagated his opinions with what Ruge not unjustly termed "crude schoolboyishness", and he sought to capture the prurient fancy of the Philistines with cynical phrases. One of his most popular phrases was "Ideas stand in the same relation to the brain as bile does to the liver or urine to the kidneys". This proved a little too much even for his hitherto staunchest supporter Ludwig Büchner, who then dissociated himself from this sort of "enlightenment work".

Approaching Marx with a view to obtaining the latter's verdict on Vogt's political programme Freiligrath received the laconic answer : "Tub-thumping," but writing to Engels Marx dealt in somewhat greater detail with the programme : "Germany abandons its non-German possessions. Does not support Austria. French despotism is temporary, Austrian despotism permanent. Both despots permitted to bleed themselves to death (whereby a certain tendency in favour of Bonaparte is visible). Armed neutrality for Germany. A revolutionary movement in Germany is not to be thought of in our lifetime (as Vogt is informed from the most reliable sources). In consequence immediately Austria is ruined by Bonaparte, a moderate liberalist-nationalist development will begin in the

Fatherland under the auspices of the Prince Regent, and Vogt may even become court jester." The suspicion that Vogt sympathized with Bonaparte which is indicated in this letter became a certainty when, although he did not issue the proposed weekly, he wrote a number of studies on the European situation which unmistakably demonstrated his intellectual relationship with the Bonapartist slogans.

Vogt also sent his programme to Karl Blind, a fugitive from Baden who had been friendly with Marx since the revolutionary years and had contributed an article to the *Neue Rheinische Revue*, but had never belonged to the inner circle of Marx's friends and political supporters. In fact, Blind was one of those portentous local patriots and republicans who regarded their own little " Canton Baden " as the centre of the universe and were often made the butt of Engels' wit, who found that the opinions of these " Statesmen " usually boiled down, for all their lofty grandeur, into an immense respect for their own persons. Blind now approached Marx and informed him that Vogt was being subsidized by Bonaparte and that he, Blind, could provide proof of these treasonable activities. Vogt had attempted to bribe a South German printer with 30,000 guilders and had also made attempts at bribery in London. In the summer of 1858 a conference had taken place in Geneva between Fazy and his friends and Prince Jerome Bonaparte to discuss the Italian war, and it had been decided that the Russian Grand Duke Constantine should be made King of Hungary.

Marx mentioned these revelations to Biskamp when the latter visited him in connection with *Das Volk*, adding that it was a South German weakness to lay the colours on heavily. Without obtaining Marx's permission Biskamp used some of Blind's revelations in a satirical article in *Das Volk* in which " the Reich's Regent " was denounced as " a traitor to the Reich ", and he sent a copy of the number in which the article appeared to Vogt. The latter answered the attack in the *Bieler Handelskurier* with a " Warning " to the workers against a " clique of fugitives " who had formerly been known in Swiss exile under various uncomplimentary names, including the " Vagabonds ", and which had now gathered in London under its chief Marx in order to hatch conspiracies amongst the German workers, conspiracies which were known from the beginning to the Continental police and led the workers into a trap. Marx did not permit " this filthy attack " to distress him unduly, and he contented himself with holding it up to general contempt in *Das Volk*.

At the beginning of June Marx went to Manchester to collect funds amongst friends and sympathizers there to support *Das*

Volk, and during his absence Liebknecht discovered the galleys of a pamphlet attacking Vogt and containing the revelations made by Blind. The compositor Vögele informed him that the manuscript of the pamphlet had been handed in by Blind himself and that the corrections on the galleys were in Blind's handwriting. A few days later Liebknecht received a copy of the printed pamphlet from the printer Hollinger and he sent it to the *Allgemeine Zeitung* in Augsburg, whose correspondent he had been for a number of years. In a covering letter he informed the editor that the pamphlet was the work of a reputable German fugitive and its accusations could all be substantiated.

The *Allgemeine Zeitung* published the material and Vogt then sued it for libel whereupon the paper turned to Liebknecht to obtain the promised proofs. Liebknecht in his turn approached Blind, but the latter declared that the troubles of the *Allgemeine Zeitung* were nothing to do with him and even denied being the author of the pamphlet, though he was compelled to admit that he had communicated the facts contained in it to Marx and that he himself had published some of them in *The Free Press*, one of Urquhart's papers. Naturally, Marx bore no responsibility in the matter at all and Liebknecht had quite made up his mind that Marx would disavow him, but the latter thought it his duty to do everything possible to expose Vogt, particularly as the latter had dragged him into the affair quite gratuitously, but even his attempts to extract an admission of authorship from Blind failed owing to the latter's obstinacy, and he had to content himself with a written statement from the compositor Vögele to the effect that the original manuscript had been in Blind's handwriting, which was thoroughly familiar to him, and that the pamphlet had been set up and printed in Hollinger's printing works. Naturally, this proved nothing at all against Vogt.

Before the case came up for trial in Augsburg the Schiller celebrations, planned for the 10th of November 1859 on the centenary of the great poet's birth, led to a new dispute in the ranks of the London exiles. To quote Lassalle, this day was celebrated by all Germans both at home and abroad as evidence of " the cultural unity " of the German people and as " a joyful promise of national resurrection ". Celebrations were also arranged in London and a great meeting was to take place at the Crystal Palace, the proceeds to be devoted to founding a Schiller Memorial Institute with a library and a course of lectures beginning annually on the anniversary of the poet's birth. Unfortunately, however, the Kinkel fraction succeeded in getting control of the preparations, and it exploited them in the

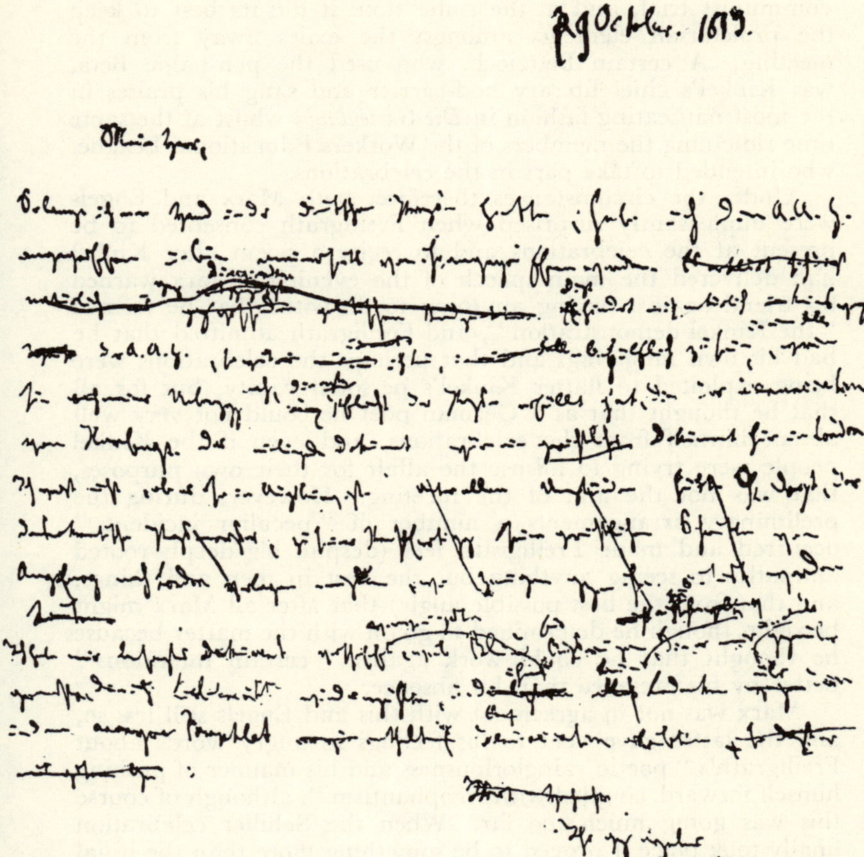

Letter Drafted by Karl Marx

most hateful and petty fashion in its own narrow interests. This group invited an official of the Prussian Embassy in London to grace the celebrations by his presence, although the man had earned a very unenviable reputation in the days of the Cologne communist trial, and at the same time it did its best to keep the proletarian elements amongst the exiles away from the meeting. A certain Bettziech, who used the pen-name Beta, was Kinkel's chief literary hod-carrier and sang his praises in the most nauseating fashion in *Die Gartenlaube* whilst at the same time ridiculing the members of the Workers Educational League, who intended to take part in the celebrations.

Under the circumstances therefore, both Marx and Engels were unpleasantly surprised when Freiligrath consented to be present at the celebrations and to recite a poem after Kinkel had delivered the main speech of the evening. Marx warned his friend against having anything to do with what he termed " the Kinkel demonstration ", and Freiligrath admitted that he had his own misgivings and that perhaps the celebrations were being exploited to flatter Kinkel's personal vanity, but for all that he thought that as a German poet he could not very well absent himself from the celebrations, and even if the Kinkel people were trying to misuse the affair for their own purposes, that was not the aim of the meeting. However, during the preliminary arrangements a number of " peculiar incidents " occurred and made Freiligrath feel (despite his deeply-rooted antipathy to seeing anything but the best in men and things, and that from the best possible angle) that after all Marx might be right, though he determined to go on with the matter because he thought that he could work against " certain intentions " better by his presence than his absence.

Marx was not in agreement with this and Engels still less so, and the latter gave vent to his feelings in angry words about Freiligrath's " poetic vaingloriousness and his manner of pushing himself forward, coupled with sycophantism ", although of course this was going much too far. When the Schiller celebration finally took place it proved to be something more than the usual superficial festivities with which the German Philistine is accustomed to celebrate the memory of the great thinkers and poets who have passed over his night-cap like high-flying cranes, and it found an echo even on the extremest left wing.

When Marx complained about Freiligrath to Lassalle the latter replied : " Perhaps it would have been better had he kept away from the meeting itself, but in any case, he did well to compose the cantata. It was by far the finest thing that appeared in connection with the celebrations." In Zürich Herwegh composed a special song for the occasion, and the centenary speech in Paris was delivered by Schily. In London the Workers Educational League took part in the meeting at the Crystal Palace after having salved its conscience the day before by a special Robert Blum memorial meeting at which Liebknecht spoke. In Manchester the celebrations were organized by a young poet named Siebel who came from Wuppertal and was a distant relative of Engels, and the latter saw nothing to object to in his activities. Writing to Marx Engels declared that he had nothing to do with the affair and that Siebel intended to deliver the oration, "the ordinary sort of declamation, of course, but quite decent. The fellow is also organizing a performance of ' Wallenstein's Camp '. I was present at two of the rehearsals, and if they can summon up sufficient audacity it ought to go off all right." Later on Engels became President of the Schiller Memorial Institute which was founded in Manchester in connection with the celebrations there, and Wilhelm Wolff mentioned it in his will for a good round sum.

Whilst all this was going on and a certain tension was making itself felt between Marx and Freiligrath, the Augsburg court heard Vogt's action against the *Allgemeine Zeitung*. It was dismissed with costs against the plaintiff, but the latter's legal defeat developed into a moral victory. The defendants, the editors and publishers of the *Allgemeine Zeitung*, were unable to bring forward any proof in support of their charges against Vogt, and they contented themselves with a defence which Marx described, all too mildly, as " politically unsavoury cant ". In fact, their attitude was worthy of the severest condemnation not only politically, but also morally, and its trump card was that the personal honour of a political opponent was fair game. How, inquired the defence, could Bavarian judges give a verdict in favour of a man who had violently attacked the Bavarian government and who was compelled to live abroad owing to his political activities ? If the court found against the defendants all the social democratic elements in Germany, who had first sought to put their dreams of freedom into execution eleven years before with the murder of Generals Latour, Gagern and Auerswald and of Prince Lichnovsky, would burst into shouts of approval. If Vogt succeeded in his action there would be no reason at all why Klapka, Kossuth, Pulski, Teleki and Mazzini should not appear before the court with equal justification and demand a verdict against their political enemies.

Despite the low cunning of this defence, or perhaps just because of it, the judges were impressed. However, their legal consciences were not quite elastic enough to permit them to give a verdict for defendants who had so utterly failed to substantiate their charges, but they were also not vigorous enough to do justice to a man who was hated by the Bavarian government and the Bavarian people. The Public Prosecutor offered a way out of the quandary and this the judges seized on eagerly. Under formal pretexts they sent the case for trial by jury, a proceeding which meant absolutely certain defeat for Vogt because at such a trial no evidence was required to substantiate the truth of the charges against him and the jurymen were not called upon to advance any reasons for their decision.

Vogt did not take up the hopeless challenge, and he is not to be blamed for that. In any case, his situation was not unfavourable, for he could now bask in the sun of double martyrdom : not only had he been falsely accused and his accusers unable to substantiate their charges against him, but the courts had refused to give him justice. One or two accompanying circumstances even heightened his triumph ; for instance, it made a most embarrassing impression on public opinion when a letter from Biskamp to the *Allgemeine Zeitung* was read in court. Biskamp was really the chief accuser of Vogt, but in this letter he admitted that he had no real proofs for his charges, advanced a few vague suppositions and concluded by asking the *Allgemeine Zeitung* whether in view of the fact that *Das Volk* was going out of existence it would care to engage him as a second London correspondent as well as Liebknecht. Even after the trial the *Allgemeine Zeitung* kept up its vague attacks on Vogt, declaring that he had been condemned by his own people, by Marx and by Freiligrath, and everyone knew that Marx was a keener and more profound thinker than Vogt whilst Freiligrath towered above him as far as political morality was concerned.

In the written statement for the defence filed by the editor Kolb Freiligrath was declared to be a contributor to *Das Volk* and one of the accusers of Vogt. These statements had been made by Kolb owing to a misunderstanding arising out of one of Liebknecht's letters, in which the latter had not expressed himself any too clearly. When the report of the *Allgemeine Zeitung* on the trial arrived in London Freiligrath immediately sent off a short statement to the effect that he had never been a contributor to *Das Volk* and that his name had been used against Vogt without his knowledge and permission. In view of the fact that Vogt and Fazy were intimate friends and that Freiligrath's employment by the Swiss bank depended on Fazy, disagreeable conclusions were drawn from this action, but they would have been justified only if it had been Freiligrath's duty to come forward openly against Vogt, but this was not the case.

Freiligrath had nothing whatever to do with the matter and he was quite entitled to protest against Kolb's attempt to shelter himself behind his name when things began to go wrong. However, the laconic and terse form in which Freiligrath's statement was couched left open the possibility of interpreting it as a disavowal of Marx also, and the latter found it strange that the statement contained not the slightest indication which might have corrected the impression that it was intended as a personal breach with him and a public disavowal of the party. The form of Freiligrath's statement may very well have been due to a certain irritability at the fact that in the name of the party Marx had wanted to forbid him publishing a harmless poem in praise of Schiller, whilst he, Freiligrath, was expected to plunge into the breach immediately on behalf of Marx when the latter had begun an unnecessary quarrel.

Appearances were made still worse when Blind published a declaration in the *Allgemeine Zeitung* condemning Vogt's policy unreservedly but declaring at the same time that it was a deliberate lie to say that he had written the pamphlet against Vogt. The statements of two witnesses were added to his letter : the printer Hollinger declared that the statement of the compositor Vögele that the pamphlet had been written by Blind and printed in Hollinger's works was " a malicious invention ", whilst a second compositor named Wiehe made a statement corroborating Hollinger's evidence.

The differences between Marx and Freiligrath were then aggravated by an unfortunate incident. Kinkel's literary hack Beta published an article in *Die Gartenlaube* praising the poet Freiligrath to the sky and ending with a scurrilous attack upon Marx, who was described as a malicious disseminator of poisonous hatred who had robbed Freiligrath of the power of song, of his freedom and of his character. Since he had come into contact with Marx's searing breath the poet had sung but little.

However, after one or two lively exchanges by letter between Marx and Freiligrath, all these things looked like being cleared up and buried with the year 1859, when they were dragged up in the New Year by Vogt, who seemed anxious to prove the truth of the old proverb that when a donkey is too well off it insists on venturing over thin ice.

4. Interludes

In the New Year of 1860 Vogt published a book entitled *My Action against the "Allgemeine Zeitung"*. It contained a stenographic report of the court proceedings and copies of all the written statements and other documents brought forward in connection with the case. All the documents were quoted in full and with perfect accuracy.

However, apart from all this the book contained a rehash in still greater detail of all the old nonsense about the "Vagabonds" Vogt had previously published in the *Bieler Handelskurier*. Marx was described as the leader of a band of blackmailers whose members lived by "so compromising people in the Fatherland" that they were compelled to purchase the silence of the band. "Not one letter, but hundreds of letters have been sent to people in Germany threatening to denounce their participation in this or that revolutionary action unless a sum of money specified was sent to a given address by a certain date," declared Vogt. That was the worst, but by no means the only libel against Marx published in the book. Although Vogt's story was thoroughly mendacious it was so mixed up with all sorts of half-truths concerning life in exile that a fairly exact knowledge of the details was necessary in order to recognize its dishonesty immediately, and naturally the German Philistine was the last person in the world likely to be in possession of such detailed knowledge.

The book therefore made a great sensation in Germany and it was welcomed with enthusiasm by the liberal press. The *National Zeitung* published two long leading articles on the basis of Vogt's statements, and when a copy of the paper arrived in London towards the end of January it created tremendous excitement in the Marx household and Frau Marx, in particular, was deeply shaken. As no copy of the book could be obtained in London Marx hurried to Freiligrath and asked him whether he had received a copy from his "friend" Vogt. Freiligrath was deeply offended and answered that Vogt was not his friend and that he had not received a copy of the book.

Although Marx was always unwilling to bother about answering scurrilous attacks upon himself, no matter how vile they might be, he realized that this time an answer was absolutely necessary, and even before a copy of Vogt's book arrived in London he decided to sue the *National Zeitung* for libel. The paper had accused him of a number of criminal and infamous actions before a public whose political prejudices made it inclined to believe anything against him, no matter how monstrous it might be, though owing to his eleven years of absence from

Germany it had no facts at all on which to judge his personal character. He felt that quite apart from political considerations he must bring the *National Zeitung* to book for defamation of character out of regard for his wife and children, and he reserved himself the satisfaction of making a literary answer to Vogt.

Marx first of all proceeded to call Blind to account on the assumption that the fellow actually held proofs against Vogt, but was unwilling to produce them out of the personal consideration which one vulgar democrat owed to another. Apparently Marx was wrong and Engels probably came nearer the truth when he declared that Blind had invented the details of Vogt's alleged attempts at bribery in order to make himself important, but that when the affair had become uncomfortable he had decided to deny everything stoutly, thereby involving himself deeper and deeper in contradictions. On the 4th of February Marx caused an announcement to be published in English in *The Free Press* declaring that the statements of Blind, Hollinger and Wiehe that the anonymous pamphlet had not been printed in Hollinger's works were untrue and that Karl Blind was an infamous liar, adding that if the latter felt himself injured he could seek recourse to the English courts. Blind was not such a fool as to accept this challenge, and he tried to defend himself by publishing a long statement in the *Allgemeine Zeitung* strongly condemning Vogt and again imputing bribery to him, but denying that he, Blind, had written the pamphlet in question.

Marx was not content with this, and he succeeded in hauling Wiehe before a magistrate and securing from him an affidavit to the effect that he, Wiehe, had set up the type of the pamphlet for reprinting in *Das Volk*, that he too had recognized Blind's handwriting in the corrections on the galleys, and that his first statement had been enticed from him by Hollinger and Blind, the former having promised him money and the latter future favours. With this Blind became amenable to the process of English criminal law and Ernest Jones offered to secure his arrest on the basis of Wiehe's affidavit, but he pointed out that once an information had been laid it would be impossible to go back on the matter and that if any attempt was made to compose the affair afterwards he, Jones, as a lawyer, would be committing a punishable offence.

Out of consideration for Blind's family Marx did not want the matter to go so far and he sent a copy of Wiehe's affidavit to Louis Blanc, who was Blind's friend, together with a letter explaining that on account of Blind's family he, Marx, would be very sorry to have to lay an information against the man, though he thoroughly deserved it. This letter had its effect and on the 15th of February 1860 the *Daily Telegraph*, which had in the meantime repeated the scurrilous libels of the *National Zeitung*, published a notice to the effect that one Schaible, a friend of Blind's family, had in fact been the author of the anonymous pamphlet and not Blind. The manœuvre was transparent enough, but Marx let it go at that because he had won his point and cleared himself of all responsibility for the pamphlet.

Before launching his counter-attack against Vogt he made an attempt to bring about a reconciliation with Freiligrath, to whom he sent a copy of his own statement against Blind and a copy of Wiehe's affidavit, but he received no reply. Despite this rebuff he made another attempt to convince Freiligrath of the importance of the Vogt case for the historical vindication of the party and for its later position in Germany. He did his best to dispel any resentment which Freiligrath might have harboured against him and declared, " If I have offended you in any way I shall be glad at any time to make amends. Nothing human is foreign to me." He was, he said, quite able to understand how extremely unpleasant the whole thing must be for Freiligrath in his present situation, but he, Freiligrath, would realize at least that it was not possible to keep his name out of the affair altogether. " We are both well aware that for years each of us in his own way, from the most unselfish motives and subordinating all private interests, has held aloft the banner of the *classe la plus laborieuse et la plus misérable* above the heads of the Philistines, and it would be a petty crime against history if we were to drift apart now on account of trifling matters due in any case to misunderstandings." The letter closed by expressing the warmest feelings of friendship for Freiligrath.

Frieligrath accepted the hand of friendship which was extended to him, but not quite so warmly as the " heartless " Marx had offered it. He declared that in the future as in the past he would remain loyal to the *classe la plus laborieuse et la plus misérable*, and that he would gladly maintain his old relations with Marx as a friend and a comrade, but, he added, " I have had nothing to do with the party now for seven years (since the dissolution of the Communist League). I have never attended its meetings, and its decisions and its actions were agreed upon without my participation. In reality, therefore, my connections with the party were broken off long ago. We were never in any doubt about it ; it was a sort of silent agreement between us. And I can only say that I still feel that I was right. My nature, like the nature of any poet, needs freedom. The party is also a cage, and it is easier to sing outside it, even for the party, than inside it. I was a poet of the proletariat and of the revolution before I became a member of the Communist League and of the editorial board of the *Neue Rheinische Zeitung*. In the future too I want to remain independent, to belong to myself alone and to order my actions as I think fit." Freiligrath's old dislike of the routine of political agitation expressed itself again in this letter, and it even caused him to see things which had no existence in fact. The party meetings he had never attended, and the party decisions and actions which had been taken without his participation had, in fact, never taken place at all.

Marx pointed this out in his reply, and after he had once again done everything he could to dispel all possible misunderstandings he referred to a favourite saying of Freiligrath in the words : " The Philistines are on us, will always be a better slogan for us than to be amongst Philistines. I have explained my attitude frankly, and I hope that you are in general agreement with me. I have also tried to clear up the misunderstanding that when I refer to the party I mean an organization which died eight years ago, or an editorial board which broke up twelve years ago. When I refer to the party I do so in an historical sense." Marx's words were both conciliatory and to the point, for in a historical sense the two men belonged together despite all differences. Marx's attitude did him all honour, for in view of the villainous attacks which Vogt had made on him he might reasonably have demanded that Freiligrath should openly dispel any appearance of solidarity with the traducer. However, Freiligrath contented himself with renewing their friendly relations and for the rest he maintained a reserved attitude which Marx henceforth facilitated by avoiding as far as possible any mention of Freiligrath's name in the matter.

A discussion with Lassalle in the Vogt affair ended differently. Marx had last written to Lassalle in November of the previous year in connection with their dispute in the Italian question and, to use his own expression, its tone had been " very blunt ". Lassalle had not replied to this letter and Marx assumed that it had wounded his feelings, but when the *National Zeitung* attacked him Marx naturally felt the need of some connections in Berlin and he requested Engels to smooth things over with Lassalle, who was after all " a first-rate fellow " compared with the others. This was indirectly a reference to a Prussian assessor named Fischel who had introduced himself to Marx as an Urquhartite and offered his services in connection with the German press. Marx sent greetings to Lassalle through Fischel, but Lassalle refused to have anything to do with " the incompetent and ignorant fellow " who, irrespective of how he may have conducted himself in London, belonged to the literary body-guard of the

Duke of Coburg in Germany, a man who had a deservedly evil reputation. Shortly after this Fischel met with a fatal accident.

Before Engels had been able to comply with Marx's request Lassalle himself wrote explaining his long silence with lack of time and demanding energetically that something should be done in "the deplorable Vogt business" which, he declared, had caused a big sensation in Germany. Naturally, those who knew Marx would not be deceived by Vogt's story, but those who did not might very well be impressed because it was cleverly supported by half-truths which the less discerning might very well accept as the whole truth. Lassalle was not prepared to acquit Marx of all responsibility in the matter, because he had accepted such serious accusations against Vogt merely on the word of a miserable liar like Blind. Unless he was really in possession of some proofs against Vogt Marx should begin his defence by withdrawing the accusation of bribery against Vogt. Naturally, he, Lassalle, was well aware that it would require a great measure of self-discipline to do justice to a man who had been guilty of such monstrous and baseless slanders, but Marx must nevertheless give this proof of his good faith unless he wanted to render his defence ineffective from the beginning. And then Lassalle objected strongly to Liebknecht's activities on behalf of such a reactionary paper as the *Allgemeine Zeitung* as they would cause astonishment amongst the general public and indignation against the party.

When Marx received this letter he had still not seen Vogt's book and was therefore not in a position to realize the situation fully, but it is not difficult to understand that Lassalle's suggestion that he should begin his defence with an *amende honorable* for Vogt did not please him, particularly as he had more reliable evidence of the latter's Bonapartist intrigues than the vague statements of Blind. He was also unable to agree with Lassalle's severe condemnation of Liebknecht's connection with the *Allgemeine Zeitung*. Marx was certainly not a friend of this paper, and whilst the *Rheinische Zeitung* had existed he had fought it energetically, but as counter-revolutionary as it might be on other fields, it at least opened its columns to various points of view with regard to foreign politics, and in this respect it enjoyed a privileged position in the German press.

Marx therefore answered somewhat ill-humouredly that the *Allgemeine Zeitung* was just as good as the *Volkszeitung*. He would sue the *National Zeitung* for libel and write an answer to Vogt, but in the introduction he would make it clear that he didn't give a damn for the opinion of the German public. On his part Lassalle then took the irritable words of Marx too seriously and protested against a democratic paper like the *Volkszeitung* being mentioned in the same breath with " the most disreputable and shameless rag in Germany ". In the main he warned Marx not to begin proceedings against the *National Zeitung*, or at least not before he had himself answered Vogt, and concluded by expressing the hope that Marx would not feel hurt by his letter and would accept an assurance of his " honest and warm friendship ".

Lassalle's hope was ill-founded. In a letter to Engels Marx used the strongest terms about Lassalle's letter and even recalled " the official accusations " which Lewy had brought to London, though he did so in order to show that he had not harboured any precipitate distrust against Lassalle, and that despite these " official accusations " he had not changed his opinion of him. However, in view of the calibre of the accusations Lassalle was unable to see any particular merit in Marx having ignored them and he revenged himself in a dignified fashion by writing a fine and convincing description of the self-sacrifice he had shown and the services he had rendered to the workers in the Rhineland during the worst days of the reaction.

Marx did not treat Lassalle as he had treated Freiligrath, and Lassalle's answer was different. He gave Marx the best advice he could give him and he did not allow his willingness to assist him to be affected by the fact that the advice was ignored.

5. *Herr Vogt*

It was not long before Lassalle's warning against appealing to the Prussian courts was shown to be well founded. Through the mediation of Fischel Marx instructed *Justizrat*[1] Weber to begin proceedings for libel against the *National Zeitung*, but he had even less success than Vogt, who had at least secured a hearing for his action. On the ground of " insufficient evidence " the court refused to permit the action to go to trial because the allegedly libellous statements had not been made in the first place by the *National Zeitung*, which had published " mere quotations from other persons ". This nonsense was rejected by the court of appeal, but only to be replaced by the still greater nonsense that it was not an insult for Marx to be termed " the directing and superior head " of a band of blackmailers and coiners. The supreme court of appeal could find " no legal error " in this

---

[1] Approximately the German equivalent of K.C.—Tr.

extraordinary decision and thus Marx's case was thrown out all along the line.

All that was left for him was to write his own answer to Vogt and this took him almost a year. In order to refute all the rumours and gossip which Vogt had revived, an extensive and protracted correspondence was necessary with people all over the world. The reply was completed on the 17th of November 1860 and Marx entitled it simply *Herr Vogt*. It is the only one of Marx's independent works which has never been reprinted,[1] and there are probably very few copies still extant. First of all, it is very long, amounting to 192 closely printed pages (Marx declared that in ordinary print it would be twice as long), and secondly it would require detailed commentary to make all the references in it clear to the present-day reader. For the most part this would not be worth while, because much of the matter with which Marx deals was forced on him by his opponent and relates to affairs which have long since been completely forgotten and rightly so. In reading the book one involuntarily experiences a sense of discomfort to hear Marx defending himself against slanderous attacks which did not touch him even remotely. On the other hand, the book offers an unusual treat to the literary gourmet. On the very first page Marx propounds a thesis which he pursues through the subsequent pages with the humour of a Shakespeare : " The original of Karl Vogt is the immortal Sir John Falstaff and in his zoological resurrection he has lost nothing of his character." Protracted as the theme is it never becomes monotonous in Marx's hands and his vast acquaintance with classic and modern literature offers him arrow after arrow which he despatches with deadly accuracy against the insolent slanderer.

In *Herr Vogt* we meet the " Vagabonds " again, but this time as a small company of light-hearted students who fled to Switzerland after the crushing of the insurrection in the Palatinate in the winter of 1849–50 and won the hearts of the Geneva beauties with their cheerfulness in adversity, and at the same time shocked and startled the local Philistines. When *Herr Vogt* was written the band had been dispersed for about ten years, but one of its members, since become a worthy merchant in the City of London, Sigismund Borkheim, gave Marx a lively description of the harmless pranks of the fugitive students, and it was published in the first chapter of *Herr Vogt*. Marx won a loyal friend in Borkheim, and it was in general a great consolation to him that numerous fugitives, not only in England, but also in France and Switzer-

[1] Except of course in the Collected Edition issued by the Marx-Engels-Lenin Institute.—Tr.

land, sprang to his assistance, although many of them hardly knew him and some of them did not know him at all. He was gratified in particular by the generous assistance granted to him by Johann Philipp Becker, a tried and trusted veteran leader of the Swiss working-class movement.

Unfortunately it is not possible to describe in detail how Marx utterly exposed the tricks and artifices of Vogt until not a vestige remained, and in fact the powerful counter-attack he delivered against Vogt was more important, for it showed that both in its perfidy and its ignorance Vogt's propaganda was nothing but an echo of the slogan issued by the false Bonaparte. The documents published later by the Government of National Defence from the archives of the Tuileries after the overthrow of the Second Empire include a receipt signed by Vogt in August 1859 for his thirty pieces of silver, in this case 40,000 francs from the secret funds of the false Bonaparte. It is possible that Vogt received this money through the mediation of the Hungarian revolutionaries and, in any case, this is the most charitable explanation, for he was very friendly with Klapka and did not realize that the position of the German democracy towards Bonaparte was different from that of the Hungarian democracy and that the latter might venture where to do so would be shameful treachery for the former.

Whatever the truth about Vogt may be, and even supposing that he did not receive cash from the Tuileries, the fact remains that Marx proved irrefutably that Vogt's propaganda was logically based on Bonaparte's slogans. These chapters throw a searchlight on the conditions existing in Europe at the time and they represent the most valuable part of the book, being highly instructive even to-day. Lothar Bucher, whose relations to Marx at that time were rather hostile than friendly, declared that the book represented a compendium of contemporary history, and Lassalle welcomed it as " a masterpiece in every respect ", declaring in his usual frank fashion that he was now able to understand why Marx had been so convinced of Vogt's corruption, for he had supported his " intrinsic proof with an immense weight of evidence ". Engels even thought that *Herr Vogt* was better than *The Eighteenth Brumaire*, simpler in style, where necessary just as effective, and in fact the finest polemical work Marx had ever written. However *Herr Vogt* has not become the most important of Marx's polemical works; on the contrary, it has receded more and more into the background, whilst *The Eighteenth Brumaire* and his polemic against Proudhon have come more and more into the foreground with the passage of time. In part that was due to the material itself, for after all the Vogt case was a comparatively unimportant incident, and in part it was due to Marx himself, to his great capacities and to his little weaknesses.

He was unable to descend to that low level of polemics which is necessary when Philistines are to be convinced, although in this case it was precisely the prejudices of the Philistines which had to be dispelled. The book convinced only those who were described by Frau Marx somewhat naïvely, but nevertheless aptly, as " people of importance ", in other words, just those people who did not require to be told that Marx was not the scoundrel Vogt tried to make him out to be, but who had sufficient good taste and understanding to read the book for its literary qualities. " Even our old enemy Ruge thinks the book is a fine piece of drollery," wrote Frau Marx. However, the book was far above the heads of the patriotic worthies in Germany and it hardly penetrated into their circles at all, and even in the days of the anti-socialist law otherwise fastidious writers like Bamberger and Treitschke disinterred Vogt's "Vagabonds" for service against the German social democracy.

In addition, Marx was not to be spared the misfortunes which invariably attended him in all business matters, though this time he was not completely without fault. Engels urged him to have the book printed and published in Germany, and in view of the conditions prevailing there at the time this would have been possible. Lassalle also advised him to do so, but merely on account of the fact that it would cost less, whilst Engels had more important arguments : " We have had the same experience with emigrant literature on a hundred occasions already. Always the same ineffectiveness, always money and work thrown into the gutter, and on top of that the annoyance. . . . What's the use of writing an answer to Vogt if no one sees it ? " However, Marx insisted on giving the manuscript to a young German publisher in London on a share and share alike basis both for profit and loss, and he advanced 25 pounds for the printing costs, 12 pounds of which came from Borkheim and 8 pounds from Lassalle, but the new firm was so shaky that it was unable to make proper arrangements for the distribution of the book in Germany and it soon ceased to exist altogether. Marx did not recover one penny of the advance he had paid and he had to pay almost as much again as the result of legal proceedings which the partner of the publisher began against him to recover the whole of the printing costs, Marx having omitted to have a written contract drawn up.

When the trouble with Vogt began Marx's friend Imandt wrote : " I shouldn't like to have to write about the affair and I shall be surprised if you can bring yourself to thrust your hand into such a muck-heap," and similar advice came to hand from Russian and Hungarian friends. To-day one almost feels inclined to wish that he had taken it. The deplorable business won him a number of new friends and, in particular, it caused him to resume friendly relations with the Workers Educational League, which immediately supported him vigorously, but it tended to hamper the great work of his life rather than further it, despite, or rather just because of, the valuable sacrifice in strength and time which it demanded without offering any commensurate gain, and at the same time it caused him serious domestic difficulties.

6. Domestic and Personal

Frau Marx, who clung to her husband with heart and soul, was even harder hit than Marx himself by " the terrible vexation at the infamous attack of Vogt ". It cost her many a sleepless night, and although she held out bravely and made a fair copy of the whole voluminous manuscript for the printer she had hardly completed this work when she suffered a breakdown. A doctor was called in and he diagnosed the trouble as small-pox and ordered the children from the house immediately.

Terrible days followed. The children were looked after by Liebknecht whilst Marx and the loyal servant of the family Lenchen Demuth attended to Frau Marx. She suffered agonies of burning pain, sleeplessness, anxiety for her husband, who never left her side, and the almost complete loss of her physical faculties, though she remained conscious all the time. A week later the saving crisis occurred, thanks to the fact that she had been vaccinated twice, and finally the doctor declared that the terrible sickness was in reality a piece of good fortune. The nervous exhaustion from which she had suffered for months had caused her system to fall victim to the poison somewhere or the other, in a shop or a bus perhaps, but without this sickness her condition would undoubtedly have led to a dangerous nervous fever or something equally serious.

Hardly had Frau Marx begun to recover when the accumulated anxiety, worries and torments which Marx had suffered caused him to fall sick also. For the first time his chronic liver trouble appeared in an acute form and in his case also the doctor declared that the cause was the ceaseless and wearing excitement through which he had gone. *Herr Vogt* had not brought in a single penny and *The New York Tribune* again placed him on half-pay so that creditors began to besiege the house. After his convalescence he decided, as his wife wrote to Frau Weydemeyer, " to make a foray into Holland, the land of his fathers, tobacco and cheese ", to see if he could persuade his uncle to part with some specie.

This letter is dated the 11th of March 1861 and its sunny good humour provides eloquent proof of the " natural vitality " which Jenny Marx possessed in her own way no less than did her husband. After long years of silence the Weydemeyers, who had suffered their share of this world's troubles during their American exile, wrote again and Frau Marx immediately poured out her heart to " the courageous and loyal companion in misfortune, the fighter and sufferer ", declaring that the one thing which gave her sufficient courage to keep going in all the misery and wretchedness, " the one bright spot in our existence, the light of our lives " was the joy in their children. The seven-year-old Jenny took after her father " with her rich, dark glossy hair, her dark, brilliant and soft eyes and her dusky Creole complexion, which shows a typically English blossom ". The fifteen-year-old Laura was more like her mother " with her wavy, curly, chestnut hair and her green iridescent eyes flashing like fire. Both girls have a really beautiful complexion and at the same time they are really so little vain that in secret I am often surprised, all the more so because I cannot say the same for their mother when she was that age and still in short skirts and frills."

However, although the two eldest daughters were a great joy to their parents, the " idolized darling of the whole house " was the youngest daughter Eleanor, or Tussy, to give her her pet name. " The child was born when our poor little Edgar died and all the love and tenderness we bore him was then transferred to his little sister, and the older girls looked after her and nursed her with almost motherly care. But then it would really be difficult to find a more lovable child, as pretty as a picture and sweet tempered. In particular, she prattles delightfully. She has learned that from the brothers Grimm, who are her constant companions day and night. We all have to read the fairy tales aloud to her until we are almost exhausted, but woe betide us if we leave out so much as a word of the story of Bluebeard or Little Snow White or Rumpelstilzchen. Thanks to these fairy tales the child has learned German, and she speaks it with remarkable accuracy and grammatical precision, and, naturally, she has learned English as a matter of course. The child is Karl's favourite and her laughter and her merry chatter dispel many of his worries." And then she praises the faithful friend and servant of the house Lenchen : " Ask your husband about her. He will tell you what a treasure we have in her. She has been with us now for sixteen years and braved all the storm and stress of our lives." The charming letter ends with a report on Karl's friends, and those who had proved themselves wanting in loyalty to him she condemns in her feminine fashion even more sternly than he would have done. " I dislike half-measures," she writes, explaining why she broke off all relations with the distaff side of the Freiligrath family.

In the meantime, the " foray " into Holland had been fairly successful, and after visiting his uncle Philips Marx went on to Berlin to see if anything could be done to found a party organ, a proposal which Lassalle had made repeatedly. The lack of such an organ had made itself felt keenly, particularly during the crisis, and, thanks to the amnesty which William, now King William, had proclaimed in January 1861 after coming to the throne, there was now a possibility of making good this deficiency. The amnesty was miserable enough in all conscience and full of traps and reservations, but at least it permitted the one-time editors of the *Neue Rheinische Zeitung* to return to Germany.

Marx was received with " the greatest friendliness " by Lassalle in Berlin, but " the place " remained " personally unsympathetic " to him. No politics of any calibre, but merely squabbles with the police, and the antagonism between the military and the civilians : " The atmosphere in Berlin is insolent and frivolous. The chambers are treated with contempt." Even compared with the conciliators of 1848, who were certainly no Titans, he found the Prussian Chamber of Deputies with its Simsons and its Vinckes " a queer mixture of bureaucracy and the school bench ". The only half-way decent figures, at least in appearance, in this gathering of pygmies were Waldeck on the one hand and Wagener and Don Quixote von Blankenburg on the other. However, he thought he could detect a general tendency towards enlightenment and, amongst a great section of the public, dissatisfaction with the bourgeois press ; people of all classes regarded a catastrophe as inevitable ; in the elections which were to take place in the autumn the former conciliators, who were regarded as red republicans by the King, were certain to be elected ; matters might then come to a head over the new military budget. Marx therefore regarded Lassalle's plan for founding a paper to be worth considering, at least in principle.

However, he was not in agreement with Lassalle in matters of detail. The latter proposed that the editorship of the paper should be in the hands of a triumvirate consisting of Marx,

Engels and himself, but with the proviso that Marx and Engels should have only one vote between them on matters of policy, as otherwise he would find himself outvoted every time. This extraordinary suggestion would have meant trouble from the beginning, and it is probable that Lassalle let it fall only in a chance conversation, but in any case this is not important in view of the fact that Marx was not inclined to give him any important say in connection with the paper at all. Writing to Engels he declared that, dazzled by the reputation he had won in certain learned circles by his *Heraclitus,* and in certain parasitic circles by his good table and wine, Lassalle was naturally unaware of the fact that he was discredited amongst the general public : " And then there is his dogmatic insistence that he is always right, his hopeless attachment to ' the speculative conception ' (the fellow is even dreaming of a new system of Hegelian philosophy raised to the second power and he is going to write it himself), his infection with old French liberalism, his boastful pen, his self-assertiveness and tactlessness, etc. Under strict discipline he could render good service as one of the editors, but otherwise he would only do us harm." This was Marx's report to Engels on his negotiations with Lassalle, and he added that in order not to wound his host he had postponed the final decision until he had discussed the matter with Engels and Wilhelm Wolff. Engels harboured the same misgivings as Marx and also opposed Lassalle's proposals.

In any case, the whole plan turned out to be what Lassalle had once prophetically termed it, a castle in Spain. Part of the cunning of the Prussian amnesty was that even when it permitted the fugitives of the revolutionary years to return to their homes under half-way tolerable conditions, it did not give them back their civil rights and their nationality which, according to Prussian law, they had lost by a stay of longer than ten years abroad. The men who returned under such conditions were liable to be hunted over the frontier at any moment at the whim of a bad-tempered police jack-in-office. Marx's own situation was even worse because several years before the revolution he had voluntarily abandoned his Prussian nationality. It is true that he was goaded into doing so by police chicanery, but this did not alter the fact that he had voluntarily abandoned his nationality. Lassalle represented him in the matter and moved heaven and earth to secure the return of his Prussian citizenship. He waited zealously on the Police President of Berlin, von Zedlitz, and on the Minister of the Interior, Count Schwerin, one of the most prominent supporters of the " New Era ", but all to no purpose. Zedlitz declared that the only objection to the renaturalization of Marx was his "republican or at least non-royalist convictions", whilst replying to Lassalle's urgent exhortations not to indulge in the same "inquisition of conscience and persecution on account of political convictions" he had so sharply condemned in his predecessors Manteuffel and Westphalen, Schwerin declared tersely : "For the moment at least there appears to be no particular reason for granting renaturalization to the person in question." A State like Prussia could not digest a man like Marx, and in this respect the obscure Ministers, Schwerin and his predecessors Manteuffel and Kühlwetter, were right.

After leaving Berlin Marx made a detour to visit old friends in Cologne and in particular to see his old mother again, who was rapidly approaching her end. In the beginning of May he was again in London, where he now hoped to be able to escape the exhausting life he had been leading and to find time and peace enough to finish his book. Whilst in Berlin he had succeeded in making arrangements with *Die Presse* in Vienna, despite his repeated earlier failures, and the paper promised to pay him a pound for each article and ten shillings for each report. At the same time his connection with *The New York Tribune* showed signs of improvement again, and it repeatedly printed his articles with express praise of their excellence. "These Yankees have a peculiar habit of handing out testimonials to their own correspondents", he wrote. The *Presse* in Vienna also "made a lot of his contributions", but still his old debts had never been completely paid off, and the fact that he had earned nothing during his sickness, coupled with the expenses of the journey to Germany, combined "to flush all the old filth to the surface again", as he put it. In his New Year's greetings to Engels he added that unless it turned out to be better than the old one it could go to the devil as far as he was concerned.

Not only was the year 1862 no better for Marx, but it was even worse. Although *Die Presse* advertized his contributions widely it treated him if anything in an even more scurvy fashion than did the American paper. In March he wrote to Engels : "I am not so much concerned about the fact that they don't print the best articles (though I always write them in such a fashion that they could very well do so), but it is financially impossible for me when they print only one out of four or five and pay only for one, that depresses me far below the standard of the penny-a-liners." During the course of the year all connections with *The New York Tribune* were broken off. The reason is not quite clear, but it seems to have been chiefly due to the American Civil War.

Although therefore this war brought him considerable personal misfortune, Marx welcomed it with the greatest sympathy. " Let there be no mistake about it," he wrote a few years later in the preface to his scientific masterpiece, " just as the American War of Independence sounded the tocsin for the European middle class in the eighteenth century, so the American Civil War sounded it for the European working class in the nineteenth century.' His letters to Engels show that he followed the course of the war with close interest. He regarded himself as a layman in military matters and gladly listened to what Engels had to say on the matter, and the latter's observations are still of the greatest value to-day, not only from the military standpoint, but also politically ; for instance, he went to the very core of the military and militia question with the words : " Only a society based on and educated in communism can approach closely to the militia system, and even then it will not completely achieve it." The words of Goethe, *in der Beschränkung zeigt sich erst der Meister*,[1] are applicable here, though in a different sense from that intended by the poet.

The mastery which Engels had achieved in military matters limited his general horizon, and the miserable military leadership of the Northern armies sometimes made him doubt their final victory. Writing in May 1862 he declared : " What makes me doubt the victory of the Yankees is not so much the military situation in itself, for that is merely the result of the general slackness and apathy which is typical of the North, but where is there revolutionary energy amongst the people ? They let themselves be drubbed and are really proud of the kicks they are getting. Where can one find throughout the North a single indication that they mean serious business in any respect ? I have never seen such a thing, not even in Germany in its worst days. The Yankees seem to extract most pleasure from the prospect of swindling their creditors." In July he was afraid that all hope was lost for the North, and in September he declared that the Southerners, who at least knew what they wanted, seemed like heroes to him in comparison with the slackness of the Northerners.

Marx, however, staunchly believed in the final victory of the Northern States, and in September he answered : " As far as the Yankees are concerned, I am still quite convinced that they will win in the end. . . . The way in which they are waging the war is quite natural for a bourgeois republic which has been ruled so long by fraud. The Southern States are ruled by an

[1] The master-hand demonstrates its skill most clearly under hampering circumstances.—Tr.

oligarchy and an oligarchy is better suited for waging war, particularly an oligarchy like the one in the Southern States where
all productive labour is performed by the Niggers and the four
million Whites are freebooters by profession, but for all that I
am prepared to stake my head that these fellows will get the worst
of it in the end. . . ." He was right and his judgment that in the
last resort war too would be decided by the economic conditions
under which the belligerents lived was vindicated.

This wonderful clarity was all the more remarkable because
the same letter revealed the pressing straits in which Marx found
himself at the time. They were so desperate, in fact, that he had
decided to do something he could never bring himself to do
previously and never did again. He informed Engels that he
was doing his best to get some sort of job and that he had every
prospect of obtaining employment in the offices of one of the
English railway companies. In the end he failed—he was unable to decide at the time whether this was a piece of misfortune
or luck—because his handwriting was not good enough. The
poverty of his family grew more and more bitter and the situation
was worsened by the fact that he repeatedly fell ill. Apart from
his old liver trouble he began to suffer from painful boils and
carbuncles, and this new trouble stayed with him on and off
for years. The general hopelessness of the situation also threatened to cause another breakdown in his wife's health. The
children had not even proper clothes and footwear to go to school
in, and whilst their school friends were amusing themselves in
the year of the Great Exhibition, they had a horror of visits on
account of their poverty. The oldest daughter, who was by this
time old enough to realize the truth of the situation, suffered
terribly under it and without her parent's knowledge she made
an attempt to train herself for the stage.

Things grew so bad that Marx finally made up his mind to a
step which he had often considered but always abandoned out
of consideration for his daughters' education. He decided to
leave his furniture to the landlord, who had already put in the
bailiffs, to inform all his other creditors that he was bankrupt,
to obtain positions for the two elder girls as governesses through
the good offices of English friends of the family, to find Lenchen
Demuth some other employment, and to move with his wife and
youngest daughter into one of those blocks of buildings which
had been run up to meet the needs of the poorer classes.

In the end, however, and thanks to Engels, this counsel of
despair was not followed. Engels' father had died in the spring
of 1860, and Engels had then been given a better position in the
firm of Ermen & Engels, with the prospect of later becoming a

partner, though this improvement meant also that he would have to live in greater style than before. In addition, the American crisis weighed heavily on the business and cut down his income considerably. In the early part of 1863 he also suffered a great personal misfortune. Mary Burns, the Irish girl with whom he had lived for ten years without the sanction of society, died and her death was a terrible blow to him. Writing to Marx he declared : " I simply cannot describe my feelings. The poor girl loved me with her whole heart," but Marx answered with less sympathy than Engels had expected and this fact alone showed more strikingly than anything else could have done how deeply he was in trouble himself. He referred to Engels' great loss with a few rather cool words and then went on to describe the desperate situation in which he found himself, declaring that unless he could get hold of a fair amount of money at once he would not be able to keep his head above water for more than a couple of weeks. It is true that he found it " disgustingly egoistical " to plague his friend with other people's troubles at such a moment, " but, after all, what can I do ? In the whole of London there is no one to whom I could even speak openly and at home I have to play the silent stoic in order to forestall an outburst from the other side."

However, Engels had been hurt by " the frosty reception " his misfortune had met with at Marx's hands and in his reply, which he delayed for a few days, he made no attempt to conceal his feelings, but at the same time he made a number of proposals to assist Marx out of his trouble, though he declared that for the moment he was not in a position to raise any large sum of money. Marx too delayed his reply for a few days, but only in order to give Engels a chance to calm down, and not in order to persist in the wrong he had done by his lack of sympathy. He denied the suggestion of " heartlessness ", but he frankly admitted that he had not expressed a proper sympathy. In this letter and in a later letter he described the situation which had put his head in a whirl. The tone he uses is tactful and conciliatory, because it is probable that Engels was wounded chiefly by the fact that Frau Marx had not sent him a word of sympathy on the death of his beloved friend. " Women are funny creatures," wrote Marx, " even the most intelligent. In the morning my wife cried over the death of Mary and your loss so much that she quite forgot our own misfortunes, which culminated on that very day, but in the evening she felt that no one in the world knew what suffering was unless he had the bailiffs in the house and children to feed."

The first words of regret had mollified Engels immediately

and he wrote : " One cannot live for years with a woman and then not feel her death terribly. I felt that my youth had been lowered into the grave with her. When I received your letter she was still unburied. Frankly, your letter was in my head for a week and I couldn't forget it. Never mind, your last letter has made up for it and I am heartily glad that I did not lose my oldest and best friend together with Mary." This was the first and last sign of tension that ever showed itself between the two men.

Thanks to " an extremely daring coup " Engels succeeded in raising a hundred pounds, and with this sum Marx was able to keep his head above water without moving into cheaper lodgings. He managed to scrape his way through the year 1863 and towards the end of it his mother died. It is unlikely that he inherited very much from her and it was in fact the eight or nine hundred pounds which he received later as the chief legatee of Wilhelm Wolff which afforded him a generous breathing space.

Wilhelm Wolff died in 1864, deeply mourned by both Marx and Engels. He was only 55 when he died, but in the storm and stress of an adventurous life he had never spared himself, and Engels even complained that his obstinate devotion to his duties as a teacher had hastened his end. Thanks to his great popularity amongst the Germans in Manchester he had worked his way up into quite comfortable circumstances, but the first years of his exile had been difficult enough. It would seem too that shortly before his death his father had left him a small inheritance. Later Marx dedicated the first volume of his immortal work to his " unforgettable friend, a brave, loyal and noble pioneer of the proletariat ", and Wilhelm Wolff's last gesture of friendship did much to give Marx the peace he needed in order to work on it.

The worries and troubles of his life had not been banished for ever, but they never returned in quite the same heart-breaking fashion of the previous years, because in September 1864 Engels signed a contract with Ermen which made him a partner in the firm, and from then on he was in a position to continue his unfailing assistance with a still more generous hand.

7. Lassalle's Agitation

In July 1862, at a time when the Marx family was in the severest straits, Lassalle made his return visit to London.

" In order to maintain certain *dehors* towards him my wife

had to take practically everything that wasn't actually nailed down to the pawnshop," wrote Marx to Engels. Lassalle had no idea how desperate the situation was and he accepted the appearances Marx and his wife presented at their face value, and the careful housekeeper Lenchen Demuth never forgot the visitor's hearty appetite. Thus " a horrible situation " developed, and it is really no reproach to Marx, particularly as Lassalle's attitude was not over modest at any time, that he could not quite overcome the feelings which once caused Schiller to say of Goethe : " How easily this man achieves all things, and how hard I have to fight for everything ! "

Only on his departure after a stay of several weeks does Lassalle seem to have realized the situation and he then offered his assistance, declaring that by the end of the year he could provide 15 pounds and that Marx could also draw bills on him to any amount, providing that Engels or someone else would stand good for them. With the assistance of Borkheim Marx then tried to obtain 400 thaler in this way, but Lassalle wrote a letter making his agreement dependent on a written undertaking by Engels to place him in possession of the necessary sum at least eight days before the bill fell due, " in order to guard against unforeseen circumstances ". The lack of confidence displayed by Lassalle in Marx's personal guarantee was naturally hurtful, but Engels urged Marx not to get excited about " such foolishness " and immediately gave the required undertaking.

The subsequent development of this financial arrangement is not quite clear. On the 29th of October Marx wrote to Engels that Lassalle was " very angry " with him and had demanded that the covering sum should be sent to his private address as he had no banker. On the 4th of November Marx wrote that Freiligrath was ready to send the 400 thaler to Lassalle, and the next day Engels answered that he would send 60 pounds to Lassalle " to-morrow ", but at the same time they both referred to a " prolongation " of the bill. Something must have gone wrong in this connection, for on the 24th of April 1864 Lassalle declared to a third party that he had not written to Marx for two years because " for financial reasons " their relations were strained. He had in fact last written to Marx at the end of 1862, sending him a copy of his pamphlet *What Now ?* This letter is no longer extant, but in a letter to Engels on the 2nd of January 1863 Marx declared that it was a request for the return of a book. In a further letter to Engels on the 12th of June Marx severely criticized Lassalle's agitation in Germany and wrote : " Since the beginning of the year I have not been able to bring myself to write to the fellow ". According to this letter, therefore,

Marx broke off his correspondence with Lassalle for political reasons.

However, there is not necessarily any real contradiction between the two versions, for one thing may very well have coincided with the other. The extremely uncomfortable circumstances under which the two men last met probably contributed to aggravating their political differences, which had certainly not grown less since Marx's visit to Berlin, to say the least of it.

In the autumn of 1861 Lassalle had visited Switzerland and Italy. In Zürich he had made the acquaintance of Rüstov, and on the island of Caprera that of Garibaldi, and whilst in London he had visited Mazzini. He seems to have been interested in a somewhat fantastic plan of the Italian Party of Action according to which Garibaldi should land his volunteers in Dalmatia and from there proceed to raise the standard of revolt in Hungary. This plan was never carried into execution and Lassalle makes no written references to it anywhere. At the utmost it was probably no more than a fleeting idea, for he had quite different affairs in his head and even before he visited London he had begun to carry his own plans into execution.

The winning of Marx as an ally was of far greater importance to him than all the Italian notions, but Marx proved even less approachable than he had been the year before. Lassalle still harboured the idea of founding a paper, but Marx declared that although he was prepared to act as its English correspondent in return for good pay, he would not take any share of the responsibility, political or otherwise, because he disagreed with Lassalle in everything except a few far-off and ultimate aims. He also showed himself no less opposed to the plans Lassalle laid before him for agitation amongst the workers. He declared that Lassalle let himself be influenced too much by the immediate circumstances of the moment. He wanted to make opposition to a pygmy like Schulze-Delitzsch the centre of his agitation : State aid against self-help, and with this he was merely resuscitating the slogan which the Catholic socialist Buchez had used against the real working-class movement in France in the 'forties. When adopting the Chartist demand for the general franchise he had overlooked the difference between English and German conditions and had quite forgotten the important lesson which the Second Empire had given the world in the question of the franchise. By denying all natural connections with the earlier movement in Germany he had fallen into the error of the sectarians, Proudhon's error, and instead of seeking the real basis in the genuine elements of the class movement he sought to lay down the lines of development of the latter according to a certain dogmatic recipe.

However, Lassalle did not permit himself to be disheartened by these criticisms and he continued his agitation as a purely working-class movement from the spring of 1863 on. He still hoped to be able to convince Marx of the value of his work and even after they had ceased corresponding he sent Marx his agitational material regularly, though its reception at Marx's hands was hardly what he had hoped for. In his letters to Engels Marx condemns Lassalle's activities with a severity which occasionally develops into bitter injustice. It is not necessary to go into the unpleasant details here and they can be read in the correspondence between Marx and Engels. Sufficient to say that the writings which have since given new hope and new life to hundreds of thousands of German workers were flung contemptuously on one side by Marx as the plagiarisms of a schoolboy, when he read them at all, and as juvenile exercises not worth reading even to kill time, when he did not read them.

Only shallow-pated Pharisees will attempt to gloss over these facts with the foolish remark that as Lassalle's teacher Marx had the right to treat him in such a fashion. Marx was not a superman and he never pretended to be anything more than a man, declaring that nothing human was foreign to him. The thoughtless repetition of the ideas of others was one of the things which annoyed him intensely. In justice to him it is as necessary to repair the wrong he did to others as it is to repair the wrong others did to him. His figure gains more in fact by an unprejudiced criticism of his relations to Lassalle than it would if we were to follow the example of his all-too-orthodox adherents and plod along the path he laid down, looking neither to left nor right and, to quote Lessing, carrying his carpet-slippers.

In one sense Marx was certainly Lassalle's teacher and in another sense he was not. From one point of view Marx might have said of Lassalle what Hegel is alleged to have said on his death-bed about his own pupils : only one of them understood me, and he misunderstood me. Lassalle was incomparably the most brilliant adherent Marx and Engels won during their lives, but he never fully grasped the alpha and omega of their new world standpoint, historical materialism. Marx was quite right when he declared that Lassalle was unable to free himself from " the speculative conception " of Hegelian philosophy, and although he thoroughly grasped the tremendous historical importance of the proletarian class struggle, he understood it only in those idealist forms of thought which were peculiar above all to the bourgeois epoch, philosophical and legal forms.

The result was that as an economist Lassalle did not approach Marx in magnitude, and he either failed to grasp the full significance of the latter's economic teachings or he misunderstood them altogether. Marx occasionally judged him too leniently in this respect, though far more often his strictures were too severe. Referring to his presentation of the Marxian theory of value Marx observed mildly that he had fallen victim to " considerable misunderstandings ", whereas it would have been nearer the truth to declare roundly that he had failed to understand it at all. Lassalle adopted only that part of Marx's theory of value which fitted in with his own legalist and philosophic way of looking at the world : the proof that general social labour-time, which determined value, made general social production necessary in order to secure for the worker the full product of his toil. For Marx, however, the theory of value represented the solution of all the mysteries of the capitalist mode of production ; it was a key to the formation of value and surplus-value as a historical process which would inevitably change the capitalist order of society into a socialist one. Lassalle overlooked the difference between labour-power which results in use-value and labour-power which results in exchange-value, the double nature of labour embodied in commodities, which for Marx was " the vital point " on which an understanding of political economy depended. The real difference between the two is revealed at this decisive point. It is the difference between the legalist-philosophical outlook and the economic materialist outlook.

In other economic questions Marx judged Lassalle's weaknesses all too harshly and particularly the two main economic pillars of Lassalle's agitation : " the iron law of wages ", so called by Lassalle, and the productive associations working with State credit, declaring that Lassalle had borrowed the one from the English economists Malthus and Ricardo, and the other from the French Catholic socialist Buchez, although as a matter of fact Lassalle had taken them both from *The Communist Manifesto*.

On the basis of the theory of population put forward by Malthus, according to which population always increases more quickly than the production of foodstuffs, Ricardo developed his law that the average wage must limit itself to the amount necessary, generally speaking, for a bare existence in the country in question, coupled with the possibility of procreation. Lassalle never accepted this justification of the law of wages by an alleged natural law, and he opposed the population theory of Malthus just as energetically as did Marx and Engels. He insisted on the " iron " character of the law of wages only for capitalist society, " under present-day conditions, under the rule of supply and demand ", and in this he was only following in the footsteps of *The Communist Manifesto*.

Lassalle had been dead three years before Marx proved the elastic character of the law of wages as it develops at the height of capitalist society, finding its highest level in the necessity for the utilization of capital and its lowest level in that depth of poverty which a worker can just tolerate without dying of starvation. Within these limits wage movements are not determined by the natural fluctuations of population, but by the degree of resistance which the workers offer to the steady tendency of capital to squeeze as much unpaid labour as possible out of their labour-power. After this the organization of the working class in trade unions was seen to have a far greater significance than Lassalle had been prepared to grant it.

In this respect therefore Lassalle was merely behind Marx in economic insight, but with regard to his productive associations he fell into a serious error. He did not borrow them from Buchez and he did not regard them as a panacea for all social evils, but as a step towards the socialization of production. In the same connection *The Communist Manifesto* mentions the centralization of credit in the hands of the State and the founding of State factories, together with a number of other measures, but at the same time it declares that these measures " appear economically insufficient and untenable, but in the course of the movement they outstrip themselves and are unavoidable as a means of entirely revolutionizing the mode of production ". On the other hand, Lassalle regarded his productive associations as "the organic seed inevitably driving forward all further development out of itself ". Here he certainly betrayed an " infection with French socialism " when he assumed that the laws of commodity production could be liquidated on the basis of commodity production.

His economic weaknesses, which can be referred to only in their main points here, were certainly calculated to upset Marx, who observed him throwing into confusion again what he, Marx, had already laboriously solved. If Marx had contented himself with an energetic and even angry protest his attitude would have been understandable, but in his justifiable annoyance he failed to observe that Lassalle's policy was fundamentally his own, despite all Lassalle's theoretical misunderstandings. Marx himself had always been in favour of seizing on the extremest edge of an existing movement as a lever to impel it still further forward and this is what he did in 1848. Lassalle was therefore no more influenced by " the immediate circumstances of the moment " than Marx himself had been in the revolutionary years. Lassalle is accused of sectarianism and of denying all natural connections with the earlier movement in Germany, but this is true only in so far as Lassalle never mentioned either the Communist League or its manifesto in his agitation, and it is just as true that in the several hundred numbers of the *Neue Rheinische Zeitung* there is just as little reference to either of them.

After the death of both men Engels indirectly, but nevertheless strikingly, justified Lassalle's tactics. In the years 1886–7 a proletarian mass movement began to develop in the United States with a very confused programme, and Engels wrote to his friend Sorge : " The first great step which must be taken in any country newly entering into the movement is to organize the workers into an independent political party, no matter how, providing it is a definite workers' party." And he went on to point out that if the programme adopted by such a party was confused and even highly deficient this was an inevitable and only temporary evil. He also wrote in a similar strain to other party friends in America, declaring that Marxist theory did not claim the monopoly of all the means of grace like the Catholic Church, that it was no dogma, but the exposition of a process of development. One should not make the inevitable confusion of the first mobilization of working-class forces worse confounded by forcing the workers to swallow ideas which for the moment they were unable to digest, but which they would willingly accept later on.

In support of his argument Engels pointed to the attitude of Marx and himself in the revolutionary years in Germany : " When we returned to Germany in the spring of 1848 we joined the Democratic Party as the only means of obtaining the ear of the working class. We were the most advanced wing of the party, but still we were a part of it." And just as the *Neue Rheinische Zeitung* had avoided all mention of *The Communist Manifesto*, so Engels warned the Americans against making it their immediate creed, pointing out that like almost all other minor works of Marx it was too difficult for the American workers to understand at the moment. They were coming into the movement for the first time and they were still somewhat clumsy, and enormously backward in theoretical matters : " We must use the practical everyday movement as a lever, and for this we need an entirely new literature. Once the American workers are more or less on the right path the manifesto will not fail to have its effect, but at the moment it would influence only very few workers." And when Sorge objected that the manifesto had exercised great influence on him when he had first read it, although he had been only a boy at the time, Engels replied : " You were Germans forty years ago with the German capacity for theory, and therefore the manifesto had its effect on you, but although it was translated into English, French, Flemish, Danish, etc., it had absolutely no effect on the other peoples."

By 1863 long years of leaden oppression had left very little of this capacity for theory amongst the German workers, and years of education were necessary before they again began to understand the manifesto. With regard to what Engels, appealing always and with complete justification to Marx, described as " the first great step ", Lassalle's agitation was beyond reproach. As an economist Lassalle was undoubtedly far behind Marx, but as a revolutionary he was Marx's equal, unless one cares to reproach him with the fact that his restless desire for revolutionary action outweighed the untiring patience of the scientific student. All his writings, with the one exception of *Heraclitus*, were written with a view to securing an immediate practical effect.

He based his agitation on the broad and firm foundation of the class struggle and he made its unswerving aim the conquest of political power by the working class. Marx's reproach that he sought to lay down the lines of development of the class struggle in accordance with a certain dogmatic recipe, was unjust, for Lassalle proceeded, in fact, from just those " genuine elements " which had naturally produced a movement amongst the German workers : the demand for the general franchise and the question of productive associations. His estimate of the general franchise as a lever of the proletarian class struggle was more correct than that of Marx and Engels, at least as far as his own day was concerned, and whatever may be said against his productive associations with State credit, they were nevertheless based on the correct fundamental idea that—to quote the words Marx himself used a few years later—" in order to save the working people co-operative labour must grow to national dimensions and logically therefore be supported by State means ". Only as a result of the great and occasionally excessive admiration his followers had for him might Lassalle have appeared on the surface as a " sectarian ", but the real and original responsibility for this was at least not his, and he went to enough trouble to avoid " the movement taking on the character of a one-man show owing to the blockheads ". He tried to win not only Marx and Engels, but also Bucher and Rodbertus, but he did not succeed and he found no equal to work with him. It was therefore natural enough when the gratitude of the workers occasionally took on the not very agreeable form of a Lassalle cult. On the other hand, it is also true that he was not the sort of man to hide his own light under a bushel and he did not possess the self-effacement with which Marx always placed himself behind the cause.

Another very important point remains to be considered, namely the apparently violent struggle of the liberal bourgeoisie against the Prussian government, and it was out of this struggle that Lassalle's agitation developed. Since 1859 Marx and Engels had again been paying closer attention to German affairs, but, as their letters up to 1866 show in various ways, they did not always succeed in obtaining a correct grasp of the situation. Despite their experience in the revolutionary years they still reckoned with the possibility of a bourgeois and even a military revolution, and as they over-estimated the German bourgeoisie so they underestimated the Greater Prussia policy. They never succeeded in overcoming the impressions of their youth, when their Rhenish homeland, proudly conscious of its modern culture, looked down with contempt on the Old Prussian provinces, and the more they concentrated their attention on the Tsarist plans for world dominance, the more they came to regard the Prussian State as nothing but a Russian province. Even in Bismarck they were inclined to see no more than the tool of a Russian tool, the puppet of " the mysterious man in the Tuileries ", of whom they declared even in 1859 that he danced only to the tune of the Russian diplomatic pipe. The idea that the Greater Prussian policy might, for all its otherwise objectionable features, lead to results which would be equally unpleasant for Paris and St. Petersburg did not occur to them. They considered a bourgeois revolution in Germany to be still possible, and therefore they necessarily found Lassalle's agitation thoroughly out of tune with development.

However, Lassalle saw things from close up and his judgment was sounder. He based his policy on the assumption that the Philistine movement of the progressive bourgeoisie would never lead to anything, " not even if we wait for centuries, for geological eras ", and he was right. Once the possibility of a bourgeois revolution was excluded he realized correctly that the unification of Germany, as far as it was possible at all, could only be the result of dynastic changes, and in his opinion the new workers' party should act as a driving wedge. He therefore opened up negotiations with Bismarck and attempted to entice the latter on to thin ice with his Greater Prussia policy, but he ventured too far himself, and although he did not violate his principles, he certainly did violate the exigencies of political tact, a proceeding which caused Marx and Engels to object strongly and with justification.

In the last resort what separated Marx and Engels from

Lassalle in the years 1863-4 was "opposing judgments on given conditions", and thus the appearance of personal rancour which seems to pervade the harsh judgments which Marx passed on Lassalle during these years must be discounted. However, Marx was never completely able to overcome his prejudice against the man whom the history of the German social democracy will always mention in the same breath with him and Engels, and even the mitigating power of death had no permanent effect.

He received the news of Lassalle's death from Freiligrath, and telegraphed it to Engels on the 3rd of September 1864 and the next day Engels answered : " You can imagine how the news surprised me. No matter what Lassalle may have been personally, and from a literary and scientific standpoint, politically he was certainly one of the finest brains in Germany. For us he was a very uncertain friend at the moment and would have been a fairly certain enemy in the future, but all the same it hits one hard to see how Germany is destroying all the more or less capable men of the extreme party. What joy there will be amongst the manufacturers and the Progressive swine—after all, Lassalle was the only man in Germany of whom they were afraid."

Marx let a few days pass and then on the 7th of September he answered : "Lassalle's misfortune has been worrying me damnably during the last few days. After all, he was one of the old guard and an enemy of our enemies. . . . But for all that I am sorry that our relations were so clouded during the past few years, although it was his fault. On the other hand I am very glad that I resisted the incitement from various quarters and refrained from attacking him during his 'jubilee year'. The devil take it, the group is becoming smaller and smaller and there are no reinforcements." In a letter of consolation to Countess Hatzfeldt he declared : " He died young—in battle—like Achilles ". And when a little later the windbag Blind tried to make himself important at Lassalle's expense Marx crushed him with the contemptuous words : " I have no intention of trying to explain the character of a man like Lassalle and the real significance of his agitation to a grotesque clown with nothing behind him but his own shadow. In any case, I feel quite convinced that Herr Karl Blind is only obeying the dictates of his own nature when he spurns the dead lion." And a few years later in a letter to Schweitzer Marx praised " the immortal service of Lassalle ", who, despite " the great mistakes " he made in his agitation, had awakened the German working-class movement to life after a slumber of fifteen years.

Unfortunately, however, days came when he judged the dead

Lassalle more bitterly and more unjustly than he had ever judged him during his lifetime. Thus an unpleasant residue remains and is resolved only in the inspiring thought that the modern working-class movement is far too tremendous for any single brain, even the most powerful, to grasp it in its entirety.

CHAPTER ELEVEN: THE EARLY YEARS OF THE INTERNATIONAL

1. The Founding of the International

THE International Working-men's Association was founded at a big meeting in St. Martin's Hall, London, on the 28th of September 1864, a few weeks after Lassalle's death.

It was not the work of one individual and it was not " a small body with a large head ". Above all, it was neither an insignificant shadow nor a terrible menace, as it was described alternately by the fantasy of the capitalist ink-slingers, in sublime indifference to the facts. The First International was a transitional form of the proletarian struggle for emancipation and it was as necessary as it was transitional.

The capitalist mode of production, an embodied contradiction, both produces and destroys modern states. It intensifies all national antagonisms to the utmost and at the same time it creates all nations in its own image. So long as the capitalist mode of production exists these contradictions are insoluble, and therefore the brotherhood of man about which all bourgeois revolutions have sung so sweetly has suffered defeat again and again. Whilst large-scale industry preached freedom and peace between nations it also turned the world into an armed camp as never before in history.

However, with the disappearance of the capitalist mode of production its contradictions will vanish also. It is true that the proletarian struggle for emancipation must develop on a national basis because the capitalist process of production develops within national limits, and in the beginning therefore the proletariat in each country finds itself face to face with its own bourgeoisie. Despite this, however, the proletariat need not submit to the merciless competition which has always destroyed all bourgeois dreams of international peace and freedom As soon as the workers realize that they must get rid of competition in their own ranks if they are to offer effective resistance to the superior power of capital—and this realization coincides with the first awakening of their class-consciousness—then it is only a step to the deeper realization that competition between the working classes of the various countries must cease too, and still further that the working classes must co-operate internationally if they are to overthrow the international dominance of the bourgeoisie.

Very early in the history of the modern working-class movement, therefore, a tendency towards internationalism made itself felt. What the bourgeoisie, thanks to the narrowing of its horizon by its profit interests, regards as unpatriotic, as ignorance and lack of understanding, is in reality a vital condition for the very existence of the proletarian struggle for emancipation. Although this struggle can solve the antagonism between nationalism and internationalism, whilst the bourgeoisie is condemned to writhe under it as long as it lives, the workers possess no magic wand in this respect any more than in any other, and they are not able to turn the hard and difficult climb into a level and easy path. The modern working class has to fight its battles under conditions created by historical development. It cannot overrun these conditions in a whirlwind charge, but can triumph over them only by understanding them in the Hegelian sense that to understand is to overcome.

This understanding was made more difficult owing to the circumstance that the beginnings of the working-class movement, and the beginnings of internationalism in it, coincided with, crossed and recrossed, the beginnings of a number of great national States, which were being founded as a result of the capitalist mode of production. The declaration of *The Communist Manifesto* that united action on the part of the proletariat in all civilized countries was a necessary condition of its emancipation was followed a few weeks later by the revolution of 1848. In England and France this revolution lined up the bourgeoisie and the proletariat against each other, but in Germany and Italy it released struggles for national independence. However, as far as the proletariat appeared in the arena as a separate force at all, it recognized quite correctly that although these struggles for national independence could not achieve its final aim, they nevertheless were a stage on the way to its achievement. The proletariat provided the national movements in Germany and Italy with their most courageous fighters, and nowhere did these movements find better advice than in the columns of the *Neue Rheinische Zeitung* which was issued by the author of *The Communist Manifesto*. However, the national struggles naturally forced the idea of internationalism into the background, particularly when the bourgeoisie of Germany and Italy began to take refuge behind reactionary bayonets. In Italy associations of workers formed themselves under the banner of Mazzini, who, although he was no socialist, was at least a republican, whilst in Germany, which was more highly developed than Italy and whose workers had realized the international implications of their cause even in the days of Weitling, a ten-year civil war took place around just this national question.

The situation in England and France when the modern proletarian movement began was quite different, for in both these countries national unity had been achieved long before, and even before the days of the March revolution the idea of internationalism was very much alive. Paris was regarded as the capital of the European revolution and London was the metropolis of the world market, but even in France and England the idea of internationalism experienced a set-back after the defeats suffered by the proletariat.

The terrible blood-letting of the June days exhausted the French working class, and the iron hand of Bonapartist despotism hampered both trade union and political organization. As a result the working-class movement in France fell back into the sectarianism of pre-revolutionary days and out of its confusion two main tendencies began to develop, separating, one might say, the revolutionary and socialist elements. One of these tendencies crystallized around Blanqui, who had no real socialist programme and aimed at seizing political power by the daring coup of a determined minority. The other and incomparably stronger tendency was under the intellectual influence of Proudhon, who sought to lead the workers away from the political struggle with his exchange-bank scheme for the provision of free credit, and similar doctrinaire experiments. Marx had already pointed out in *The Eighteenth Brumaire* that this movement abandoned all attempts to transform the old world with the tremendous means the latter offered for such purpose, whilst seeking salvation by backstair methods, by private means, and within its own limited conditions of existence.

After the collapse of the Chartist movement a process of development which was in many respects similar began in England also. The great utopian Robert Owen was still alive, though very old, and his school had degenerated into a sort of religious free-thought association. Side by side with Owen's school was the Christian socialism of Kingsley and Maurice, and although it must not be tarred with the same brush as its continental caricatures it too pursued educational and co-operative aims, and refused to have anything to do with the political struggle. Even the trade unions, in which respect England was in advance of France, remained politically indifferent and confined their activities to satisfying their immediate interests, a policy which was facilitated by the feverish industrial activities of the 'fifties in England and by the latter's dominating position on the world market.

Despite all this, the international working-class movement on English territory sank only very slowly into a torpor and its traces can be followed into the end of the 'fifties. The Fraternal Democrats had dragged on into the days of the Crimean War, and even when they finally disappeared an international committee was formed and after that an international association, thanks chiefly to the energies of Ernest Jones. These two organizations were never of any great significance, but at least they showed that the idea of internationalism had not died out completely and that its fire still glowed and might be fanned into leaping flames again by a strong breeze.

This breeze sprang up in the form of the commercial crisis of 1857, the war of 1859 and in particular the civil war which broke out between the Northern and Southern States in America in 1860. The commercial crisis of 1857 struck the first serious blow at Bonapartist rule in France, and the attempt to counter its effects by launching a foreign political adventure was by no means completely successful. The game which the false Bonaparte started quickly slid out of his hands. The movement for Italian unity grew too strong for him to control whilst the French bourgeoisie showed little inclination to let itself be fobbed off with the somewhat sparse laurels of Magenta and Solferino. Under the circumstances the idea of curbing the growing insolence of the bourgeoisie by giving the working class a little more leeway was a fairly obvious one, and in fact the very existence of the Second Empire depended on Bonaparte's successful solution of the problem of playing off the bourgeoisie and the proletariat against each other whilst holding both in check.

Naturally, Bonaparte intended to make only trade-union concessions to the working class and not political concessions. Proudhon, who enjoyed great influence on the working-class movement, was opposed to the Second Empire, although some of his paradoxical utterances might very easily have awakened the contrary impression, but he was also an opponent of strikes. However, this was just the point on which the French workers were getting out of hand, and despite Proudhon's warnings and despite the severe anti-combination laws no less than 3,909 workers were convicted from 1853 to 1866 for offences against these laws and no less than 749 combinations were involved. The imitation Cæsar then began to pardon the convicted men, and he also supported the sending of French workers to the Great Exhibition in London in 1862, and it must be admitted that he did it in a much more effective and thorough fashion than did the German *Nationalverein*, which put the same ingenious idea into operation. The delegates were elected by their fellow-workers in the same trades. Fifty polling booths for 150 trades were established in Paris, and 200 delegates were elected and sent to London, the expenses of the journey being borne partly by voluntary subscription and partly by subsidies from the imperial and municipal treasuries, which contributed 20,000 francs each. On their return the delegates were permitted to publish detailed reports, and generally speaking, these reports went far beyond the limits of trade affairs. Under the conditions existing in France at the time the affair represented a first-class State action and it caused the Police Prefect of Paris, prophetic in his presentiments, to sigh that before the Emperor went in for such experiments it would be better to abolish the anti-combination laws altogether.

In fact, the French workers rewarded their self-seeking patron not in the way he expected, but in the way he deserved. During the elections of 1863 the government candidates in Paris received only 82,000 votes as against 153,000 for the candidates of the opposition, whereas in the elections of 1857 the government candidates had received 111,000 votes and the candidates of the opposition only 96,000 votes. It was generally assumed that this was due only in a slight degree to the changed attitude of the bourgeoisie and chiefly to the changed attitude of the working class, which proclaimed its independence just at the moment when the false Bonaparte began to flirt with the workers, though it still marched under the banner of bourgeois radicalism. This assumption was confirmed by subsequent by-elections in Paris in 1864 when sixty workers put forward the engraver Tolain as their candidate and issued a manifesto announcing the rebirth of socialism. The socialists had learned from past experience, it declared. In 1848 the workers had possessed no clear programme and had adopted this or that social theory more by instinct than deliberation, but to-day they rejected all utopian exaggerations and sought relief in social reforms such as the freedom of the press, the right to organize, the repeal of the anti-combination laws, general and free education, and the abolition of the religious budget.

At the election, however, Tolain received only a few hundred votes. Proudhon was in agreement with the contents of the manifesto but condemned participation in the election, regarding the polling of blank ballot papers as a more effective protest against the Second Empire régime. The Blanquists found the manifesto too moderate for them, whilst the bourgeoisie in all its liberal and radical shades, with one or two exceptions, attacked Tolain with mockery and gibes, though in reality there was nothing in his programme to give them any cause for anxiety. It was a phenomenon similar to the one which was taking place at the same time in Germany. Encouraged by this Bonaparte ventured a step further, and in May 1864 a law was passed which, although it did not withdraw the prohibition of trade unions (which was done only four years later), at least repealed the paragraphs of the penal code which provided punishments for workers convicted of joining combinations with a view to improving their working conditions.

In England the anti-combination laws had been repealed in 1825, but the existence of the trade unions was still not absolutely secure either legally or actually, whilst the masses of their members had not the franchise, which would have permitted them to abolish the legal hindrances which hampered their struggle for better working conditions. The development of continental capitalism destroyed innumerable existences and created dangerous competition for the English workers in the form of sweated labour, and every time they made an attempt to secure higher wages or shorter working hours the English capitalists threatened to import cheap foreign labour-power from France, Belgium, Germany and other countries. In this situation the American Civil War aroused the workers and produced a cotton crisis which caused great misery amongst the English textile workers.

In this way the English trade unions were shaken out of their comfortable torpor and the " New Unionism " developed, represented by a number of experienced leaders of the older unions : Allan of the engineers, Applegarth of the carpenters, Lucraft of the joiners, Cremer of the builders, Odger of the shoemakers, and others. These men recognized the necessity of a political struggle on behalf of the trade unions, and they turned their attention to the question of reforming the franchise. They were the moving spirits behind a monster meeting which took place in St. James's Hall under the chairmanship of the Radical leader, John Bright, and registered a fierce protest against Palmerston's intention of intervening in the American Civil War on the side of the Southern States, and when Garibaldi came to London on a visit in the spring of 1864 they organized a tremendous reception for him.

The political reawakening of the English and French working classes also revived the idea of internationalism. A " fraternal celebration " had taken place in 1862 at the Great Exhibition in London between the English workers and the French delegates,

and this bond was strengthened still further by the Polish insurrection of 1863. The Polish cause had always been extremely
popular amongst the revolutionary elements in the countries of
Western Europe. The oppression and dismemberment of Poland
had made the three Eastern European powers into a reactionary
block, and the restoration of Polish independence would have
struck a deadly blow against Russian hegemony in Europe.
The Fraternal Democrats had always celebrated the anniversary
of the Polish Revolution of 1830, and these celebrations had been
enthusiastic demonstrations in favour of a united and independent
Poland, but always with the basic idea that the restoration of a
free and democratic Poland was a necessary condition for the
proletarian struggle for emancipation. This was also the case
in 1863, and the social note was sounded very sharply at the
celebrations which took place in London in the presence of
representatives of the French workers. The social question was
also at the basis of an address which a committee of English
workers under the chairmanship of Odger sent to the French
workers to thank them for having sent representatives to the
celebrations in London, and it pointed out in particular that
English capital was able to hold the English workers in check
by importing sweated foreign labour, only because the working
classes in the various countries had not yet established close and
fraternal relations with each other.

    This address was translated into French by Professor Beesly,
a Professor of History at London University who had rendered
many services to the workers, and it met with a powerful echo
in the workshops of Paris, where the workers decided to send
their answer to London in the hands of a special deputation. A
meeting took place in St. Martin's Hall, London, on the 28th of
September 1864 under the chairmanship of Professor Beesly to
welcome this French deputation. The hall was packed to the
doors, and the English workers heard Tolain read the answer of
the French workers, which referred to the Polish insurrection in the
words : " Once again Poland has been drenched with the blood
of its best sons and we were helpless spectators," and went on to
demand that the voice of the people should be heard in all
important political and social questions. The despotic power of
capital must be broken. Owing to the division of labour the
worker had been turned into a mechanical tool, and free trade
without international proletarian solidarity must develop into
a form of industrial serfdom more merciless and more terrible
that the serfdom which the Great French Revolution had
destroyed. The workers of the world must unite in order to
offer stern resistance to such a terrible system.

After a lively debate in which Eccarius spoke on behalf of the German workers the meeting adopted the proposal of the trade unionist Wheeler to elect a committee with the power of co-option, and to instruct it to draw up the statutes of an international workers association for use until an international congress in Belgium should decide finally on them. The committee was elected and consisted of numerous trade unionists and representatives of foreign workers, including for the German workers Karl Marx, whose name the newspaper reports mentioned last of all.

2. *The Inaugural Address*

Up to this meeting Marx had taken no active part in the movement, but he had been called upon by the Frenchman le Lubez to be present at it on behalf of the German workers and to name a German worker as a speaker. Marx put forward Eccarius whilst he remained a silent observer on the platform.

He estimated the importance of his scientific work highly enough to place it before any frivolous or hopeless organizational efforts, but he willingly placed it on one side when there was really useful practical work to be done for the cause of the proletariat, and this time he recognized that " affairs of importance " were at stake. He wrote in the same strain to Weydemeyer and other friends : " The recently formed International Workers Committee is not unimportant. Its English members consist chiefly of the heads of the trade unions, that is to say, the real labour lords of London, the men who organized the tremendous reception for Garibaldi and the monster meeting in St. James's Hall (under Bright's chairmanship) which prevented Palmerston declaring war on the Northern States as was his intention. As far as the French are concerned the members of the committee are not very important but they are the direct representatives of the workers in Paris. Connections have also been established with the Italian associations which held their congress in Naples recently. Although for years I have systematically refused to take part in any ' organizations ' I accepted this time because here there is a possibility of doing some real good." Writing to Engels he declared : " There is now evidently a revival of the working classes taking place," and he considered it his primary duty to guide it along right lines.

Fortunately the circumstances gave him the intellectual leadership automatically. The committee co-opted new members until it was about fifty strong, half of the members being English workers, whilst the strongest single group after the English was the German group, which included Marx, Eccarius, Lessner, Lochner and Pfänder, all of whom had been members of the Communist League. France had 9 representatives, Italy 6, and Poland and Switzerland 2 each. After constituting itself, the committee then appointed a sub-committee to draw up a programme and statutes.

Marx was also elected on to this sub-committee, but owing to illness and the fact that the invitations were sometimes sent out too late he was unable to attend many of its meetings. In the meantime Major Wolf, the private secretary of Mazzini, the Englishman Weston and the Frenchman le Lubez had vainly tried to perform the task which the sub-committee had been set. Although Mazzini was very popular amongst the English workers at the time he understood far too little about the modern working-class movement to impress trained trade unionists with the draft he drew up. He simply did not understand the proletarian class struggle and therefore he hated it. His programme contained a few socialist phrases, but they were the sort which the proletariat had already abandoned in the 'sixties, and the statutes he drew up were also conceived in the spirit of a bygone era and provided for a high degree of centralization such as was demanded by the exigencies of political conspiracies. As a result Mazzini's attempt was utterly foreign not only to the conditions of trade unionism in general, but to the aims of an international association of workers in particular, whose aim was not to create any new movement, but merely to link up the working-class movements which already existed in the various countries. The drafts which le Lubez and Weston put forward also represented little more than collections of general phrases.

The situation was hopeless therefore until Marx took it in hand. He was determined to throw the whole of the previous efforts overboard if possible and in order to emancipate himself from them completely he drew up an address to the working class—an idea which had not occurred to the meeting in St. Martin's Hall—a sort of review of working-class history since 1848, to serve as an introduction to the statutes of the new organization which might then be clearer and briefer. The sub-committee accepted Marx's proposals immediately and all it demanded was the addition of a few phrases about " right and duty, truth, morality and justice ", but as Marx pointed out in a letter to Engels, he succeeded in inserting them in such a way that they did no harm. The committee then unanimously and enthusiastically adopted *The Inaugural Address and Provisional Rules.*

Referring to this document later Professor Beesly declared that it was probably the most tremendous and impressive representation of the working-class case against the middle class ever pressed into a dozen pages. It opens by recording the impressive fact that in the years from 1848 to 1864 the misery of the working class did not diminish although just this period had gone into history as one of unparalleled industrial development and commercial growth, and it proves its point by comparing the frightful statistics published in the official Blue Books concerning the misery of the English proletariat with the official figures used by the Chancellor of the Exchequer, Gladstone, in a budget speech to show " the intoxicating augmentation of wealth and power " which had taken place in the same period but had been " entirely confined to classes of property ". The Address exposed this crying contradiction of the basis of English conditions because England was the foremost country of European trade and industry, but it pointed out that similar conditions existed on a somewhat smaller scale, and making allowances for local differences, in all continental countries where large-scale industry was beginning to develop.

All over the world this " intoxicating augmentation of wealth and power " was " entirely confined to classes of property " with the one exception perhaps that a small section of the workers, as in England, were receiving somewhat higher wages, though even this improvement was cancelled out by the general increase in prices. " Everywhere the great mass of the working classes sank into ever deeper misery at least to the same extent as the upper classes rose in the social scale. In all the countries of Europe it is now an irrefutable fact, undeniable for every unprejudiced inquirer and denied only by those who have an interest in awakening deceptive hopes in others, that neither the perfection of machinery nor the application of science to industry and agriculture, neither the resources and artifices of communication nor new colonies and emigration, neither the conquest of new markets nor free trade, or all these things combined can succeed in abolishing the misery of the working masses, and that on the contrary, every new development of the creative power of labour is calculated, on the false basis of existing conditions, to intensify the social antagonisms and aggravate the social conflict. During this intoxicating period of economic progress starvation raised itself almost to the level of a social institution in the capital of the British Empire. This period is characterized in the annals of history by the accelerated return, the extended compass and the deadly effects of the social pest known as industrial and commercial crisis."

The Address then glanced at the defeat of the working-class movement in the 'fifties, and came to the conclusion that even this period had its compensating characteristics. Two facts in particular were stressed, first of all the legal enactment of the ten-hour day with its salutary effects on the English proletariat. The struggle for the legal limitation of the working day had been a direct intervention in the great conflict between the blind forces of the law of supply and demand, which summed up the political economy of the bourgeoisie, and production regulated by social welfare as represented by the working class. " And therefore the Ten Hour Bill was not only a great practical success, but also the victory of a principle ; for the first time the political economy of the bourgeoisie was defeated by the political economy of the working class."

The political economy of the proletariat had won a still greater victory through the co-operative movement and by the establishment of factories based on the principle of co-operation and made possible by the tireless work of a few men without outside assistance. The value of these great social experiments could not be estimated too highly. " In practice instead of by reasoning they have proved that production on a large scale and in accordance with the laws of modern science is possible without the existence of a class of employers giving employment to a class of workers ; that in order to produce wealth the tools of labour need not be monopolized as the instruments of an exploiting domin-ance over the workers ; that wage-labour, like slave-labour and serfdom, is only a subordinate and temporary form doomed to disappear before co-operative labour, which performs its difficult task with a willing hand, a joyful spirit and a light heart." How-ever, co-operative labour limited to occasional attempts would not be able to break the monopoly of capital. " Perhaps just for this reason aristocrats, apparently high-minded in their ideas, philanthropic rhetoricians of the bourgeoisie and even hard-headed economists have suddenly begun to pay loathsome compli-ments to the co-operative labour system, which they tried vainly to suppress in its infancy, mocked at as the utopianism of dreamers or condemned as the madness of socialists ". Only the develop-ment of co-operative labour to national dimensions could save the working masses, but the owners of land and capital would always mobilize their political privileges to perpetuate their economic monopoly indefinitely, and it was therefore the great duty of the working class to conquer political power.

The workers seemed to have grasped the necessity of this,

as was proved by the simultaneous revival of the working-class movement in England, France, Germany and Italy, and by the simultaneous efforts to reorganize the workers politically. "They possess one element of success—numbers. But numbers are weighty in the scales only when they are united in an organization and led towards a conscious aim." Past experience had shown that to ignore the fraternity which should exist between the workers of all countries and spur them on to stand shoulder to shoulder in all the struggles for their emancipation, always revenged itself in a general failure of all their unrelated efforts. This consideration had moved the meeting in St. Martin's Hall to found the International Working-men's Association.

A further conviction had impelled the meeting : the emancipation of the workers demanded fraternal relations between the workers of all countries, but how could this high aim be achieved in face of a foreign policy on the part of the various governments pursuing criminal aims, exploiting national prejudices, and shedding the blood and wasting the substance of the peoples in predatory wars ? Not the wisdom of the ruling classes but the heroic resistance of the proletariat against criminal folly had saved the countries of Western Europe from an infamous crusade to perpetuate slavery on the other side of the Atlantic. The shameless applause, the hypocritical sympathy or the stupid indifference with which the ruling classes had watched Tsarist Russia conquer the mountain fastnesses of Caucasia and slaughter the heroic Poles indicated to the working classes their duty to penetrate into the secrets of international politics, to watch the diplomatic tricks of their governments closely, to oppose them with all possible means and, should it prove impossible to frustrate them, to organize great demonstrations to demand that the simple laws of morality and justice which governed the relations between individuals should also be the supreme laws governing the relations between nations. The struggle for such a foreign policy was part and parcel of the general struggle for the emancipation of the working class. The address then concluded, as *The Communist Manifesto* had concluded, with the words : "Workers of the World Unite ! "[1]

The provisional rules began with reflections which may be summed up as follows : the emancipation of the working class must be the task of the workers themselves. The struggle for the emancipation of the working class is not a struggle for the establishment of new class privileges, but for the abolition of class rule altogether. The economic subjugation of the worker to those who have appropriated the tools of labour, i.e., the source of life, results in servitude in all its forms : social misery, intellectual

---

[1] The actual words, written by Marx in English, were the less commonly used expression: "Proletarians of all countries unite!"

atrophy and political dependence. The economic emancipation of the working class is therefore the great aim for which all political movements must serve as a means. Up to the present all attempts to realize this great aim have been unsuccessful owing to the lack of unity between the various working-class groups in each country and between the working classes of the various countries. The emancipation of the workers is neither a local nor a national task, but a social one. It is a task which embraces all countries in which modern society exists and it can be achieved only by systematic co-operation between all these countries. The moral platitudes about justice and truth, duties and rights which Marx had embodied in his text so unwillingly were then hung on to these clear and trenchant passages.

The head of the new association was a General Council composed of workers from the various countries represented in the association, but until the first congress the committee elected by the meeting in St. Martin's Hall exercised the functions of the General Council. The tasks of this council were : to establish international relations between the working-class organizations in the various countries, to inform the workers of each country regularly concerning the activities of their fellow workers in other countries, to collect statistics on the situation of the working classes in the various countries, to discuss questions of general interest to all working-class organizations, to secure uniform and simultaneous action on the part of all affiliated organizations in the event of international disputes, to publish regular reports on the work of the association, and other similar tasks.

The General Council was to be elected by the congress, which was to meet once a year and determine the seat of the council and the place and time of the next congress. The General Council had the right to co-opt new members and, if necessary, to alter the venue of the next congress, but not to postpone it. The workers' organizations in the various countries which affiliated to the International were to retain their organizational independence completely and any independent local organization might take up direct relations with the General Council, although in the interests of effectiveness it was regarded as desirable that the various organizations in the individual countries should unite as far as possible on a national basis and under central bodies.

Although it would be quite wrong to describe the International as the work of " one great brain ", it is nevertheless true that when it was founded it had a great brain at its disposal which saved it long and tedious wanderings on the wrong track by pointing out the right one from the beginning. Marx did no more than this, and it was never his intention to do any more. The incomparable mastery which the *Inaugural Address* reveals is derived from the fact that it was based on the given situation and, as Liebknecht aptly pointed out, contained the final implications of communism no less than *The Communist Manifesto*.

However, *The Inaugural Address and Provisional Rules* differed from *The Communist Manifesto* not only in the form : " Time is necessary ", Marx wrote to Engels, " before the revived movement can permit itself the old audacious language. The need of the moment is : bold in matter, but mild in manner." It also had a very different task. The aim of the International was to unite the whole of the fighting proletariat of Europe and America into one great army, and to give it a programme which, in the words of Engels, would leave the door open for the English trade unions, the French, Belgian, Italian and Spanish Proudhonists, and the German Lassalleans. Marx relied exclusively on the intellectual development of the working class which would result from its united action to guarantee the final victory of scientific socialism as set out in *The Communist Manifesto*.

It was not long before his hopes were subjected to a severe test, for hardly had the propaganda work of the International begun when it came into severe conflict with that section of the European working class which understood the principles of the International better than any other.

3. The Breach with Schweitzer

It is a legend, but neither a true nor an agreeable one, that the German Lassalleans refused to affiliate to the International and took up a hostile attitude towards it from the beginning.

In the first place, it is quite impossible to find any reason which might have caused them to take up such an attitude. It is true that they attached great importance to strict discipline in their own ranks, but the Provisional Rules of the International threatened no sort of interference and, above all, they could subscribe to the *Inaugural Address* from beginning to end, and with particular satisfaction to that section which declared that only the development of the co-operatives to national dimensions and their furtherance by State means could save the working masses.

The truth is that from the very beginning the Lassalleans

in Germany took up a friendly attitude towards the International, although at the time of its foundation they were deeply engrossed in their own troubles. After the death of Lassalle, and at his testamentary recommendation, Bernhard Becker was elected President of the *Allgemeiner Deutscher Arbeiterverein*, but he soon proved himself so incompetent that hopeless confusion resulted and all that held the organization together was its organ the *Sozialdemokrat*, which had been appearing since the end of 1864 under the intellectual leadership of J. B. von Schweitzer, an energetic and capable man who had done his best to secure the co-operation of Marx and Engels. Without any pressure having been exerted on him he made Liebknecht a member of the editorial board and in the second and third numbers of the papers he published the *Inaugural Address*.

The Paris correspondent of the paper, Moses Hess, cast suspicion on Tolain, declaring him to be a friend of the Palais Royal, in which Jerome Bonaparte was playing the rôle of red demagogue, but Schweitzer published the letter only after having secured the express agreement of Liebknecht, and when Marx complained he did his utmost to settle the affair amicably and ordered that Liebknecht should first edit everything the paper published concerning the International. On the 15th of February 1865 Schweitzer wrote to Marx informing him that he intended to put forward a resolution declaring his organization completely in agreement with the principles of the International and deciding to send delegates to its congresses. His organization would not, however, affiliate formally to the International, but solely on account of the German federal laws which prohibited the establishment of any connections between working-class organizations. Schweitzer received no answer to this letter and instead Marx and Engels issued a public declaration breaking off all connections with the *Sozialdemokrat*.

These facts show clearly enough that the unfortunate breach had nothing whatever to do with disagreements in connection with the International, and its real cause is explained quite frankly by Marx and Engels in their declaration. They had never failed to take the difficult situation of the *Sozialdemokrat* into consideration, they declared, and they had never put forward any demands unsuited to the Berlin meridian, but they had repeatedly demanded that the paper should not be less audacious towards the government and the feudal-absolutist party than towards the Progressives. The tactics pursued by the *Sozialde-mokrat* made it impossible for them to contribute any further to it. They still subscribed word for word to what they had once written in the *Deutsche Brüsseler Zeitung* on royal Prussian governmental socialism and the attitude of a working-class party to such a tawdry deception when answering the *Rheinischer Beobachter*, which had proposed " an alliance of the proletariat with the government against the liberal bourgeoisie ".

As a matter of fact, the tactics pursued by the *Sozialdemokrat* had nothing to do with any such " alliance " or with any " royal Prussian governmental socialism ". When Lassalle's first hope of arousing the German working class in one powerful onset proved to be a vain one, the *Allgemeiner Deutscher Arbeiterverein* with its few thousand members found itself wedged in between two opponents, each of which was strong enough to crush it. From the bourgeoisie the young workers' party had nothing to expect but stupid hatred, whereas it might reasonably expect that the cunning diplomat Bismarck would not be able to carry out his Greater Prussia policy without making certain concessions to the masses of the people. Schweitzer never harboured any illusions about the value or the aim of such concessions, but at a time when the German working class was practically deprived of the right to organize, when it enjoyed no effective franchise, and when the freedom of the press, of association and of meeting was at the mercy of bureaucratic arbitrariness, the Social Democracy could not hope to make progress by attacking both its opponents simultaneously and with equal energy, but only by playing one off against the other, though naturally an absolutely necessary condition for such a policy was the complete independence of the young workers' party towards both sides and a firm consciousness of this independence amongst the working masses.

Schweitzer pursued this policy with vigour and success, and it is impossible to find anything in the columns of the *Sozialdemokrat* which savours of an " alliance " with the government against the Progressives. An examination of his activities against the general political background of the day will reveal some mistakes—admitted by himself—but on the whole a sagacious and logical policy guided exclusively by the interests of the working class, and certainly not dictated by Bismarck or any other reactionary.

Although in other respects Schweitzer was not the equal of Marx and Engels, he had at least one advantage over them and that was a thorough knowledge of conditions in Prussia. They had no first-hand knowledge of the situation, whilst Liebknecht, upon whom the task of making good this deficiency naturally devolved, did not perform it at all satisfactorily. Liebknecht had returned to Germany in 1862 to found the *Norddeutsche Allgemeine Zeitung*, together with the red republican Brass, but hardly had his editorial work begun when he discovered that Brass had sold the paper to Bismarck. He immediately parted company with the paper, but this first experience on German territory was unfortunate not only in the sense that it left him once again in a critical financial situation reminiscent of the days of his exile, though this did not worry him unduly because he was accustomed to placing the cause above his own personal interests, but also because it prevented him from obtaining an unprejudiced view of the new conditions he found in Germany.

When he returned he was fundamentally still the old '48er in the spirit of the *Neue Rheinische Zeitung*, which paid much less attention to socialist theory and even to the class struggle than it did to the revolutionary struggle of the nation against the rule of the reactionary classes. Although he was well versed in the fundamental ideas of socialist theory, Liebknecht was never a profound socialist theorist, and the chief thing he had learned from Marx during the years of exile was the latter's tendency to search the wide fields of international politics for any signs of revolutionary developments. As Rhinelanders Marx and Engels were inclined to regard everything East Elbian too contemptuously, and they therefore underestimated the importance of the Prussian State ; but Liebknecht was still worse, for he had been born in South Germany, and in the early years of the movement he had been either in Baden or in Switzerland, the two strongholds of particularism. He regarded Prussia as the Russian vassal of pre-March days, as a reactionary State which fought against historical progress with the contemptible weapon of corruption, a State which must be defeated before it would be possible to think of any modern class struggle in Germany. He failed to recognize how much the economic development of the 'fifties had changed the Prussian State and created circumstances which made the separation of the working class from bourgeois democracy a historical necessity.

In consequence any permanent understanding between Liebknecht and Schweitzer was impossible, and in the eyes of the former it was the last straw when the latter published a series of five articles on Bismarck's Ministry, drawing a masterly parallel between the Greater Prussia policy and the proletarian revolutionary policy in the question of German unity, but committing the " error " of describing the dangerous energy of Bismarck's policy so eloquently that the description seemed almost a glorification. On the other hand, in a letter to Schweitzer on the 13th of February, Marx committed the " error " of declaring that although the Prussian government might adopt all sorts of frivolous experiments with the idea of productive co-operatives, it would not repeal the anti-combination laws and curb bureaucracy and police arbitrariness. However, Marx was inclined to overlook what he had so eloquently put forward against Proudhon, namely that governments could not control economic circumstances but were themselves controlled by them, and a few years later the Bismarck Ministry was compelled willy-nilly to repeal the anti-combination laws. In his answering letter of the 15th of February, the letter in which he promised to work for the International in the *Allgemeiner Deutscher Arbeiterverein* and again informed Marx that Liebknecht was being entrusted with the editorship of all matters relating to the International, Schweitzer declared that he would gladly listen to any theoretical advice Marx might have to give, but that in order to decide on practical questions and immediate tactics one must be in the centre of the movement itself and have a thorough knowledge of existing conditions. Marx and Engels then broke with him.

These misunderstandings and complications can be fully understood only in connection with the unfortunate activities of Countess Hatzfeldt, who sinned grievously against the memory of the man who had once saved her name from obloquy. She sought to turn Lassalle's creation into an orthodox sect honouring the word of the master as its supreme law, but even then it was not so much the word of the master as the interpretation Countess Hatzfeldt put upon it which was to be the supreme law. The mischief she did can be seen from a letter written by Engels to Weydemeyer on the 10th of March in which after a few words on the founding of the *Sozialdemokrat* he declares : " An intolerable Lassalle cult developed in the paper, and in the meantime we learned definitely (old Countess Hatzfeldt informed Liebknecht and appealed to him to act in the same spirit) that Lassalle was much more deeply involved with Bismarck than we had thought. A formal alliance existed between the two and things had gone so far that Lassalle was to go to Sleswig-Holstein to support the annexation of the Duchies whilst in return Bismarck made a vague promise to introduce a sort of general franchise and a rather more definite promise to grant the right to organize, to make social concessions, to give State support to the workers organizations, etc. The foolish Lassalle had no guarantees at all that Bismarck would keep his part of the agreement and he would certainly have been packed off to gaol the moment he made himself a nuisance. The editors of the *Sozialdemokrat* know this perfectly well, and yet they are keeping up the Lassalle cult more vigorously than ever. In addition, they let themselves be intimidated by Wagener (of the *Kreuz-Zeitung*) and paid court to Bismarck, flirted with his ideas, etc., etc. We published a

declaration and broke off relations and Liebknecht did the same."
It is difficult to understand how Marx and Engels, who both knew
Lassalle well and both read the *Sozialdemokrat*, could have been
taken in by the fantastic stories of Countess Hatzfeldt, but as
they were it is only logical that they broke off all relations with
the movement which Lassalle had founded.

However, their action had no practical effects on that movement and even old members of the Communist League like
Röser, who had defended the principles of *The Communist Manifesto* so brilliantly before the Cologne Assizes, declared themselves
in favour of Schweitzer's tactics.

4.　The First Conference in London

The German Lassalleans were thus excluded from the sphere
of the International from the beginning and at first the propaganda amongst the English trade unionists and the French
Proudhonists made very slow progress.

After all, it was only a small circle of trade-union leaders
who had realized the necessity of the political struggle and even
they regarded the International more as a means to attain trade-
union ends than anything else. But at least they possessed a
great amount of practical experience in organizational questions,
whereas the French Proudhonists had neither this nor any insight into the historical character of the working-class movement.
The new organization had, in fact, set itself a tremendous task,
and it needed both tremendous energy and tremendous industry
to perform it.

Although Marx was plagued again and again by painful
illnesses, and although he was itching to complete his scientific
work, he spared neither energy nor industry in the cause of the
International. On one occasion he sighed : " The worst part
about such agitation is that it disturbs one's work," and on
another occasion he declared that the International and everything connected with it weighed on him " like an incubus " and
he would be glad to shake it off. However, he realized that
once having put his hand to the plough he could not look back,
and in reality it would not have been Marx had not the carrying
of this burden made him happier and more hopeful than its
abandonment could possibly have done.

It soon became clear that Marx was the actual " head " of
the movement. Not that he pushed himself forward in any way,

for he had an unlimited contempt for all cheap popularity, and unlike those Democrats who made themselves look important in public whilst in reality doing nothing, he did a tremendous amount of work behind the scenes whilst at the same time keeping himself well out of the public view. However, there was not another man in the organization who possessed the unusual qualities necessary for its great tasks : the clear and deep insight into the laws of historical development, the energy to pursue the necessary unswervingly, the patience to be satisfied within the limits of the possible, the forbearance with honest error and the masterful ruthlessness with obstinate ignorance. To a far greater extent than in Cologne Marx was now in a position to exercise his incomparable gift of mastering men by teaching and leading them.

The personal disputes and quarrels which are inevitably part and parcel of the beginnings of all such movements cost him " an enormous amount of time ", and the Italian and in particular the French members caused him a lot of unnecessary difficulties. Since the revolutionary years there had existed a deep antipathy between the " hand and brain workers " in Paris. The proletarians found it difficult to forget the all too frequent treachery of the intellectuals, and the latter decried all working-class movements which wanted to have nothing to do with them, whilst under the stifling pressure of Bonapartist military despotism, which made every means of contact through newspapers or organizations impossible, the suspicion of Bonapartist trickery was rife even in the ranks of the working class itself. The bubbling and simmering of this " French stew " cost the General Council many a valuable evening and the adoption of many a long-winded resolution.

Marx's activities in connection with the English section of the International were more agreeable and fruitful. The English workers had strenuously opposed the intention of their government to intervene in the American Civil War on the side of the rebellious Southern States, and when Abraham Lincoln was re-elected President they sent him a message of greetings and congratulation. Marx drew up this address to the " son of the working class " who had been entrusted with the task of leading his country in a noble struggle to emancipate an enslaved race. So long as the white workers of America failed to realize that the existence of human slavery was a shame to the republic, so long as they boasted to the Negro, who was sold without his previous agreement, of their own inestimable privilege of selling themselves and choosing their masters, they would be incapable of winning real freedom or of supporting the struggle of their European brothers for freedom. However, the sea of bloodshed during the civil war had swept away this barrier.

Like Lessing, Marx always spoke of his own work in derogatory terms, but he obviously put his whole heart into this address, although writing to Engels he declared that he had been instructed to give the address its form, which was a more difficult task than if he had been made responsible for the content as well, and that he had done so in order that the phrases which were the usual stock-in-trade of such documents should at least be different from the usual vulgar democratic phraseology. Lincoln did not fail to observe the difference and, much to the surprise of the London newspapers, for " the old man " invariably replied to all congratulations from bourgeois democratic circles with a few formal compliments, he answered the address in a warm and friendly tone.

In view of its content an address read by Marx on " Value, Price and Profit " on the 26th of June 1865 to the General Council of the International was much more important. Its aim was to refute the contention of a number of members of the council that a general rise in wages could be of no real use to the workers and that therefore the trade unions were harmful. This was based on the erroneous assumption that wages determined the value of commodities and that if the capitalists pay 5 instead of 4 shillings in wages to-day, they will sell their commodities for 5 instead of 4 shillings to-morrow, as a result of the increased demand. Marx declared that although this was very shallow reasoning and took only the most superficial appearance of things into account, it was nevertheless not easy to explain all the economic questions involved to ignoramuses. It was impossible to compress a course of political economy into one hour. However, he in fact succeeded in doing so admirably and he was thanked by the trade unions for having rendered them a valuable service.

It was chiefly the growing movement for a reform of the franchise which brought the International its first signal successes, and on the 1st of May 1865 Marx reported to Engels : " The Reform League is our work. In the inner committee of twelve (six representatives each of the middle class and the working class) all the working-class representatives are members of our General Council, including Eccarius. We have foiled all the middle-class attempts to deceive the workers. . . . If this attempt to regenerate the political working-class movement in England succeeds then our association will have done more for the European working class than would have been possible in any other fashion, and without making a noise about it. And there is every prospect of success." On the 3rd of May Engels answered : "In a very short space of time and with very little to-do the international association has really won a tremendous amount of ground. It is a good thing that it is now so busily engaged in England instead of bothering its head with French cliquism. At least you have some compensation for your lost time." However, it was soon to become evident that even this success had its unsatisfactory side.

Marx considered that on the whole the political situation was not yet mature enough to justify the holding of the public congress which had been arranged to take place in Brussels in 1865, and he feared, not without good reason, that it would degenerate into a Babel of tongues. With great difficulty and against particularly energetic opposition from the French he succeeded in securing agreement for the holding of an internal conference in London instead of the public congress in Brussels, a conference to be attended only by the representatives of the leading committees and to be no more than a preliminary to the future congress. In support of his standpoint Marx advanced the following reasons : the necessity of previous agreement and discussion, the reform movement in England, the wave of strikes springing up in France, and finally the legislation against foreigners being introduced in Belgium, which would make it impossible to hold the congress there.

The conference took place in London from the 25th to the 29th of September 1865. The General Council was represented by its President Odger, its General Secretary Cremer, a number of English members, and Marx and his two chief assistants in the affairs of the International, Eccarius and Jung, a Swiss watchmaker who lived in London and spoke English, German and French equally well. France was represented by Tolain, Fribourg and Limousin, all of whom were to abandon the International, Marx's old friend Schily of 1848 and Varlin, who was later to be one of the heroes and martyrs of the Paris Commune. Switzerland sent two representatives, the bookbinder Dupleix for the Franco-Italian Swiss workers and Johann Philipp Becker, a former brush-maker and now a tireless revolutionary agitator, for the German Swiss workers. Belgium was represented by Cæsar de Paepe, who had begun to study medicine as a compositor's apprentice and had succeeded in becoming a doctor.

The conference dealt first of all with the finances of the association, and it was revealed that the total income for the first year had been about 33 pounds. No agreement was come to with regard to regular membership subscriptions, but it was agreed to raise 150 pounds for propaganda purposes and to cover the expenses in connection with the forthcoming congress : 80 pounds to be raised in England, 40 pounds in France and 10 pounds each in Belgium and Switzerland. The budget of the International was never its most impressive feature nor did money ever represent the sinews of its war. Years later Marx declared with grim humour that the finances of the International had always been steadily growing negative quantities, and still later Engels wrote that the famous " millions of the International " had been chiefly debts, and that in all probability so much had never been achieved with so little money.

The report on the situation in England was delivered by the General Secretary Cremer, who declared that although it was generally believed on the Continent that the English trade unions were very rich and well able to support a cause they felt to be their own, they were in fact bound down by petty statutes which kept their expenditure within very narrow limits. With very few exceptions English trade unionists knew nothing about politics and it was very difficult to enlighten them. However, a certain amount of progress was being made. A few years ago representatives of the International would have been unable to obtain even a hearing, whereas to-day they received a friendly reception and their principles met with approval. It was the first time that an organization connected with politics had succeeded in establishing such relations with the trade unions.

Fribourg and Tolain reported that the International was meeting with a good reception in France. Apart from Paris, members had been won in Rouen, Nantes, Elbeuf, Caen and other places, and a considerable number of membership cards had been sold at 1.25 francs for the annual subscription. Unfortunately the proceeds had been exhausted by the setting up of a bureau in Paris and by the expenses of the delegates to the conference. However, the General Council was offered the consoling prospect of the sale of the remaining 400 membership cards. The French delegates complained that the postponement of the congress had been a great hindrance to the development of the movement. The French workers were intimidated by the Bonapartist police régime and one met continually with the objection : show us what you can do first of all, and then we will join you.

The reports which Becker and Dupleix made for Switzerland were very favourable, although the agitation there had been going on only for six months. In Geneva there were 400 members and in Lausanne and Vevey 150 members each. The monthly membership subscription had been fixed at 50 pence, but the members would gladly pay double that amount because they were thoroughly convinced of the necessity of supporting the General Council financially also. Despite this the Swiss delegates also brought no money, and instead they offered the conference the consoling reflection that there would have been a nice round sum available if the delegates had not had to pay the expenses of their journey to England.

The agitation in Belgium had been going on for a month only, but de Paepe reported that 60 members had already been won and that an agreement had been made for an annual membership subscription of at least 3 francs, of which one-third would go to the General Council.

In the name of the General Council Marx proposed that the congress should be held in Geneva in September or October 1866. The place of the congress was agreed to unanimously, but at the vigorous insistence of the French delegates the date was put forward to the last week in May. The French delegates also demanded that anyone in possession of a membership card of the International should be given a seat and a vote at the congress, declaring that this was a matter of principle and the real meaning of the general franchise. Exclusively delegate representation at the congress, as demanded by Cremer and Eccarius, was secured only after a lively debate.

The General Council had drawn up a very big agenda for the congress : co-operative work, the shortening of working hours, female and child-labour, the past and future of the trade unions, the influence of the standing army on the interests of the working classes, etc., but only two points produced differences of opinion, and one of them was not put forward by the General Council at all, but by the French delegates. They demanded that " Religious ideas and their influence on the social, political and cultural movement " should be made a special point on the agenda. How they came to put forward this suggestion, and what attitude Marx took up towards it, can perhaps best be seen in a few sentences in the obituary article on Proudhon written by Marx a few months later and published in Schweitzer's *Sozialdemokrat*, the only contribution he ever made to the latter paper, by the way. " Proudhon's attack on religion and on the churches, etc., rendered a great local service at a time when the French socialists considered it necessary to prove their superiority to the bourgeois Voltairism of the eighteenth century and the German Godlessness of the nineteenth century by their religiousness. Peter the Great defeated Russian barbarism with barbarism, and Proudhon did his best to defeat French phraseology with the phrase." The English delegates also warned the conference against having anything to do with this " apple of discord ", but the French delegates insisted and their motion was adopted with 18 against 13 votes.

The other point on the agenda which produced disagreement was put forward by the General Council and dealt with a question of European politics which Marx considered of particular importance, namely " the necessity of opposing the growing influence of Russia in European affairs by re-establishing the independence of Poland on a democratic and socialist basis in accordance with the right of self-determination for all nationalities ". The French delegates in particular were opposed to this : Why mix up political with social questions ? Why wander so far afield when there was so much oppression to be fought at home ? Why bother so much about the influence of the Russian government when that of the Prussian, Austrian, French and English governments was no less evil ? The Belgian delegate Cæsar de Paepe was particularly energetic in his opposition, declaring that the restoration of an independent Poland would benefit three classes only : the higher aristocracy, the lower aristocracy and the clerics.

Proudhon's influence made itself clearly felt here. He had repeatedly opposed the restoration of Polish independence, the last occasion having been in connection with the Polish insurrection in 1863 when, as Marx pointed out frankly in the obituary article, he indulged in idiotic cynicism to the advantage of the Tsar. At the same time the insurrection had awakened all the old sympathies of Marx and Engels in the revolutionary years for the Polish cause and they had intended to issue a joint manifesto on the insurrection, but in the end this intention was not carried out.

Their sympathy for Poland was certainly not uncritical. On the 21st of April 1863 Engels had written to Marx : " I must say that to summon up any enthusiasm for the Polacks of 1772 needs a hide like an ox. In the greater part of Europe the aristocracy of the day went down decently and even with wit, although its general maxim was that materialism represented what one ate, on what one slept, what one gained at the gaming tables or received for hard work, but no aristocracy was quite so stupid as the Polish in the way it sold itself to the Russians." However, so long as there was no possibility of a revolution in Russia itself the restoration of Polish independence offered the only possibility of checking Russian influence in Europe and therefore Marx regarded the brutal suppression of the Polish insurrection and the simultaneous drive of Tsarism into Caucasia as the most important events in Europe since 1815. In that part of *The Inaugural Address* which dealt with the foreign policy of the proletariat he had laid the greatest stress on the Polish question, and the resistance put up by Tolain, Fribourg and others on just this point caused him to refer with bitterness to their opposition for a long time afterwards. However, with the assistance of the English delegates he succeeded in breaking down the opposition and the item remained on the agenda.

The conference held private sessions in the morning, under the chairmanship of Jung, and semi-public meetings in the evening, under the chairmanship of Odger. Those questions which had already been thrashed out and agreed upon in the private sessions were then brought up for discussion in these evening meetings before a larger audience which consisted chiefly of workers. On their return to Paris the French delegates published a report of the conference and the agenda which had been drawn up for the congress, and this met with a lively echo in the Paris press. Marx observed with obvious satisfaction : " Our Parisians have been somewhat surprised to discover that just the paragraphs on Russia and Poland which they wanted to have deleted created the biggest sensation." And many years afterwards he still recalled with lively satisfaction " the enthusiastic comments " which these passages in particular and the congress agenda in general had produced from the famous French historian Henri Martin.

5. The Austro-Prussian War

The time and energy which Marx devoted to the cause of the International had the disagreeable result that his efforts to earn a living were interfered with and his old financial troubles arose again.

On the 31st of July he was again compelled to write to Engels informing him that for the last two months the family had been living on the pawnshop : " I assure you I would sooner cut off my finger than write this letter. It is truly crushing to have to live half one's life in dependence. The only consolation which sustains me is that you and I are in partnership and that my job is to give my time to theoretical and party business. I am afraid this house is rather above my means and this year we have lived a little better than usual, but it was the only way to give the children an opportunity of establishing connections which might offer them some security for their future, not to mention the fact that it was some little recompense for all they have gone through. I think you will agree with me that even purely from the business point of view a completely proletarian household would be unsuitable here, although as far as my wife and I are concerned it would be all right, or if the girls were boys." Engels assisted his friend immediately, but the petty worries and troubles of securing a bare existence again began to plague Marx and his family and they continued to do so for a number of years.

A few months later, on the 5th of October 1865, a letter from Lothar Bucher offered Marx an unexpected opportunity of earning money, and in a most peculiar fashion. Bucher had lived as an emigrant in London, but the two men had maintained no relations and certainly not friendly ones. Even when Bucher began to take up an independent position in the general emigrant tangle and joined Urquhart as the latter's enthusiastic supporter, Marx remained critical towards him, but Bucher spoke very favourable to Borkheim of Marx's answer to Vogt and wanted to review it for the *Allgemeine Zeitung*. No such review ever appeared, but whether this was because Bucher did not write it or because the *Allgemeine Zeitung* refused to print it there is now no means of telling. After the granting of the Prussian amnesty Bucher returned to Germany and in Berlin he made friends with Lassalle. With the latter he visited the Great Exhibition in London in 1862, and through him he became acquainted with Marx, who described him as " a fine but rather confused chappie " and thought it unlikely that he was in agreement with Lassalle's " foreign policy ". After Lassalle's death Bucher had entered the service of the Prussian government, and in a letter to Engels Marx had dismissed him and Rodbertus with the round abuse : " A miserable pack, all that rabble from Berlin, Brandenburg and Pomerania ! "

And now Bucher wrote : " First of all to business : the *Staatsanzeiger* would like a monthly report on the movements of the money-market (and naturally of the commodity market also as far as the two cannot be separated), and I was asked whether I could recommend anyone. I replied that I knew of no one better suited to the job than you, and in consequence I have been asked to approach you in the matter. You would not be limited with regard to the length of the articles ; the more thorough and comprehensive the better. With regard to the content you would naturally follow only the dictates of your scientific convictions. However, consideration for the readers (*haute finance*) and not for the editorial board would make it advisable to leave the inner core of the matter visible only to experts, and to avoid all polemics." A few business observations then followed, a reference to a joint outing with Lassalle, whose end would always remain " a psychological riddle " to the writer, and then the remark that he, Marx, was no doubt aware that the writer had since returned to his first love, the files. " I never shared Lassalle's opinions and always thought he saw things developing more quickly than really was the case. Progress will shed its skin many times before it dies, and therefore anyone who wants to work within the State during his lifetime must rally round the government." After recommendations to Frau Marx and greetings to the young ladies, and in particular the little one, the letter closed with the traditional flourish : " Your obedient and respectful servant."

Marx rejected the offer, but no detailed information is obtainable as to what he actually wrote, and what he actually thought about Bucher's letter. Immediately after having received it he went to Manchester where no doubt he discussed the matter with Engels, but there is no mention of the affair at all in their letters to each other and only one passing reference in Marx's letters to his other friends, as far as they are known. Fourteen years later when the terrorist attempts of Hödel and Nobiling let loose a fierce campaign of incitement against the socialists, he published Bucher's letter, and its effect was like a bomb-shell in the camp of the socialist-baiters. At the time of the publication Bucher was secretary to the Berlin Congress, and according to the statement of his semi-official biographer it was he who drew up the first anti-socialist bill which was brought forward after the Hödel and Nobiling outrages but rejected by the Reichstag.

Since then there has been much discussion as to whether Bucher's letter was an attempt by Bismarck to buy Marx, and it is certain at least that in the autumn of 1865, after the signing of the Treaty of Gastein had ineffectively patched up the threatening breach with Austria, Bismarck was inclined, to use his own hunting simile, " to let loose any dog willing to bark ". Bismarck himself was far too much an inveterate East Elbian Junker to flirt with the working class in the way Disraeli, or even Louis Bonaparte, did, and the droll ideas he formed about Lassalle, whom he met personally on a number of occasions, are sufficiently known, but at least in his immediate entourage he had two people who were better equipped to deal with this delicate question, and they were Lothar Bucher and Hermann Wagener. It is a fact that at the time Wagener was doing his best to decoy the German working-class movement, and as far as Countess Hatzfeldt had any say in the matter he succeeded. As the intellectual leader of the Junkers and an old friend of Bismarck from the pre-

March days, Wagener was in an incomparably stronger position than Bucher, who was completely dependent on Bismarck's good-will owing to the fact that the bureaucracy regarded him with suspicion as an intruder whilst the King refused to have anything whatever to do with him on account of 1848. And in any case, Bucher was a weakling, " a fish without bones ", as his friend Rodbertus declared.

If Bucher's letter was really an attempt to buy Marx, it was certainly not made without Bismarck's knowledge, but it is doubtful whether it actually was such an attempt. The way in which Marx used the letter in 1878 during the anti-socialist campaign was irreproachable and it was a clever move, but it does not even prove that Marx himself thought the letter to have been an attempt to buy him, much less that the letter was such an attempt. Bucher was well aware that since Marx had broken off relations with Schweitzer the German Lassalleans had no very high opinion of him, and further, a monthly report on the movements of the money-market in the most boring of all German newspapers can hardly have recommended itself as an effective means to pacify the general discontent with Bismarck's policy, not to speak of winning the support of the workers for that policy. Under the circumstances therefore there is more than a little to be said in favour of Bucher's statement that he recommended his old companion in exile to the Curator of the *Staatsanzeiger* without any ulterior political motive, though perhaps with the proviso that the Curator had already refused to accept a representative of the Manchester school. Having suffered a rebuff at Marx's hands Bucher then approached Dühring, who agreed to take over the work but very soon gave it up when it turned out that the Curator of the *Staatsanzeiger* was very far from possessing that respect for " scientific convictions " with which Bucher had credited him.

Worse even than the increasing economic difficulties with which Marx had to contend as a result of his active work for the International and his own scientific work was the fact that his health began to suffer more and more. On the 10th of February 1866 Engels wrote : " You must really do something to get rid of this carbuncle business. . . . Stop your night work for a time and lead a more regular life." And on the 13th of February Marx replied : " Yesterday I was on my back again with a malignant boil which formed in my left groin. If I had money enough for my family and my book were finished I shouldn't care in the least whether I went to the knacker's yard to-day or to-morrow, as it is, however, I do care." And a week later Engels received the alarming information : " This time it was touch and go. My family didn't know how serious the matter really was. If the thing breaks out again three or four times in the same fashion I am a dead man. I have fallen away terribly and still feel damned weak, not so much in my head as in my loins and legs. The doctors are right of course when they say that excessive night work was the cause of the relapse, but I can't tell them what compels me to commit such extravagances, and it would be no use if I could." However, Engels now insisted that his friend should give himself a rest for a few weeks and Marx went to Margate.

In Margate he soon recovered his spirits and in a cheerful letter to his daughter Laura he wrote : " I am really glad that I went to a private house and not to a hotel where I should inevitably have been bothered with local politics, domestic scandals and neighbourly tittle-tattle, but still, I can't sing with the Miller of Dee that I care for nobody and nobody cares for me, because after all there is my landlady, who is as deaf as a post, and her daughter, who is troubled with chronic hoarseness. However, they are nice people, attentive and not intrusive. I have developed into a perambulating walking-stick. The greater part of the day I am out in the air and at ten o'clock I go to bed. I read nothing, write less and am gradually working myself into that state of Nirvana which Buddhism regards as the consummation of human bliss." And at the foot of the letter there is a teasing remark which apparently foreshadows coming events : " That little devil Lafargue is still plaguing me with his Proudhonism, and I suppose he won't be satisfied until I've knocked some sense into his Creole skull."

Whilst Marx was still in Margate the first lightning flashes pierced the war-clouds which had gathered over Germany. On the 8th of April Bismarck concluded an offensive alliance with Italy against Austria, and the next day he approached the Germanic Diet with the request that a German parliament should be convened on the basis of the general franchise to discuss a reform of the League for presentation to the German governments. The attitude which Marx and Engels took up to these events reveals how far they had lost touch with the German situation. Their judgment vacillated. Referring to Bismarck's proposal to convene a German parliament Engels wrote on the 10th of April : " What an ass the fellow must be to believe that will help him in the least ! If things really come to a head then for the first time in history future developments will depend on the attitude of Berlin. If the Berliners deliver their blow at the right moment then things may develop favourably—but who can rely on them ? "

Three days later he wrote again, but this time with extra-ordinarily clear foresight : " It looks as though the German bourgeoisie will agree to the proposal (the general franchise) after a little resistance, for, after all, Bonapartism is the real religion of the bourgeoisie. I am beginning to realize more and more clearly that the bourgeoisie is not cut out to rule directly, and that therefore where there is no oligarchy (like the one in England) prepared to govern in the interests of the bourgeoisie in return for liberal rewards, a Bonapartist semi-dictatorship is the normal form of bourgeois rule. Such a form carries through the great material interests of the bourgeoisie even against the bourgeoisie, but refuses to give the latter a share in the government. On the other hand this dictatorship itself is compelled against its will to further these material interests of the bourgeoisie, and thus we now observe Monsieur Bismarck adopting the pro-gramme of the *Nationalverein*. Carrying it out is, of course, quite another matter, but he is hardly likely to come to grief on account of the German bourgeoisie." Engels thought that Bismarck would fail because of the Austrian army. Benedek was in any case a better general than Prince Friedrich Karl. Austria was strong enough to force Prussia to sue for peace, but Prussia was not strong enough to force Austria to do so, and there-fore every Prussian success would be an invitation to Bonaparte to intervene.

In a letter to his new friend Doctor Kugelmann of Hannover Marx described the situation in almost the same words. Whilst he was still a lad in 1848 Kugelmann had been an enthusiastic supporter of Marx and Engels, and he had carefully collected all their writings, but it was not until 1862 that, thanks to Freili-grath's mediation, he made the acquaintance of Marx and soon became one of his confidants. Marx subordinated himself to Engels' judgment absolutely in all military questions and with a lack of criticism unusual for him.

Still more astonishing than his over-estimation of the Austrian army was Engels' idea of the condition of the Prussian army, because he had just dealt with the army reform, which had been the occasion of the Prussian constitutional conflict, and in this work he had shown far greater insight than the bourgeois demo-cratic tub-thumpers. On the 25th of May he wrote : " If the Austrians are clever enough not to attack then the trouble in the Prussian army will certainly come to a head. The men were never so rebellious as they have proved themselves during this mobilization. Unfortunately we hear of only a small part of what is really happening, but even that is enough to show that an offensive war is impossible with such an army." And on the

11th of June he wrote : " The *Landwehr* [1] will be as dangerous to Prussia in this war as the Poles were in 1806, when they represented over a third of the army and disorganized everything, with the exception that this time the *Landwehr* will not disband after the defeat, but revolt." That was written three weeks before the decisive battle of Königgrätz.

Königgrätz dispelled all misunderstandings immediately and the day after the battle Engels wrote : " What do you think of the Prussians ? They followed up their success with enormous energy. Such a decisive battle all over in eight hours is unparalleled ; under other circumstances it would have lasted two days, but the percussion gun is a deadly weapon, and then the fellows fought with a bravery seldom seen in peace-time soldiers." Marx and Engels might make mistakes and they often did so, but they never resisted the recognition of error when the events themselves compelled it. The Prussian victory was an unpleasant pill for them to swallow, but they made no attempt to avoid their medicine and on the 25th of July Engels, who still retained the leadership in this question, summed up the situation as follows : " The situation in Germany now seems fairly simple to me. From the moment Bismarck carried out his plan with the Prussian army and met with such colossal success, the development in Germany took such a decided trend in his direction that, like everyone else, we must now recognize accomplished facts whether we like them or not. . . . There is at least one good side to the matter and that is that it simplifies the situation and makes the revolution easier by abolishing petty-capital brawling and will in any case accelerate development. After all, a German parliament is quite a different thing from a Prussian chamber. The whole petty-State particularism will be dragged into the movement, the worst localizing influences will be destroyed, and the parties will become really national instead of merely local." And two days later Marx answered with dry composure : " I agree with you entirely that we must take the mess as it is. Still, it is pleasant to be at a distance during this first period of young love."

At the same time Engels wrote, " Brother Liebknecht is spurring himself into fanatical pro-Austrianism " and he did not mean this as praise. He, Liebknecht, was responsible obviously for " an outburst of anger " from Leipzig which had appeared in the *Frankfurter Zeitung*. This regicidal paper had even trimmed its sails so far as to reproach Prussia for its shameful treatment of " the noble Prince of Hesse " and its heart was warming to the poor blind Guelph. At the same time Schweitzer in Berlin

[1] The Reserve.—Tr.

was taking up the same attitude as Marx and Engels, and almost in the same words, and for this " opportunist policy " the memory of the unfortunate man still suffers from the moral indignation of those ponderous " Statesmen " who swear by Marx and Engels, but do not understand them.

6. The Geneva Congress

Despite the original plan, the first congress of the International had not taken place when the battle of Königgrätz decided the fate of Germany. It had been necessary to postpone the congress until September, although in the second year of its existence the organization had made much quicker progress than in the first.

Geneva began to develop into the most important centre of the movement on the Continent, and both the German Swiss and the Franco-Italian ·Swiss sections founded party organs. The German Swiss section issued *Der Vorbote*, a monthly ·publication founded and edited by the veteran revolutionary Becker, and even to-day its columns represent one of the most important sources of information concerning the First International. It first appeared in January 1866 and styled itself the " Central Organ of the German Language Group ", for the German members of the International also regarded Geneva as their centre owing to the fact that the laws of Germany prevented the formation of a specifically German section, and for much the same reason the influence of the Franco-Italian Swiss section in Geneva extended into France.

The movement in Belgium also issued a paper of its own entitled *le Tribune du Peuple*, and Marx recognized it as the official organ of the International equally with the two Geneva papers, but there were one or two papers issued in Paris and representing the cause of the workers in their own way which he did not recognize as official mouthpieces of the International. The cause of the International made good progress in France also, but it was more like a fire sweeping over stubble than a steady blaze. Owing to the complete absence of any freedom of the press or any right to meet, it was difficult to found any real centres of the movement, and the ambiguous toleration of the Bonapartist police tended to sap the energy of the workers rather than encourage it. Further, the dominating influence of Proud-honism was not favourable to any development of working-class organizational strength.

"Young France", as the fugitives in Brussels and London styled themselves, made a deal of noise and trouble. In February 1866 a French section of the International which had been founded in London violently opposed the General Council for having placed the Polish question on the agenda of the congress. Under the influence of Proudhonism its representatives asked how one could possibly think of opposing Russian influence by the restoration of Polish unity at a time when Russia was freeing the serfs whilst the Polish aristocracy and clergy obstinately refused to do so. And at the outbreak of the Austro-Prussian War the French members of the International caused the General Council a lot of trouble with what Marx described as their " Proudhonised-Stirnerism ". They announced that the nation as an idea was obsolete. The nations should be dissolved into little " groups " which would then form an " association " in place of the State. " And this ' individualization ' of humanity and the corresponding *mutualisme* will proceed whilst in all countries history conveniently comes to a full stop and the whole world waits until the individuals are ripe to make a social revolution. They will then carry out this experiment and the rest of the world will be overwhelmed by the force of their example and will proceed to do the same." This sarcasm was directed against Marx's " very good friends " Lafargue and Longuet, who were later to become his sons-in-law, but who at the time were making themselves a nuisance as " apostles of Proudhon ".

Much to Marx's satisfaction the main strength of the International was still in the English trade unions, and in a letter to Kugelmann on the 15th of January 1866 he expresses delight at the fact that it had been possible to draw these, the only really big working-class organizations, into the movement. He was particularly pleased with a monster meeting which had taken place a few weeks earlier in St. Martin's Hall under the intellectual leadership of the International in favour of the reform of the franchise. In March 1866 Gladstone's Whig Cabinet brought in a Bill for electoral reform, but it proved too radical for a section of Gladstone's own party, which went over to the Tories and caused the fall of the government and its replacement by a Tory Ministry with Disraeli as Prime Minister. When Disraeli then attempted to postpone the question of electoral reform indefinitely the movement in its favour grew more and more vigorous. Writing to Engels on the 7th of July Marx declared : " The workers' demonstrations in London, marvellous compared with anything we have seen in England since 1849, are purely the work of the International. Lucraft, for instance, the leader of the Trafalgar Square demonstration, is a member of our council." At a meeting of 20,000 people in Trafalgar Square Lucraft proposed a demonstration in Whitehall Gardens, " where we once chopped off the head of a King ", and shortly afterwards a great demonstration of 60,000 people in Hyde Park almost developed into an insurrection.

The trade unions freely recognized the services of the International in furthering the movement which was sweeping the country, and a delegate conference in Sheffield representing all the big trade unions adopted a resolution : " That this conference fully recognizes the services of the International Working-men's Association in furthering fraternal solidarity between the workers of all countries and urgently recommends all the societies represented at its deliberations to affiliate to this body in the conviction that such affiliation is of great importance for the progress and welfare of the whole working class." As a result of this resolution many trade unions then affiliated to the International, but although this was a great moral and political success it did not yield proportionate material advantages. It was left to the unions to pay what affiliation subscriptions they thought fit or none at all, and when they did decide to pay anything their contributions were extremely modest, for instance, the boot and shoemakers with 5,000 members paid an affiliation subscription of five pounds annually, the carpenters with 9,000 members paid two pounds annually, whilst the bricklayers with from 3,000 to 4,000 members paid only a pound.

However, Marx was very soon compelled to recognize that " the damned traditional character of all English movements " was making itself felt in the Reform movement too. Before the founding of the International the trade unions had approached the bourgeois Radicals in connection with the reform movement, and the more the latter promised to yield tangible fruits the closer these relations became. " Payments on account ", which would formerly have been rejected with great indignation, now appeared as acceptable prizes in the struggle. Marx missed the fiery spirit of the old Chartists and deeply regretted the incapacity of the English to do two things at once, pointing out that the more progress the reform movement made the cooler the trade-union leaders became " in our own movement ", and that " the reform movement in England, which was brought into being by us, has almost killed us ". A strong bulwark against the advance of this tendency was removed owing to the fact that Marx's illness and his convalescence in Margate prevented him from intervening in person.

The Workman's Advocate, a weekly paper which the conference of 1865 had raised to the dignity of an official organ of the International and which changed its name to *The Commonwealth* in February 1866, caused him a lot of trouble and worry. He was a member of the management of the paper, which was compelled to fight ceaselessly against financial difficulties and was therefore dependent on the assistance of the bourgeois electoral reformers. He did his utmost to counteract this bourgeois influence and at the same time he had to compose the jealous disputes which arose in connection with the editorial work. For a time Eccarius was the editor of the paper and he published his famous polemic against John Stuart Mill in it.[1] Marx rendered him very much assistance in the writing of this work. In the end, however, Marx was unable to prevent *The Commonwealth* from degenerating " into a purely reform organ for the moment . . . partly for economic and partly for political reasons ", as he wrote to Kugelmann.

This general situation explains completely why he harboured lively misgivings concerning the coming congress of the International and feared that it would " expose us to European ridicule ". The French members insisted that the decision of the General Council to hold the congress in May should be adhered to and Marx wanted to go to Paris to convince them of the impossibility of this date, but Engels declared that the whole affair was not worth the risk of falling into the hands of the Bonapartist police where he, Marx, would be without protection. It was not so important whether the congress made any valuable decisions or not so long as a public scandal was avoided and that would be possible somehow. In a certain sense, of course—at least, towards themselves—any such demonstration would be a failure, but it need not necessarily be one which would ridicule them in the eyes of Europe.

The matter was finally settled by the Geneva organization. which had not completed its preparations for the congress and therefore decided to postpone it until September, and this was agreed to everywhere except in Paris. Marx had no intention of attending the congress, for his scientific work no longer permitted any considerable interruption and he felt he was doing something more important for the working class than anything he might be able to do at the congress, but for all that he devoted very much of his time to assuring the best possible auspices for the congress. He drew up a memorandum for the London delegates and deliberately limited it to such points as would " permit immediate co-operation and understanding between the workers and serve the immediate needs of the class struggle and the organization of the workers as a class ". One can pay

---

[1] *A Working-man's Refutation of J. S. Mill.*—Tr.

this memorandum the same compliment which Professor Beesly paid to *The Inaugural Address*: it sums up the immediate demands of the international proletariat more thoroughly and more strikingly than ever before in a few pages.

The President of the General Council, Odger, and its General Secretary, Cremer, went to Geneva as the representatives of the Council together with Eccarius and Jung, and it was on the two last named that Marx chiefly relied.

The congress took place from the 3rd to the 8th of September under the chairmanship of Jung and in the presence of 60 delegates. Marx found that it had been " better than I expected ", but he expressed himself bitterly about " the gentlemen from Paris ". Their heads were "full of the emptiest Proudhonist phrases. They babble about science and they are uttely ignorant. They scorn all revolutionary action, that is to say, action arising out of the class struggle, and all concentrated social movements, movements which can be carried out with political means (for instance, the legal limitation of the working day). Under the pretext of freedom and anti-governmentalism or anti-authoritarian-individualism these gentlemen, who have meekly tolerated sixteen years of the blindest despotism and are still tolerating it, actually preach a vulgar bourgeois economic system idealized a little by Proudhonism." And so on in even harsher terms.

Marx's judgment was severe, but a few years later Johann Philipp Becker, who was present at the congress and one of its foremost delegates, expressed himself even more harshly concerning the chaos which marked its sessions, except that he did not forget the Germans on account of the French, or the supporters of Schulze-Delitzsch on account of the Proudhonists : " How much politeness we had to waste on the good people in order to avoid with decency the danger of their enthusiasm running away with the congress ". The reports published at the time in *Der Vorbote* on the deliberations of the congress are written in a different tone and they must be read with all the critical faculties alert.

The French were relatively strong at the congress and they controlled about one-third of the mandates. In the upshot they did not achieve very much, but they spared no eloquence. Their proposal that only manual workers should be accepted as members of the International and that all others should be excluded was turned down, as was also their proposal to deal with the religious question in the programme of the International, a rebuff which marked the end of this abortion. On the other hand, a fairly harmless resolution calling for the study of international credit was adopted. Its aim was to secure later on the founding of a central bank for the International along Proudhonist lines. Much more disagreeable was the adoption of a resolution, brought forward by Tolain and Fribourg, declaring that female labour represented a " principle of degeneration " and that a woman's place was in the home. However, this resolution was opposed even by other French delegates, including Varlin, and it was adopted together with a resolution of the General Council on female and child labour which in effect killed it. For the rest the French delegates succeeded in smuggling a little Proudhonism into the resolutions of the congress here and there, but although these blemishes which disfigured his hard work annoyed him Marx did not fail to recognize that on the whole the congress had been fairly satisfactory.

Only in one point did he suffer a rebuff which might be considered painful, and probably was, and that was in the Polish question. Thanks to his experience with the London conference, he had carefully worked out this point in the memorandum he drew up for the London delegates. He declared that the European working class must take up the question because the ruling classes suppressed it (despite their effusive enthusiasm for every other sort of nationality) because the aristocracy and the bourgeoisie regarded the threatening Asiatic power in the background as the final bulwark against the advancing working class. This power could be checked only by the restoration of Polish unity on a democratic basis. Whether Germany remained an outpost of the Holy Alliance or became an ally of republican France would depend on the solution of this question. So long as this great European question remained unsolved the working-class movement would be continually hampered, held up and interrupted in its development.

The English delegates supported the proposal vigorously, but it met with an opposition no less vigorous from the French delegates and a number of the Franco-Italian Swiss delegates. In the end Becker, who had supported the resolution but was anxious to avoid a split on the question, put forward a compromise resolution declaring that the International was opposed to any form of rule by violence and that therefore it would strive for the abolition of Russian imperialist influence in Europe and for the restoration of Polish independence on a social democratic basis, and this evasive solution was adopted. Apart from this, the English memorandum triumphed all along the line. The provisional rules were adopted with one or two alterations and no debate at all took place on the inaugural address, which thenceforth was invariably referred to in the decisions and proclamations of the International as a fundamental official document.

The General Council was re-elected with its seat in London, and it was instructed to collect detailed statistics on the situation of the working classes all over the world and to issue reports as often as its means allowed on all matters of interest to the International. In order to provide it with the necessary funds the congress decided that every member of the International should be levied 30 centimes for the coming year, and it recommended that a regular annual subscription of one-halfpenny or one penny should be paid by all members in addition to the fee for the membership card.

The most important programmatic announcements of the congress were its decisions concerning legislation for labour protection and the trade unions. It accepted the principle of a struggle for labour protection legislation and pointed out that " by compelling the adoption of such laws the working class will not consolidate the ruling powers, but, on the contrary, it will be turning that power which is at present used against it into its own instrument ". With general legislation it would be able to obtain what it would be useless to attempt to obtain by isolated and individual efforts. The congress recommended the shortening of the working day as a necessary condition without which all the other efforts of the proletariat in the struggle for emancipation must fail. The shortening of the working day was necessary in order to restore the physical energy and health of the workers and to give them the possibility of intellectual development, social intercourse and social and political activities. As the legal maximum working day the congress proposed eight hours, the working time to be arranged in such a way as to comprise only the actual working hours and reasonable pauses for meals. This maximum eight-hour day should apply to all adult workers, both men and women, adults being all persons having completed their eighteenth year. Night work was condemned on principle as dangerous to the health of the workers, unavoidable exceptions to be laid down by law. Women workers should be strictly excluded from night work and from all forms of work harmful to the female constitution or morally objectionable for the female sex.

The congress regarded the tendency of modern industry to draw children and young persons of both sexes into the process of social production as salutary and legitimate progress, although it condemned the form in which this took place in capitalist society as revolting. In any reasonable system of society, it declared, each child would become a productive worker from its ninth year on, whilst at the same time no adult person would be excepted from the general law of nature which prescribed that in order to eat a man must first work, and furthermore all men should work not only with their brains, but also with their hands. In the prevailing system of society it was desirable to divide children and young people into three categories and treat them accordingly : children from 9 to 13 years old, children from 13 to 15 years, and young people from 15 to 17 years old. The working hours of the first category should not exceed two per day, whether in household or workshop, of the second category not more than four hours, and of the third category not more than six hours, whereby there must be a break of one hour in the working time for meals and recreation. However, productive labour on the part of children and young persons should be permitted only when combined with educational training, including mental, physical and technical training giving them instruction in the general scientific principles of all processes of production and at the same time acquainting them with the practical use of the simpler forms of tools.

With regard to the trade unions the congress decided that their activity was not only legitimate, but necessary. The trade unions were a means of using the only social power of the proletariat, namely its numbers, against the centralized social power of capitalism, and so long as the capitalist mode of production existed it would not be possible to do without trade unions. On the contrary, the trade unions would generalize their activities by establishing international connections. By consciously opposing the ceaseless excesses of capitalism they would unconsciously become the organizational centre for the working class in the same way as the mediæval communes had become such a centre for the rising bourgeoisie. Conducting a ceaseless guerilla warfare in the everyday struggle between capital and labour, the trade unions would become still more important as a lever for the organized abolition of wage-labour. In the past the trade unions had concentrated their activities too exclusively on the immediate struggle against capital, but in the future they ought not to hold themselves aloof from the general political and social movement of their class. Their influence would grow stronger to the extent that the great masses of the workers realized that their aim was not narrow and selfish, but directed to securing the general emancipation of the downtrodden millions.

Shortly after the congress in Geneva and in the spirit of the above resolution Marx took a step from which he hoped great things. Writing to Kugelmann on the 13th of October 1866 he declared : " The London Trades Council (its secretary is our President Odger) is now considering a proposal that it should

CHAPTER TWELVE: "DAS KAPITAL"

1. Birth Pangs

WHEN Marx refused to be present at the Geneva congress on the ground that the completion of his main work—up to the moment he had done only minor things, he thought—seemed more important for the cause of the workers ·than anything he could do at the congress, he was engaged in polishing and putting the final touches to the first volume. At first this final work, which began on the 1st of January 1866, proceeded quickly, for " naturally it gave me pleasure to lick the club clean after so many birth pangs ".

These birth pangs had lasted approximately twice as many years as Nature needs months for the production of a human being, and Marx was justified in saying that probably no work of the sort had ever been written under more difficult circumstances. Again and again he had fixed a time limit for its completion. In 1851 it was " five weeks ", and in 1859 it was " six weeks ", but always the time limit had been ignored owing to his merciless self-criticism and the tremendous conscientiousness which continually drove him to make new investigations, neither of which could be shaken by even the most impatient exhortations of his best friend.

At the end of 1865 the work was finished, but only in the form of an enormous manuscript which could have been prepared for publication by no one apart from himself, not even by Engels. From January 1866 to March 1867 Marx turned out the first volume of *Capital* in the classic form in which we have it to-day, as an " artistic whole " out of this tremendous mass of material. It was a feat which bore eloquent witness to his magnificent working capacity, for the year and a quarter in which it was performed was troubled by chronic ill-health and even really dangerous illnesses, such as the one in February 1866, by an accumulation of debts which threatened to overwhelm him, and not least by the wearisome preparations for the Geneva congress of the International.

In November 1866 the first bundle of manuscript was sent

off to Otto Meissner in Hamburg, a publisher of democratic literature who had previously issued a small work of Engels on the Prussian military question. In April 1867 Marx himself took the rest of the manuscript to Hamburg and found Meissner " a decent fellow ". Short negotiations proved sufficient to settle all the arrangements. Marx was anxious to remain in Germany until the first proofs arrived from Leipzig, where the book was to be printed, and in the meantime he visited his friend Kugelmann in Hannover, where he was most hospitably received. He spent a number of pleasant weeks with Kugelmann and his family, and afterwards referred to this period as " one of the happiest and most agreeable oases in the desert of life ".

His good spirits were certainly heightened to some extent by the fact that he was treated with respect and sympathy in educated circles in Hannover, treatment to which he was unaccustomed from such quarters, and on the 24th of April he wrote to Engels : " You know, we two have a much better reputation amongst the ' educated bourgeoisie ' than we thought." And on the 27th of April Engels answered : " I have always felt that the damned book on which you have worked so long was the real reason for all your misfortunes and that you would never be able to overcome them as long as you had not shaken it off. Its incompletion dragged you down physically, intellectually and financially, and I can well understand that you feel a different fellow altogether now that you have finally got rid of it, particularly as you will find when you come back into the world that it is no longer quite so depressing as it was." And for himself Engels expressed the hope that he would soon be able to emancipate himself from " this damned business ", because so long as he was in it up to his eyes he would be unable to do anything worth while, and now that he had become a partner in the firm the situation had grown worse owing to his increased responsibility.

On the 7th of May Marx wrote : " I firmly hope and trust that by the end of the year I shall be a made man, at least in the sense that I hope to be able to reform my financial situation thoroughly and stand upon my own feet finally. Without you I could never have finished my work and I assure you that it has always been a weight on my conscience that you have had to waste your splendid abilities in commercial affairs and let them go rusty on my account, and that on top of that you have had to suffer all my miserable worries with me." As a matter of fact, Marx did not become " a made man " by the end of the year or at any time, and Engels had to keep his nose to the grindstone for a few years more, but nevertheless the horizon did begin to clear up a little.

Whilst he was in Hannover Marx finally paid a long-post-poned debt in the shape of a letter to one of his supporters, a mining engineer named Siegfried Meyer who had been living in Berlin but was about to emigrate to America. The way in which he did so offers us another striking example of his " heartless-ness " : " You must think very badly of me, and still more so when I tell you that your letters were not only a great pleasure to me but a real consolation in the troubled period in which I received them. The knowledge that a capable man of high principles was securely won for our party compensated me for much. In addition, your letters were always couched in such warm terms of friendship for me personally, and you will realize that a man who is constantly engaged in a bitter struggle with the world (the official world) does not underestimate such a thing. Well then, you will ask, why didn't I answer you ? Because I was constantly hovering on the edge of the grave and was com-pelled to use every minute of the time in which I was fit to work to finish my book, to which I have sacrificed my health, my happiness and my family. I hope that this explanation requires no further enlargement. I have to laugh at the so-called ' practical ' men and their wisdom. If one had a hide like an ox one could naturally turn one's back on the sufferings of humanity and look after one's own skin, but as it is I should have considered myself very unpractical if I had died without com-pleting my book, at least in manuscript form."

In the buoyant spirits of his Hannover days Marx took it quite seriously when an advocate named Warnebold, a man quite unknown to him, approached him with the alleged informa-tion that Bismarck wished to win him and his great talents for the German people. Not that Marx was in the least way tempted by the proposal, and he certainly agreed with Engels who wrote : " It is typical of the fellow's intellectual horizon and of his way of thinking that he judges everybody by himself." But in a sober everyday mood Marx would hardly have taken Warne-bold's message at its face value, for the North German League was barely completed and war with France had been narrowly averted in connection with the Luxemburg affair, and Bismarck could not possibly have risked offending the bourgeoisie by taking the author of *The Communist Manifesto* into his service, for the bourgeoisie had only just come over to his side and it looked askance even at such collaborators as Bucher and Wagener.

On his journey back to London Marx had an adventure, not with Bismarck, but with a relation of Bismarck, and he related the affair to Kugelmann with some gratification. On the boat a German girl, whom he had already noticed on account of her upright almost military carriage, asked him for information concerning the railway connections in London. It turned out that she had a few hours to wait before her train left and Marx gallantly assisted her to pass the time by taking her for a walk in Hyde Park : " It appeared that her name was Elisabeth von Puttkamer and that she was a niece of Bismarck, with whom she had been staying for a few weeks in Berlin. She had the whole Army List at her finger tips, for her family supplies our army liberally with gentlemen of honour and wasplike waists. She was a cheerful and well-educated girl, but aristocratic and black-white to the marrow.[1] She was not a little surprised when she learned that she had fallen into red hands." However, the young lady did not lose her good spirits on that account, and in a neat little letter she expressed " girlish respect " and " heartfelt thanks " to her cavalier for all the trouble he had taken with " such an inexperienced creature ", and her parents also wrote a letter of thanks in which they informed him how happy they had been to learn that one could still meet good men on a journey.

On his arrival on London Marx corrected the proof-sheets of his book, but even this time not without a certain amount of occasional abuse on account of the dilatoriness of the printer, and at two o'clock in the morning of the 16th of August 1867 he wrote to Engels informing him that the last printer's sheet had just been corrected : " So this volume is now finished. I must thank you alone that it was possible. Without your sacrifices for me I could never possibly have done the enormous amount of work for the three volumes. I embrace you with heartfelt thanks. Greetings, my dearly beloved friend."

2. The First Volume

The first chapter of Marx's book summed up once again what he had already written in 1859 in his *Critique of Political Economy* concerning the nature of commodities and money. This was done not merely for the sake of completeness, but because even intelligent readers had often failed to grasp his ideas thoroughly, so that he assumed that there must have been something wrong with his presentation of them and in particular with his analysis of the nature of a commodity.

The professorial luminaries of Germany could certainly not be counted amongst his intelligent readers and they execrated

[1] Black and white are the Prussian colours.—Tr.

the first chapter in particular on account of its "involved mysticism". "At first glance a commodity seems a trivial, easily understood thing. However, its analysis shows that it is a very eccentric thing, full of metaphysical subtleties and theological tricks. As far as it is a use-value there is nothing mysterious about it. . . . The form of wood is changed when we make a table out of it. Nevertheless, the table remains wood, an ordinary perceptible thing. But as soon as it appears as a commodity it becomes transcendental as well as perceptible. It not only stands with its four feet firmly on the ground, but towards other commodities it stands upside down and its wooden head develops whimsicalities far stranger than if it began to dance without human agency." This argument was taken amiss by all those blockheads who could produce metaphysical subtleties and theological quibbles *ad lib.*, but not anything as material and ordinary as a simple wooden table.

Considered purely from the literary point of view, the first chapter of *Capital* is one of the finest things Marx ever wrote. After dealing with commodities he then proceeded to show how money is transformed into capital. If equal values exchange against equal values in commodity circulation how can the moneyed man buy commodities at their value and sell them at their value and nevertheless receive greater value than he gave? He can do this because under prevailing social relations he finds a commodity of such a peculiar nature on the commodity market that its consumption is a source of new value. That commodity is labour-power.

It exists in the shape of the living worker, who needs a certain quantity of foodstuffs for the maintenance of his life and that of his family, the latter guaranteeing the perpetuation of living labour-power after his death. The labour-time necessary to produce this quantity of foodstuffs, etc., represents the value of labour-power. However, this value, which is paid in the form of wages, is much less than the value which the purchaser of labour-power is able to extract from it. The surplus-labour of the worker over and above the labour-time necessary to replace the value represented by his wages is the source of surplus-value, the source of the ceaselessly growing accumulation of capital. This unpaid labour of the worker is distributed amongst all the non-labouring members of society, and the whole social system in which we live is based on it.

In itself unpaid labour is certainly not an exclusive characteristic of modern bourgeois society. As long as possessing and dispossessed classes have existed the latter have always had to perform unpaid labour. As long as one section of society possesses a monopoly of the means of production then the worker, whether free or unfree, will have to work longer than the time necessary to maintain his own existence in order to provide foodstuffs, etc., for the owners of the means of production. Wage-labour is only a particular historical form of the system of unpaid labour, which has existed since the division of society into classes, and it must be examined as such if it is to be understood correctly.

In order to be able to transform his money into capital the moneyed man must find free workers on the market, free in the double sense that first of all they are free to dispose of their own labour-power as a commodity and that they have no other commodities to dispose of, and free in the sense that they possess none of the means necessary to apply their labour-power independently. This is a relation with no basis in the laws of Nature, for Nature does not produce on the one hand the owners of commodities, of money, and on the other hand those who own nothing but their labour-power. It is further not a social relation common to all periods of history, but the result of a long period of historical development, the product of many economic changes and of the decline and disappearance of a whole series of earlier forms of social production.

Commodity production is the starting-point of capital. Commodity production, commodity circulation and developed commodity circulation, trade, form the historical conditions under which capital develops. The history of modern capital dates from the creation of modern world trade and of the modern world market in the sixteenth century. The delusion of the vulgar economists that once upon a time there was an élite of industrious men who accumulated riches, and a mass of lazy good-for-nothings who finally had nothing left to sell but their own skins, is stuff and nonsense, and the semi-enlightened fashion in which bourgeois historians describe the dissolution of the feudal mode of production as the emancipation of the worker, but not at the same time as the development of the feudal into the capitalist mode of production, is no better. The worker ceased to belong to the category of the means of production like the slave and the serf, but he also ceased to possess the means of production like the peasant or artisan working on his own account.

The great mass of the people was deprived of land, food and the means of production by a series of violent and brutal measures, which Marx describes in detail on the basis of English history in the chapter on primary accumulation. In this way the free worker needed by the capitalist mode of production was created.

Capital came into the world oozing mud and blood from every pore, and as soon as it was able to stand on its own feet it not only maintained the separation of the worker from the means necessary to apply his labour-power, but it reproduced this separation on an ever-increasing scale.

Wage-labour differs from earlier forms of unpaid labour as a result of the fact that the movement of capital is boundless and its voracious appetite for surplus-labour insatiable. In societies in which the use-value of a commodity is more important than its exchange-value, surplus-labour is limited to a more or less wide circle of needs, but the nature of this form of production does not result in an unlimited demand for surplus labour. Where the exchange-value of a commodity is more important than its use-value the situation is different. As a producer with alien labour-power, as a sucker of surplus labour and an exploiter of labour-power, capital outdoes all previous modes of production based on direct forced labour in point of energy, recklessness and effectiveness. The main thing for capital is not the labour process, not the production of use-values, but the process of utilization, the production of exchange-values from which it can extract a greater value than it put in. The demand for surplus-value knows no satiety. The production of exchange-values knows no such limits as are drawn for the production of use-values by the satisfaction of immediate needs.

Just as a commodity is a combination of use and exchange values so the process of commodity production is a combination of the labour process and the value-creating process. The value-creating process lasts up to the point where the value of labour-power paid in wages is replaced by an equal amount of value, and beyond this point it develops into the process of producing surplus-value, the process of utilization. As a combination of the labour process and the process of utilization it becomes the process of capitalist production, the capitalist form of commodity production. In the labour process labour-power and the means of production work together. In the process of utilization the same capital components appear as constant and variable capital. Constant capital is transformed in the process of production into means of production, raw materials, auxiliary materials and tools of production, and does not change its value. Variable capital is transformed in the process of production into labour-power and its value changes : it reproduces its own value and then produces a surplus over and above that value, a surplus-value which may vary in volume and be larger or smaller according to circumstances. Marx thus clears the way for an examination of surplus-value, which appears in two forms, relative and absolute surplus-value, which have played a different, but each a decisive rôle in the history of the capitalist mode of production.

Absolute surplus-value is produced when the capitalist causes the worker to work beyond the time neçessary for the reproduction of his labour-power. If the capitalist had his way the working day would comprise twenty-four hours, for the longer the working day the more surplus-value it produces. On the other hand, the worker has the justifiable feeling that every hour of labour-time which he is compelled to perform over and above that necessary to reproduce his wages is unfairly extracted from him and that he has to pay with his own health for excessive labour-time. The struggle between capitalist and worker concerning the length of the working day began with the first historical appearance of free workers on the market, and it has lasted down to the present day. The capitalist fights for profit, and, whether he is personally a good fellow or a blackguard, the competition of his fellow capitalists compels him to do everything possible to extend the working day to the limits of human endurance. The worker, on the other hand, fights to maintain his health and to secure a few free hours a day in which he can engage in other human activities apart from working, eating and sleeping. Marx describes powerfully the fifty years of civil war between the working class and the capitalist class in England from the birth of large-scale industry, which drove the capitalists to break down every limit placed on the exploitation of the proletariat by nature and custom, age and sex, and day and night, up to the passing of the Ten Hour Bill, won by the working class in the struggle against capital as a powerful social obstacle preventing the workers selling themselves and their kind into death and slavery by free contract with capital.

Relative surplus-value is produced when the labour-time necessary for the reproduction of labour-power is reduced to the benefit of surplus-labour. The value of labour-power is reduced by an increase in the productivity of labour-power in those industries whose products determine the value of labour-power, and to this end a constant revolutionization of the mode of production, of the technical and social conditions of the labour process is necessary. The historical, economic, technological and socio-psychological observations which Marx then makes in a series of chapters dealing with co-operation, the division of labour and manufacture, and machinery and large-scale industry have been recognized, even by the representatives of the bourgeoisie, as a rich mine of scientific facts.

Marx not only shows that machinery and large-scale industry have created greater misery than any previous mode of production known to history, but also that in their ceaseless revolutionization of capitalist society they are preparing the way for a higher social form. Factory legislation was the first conscious and methodical reaction of society to the unnatural form of its own process of production. When society regulates labour in factories and workshops it appears for the moment only as an interference with the exploiting rights of capital.

However, the force of circumstances soon compels society to regulate household labour also and to interfere with parental authority, and with this it recognizes that large-scale industry liquidates the old family relations together with the economic basis of the old family system and the family labour which corresponded to it. " However terrible and revolting the dissolution of the old family system within the capitalist system may appear, nevertheless, by granting a decisive rôle in the social process of production to women, young people and children beyond the sphere of the household, large-scale industry creates a new economic basis for a higher form of the family and for the relation of the sexes. Naturally, it is just as stupid to regard the Christian-Germanic form of the family as absolute, as it would have been to regard the classical Roman form, or the classical Greek form, or the Oriental form as absolute, forms which by the way represent together a historical series of development. It is equally clear that the composition of the combined labour personnel out of individuals of both sexes and various ages must change into a source of humane progress under suitable conditions, although in its untrammelled and brutal capitalist form (in which the workers exist for the process of production and not the process of production for the workers) it is the foul source of corruption and slavery." The machine which degrades the worker to its mere appendage creates at the same time the possibility of increasing the productive forces of society to such an extent that all members of society without exception could enjoy the same possibilities of a development worthy of human beings, a consummation for which all former societies were too poor.

After examining the production of absolute and relative surplus-value Marx then proceeds to develop the first rational theory of wages known to the history of political economy. The price of a commodity is its value expressed in money, and wages represent the price of labour-power. Labour itself does not appear in the commodity market, but the living worker who offers his labour-power for sale, and labour appears only in the consumption of the commodity labour-power. Labour is the substance and the immanent measure of values, but it has no value itself. However, labour appears to be paid for in wages because the worker receives his wages only after he has performed his labour. The form in which wages are paid effectively conceals every trace of the division of the working day into paid and unpaid labour-time. With slaves it is exactly the opposite. The slave appears to be working for his master all the time even when he is working to reproduce the value of his own foodstuffs, and all his labour appears to be unpaid labour. With wage-labour, however, all the labour, including even the unpaid labour, seems to be paid. In the one case the property relation conceals the fact that the slave is working part of the time for himself, whilst in the other case the money relation conceals the fact that the wage-worker is working part of the time for nothing. We realize therefore, points out Marx, the decisive importance of the transformation of the value and price of labour-power into the form of wages, or into the value and price of labour itself. All the legal conceptions of both the capitalists and the workers, all the mystifications of the capitalist mode of production, all its illusions of freedom and all the extenuating humbug of vulgar political economy are based on this appearance, which conceals the real state of affairs and suggests exactly the contrary.

The two chief forms of wages are time-wages and piece-wages. On the basis of the laws governing time-wages Marx demonstrates the emptiness of the contentions that the shortening of the working day must lower wages, as put forward by people with an axe to grind, and shows that exactly the contrary is true : a temporary shortening of the working day lowers wages, but a permanent shortening raises wages. The longer the working day the lower the wage.

Piece-wages are nothing but a changed form of time-wages, and they are the form of wages best suited to the capitalist mode of production. This form of wages spread widely during the actual manufacturing period, and in the storm and stress period of English large-scale industry it served as a lever to lengthen the working day and lower wages. Piece-wages are very advantageous for the capitalist because they render supervision of the workers almost unnecessary and at the same time offer many opportunities for making deductions from wages, and practising other forms of cheating. On the other hand, this form of wages possesses many big disadvantages for the worker : physical exhaustion as the result of excessive efforts to raise the level of wages, efforts which in fact tend rather to lower wages, increased competition amongst the workers with the resultant weakening of their solidarity, the appearance of parasitic elements between the capitalists and the workers, of middle-men who pocket a substantial part of the workers' wages, and similar disagreeable phenomena.

The relation of surplus-value and wages causes the capitalist mode of production to reproduce constantly not only the capital of the capitalist, but also the poverty of the worker. On the one hand there is the capitalist class owning all the foodstuffs, all the raw materials and all the means of production, and on the other hand there is the working class, the great mass of human beings, who are compelled to sell their labour-power to the capitalists in return for that quantity of food which in the best case is sufficient to maintain them in working condition and permit the production of a new generation of working proletarians. But capital does not merely reproduce itself, it increases its volume constantly, and Marx devotes the final part of his first volume to examining this " Process of Accumulation ".

Not only does surplus-value result from capital, but capital results from surplus-value. A part of the annually produced surplus-value which is distributed amongst the possessing classes is consumed by them as income, but another part is accumulated as capital. The unpaid labour which has been extracted from the workers now serves as a means to extract still further unpaid labour from them. In the stream of production all the originally advanced capital becomes a vanishing quantity compared with the directly accumulated capital, that is to say, that surplus-value or surplus-product which is changed back into capital, whether it is still functioning in the hands of him who originally accumulated it or in the hands of another. The law of private property based on commodity production and commodity circulation transforms itself into its direct opposite, thanks to its own internal and inevitable dialectic. The laws of commodity production seem to justify a property right in individual labour. Commodity owners with equal rights face each other. The means to obtain the other commodity is only the sale of one's own commodity, and one's own commodity can be produced only by labour. Property, on the side of the capitalist, now appears as the right to appropriate the unpaid labour of others or its produce, and on the side of the worker as the impossibility of appropriating his own product.

When the modern proletariat began to grasp the meaning of this, when the urban proletariat in Lyons sounded the tocsin and the rural proletariat in England laid fire to the houses of their oppressors, the vulgar political economists invented the " abstinence theory " according to which capital was accumulated by the " voluntary abstinence " of the capitalists, a theory which Marx scourged as mercilessly as Lassalle had done before him. An instance of "abstinence" really contributing to the accumulation of capital is the compulsory "abstinence" of the workers, the brutal depression of wages below the value of labour-power in order to turn the necessary consumption funds of the workers into the accumulation funds of the capitalists, at least in part. This is the real origin of all the lamentations about the "luxurious" life of the workers, the endless jeremiad about the grand pianos which some workers are alleged to have purchased at some time or the other, all the cheap and nasty cookery recipes of the Christian social reformers, and all the other related tricks and frauds used by the intellectual hod-carriers of capitalism.

The general law of capitalist accumulation is as follows : The growth of capital includes the growth of its variable section, or that part which is changed into labour-power. If the composition of capital remains unchanged, if a certain quantity of the means of production demands always the same quantity of labour-power to set it into motion, then obviously the demand for labour-power will grow in proportion with the growth of capital, as will also the subsistence funds of the workers ; the quicker capital grows the quicker they must grow also. As simple reproduction constantly reproduces the capital relation itself, so accumulation reproduces the capital relation on a larger scale : more capitalists or bigger capitalists on the one hand, and more wage-workers on the other. The accumulation of capital is therefore the increase of the proletariat also, and in the case supposed this increase takes place under the most favourable conditions for the workers. A larger part of their own increasing surplus-product, which increasingly changes into capital, returns to them in the form of means of payment so that they are able to increase their consumption and to equip themselves more generously with clothing, furniture, etc. However, their relation of dependency towards the capitalist does not change in any way, just as a slave does not cease to be a slave if he is well-fed and well-clothed. They must always provide a certain quantity of unpaid labour, and although this may diminish it can never do so to an extent seriously endangering the capitalist character of the process of production. If wages rise above this point then the profit incentive is blunted and the accumulation of capital slackens until wages sink again to a level corresponding to the needs of its utilization.

However, only when the accumulation of capital takes place without any change in the relation between its constant and variable components can the golden chain which the wage-worker himself forges grow lighter and less irksome, but in reality the process of accumulation is accompanied by a great revolution in what Marx calls the organic composition of capital. Constant capital grows at the expense of variable capital. The growing productivity of labour causes the mass of the means of production to increase more quickly than the mass of labour-power embodied in them. The demand for labour-power does not rise proportionately with the accumulation of capital, but sinks relatively. The same effect is produced in another form by the concentration of capital which takes place, quite apart from its accumulation, owing to the fact that the laws of capitalist competition lead to the swallowing up of the smaller capitalists by the larger ones. Whilst the supplementary capital formed in the process of accumulation demands fewer and fewer workers in comparison with its quantity, the old capital which is reproduced in a new composition disposes more and more of the workers formerly employed by it. In this way there develops a relative surplus mass of workers, relative that is to the needs of the utilization of capital, an industrial reserve army which is paid below the value of its labour-power in bad or middling business periods, which is employed irregularly and which at other times is dependent on public assistance, but which at all times serves to lower the resistance of the employed workers and to depress their wage standards.

This industrial reserve army is a necessary product of the process of accumulation, or of the development of wealth on a capitalist basis, and at the same time it develops into a lever of the capitalist mode of production. With accumulation and the accompanying development of the productivity of labour, capital's power of sudden expansion also grows and demands large masses of workers who can be employed at a moment's notice in new markets or in new branches of production without interrupting the work of production in other spheres. The characteristic course of modern industry, the form of a decennial cycle (broken only by minor vacillations) of periods of average activity, of production at high pressure, of crisis and stagnation is based on the continous formation, the greater or lesser absorption, and reconstitution of the industrial reserve army. The greater social wealth, the amount of capital at work, the extent and energy of its growth, and the greater therefore the absolute size of the working population and the productivity of its labour, the greater is relative over-population or the industrial reserve army. Its comparative size increases with the increase of wealth. The larger is the industrial reserve army in relation to the active industrial army, the larger are those sections of workers whose poverty is in inverse ratio to their labour torment. And finally, the larger is the Lazarus section of the working class and the larger is the industrial reserve army, the greater are the numbers of those who are officially acknowledged paupers. This is the absolute general law of capitalist accumulation.

The historical tendency of capitalist accumulation develops from this law. Hand in hand with the accumulation and concentration of capital develops the co-operative form of the labour process on a steadily growing scale, the conscious technological application of science to production, the organized and joint cultivation of the land, the transformation of the means of production into forms usable only jointly, and the economizing of the means of production by their use as joint means of production of combined social labour. With the steadily diminishing number of those capital magnates who usurp and monopolize all the advantages of this process of transformation, there is a corresponding increase in the volume of misery, oppression, slavery, degradation and exploitation, but at the same time also in the indignation of the working class, which steadily grows in size and is trained, united and organized by the mechanism of the capitalist process of production itself. The monopoly of capital becomes a fetter to the mode of production which has grown up with and under it. The centralization of the means of production and the socialization of labour reach a point where they become incompatible with their capitalist shell. The knell of capitalist private property sounds and the expropriators are expropriated.

Individual property based on individual labour is restored, but on the basis of the achievements of the capitalist era, as the co-operation of free workers and as their common property in the land and the means of production produced by labour. Naturally, the transformation of capitalist property, which is already practically based on a social mode of production, into social property is by no means as wearisome and difficult as was the transformation of scattered property based on individual labour into capitalist property. In the one case it was the expropriation of the masses of the people by a few usurpers, and in the other case it will be the expropriation of a few usurpers by the masses of the people.

3. The Second and Third Volumes

The fate of the second and third volumes of *Capital* was similar to that of the first. Marx hoped to be able to publish them soon after the appearance of the first, but in fact many years passed and in the end he did not succeed in preparing them for print.

Ever new and deeper studies, lingering illness and finally death prevented him from completing the whole work, and it was Engels who prepared the second and third volumes from the unfinished manuscripts his friend left behind. The wealth of material which he found consisted of drafts, jottings and the brief notes made by a scientific student for his own eyes alone, with here and there long and connected passages. All in all it represented the results of tremendous intellectual labours extending, with considerable interruptions, from 1861 to 1878.

In these circumstances we must not look to the last two volumes of *Capital* to provide us with a final and completed solution of all economic problems. In some cases these problems are merely formulated, together with an indication here and there as to the direction in which one must work to arrive at a solution. In accordance with Marx's whole attitude, his *Capital* is not a Bible containing final and unalterable truths, but rather an inexhaustible source of stimulation for further study, further scientific investigations and further struggles for truth.

The same circumstances also explain why the second and third volumes are not so perfected in their form as the first volume, why they do not sparkle with quite the same intellectual brilliance. However, they give even greater pleasure to some readers just because they present sheer intellectual problems without bothering greatly about the form. The contents of the two volumes represent an essential supplement to and development of the first volume, and they are indispensable for an understanding of the Marxian system as a whole. Unfortunately they have not been treated in any popularization up to the present and they are therefore still unknown to the broad masses of even the enlightened workers.

In the first volume Marx deals with the cardinal question of political economy : what is the origin of wealth ? What is the source of profit ? Before his investigations this question was answered in two different ways.

The " scientific " defenders of the best of all worlds in which we live, some of them men like Schulze-Delitzsch, who enjoyed respect and confidence even amongst the workers, explained capitalist wealth by a series of more or less plausible vindications and cunning manipulations : as the result of a systematic addition to the prices of commodities in order to " compensate " the employer for his generosity in " giving " his capital for productive purposes, as compensation for the " risk " every employer runs, as a reward for the " intellectual management " of business, and so on in the same strain. These explanations have all one common aim, that of presenting the wealth of the one and therefore the poverty of the other as something " just " and in consequence unalterable.

On the other hand, the critics of bourgeois society, that is to say, all the socialist schools of thought which existed prior to Marx, declared capitalist wealth to be simply the result of swindling, theft from the workers made possible by the intervention of money or by deficiencies in the organization of the process of production. Proceeding from this standpoint, these socialists developed various utopian plans for abolishing exploitation by doing away with money, by " the organization of labour ", and similar plans.

The real source of capitalist wealth was revealed for the first time in the first volume of *Capital*, which wasted no time either in finding justifications for the capitalists or in reproaching them with their injustice. Marx showed for the first time how profit originated and how it flowed into the pockets of the capitalists. He did so on the basis of two decisive economic facts : first, that the mass of the workers consists of proletarians who are compelled to sell their labour-power as a commodity in order to exist, and secondly that this commodity labour-power possesses such a high degree of productivity in our own day that it is able to produce in a certain time a much greater product than is necessary for its own maintenance in that time. These two purely economic facts, representing the result of objective historical development, cause the fruit of the labour-power of the proletarian to fall automatically into the lap of the capitalist, and to accumulate, with the continuance of the wage system, into ever-growing masses of capital.

Thus capitalist wealth is explained not as any compensation to the capitalists for imaginary sacrifices or benefits granted, or as the result of cheating or theft in the generally accepted sense of the words, but as an exchange between capitalist and worker, as a transaction of unimpeachable legal equity proceeding exactly according to those laws which govern the sale and purchase of all other commodities. In order to explain thoroughly this unobjectionable transaction which gives the capitalist the golden fruits of labour, Marx had to develop the law of value discovered by the great English classical economists Adam Smith and David Ricardo at the end of the eighteenth and the beginning of the nineteenth centuries, i.e., the explanation of the inner laws of commodity exchange, to its logical conclusion and apply it to the commodity labour-power. The first volume deals chiefly with the law of value, and, resulting from it, wages and surplus-value, i.e. the explanation of how the product of wage-labour divides itself naturally and without any violence or cheating into a pittance for the wage-worker and effortless wealth for the capitalist. And here lies the great historical significance of the first volume of *Capital*. It demonstrated that exploitation can be abolished only by abolishing the sale of labour-power, that is by abolishing the wage system.

In the first volume we are all the time at the point of production, in a factory, in a mine or in a modern agricultural undertaking, and what is said applies equally to all capitalist undertakings. We are given an individual example as the type of the whole capitalist mode of production. When we close the volume we are thoroughly acquainted with the daily creation of profit and with the whole mechanism of exploitation in all its details. Before us lie piles of commodities of all sorts still damp with the sweat of the workers as they come from the factories, and in all of them we can clearly discern that part of their value which results from the unpaid labour of the workers and which belongs just as equitably to the capitalist as the whole commodity. The root of capitalist exploitation is laid bare before our eyes.

However, at this stage the capitalist has his harvest by no means safely in the barn. The fruit of exploitation is present, but it is still in a form unsuitable for appropriation. So long as the fruit of exploitation takes the form of piled-up commodities the capitalist can derive but little pleasure from the process. He is not the slave-owner of the classical Græco-Roman world, or the feudal lord of the Middle Ages, who ground the faces of the working people merely to satisfy their own craving for luxury and to maintain an imposing retinue. In order to maintain himself and his family " in a manner befitting his social station " the capitalist must have his riches in hard cash, and this is also necessary if he is to increase his capital ceaselessly. To this end therefore he must sell the commodities produced by the wage-workers together with the surplus-value contained in them. The commodities must leave the factory and the warehouse and be thrown on to the market. The capitalist follows his commodities from his warehouse and from his office into the stock exchange and into the shops, and in the second volume of *Capital* we follow the capitalist.

The second stage in the life of the capitalist is spent in the sphere of commodity exchange, and here he meets with a number of difficulties. In his own factory the capitalist is undisputed master, and strict organization and discipline prevail there, but on the commodity market complete anarchy prevails under the name of free competition. On the commodity market no one bothers about his neighbour and no one bothers about the whole, but for all that it is precisely here that the capitalist feels his dependence on the others and on society as a whole.

The capitalist must keep abreast of his competitors. Should he take more time than absolutely necessary in selling his commodities, should he fail to provide himself with sufficient money to purchase raw materials and all the other things he needs at the right moment in order to prevent his factory coming to a standstill for lack of supplies, should he fail to invest promptly and profitably the money he receives for the sale of his commodities, he is bound to fall behind in one way or the other. The devil takes the hindmost, and the individual capitalist who fails to ensure that his business is managed as effectively in the constant exchange between the factory and the commodity market as it is in the factory itself will not succeed in obtaining the normal rate of profit no matter how zealously he may exploit his workers. A part of his " well-earned " profit will be lost somewhere on the way and will not find its way into his pocket.

However, this alone is not enough. The capitalist can accumulate riches only if he produces commodities, i.e. articles for use. Further, he must produce precisely those kinds and sorts of commodities which society needs, and he must produce them in just the quantities required, otherwise his commodities will remain unsold and the surplus-value contained in them will be lost. How can the individual capitalist control all these factors ? There is no one to tell him what commodities society needs and how many of them it needs, for the simple reason that no one knows. We are living in a planless, anarchic society, and each individual capitalist is in the same position. Nevertheless, out of this chaos, out of this confusion, a whole must result which will permit the individual business of the capitalist to prosper and at the same time satisfy the needs of society and permit its continued existence as a social organism.

To be more exact, out of the anarchic confusion of the commodity market must develop the possibility of the ceaseless circular movement of individual capital, the possibility of producing, selling, purchasing raw materials, etc., and producing again, whereby capital constantly changes from its money form into its commodity form and back again. These stages must dovetail accurately : money must be in reserve to utilize every favourable market opportunity for the purchase of raw materials, etc., and to meet the current expenses of production, and the money which comes flowing back as the commodities are sold must be given an opportunity of immediate utilization again. The individual capitalists, who are apparently quite independent of each other, now join together in fact and form a great brotherhood, and thanks to the credit system and the banks they continually advance each other the money they need and take up the available money so that the uninterrupted progress of production and the sale of commodities is ensured both for the individual capitalist and for society as a whole.

Bourgeois economists have never found any explanation for the credit system beyond calling it an ingenious institution for "facilitating commodity exchange", but in the second volume of *Capital* Marx demonstrates, quite incidentally, that the credit system is a necessary part of capitalist life, the connecting link between two phases of capital, in production and on the commodity market, and between the apparently arbitrary movements of individual capital.

And then the permanent circulation of production and consumption in society as a whole must be kept in movement in the confusion of individual capitals, and this must be done in such a fashion that the necessary conditions of capitalist production are assured : the production of the means of production, the maintenance of the working class and the progressive enrichment of the capitalist class, i.e. the increasing accumulation and activity of all the capital of society. The second volume of *Capital* investigates how a whole is developed from the innumerable deviating movements of individual capital, how this movement of the whole vacillates between the surplus of the boom years and the collapse of the crisis years, but is wrenched back again and again into correct proportions only to swing out of them again immediately, and how out of all this there develops in ever more powerful dimensions that which is only a means for present-day society, its own maintenance and economic progress, and that which is its end, the progressive accumulation of capital. Marx offers us no final solution, but for the first time in a hundred years, since Adam Smith, the whole is presented on the firm foundations of definite laws.

But even with this the capitalist has not completely traversed the thorny path before him, for although profit has been turned and is being turned in increasing measure into money, the great problem now arises of how to distribute the booty. Many different groups of capitalists put forward their demands. Apart from the employer there is the merchant, the loan capitalist and the landowner. Each of these has done his share to make possible the exploitation of the wage-worker and the sale of the commodities produced by the latter, and each now demands his share of the profit. This distribution of profit is a much more complicated affair than it might appear to be on the surface, for even amongst the employers themselves big differences exist, according to the type of undertaking, in the profits obtained, so to speak, fresh from the factory.

In one branch of production commodities are produced and sold quickly, and capital plus the normal addition returns to the undertaking in a short space of time. Under such circumstances business and profits are made rapidly. In other branches of production capital is held fast in production for years and yields profit only after a long time. In some branches of production the employer must invest the greater part of his capital in lifeless means of production, in buildings, expensive machinery, etc., i.e. in things which yield no profit on their own account no matter how necessary they may be for profit-making. In other branches of production the employer need invest very little of his capital in such things and can use the greater part of it for the employment of workers, each of whom represents the industrious goose that lays the golden egg for the capitalist.

Thus in the process of profit-making big differences develop as between the individual capitalists, and in the eyes of bourgeois society these differences represent a much more urgent " injustice " than the peculiar " exchange " which takes place between the capitalist and the worker. The problem is to come to some arrangement which will ensure a " just " division of the spoils, whereby each capitalist gets " his share ", and what is more, it is a problem which has to be solved without any conscious and systematic plan, because distribution in present-day society is as anarchic as production. There is in fact no " distribution " at all in the sense of a social measure and what takes place is solely exchange, commodity circulation, buying and selling. How therefore does unregulated commodity exchange permit each individual exploiter and each category of exploiters to obtain that share of the wealth produced by the labour-power of the proletariat which is his or its " right " in the eyes of capitalist society ?

Marx gives the answer to this question in the third volume of *Capital*. In the first volume he deals with the production of capital and lays bare the secret of profit-making. In the second volume he describes the movement of capital between the factory and the market, between the production and consumption of society. And in the third volume he deals with the distribution of the profit amongst the capitalist class as a whole. And all the time he proceeds from the basis of the three fundamental principles of capitalist society : firstly, that everything that happens in capitalist society is not the result of arbitrary forces, but the result of definite and regularly operating laws, although these laws are unknown to the capitalists themselves; secondly, that economic relations in capitalist society are not based on violence, robbery and cheating; and, thirdly, that no social reason is at work controlling the movements of society as a whole. He analyses and systematically lays bare one after the other all the phenomena and all the relations of the capitalist economic system exclusively on the basis of the exchange mechanism of capitalist society, i.e. the law of value and the surplus-value which results from it.

Taking his great work as a whole we can say that the first volume, which develops the law of value, wages and surplus-value, lays bare the foundations of present-day society, whilst the second and third volumes show us the house which is based on these foundations. Or, to use a different comparison, we can say that the first volume shows us the heart of the social organism, which generates the living sap, whilst the second and third volumes show us the circulation of the blood and the nourishment of the body from the centre out to the cutaneous cells.

The contents of the second and third volumes take us on to a different plane. In the first volume we are in the factory, in the deep social pit of labour where we can trace the source of capitalist wealth. In the second and third volumes we are on the surface, on the official stage of society. Department stores, banks, the stock exchanges, finance and the troubles of the " needy " agriculturalists take up the foreground. The worker has no rôle on this stage, and in fact he shows little interest in the things which happen behind his back after he has been skinned. We see the workers in the noisy mob of business people only when they troop off to the factories in the grey light of the early morning or hurry home again in the dusk when the factories eject them in droves after the day's work.

At first glance therefore it may not be clear why the workers should concern themselves with the private worries of the capitalists and with the squabbles which take place over the division of the spoils. However, both the second and the third volumes are as necessary to a thorough understanding of present-day economic mechanism as is the first volume. It is true that they do not play the same decisive and fundamental historic rôle for the modern working-class movement as the first volume does, but nevertheless they offer a wealth of insight into the workings of capitalism which is invaluable to the intellectual equipment of the proletariat in the practical struggle for its emancipation. Two examples will suffice.

When dealing with the process by which the regular maintenance of society results from the chaotic movement of individual capitals, in the second volume, Marx naturally touches on the problem of the crises. One must not expect any systematic and didactic dissertation on this phenomenon. There are in fact only a few incidental observations, but the utilization of these observations would be of the greatest value for all enlightened and thinking workers. For instance, it is one of the main planks in the agitation of the social democrats, and above all of the trade-union leaders, that economic crises take place chiefly as the result of the short-sightedness of the capitalists, who simply will not grasp the fact that the masses of the workers are their best customers and that all they need do is to pay these workers higher wages in order to ensure the existence of unfailing purchasing power for their goods and thus avoid all danger of crises.

This argument is a very popular one, but it is wholly fallacious, and Marx refutes it in the following words : " It is sheer tautology to say that crises are produced by the lack of paying consumption or paying consumers. The capitalist system recognizes only paying consumers, with the exception of those in receipt of poor law support or the ' rogues '. That commodities are unsaleable means no more than that there are no purchasers, or consumers, for them. And if people are inclined to give this tautology an appearance of some deeper meaning by saying that the working class does not receive enough of its own product and that the evil would be dispelled immediately it received a greater share, i.e. if its wages were increased, all one can say is that crises are invariably preceded by periods in which wages in general rise and the working class receives a relatively greater share of the annual product intended for consumption. From the standpoint of these valiant upholders of ' plain common sense,', such periods should prevent the coming of crises. It would appear therefore that capitalist production includes conditions which are independent of good will or bad will and which permit such periods of relative prosperity for the working class only temporarily and always as the harbingers of the coming crises."

The investigations which Marx pursues in the second and third volumes of *Capital* offer a thorough insight into the nature of crises, which are seen to be the inevitable result of the movement of capital, which in its impetuous and insatiable urge to accumulation and growth quickly plunges beyond the limits of consumption, no matter how wide these limits may be set as the result of increased purchasing power of one section of society or by the opening up of new markets. Thus the idea of a harmony of interests between capital and labour which lurks behind the popular agitation of the trade unions. harmony which is prevented only by the short-sightedness of the capitalists, is refuted, and all hope of palliative measures to patch up the economic anarchy of capitalism must be abandoned. The struggle to improve the material conditions of life of the proletariat has a thousand brilliant arguments in its favour in the intellectual armoury of the modern working-class, and it certainly does not need the help of a theoretically untenable and practically ambiguous argument such as the one dealt with above.

A second example : in the third volume of *Capital* Marx provides for the first time a scientific explanation of a phenomenon which has puzzled bourgeois economic science since its inception, namely that, although invested under varying conditions, capital in all branches of production yields as a general rule only the so-called " customary rate of profit ". At first glance this phenomenon would seem to contradict a statement which Marx himself makes, i.e. that capitalist wealth arises exclusively from the unpaid labour of the wage-workers. How can the capitalist who is compelled to invest comparatively large proportions of his capital in lifeless means of production secure the same profit as his colleague who need invest far less of his capital in such things and can therefore use proportionately larger quantities of living labour-power ?

Marx solves this riddle with extraordinary simplicity by showing that with the sale of one sort of commodity above its value and other sorts of commodities below their value the differences in profit are levelled out and an " average rate of profit " developed for all branches of production. Quite unconsciously, and without any agreement amongst themselves, the capitalists exchange their commodities in such a fashion that each capitalist contributes the surplus-value which he has extracted from his workers to a general pool, and the total result of their combined exploitation is then divided fraternally amongst the capitalists, each of whom receives a share in accordance with the size of his capital. The individual capitalist therefore does not enjoy the profit which he directly extracts from his workers, but only his share of that total profit which he and his capitalist colleagues together have extracted from the workers. " As far as profit is concerned, the various capitalists play the rôle of mere shareholders in a joint-stock company distributing its profits in equal percentages so that the shares of the various capitalists differ only according to the amount of capital invested by each in the joint undertaking, according to the proportionate participation of each in the undertaking as a whole."

What penetrating insight into the real and material basis of capitalist class-solidarity are we offered by this apparently

dry-as-dust law of the " average rate of profit " ! We observe
that although the capitalists are hostile brothers in their daily
activities, nevertheless, as far as the working class is concerned
they represent a sort of Freemasonry interested intensely and
personally in the total result of all the exploitation conducted
by all its members. Although the capitalists have naturally not
the least idea of these objective economic laws, their unfailing
instinct as members of a ruling class shows itself in an appreciation of their own class interests and of their antagonism to the
proletariat, and unfortunately it has persisted far more firmly
through the storms of history than has the class-consciousness of
the workers, whose scientific basis is revealed in the works of
Marx and Engels.

These two short and arbitrarily chosen examples must suffice
to give the reader some idea of what treasures still remain un-
mined in the second and third volumes of *Capital* and awaiting
a popularization, and what a wealth of intellectual stimulation
and intellectual profundity they offer the enlightened workers.
Incomplete as the two volumes are, they offer more than any final
truth could : an urge to thought, to criticism and self-criticism,
and this is the essence of the lessons which Marx gave the working
class.

4. The Reception of *Capital*

The hope expressed by Engels that after having completed
the first volume and got rid of the " incubus " Marx would " feel
a different fellow altogether " was fulfilled only in part.

The improvement in the latter's health was unfortunately
not permanent whilst his pecuniary situation remained embar-
rassingly uncertain. At about this time he even considered
moving to Geneva, where he would have been able to live much
more cheaply, but circumstances bound him to London and the
treasures of the British Museum. He hoped to find a publisher
for an English translation of his work, and he was unable and
unwilling to surrender the intellectual leadership of the International before he had seen it safely started along the correct
path.

The marriage of his second daughter Laura to his " medical
Creole " Paul Lafargue was a happy domestic event. The young
couple had become engaged in August 1866, but it had been
agreed that Lafargue should first complete his medical studies

before they married. He had been struck off the rolls of the University of Paris for a period of two years owing to his participation in a students' congress in Liège, and he then went to London in connection with the International. At first he was a follower of Proudhon and had no relations with Marx beyond visiting him as a matter of politeness to leave a card from Tolain, but fate took a hand in the usual fashion and not long afterwards Marx wrote to Engels : " At first the young fellow attached himself to me, but it was not long before he found the daughter more attractive than the father. He is the only child of a former planter's family and his economic position is tolerably good." According to Marx's description Lafargue was good-looking, intelligent, energetic, physically well-developed and good-hearted, but a little spoiled and nevertheless somewhat too unsophisticated.

Lafargue was born in Santiago on the island of Cuba, but when he was nine his parents took him to France. His paternal grandmother was a Mulattress and through her he had Negro blood in his veins, a fact to which he referred willingly and which accounted for the subdued duskiness of his complexion and for the great whites of his eyes, though otherwise his features were very regular. It was probably this Negro strain in him which accounted for a certain obstinacy which occasionally caused Marx to reproach him, half in annoyance and half in amusement, for his " Nigger skull ". However, the tone of good-humoured banter which they used towards each other is sufficient proof of how well they got on together. For Marx Lafargue became not only a son-in-law who brought happiness to his daughter Laura, but also a capable and dexterous assistant who proved a loyal defender of his intellectual legacy.

Marx's chief worry in this period was his anxiety about his book, and on the 2nd of November 1867 he wrote to Engels : " The fate of my book makes me nervous. I hear and see nothing. The Germans are fine fellows ! Their achievements on this field as the lackeys of the English and the French and even of the Italians no doubt give them the right to ignore my work. Our friends over there don't know how to agitate. And in the meantime one must follow the Russian policy and wait. Patience is the secret of Russian diplomacy and success, but we poor creatures who live only once can starve the while." The impatience these lines betray is understandable enough, but it was not quite justified.

The book had hardly been published two months, and in such a short space of time it was impossible to write any really thorough criticism, but both Engels and Kugelmann had done everything possible to " make a noise about the book ", and even

Marx thought that this was the most necessary thing at the moment in the hope of producing some effect in England also. It cannot be said that Engels and Kugelmann were over-punctilious in their efforts, but they met with a certain amount of success. They secured the publication of advance notices of the book in quite a number of papers, including bourgeois publications, and even a reprint of the introduction. And in addition they had even prepared a piece of advertisement which was quite sensational for those days, namely the publication of a biographical article in *Die Gartenlaube*, when Marx requested them to stop such " nonsense " :. " I consider that that sort of thing is likely to do more harm than good and, in any case, it is beneath the dignity of a man of science. For instance, long ago Meyer's *Encyclopædia* asked me for biographical notes, but I did not even answer their letter, much less give them the information they wanted. Every man to his taste."

The article which Engels had written for *Die Gartenlaube*, " a blurb, written in great haste, which would have done justice to Beta ",[1] as its author described it, was finally published in *Die Zukunft*, Johann Jacoby's organ which Guido Weiss had been publishing in Berlin since 1867, and then reprinted by Liebknecht in the *Demokratisches Wochenblatt*, but much shortened, a fact which caused Engels to observe disagreeably : " Wilhelm has now happily arrived at a stage where he dare not even say that Lassalle copied you and did it badly. He has completely emasculated the article, and why he thought it worth while printing at all after that only he can know." Liebknecht was, in fact, completely in agreement with the passages he cut out of the article, but he cut them out nevertheless in order to avoid giving offence to a number of Lassalleans who had just fallen away from Schweitzer and were helping to found the Eisenach fraction.

Later on Marx's work received some excellent criticisms, for instance, a review by Engels in the *Demokratisches Wochenblatt*, one by Schweitzer in the *Sozialdemokrat*, and a second review by Joseph Dietzgen in the former publication. Apart from Engels' review, which naturally showed a thorough understanding of the points at issue, Marx was compelled to recognize that despite a number of errors Schweitzer had certainly studied the book and understood its importance. Marx heard of Dietzgen for the first time after the publication of *Capital*, and he welcomed him as a capable philosophic brain, but without forming any excessively high opinion of him.

[1] This is a reference to the oily Bettziech, who used that pen-name when fulsomely praising his idol Kinkel.—Tr.

The first "expert" also took the floor in 1867. This was Eugen Dühring, who reviewed the book in one of the supplements to Meyer's *Encyclopædia*. Although Marx felt that Dühring had not grasped the fundamentally new elements in his work, he was on the whole not dissatisfied with the review, declaring it "quite decent", though he suspected that Dühring's attitude had been determined more by his hatred of Roscher and the other university luminaries than by any real interest for or understanding of the points at issue. Engels' opinion of Dühring's review was much less favourable, and in fact his judgment was the keener, for it was not long before Dühring turned round completely and did his best to tear the book to pieces.

Marx had no better luck at the hands of the other "experts", and eight years later one of these worthies, who cautiously concealed his name, oracularly informed the world that Marx was an "Autodidact" who had overlooked a whole generation of scientific progress. After such and similar achievements on the part of the "experts" the bitterness which Marx invariably showed towards them was thoroughly justified, although he probably set down much to their malice which should have been set down to their ignorance, for they were utterly unable to grasp his dialectical method. This was also the case with men who lacked neither good-will nor economic knowledge, but who nevertheless found it difficult to understand the book, whilst on the other hand men who were by no means familiar with economic matters and who were more or less hostile to communism, but who had passed through the Hegelian school, spoke with the greatest enthusiasm of it.

For instance, Marx was unconscionably severe in his judgment on the second edition of F. A. Lange's book on the labour question,[1] in which the author dealt in detail with the first volume of *Capital*, declaring : "Herr Lange is loud in his praises, but only in order to make himself important." This was certainly not true, for Lange's honest interest in the labour question was beyond all doubt, though Marx was right enough when he observed that Lange knew nothing of the Hegelian method and even less of the critical way in which he, Marx, had applied it. In fact, Lange turned the truth upside down when he declared that, speculatively considered, Lassalle was freer and more independent of Hegel than was Marx, whose speculative form adhered closely to the manner of its philosophic model and in certain sections of the book mastered its matter only with difficulties, for instance, with regard to the theory of value, to which, by the way, Lange credited no permanent worth.

[1] *Die Arbeiterfrage.*

Freiligrath's verdict on the first volume, a copy of which Marx had presented him, was even more peculiar. Friendly relations had existed between the two men since the year 1859, although occasionally they had been overclouded through the fault of third persons, and Freiligrath was about to return to Germany where a collection on his behalf promised him a carefree old age after the closing down of the London branch of the bank for which he worked had deprived the almost sixty-year-old man of his livelihood. The last letter he wrote to his old friend—no further correspondence passed between them—contained hearty congratulations on the marriage of Marx's daughter Laura to young Lafargue and no less hearty thanks for a copy of the first volume of *Capital* which Marx had sent him. The study of the book had enlightened him in many ways, he declared, and had been a source of great pleasure. The success of the book would probably not be sudden and sensational, but its effect would be all the deeper and more permanent. So far so good, but then he declared : " I know that many young merchants and manufacturers in the Rhineland are enthusiastic about the book, and in such circles it will fulfill its real aim, and besides it will prove an indispensable work of reference for the scholar ". It is true that Freiligrath never claimed to be anything but " an economist by instinct ", and all his life he hated " heckling and Hegeling ", as he put it, but after all, he had spent almost two decades in the pulsating life of the English metropolis, and it was therefore an extraordinary performance on his part when he regarded the first volume of *Capital* as a sort of guide-book for young merchants and manufacturers, and at the utmost, " besides ", a reference work for scholars.

Ruge's judgment, on the other hand, was quite different. Although he hated communism like poison and was not burdened with any knowledge of economics, he had once fought courageously as a Young Hegelian. " It is an epoch-making work and it sheds a brilliant, sometimes dazzling, light on the development, decline, birth pangs and the horribly painful maladies of social periods. The passages on the production of surplus-value by unpaid labour, the expropriation of the workers who work for themselves, and the approaching expropriation of the expropriators are classic. Marx's knowledge is wide and scholarly, and he possesses splendid dialectical talent. The book is far above the intellectual horizon of many people and many newspaper writers, but it will certainly make its way despite the breadth of its plan, or perhaps it will exercise a powerful influence just for this reason." Ludwig Feuerbach passed a similar judgment with the difference, in accordance with his own development, that he was less interested in the dialectics of the author than the fact that the book was "rich in undeniable facts of the most interesting, but at the same time most horrible nature", which, he thought, went to prove the truth of his moral philosophy that where the necessities of life were absent moral compulsion was also absent.

The first translation of the first volume appeared in Russia. On the 12th of October 1868 Marx reported to Kugelmann that a publisher in St. Petersburg had surprised him with the information that a translation was already in print, and with a request for a photo to be used as a frontispiece. He was unwilling to refuse his "good friends" the Russians this little favour and found it one of the ironies of fate that the Russians, against whom he had fought in German, French and English for 25 years, should always have been his "patrons". His reply to Proudhon and his *Critique of Political Economy* had sold nowhere so well as in Russia. Still, he was not prepared to give them all too much credit for this and declared that it was pure Epicureanism, a desire for the extremist products that the Western world could offer.

However, this was not really true. The translation appeared only in 1872, but it proved to be a serious scientific undertaking and a great success, and Marx himself declared it "masterly". The translator was Danielson, better known under his pen-name Nikolai-on, and he was assisted in the translation of a number of the most important chapters by Lopatin, a daring young revolutionary, "a very wide-awake and critical brain, a cheerful character and as stoical as a Russian peasant, taking everything as he finds it", as Marx described him after making his acquaintance in the summer of 1870.

Permission to publish the translation was given by the Russian censorship authorities with the following explanation : "Although the political convictions of the author are completely socialist and although the whole book is of a very definitely socialist character, the manner of its presentation is certainly not such as to make the book open to all and in addition it is written in a strictly scientific fashion so that in the opinion of the committee it should not be prosecuted." The translation was published on the 27th of March and by the 25th of May a thousand copies, or one third of the total edition, had been sold.

At the same time a French translation began to appear and also a second edition of the German original, both in two parts. The French edition was prepared by J. Roy, with considerable assistance from Marx himself, who had "the devil's own job" with it and often complained that it cost him more time and trouble than if he had done the whole thing himself. However, as a consolation he was able to credit the French translation with a particular scientific value apart from the original. The first volume of *Capital* met with less success in England than in Germany, Russia and France. Apparently only one short review was published (in *The Saturday Review*), but this declared that Marx had the gift of lending even the dryest economic questions a certain fascination. A longer review which Engels wrote for *The Fortnightly Review* was rejected on the ground that it was " too dry ", although Professor Beesly, who was closely connected with the magazine, did his best to get it accepted. Marx set great hopes on an English translation, but none appeared during his lifetime.

CHAPTER THIRTEEN:
THE INTERNATIONAL AT ITS
ZENITH

1. England, France and Belgium

THE second congress of the International took place in Lausanne from the 2nd to the 8th of September 1867, shortly after the appearance of the first volume of *Capital*. Its level was not as high as that of the first congress in Geneva.

Even the appeal issued by the General Council in July calling for the sending of strong delegations to the congress was noticeably less interesting in its survey of the third year of the existence and activity of the International. Only Switzerland and Belgium, where a massacre of striking workers in Marchienne had roused the feelings of the proletariat, were able to report steady progress, and for the rest the document complains of obstacles placed in the way of propaganda in various countries by various circumstances. Prior to 1848 Germany had shown a deep interest in social questions, but now it was fully occupied with the question of national unity. Despite the energetic support it had given to the strikes of the French workers, the International had not made the expected progress in France owing to the prevailing lack of freedom. The reference here is to the great lock-out of the bronze workers in Paris in the spring of 1867, which had developed into a fight for the right to organize and had ended in a victory for the workers.

England also received a mild rebuke, the appeal pointing out that it was so taken up with the movement for the reform of the franchise that for the moment it had lost sight of economic questions. However, under the pressure of the masses Disraeli had been compelled to grant an even wider franchise than Gladstone had originally intended and now every tenant of a town house received the vote no matter what its annual rental might be. The General Council then expressed the hope that the time had now arrived for the English workers to realize the usefulness of the International. In conclusion it referred to the United States, where the workers had won the eight-hour day in a number of States.

Every section of the International, irrespective of its size, was entitled to send a delegate to the congress. Larger sections were entitled to send a delegate for the first five hundred members and a further delegate for every subsequent five hundred. The tasks before the congress were drawn up as follows : (1) What practical steps must be taken by the International to create a joint centre for the working class in its struggle for emancipation ? And (2) How can the credit given by the working class to the bourgeoisie and the government be used in the interests of the proletarian struggle for emancipation ?

This programme was very general, and to make matters worse it was not accompanied by any memorandum which might have provided it with a detailed basis. Eccarius and Dupont, a music instrument maker, went to Lausanne as the representatives of the General Council. Dupont was the corresponding secretary for France and a very capable man. In the absence of Jung he took the chair at the congress, at which 71 delegates were present. Amongst the German delegates were Kugelmann, F. A. Lange, Ludwig Büchner and Ladendorff, a good bourgeois democrat but a violent opponent of communism. The Franco-Italian group far outnumbered the Teutonic group and, apart from a few Belgians and Italians, it was composed chiefly of French and Swiss-French delegates.

This time the Proudhonists had prepared themselves more thoroughly and more rapidly than the General Council, and three months before the latter issued its congress appeal they drew up an agenda for the congress containing such points as : mutuality as the basis of social relations, equal compensation for social services rendered, credit and people's banks, mutual insurance associations, the position of man and woman in society, collective and individual interests, the State as guardian and dispenser of justice, the right to punish, and a dozen similar questions. The result was unholy confusion, but it is not necessary to go into details, because Marx had nothing to do with it all, and in any case the decisions, many of them mutually contradictory, adopted by the congress existed on paper only.

The practical work of the congress was more fruitful than its theoretical deliberations. It confirmed the General Council with headquarters in London and decided on an annual contribution of 10 centimes per member, determining that the prompt payment of this sum for all members should be an essential condition of the right to send delegates to the annual congresses. It also decided that the social emancipation of the working class was indivisible from political action, and that the fight for political freedom was a preliminary and absolute necessity. It attached such importance to this statement that it decided to repeat it solemnly at every subsequent congress. It also adopted a correct attitude to the bourgeois League for Peace and Freedom, which had recently developed out of the loins of the radical bourgeoisie and shortly afterwards held its first congress in Geneva. All the attempts of the League to secure the support of the workers were answered with the simple statement : we shall support you gladly whenever our own interests can be advanced thereby.

Strangely enough, this less important congress attracted much more attention in the bourgeois world than its predecessor, although of course it must not be forgotten that the first congress had taken place whilst the reverberations of the Austro-Prussian War were still disturbing Europe. The English press in particular, and above all *The Times*, for which Eccarius reported, showed a lively interest in the Lausanne congress, although it had completely ignored its predecessor. Naturally, there was no lack of mockery, but nevertheless the bourgeoisie began to take the International seriously. In a letter to *Der Vorbote* Frau Marx wrote : " When our congress was compared with its step-brother the Peace Congress the comparison was always in favour of the elder brother, for the latter was regarded as a serious threat whilst the former was treated as a farce and a burlesque." Marx consoled himself in a similar fashion, for of course it was impossible for him to feel any satisfaction with the Lausanne debates : " Things are on the move. And without funds ! And with the intrigues of the Proudhonists in Paris and of Mazzini in Italy. With the jealous Odger, Cremer and Potter in London, and Schulze-Delitzsch and the Lassalleans in Germany. We are entitled to be very satisfied." And Engels declared that it was immaterial what the congress decided in Lausanne so long as the General Council remained in London. This was very true, for with the third year of its existence the period of peaceful development ceased and a time of fierce struggles began for the International.

A few days after the conclusion of the Lausanne congress an incident occurred which had far-reaching consequences. On the 18th of September 1867 armed Fenians held up a prison waggon in which two Fenian prisoners were being transported. They made their attack in broad daylight, broke open the doors of the waggon and released their comrades after having shot dead one of the police escort. The men actually engaged in the coup were never captured, but a number of men[1] were chosen from amongst the masses arrested afterwards and brought before the courts on a charge of murder. The trial was preju-

---

[1] Four—Allen, Larkin, O'Brien, and O'Meagher Condon.

diced from the beginning and no real evidence was produced against the accused, but for all that they were sentenced to death and hanged.[1] The affair caused a great sensation in England, and a " Fenian panic " took place when in December the wall of the prison in Clerkenwell, a district inhabited almost exclusively by workers and members of the lower middle-class, was blown up by Fenians, causing the death of twelve people and wounding over a hundred others.

The International of course had nothing whatever to do with the Fenian conspiracy, and both Marx and Engels condemned the Clerkenwell outrage as a piece of folly which would do the Fenians more harm than anyone else, because it would cool off or perhaps entirely destroy the sympathies of the English workers for the Irish cause, but the way in which the English government treated the Fenians as common criminals although they were political rebels against shameless and century-old oppression roused indignation in all revolutionary breasts. Even in June 1867 Marx had written to Engels : " These revolting swine boast of their English humanity because they do not treat their political prisoners any worse than murderers, footpads, forgers and sodomists." And Engels was influenced by the additional factor that Elizabeth Burns, to whom he had transferred his affection for her dead sister Mary, was a staunch Irish patriot.

However, the lively interest which Marx showed for the Irish question was caused by something even deeper than sympathy for an oppressed people. His studies had led him to the conclusion that the freedom of the Irish people was a necessary condition for the emancipation of the English working class, on which, in its turn, the emancipation of the European proletariat depended. He felt that the overthrow of the English landed oligarchy would be impossible so long as it held such a strongly entrenched position in Ireland, but immediately the Irish people took charge of its own destiny, elected its legislators, appointed its government and became autonomous, the destruction of the landed aristocracy, which consisted for the most part of English landlords, would be much easier than in England because in Ireland it was not merely an economic, but a national question. In England the landlords were the traditional dignitaries, but in Ireland they were the bitterly hated representatives of national oppression. With the disappearance of the English troops and the English police from Ireland an agrarian revolution would take place.

As far as the English bourgeoisie was concerned, it had a common interest with the English aristocracy in turning Ireland into a mere pasture-land to provide the English market with

[1] Allen, Larkin, and O'Brien were hanged. Condon, who was a U. S. citizen, was reprieved.

meat and wool at the lowest possible prices. But apart from that it had still more important reasons for desiring the continuation of the existing Irish régime. Owing to the steadily increasing concentration of tenant farming Ireland provided a steady surplus of its population for the English labour market, thus depressing wages and the material and moral position of the English working class. In all the industrial and commercial centres of England the working class was divided into two hostile camps : the English workers on the one hand and their Irish fellow-workers on the other. The ordinary English worker hated the Irish worker as a competitor, and felt himself superior as a member of a dominant race, thus becoming a tool of the aristocrats and capitalists against Ireland and at the same time strengthening the dominance of those classes over himself. The English worker harboured religious, social and national prejudices against the Irish worker and regarded him much in the same way as the " poor whites " regarded the " Nigger " in the former slave States of the Union. On the other hand, the Irish worker paid him back in his own coin and with interest. He regarded the English worker as at once the accomplice and the stupid tool of English dominance in Ireland. The impotence of the working class in England despite its organization was rooted in this antagonism, which was artificially kept alive by the press, the pulpit and the comic papers—in short, by every means at the disposal of the ruling classes.

Further, the evil was kept alive on the other side of the Atlantic, where the antagonism between the English and Irish prevented any honest and effective co-operation between the working classes of England and America. The most important task of the International was to accelerate the development of the social revolution in England, the metropolis of capital, and the only means to this end was to secure the independence of Ireland. The International must come out openly on the side of Ireland on every possible occasion and the General Council must make it its special task to convince the English workers that the national independence of Ireland was not merely a question of abstract justice and human sympathy, but the preliminary condition for their own social emancipation.

In the years that followed Marx devoted all his energies to this task. Just as he regarded the Polish question (which had disappeared from the agenda of the International since the Geneva congress) as a lever for the overthrow of Russian dominance, so he regarded the Irish question as a lever for the overthrow of English world dominance, and his attitude was not affected by the fact that it offered the " intriguers " in the working-class movement who were anxious to become members of the next parliament (he counted even Odger, the President of the General Council, amongst them) an excuse for joining the bourgeois Liberals, for, in the hope of securing office again, Gladstone was exploiting the Irish question as an election slogan and it had become one of the burning questions of the day. The General Council organized a petition to the English government against the execution of the three convicted Manchester Fenians, naturally without success, and condemned the executions as legal murder, and it also organized public meetings in London in support of the Irish cause.

This activity gave offence to the English government, and it was seized upon by the French government for an attack upon the International. For three years Bonaparte had watched the development of the International without interfering with it, hoping thereby to frighten the refractory bourgeoisie. When the French members of the International opened a bureau in Paris they informed the Prefect of Police and the Minister of the Interior, but these two dignitaries did not even acknowledge the receipt of the letters. However, there had been minor pieces of sharp practice and trickery on the part of the authorities. The Geneva congress of the International sent its minutes to the General Council in the hands of a born Swiss who had become a naturalized Englishman, it being unwilling to trust its documents to the tender mercies of Bonaparte's *cabinet noir*, but on the French frontier they were pilfered by the police, and the French government remained deaf to all protests. However, the Foreign Office in London took up the case and the thieves were then compelled to disgorge their booty.

The Emperor's confidant Rouher was snubbed by the International when he declared himself prepared to allow the publication of a manifesto drawn up by the French delegates to the Geneva congress only on condition that " a few words of thanks to the Emperor, who had done so much for the workers, should be inserted ". This was refused, although the general policy of the French members of the International was to avoid as far as possible giving any offence to the lurking beast, knowing full well that it was only biding its time, and this caused the bourgeois radicals to suspect them of being camouflaged Bonapartists.

Some French writers assert that they permitted this suspicion to provoke them into giving their support to one or two tame proclamations which the radical bourgeoisie issued against the Empire, but this is unimportant, for the reasons which caused Bonaparte to break openly with the working class lay much deeper. The strike movement which followed on the devastating crisis of 1866 developed to an extent which seriously disturbed him, and then, in the spring of 1867 when war with the North German League threatened on account of the Luxemburg dispute, the workers of Paris, under the influence of the International, ex changed peace addresses with the workers of Berlin, and finally the French bourgeoisie was making such an ear-splitting noise with its demand for " Vengeance for Sadova " [1] that the denizens of the Tuileries conceived the brilliant notion of stopping the noise with " liberal " concessions.

In these circumstances Bonaparte imagined that he would be killing two birds with one stone when he prepared a blow against the Paris bureau of the International under the pretext that it was the centre of a Fenian conspiracy. The homes of the members of the bureau were raided without warning and in the dead of night, but naturally not the faintest vestige of any conspiracy was found, and in order to prevent Bonaparte's discomfiture from covering him with public ridicule nothing remained but to take proceedings against the arrested men for being members of an unauthorized society of more than twenty members. On the 6th and 20th of March 15 members of the International were tried and found guilty. They were fined 100 francs each and the bureau was declared dissolved. An appeal against the verdict proved fruitless.

However, before the appeal had been heard new proceedings had been commenced. The public prosecutor and the court itself had treated the accused with unusual consideration whilst Tolain had defended them and himself with great moderation, but two days after the opening of the trial a new bureau had been formed and this defiant and open mockery robbed Bonaparte of his last illusions. On the 22nd of May 9 members of the new bureau were hauled before the courts, and after a brilliant and caustic defence by Varlin they were sentenced to three months imprisonment each. With this the real relations between the Empire and the International were clearly revealed and the French section of the latter won new strength from this final and open breach with the December butcher.

The International also came to grips with the Belgian government. The mineowners in the Charleroi Basin goaded their miserably paid workers into revolt by persistent chicanery and then let loose the armed forces of the State against them. In the panic-stricken reign of terror which followed the International championed the cause of the brutally maltreated workers. It

[1] Sadova—a Bohemian village and the name used by the Austrians for the Battle of Königgrätz at which they were decisively defeated by the Prussians on the 3rd of July 1866.—Tr.

made their case known to the general public in the press and at public meetings ; it supported the dependants of the killed and wounded workers, and provided the arrested men with legal assistance which subsequently secured their acquittal.

The Belgian Minister of Justice, de Bara, launched a flood of fierce abuse against the International in the Belgian Chamber and threatened repressive measures, including the prohibition of the next congress of the International, which had been arranged to take place in Brussels. However, these threats did not intimidate the Belgian members of the International and they answered the Minister in a defiant open letter which concluded with the assurance that the next congress of the International would take place in Brussels whether the Minister of Justice liked it or not.

2.   Switzerland and Germany

The most effective lever of the great forward movement made by the International in these years was the general wave of strikes which swept over all the more or less developed capitalist countries as a result of the economic crash in 1866.

The General Council was in no way responsible for the outbreak of these strikes, but it supported the strikers with advice and assistance, and it mobilized the international solidarity of the proletariat in their favour. In this way the International deprived the capitalist class of a very effective weapon, and employers were no longer able to check the militancy of their workers by importing cheap foreign labour. Still further, the International recruited self-sacrificing allies from amongst the unconscious auxiliaries of the common enemy. Wherever its influence was felt it sought to convince the workers that their own interests demanded that they should support the wage struggles of their foreign comrades.

This activity of the International proved to be of permanent value and won it a European reputation far in excess of the real increase in its power. The bourgeois world either would not or could not realize that the origin of the strike wave must be looked for in the miserable situation of the workers, and it therefore sought to explain the strikes as the result of the secret machinations of the International. In consequence the latter developed into a demoniacal monster which the bourgeoisie sallied out to destroy in every strike struggle. Each big strike quickly became a struggle around the International and from each strike it emerged with increased power.

Typical struggles of this kind were the strike of the building workers in the spring of 1868 in Geneva and the strike of the ribbon weavers and silk dyers which broke out in the autumn of the same year in Basle and continued until the following spring. The strike of the building workers in Geneva began with a demand for higher wages and a shorter working day, but the employers soon altered its character by demanding that the workers should sever all connections with the International as the preliminary condition to the conclusion of any agreement. The striking workers immediately rejected this piece of insolence, and thanks to the assistance which the General Council secured on their behalf in England, France and other countries they were able to carry through their original demands. In Basle capitalist arrogance played a still more brutal game. The ribbon weavers of a factory in the town were informed that this year they would not be granted the few hours' holiday which they had enjoyed traditionally for many years on the last day of the autumn fair, and that any workers who took time off despite the warning would be instantly dismissed. A section of the workers insisted on their traditional rights, and the next day they were turned away from the factory gates by the police, despite the fact that they were entitled to fourteen days' notice. This piece of capitalist brutality and insolence aroused the workers of Basle, and a struggle began which lasted many months and culminated in an attempt on the part of the Cantonal government to intimidate the workers with military measures, including the imposition of regulations amounting practically to martial law.

The aim of this fierce attack soon proved to be an attempt to destroy the International. The capitalists did everything possible to crush the workers, from brutalities such as the eviction of strikers' families from their homes and the stopping of credit at the shops, to such ludicrous measures as the despatch of an emissary to London to investigate the financial sources of the International. "If these good and orthodox Christians had lived in the early days of Christianity they would have instituted inquiries concerning the banking account of the apostle Paul in Rome," jested Marx, following up a comparison made by *The Times* between the sections of the International and the early Christian communities. Despite all the efforts of the capitalists, the workers of Basle remained staunch to the International, and when they finally won the victory they celebrated it with a great procession through the town and a mass meeting on the market square. They received generous support from the workers in other countries, and the effects of their struggle were felt even in the United States, where the International was beginning to establish a firm footing and where F. A. Sorge, one of the fugitives of 1848 and now a teacher of music in New York, began to take a position similar to that of Johann P. Becker in Geneva.

Above all, the strike movement opened up Germany for the International, where it had possessed only isolated groups. After difficult struggles and much confusion the *Allgemeiner Deutscher Arbeiterverein*, had developed into a solid organization, and it continued to make very satisfactory progress, particularly after Schweitzer had been elected its leader. Schweitzer was a member of the North German Reichstag for Elberfeld-Barmen whilst his old opponent Liebknecht was a member for Stollberg-Schneeberg. Thanks to their opposing attitudes in the national question they very quickly came to grips in the Reichstag. Like Marx and Engels, Schweitzer accepted the situation which had been irrevocably created by the battle of Königgrätz, whilst Liebknecht obstinately opposed the North German League as a product of lawless and infamous violence, and as a creation to be destroyed ruthlessly even if it were necessary to abandon for the moment the social aims of the working class in the process. In the autumn of 1856 Liebknecht helped to found the Saxon People's Party, which adopted a radical-democratic, but not a socialist programme, and in 1868 he issued the *Demokratisches Wochenblatt* in Leipzig as the organ of this party, which recruited its members chiefly from the ranks of the workers, differing happily in this respect from the German People's Party, which, apart from a handful of honest intellectuals like Johann Jacoby, consisted chiefly of Frankfort stock-exchange democrats, Swabian particularist republicans and those elements whose moral indignation had been aroused at the wanton violation of legality committed by Bismarck when he brusquely dismissed a few of the pocket princes. A more agreeable neighbour was the Association of German Workers Organizations, which had been founded by the progressive bourgeoisie immediately after Lassalle began his agitation and as a counterblast to it. However, the very fact that it fought against the Lassalleans forced it to the left, and this tendency was strengthened by the election of August Bebel as chairman of the association, in whom Liebknecht found a loyal ally.

In the very first number of the *Demokratisches Wochenblatt* Liebknecht referred to Schweitzer as a man who had been disavowed by all the pioneers of the social democratic cause, but on the whole this attack was rather stale and ineffective because

Schweitzer had not let himself be disturbed for one moment by the rebuff he had received three years before from Marx and Engels, but had steadfastly pursued his aim of leading the German working-class movement in the spirit of Lassalle whilst not permitting it to degenerate into an orthodox sect slavishly subject to the literal word of the master. Schweitzer had done his best to make the first volume of Marx's *Capital* known to the German workers, and he had done so earlier and more thoroughly than Liebknecht. In April 1868 he even approached Marx for advice concerning the reduction of import duties on iron which the Prussian government was planning.

The mere fact that Marx was the corresponding secretary of the General Council for Germany would have been sufficient to compel him to answer any questions put to him by the parliamentary representative of the workers of a big industrial constituency, but in addition he had in the meantime come to quite another conclusion concerning Schweitzer's activities. Although Marx could see things only from a distance he did not fail to recognize " the intelligence and energy " with which Schweitzer led the working-class movement, and at the meetings of the General Council he invariably referred to him as a man of the party and never mentioned their differences.

Even now there were still enough differences between them. Neither Marx nor Engels had fully abandoned their personal mistrust of Schweitzer, and although they no longer suspected him of intriguing with Bismarck they did suspect that his approaches to Marx were chiefly intended to oust Liebknecht. Above all, neither of them could quite get rid of the idea that the *Allgemeiner Deutscher Arbeiterverein* was a " sect " and that Schweitzer wanted " his own working class movement ", but for all that they always recognized that Schweitzer's policy was far better than that of Liebknecht.

Marx declared that Schweitzer was undoubtedly the most intelligent and the most energetic of all the workers' leaders in Germany, and that only through Schweitzer was Liebknecht compelled to remember the existence of a working-class movement independent of the petty-bourgeois democrats. Engels was of a very similar opinion and declared that the " fellow " understood and could explain the general political situation and the attitude of the workers to other parties much better than anyone else. " He declared that compared with us all other parties represented a reactionary mass whose differences were hardly of any weight for us ! He recognizes, it is true, that 1866 and its consequences ruined the princelets, undermined the principle of legitimacy, shook the reaction to the core and brought the people into movement, but—now—he is attacking the other consequences, tax impositions, etc., and he conducts himself far more ' correctly ', as the Berliners say, towards Bismarck than does Liebknecht towards the ex-princes." Referring to Liebknecht's tactics on another occasion, Engels declared that he was sick and tired of being told again and again, " we must not make any revolution until the Germanic Diet, the blind Guelph and the worthy Elector of Hesse have been restored, and just but merciless vengeance wrought on the Godless Bismarck ". Engels was guilty of a certain amount of impatient exaggeration here, but at the same time there was a great deal of truth in what he said.

At a later date Marx declared that at one time it had been supposed that the development of Christian mythology under the Roman Empire had been possible only because of the absence of the printing press, but to-day exactly the contrary was true. The daily papers and the telegraph spread their inventions over the whole world in a trice and invented more myths in a single day (myths which the bourgeois donkeys believed and passed on) than would have been possible previously in a century. A particularly striking confirmation of this observation is the fact that for decades credence was attached (and not only by " bourgeois donkeys ") to the myth that Schweitzer had tried to sell the German working class to Bismarck, and that it had been saved thanks only to the intervention of Liebknecht and Bebel.

The exact contrary is true. Schweitzer championed a fundamental socialist standpoint, whilst the *Demokratisches Wochenblatt* flirted with the particularist supporters of the " ex-princes " and with the liberal corruptionist régime in Vienna in a fashion which it was impossible to justify on socialist grounds. In his memoirs Bebel declares that the victory of Austria over Prussia would have been desirable because the revolution could have disposed more easily of an internally weak State like Austria than of an internally strong State like Prussia, but this is an afterthought and, quite apart from the value of this idea, not a trace of any such standpoint can be found in the literature of the day.

Despite his personal friendship with Liebknecht and his personal mistrust of Schweitzer, Marx did not fail to realize the true state of affairs. His answer to Schweitzer on the question of the iron import duties is marked with cautious reserve in the form, but it is exhaustive and objective in content. Schweitzer then did a thing he had suggested three years before, and at the General Meeting of the *Allgemeiner Deutscher Arbeiterverein* which took place in Hamburg at the end of August 1868 he proposed affiliation to the International. In view of the anti-combination laws the affiliation was to take the form of a declaration of sympathy with the aims of the International and not to be a formal organizational tie. Marx was invited to attend the General Meeting to receive the thanks of the German workers for his scientific services to the working-class cause, and a preliminary inquiry made by Schweitzer was answered in a friendly spirit by Marx, who, however, did not attend the meeting in the end, despite Schweitzer's urgent invitation.

In a letter of thanks for the " honour " done him he excused himself on the ground that the preparations of the General Council for the forthcoming congress of the International in Brussels prevented his leaving London, and at the same time he observed " with pleasure " that the agenda of the General Meeting contained those items which were essential as the starting-point of any serious working-class movement : agitation for full political rights, the legal regulation of the working day, and systematic international working-class co-operation. Writing afterwards to Engels, Marx declared that in this letter he had really congratulated the Lassalleans on having abandoned Lassalle's programme, but frankly it is difficult to see what possible objection Lassalle could have had to the three points mentioned.

The real breach with the traditions of Lassalle was made by Schweitzer himself at the General Meeting when, in the teeth of violent opposition and only by threatening to resign, he succeeded in obtaining a mandate for himself and his Reichstag's colleague Fritzsche to call a general congress of the working class in Berlin at the end of September with a view to forming an all-embracing working-class organization for the purpose of conducting strikes. Schweitzer had learned from the European strike movement. He did not overestimate its importance, but he realized that a working-class party which wished to remain worthy of its tasks could not possibly let the strikes which were breaking out everywhere with elementary violence degenerate into unorganized confusion. He therefore did not hesitate to found trade unions, though he failed to realize the particular conditions of their existence and wished to organize them as strictly as the *Allgemeiner Deutscher Arbeiterverein* itself and more or less as mere auxiliary organizations of the latter.

Marx warned him in vain against committing this serious error. All the letters written by Schweitzer to Marx are still available, but only one from Marx to Schweitzer, though it is probably the most important, namely the letter of the 13th of October 1868.[1] This letter shows a friendly consideration for Schweitzer's point of view, and its form is irreproachable. It marshals the most important objections to Schweitzer's scheme of trade-union organization, but it weakens its own case by referring to the organization founded by Lassalle as a " sect " which must finally decide to merge itself into the general working-class movement. In his answer, the last letter he wrote to Marx, Schweitzer replied with justice that he had always done his best to keep pace with the general working-class movement in Europe.

A few days after the General Meeting of the *Allgemeiner Deutscher Arbeiterverein* in Hamburg the Association of German Workers Organizations held its congress in Nuremberg. This congress also proved able to read the signs of the times, and its majority adopted the main passages from the Rules of the International as a political programme and the *Demokratisches Wochenblatt* as its organ, whereupon the minority withdrew and disappeared for ever. After this the majority rejected a proposal for old-age pensions on an insurance basis under State control in favour of one for the establishment of trade associations, on the ground that experience had shown that such associations were best suited to administer old-age pensions, health benefits and support for travelling journeymen. This argumentation in favour of the founding of trade unions was not so vigorous as the appeal made by the Hamburg congress to the class struggle between capital and labour which was expressing itself in a wave of strikes. The Hamburg congress justified its affiliation to the International on the grounds that all working-class parties had joint interests, whereas the Nuremberg congress was much less clear and energetic in its attitude. A few weeks later the *Demokratisches Wochenblatt* announced in heavy print that the congress of the German People's Party in Stuttgart had decided to adopt the Nuremberg programme.

However, the *Allgemeiner Deutscher Arbeiterverein* and the Association of German Workers Organizations had come closer to each other, and Marx did his best as a neutral mediator between Liebknecht and Schweitzer to bring about the unification of the German working-class movement, though he did not succeed. With an empty pretext the Nuremberg Association refused to send delegates to the trade-union congress called by Schweitzer and Fritzsche in Berlin, but the congress was well attended and led to the formation of numerous " workers clubs " which were co-ordinated in a " Workers Union " led by Schweitzer.

[1] There are more letters than this one extant, for instance a long letter of Marx to Schweitzer dated the 24th of January 1865 and dealing with Proudhon.—Tr.

The Nuremberg Association then began to form what it rather pompously called " International Trade Co-operatives ", on the basis of statutes drawn up by Bebel which were far more in accordance with the needs of trade-union life than Schweitzer's proposals, and afterwards it offered to negotiate with the other organizations with a view to securing unity, but this offer was brusquely rejected. The Nurembergers were informed that they were responsible for the disunion and that they could save themselves the trouble of establishing the unity they had prevented. If they were really serious in their desire for unity they could affiliate to the Workers Union and work within its ranks for any changes they might think desirable.

Marx was unable to prevent the disruption of the German working-class movement, but still, the support given by both tendencies to the International represented a gain. The International was now beginning to mark down the spheres of its influence everywhere, though here and there its limits were still hazy, and he considered moving the headquarters of the General Council from London to Geneva. The annoyance caused by the French section in London had something to do with his attitude. This section was not numerically very strong, but it made a lot of noise and caused the International particular embarrassment by its loud applause of the pitiful clown Pyat, who was advocating the assassination of Louis Bonaparte. Naturally the General Council did its best to curb this folly, and its " dictatorship " was dramatically denounced by the section, which also began to prepare an attack on the council at the coming congress of the International in Brussels.

Fortunately Engels strongly advised Marx against taking such a dangerous step, declaring that after all, merely because a pack of fools were making themselves a nuisance, it was not possible to hand over the leadership of the movement to men who, for all their goodwill and natural instinct, were not cut out for the rôle of leadership. The bigger the movement became, and particularly now that it was making progress in Germany, the more important it was that Marx should keep the reins in his hands. And it was not long before it was demonstrated, precisely in Geneva, that good-will and mere instinct were certainly not sufficient in themselves.

3.   Bakunin's Agitation

The third congress of the International took place in Brussels from the 6th to the 13th of September 1868.

It was better attended than any other congress either before or afterwards, but it was strongly local in character, more than half of those present being from Belgium. About one-fifth of the delegates came from France. Eleven delegates represented England, six of them being members of the General Council, including Eccarius, Jung, Lessner and the trade unionist Lucraft. Eight delegates were present from Switzerland but from Germany only three, including Moses Hess of the Cologne section. Schweitzer had received an official invitation but was unable to attend owing to the fact that legal business required his presence in Germany. Instead he sent a message declaring the agreement of the *Allgemeiner Deutscher Arbeiterverein* with the aims of the International and explaining that formal affiliation was prevented only by the anti-combination laws of Germany. Italy and Spain sent one representative each.

The more vigorous life of the International in the fourth year of its existence made itself very definitely felt in the proceedings of the congress. The resistance which the Proudhonists had offered to trade unionism and strikes at the Geneva and Lausanne congresses had almost turned into its contrary, but they still clung to their old ideas of " free credit " and the " exchange bank ", and succeeded in securing the adoption of an academic resolution in their favour, although Eccarius demonstrated the practical impossibility of these Proudhonist remedies on the basis of English experience, whilst Hess demonstrated their theoretical untenableness on the basis of Marx's reply to Proudhon twenty years earlier.

In the " property question " the French delegates suffered complete eclipse. At the proposal of de Paepe a long resolution on the subject was adopted demanding that a well-organized system of society should take over and administer the mines and the railways in the interests of the whole of society, i.e. a new State based on canons of justice, and that until that time they should be run by companies of workers affording the necessary guarantees to society as a whole. The land and the forests were also to be taken over by the State and entrusted to similar companies of workers offering the same guarantees. And finally, all canals, roads, telegraphs, and in short all the means of transport and communication were to become the common property of society as a whole. The French delegates protested violently against this " primitive communism ", but all they could secure was an agreement that the next congress, which it was decided should take place in Basle, should discuss the question anew.

We have Marx's word that he had no part in drawing up the resolutions of the Brussels congress, but he was not dissatisfied with the proceedings. First of all, the congress followed the example of the Hamburg and Nuremberg congresses and thanked him in the name of the international proletariat for his scientific work on its behalf, a fact which afforded him both personal and political satisfaction, and secondly the attack launched by the French section in London against the General Council was repulsed. However, a resolution proposed by the Geneva section and adopted by the congress to the effect that threatening wars should be warded off by general strikes, by a general strike of the peoples, he described as " nonsense ", but he approved of a decision to break off relations with the League for Peace and Freedom, which held its second congress a little while later in Berne. The League proposed an alliance to the international, but it received the terse answer from Brussels that there seemed no obvious reason for its continued existence and that the best thing it could do would be to liquidate itself and advise its members to join the various sections of the International.

The idea of this alliance was supported chiefly by Michael Bakunin, who had been present at the first congress of the League for Peace and Freedom in Geneva and had joined the International a few months before the Brussels congress. When the International rejected his proposal for an alliance between the two organizations he did his best to persuade the Berne congress of the League for Peace and Freedom to advocate the destruction of all States and the establishment of a federation of free productive associations of all countries on the ruins. However, he was in the minority at the congress of the League also, together with Johann Philipp Becker and others, and with this minority he then founded the International Alliance of Socialist Democracy. This body was to join the International without reservation in order to work within it to further the study of all political and philosophic questions on the basis of the great principle of the general and moral equality of all human beings throughout the world.

The coming of the Alliance was announced by Becker in the September number of *Der Vorbote*, and its aim was declared to be the formation of sections of the International in France, Italy and Spain and wherever it had influence, but it was three months later, on the 15th of December 1868, that Becker formally requested the General Council to accept the Alliance into the International, and in the meantime this request had been made to and rejected by the French and Belgian Federal Councils. A week later, on the 22nd of December, Bakunin wrote to Marx from Geneva : " My dear friend, I understand more clearly than ever now how right you were to follow the great path of economic revolution, inviting us to go with you and condemning those of us who frittered away our energies in the by-paths of partly national and occasionally wholly political ventures. I am now doing what you have been doing for the last twenty years. Since my solemn and public breach with the bourgeoisie at the Berne congress I know no other society and no other environment than the world of the workers. My Fatherland is now the International, to whose prominent founders you belong. You see therefore, my dear friend, that I am your pupil, and I am proud of it. So much for my attitude and my personal opinions." There is no reason to doubt the honesty of these assurances.

A rapid and fundamental grasp of the relations between the two men can be gained from a comparison between Marx and Proudhon made several years later by Bakunin at a time when he was already in violent opposition to Marx : " Marx is a serious and profound economic thinker and he has the tremendous advantage over Proudhon of really being a materialist. Despite all his efforts to free himself from the traditions of classical idealism, Proudhon remained an incorrigible idealist all his life, swayed at one moment by the Bible and the next by Roman Law (as I told him two months before he died) and always a metaphysician to his finger-tips. His great misfortune was that he had never studied natural science and never adopted its methods. He possessed sound instincts and they fleetingly showed him the correct path, but misled by the bad or idealist habits of his intellect he fell back again and again into his old errors. Thus Proudhon became a permanent contradiction, a powerful genius and a revolutionary thinker who fought ceaselessly against the illusions of idealism but never succeeded in defeating them for good." Thus Bakunin on Proudhon.

He then proceeded to describe the character of Marx as it appeared to him : " As a thinker Marx is on the right path. He has set up the principle that all religious, political and legal developments in history are not the cause but the effects of economic developments. That is a great and fruitful idea, but not all the credit for it is due to him. Many others before him had an inkling of it and even expressed it in part, but in the last resort credit is due to him for having developed the idea scientifically and having made it the basis of his whole economic teachings. On the other hand, Proudhon understood and appreciated the idea of freedom better than Marx. When not engaged in inventing doctrines and fantasies Proudhon possessed the authentic instinct of the revolutionary ; he respected Satan and proclaimed anarchy. It is quite possible that Marx will develop an even more reasonable system of freedom than did Proudhon, but he lacks Proudhon's instinct. As a German and a Jew he is authoritarian from head to heels." So much for Bakunin on Marx.

The conclusion which he drew for himself from this comparison was that he incorporated the higher unity of both these systems. He thought to have developed the anarchist system of Proudhon, freed it from all doctrinaire, idealist and metaphysical dross, and given it a basis of materialism in science and of social economics in history, but he was sadly deceiving himself. He developed far beyond Proudhon, possessing a far wider European education and understanding Marx far better, but unlike Marx he had neither gone through the school of German philosophy thoroughly, nor closely studied the class struggles of the Western European peoples. And above all, his ignorance of economics was even more damaging to him than ignorance of natural science had been to Proudhon. This deficiency in Bakunin's education was due to the fact that his revolutionary activities had caused him to spend many of the best years of his life in Saxon, Austrian and Russian prisons and in the icy wastes of Siberia, but as honourable as this explanation is it did not make the deficiency any the less serious.

The " Inner Satan " was at once his strength and weakness, and what he meant with this favourite expression of his has been explained aptly and in noble words by the famous Russian critic Bielinski : " Michael is often guilty and sinful, but there is something in him which outweighs all his deficiencies—that is the eternally active principle which lives deep within his spirit." Bakunin was a thoroughly revolutionary character and like Marx and Lassalle he possessed the gift which caused men to listen to his voice. It was no mean achievement for a penniless fugitive with nothing but his indomitable will to have laid the basis of the international working-class movement in a number of European countries, in Spain, Italy and Russia. However, it is only necessary to mention these countries in order to realize the difference between him and Marx. Both men observed the approaching revolution, but whereas Marx realized that the industrial proletariat, which he had studied in Germany, France and England, was the backbone of the revolution, Bakunin thought to snatch the victory with the masses of the declassed youth, the peasantry and even the slum proletariat. Although he recognized Marx's superiority as a scientific thinker, in his own actions he fell back again and again into errors which were typical of "the revolutionaries of a past generation". He accepted his fate and consoled himself with the reflection that although science might be the compass of life it was not life itself and only life could create real things and beings.

It would be folly and at the same time an injustice both to Marx and Bakunin to judge their relations solely on the basis of the irreconcilable quarrel which ended them. It is of far greater value politically, and particularly psychologically, to trace how they were drawn to each other again and again only to fall asunder throughout the course of thirty years. Both began their revolutionary careers as Young Hegelians and Bakunin was also one of the founders of the *Deutsch-Französische Jahrbücher*. When the breach took place between Marx and Ruge, Bakunin supported Marx against his old patron, but later on when he was able to see at first hand in Brussels what Marx meant by communist propaganda he was horrified, and a few months later he enthusiastically supported Herwegh's adventurous volunteer crusade into Germany only to realize the folly of the venture and acknowledge his error openly.

Soon afterwards, in the summer of 1848, the *Neue Rheinische Zeitung* accused him of being a tool of the Russian government, but its subsequent reparation for an error into which it had been led by two independent sources was magnanimous enough to satisfy Bakunin completely. Marx and Bakunin met again in Berlin and renewed their old friendship, and when Bakunin was expelled from Prussia the *Neue Rheinische Zeitung* championed his cause energetically. His subsequent Pan-Slav agitation came in for severe criticism, but an introductory remark declared, "Bakunin is our friend", pointed out that he was acting from democratic motives and granted that his self-deception in the Slav question was very understandable. And for the rest, Engels, who was the author of this article, was wrong in his chief objection to Bakunin's propaganda, for the Slav peoples then under Austrian domination have since proved that they did in fact possess the historical future which Engels denied them. Bakunin's revolutionary participation in the Dresden insurrection was appreciated by Marx and Engels sooner and more enthusiastically than anyone else.

Bakunin was taken prisoner during the retreat from Dresden and twice sentenced to death, first by a Saxon and then by an Austrian court martial. In both cases the sentence was commuted to life-long hard labour and in the end he was extradited to Russia, where he spent many terrible years in the fortress of St. Peter-Paul. During his incarceration an idiotic Urquhartite again brought forward the exploded accusation that Bakunin was an agent of the Russian government and declared in an article in *The Morning Advertiser* that he was in fact not in prison at all. The same paper was then compelled to publish letters of protest from Herzen, Mazzini, Ruge and Marx. An unfortunate coincidence was the fact that Bakunin's slanderer was also called Marx and this became known to a few people although he obstinately refused to abandon his public anonymity. This coincidence was later exploited by the sham revolutionary Herzen to launch a shameful intrigue. In 1857 Bakunin was sent from the St. Peter-Paul fortress to Siberia, and in 1861 he succeeded in making his escape over Japan and the United States to London, where Herzen persuaded him that Marx had denounced him in the English press as a Russian spy during his imprisonment. This was the beginning of that infamous scandal-mongering which caused much of the trouble between the two men.

Bakunin had been completely isolated from European life for over a decade, and it is therefore understandable that on his arrival in London he first sought contact with Russian fugitives of the Herzen type, though fundamentally he had little in common with them. Even in his Pan-Slavism, as far as it is possible to give his aims such a name, Bakunin always remained a revolutionary, whereas Herzen was in reality playing the game of Tsarism under a mildly liberalist mask with his attacks on the " degenerate West " and his mystic cult of the Russian village community. It is nothing against Bakunin that he maintained friendly personal relations with Herzen up to the latter's death, for Herzen had been of assistance to him in his youthful troubles, but the political breach between the two was brought about by Bakunin in 1866 in a letter to Herzen reproaching him for wanting a social transformation without a political one and with being prepared to forgive the State everything provided it left the Russian village community intact, because this was the basis of Herzen's hopes for the regeneration not only of Russia and the Slav countries, but of the whole world. Bakunin subjected this fantasy to annihilating criticism.

However, after his successful flight from Siberia he stayed in Herzen's house and was thus kept apart from any contact with Marx, but despite this fact he translated *The Communist Manifesto* into Russian and secured its publication in Herzen's *Kolokol*, and this was typical of him.

During Bakunin's second stay in London, at the time when the International was founded, Marx broke the ice and visited him. He was able to assure Bakunin truthfully that far from having been the originator of the slander he had expressly opposed it. After this explanation the two parted as friends. Bakunin was enthusiastically in favour of the plan for an international working-class organization, and on the 4th of November Marx wrote to Engels : " Bakunin sends you his greetings. He left for Italy to-day, where he is now living (Florence). I must say that he impressed me favourably, more so than formerly. . . . On the whole he is one of the few people I have met during the past sixteen years who have progressed and not retrogressed."

The enthusiasm which Bakunin felt for the cause of the International did not last very long and his stay in Italy soon awakened " the revolutionary of a past generation " in him. He had chosen Italy to live in on account of its agreeable climate and its cheapness, but also for political reasons and because both France and Germany were closed to him. He regarded the Italians as the natural allies of the Slavs in the struggle against Austrian oppression, and whilst he was still in Siberia the exploits of Garibaldi had stirred his imagination. His first conclusion from these exploits was that the revolutionary movement was once again resurgent. In Italy he found numerous political secret societies, a declassed intelligentsia prepared to plunge at a moment's notice into all sorts of conspiratorial adventures, a mass of peasants always on the verge of starvation, and finally an eternally seething slum proletariat. This latter was particularly strongly represented by the Lazzaroni of Naples, where Bakunin went to live after a short stay in Florence. These classes appeared to him as the real driving forces of the revolution, and he regarded Italy as the country in which the social revolution was probably nearest, though he was soon compelled to recognize his error. Mazzini's propaganda was still the dominant factor in Italy and Mazzini was an opponent of socialism. The sole aim of his vague religious battle-cries and of his strictly centralized movement was to secure a united bourgeois republic.

During the years he spent in Italy Bakunin's revolutionary agitation took on a more definite form. Owing to his lack of theoretical knowledge, his surplus of intellectual agility and his impetuous desire for action, he was always very strongly under the influence of his environment. The politico-religious dogmatism of Mazzini drove Bakunin to stress his own atheism and anarchism and his denial of all State authority. And on the other hand, the revolutionary traditions of those classes which he regarded as the pioneers of the general transformation of society greatly influenced his own inclination to indulge in secret conspiracies and local insurrections. Bakunin therefore founded a revolutionary socialist secret society which in the beginning was composed chiefly of Italians and aimed at combating " the disgusting bourgeois rhetoric of Mazzini and Garibaldi ", but which soon extended its influence internationally.

In the autumn of 1867 he moved to Geneva, where he first tried to influence the League for Peace and Freedom in favour of his secret society, and when he failed to do so he did his best to secure the acceptance of its affiliation to the International, an organization about which he had not bothered his head for four years.

4. The Alliance of Socialist Democracy

Marx continued to harbour feelings of friendship for the old revolutionary Bakunin and he opposed various attacks which were made or planned against him amongst his, Marx's, immediate circle.

The originator of these attacks was Sigismund Borkheim, an honest democrat to whom Marx was indebted in connection with the Vogt affair and other matters. Borkheim had two weaknesses : first of all he thought himself a brilliant writer, and this was not the case, and secondly he suffered from an eccentric hatred of the Russians, a hatred which was no less intense than Herzen's equally eccentric hatred of the Germans.

Herzen was Borkheim's pet aversion, and he belaboured him thoroughly in a series of articles which appeared at the beginning of 1868 in the *Demokratisches Wochenblatt* shortly after its appearance. Although at that time Bakunin had already broken with Herzen politically he was attacked by Borkheim as one of Herzen's " cossacks " and pilloried with him as an " indestructible negation ". Borkheim had read in one of Herzen's articles that years before Bakunin had made " the peculiar observation " that " active negation is a creative power ", and in his moral indignation Borkheim asked rhetorically whether such an idea had ever occurred to anyone on the European side of the Russian frontier, and added that it would be laughed out of court by thousands of German schoolboys. The worthy Borkheim was unaware that Bakunin's often-quoted declaration, " the lust for destruction is a creative lust", came from an article in the *Deutsche Jahrbücher*, published at a time when Bakunin moved in Young Hegelian circles and co-operated with Marx and Ruge in founding the *Deutsch-Französische Jahrbücher*.

It is easy to realize that Marz regarded this and similar efforts with secret horror, and that he opposed Borkheim tooth and nail when the latter proposed to use Engels' articles against Bakunin in the *Neue Rheinische Zeitung* as the basis for his own gibberish because he felt that they " suited his own book so splendidly ". Marx insisted that if the articles were used at all they must not be used insultingly, because Engels was an old personal friend of Bakunin, and when Engels supported Marx Borkheim abandoned his plan. Johann Philipp Becker also wrote to Borkheim asking him not to attack Bakunin, but he received a petulant reply in which Borkheim declared, " with his usual delicacy ", as Marx wrote to Engels, that he was prepared to continue his friendship for Becker and also his financial support (not very considerable, by the way) but that in the future politics must be avoided in their correspondence. With all his friendship for Borkheim Marx found that the former's " Russophobia " had taken on dangerous dimensions.

Marx's feelings of friendship for Bakunin were not affected by the fact that the latter took part in the congresses of the League for Peace and Freedom. The first congress of the League had already taken place in Geneva when Marx sent a copy of the first volume of his *Capital* with a personal dedication to Bakunin. Receiving no word of thanks he made inquiries of a Russian emigrant in Geneva, to whom he had written on another matter, concerning his " old friend Bakunin ", although he already harboured a faint doubt as to whether Bakunin was still his friend or not. The answer to this indirect inquiry was Bakunin's letter of the 22nd of December in which he promised to follow Marx along the path which the latter had been pursuing for twenty years.

On the day Bakunin wrote this letter the General Council had already decided to reject the request of the Alliance of Socialist Democracy, forwarded through Becker, for permission to affiliate to the International. Marx was the prime mover in this rejection. He had known of the existence of the Alliance, which had been announced in *Der Vorbote*, but he had regarded it up to then as a stillborn local growth and not of any importance. He knew Becker as an otherwise reliable comrade, but inclined to indulge in organizational dabblings. Becker forwarded the programme and the statutes of the Alliance and declared in an accompanying letter to the General Council that the Alliance was anxious to make good the lack of " idealism " in the International.

This unfortunate observation caused " great wrath " amongst the members of the General Council, " and particularly amongst the French ", as Marx wrote to Engels, and the rejection of the application of the Alliance was decided on immediately. Marx was instructed by the General Council to write the letter conveying its decision in the matter. The letter which he wrote to Engels " after midnight " on the 18th of December to obtain the latter's advice indicates that he himself was somewhat indignant about the affair. " Borkheim was right this time," he added. He was exercised not so much by the programme of the Alliance as by its statutes. The programme declared above all that the Alliance was atheist. It demanded the abolition of all religions, the replacement of belief by science, and of divine justice by human justice. It then demanded political, economic and social equality for all classes and all individuals of both sexes, and a beginning was to be made with the abolition of the right of inheritance. It further demanded that all children of both sexes should receive equal opportunities for development from birth on, that is to say, material care and education on all fields of science, industry and the arts. And finally the programme condemned all forms of political activity which did not aim directly at securing the victory of labour over capital.

Marx's verdict on this programme was not a flattering one. A little while afterwards he referred to it as " an olla podrida of worn-out platitudes, an empty rigmarole, a rosary of pretentious notions to make the flesh creep, a banal improvization aiming at nothing more than a temporary effect ". However, in theoretical matters the International was prepared to tolerate much, for its historical task was to develop a joint programme for the international proletariat out of its practical activity, but just for this reason its organization was of paramount importance as the preliminary condition for all successful practical activity, whereas the statutes of the Alliance made dangerous encroachments precisely on this field.

The Alliance declared itself a branch of the International and accepted all its general statutes, but it wanted to remain a separate organization. Its founders set themselves up in Geneva as a provisional central committee. National offices were to be opened in each country and to form groups everywhere, which should then be affiliated to the International. At the annual congresses of the International the representatives of the Alliance, as a branch of the International, proposed to hold their own public sessions in a special room.

Engels decided immediately. Acceptance was impossible. The result would be two General Councils and two congresses. At the first opportunity the practical General Council in London would find itself at loggerheads with the " idealist " General Council in Geneva. For the rest he advised coolness in dealing with the matter. Any violent rejection would excite the very numerous Philistines amongst the workers (particularly in Switzerland) and do the International harm. One should reject the application of the Alliance calmly and firmly, and point out that it had chosen a special field for its activities and that the International would wait and see what success it had. In the meantime there was no reason why the members of the one association should not also be members of the other if they wanted to. His verdict on the programme of the Alliance was very much like Marx's. He had never read anything so miserable in his life. Bakunin must have become a "perfect donkey", an observation which indicated no particular resentment against Bakunin, or at least no more than when Marx referred to his old and loyal friend Becker as "an old confusionist". In their private correspondence the two friends made generous use of such hearty invective.

In the meantime Marx had simmered down and he drew up the decision of the General Council refusing permission for the Alliance to affiliate to the International in a form to which no objection could be taken. An indirect sally at Becker was contained in the statement that actually a number of the founders of the Alliance had already settled the question by their co-operation as members of the International in the adoption of the decision of the Brussels congress not to amalgamate with the League for Peace and Freedom. The main reason given for the negative decision of the General Council was that to accept the affiliation of a second international body existing both inside and outside the International would be the best means of destroying the organization.

It is very unlikely that Becker fell into a great rage when he received the decision of the General Council. More credible is the statement of Bakunin that he was opposed from the beginning to the formation of the Alliance, but was outvoted by the members of his secret society. He had wished to maintain this secret society, whose members were to work within the International for the aims of the society, and he had wished for the immediate affiliation of the organization to the International in order to prevent all rivalries. In any case the central committee of the Alliance in Geneva answered the letter of the General Council refusing affiliation with an offer to turn the sections of the Alliance into sections of the International if the General Council would recognize the theoretical programme of the Alliance.

In the meantime Marx had received Bakunin's friendly letter of the 22nd of December, but by this time his suspicions had been so aroused that he disregarded this "sentimental entrée". The new proposal of the Alliance also aroused his mistrust, but he did not permit his feelings to cause him to answer it in any but a thoroughly objective fashion. At his proposal the General Council decided on the 9th of March 1869 that it was not within its province to examine the theoretical programmes of the various workers' organizations affiliated to the International. The working classes in various countries was at various stages of development and in consequence their practical activity found theoretical expression in varying forms. Joint action, which was the aim of the International, the exchange of ideas between the various sections of the International and finally the direct discussions at the annual congresses, would gradually result in the development of a joint theoretical programme for the whole of the working-class movement, but for the moment the task of the General Council was to determine only whether the general tendency of the various programmes was in accordance with the general tendency of the International, that is to say, the struggle for the complete emancipation of the working class.

In this connection, the decision pointed out, the programme of the Alliance contained a phrase which was open to dangerous misunderstanding : political, economic and social equality for all classes when taken literally meant nothing but harmony between capital and labour such as was preached by bourgeois socialists. The real secret of the proletarian movement and the great aim of the International was rather the destruction of all classes. However, as the context indicated, the phrase concerning " the equality of the classes " was probably due to a slip of the pen, and the General Council had no doubt that the Alliance would be prepared to abandon this dangerous phrase and then there would be no obstacle to the transformation of its sections into sections of the International. When this was finally done the General Council, according to the Statutes of the International, should be informed of the place and the membership figures of all new sections.

The Alliance then altered the phrase objected to by the General Council and announced on the 22nd of June that it had dissolved itself and called upon its sections to transform themselves into sections of the International. The Geneva section of the Alliance, which was led by Bakunin, was accepted into the International by a unanimous vote of the General Council. Allegedly Bakunin's secret society had also dissolved itself, but it continued to exist in a more or less loose form and Bakunin himself continued to work for the programme which the Alliance had set itself. From the autumn of 1867 to the autumn of 1869 he lived on the shores of Lake Geneva, sometimes in Geneva and sometimes in Vevey or Clarens, and won considerable influence amongst the Franco-Italian Swiss workers.

He was supported in his activity by the peculiar circumstances in which these workers lived. In order to understand the situation it is necessary to remember that the International was not an organization with a definite theoretical programme, but one which tolerated all sorts of tendencies within its fold, as the General Council had pointed out in its letter to the Alliance. A glance through the columns of *Der Vorbote* will show that even such a zealous and meritorious pioneer of the International as Becker never bothered himself unduly about theoretical questions. And in fact there were two very different tendencies in the Geneva sections of the International. On the one hand there was the *fabrique*, as the highly-skilled and well-paid workers of the jewellery and watchmaking industries were called in the Geneva dialect. These workers were almost exclusively of local origin. And on the other hand there was the *gros métiers*, which consisted chiefly of building workers, almost exclusively foreign-born, mostly German, and was compelled to fight one strike after the other to maintain tolerably decent working conditions. The former possessed the franchise and the latter did not, but the numbers of the *fabrique* were not sufficient for them to hope for electoral successes on their own and in consequence they were very much inclined to make electoral compromises with the bourgeois radicals. The workers of the *gros métiers* were subjected to no such temptation and they were much more in favour of direct revolutionary action of the kind propagated by Bakunin.

Bakunin found an even more favourable recruiting field amongst the watchmakers of the Jura. These workers were not highly-skilled men engaged in the luxury trades, but chiefly domestic workers, whose already miserable conditions of life were being threatened by American mass production. They were scattered in little villages all over the mountains and little suited to a mass movement with political aims. In addition they had been made shy of politics by a number of unfavourable experiences. The first man to agitate amongst them for the cause of the International was a doctor named Coullery, an honest man of humanitarian instincts, but politically hopelessly confused. He had led these workers into electoral alliances not only with the bourgeois radicals, but even with the monarchist liberals in Neufchâtel, whereby the workers had invariably got the worst of the bargain. After Coullery had been completely discredited in their eyes the workers of the Jura found a new leader in James Guillaume, a young teacher in the industrial centre of Locle, who had thoroughly assimilated their ideas and issued a little paper entitled *Le Progrès* and preaching an ideal anarchist society in which all men would be free and equal. When Bakunin went into the Jura for the first time he found the ground thoroughly prepared for his seed, but the poor devils there probably had a greater effect on him than he had on them, for from that time onward his condemnation of all forms of political activity became stronger than ever.

For the moment, however, peace reigned in the Franco-Italian Swiss sections of the International and in January 1869, chiefly at Bakunin's instance, they formed a joint federal council and issued a fairly influential weekly newspaper entitled *L'Égalité*, to which Bakunin, Becker, Eccarius, Varlin and other prominent members of the International contributed. It was Bakunin who persuaded the federal council to put forward the question of the right of inheritance for discussion at the next congress of the International in Basle. He was perfectly within his rights in doing so, for it was one of the chief tasks of the congress to discuss such questions and the General Council immediately agreed.

Marx, however, regarded the action as a challenge from Bakunin, and as such he welcomed it.

5. The Basle Congress

The fourth congress of the International took place on the 5th and 6th of September in Basle and the International reviewed the fifth year of its existence.

It had proved the most lively year of all and had been shaken by "the guerilla fights between capital and labour", strikes which the ruling classes of Europe began to explain more and more not as the result of the misery of the proletariat or the despotism of capital, but as the result of the secret machinations of the International.

In consequence the brutal lust to smash the International by force of arms grew rapidly. Even in England bloody collisions took place between striking miners and the military. In the mining district of the Loire drunken soldiery carried out a blood-bath near Ricamarie and twenty people were shot down, including two women and a child. Once again Belgium distinguished itself most horribly—" the model State of Continental constitutionalism, the comfortable carefully-fenced paradise of land-owners, capitalists and priests ", as it was called in a powerful appeal drawn up by Marx and issued by the General Council to the workers of Europe and the United States on behalf of the victims shot down in Seraing and in the Borinage by the ruthless fury of the profit-hunters. "The earth completes its annual revolution no more certainly than the Belgian government its annual slaughter of the workers," declared Marx.

The bloody seed ripened into the harvest of the International. In the autumn of 1868 the first elections took place in England on the basis of the reformed franchise, but the results confirmed the warnings which Marx had given the workers against the one-sided policy of the Reform League. Not a single workers' representative was elected. The "big money-bags" were victorious and Gladstone again came to the helm, but he had no intention of bringing about a thorough settlement of the Irish question or redressing the just complaints of the trade unions, and as a result the New Unionism caught fresh wind in its sails.

At the annual congress of the trade unions which took place in Birmingham in 1869 an urgent appeal was issued to all working-class organizations in the United Kingdom to affiliate to the International, not only because the interests of the working class were everywhere the same, but because the principles of the International were calculated to secure permanent peace amongst the peoples of the world. In the summer of 1869 war had threatened between England and the United States, and an address was drawn up by Marx to the National Labor Union in the United States declaring : " It is now your turn to prevent a war whose inevitable result would be to throw back the advancing working-class movements on both sides of the Atlantic." The Address met with a lively echo in the United States.

In France also the cause of the working class was making good progress and the police persecutions had the usual result of recruiting new supporters for the International. The helpful intervention of the General Council in numerous strikes led to the formation of trade unions which could not be suppressed no matter how obviously the spirit of the International lived in them. The workers took no part in the elections of 1869 by putting forward candidates of their own, but they supported the candidates of the extreme bourgeois left, which came forward with a very radical election programme. In this way the workers contributed at least indirectly to the heavy defeat which Bonaparte suffered, particularly in the big towns, although the fruits of their efforts fell for the moment into the lap of bourgeois democracy. The Second Empire began to crack ominously, and from outside it received a heavy blow as the result of the revolution which took place in Spain in the autumn of 1868 and drove Queen Isabella from the country.

The course of development in Germany was somewhat different, for there Bonapartism was still advancing and not yet on the decline. The national question split the German working class, and this split represented a great obstacle to the progress of the developing trade-union movement. Thanks to his wrong policy in the trade-union agitation Schweitzer had slithered into a situation which he could no longer control. The baseless attacks which were continuously directed against his personal honesty caused even some of his own followers to doubt him and he was ill advised enough to endanger his reputation, which had not been seriously damaged, by a little *coup d'état*.

A minority in the *Allgemeiner Deutscher Arbeiterverein* therefore turned its back on the organization and amalgamated with the Nuremberg associations into a new Social Democratic Party, whose members became known as the Eisenachers, owing to the fact that their inaugural congress took place in Eisenach. In the beginning both fractions fought each other violently, but they took up more or less the same attitude towards the International. They were in agreement in principle, but disagreed in form as long as the German combination laws existed. Marx and Engels were very much annoyed when Liebknecht played off the General Council of the International against Schweitzer, a thing he had no right to do. Although they welcomed " the dissolution of the Lassallean Church ", they could not do much with the other group until it had separated itself definitely from the German People's Party or maintained at the utmost a loose cartel arrangement with the latter. For the rest, they were still of the opinion that as a debater Schweitzer was superior to all his opponents.

The progress of the Austro-Hungarian working-class movement, which had begun to develop only since the defeats of 1866, was more harmonious. Lassallean tendencies found no foothold and the masses of the workers began to rally to the standard of the International, as the General Council pointed out in its report to the Basle congress.

The congress thus met under favourable circumstances. Only 78 delegates were present, but the congress was much more " international " than the previous congresses had been. Nine countries were represented. The General Council was represented as usual by Eccarius and Jung, and apart from them by two of the most prominent English trade-union leaders, Applegarth and Lucraft. France sent 26 delegates, Belgium 5, Germany 12, Austria 2, Switzerland 23, Italy 3, Spain 4 and the United States 1 delegate. Liebknecht represented the Eisenach fraction and Moses Hess the Berlin section. Bakunin had both a French and an Italian mandate and Guillaume had been delegated from Locle. The chair at the congress was again taken by Jung.

In the beginning the congress dealt with organizational questions. At the proposal of the General Council it unanimously decided to recommend all its sections and affiliated bodies to abolish the office of President, an action which the General Council had taken on its own account several years previously, on the ground that it was not in accordance with the dignity of a working-class organization to maintain a monarchical and authoritarian principle within its ranks, for even where the presidency was only an honorary office it represented a violation of the democratic principle. On the other hand, the General Council proposed that its own executive powers should be extended and that it should have the right to suspend any section from membership of the International, pending the decision of the next congress, where such section acted against the spirit of the International. The proposal was adopted with the amendment that where Federal Councils existed they should be consulted before the General Council took any such action. Both Bakunin and Liebknecht vigorously supported the proposal. As far as Liebknecht was concerned this was natural, but not so with Bakunin, who thereby violated his own anarchist principle, whatever his opportunist motives for so doing may have been. It is probable that he thought to drive out the devil with Beelzebub and counted on the assistance of the General Council against all parliamentary-political activity, which he considered purely opportunist. Perhaps he was supported in this idea by Liebknecht's well-known attack on the participation of Schweitzer and Bebel in the work of the North German Reichstag. However, Marx disapproved of Liebknecht's speech, and Bakunin, who had reckoned without his host, was soon to learn that violations of principle always revenge themselves.

The most important theoretical problems on the agenda of the congress were the question of common ownership of the land and the question of the right of inheritance. The former question had actually already been settled at the Brussels congress, and this time it was disposed of summarily. With 54 votes the congress decided that society had the right to establish common ownership of the land, and with 53 votes that such an action was necessary in the interests of society as a whole. For the most part the minority abstained from voting. Eight delegates voted against the second decision, and four against the first. A variety of opinions resulted as to the practical measures for putting the decisions into effect, and it was left to the next congress in Paris to discuss the question thoroughly.

In the question of the right of inheritance the General Council had drawn up a report which summed up the most important points in a few words in the masterly fashion typical of Marx. Like all other bourgeois legislation, the inheritance laws were not the cause, but the effect, the legal consequence of the economic organization of a society based on private property in the means of production. The right to inherit slaves had not been the cause of slavery. On the contrary, slavery had been the cause of the right to inherit slaves. If the means of production were turned into common property then the right of inheritance would disappear as far as it was of social importance, because a man could leave to his heirs only that which he had possessed during his life. The great aim of the working class was therefore to abolish those institutions which gave a few people the economic power to appropriate the fruits of the labour of the many. To proclaim the abolition of the laws of inheritance as the starting point of a social revolution would therefore be just as absurd as to proclaim the abolition of the laws of contract between buyers and sellers so long as the present system of commodity exchange prevailed. It would prove false in theory and reactionary in practice. The right of inheritance could be altered only in a period of transition when on the one hand the existing economic basis of society had not yet been altered whilst on the other hand the working class already possessed sufficient power to carry through measures preparatory to a thorough transformation of society. As such transitional measures the General Council recommended the extension of death duties and the limitation of testamentary inheritance rights, which, as distinct from the right of family inheritance, exaggerated the principles of private property in a superstitious and arbitrary fashion.

However, the commission to which the question had been delegated for discussion proposed that the abolition of the right of inheritance should be proclaimed as one of the fundamental demands of the working class, although it could produce nothing in support of its proposal apart from a few ideological phrases about " privileges ", " political and economic justice " and " social order ". In the comparatively brief discussion which followed, Eccarius, the Belgian delegate de Paepe and the French delegate Varlin spoke in favour of the report of the General Council, whilst Bakunin spoke on behalf of the commission's proposal, whose spiritual father he was. He recommended the adoption of the proposal for reasons which were allegedly practical, but which were in reality quite illusory. It would be quite impossible to establish common property without first abolishing the right of inheritance. If one tried to take the land away from the peasants they would resist, but they would not feel themselves directly affected by the abolition of the right of inheritance, and thus private property would gradually die out. When a vote was taken it was seen that there were 32 in favour of the proposal of the commission, 23 against, 13 abstentions and 7 delegates absent. The report of the General Council received 19 votes, 37 against, 6 abstentions and 13 delegates absent. Thus neither the report of the General Council nor the proposal of the commission received a clear majority so that the discussion remained without any tangible result.

The Basle congress produced a louder echo than any of its predecessors both in the bourgeois and in the proletarian world. The most learned representatives of the bourgeoisie observed, half with horror and half with malicious satisfaction, that at last the communist character of the International had been revealed, whilst in the proletarian world the decisions in favour of the common ownership of the land were welcomed with joy. In Geneva the German-language section published a manifesto to the agricultural population which was translated into French, Italian, Spanish, Polish and Russian and widely distributed. In Barcelona and in Naples the first sections of agricultural workers arose. In London the Land and Labour League was formed at a big public meeting with the slogan, " The Land for the People ! " Ten members of the General Council of the International were also members of its committee.

In Germany the worthy gentlemen of the German People's Party were furious at the decisions of the Basle congress and at first Liebknecht permitted himself to be intimidated by their fury, even issuing a declaration to the effect that the Eisenach fraction was not bound by the decisions of the congress. Fortunately, however, the indignant and highly respectable leaders of the German People's Party were not content with this and demanded that the decisions of the congress should be expressly disavowed, whereupon Liebknecht finally broke off relations with them, a step to which Marx and Engels had urged him long before. However, his initial hesitation had brought grist to Schweitzer's mill, for Schweitzer had " preached " the common ownership of the land in the *Allgemeiner Deutscher Arbeiterverein* for years and had not just adopted it in order to ridicule his opponents, as Marx assumed, finding it " a piece of insolence ". Engels controlled his anger over the " blackguard " sufficiently to recognize that it was " very clever " of Schweitzer always to maintain a correct theoretical attitude, well knowing that his opponents were hopelessly lost immediately any question of theory arose.

For that moment therefore the Lassalleans remained not only

the most firmly organized, but theoretically the most progressed of all the German working-class parties.

6. Confusion in Geneva

In so far as the discussion at the Basle congress on the right of inheritance had been a sort of intellectual duel between Bakunin and Marx it had brought no final decision, but it had been rather unfavourable than favourable for the latter. However, it would be incorrect to assume from this that Marx was heavily hit and then prepared for a powerful counterblast against Bakunin. Such a contention would not be in accordance with the facts.

Marx was quite satisfied with the result of the Basle congress. At the time he was with his daughter Jenny on a journey through Germany for the benefit of his health and on the 25th of September he wrote to his daughter Laura from Hannover : " I am glad that the Basle congress is now over and that its results were comparatively good. Such open displays of the party with all its sores always worry me. None of the actors was up to the level of his principles, but the idiocy of the upper class repairs the errors of the working class. Even the obscurest sheets in the smallest German towns through which we have passed were full of the deeds of this ' terrible congress '."

Bakunin was no more disappointed with the results of the Basle congress than was Marx. It has been said that with his proposal concerning the right of inheritance Bakunin wished to defeat Marx and obtain the removal of the General Council from London to Geneva as the fruit of his theoretical victory, and that when he did not succeed in this, he attacked the General Council with increased violence in *L'Égalité*. These statements have been made so often that they have crystallized into a sort of legend, but nevertheless there is not a word of truth in them. After the Basle congress Bakunin did not write a line for *L'Égalité* ; before the Basle congress he was its chief editor, but one will look in vain through the long series of articles he published in it for any trace of hostility towards the General Council or towards Marx. Four articles in particular written on " The Principles of the International " were completely in the spirit in which the International was founded. It is true that in these articles he expresses misgivings concerning the disastrous influences of what Marx termed " parliamentary cretinism " on the parliamentary representatives of the workers, but first of all such misgivings have been justified again and again since, and secondly his remarks were quite harmless compared with the violent attacks which Liebknecht was then making on the participation of the working class in bourgeois parliamentarism.

Further, Bakunin's ideas on the inheritance question may have been eccentric, but it was nevertheless his right to put them forward for discussion at the congress, and in fact the congresses of the International have discussed much more eccentric ideas without those who put them forward being credited with any ulterior motives. The accusation that he had planned to secure the removal of the General Council from London to Geneva was answered briefly and strikingly by Bakunin immediately it was uttered publicly : " If such a proposal had been put forward I should have been the first to oppose it and with all possible energy because it would have seemed to me to be fatal for the future of the International. It is true that the Geneva sections have made tremendous progress in a very short space of time, but the atmosphere of Geneva is still too specifically local for it to be a good spot for the General Council. Apart from that, it is clear that so long as the present political organization of Europe exists London will remain the only place suitable for the seat of the General Council and one would be a fool or an enemy of the International to propose to move it anywhere else."

There are people who consider that Bakunin was a liar from the very beginning and that his reply to the accusation against him was a subsequent excuse, but this theory collapses immediately in face of the fact that prior to the Basle congress Bakunin had arranged to move after the congress from Geneva to Locarno. His decision was taken for reasons over which he had no control. He was in urgent financial straits and his wife was expecting a child. He wished to settle down in Locarno and translate the first volume of Marx's *Capital* into Russian. A young admirer named Liubavin had persuaded a Russian publisher to pay 1,200 roubles for the translation, and of this sum Bakunin received an advance of 300 roubles.

Although in the light of these facts all the intrigues which Bakunin is alleged to have set on foot before and after the Basle congress are seen to be non-existent, nevertheless the congress left a bitter taste in his mouth because under the influence of Borkheim's incitement Liebknecht had declared in the presence of third parties that he held proofs showing that Bakunin was an agent of the Russian government. Bakunin demanded that Liebknecht should support his accusations before a party court of honour and this Liebknecht was unable to do, with the result that the court sternly reprimanded him. After the Cologne communist trial and his experiences in exile Liebknecht was rather inclined to suspect spies everywhere, but he accepted the verdict of the court and offered Bakunin his hand as a sign of reconciliation, and the latter accepted it.

Bakunin was therefore all the more embittered when a few weeks later on the 2nd of October Moses Hess revived the old slanders in the Paris *Reveil*. Hess, who was present at the Basle congress as a German delegate, was giving the secret history of the congress, and in this connection he dealt with Bakunin's alleged " intrigues " to undermine the fundamental basis of the International and secure the removal of the General Council from London to Geneva. He declared that Bakunin's plans had come to nothing at the congress and concluded with the baseless insinuation that he, Hess, did not want to impugn Bakunin's revolutionary honesty, but that the Russian was closely related to Schweitzer, who had been accused by the German delegates at the Basle congress of being an agent of the German government. The malicious intent of this denunciation was made all the clearer by the fact that it was quite impossible to establish any " close relation " between the agitation of Schweitzer and the agitation of Bakunin, and that personally the two men had never had anything whatever to do with each other.

It would certainly have been wiser for Bakunin to have ignored this article, which was ignoble enough in all conscience, but it is easy to understand that he was provoked to anger by the repeated attacks on his political honesty, particularly when the attacks were underhanded and malicious. He therefore wrote a reply, but in his initial anger the reply became so long that he realized himself that the *Reveil* could not possibly publish it. He attacked the " German Jews " with particular violence, but expressly excepted " giants " like Lassalle and Marx from the race of pygmies *à la* Borkheim and Hess. He then decided to use this long reply as an introduction to a book on his revolutionary beliefs and he sent it to Herzen in Paris with the request that the latter should try to find a publisher, and he added a shorter reply for the *Reveil*. However, Herzen feared that even this would not be published and he himself wrote a defence of Bakunin against Hess, and this defence was published by the *Reveil* together with an editorial comment which completely mollified Bakunin.

Herzen was not at all satisfied with the longer reply. He disapproved of the attacks on the " German Jews ", and was surprised that Bakunin attacked little known people like Borkheim and Hess instead of challenging Marx. Bakunin answered on the 28th of October declaring that although he considered Marx responsible for the attacks made on him he had refrained from attacking him for two reasons and had even called him a " giant ". The first reason was one of justice. " Apart from all the nasty tricks he has played us, we, or at least I, cannot ignore his tremendous services to the cause of socialism, which he has served for almost twenty-five years with insight, energy and disinterestedness, and in which he has undoubtedly excelled us all. He was one of the founders, the chief founder in fact, of the International and in my eyes that is a tremendous service and one which I shall always recognize no matter what he may have done against us."

And then he was guided by political and tactical considerations towards Marx, " who cannot stand me and loves no one but himself and perhaps those who are nearest to him. Marx's influence in the International is undoubtedly very useful. He has exercised a wise influence on his party down to the present day and he is the strongest support of socialism and the firmest bulwark against the invasion of bourgeois ideas and intentions. I should never forgive myself if I had even tried to destroy or even weaken his beneficial influence merely in order to revenge myself on him. However, a situation may arise, and shortly at that, in which I shall take up the struggle against him, though certainly not in order to attack him personally, but on a question of principle, on account of the State communism which he and the English and Germans he leads support so enthusiastically. That would be a life-and-death struggle, but everything comes in its own good time and the hour of conflict has not yet arrived."

And finally Bakunin mentions a tactical reason which prevented him from attacking Marx. If he attacked Marx openly then three-quarters of the International would be against him, but on the other hand if he attacked the ragtag and bobtail that crowded around Marx the majority of the International would be on his side and Marx himself would find a certain amount of malicious pleasure in it—" *Schadenfreude* " is the German word which Bakunin uses in his letter to Herzen, which is otherwise written in French.

Immediately after writing this letter Bakunin moved to Locarno. He was so occupied with his personal affairs that during the last few weeks he spent in Geneva after the Basle congress he took no part at all in the working-class movement and did not write a line for *L'Égalité*. His successor on the editorial board was Robin, a Belgian teacher who had moved to Geneva about a year previously, and together with him Perron, the enameller who had edited the paper before Bakunin. Both were supporters of Bakunin, but they did not act on his instructions. Bakunin's aim was to enlighten the workers of the *gros métiers*, in whom the revolutionary proletarian spirit was much more alive than in the workers of the *fabrique*, and to encourage them to undertake independent action. In this he found himself in opposition to their own committees—and what he has to say about the objective dangers of such a " departmental policy " as we should call it nowadays, is well worth reading even now—not to speak of the *fabrique*, which had supported the workers of the *gros métiers* in their strikes and drew from this undeniable service the false conclusion that the workers of the *gros métiers* should follow faithfully every step of their colleagues of the *fabrique*. Bakunin had fought against these tendencies, particularly in view of the incurable leanings of the *fabrique* towards alliances with bourgeois radicalism. However, Robin and Perron thought that they could whitewash and patch up the differences between the *gros métiers* and the *fabrique*, differences which had not been created by Bakunin, but which had their basis in a social antagonism. As a result they slithered into a see-saw system which satisfied neither the *gros métiers* nor the *fabrique* and opened the door to all sorts of intrigues.

A master of such intrigues was a Russian fugitive named Nikolas Utin, who lived in Geneva at the time. He had taken part in the Russian student disturbances at the beginning of the 'sixties, and when the country grew too hot for him he fled abroad, where he lived comfortably on a considerable income—from twelve to fifteen thousand francs have been mentioned—which he derived from his father's trading in spirits. This fact won him a position which the intellectual capacities of the vain and garrulous fellow could never have obtained for him. His successes were exclusively on the field of tittle-tattle where, as Engels once said, " the man with something serious to do can never compete with those who have all day to gossip in ". In the beginning Utin had made up to Bakunin, only to be thoroughly snubbed by him, and when the latter left Geneva Utin seized the opportunity to revenge himself for his wounded vanity by pursuing him with underhand slander. His efforts to this edifying end were not without result, and afterwards he cast himself humbly at the feet of the Tsar and begged for mercy. The Tsar was not adamant, and during the Russo-Turkish war of 1877 Utin became a contractor to the Tsarist army, in which capacity he no doubt worshipped mammon even more successfully than he had done through the paternal spirits business.

People like Robin and Perron were easy game for Utin because although their personal honesty was above reproach they were almost incredibly clumsy, and to make matters worse they began a squabble with the General Council on questions which were certainly not of any urgent interest to the Franco-Swiss workers. *L'Égalité* complained bitterly that the General Council paid far too much attention to the Irish question, that it failed to set up a Federal Council for the English sections, that it did not arbitrate in the conflict between Liebknecht and Schweitzer, etc. Bakunin had nothing to do with all this, and the wrong impression that he approved of these attacks on the General Council or even instigated them was caused exclusively by the fact that Robin and Perron were his supporters and that Guillaume's paper took up the same attitude.

The General Council replied to Robin's attacks in a private circular dated the 1st of January 1870 and addressed, apart from Geneva, only to the French-speaking Federal Councils. Although this circular was sharp in its tone it remained well within the limits of objective argument. The reasons which the General Council gave for not forming a Federal Council in England are interesting still. It declared that although the revolutionary initiative would probably come from France, nevertheless only England could serve as the lever for any serious economic revolution. It was the only country where there were no longer any peasants and where the ownership of the land was concentrated in the hands of a few landowners. It was the only country where the capitalist mode of production had established itself in almost the whole of production and where the great mass of the population consisted of wage-workers. It was the only country where the class struggle and the organization of the workers had reached a certain degree of universality and maturity. And finally, thanks to the dominant position of England on the world market, any revolution in its economic conditions would immediately react on the whole world.

Although therefore all the necessary material conditions for a social revolution existed in England, nevertheless the English workers did not possess either a capacity for generalization or revolutionary ardour. The task of the General Council was to give the English workers this spirit and this ardour, and the fact that it was performing its task successfully could be seen from the complaints of the big bourgeois newspapers in London that the General Council was poisoning the English spirit of the workers and driving them towards revolutionary socialism. An English Federal Council would come between the General Council of the International and the General Council of the trade unions and enjoy no prestige, whilst the General Council of the International would lose its influence on the great lever of the proletarian revolution. It therefore refused to commit the folly of placing this lever in English hands and contenting itself with bombastic mouthings in the place of serious and unseen work.

Before this circular arrived at its destination the trouble came to a head in Geneva itself. Seven members of the editorial board of *L'Égalité* were supporters of Bakunin and only two were his opponents. Arising out of a subordinate and politically unimportant incident the majority raised the question of confidence, and it was then seen that with their vacillating policy Robin and Perron had sat down between two stools. The minority was supported by the Federal Council and the seven members of the majority had to resign, including Becker, who had been very friendly with Bakunin whilst the latter lived in Geneva, but who had found many things to object to in the policy of Robin and Perron. The control of *L'Égalité* then went over into the hands of Utin.

7. The "Confidential Communication"

In the meantime Borkheim continued his incitement against Bakunin. On the 18th of February he complained to Marx that *Die Zukunft*, the organ of Johann Jacoby, had refused to publish what Marx described in a letter to Engels as "a monster epistle on Russian affairs, an indescribable hodge-podge of minute details all tumbling one over the other". At the same time Borkheim cast suspicion on Bakunin "in connection with certain financial transactions", on the authority of Katkoff, who in his youth had been a follower of Bakunin but later went over to the reaction. Marx paid little attention to this accusation, and Engels remarked philosophically: "Borrowing money is too typical a Russian means of existence for one Russian to be able to reproach another about it."

After informing Engels about Borkheim's continued incitement against Bakunin Marx declared that the General Council had been called upon to decide whether a certain Richard (who later really turned out to be a bad hat) had been expelled from the International in Lyon with justification, and added that as far as he could see the man could be accused of nothing more than a slavish support of Bakunin and an accompanying priggishness. "It appears that our last circular made a sensation and that in France and Switzerland a regular hunt against the

Bakuninists has begun. However, there must be moderation in all things and I shall see to it that no injustice is done."

A confidential communication which Marx made a few weeks later on the 28th of March through the mediation of Kugelmann to the Brunswick committee of the Eisenachers was in strong contrast with the good intentions with which he had concluded his letter to Engels. The basis of this confidential communication was the circular of the General Council intended only for Geneva and for the French-speaking Federal Councils, which had long since served its purpose and which had in fact let loose the " regular hunt " against the Bakuninists of which Marx had expressed his disapproval. It is difficult to see why Marx communicated the contents of this circular to Germany in face of the unpleasant result it had already had elsewhere, particularly as Bakunin had no supporters in Germany at all.

It is still more difficult to understand why he provided the circular with an introduction and a close which were even more calculated to let loose a " regular hunt ", particularly against Bakunin. The introduction began with bitter reproaches against Bakunin, who had first of all attempted to smuggle himself into the League for Peace and Freedom, but in whose executive committee he had been watched as a " suspected Russian ". After having failed to secure the adoption of his programmatic absurdities in the League he had then turned his attention to the International in order to make it into his private instrument. To this end he had founded the Alliance of Socialist Democracy. After the General Council had refused to recognize the Alliance the latter had nominally been dissolved, but in fact it had continued to exist under Bakunin's leadership, who had then sought to attain his ends with other means. He had put forward the question of the right of inheritance at the Basle congress in the hope of defeating the General Council on the theoretical field and causing its removal from London to Geneva. He had organized " a downright conspiracy " in order to secure a majority at the Basle congress ; however, he had not been successful and the General Council had remained in London. " Bakunin's anger at the failure of his plan—perhaps he had attached all sorts of private speculations to its success—" had then expressed itself in the attacks of *L'Égalité* on the General Council, attacks which had been answered in the circular of the 1st of January.

Marx then inserted the full text of the circular in his confidential communication and continued : even before the arrival of the circular the crisis had come to a head in Geneva. The Franco-Italian Swiss Federal Council had disapproved of the attacks made by *L'Égalité* on the General Council and decided to keep a close control over the paper for the future. Bakunin had then retired from Geneva to Tessin. "Soon afterwards Herzen died. Bakunin, who had disavowed his old friend and patron from the moment he wished to put himself forward as the leader of the European working-class movement, then immediately began to sound a fanfare in Herzen's praise. Why? Despite his own wealth Herzen had been in receipt of an annual sum of 25,000 francs for propaganda from the pseudo-socialist Pan-Slavist party in Russia, with which he was friendly. Thanks to his lavish praise Bakunin succeeded in obtaining this money himself and then 'took over Herzen's heritage' unreservedly, as much as he hated it." In the meantime a colony of young Russian fugitives had established itself in Geneva, students who were really honest in their endeavours and who had made the struggle against Pan-Slavism the chief point in their programme. They had asked to be admitted as a section of the International, proposing that Marx should be their provisional representative on the General Council, and both these requests had been granted. They had also declared that they were about to tear the mask from Bakunin's face publicly. In this way the game of this highly dangerous intriguer would be up, at least as far as the International was concerned.

It is hardly necessary to enumerate the many errors this document contains. Generally speaking, the more incriminating the accusations it makes against Bakunin appear to be the more baseless they are in reality. This is true in particular of the accusation of legacy-hunting. No pseudo-socialist Pan-Slavist party in Russia ever paid Herzen 25,000 francs annually for propaganda. The unsubstantial basis of this fairy-tale was that in the revolutionary years a young Russian named Batmetiev had given 20,000 francs to start a revolutionary fund and that Herzen had administered this fund. There is no reason whatever to believe that Bakunin ever showed any inclination to pocket this fund on his own behalf and certainly the warm obituary he wrote for Rochefort's *Marseillaise* on a political opponent who had been a friend of his youth cannot be quoted in support of such a statement. At the utmost the obituary might offer an opportunity for an accusation of sentimentality, just as all the errors and weaknesses of Bakunin, no matter how numerous they may have been, were due to characteristics which were generally speaking the opposite of those which go to the make-up of a "highly dangerous intriguer".

The concluding passages of the confidential communication show how Marx came to fall into these errors concerning Bakunin. His information was obtained from the Russian fugitives committee in Geneva, in other words from Utin, or through him from Becker. At least, a letter from Marx to Engels seems to indicate that he obtained the most serious of the accusations, that of legacy-hunting, from Becker. However, this does not rhyme with a contemporary letter from the latter to Jung, which is still extant, in which Becker complains about the confusion prevailing in Geneva, about the antagonism between the *fabrique* and the *gros métiers*, about " weak-nerved illusionists like Robin and obstinate cranks like Bakunin ", but ends up by praising Bakunin and declaring that he was much better and more useful than he had been. The letters of Becker and the Russian fugitives committee in Geneva to Marx are no longer extant, and in both his official and private answers to this new section of the International Marx apparently thought it better to say nothing about Bakunin at all. He advised the Russian section to work chiefly for Poland, that is to say, to free Europe from its own proximity, and he did not fail to see the humour of being the representative of young Russia, declaring that a man could never know in what strange company he might fall.

Although he treated the matter with a certain amount of humour it was obviously a great satisfaction to him to observe that the International was beginning to find a foothold amongst the Russian revolutionaries, and otherwise it would be impossible to understand why he was prepared to believe accusations against Bakunin when Utin, who was completely unknown to him, made them, although he had refused to credit them from his old friend Borkheim. By a peculiar coincidence Bakunin fell victim just at that time to an error of judgment with regard to a Russian fugitive, whom he regarded as the first swallow of the coming Russian revolutionary summer, and even let himself be drawn into an adventure which was to do his reputation more harm than any other incident in his whole adventurous life.

A few days after the confidential communication had been written the second annual congress of the Franco-Italian Swiss Federation took place on the 4th of April in La Chaux-de-Fonds, and an open breach occurred. The Geneva section of the Alliance, which had already been accepted into the International by the General Council, demanded that it should also be accepted into the Federation and that its two delegates should be given representation at the congress. Utin opposed this and made violent attacks on Bakunin, denouncing the Geneva section of the alliance as his intriguing tool, but he was vigorously opposed by Guillaume, a narrow-minded fanatic who in later years treated Marx as badly as Utin treated Bakunin, but a man whose education and capacity put him in a different class altogether from that of his pitiful opponent. Guillaume was victorious with a majority of 21 against 18 votes. However, the minority refused to recognize the decision of the majority and split the congress. Two congresses then met simultaneously. The majority congress decided to move the seat of the Federal Council from Geneva to La Chaux-de-Fonds and to make *Solidarité*, which Guillaume issued in Neufchâtel, the organ of the Federal Council.

The minority justified its attitude by declaring that the majority was a purely accidental one, because only 15 sections had been represented at La Chaux-de-Fonds, whilst Geneva alone had thirty sections which all or almost all opposed the acceptance of the Alliance into the Franco-Italian Swiss section. The majority on the other hand insisted that a section which had been admitted by the General Council could not be rejected by a Federal Council. Becker declared in *Der Vorbote* that the whole affair was much objectionable ado about nothing and had been possible only thanks to a lack of fraternal feelings on both sides. The section of the Alliance was chiefly interested in the propaganda of theoretical principles and could therefore not attach much importance to being accepted into a national organization, all the more so as it was regarded in Geneva as the intriguing tool of Bakunin, who had long been unpopular there. On the other hand, if the Alliance really wanted to be accepted it was narrow-minded and childish to refuse or to make its acceptance the reason for a split.

However, the situation was not quite so simple as Becker described it. The decisions which the two separate congresses adopted were similar in many respects, but they differed just in the cardinal question—the antagonism out of which the whole confusion in Geneva had developed. The majority congress completely adopted the standpoint of the *gros métiers* and condemned all forms of politics which aimed merely at social changes through national reforms, declaring that every politically organized State was nothing but a means of capitalist exploitation on the basis of bourgeois law, and therefore any participation of the proletariat in bourgeois politics consolidated the existing system and paralysed revolutionary proletarian action. The minority congress, on the other hand, adopted the standpoint of the *fabrique*. It condemned political abstinence as damaging to the cause of the working class, and recommended participation in the elections, not because it would be possible to secure the emancipation of the workers in this way, but because the parliamentary representation of the workers was a means of agitation and propaganda which it would not be tactical to ignore.

The newly-formed Federal Council in La Chaux-de-Fonds demanded recognition from the General Council as the leader of the Federation. However, the General Council refused to give this recognition, and on the 28th of June it declared that the Federal Council in Geneva, which was supported by the majority of the Geneva sections, should continue to exercise its old functions, whilst the new Federal Council should adopt a local name. Although this decision was fair enough and had been provoked by the new Federal Council, the latter refused to submit to it and protested vigorously against the dictatorial tendencies, against the " authoritarianism " of the General Council, thus giving the opposition within the International the second plank in its platform—the first being political abstinence. The General Council then severed all relations with La Chaux-de-Fonds.

8. The Irish Amnesty and the French Plebiscite

The winter of 1869–70 was again a period of numerous physical ailments for Marx, but at least he had got rid of his constant money troubles. On the 30th of June 1869 Engels had finally freed himself from his " damned business ", and six months before he had asked Marx whether the latter thought he could get along on 350 pounds a year. Engels wanted to liquidate his affairs with his partner in such a fashion that this sum would be available for Marx for a period of five or six years. The correspondence between the two friends does not show what arrangements were made in the end, but in any case Engels banished Marx's financial troubles not only for a period of five or six years, but up to the latter's death.

In this period both of them occupied themselves very much with the Irish question. Engels conducted detailed studies into the historical development of the movement, but unfortunately the fruits of his studies were never published, whilst Marx urged the General Council to support the Irish movement, which demanded an amnesty for the irregularly condemned Fenians, who were being infamously treated in prison. The General Council expressed its admiration for the firm, great-hearted and courageous fashion in which the Irish people fought for its rights, and it condemned the policy of Gladstone, who despite all the promises he had made at the elections refused to grant an amnesty or made its granting subject to conditions which were an insult to the victims of English misgovernment and to the Irish people.

The Prime Minister was reproached in the sharpest terms for preaching the doctrine of subjugation to the English people after he had, despite his position of responsibility, expressed his enthusiastic approval of the revolt of the American slave-owners, and the General Council declared that his whole attitude in the question of the Irish amnesty was an authentic product of that " policy of conquest " whose flaming denunciation by Gladstone had driven his Tory rivals from office. In a letter to Kugelmann, Marx declared that he was now attacking Gladstone as he had once attacked Palmerston, and added : " The democratic fugitives here love to attack continental despots from a safe distance. I like to attack only when I can see my enemy face to face."

Marx was particularly delighted by the fact that his eldest daughter won a signal success in the Irish campaign. The English press obstinately remained silent about the barbarities committed against the imprisoned Fenians, so Jenny Marx sent a number of articles to Rochefort's *Marseillaise* under the pseudonym of Williams, a name which her father had used quite a lot in the 'fifties. In these articles she passionately described how democratic England treated its political prisoners, and these revelations in a paper which was probably more read than any other on the continent were too much for Gladstone, and a few weeks later most of the imprisoned Fenians were free and on their way to America.

The *Marseillaise* had won its European reputation as the result of its intrepid attacks on the false Bonaparte, whose régime was by this time crackling at all its joints. At the beginning of 1870 Bonaparte made a last desperate attempt to save his bloody and shabby régime by making concessions to the bourgeoisie, and he appointed the garrulous liberal Ollivier Prime Minister. Ollivier did his best by means of so-called reforms, but, as the leopard cannot change its spots at will, Bonaparte demanded that these " reforms " should receive the typically Bonapartist blessing of a plebiscite. Ollivier was weak enough to give way and even recommended the Prefects to do their utmost to make the plebiscite a success, but the Bonapartist police knew better than the vain chatterer how to secure the success of a plebiscite, and on the eve of the voting it discovered an alleged bomb plot on the part of members of the International against the life of Napoleon. Ollivier was cowardly enough to submit to the police, particularly as the action was chiefly directed against workers, and everywhere in France the " leaders " of the International, as far as they were known to the police, were surprised by searches and arrests.

The General Council lost no time in parrying the blow, and a protest was published on the 3rd of May declaring : " Our statutes make it the duty of all sections of our association to act openly, and even if the statutes were not clear on the point, the character of an association which identifies itself with the working class excludes any possibility of such an association taking on the form of a secret society. If the working class, which forms the great majority of any nation and produces all riches and in whose name even the usurping powers allegedly rule, conspires, then it conspires publicly in the same way as the sun conspires against darkness, and in the full consciousness that no legitimate power exists outside its own orbit. . . . The loud and violent measures taken against our French sections have been calculated exclusively to serve one purpose, as a manipulation to support the plebiscite." This was the plain truth, but the contemptible means once again served their contemptible end, and the " liberal empire " was ushered in with seven million votes against one and a half million.

After that, however, the authorities had to let their bomb-plot swindle drop. The police declared that they had found a code dictionary in the possession of the members of the International, but all they could make out of it was one or two names like Napoleon and one or two chemical expressions such as Nitroglycerine, and this was rather too much to ask even the Bonapartist courts to swallow. The indictment therefore shrank to the same alleged offence for which French members of the International had twice been tried and convicted previously : membership of a secret or unlawful society.

After a brilliant defence conducted this time by the coppersmith Chatain, who was later a member of the Paris Commune, a number of convictions were secured by the prosecution on the 9th of July, the maximum sentence being one year's imprisonment and one year's loss of all civil rights, but simultaneously the storm broke which was to sweep the Second Empire off the face of the earth.

CHAPTER FOURTEEN: THE DECLINE OF THE INTER-NATIONAL

1. Sedan

VERY much has been written about the attitude of Marx and Engels to the Franco-Prussian War, although fundamentally there is very little to be said about it. Unlike Moltke they did not regard war as an element of God's dispensation, but as an element of the devil's dispensation, as an inseparable accompaniment of class society and in particular of capitalist society.

As historians they naturally did not adopt the utterly un-historical attitude that war is war and that every war is tarred with the same brush. For them every war had its own definite causes and consequences and upon those causes and conse-quences must depend the attitude taken up by the working class towards the war. That was also the attitude of Lassalle, with whom they disputed in 1859 on the actual determining conditions of the war, whilst all three of them adopted the same funda-mental attitude towards it, i.e., all three aimed at utilizing the war as thoroughly as possible in the interests of the proletarian struggle for emancipation.

The attitude of Marx and Engels to the war of 1866 was determined by the same consideration. After the failure of the German revolution of 1848 to establish national unity the Prussian government sought to exploit the German movement for unity (which was awakened again and again by the course of economic development) in its own interests and to establish instead of a united Germany an extended Prussia, as old Kaiser Wilhelm had put it. Marx and Engels, Lassalle and Schweitzer, Liebknecht and Bebel were all completely in agreement about the fact that German unity, which the German proletariat needed as a preliminary stage in its own struggle for emanci-pation, could only come through a national revolution, and they therefore sharply opposed all the dynastic-particularist tendencies of the Greater-Prussian policy. However, after the decision had been fought out at Königgrätz they all sooner or later, according to the measure of their insight into the "actual conditions", swallowed the unpleasant pill, i.e. when it became clear that a national revolution was no longer possible, owing to the cowardice of the bourgeoisie and the weakness of the proletariat, and that Greater Prussia, built up with "blood and iron", offered more favourable conditions to the class struggle of the proletariat than the restoration—impossible in any case—of the Germanic Diet with its pitiful hole-and-corner policy. Marx and Engels immediately came to this conclusion, as also did Schweitzer as the successor of Lassalle. They accepted the North German League, despite its crippled and stunted form, as a given fact which offered the struggle of the German working class a firmer basis than the ghastly mismanagement of the Germanic Diet, though their acceptance was not even a willing, much less an enthusiastic one. On the other hand, Liebknecht and Bebel still maintained their Greater-German revolutionary outlook, and even after 1866 they continued to work for the destruction of the North German League.

After the decision to which Marx and Engels came in 1866 their attitude towards the war of 1870 was already more or less settled. They never expressed any opinions on the immediate happenings which led up to the war, either on Bismarck's Spanish throne candidature on behalf of a Hohenzollern prince against Bonaparte, or on Bonaparte's policy of a Franco-Austro-Italian alliance against Bismarck. In any case, it was at that time hardly possible to express any reasonable judgment on either. However, as far as Bonaparte's war policy was directed against the national unity of Germany, they both recognized that Germany was on the defensive.

In an address issued by the General Council of the International on the 23rd of July and drawn up by Marx the latter gave detailed reasons for this standpoint. He declared that the war plot of 1870 was an improved edition of the *coup d'état* of 1851, but it sounded the death-knell of the Second Empire, which would end as it had begun, as a parody. However, one must not forget that it was the ruling classes and the governments of Europe which had made it possible for Bonaparte to play the brutal farce of a restored empire for eighteen years. The war was a defensive war as far as Germany was concerned, but who had forced Germany into such a situation, who had made it possible for Louis Bonaparte to make war on Germany? Prussia. Before Königgrätz Bismarck had conspired with Bonaparte, and after Königgrätz Bismarck had not established a free Germany in contrast to an enslaved France, but had crowned all the native perfidies of the old system with all the underhand tricks of the

Second Empire, so that the Bonapartist régime flourished on both banks of the Rhine. What other result could there have been but war? "If the German working class permits the present war to lose its strictly defensive character and to degenerate into a war against the French people then both defeat and victory will be equally fatal. All the misery which Germany suffered as the result of the so-called wars for independence would return with increased intensity." The Address pointed out that the demonstrations of the German and French workers against the war made it unnecessary to fear such a sad result, and reminded the workers that in the background of the suicidal struggle the evil figure of Russia was on the watch. All the sympathies which the Germans could demand as their right in their defensive struggle against the Bonapartist attack would be flung away if they permitted the Prussian government to call for or accept the assistance of the Cossacks.

On the 21st of July, two days before this address was issued, the North German Reichstag had voted a war credit of 120 million thaler. In accordance with their policy since 1866 the Lassallean parliamentary representatives had voted for the credit, whilst Liebknecht and Bebel, the parliamentary representatives of the Eisenachers, had abstained from voting, because a vote in favour of the credit would have been a vote of confidence in the Prussian government which had sown the seeds of the present war by its attitude in 1866, whilst a vote against the credit might have been interpreted as expressing approval of the atrocious and criminal policy of Bonaparte. Liebknecht and Bebel regarded the war chiefly from the moral point of view, as Liebknecht demonstrated later in his work on the Ems despatch and Bebel in his Memoirs.

Their attitude met with vigorous opposition in their own fraction and in particular from its leadership, the Brunswick Committee. In reality the abstention of Liebknecht and Bebel was not practical politics, but a moral protest which, irrespective of how justified it might be in itself, was not in accordance with the political exigencies of the situation. Although it may be possible and perhaps effective in private life to declare to two opponents : you are both wrong and I refuse to have anything to do with your quarrel, it is not possible in the life of States when whole peoples have to suffer from the quarrels of Kings. The practical consequences of this impossible neutrality were revealed during the very first weeks of the war in the unclear and illogical attitude of the *Volksstaat* in Leipzig, the organ of the Eisenach fraction. As a result the conflict between the editorial board, that is to say, Liebknecht, and the Brunswick Committee was intensified and the latter appealed to Marx for advice and support.

On the 20th of July, immediately after the outbreak of war and before the abstention of Liebknecht and Bebel, Marx had written to Engels sharply criticising " republican chauvinism " in France : " The French need a drubbing. If the Prussians are victorious then the centralization of the State power will be favourable to the centralization of the working class. German preponderance will shift the centre of the working-class movement in Western Europe from France to Germany, and one has only to compare the movement of 1866 in both countries to see that the German working class is theoretically and organizationally superior to the French. The superiority of the Germans over the French in the world arena would mean at the same time the superiority of our theory over Proudhon's, etc." When Marx received the appeal of the Brunswick Committee he approached Engels as he always did in all important questions to secure his his advice, and, as in 1866, it was Engels who decided the details of the tactics adopted.

In his reply on the 15th of August Engels writes : " The situation seems to me to be as follows : Germany has been forced into a war to defend its national existence by Badinguet (Bona-parte). If Germany is defeated then Bonapartism will be consoli-dated for years and Germany broken for years, perhaps for generations. Under such circumstances there could be no question of any independent German working-class movement. The struggle for the establishment of national unity would absorb all energies, and in the best case the German workers would be taken in tow by the French. If Germany is victorious then French Bonapartism is destroyed in any case, the eternal squabbling about the establishment of German unity will be ended at last, the German workers will be able to organize themselves on a far broader basis than previously, whilst the French workers will also have much greater freedom of move-ment than under Bonapartism no matter what sort of a govern-ment may follow there. The great masses of the German people, all classes, have realized that the national existence of Germany is at stake and they have therefore immediately sprung into the breach. Under these circumstances it seems impossible to me that a German political party can preach total obstruction à la Wilhelm (Liebknecht) and place all sorts of subordinate con-siderations before the main issue."

Engels condemned French chauvinism, which made its influence felt even deep in the ranks of the republican elements, as severely as Marx : " Badinguet could never have begun this war without the chauvinism of the masses of the French people, the bourgeoisie, the petty-bourgeoisie, the peasants and the imperialist Haussmann building proletariat created by Bonaparte in the big towns and recruited chiefly from the peasantry. Peace between France and Germany is impossible so long as this chauvinism has not been crushed, and thoroughly at that. One might have expected a proletarian revolution to undertake this task, but now that the war has begun the Germans have no alternative but to do it themselves and at once."

The " subordinate considerations ", namely that the war had been planned by Bismarck and company, and that a German victory would reflect glory on Bismarck's system, were due to the miserable quality of the German bourgeoisie. It was all very unpleasant, but nothing could be done about it : " But to raise anti-Bismarckism to a guiding principle for this reason would be absurd. First of all, just as in 1866, Bismarck is doing a share of our work ; he is doing it in his own way and without wanting to, but nevertheless he is doing it. He is giving us a clearer field than we had before. And then we are no longer living in A.D. 1815. The South Germans must now necessarily enter the Reichstag and with their entry a counter-weight to Prussia is established. . . . In any case, Liebknecht's desire to turn back the whole course of history since 1866 just because it doesn't please him is nonsense, but there, we know our exemplary South Germans."

In this letter, Engels once again returns to Liebknecht's policy : " Wilhelm's contention that because Bismarck was once an accomplice of Badinguet the correct attitude is therefore one of neutrality is amusing. If that opinion were generally prevalent in Germany we should soon have the Rhenish League again and the noble Wilhelm would be hard pressed to find what rôle he could play in it, not to speak of the working-class movement. A people used only to blows and kicks is just the right stuff to make a social revolution, particularly in Wilhelm's beloved Statelets ! Wilhelm obviously reckons with the victory of Bonaparte merely in order to put paid to Bismarck. You can remember how he always used to threaten him with the French. You are on Wilhelm's side, of course." The last remark was intended ironically because Liebknecht had declared that Marx had been in agreement with his and Bebel's abstention in the war-credit vote.

Marx admitted that he had expressed approval of the " declaration " of Liebknecht. It had been made at a " moment " when a certain stickling for principles was an *acte de courage*, but one must not conclude from this that the moment would continue and still less that the attitude of the German proletariat in a war which had become national, could be summed up in Liebknecht's antipathy towards Prussia. Marx had good reason for referring to the " declaration " and not to the abstention itself. Whilst the Lassalleans had voted for the war credit in the general chorus of the bourgeois majority without stressing in any way their socialist standpoint, Liebknecht and Bebel had made a declaration giving the reasons for their abstention. They not only gave the reasons for their attitude, but " as social republicans and members of the International which fought against all oppressors irrespective of their nationality and sought to unite all the oppressed in a fraternal alliance " they added a protest on principle against the war and all dynastic wars, and expressed the hope that the peoples of Europe would learn from their present disastrous experiences and do everything possible to win the right of self-determination for themselves and to abolish the existing jackboot and class rule which was the cause of all State and social evils. Naturally, Marx was very satisfied with this " declaration " which for the first time in history defiantly and openly raised the banner of the International in a European parliament and at that in a question of world historic importance.

That his approval referred to this declaration can be seen from his choice of words. The abstention itself was not at all " a stickling for principles ", but rather a compromise, for Liebknecht had in fact intended to vote against the credit, but had been persuaded by Bebel to abstain from voting instead. Further, as every issue of the *Volksstaat* showed, the abstention was not an action which determined their policy merely for " the moment ". And finally, it was not an " *acte de courage* " in the sense that it contained its own justification. If Marx had meant his " *acte de courage* " in that sense then he would have had to praise the worthy Thiers still more highly, for Thiers spoke vigorously against the war in the French Chamber, although the Mamelukes of the Second Empire raged against him and overwhelmed him with the wildest abuse, or the bourgeois democrats of the Favre-Grevy school, who did not abstain from voting but refused to grant the credits point-blank, although the patriotic storm was at least as violent in Paris as in Berlin.

The conclusion which Engels drew for the policy of the German working-class from his estimate of the situation may be summed up as follows : to join the national movement as long as it limited itself to the defence of Germany (an action which did not under certain circumstances exclude the conduct of an offensive until the signing of peace) ; to stress the difference between German national interests and the dynastic-Prussian interests; to oppose any annexation of Alsace and Lorraine; immediately a republican government had taken the place of the chauvinist government in Paris to work with it to secure an honourable peace; and always to stress the unity of interests between the French and German workers, who had not approved of the war and who were not fighting against each other.

Marx declared himself completely in agreement with this summing up, and he wrote to the Brunswick Committee in this sense.

2. After Sedan

Before the Brunswick Committee was able to make any practical use of the advice it received from London the situation had completely changed. The battle of Sedan had taken place, Bonaparte was a prisoner of war, the Second Empire lay in ruins and a bourgeois republic had been declared in Paris. The former deputies of the French capital placed themselves at the head of the republic and proclaimed themselves a " Government of National Defence ".

As far as the Germans were concerned therefore the war had ceased to be one of national defence. The King of Prussia, as the leader of the North German League, had declared repeatedly and solemnly that he was waging war not against the French people, but against the government of the French Emperor, whilst the new rulers in Paris declared themselves prepared to pay any amount of money as an indemnity for the German losses. However, Bismarck demanded that France should make territorial concessions and he continued the war for the conquest of Alsace and Lorraine, ignoring the fact that he thereby made Germany's contention that it was conducting a defensive war a mockery.

By this action he followed in the footsteps of Bonaparte and also in the arrangement of a sort of plebiscite which was to free the King of Prussia from his solemn undertakings. Even on the eve of Sedan " notabilities " of all sorts issued " mass addresses " to the King putting forward the demand for " protected frontiers ". The " unanimous will of the German people " made such an impression on the old gentleman that on the 6th of September he wrote home : " If the ruling houses were to oppose this feeling they would risk their thrones ", and on the 14th of September the semi-official *Provinzial-Korrespondenz* declared it

" a naïve and unreasonable demand " that the head of the
North German League should stand by undertakings he had given
expressly and of his own free will.

In order to enhance the " unanimous will of the German
people ", the authorities proceeded to crush all opposition ruthlessly. On the 5th of September the Brunswick Committee
had issued an appeal calling for working-class demonstrations
in favour of an honourable peace with the French Republic and
against the annexation of Alsace and Lorraine. The appeal
contained parts of the letter which Marx had sent to the Committee. On the 9th of September the signatories to the appeal
were arrested by the military authorities and taken in chains
to the fortress of Lötzen. Johann Jacoby was also sent as a
prisoner of State to the same place, because at a meeting in
Königsberg he had also protested against the annexation of
French territory and uttered the heretical opinion : " A few
days ago we were waging a defensive war, a holy war for our
beloved Fatherland, but to-day it is a war for conquest, a war to
establish the hegemony of the Germanic race in Europe." A
wave of confiscations and prohibitions, searches and arrests
completed the military reign of terror, whose aim it was to place
" the unanimous will of the German people " beyond all doubt.

On the day on which the members of the Brunswick Committee were arrested the General Council of the International
again came forward with an Address drawn up by Marx and
partly by Engels on the new situation. It was able to point out
how quickly its prophecy that the war would sound the death-
knell of the Second Empire had been fulfilled, and also how
quickly its doubts as to how long the war would remain a defensive
war for Germany had been confirmed. The Prussian military
camarilla had decided in favour of a war of conquest. How had
it released the Prussian King from the solemn undertakings he
had himself made with regard to the defensive war ? " The
wire-pullers had to present him as giving way to an overwhelming
demand on the part of the German nation, and it immediately
gave the cue to the German liberal middle-class with its professors,
its capitalists, its town councillors and its newspaper men. The
middle-class, which had offered an unexampled spectacle of
indecision, incompetence and cowardice in the struggles for civil
freedom during the years from 1846 to 1870, was naturally highly
delighted at the opportunity of appearing on the European
stage in the rôle of the roaring lion of German patriotism. It
accepted the deceitful appearance of civil independence in order
to pretend that it was forcing something on to the Prussian
government—what ? The secret plans of the Prussian govern-

ment, no more no less. It did penance for its long and almost religious belief in Louis Bonaparte's infallibility by demanding loudly the dismemberment of the French Republic."

The address then examined the " plausible excuses " which " these stout patriots " put forward to justify the annexation of Alsace and Lorraine. They did not dare to contend that the inhabitants of these provinces were longing for the embrace of Germany, but they pointed out that long, long before the territory of the two provinces had been a part of the long-since deceased German Empire. " If the map of Europe is to be remodelled according to old historical rights then we must not forget that the Elector of Brandenburg was once the vassal of the Polish Republic as far as his Prussian possessions were concerned."

" Many weak-minded people " were led astray by the fact that " the cunning patriots " demanded Alsace and Lorraine as " a material guarantee " against future French attacks. In a military-scientific dissertation, which was Engels' contribution to the Address, it pointed out that Germany did not need this strengthening of its frontiers against France, as the experience of the present war had clearly shown. " If the present campaign has proved anything so it has proved how easy it is to attack France from Germany." But was it not an absurdity, an ana-chronism, to put forward military considerations as the principle determining national frontiers ? " If this principle were estab-lished then Austria would have a right to the province of Venice and to the Mincio line, and France would be entitled to claim the Rhine as a protection for Paris, which is certainly more open from attacks from the North-West than Berlin is from the South-West. If national frontiers are to be determined by military considerations then there will be no end of the various claims established, for every military position is necessarily weak some-where and could always be strengthened by the annexation of still further territory. And finally, frontiers laid down in this fashion can never be final, just because they would always be forced on the vanquished by the victors and would therefore bear in them the seeds of new wars."

The address recalled the " material guarantees " which Napoleon had taken in the Peace of Tilsit. And nevertheless a few years later his whole gigantic power had collapsed like a rotten reed before the onslaught of the German people. " What are the ' material guarantees ' which Prussia could or dare force on France even in its wildest dreams compared with those which Napoleon forced on Prussia ? The result will be no less disastrous this time."

The mouthpieces of German patriotism declared that one

must not confuse the Germans with the French. The Germans wanted not military glory but security. They were essentially a peace-loving people. " Naturally, it was not Germany which invaded France in 1792 with the noble aim of destroying the revolution of the eighteenth century with bayonets. Was it not Germany which soiled its hands with the subjugation of Italy, the suppression of Hungary and the dismemberment of Poland ? Its present military system, which divides the whole of the physically fit adult male population into two parts—a standing army on duty and a second standing army on leave—both of them equally enjoined to passive obedience to the orders of the Regent by the Grace of God, such a military system is naturally a ' material guarantee ' of world peace and beyond that the highest aim of civilization ! In Germany as in all other countries the flunkeys of the ruling power poison public opinion with incense and lying self-praise. They wax indignant at the sight of the French fortifications around Metz and Strassburg—these German patriots—but they see no harm in the tremendous system of Muscovite fortifications around Warsaw, Modlin and Ivangorod. Whilst they shudder at the thought of Bonapartist attacks they close their eyes to the scandal of Tsarist protectorship."

Pursuing this train of ideas the Address then declared that the annexation of Alsace and Lorraine would drive the French Republic into the arms of Tsarism. Did the Teutonists really believe that this would offer any guarantee for the peace and freedom of Germany ? " If the fortunes of war, the arrogance of victory, and dynastic intrigues mislead Germany into seizing French territory then only two ways will be left open. Either it will have to submit to being the obvious slave of Russian pene-tration, no matter what the result may be, or, after a short breathing space, it will have to prepare itself for a new ' defensive ' war, not for one of those new-fangled " localized ' wars, but for a racial war against the combined forces of the Slavs and the Neo-Latin peoples."

The German working-class, which had been unable to prevent the war, had supported it energetically as a war for Germany's independence and for the emancipation of Germany and Europe from the crushing incubus of the Second Empire. " It was the German industrial workers together with the agricultural workers who provided the sinew and muscle of heroic armies, whilst behind them they left half-starving families." Decimated in battle, they were once again decimated by misery and impoverishment at home. They then demanded guarantees that the tremendous sacrifices which they had made should not have been made in vain, that they should win their freedom, that the victories which they had won over the Bonapartist armies should not be turned into a defeat of the people as in 1815. As the first of these guarantees they demanded " an honourable peace for France " and " the recognition of the French Republic ". The address pointed to the appeal issued by the Brunswick Committee. Although, unfortunately, it was not possible to reckon with any immediate success, history would show that the German working-class was not made of the same pliable stuff as the German middle-class. It would do its duty.

The address then turned its attention to the French side of the situation. The republic had not overturned the throne but merely taken the empty seat. It had been proclaimed not as a social achievement, but as a measure of national defence. The republic was in the hands of a provisional government composed in part of notorious Orléanists and partly of bourgeois republicans, in whose ranks there were a number who had been branded indelibly by the June insurrection of 1848. The distribution of offices in the new government boded little good. The Orléanists had secured the strongest positions—the army and the police—whilst the alleged republicans had received the talking posts. The very first actions of the new government proved fairly clearly that it had inherited not only a heap of ruins from the Second Empire, but also the latter's fear of the working class.

" Thus the French working class finds itself in an extremely difficult position. Any attempt to overthrow the new government with the enemy at the gates would be desperate folly. The French workers must do their duty as citizens, but they must not let themselves be dominated by the national memories of 1792 as the French peasants were deceived by the national memories of the First Empire. They have not to repeat the past but to build up the future. Let them with calmness and determination utilize the means which republican freedom offers in order to organize their own class thoroughly. That will give them Herculean strength for the resuscitation of France and for our joint task—the emancipation of the proletariat. The fate of the republic depends on their strength and their wisdom."

This address met with a lively echo amongst the French workers, who abandoned their struggle against the provisional government and did their duty as citizens, particularly the proletariat of Paris, which, organized in the National Guard, took a prominent part in the heroic defence of the French capital, but did not let itself be blinded by the national memories of 1792 and worked zealously to organize itself as a class. The German workers showed themselves no less capable of carrying out their tasks. Despite threats and persecutions both the

Lassalleans and the supporters of the Eisenach fraction demanded an honourable peace with the French Republic, and when the North German Reichstag met again in December to vote new war credits the parliamentary representatives of both fractions voted with determination against any new credits. Liebknecht and Bebel in particular carried on this struggle with burning zeal and challenging courage, and it is for this reason that the credit for it is chiefly connected with their names, and not on account of their abstention in July, as a widespread legend would have it. At the end of the Reichstag term they were both indicted for high treason.

During the winter Marx had again been overburdened with work. In August the doctors had sent him to the seaside, but he had been " laid on his back " there by a violent cold, and on the last day of the month he had returned to London with his health by no means restored. However, he had to take over almost all the international correspondence of the General Council because the greater number of its foreign correspondents had gone to Paris. In a letter to his friend Kugelmann on the 14th of September he complained that he was never able to go to bed before three o'clock in the morning, but that he hoped for some relief in the future because Engels was now settling down in London for good.

There is no doubt that Marx hoped that the French Republic would be able to offer successful resistance to the Prussian war of conquest. The conditions in Germany filled him with bitterness, and they were in fact in such a state that even Windthorst, the leader of the ultra-montane Guelph party, made the scathing suggestion that if Bismarck must annex something or the other then he would find Cayenne better suited to his form of statesmanship. On the 13th of December Marx wrote to Kugelmann : " It would appear that Germany has swallowed not only Bonaparte, his generals and his army, but with them the whole system of imperialism, which is now making itself at home with all its sores in the land of the oak and the lime." In this letter he records with obvious satisfaction that public opinion in England, which in the beginning had been ultra-Prussian, had now changed into the contrary. Apart from the decisive sympathies of the masses of the people for the Republic and other circumstances, " the way in which the Germans have waged the war—the system of requisitions, the burning down of villages, the execution of the *francs-tireurs*, the seizing of hostages, and similar recapitulations from the Thirty Years War—has caused general indignation. Naturally, the English have done the very same thing in India, Jamaica, etc., but the French are not Hindus or Chinese or

Negroes, and the Prussian are not heaven-sent English. It is a typically Hohenzollern idea that a people which continues to defend itself after its standing army has been destroyed is committing a crime." Frederick William III had suffered from this idea during the Prussian war against the first Napoleon.

Marx called Bismarck's threat to bombard Paris " a mere trick ". " According to all the laws of probability such an action could have no serious effect on Paris. Supposing a few out-works are blown down and a few breaches made—how much use is that in a case where the numbers of the beleaguered are greater than those of the beleaguerers? The only real means of subduing Paris is to starve it out." A pretty picture by the way : this " man without a Fatherland " who made no claim to any independent judgment in questions of military science declared Bismarck's threat to bombard Paris to be a " mere trick " for exactly the same reason that all the prominent Generals of the German army, with the exception of Roon, condemned the proposal as a " cadet's escapade " in a furious discussion which lasted for weeks behind the scenes at the German headquarters ; whilst the whole camp-following of patriotic professors and newspaper men let themselves be incited by Bismarck's agents into paroxysms of moral indignation at the attitude of the Prussian Queen and the Prussian Crown Princess because these ladies allegedly prevented their henpecked heroes from bombarding Paris, either for sentimental reasons or perhaps for treasonable considerations.

When Bismarck then declared grandiloquently that the French government was preventing the free expression of opinion in the press and in parliament, Marx answered "this Berlin humour " in the *Daily News* of the 16th of January 1871 by de-scribing caustically the régime of police oppression which was gagging Germany. He concluded his description with the words : " France—and its cause is happily far removed from being lost— is fighting at the moment not only for its own national indepen-dence, but for the freedom of Germany and of Europe." This sentence sums up the attitude which Marx and Engels adopted to the Franco-Prussian War after Sedan.

3. *The Civil War in France*

Paris capitulated on the 28th of January. The agreement which was drawn up between Bismarck and Jules Favre to define the terms of the capitulation provided expressly that the Paris National Guard should retain its arms.

The elections to the National Assembly resulted in a monarchist-reactionary majority, which then elected the old intriguer Thiers as President of the Republic. His first care after the adoption of the peace preliminaries—the cession of Alsace and Lorraine and the payment of five milliard francs as a war indemnity—by the National Assembly was to disarm Paris, for the ingrained bourgeois Thiers, and also the reactionary landowners, regarded Paris in arms as no less than the revolution.

On the 18th of March Thiers attempted to seize the guns of the National Guard with the insolent lie that they were the property of the State, although they had been cast during the siege at the cost of the National Guard and were recognized as the property of the National Guard in the agreement of the 28th of January. The attempt met with resistance and the troops detailed for the coup went over to the people. The civil war had begun. On the 26th of March Paris elected the Commune whose history is as rich in heroism and sacrifices on the part of the workers of Paris as it is in cowardly brutality and malice on the part of the Versailles parties of law and order.

It is unnecessary to stress the burning interest and sympathy with which Marx followed the development of these events. On the 12th of April he wrote to Kugelmann : " What resilient vigour, what historic initiative and what self-sacrifice these Parisians are showing ! After six months of starvation and ruin brought about more by internal treachery than by the open enemy, they rise in revolt as though there had never been a war between France and Germany, as though Prussian bayonets did not exist, as though the enemy were not at the gates. History can show no similar example of such magnificence ! " If the Parisians were defeated it would be due to their " good-nature ". After the troops and the reactionary section of the National Guard left the field they should have marched on Versailles at once, but conscientious scruples made them wish not to open the civil war. As though the malicious abortion Thiers had not already opened it by his attempt to disarm Paris ! But even if the Parisians should be defeated their insurrection would remain the most glorious achievement of our party since the June revolt. " Compare these heaven-storming Titans with the pious slaves of the Prusso-German Holy Roman Empire with its posthumous masquerades exuding a stale air of barracks, churches, rural obscurantism and above all Philistinism."

When Marx referred to the Paris Commune as an achievement of " our party " he was entitled to do so both in the general sense that the working class of Paris was the backbone of the Commune, and in the particular sense that the Parisian members of the International were amongst the most capable and gallant fighters for the Commune, although they represented only a minority on its council. The International was already notorious as the cause of all the troubles of the bourgeoisie, and it served the ruling classes of all countries as the scapegoat for all unpleasant events. It was very natural therefore that the bourgeoisie regarded the machinations of the International as responsible for the Paris Commune, also. Curiously, however, one of the organs of the Paris police press sought to absolve the " *Grand chef* " of the International from any responsibility in the matter, and on the 19th of March it published a letter alleged to have been sent by him to the Paris sections reproaching them for paying too much attention to political and too little attention to social questions. Marx immediately sent a letter to *The Times* characterizing this document as " an insolent forgery ".

No one knew better than Marx that the International had not made the Commune, but from the beginning he regarded it as flesh of its flesh and blood of its blood. Naturally, however, only in the spirit of the programme and statutes of the International according to which all working-class movements aiming to emancipate the proletariat belonged to it. Neither the Blanquist majority in the Council of the Commune nor the minority which, although it belonged to the International, was influenced chiefly by the ideas of Proudhon, could be counted amongst Marx's immediate supporters. During the period of the Commune he kept in touch with this minority as far as the situation permitted, but unfortunately very little evidence of this is still extant.

Replying to a letter from Marx which has not been preserved, Leo Frankel, a delegate for the Department of Public Works, wrote on the 25th of April : " I should be very glad if you would assist me with your advice as far as possible because at the moment I am responsible, completely responsible in fact, for all the reforms which I wish to introduce in the Department for Public Works. One or two lines from your last letter are sufficient to indicate that you will do everything possible to make all peoples and all workers, and in particular the German workers, understand that the Paris Commune has nothing in common with the antediluvian German commune. In any case, you will be doing our cause a good service in this respect." If Marx replied to this letter or gave Frankel any advice we have no evidence of it.

A letter sent by Frankel and Varlin to him has also been

lost, but on the 13th of May Marx replied to it : " I have spoken with the bearer. Wouldn't it be a good idea to put papers of such a compromising nature for the Versailles *canaille* in a safe place ? Such precautionary measures never do any harm. I have received a letter from Bordeaux informing me that at the last municipal elections four members of the International won seats. Things are beginning to move in the provinces too, though unfortunately their action is localized and peaceable. I have written several hundred letters to all corners of the world where we have connections in your affair. In any case, the working class was in favour of the Commune from the beginning. Even the English bourgeois newspapers have now abandoned their preliminary hostility. Occasionally I have succeeded in smuggling a favourable article into their columns. It seems to me that the Commune is wasting too much time on unimportant details and personal disputes. Obviously there are other influences apart from those of the proletariat at work. But all this would not matter if you could make up for lost time." Finally he pointed out that speedy action was necessary in view of the fact that three days previously the definitive treaty of peace had been signed between Germany and France in Frankfort on Main, and that Bismarck now had the same interest as Thiers in the suppression of the Commune, particularly in view of the fact that with the signing of the treaty the war indemnity payments were to commence.

As far as Marx gave any advice in this letter one can feel a certain reserve, and without a doubt everything he wrote to members of the Commune was couched in the same tone. It was not that he was unwilling to take complete responsibility for the actions and omissions of the Commune, for he did that immediately after its defeat in full public and in all detail, but because he felt no inclination to play the rôle of dictator and to determine from afar what was to be done on the spot by those who could best see what should be done and what not.

On the 28th of May the last defenders of the Commune had fallen and two days later Marx presented the General Council with the Address on *The Civil War in France*, one of the most brilliant documents that ever came from his pen and all in all even to-day the crowning contribution to the voluminous literature which has been published on the Commune. On the basis of this difficult and complicated problem he demon-strated once again his extraordinary capacity to recognize the historic essence of a situation under the deceptive surface of apparently insoluble confusion and in the middle of a hundred conflicting rumours. As far as the Address dealt with facts—

and its two first and its fourth and last sections describe the actual course of events—it recognized the truth in every instance and has never been refuted in any single point.

The Address certainly gives no critical history of the Commune, but that was not its aim. It was written to defend the honour of the Commune and to justify it against the villification and injustice of its enemies, and it did so brilliantly. It was written as a polemic and not as an historical judgment, and since then the weaknesses and errors of the Commune have been subjected often enough to severe criticism on the part of socialists, sometimes too severe. At the time Marx contented himself with the following hint : " In every revolution people of a character very different from that of the real representatives of the revolution push themselves forward side by side with the latter. Some of these people are survivors from earlier revolutions with which they are completely bound up ; they have no understanding of the present revolution, but, thanks to their well-known courage and high character, or perhaps to mere tradition, they still enjoy considerable influence on the masses of the people. Others again are mere bawlers who have repeated the same declamations against the government of the day for years and thus by false pretences won the reputation of being revolutionaries of the first water. Such people also appeared on the scene after the 18th of March and in a number of cases they even played a prominent rôle. As far as lay in their power they obstructed the real action of the working class just as they had obstructed the full development of all earlier revolutions." Such elements, the Address pointed out, represented an unavoidable evil. Given time it was possible to shake them off, but the Commune had not been granted the necessary time.

The third section of the Address, which deals with the historical character of the Commune, is of particular interest. With great discernment Marx demonstrates the difference between the Commune and earlier historical forms which might appear similar to it—from the mediæval commune to the Prussian urban municipal system : " Only a Bismarck (who, were he not fully occupied with his blood-and-iron intrigues, would gladly return to his old handiwork as contributor to the *Kladderadatsch*, so perfectly was it suited to his mental calibre), only such a mentality, could conceive the idea of crediting the Paris Commune with any yearning for that caricature of the old French municipal constitution of 1791, the Prussian urban municipal system which debases the urban administration to a mere subordinate cog of the Prussian State machinery." In the manifold nature of the interpretations placed on the Commune and in the manifold nature of the interests expressed in it the Address recognized the fact that it was a political form easily capable of extension, whereas all previous governmental forms had been chiefly of an oppressive nature : " Its real secret was that it was essentially a government of the working class, the result of a struggle between the producing and the expropriating classes, the finally discovered political form under which the economic emancipation of labour could take place."

The address was unable to offer proof of this statement by producing a detailed governmental programme of the Commune, for the latter did not develop thus far and could not do so owing to the fact that from the first day of its existence to the last it was compelled to fight a life-and-death struggle with its enemies. However, the Address proved its point on the basis of the practical policy which the Commune had pursued, a policy whose inner essence consisted in the destruction of the State, which in its most prostituted form (the Second Empire) represented no more than " a parasitic growth " on the social body, sapping its strength and preventing its free development.

The first decree issued by the Commune abolished the standing army and replaced it by the people in arms. The Commune deprived the police force, up to then the mere tool of the government, of all political functions and turned it into an instrument responsible to the Commune. After having abolished the standing army and the police force as the material weapons of the old government, the Commune proceeded to break its spiritual weapon of oppression, the power of the clergy. It decreed the dissolution and expropriation of all the churches as far as they were property-owning bodies. It opened up all educational institutions to the people without charge and freed such institutions from all interference on the part of the State and church. And finally, it tore up the old State bureaucracy by the roots by making all State officials, including judges, subject to election and deposition at any time, and by fixing the maximum rate of pay for State servants at 6,000 francs.

The way in which the Address dealt with these details was brilliant, but there was a certain contradiction between them and the opinions previously held by Marx and Engels for a quarter of a century and set down in *The Communist Manifesto*. They held that one of the final results of the future proletarian revolution would certainly be the dissolution of that political institution known as the State, but this dissolution was to have been gradual. The main aim of such an institution was always to protect by force of arms the economic oppression of the working majority of the population by a minority in exclusive possession of the wealth of society. With the disappearance of this minority of wealthy persons the necessity for an armed repressive institution such as the State would also disappear. At the same time, however, they pointed out that in order to achieve this and other still more important aims of the future social revolution the working class must first of all seize the organized political power of the State and use it to crush the resistance of the capitalists and reorganize society. These opinions of *The Communist Manifesto* could not be reconciled with the praise lavished by the Address of the General Council on the Paris Commune for the vigorous fashion in which it had begun to exterminate the parasitic State.

Naturally, both Marx and Engels were well aware of the contradiction, and in a preface to a new edition of *The Communist Manifesto* issued in June 1872 under the immediate influence of the Paris Commune they revised their opinions, appealing expressly to the Address of the General Council and declaring that the workers could not simply lay hold of the ready-made State machinery and wield it for their own purposes. At a later date, and after the death of Marx, Engels was compelled to engage in a struggle against the anarchist tendencies in the working-class movement, and he let this proviso drop and once again took his stand on the basis of the Manifesto. It is not difficult to realize that the supporters of Bakunin interpreted the Address of the General Council in their own way, and Bakunin declared mockingly that although the Commune had overthrown all Marx's ideas, the latter had doffed his hat to it in violation of all logic and been compelled to accept its programme and its aims as his own. And in fact, if an insurrection which had not even been prepared but forced on the workers by a sudden and brutal attack was able to abolish the whole oppressive machinery of the State by means of a few simple decrees, was not that a confirmation of Bakunin's steadfastly maintained standpoint? It was not difficult for those who wanted to believe this to find support for their attitude in the Address, which tended rather to present as already existing something which in reality was no more than a possibility developing from the character of the Commune. In any case, the fact that Bakunin's agitation began to meet with greater approval in 1871 than ever before was due to the powerful impression made by the Paris Commune on the European working class.

The Address concluded with the words : " The Paris of the workers with its Commune will be commemorated for ever as the glorious herald of a new society. Its martyrs are enshrined in the great heart of the working class. Its destroyers have already been pilloried by history, and not all the prayers of their priests and parsons will be able to set them free." The Address immediately created a tremendous sensation, and in a letter to Kugelmann Marx declared : "It has kicked up the devil's own rumpus, and at the moment I have the honour of being the most slandered and most threatened man in London. It is doing me good after twenty long and boring years of idyllic isolation like a frog in a swamp. The government organ—*The Observer*— is even threatening me with prosecution. Let them try it ! I snap my fingers at the *canaille*." Immediately after the first howl of wrath had gone up Marx had proclaimed himself as the author of the Address.

In later years he was reproached, even from social democratic sources, with having endangered the International by burdening it with the responsibility for the Commune, although it had not been the duty of the International to shoulder any part of the responsibility. To defend the Commune against unjust attacks was all very well, but he should have crossed himself in face of its defects and errors. In any case, such opinions were not widely held and the tactic proposed might have been good for a liberal "Statesman", but not for Marx just because he was Marx. It never occurred to him to endanger the future of his cause in the deceptive hope that he could thereby diminish the dangers which threatened it in the immediate present.

4. The International and the Paris Commune

By taking over the heritage of the Commune without previously sorting over the remains, the International faced a world of enemies.

Least important were the slanderous attacks with which it was overwhelmed by the bourgeois press of all countries. On the contrary, as a result of these attacks it won, in a certain sense and to a certain degree, a propaganda weapon because the General Council was able to reply to such attacks openly and thus at least secured a hearing in the English press.

A much greater problem for the International was that presented by the necessity of assisting the numerous fugitive communards who fled to Belgium and to Switzerland, but chiefly to London. Owing to the fact that the state of its finances grew more and more unfavourable the collection of the necessary funds to assist the fugitives met with great difficulties and necessitated great efforts, and for many months it was compelled to devote its chief energies and the greater part of its time to this problem to the detriment of its normal tasks, although the latter became more and more urgent as almost all governments now began to mobilize their forces against the International.

However, even this war of the governments against the International was not its chief trouble. The campaign against the International was carried on with more or less energy in the various continental countries, but the attempts to unite all governments in a joint campaign of repression against the class-conscious proletariat failed for the moment. The first attempt of this nature was made by the French government on the 6th of June 1871 in a circular issued by Jules Favre, but the document was so stupid and mendacious that it made little impression on the other governments, even on Bismarck, who was invariably willing to listen to any reactionary suggestion, particularly when it was directed against the working class, and who had been startled out of his megalomania by the support accorded to the Commune by the German Social Democracy, including both the Lassallean and the Eisenach fractions.

A little later the Spanish government made a second attempt to unite the governments of Europe against the International, this time also by means of a circular, issued to all governments by its Minister for Foreign Affairs. It was not sufficient, this circular declared, that individual governments should take the severe measures necessary against the International and its sections in their own territories. All governments should unite to exterminate the evil. This inducement might have met with greater success but for the fact that the English government immediately scotched it. Lord Granville replied that " in this country " the International had limited its operations chiefly to giving advice in strikes, and had only very limited funds with which to support such actions, whilst the revolutionary plans which formed a part of its programme represented rather the opinions of its foreign members than those of the British workers, whose attention was directed chiefly to wage questions. However, foreigners in England enjoyed the protection of the laws of the country in the same way as British subjects. If they violated these laws by conducting warlike operations against any country with which Great Britain maintained friendly relations they would be punished, but for the present there was no reason for taking any special measures against foreigners on British soil. This reasonable rejection of an unreasonable demand caused Bismarck's semi-official mouthpiece to snarl that any measures

taken against the International would for the most part remain ineffective so long as British territory represented an asylum from which all the other States of Europe could be disturbed with impunity and under the protection of the British law.

Although its enemies did not succeed in organizing a joint crusade on the part of the various governments against the International, the International itself did not succeed in organizing a solid phalanx of resistance to the persecutions suffered by its sections in the various continental countries. This was its chief cause of anxiety, and it was made still more serious by the fact that the International felt the ground trembling under its feet in just those countries whose working classes it had regarded as its firmest bulwarks : England, France and Germany, where large-scale industrial development was furthest progressed and whose workers possessed a more or less limited franchise. The importance of these countries for the International was reflected in the fact that there were twenty Englishmen, fifteen Frenchmen and seven Germans on its General Council as against only two representatives each from Switzerland and Hungary and one representative each from Poland, Belgium, Ireland, Denmark and Italy.

From the very beginning Lassalle had organized his agitation amongst the German workers as a national affair, and this had brought him in bitter reproaches from Marx, but it was soon seen that this fact helped the German workers movement over a crisis which severely shook the socialist movement in all other continental countries. For the moment the war against France had resulted in the temporary standstill of the German working-class movement. The two fractions had enough to occupy them in their own affairs to prevent them bothering much about the International. Although both fractions had declared themselves against the annexation of Alsace-Lorraine and in favour of the Paris Commune, the Eisenach fraction, which alone was recognized by the General Council as a section of the International, had come so much into the foreground that it had been harrassed by the authorities with indictments for high treason and similar disagreeable matters far more than the Lassallean fraction. It was Bebel, who, according to Bismark's own evidence, first awakened the suspicion of the latter by his fiery speech in the Reichstag in which he declared the German Social Democracy in solidarity with the Paris communards, and caused Bismarck to deliver increasingly violent blows against the German working-class movement. However, much more decisive for the attitude of the Eisenach fraction towards the International was the fact that since it had constituted itself as an independent

party on a national basis it had become more and more estranged
from the International.

In France Thiers and Favre had caused the monarchist-
reactionary National Assembly to adopt a draconic exceptional
law against the International and this law completely paralysed
the French working class, which had already been weakened
to the point of utter exhaustion by the fearful blood-letting of the
Versailles massacres. In their fierce desire for revenge these
upholders of law and order even went so far as to demand from
Switzerland, and even from England, the extradition of the
fugitive communards as common criminals, and as far as Switzerland was concerned they came within an ace of being successful.
Under these circumstances the connections of the General Council
in France were completely broken off. In order to secure the
representation of the French workers on its General Council the
International co-opted a number of fugitive communards (partly
men who had already been members of the International and
partly men who had distinguished themselves by their revolutionary energy in the cause of the Commune), its aim being to
honour the Commune. This was a good idea as far as it went,
but it weakened the General Council rather than strengthened
it, for the fugitive communards suffered the inevitable fate of all
emigrants and exhausted their energies in internal struggles.
Marx now had to go through those troubles and difficulties with
the French emigrants which he had experienced with the German
emigrants twenty years previously. He was certainly the last
man to demand any recognition for doing what he, in any case,
considered it his duty to do, but in November 1871 the constant
bickerings of the French fugitives caused him to sigh regretfully :
" And that's my reward for having wasted almost five months
of my time on their behalf and for having vindicated their honour
in the Address ! "

And finally, the International lost the support which it had
previously enjoyed from the English workers. Externally the
breach first appeared when two reputable leaders of the trade-
union movement, Lucraft and Odger, who had been members
of the General Council since its inception, Odger even as President so long as that office had existed, resigned from the council
on account of the Address on the Civil War in France. This
action gave rise to the legend that the trade unions parted
company with the International owing to their moral abhorrence
of the latter's defence of the Commune. The grain of truth which
this legend contains by no means represents the real issue. The
breach was due to much more important and deep-lying reasons.

From the beginning the alliance between the International

and the trade unions was a *mariage de convenance*. Both parties needed each other, but neither of them ever intended to bind itself up with the other for better or for worse and till death, etc. With masterly dexterity Marx had drawn up a joint programme in the Inaugural Address and the Statutes of the International, but although the trade unions were thus able to accept the programme, in practice they never used any more of it than suited their purpose. In his answering despatch to the Spanish government Lord Granville correctly describes the relation between the English trade unions and the International. The aim of the trade unions was to improve working conditions on the basis of capitalist society, and in order to further this aim they did not scorn the political struggle, but in the choice of their allies and their weapons they were guided by no fundamental considerations, so far as such considerations did not apply immediately to their actual aim.

Marx was soon compelled to recognize that this egoistic peculiarity of the trade unions, which was deeply rooted in the history and the character of the English proletariat, could not be broken so easily. The trade unions needed the International in order to carry the Reform Bill, but once this was achieved they began to flirt with the Liberals, for without the assistance of the latter they could not hope to win seats in parliament. Even in 1868 Marx had complained of these " intriguers " and had mentioned Odger, who put up for parliament on several occasions, as one of them. On another occasion Marx justified the presence of a number of the supporters of the Irish sectarian Bronterre O'Brien in the General Council with the following significant words : " Despite their follies these O'Brienites represent a (very often necessary) counter-weight to the trade unionists in the General Council. They are more revolutionary, more definite in their attitude to the land question, less national and not open to corruption in any shape or form ; but for that they would have been turned out long ago." He also opposed the repeated proposal that a special Federal Council should be formed for England, chiefly on the ground, given for instance in the circular of the General Council issued on the 1st of January 1870, that the English lacked revolutionary ardour and the capacity to generalize, so that any such Federal Council would become a tool in the hands of Radical members of parliament.

After the secession of the English working-class leaders Marx accused them bluntly of having sold themselves to the Liberal Ministry. This may have been true of some of them, but it was not true of all, even if one assumes " corruption " to include other forms than that of cash payment. As a trade-union leader

Applegarth enjoyed at least as big a reputation as Odger and Lucraft, and was in fact considered by both Houses of Parliament as the official representative of trade unionism. Immediately after the Basle congress of the International he had been questioned by his parliamentary patrons as to his attitude towards the decisions of the congress in the question of the common ownership of the land, etc., but he had refused to let himself be intimidated by their scarcely veiled threat. In 1870 he was appointed a member of the Royal Commission upon the Contagious Diseases Acts, thus becoming the first worker to be styled by his Sovereign " Our Trusty and Well-beloved ", nevertheless he signed the Address of the General Council on the Civil War in France and remained a member of the council to the end.

The attitude of Applegarth, whose personal character is above reproach and who later refused an appointment on the Board of Trade, indicates clearly the real reasons for the secession of the trade-union leaders. The immediate aim of the trade unions was to secure legal protection for themselves and their funds. This aim appeared to have been achieved when in the spring of 1871 the government brought in a Bill giving every trade union the right to register itself as an approved society, thereby receiving legal protection for its funds providing that its statutes did not conflict with the law. However, what the government gave with one hand it immediately took away with the other, for the Bill contained a lengthy clause which practically abolished the right of combination by confirming all the old elastic terms aimed at preventing strikes by prohibiting " violence ", " threats ", " intimidation ", " molesting ", " obstruction ", etc. It was, in fact, nothing but an exceptional law against the trade unions, and every action taken by them, or by anyone else, with a view to furthering their cause was declared punishable, whilst the same actions when committed by other bodies remained legal. With politeness and restraint the historians of British trade unionism declare : " It seemed of little use to declare the existence of trade societies to be legal if the criminal law was so stretched as to include the ordinary peaceful methods by which these societies attained their ends."[1] For the first time, therefore, the trade unions were legally recognized and afforded protection, but at the same time all the provisions of the laws against trade-union action were expressly confirmed and even intensified.

Naturally, the trade unions and their leaders rejected this Greek gift, but their protests succeeded only in persuading the

---

[1] *The History of Trade Unionism*, by Sidney and Beatrice Webb. London : Longmans, Green & Co., 1894, pp. 263–4.

government to divide its bill into two separate parts : a Bill legalizing the existence of the trade unions and a Criminal Law Amendment Bill embracing all the clauses against trade-union activity. That was of course no real success, but merely a trap into which the trade-union leaders were invited to fall, and into which, in fact, they did fall because their anxiety for their funds was greater than their loyalty to trade-union principles. All of them, and Applegarth was even in the van, registered their organizations under the new law, and in September 1871 the Conference of Amalgamated Trades, the representative body of the " New Unionism ", which had once been the link between the International and the unions, formally dissolved itself, " having discharged the duties for which it was organized ".

Owing to the fact that in their gradual approach towards middle-class respectability the leaders of the trade unions had come to regard strikes as one of the more primitive methods of trade-union activity it was not difficult for them to salve their consciences. As early as 1867 one of them had declared in giving evidence before a Royal Commission that strikes were a sheer waste of money and energies both for the workers and their employers. Therefore in 1871 when a powerful movement in favour of the nine-hour day swept over the country the trade-union leaders did their utmost to hold back the workers, who had not participated in the " statesmanlike " development of their leaders and who were fiercely indignant at the new Criminal Law Amendment Bill against trade-union activities. This movement began on the 1st of April with a strike of the engineering workers in Sunderland, spread rapidly throughout the engineering centres and culminated in the Newcastle strike which lasted five months and ended in a complete victory for the workers. The great engineering union, the Amalgamated Society of Engineers, was definitely opposed to this mass movement on the part of the workers, and only after the strike had been proceeding for four-teen weeks did those strikers who were members of the union receive strike support, which was fixed at five shillings a week. With this and the usual unemployment support they had to carry on their struggle. The movement, which quickly spread to a number of other trades and industries, was led exclusively by the " Nine Hours League ", which had been formed for this purpose and had a very capable leader in John Burnett.

On the other hand, the Nine Hours League received vigorous support from the General Council of the International, which sent its members Cohn and Eccarius to Belgium and Denmark to prevent the agents of the employers recruiting blacklegs there, a task which they both performed with a considerable degree of success. Whilst negotiating with Burnett Marx was unable to suppress the bitter remark that it was a peculiar misfortune that the organized bodies of workers remained aloof from the International until they were in trouble, whereas if they came in good time it would be easier to take effective precautionary measures. For the moment, however, the course of development made it appear as though the International were about to be richly compensated by the masses for what it had lost in their leaders. New sections were formed and the existing sections greatly increased their strength, but at the same time the demand that a special Federal Council should be formed for England was raised with increasing urgency.

Marx then finally made the concession he had refused for so long. With the fall of the Paris Commune the possibility of a new revolution had receded into the background and apparently therefore he no longer attached such importance to the General Council keeping its hand directly on the strongest lever of the revolution. However, his old misgivings soon proved to be justified and with the establishment of the Federal Council the traces of the International began to disappear more rapidly in England than in any other country.

5.　The Bakuninist Opposition

After the fall of the Paris Commune the International had difficulties enough to face in Germany, France and England, but they were nothing compared to the troubles in those countries in which its foothold was weak. The small centre of trouble which had formed in Switzerland even before the Franco-Prussian War now spread to Italy, Spain, Belgium and other countries, and it began to look as though Bakunin's ideas would be victorious over those of the General Council.

Not that this development was due to Bakunin's intrigues as the General Council assumed. It is true that in the beginning of 1871 he interrupted his work on the translation of the first volume of *Capital* in order to devote his attention completely to new political activities, but these latter had nothing to do with the International, and in the end they seriously damaged his own political reputation. It was the notorious Netchayeff affair, and it cannot be disposed of as easily as the enthusiastic admirers of Bakunin would like when they ascribed his errors to " too great trust as a result of too great goodness ".

At the time Netchayeff was a young man in the twenties. He had been born as a serf, but thanks to the patronage of liberal-minded persons he had been able to attend a seminary to be trained as a teacher. He fell in with the Russian students' movement of the day and won a certain position in it, not as the result of his education, which was scanty, or his brain, which was mediocre, but on account of the fierce energy and his boundless hatred of Tsarist oppression. His chief characteristic was his complete freedom from all moral considerations when he thought to further his cause. Personally he asked for nothing, and when it was necessary he did without everything, but when he thought he was acting in a revolutionary fashion he was prepared to stop at nothing, no matter how reprehensible it might be.

He first appeared in Geneva in the spring of 1869 demanding double admiration as a prisoner of State escaped from the fortress of St. Peter-Paul and as a delegate from an all-powerful committee which was supposed to be secretly preparing the revolution throughout Russia. Both statements were inventions ; Netchayeff had never been in St. Peter-Paul and no such committee existed. After the arrest of a number of his immediate companions he had left Russia in order, as he declared, to influence the older emigrants to use their names and their writings to stir up the enthusiasm of the Russian youth. As far as Bakunin was concerned he succeeded in an almost incredible fashion. Bakunin was deeply impressed by " the young savage ", " the young tiger " (as he used to call Netchayeff), as the representative of a new generation whose revolutionary energy would overthrow Tsarist Russia. Bakunin believed so firmly in the " committee " that he placed himself unconditionally at its orders, which were given to him through Netchayeff, and immediately declared himself ready to publish a number of extreme revolutionary writings together with the latter and to send them over the Russian frontier.

There is no doubt about Bakunin's responsibility for this literature, and it is of no decisive importance whether he or Netchayeff was directly responsible for a number of its worst examples. And further, Bakunin's authorship has never been denied in connection with the appeal issued to the officers of the Tsarist army calling on them to place themselves at the disposal of the " committee " as unconditionally as Bakunin had done, or with the leaflet which idealized banditry in Russia, or with the so-called revolutionary catechism in which Bakunin's love of grisly ideas and fierce words was given full rein to the point of surfeit. On the other hand, it has never been proved that

Bakunin had any part in Netchayeff's reckless actions. In fact, he was himself one of their victims, and it was his realization of them, all too late, that caused him to show " the young tiger " the door.

Both Bakunin and Netchayeff were accused by the General Council of the International of having sent innocent persons to their doom in Russia by sending them letters, material or telegrams in such a form as inevitably to draw down on them the attention of the Russian police, although Bakunin's reputation might reasonably have been expected to protect him from such accusations. After his exposure Netchayeff admitted the real state of affairs. He acknowledged openly and with the utmost impudence that it was his custom to compromise deliberately all those who were not completely in agreement with him in order either to destroy them or to draw them into the movement completely. In accordance with the same reprehensible principles he would persuade people to sign compromising declarations in a moment of excitement, or he would steal compromising letters in order afterwards to be able to exercise extortionate pressure on their authors.

When Netchayeff returned to Russia in the autumn of 1869 Bakunin had not yet learnt of these methods, and Netchayeff was provided with a written authorization from Bakunin which declared that he was the " accredited representative ", naturally not of the International and not even of the Alliance of Socialist Democracy, but of a European Revolutionary Alliance which Bakunin's inventive genius had founded as a sort of branch of the Alliance for Russian affairs. This organization probably existed only on paper, but in any case Bakunin's name was enough to secure a certain support from amongst the students for Netchayeff's agitation. His chief method of obtaining influence was still the myth of the " committee ", and when one of his newly won supporters, the student Ivanov, began to doubt the existence of this secret authority, he disposed of the inconvenient sceptic by assassination. The finding of Ivanov's body led to numerous arrests, but Netchayeff succeeded in slipping over the frontier.

At the beginning of January 1870 he again appeared in Geneva and the old game started anew. Bakunin came forward as his fiery defender and declared that the murder of Ivanov was a political and not a common crime and that the Swiss government should therefore not grant the request of the Tsarist government for his extradition. For the moment Netchayeff kept so closely to hiding that the Swiss police could not find him, but he played his protector a nasty trick. He persuaded him to abandon the translation of the first volume of *Capital* in order to devote himself completely to revolutionary propaganda and promised to come to an agreement with the publisher in the question of the advance which had already been paid. Bakunin, who was living in the narrowest of straits at the time, could only assume that this promise meant that either Netchayeff or the mysterious " committee " would refund the 300 roubles advance to the publisher. However, Netchayeff sent an " official " letter on a piece of notepaper bearing the name of the " committee " and decorated with an axe, a dagger and a revolver, not to the publisher but to Liubavin, who had acted as intermediary between Bakunin and the publisher. Liubavin was forbidden to demand the repayment of the advance from Bakunin on pain of death. An insulting letter from Liubavin was the first intimation Bakunin had of the business. He immediately sent Liubavin a new acknowledgment of the debt and repeated his promise to pay it back as soon as his means permitted, and at last he broke off his relations with Netchayeff, about whom he had in the meantime discovered still worse things, such as the plot to hold up and rob the Simplon post.

The incredible, and for a political leader unpardonable, gullibility which Bakunin displayed in this, the most adventurous episode of his life had very unpleasant results for him. Marx heard about the affair in July 1870, and this time from an irreproachable source, namely the thoroughly reliable Lopatin, who during his stay in Geneva in May had vainly tried to convince Bakunin that no such " committee " existed in Russia, that Netchayeff had never been a prisoner in St. Peter-Paul, and that the throttling of Ivanov had been an utterly senseless murder. If anyone was in a position to know the truth it was Lopatin, and it was only natural that his information confirmed the unfavourable opinion Marx now had of Bakunin. After the Russian government had discovered the truth about Netchayeff's activities as a result of the numerous arrests which were made in connection with the murder of Ivanov it exploited the favourable opportunity to the full, and in order to ridicule and expose the Russian revolutionaries in the eyes of the world it arranged for the first time a political trial in public and before a jury. The proceedings in the so-called Netchayeff process opened in St. Petersburg in July 1871. There were over eighty accused, most of them students, and the majority of them were sentenced to long terms of imprisonment or of forced labour in the Siberian mines.

Netchayeff himself was still at liberty, and he remained variously in Switzerland, London and Paris, where he went through the siege and the Commune. He fell into the hands of the police only in the autumn of 1872 as the victim of a spy. Bakunin and his friends issued a leaflet on his behalf, published by Schabelitz in Zürich, opposing his extradition as a common criminal. This action does Bakunin no dishonour, and this is also true of a letter he wrote to Ogarev, a man who had also been completely deceived by Netchayeff, so much so in fact that he had handed over either wholly or in part the Batmetiev funds which he had administered after the death of Herzen : " Something within me tells me that this time Netchayeff, who is utterly lost and certainly knows it, will retrieve all his old energy and steadfastness from the depths of his character, which may be confused and vitiated but is not low. He will go under as a hero and this time he will betray no one and nothing ". In ten long years of suffering in a Tsarist prison up to the day of his death Netchayeff justified these expectations. He did everything he could to repair his earlier errors and maintained an iron energy which even made his warders give way to him.

The Franco-Prussian War broke out just as Bakunin had parted company with him. It immediately gave Bakunin's ideas another direction. The old revolutionary reckoned that the invasion of France by German troops would give the signal for the social revolution in France. The French workers could not remain inactive in the face of an aristocratic, monarchist and military invasion unless they wished to betray not only their own cause but the cause of socialism. A victory for Germany would be a victory for European reaction. Bakunin was right in declaring that a revolution at home need not paralyse the resistance of the French people to the foreign enemy, and he appealed to French history in particular to prove his point, but his proposals to persuade the Bonapartist and reactionary peasant class into joint revolutionary action with the urban workers were thoroughly fantastic : one must not approach the peasants with any decrees or communist proposals or organizational forms, as that would cause them to revolt against the towns, instead one should draw the revolutionary spirit from out of the depths of their souls—and other similarly fantastic phrases.

After the fall of the Second Empire Guillaume published an appeal in the *Solidarité* calling for the formation of armed bands of volunteers to hurry to the assistance of the French Republic. It was a downright act of folly, particularly coming from a man who had opposed with nothing short of fanaticism any participation of the International in politics, and it produced no result but laughter. However, Bakunin's attempt to proclaim a revolutionary commune in Lyon on the 28th of September must not be placed in the same category. Bakunin had been called to Lyon by the revolutionary elements there. The Town Hall had been occupied, the "administrative and governmental machinery of the State" abolished and the "Revolutionary Federation of the Commune" proclaimed in its place, when the treachery of General Cluseret and the cowardice of a number of other persons gave the National Guard an easy victory. Bakunin had vainly urged that energetic measures should be taken and that, above all, the representatives of the government should be arrested. He was taken prisoner himself, but released almost immediately by a detachment of volunteers. He remained a few weeks in Marseilles in the hope that the movement would revive, but when this hope proved baseless he returned at the end of October to Locarno.

The ridiculing of this unsuccessful attempt might reasonably have been left to the reaction, and an opponent of Bakunin whose opposition to anarchism did not rob him of all capacity to form an objective judgment wrote : "Unfortunately mocking voices have been raised even in the social democratic press, although Bakunin's attempt certainly does not deserve this. Naturally, those who do not share the anarchist opinions of Bakunin and his followers must adopt a critical attitude towards his baseless hopes, but apart from that, his action in Lyon was a courageous attempt to awaken the sleeping energies of the French proletariat and to direct them simultaneously against the foreign enemy and the capitalist system. Later the Paris Commune attempted something of the sort also and was warmly praised by Marx." That is certainly a more objective and reasonable attitude than that of the Leipzig *Volksstaat*, which, adopting a well-worn tactic, declared that the proclamation issued by Bakunin in Lyon could not have been better suited to Bismarck if it had been drawn up in the latter's own press bureau.

The failure of the movement in Lyon deeply depressed Bakunin. Believing the revolution to be on the threshold he saw it disappear into the distant future, particularly after the overthrow of the Paris Commune, which had filled him with new hope for the moment. His hatred against the revolutionary propaganda carried on by Marx increased because he thought it chiefly responsible for the indecisive attitude of the proletariat. In addition his personal situation was very pressing. He received no assistance from his brothers and there were days when he had not even five centimes in his pocket to purchase his usual cup of tea. His wife was afraid that he would lose his energy and go to seed. However, he decided to set down his opinions on the development of humanity, philosophy, religion, the State and anarchy in a work which was to be written piecemeal in his free moments and to represent his political testament.

This work was never concluded. His unruly spirit was not permitted much peace. Utin had continued his incitement in Geneva, and in August 1870 he had secured the expulsion of Bakunin and a number of his friends from the central section in Geneva on the ground that they were members of the Alliance section. Utin had then spread the lie that the Alliance had in fact never been admitted into the International by the General Council, and that the documents in the possession of the Alliance bearing the signatures of Jung and Eccarius were forgeries. In the meantime, however, Robin had emigrated to London and had been made a member of the General Council despite the fact that he had attacked it so vigorously in *L'Égalité*. With this action the General Council gave a proof of its objectivity, for Robin had never ceased to be a sworn supporter of the Alliance. On the 14th of March 1871 he had proposed that the International should call a private conference to settle the dispute in Geneva. On the eve of the Paris Commune the General Council had thought it desirable to reject this proposal, but on the 25th of July it decided to call a conference on the Geneva dispute for the following September. In the same session it confirmed, at the instance of Robin, the authenticity of the documents signed by Jung and Eccarius informing the Alliance of its admission to the International.

This letter had hardly arrived in Geneva when the Alliance section voluntarily dissolved on the 6th of August and informed the General Council of this step immediately. The idea was to create a good impression ; after the section had been vindicated by the General Council against the lies of Utin, it sacrificed itself in the interests of peace and reconciliation. As a matter of fact, however, as Guillaume later admitted, other motives had been decisive. The Alliance section had sunk into complete un-importance and appeared, particularly to the Commune fugitives in Geneva, as nothing but the dead remnant of personal squabbles. Now Guillaume regarded these fugitives as suitable elements for the conduct of the struggle against the Federal Council in Geneva on a broader basis. Therefore the Alliance section was dissolved and its remnants united a few weeks later together with the Communards in a new " Section of Revolutionary Socialist Propaganda and Action ", which declared itself in agreement with the general principles of the International, but reserved itself the right to make full use of the freedom which the statutes and the congresses of the International afforded.

In the beginning Bakunin had nothing to do with this at all. It is significant of his alleged omnipotence as the leader of the Alliance that its section in Geneva had not even bothered to ask him, although he was near at hand in Locarno, before it dissolved itself. However, it was not wounded sensibility, but because he felt that, under the circumstances, the dissolution of the section was a cowardly and underhand trick which caused him to protest sharply : " Let us not be cowards under the pretext of saving the unity of the International." At the same time he began to work on a detailed description of the Geneva confusion in order to demonstrate the principles which in his opinion were at stake in the dispute, and this was to serve as a guide to his supporters at the London conference.

Considerable fragments of this work are still extant and they differ very favourably from the Russian leaflets drawn up by him together with Netchayeff a year before. With the exception of one or two forceful expressions they are written calmly and objectively, and no matter what attitude one may take up to Bakunin's particular ideas, they certainly do prove convincingly that the cause of the confusion in Geneva was more deeply rooted than in the shifting sands of personal squabbles, and that as far as the latter played a rôle at all the greater part of the responsibility rested on the shoulders of Utin and his friends.

Bakunin never for one moment denied the fundamental differences between him and Marx on the question of the latter's " State communism ", and he did not handle his opponents with kid gloves. However, Bakunin did not present Marx as a worthless fellow pursuing nothing but his own reprehensible ends. He described the development of the International from out of the masses of the people with the assistance of capable men devoted to the cause of the people and added : " We seize this opportunity of paying our respects to the famous leaders of the German Communist Party, citizens Marx and Engels in particular, and also citizen Ph. Becker (our former friend and now our irreconcilable enemy), who, as far as it is given to individuals to create, are the real creators of the International. We acknowledge their services all the more readily because soon we shall be compelled to fight against them. Our respect for them is deep and wholehearted, but it does not go so far as to idolize them, and we shall never consent to play the rôle of their slaves. And although we do full justice to the tremendous service which they have done and are still doing the cause of the International, nevertheless we shall fight to the hilt against their false authoritarian theories, against their dictatorial presumption and against their methods of underground intrigues and vainglorious machinations, their introduction of mean personalities, their foul insults and infamous slanders, methods which characterize the political struggles of almost all Germans and which they have unfortunately introduced into the International." That was certainly frank enough, but Bakunin never let himself be provoked into denying the immortal services which Marx had rendered to the working-class movement as the founder and leader of the International.

However, Bakunin did not finish this work either. He was engaged on it when Mazzini published violent attacks on the Commune and on the International in a weekly publication which he issued in Lugano. Bakunin immediately came to grips with him in " The Answer of an Internationalist to Mazzini ", and when Mazzini and his supporters took up the gauntlet this was followed by other leaflets in the same tone. After all his recent failures Bakunin now enjoyed complete success : the International, which up to then had found only a very narrow foothold in Italy, began to gain ground rapidly. This success was achieved by Bakunin not as the result of his " intrigues ", but as the result of the eloquent words with which he released the tension which the Paris Commune had caused amongst the Italian youth.

Large-scale industry was still undeveloped in Italy and the developing proletariat was awakening to class-consciousness only very slowly, and it possessed no legal weapons either of offence or defence. On the other hand, the struggles of half a century for national unity had developed and maintained a revolutionary tradition amongst the bourgeois classes. Innumerable insurrections and conspiracies had tried to win national unity until finally it had been obtained in a form which necessarily represented a great disappointment to all revolutionary elements. Under the protection first of all of French and then of German arms the most reactionary State in the country had founded an Italian monarchy. The heroic struggles of the Paris Commune roused the revolutionary youth of Italy from the depression into which it had fallen. On the edge of the grave Mazzini turned away from the new light which inflamed his old hatred of socialism, but Garibaldi, who was a national hero to a far greater extent, honestly welcomed the " rising sun of the future " in the International.

Bakunin knew perfectly well from what sections of the population his supporters flocked, and in April 1872 he wrote : " What Italy has lacked up to the moment was not the correct instinct, but the organization and the idea. Both are now developing so rapidly that together with Spain Italy is perhaps at this moment the most revolutionary country. Something exists in Italy which is lacking in other countries : an ardent, energetic youth, without hope of a career, work or a solution ; a youth which despite its bourgeois origin is not morally and intellectually exhausted like the bourgeois youth in other countries. To-day it is plunging head first into revolutionary socialism with our whole programme, the programme of the Alliance." These lines were written by Bakunin to a Spanish supporter and were intended as encouragement to further action. However, it was not an amiable illusion, but an undeniable fact when Bakunin estimated his successes in Spain, where he exercised influence only through friends and not by his presence, just as high, if not higher, than his successes in Italy.

In Spain also industrial development was still very backward and where any proletariat in the modern sense existed it was bound hand and foot, and without any legal rights so that all that remained to it in its desperation was the weapon of armed insurrection. The great Spanish manufacturing town Barcelona has more barricade struggles in its history than any other town in the world. In addition, long years of civil war had disturbed the country, and, after having driven out the Bourbon dynasty in the autumn of 1868, all revolutionary elements had been greatly disappointed to find themselves under the (very shaky) dominance of a foreign King. In Spain also the sparks flung into the air from the revolutionary conflagration in Paris fell on heaped-up combustible material. The situation in Belgium was somewhat different from the situation in Italy and Spain because in Belgium there was already a proletarian mass movement in being, although it was limited almost exclusively to the Walloon districts. The extremely revolutionary miners of the Borinage formed the backbone of this movement, and any idea of improving their class situation by legal means had been crushed in its infancy by the blood-baths in which their strikes were drowned year after year. Their leaders were Proudhonists and therefore inclined towards the opinions of Bakunin.

If one follows the development of the Bakuninist opposition in the International after the fall of the Paris Commune one finds that it came forward under Bakunin's name because it hoped to solve with his ideas the social antagonisms and tensions from which it really sprang.

6. The Second Conference in London

The conference which the General Council decided to call for September in London was intended to take the place of the annual congress which was about to fall due.

The congress in Basle in 1869 had decided that the next congress should take place in Paris, but the campaign of incitement which Ollivier organized against the French sections of the International to celebrate the plebiscite caused the General Council to use its authority to alter the venue of the congress, and in July 1870 it decided that the congress should be held in Mayence. At the same time the General Council proposed to the National Federations that its seat should be moved from London to some other place, but this proposal was unanimously rejected. The outbreak of the Franco-Prussian War made it impossible to hold the congress in Mayence and the Federations then instructed the General Council to convene the congress at its own discretion and in accordance with the circumstances of the moment.

The development of events made it appear undesirable to call the congress for the autumn of 1871. The pressure exerted on the members of the International in the various countries made it appear likely that they would not be able to send delegates to the congress as freely as was desirable, and that those few members who were able to attend the congress would be exposed to the visitations of their governments more than ever upon their return. The International was very unwilling to do anything which might increase the number of victims because it already had more than enough to do to assist its persecuted members, and this task made the greatest demands on its energies and its resources.

The General Council therefore decided that for the moment it would be better to call a private conference in London, similar to the one which had taken place in 1865, rather than a public congress. The poor attendance at this conference completely confirmed the misgivings of the General Council. The conference took place from the 17th to the 23rd of September and only 23 delegates were present, including six from Belgium, two from Switzerland and one from Spain. Thirteen members of the General Council were also present, but six of them had only advisory votes. Amongst the extensive and numerous decisions of the conference were a number dealing with working-class statistics, the international relations of the trade unions, and agriculture, which under the existing circumstances had only an academic significance. The chief tasks of the conference were to defend the International against the furious attacks of the external enemy and to consolidate it against the elements which threatened to undermine it from within, tasks which, on the whole, coincided.

The most important decision of the conference referred to the political activity of the International. It appealed first of all to the *Inaugural Address*, the statutes, the decision of the Lausanne congress and other official announcements of the International declaring the political emancipation of the working class to be indissolubly bound up with its social emancipation, and then pointed out that the International was faced with a ruthless reaction which shamelessly suppressed every effort of the working class towards its emancipation and sought by brute force to perpetuate class differentiation indefinitely and the rule of the possessing classes based upon it. It declared that the working class could resist this violence offered to it by the ruling classes only by acting as a class, by constituting itself into a special political party against all the old party organizations of the possessing classes, that this constitution of the working class as a special political party was indispensable for the victory of the social revolution and its final aim, the abolition of all classes, and finally, that the unification of isolated forces which the working-class had already carried out up to a point by means of its economic forces must also be used as a weapon in the struggle against the political power of the exploiters. For all these reasons the conference reminded all members of the International that the economic movement and the political movement of the fighting working class were indissolubly connected.

In organizational matters the conference requested the General Council to limit the number of members which it co-opted and at the same time not to favour one nationality more than another. The title General Council was to apply exclusively to the General Council, the Federal Councils were to take their names according to the countries they represented and the local sections were to be known according to the name of their particular locality. The conference prohibited the use of any sectarian names such as Positivists, Mutualists, Collectivists and Communists. Every member of the International would continue, as previously decided, to pay one penny per year towards the support of the General Council.

For France the conference recommended vigorous agitation in the factories and the distribution of leaflets ; for England the formation of a special Federal Council to be confirmed by the General Council as soon as it had been recognized by the branches in the provinces and by the trade unions. The conference declared that the German workers had fulfilled their proletarian duty during the Franco-Prussian War, and it rejected all responsibility for the so-called Netchayeff conspiracy. At the same time it instructed Utin to prepare a *résumé* of the Netchayeff process from Russian sources and to publish it in *L'Égalité*, but to present it for the approval of the General Council before publication.

The conference declared that the question of the Alliance was settled now that the Geneva section had voluntarily dissolved itself, and the adoption of sectarian names, indicating a special mission apart from the general aims of the International, had been prohibited. With regard to the Jura sections the conference confirmed the decision of the General Council of the 29th of June 1870 recognizing the Federal Council in Geneva as the only representative body for the Neo-Latin Swiss members, but at the same time it appealed to the spirit of unity and solidarity which must inspire the workers more than ever now that the International was being persecuted from all sides. It therefore advised the workers of the Jura sections to affiliate once again to the Federal Council in Geneva and suggested that if they found this impossible they should call themselves the Jura Federation. The conference also gave the General Council authority to disavow all alleged organs of the International which, like the *Progrès* and the *Solidarité* in the Jura, discussed internal questions of the International before the bourgeois public.

Finally the conference left it to the discretion of the General Council to decide the time and place of the next congress or to replace–it by a further conference.

On the whole it cannot be denied that the decisions of the conference were guided by a spirit of objective moderation. The solution it offered the Jura sections, namely to call themselves the Jura Federation, had already been considered by the sections themselves. Only the decisions with regard to the Netchayeff affair contained a personal note of hostility which could not be justified by objective considerations. Naturally, the bourgeois press exploited the revelations in the Netchayeff affair against the International, but this represented no more than the usual slanders which were flung at the International day in and day out, and there was no particular necessity to refute them. In similar cases the International had contented itself with kicking the rubbish contemptuously into the gutter, but if it wished to make an exception in the Netchayeff case it should not have chosen a hateful intriguer like Utin as its representative, a man from whom Bakunin might expect just about as much regard for truth as from the bourgeois press.

Utin began the task entrusted to him with one of his usual

blood-and-thunder stories. In Zürich, where he intended to carry out his task and where according to his own statement his only enemies were a few Slav supporters of the Alliance under Bakunin's orders, eight Slavs allegedly attacked him one fine day in a quiet place near a canal. They beat him, flung him to the ground and would have finished him off completely and flung his body into the water, but for the fact that four German students happened to come along and save his precious life, thus making possible his future services to the Tsar.

With this one exception, the decisions of the conference undoubtedly offered the basis for an agreement, all the more so as the whole working-class movement was surrounded by enemies and internal agreement was absolutely necessary. On the 20th of October the new Section for Revolutionary Socialist Propaganda and Action, which had been formed in Geneva from amongst the remnants of the Alliance and a number of fugitive Communards, approached the General Council with a request for affiliation. After the General Council had consulted the Federal Council in Geneva the request was rejected whereupon *La Révolution Sociale*, which had taken the place of the *Solidarité*, began a vigorous attack on the " German Committee led by a brain *à la Bismarck* ", this being in the opinion of the editors of *La Révolution Sociale* a correct description of the General Council of the International. However, this slogan quickly found an echo so that Marx wrote to an American friend : " It refers to the unpardonable fact that I was born a German and that I do in fact exercise a decisive intellectual influence on the General Council. *Nota bene :* the German element in the General Council is numerically two-thirds weaker than the English and the French. The crime is therefore that the English and French elements are dominated (!) in matters of theory by the German element and find this dominance, i.e. German science, useful and even indispensable."

The Jura sections made their general attack at a congress which they held on the 12th of November in Sonvillier, although only 9 out of 22 sections were represented by 16 delegates, and most of this minority suffered from galloping consumption. However, to make up for this they made more noise than ever. They felt deeply insulted at the fact that the London conference had forced a name on them which they had themselves already considered, but nevertheless they decided to submit and call themselves the Jura Federation in future, whilst revenging themselves by declaring the Neo-Latin Federation to be dissolved, a decision which of course was without any practical significance. However, the chief achievement of the congress was the drafting and despatch of a circular to all the Federations of the International attacking the validity of the London conference and appealing from its decisions to a general congress to be called as quickly as possible.

This circular, which was drawn up by Guillaume, proceeded from the assumption that the International was on a fatal and downward path. Originally it had been formed as " a tremendous protest against any kind of authority ", and in the statutes each section and each group of sections had been guaranteed complete independence, whilst the General Council as an executive group had been given definitely limited powers. Gradually, however, the members had come to place a blind confidence in the General Council and this had led in Basle to the abdication of the congress itself as a result of the fact that the General Council had been given authority to accept, reject or dissolve sections pending the decisions of the next congress. The author of the circular made no reference to the fact that this decision had been adopted after Bakunin had spoken vigorously in its favour, and with Guillaume's own approval.

The General Council, continued the circular, which had consisted of the same men and sat in the same place for five years, now regarded itself as the " legitimate head " of the International. As in its own eyes it was a sort of government it naturally regarded its own peculiar ideas as the official theory of the International and the only one permissible. The differing opinions which arose in other groups were regarded by the General Council as heresy pure and simple. Thus an orthodoxy had gradually developed in the International with its seat in London and its representatives in the members of the General Council. It was not necessary to complain of their intentions because they were acting according to the opinions of their own particular school, but one must fight against them vigorously because their omnipotence necessarily had a corrupting effect. It was quite impossible that a man who held such power over his equals could remain a moral character.

The London conference had continued the work of the Basle congress and taken decisions which were intended to transform the International from a free association of independent sections into an authoritarian and hierarchical organization in the hands of the General Council. And to crown it all the conference had decided that the General Council should have power to determine the time and place of the next congress, or of a conference to replace it. Thus it was being left to the arbitrary discretion of the General Council to replace the general congresses, the great open sessions of the International, by secret conferences. There-

fore it had become necessary to limit the powers of the General
Council to the fulfilment of its original mission, namely that of a
simple bureau for correspondence and the collection of statistics,
and to obtain by the free association of independent groups that
unity which the General Council wished to establish by means
of dictatorship and centralization. In this respect, however, the
International must be the precursor of the future society.

Despite the gloomy colours in which it painted the situation,
or perhaps just because of them, this circular of the Jura sections
did not achieve its real aim. Even in Belgium, Italy and Spain
its demand for the calling of a congress as quickly as possible
met with no support. In Spain the sharp attacks on the General
Council gave rise to the suspicion that jealousy between Marx
and Bakunin was behind it all. In Italy the members felt no
more inclined to let themselves be ordered about by the Jura
than by London. Only in Belgium was a decision adopted for
an alteration of the statutes of the International, in the sense that
the latter should declare itself expressly an association of completely independent federations and its General Council as " a
Centre for Correspondence and Information ".

To make up for this lack of appreciation, however, the
circular of Sonvillier was welcomed enthusiastically by the
bourgeois press, which pounced on it as a rare titbit. All the
lies which it had spread, particularly since the fall of the Paris
Commune, about the sinister power of the General Council were
now confirmed from within the ranks of the International. The
Bulletin Jurassien, which in the meantime had taken the place of the
short-lived *Révolution Sociale*, had at least the pleasure of printing
enthusiastic articles of approval from the bourgeois newspapers.

The noisy echo of the Sonvillier circular caused the General
Council to issue an answer to it, also in the form of a circular,
entitled : *Les prétendues Scissions dans l'Internationale.*[1]

7. The Disintegration of the International

As far as the circular of the General Council dealt with the
accusations made in Sonvillier and other places on account of
alleged violations or even falsification of the statutes, fanatical
intolerance and similar accusations, it conducted a thoroughly
victorious polemic and one can only regret that for the greater
part it was wasted on quite unimportant matters.

[1] The Alleged Disruption in the International.

To-day it is necessary to overcome a good deal of reluctance in order to bother one's head at all about such insignificant affairs. For instance, when the International was founded its Paris members had omitted a phrase from its statutes in order to avoid trouble with the Bonapartist police. One passage of the statutes read that all political movements of the working class must subordinate themselves as a means to securing the economic emancipation of the working class. The expression " as a means " had been left out in the French text. The situation was perfectly clear, but again and again the lie was spread to the point of surfeit that the General Council had afterwards interpolated the expression " as a means ". And when the London conference acknowledged that the German workers had done their proletarian duty during the Franco-Prussian War this was used as an excuse for the accusation of " Pan-Germanism ", which was alleged to dominate the General Council.

The circular tore these ridiculous charges to pieces, and when one considers that they were brought forward in order to undermine the centralization of the International, although the maintenance and consolidation of this centralization was the only possibility of saving the tottering organization from succumbing to the attacks of the reaction, it is easy to understand the bitterness of the concluding passages of the circular which accuse the Alliance of playing into the hands of the international police. " It proclaims anarchy in the ranks of the proletariat as the infallible means of breaking the powerful concentration of political and social forces in the hands of the exploiters. Under this pretext and at a moment when the old world is seeking to destroy the International it demands that the latter should replace its organization by anarchy." The more the International was attacked by its external enemies, the more frivolous appeared the attacks made on it from within, particularly when those attacks were so baseless.

However, the clarity with which the General Council realized this side of the question was set off by its failure to see clearly the other side of the question. As its title indicated, the circular was prepared to admit no more than " alleged disruption " in the International. It put down the whole conflict, as Marx had already done in his Confidential Communication, to the machinations of " certain intriguers ", and in particular Bakunin. It brought forward the old accusations against him in connection with " the equalization of the classes " and in connection with the Basle congress, etc., and accused him of having been responsible together with Netchayeff for betraying innocent people to the Russian police. It also devoted a special passage to the fact that two of his supporters had turned out to be Bonapartist police spies, a fact which was certainly extremely unpleasant for Bakunin, but no more compromising for him than it was for the General Council when, a few months later, it suffered the same misfortune with two of its own supporters. The circular also accused " young Guillaume " of having denounced " the factory workers " of Geneva as hateful " bourgeois ", without taking the least notice of the fact that amongst the *fabrique* in Geneva there was a section of highly paid workers in the luxury trades which had concluded more or less deplorable election compromises with the bourgeois parties.

However, by far the weakest point in the circular was its defence of the General Council against the accusation of " orthodoxy ". It appealed to the fact that the London conference had prohibited the adoption of sectarian names by any of the sections. That was certainly justifiable in view of the fact that the International was a highly diverse conglomeration of trade-union organizations, co-operatives, and educational and propaganda associations, but the interpretation the circular of the General Council placed upon this decision was highly contestable.

The circular declares : " The first stage in the struggle of the proletariat against the bourgeoisie is characterized by the development of sects. These sects have a justifiable existence at a time when the proletariat is not sufficiently developed to act as a class. Individual thinkers begin to criticize social contradictions and seek to overcome them by fantastic solutions which the masses of the workers are expected to accept, spread and carry out. It lies in the nature of the sects which form around such pioneers that they are exclusive and that they hold themselves aloof from all practical activities, from politics, strikes, trade unions, in a word from every form of mass movement. The masses of the workers remain indifferent, or even hostile to their propaganda. The workers of Paris and Lyon wanted no more to do with the St. Simonists, the Fourierists and the Icarians, than the English Chartists and trade unionists with the Owenites. Originally one of the levers of the working-class movement, they become a hindrance and reactionary immediately the movement overtakes them. Examples of this are the sects in France and England, and later on the Lassalleans in Germany, who, after having hampered the organization of the proletariat for years, have finally become simply tools in the hands of the police." And in another passage the circular refers to the Lassalleans as " Bismarck socialists " who wear the white blouse of the Prusso-German Empire outside their police organ, *Der Neue Sozial-demokrat*.

There is no express proof that Marx drew up this circular. To judge by content and style Engels may have had a big hand in it, but the passages on the rôle of sectarianism are certainly from Marx and the same ideas can be found in his contemporary correspondence with party friends, having been developed for the first time in his polemic against Proudhon. On the whole the historic significance of socialist sectarianism is aptly characterized, but Marx made a mistake when he tarred the Bakuninists, not to speak of the Lassalleans, with the same brush as the Fourierists and the Owenites.

One can judge as contemptuously of anarchism as one likes and regard it simply as a disease of the working-class movement wherever it shows itself, but it is impossible—and certainly to-day with the experiences of half a century behind us—to imagine that this disease was communicated from outside. On the contrary, it is obvious that it is a disease to which the working class shows a natural disposition and which develops in favourable, or rather unfavourable circumstances. It is difficult to understand such an error even for 1872. Bakunin was the last man to come forward with a complete and stereotyped system, and expect the workers to accept it and put it into operation without demur. Marx himself never tired of repeating that Bakunin was a cipher in theoretical matters and only in his element when intriguing, and that his programme was a hodge-podge of superficial ideas collected right and left.

The decisive characteristic of all sectarianism is its hostility to all forms of the proletarian mass movement, hostile both in the sense that sectarianism has no use for such a movement and such a movement has no use for sectarianism. Even if it were true that Bakunin wished to obtain control of the International merely in order to serve his own ends, he would even then have proved that as a revolutionary he reckoned with the masses. Although his struggle against Marx developed with extraordinary bitterness he always, practically to the end, counted it Marx's immortal service that in the International he had created the framework for a proletarian mass movement. The differences between the two referred to the tactics which this mass movement must adopt in order to achieve its aim. No matter how wrong Bakunin's views may have been, they certainly had nothing in common with sectarianism.

And then the Lassalleans! In 1872 they were certainly not up to the full level of socialist principles, but they were superior to every other contemporary working-class party in Europe both with regard to theoretical insight and organizational strength, not excepting the Eisenach fraction, whose chief intellectual resources were still the popular writings of Lassalle. Lassalle built up his agitation on the broad basis of the proletarian class-struggle, thereby excluding any possibility of sectarianism. His successor Schweitzer was so thoroughly convinced of the indissolubility of the political and the social struggle of the proletariat that he earned the reproach of " parliamentarism " from Liebknecht. It is true that Schweitzer ignored the warnings of Marx in the trade-union question, to his own misfortune, but when the circular of the General Council was written he had been out of the movement for years, whilst the Lassalleans had already begun to make good their errors in this respect—for instance, in the strikes of the building workers in Berlin. They had overcome the short interruption of their agitation caused by the war, and the workers began to stream into their ranks in increasing numbers.

It is not necessary to stress particularly the attacks made by the circular on the Lassalleans, for Marx harboured an invincible dislike for Lassalle and everything Lassallean, but the connection in which these attacks were made gave them a particular significance. They threw a clear light on the real cause for the dissolution of the International, on the indissoluble contradiction which had developed in the great association after the fall of the Paris Commune. After the fall of the Commune the whole reactionary world mobilized its forces against the International, and the only way in which the latter could hope to defend itself was by centralizing its forces still more strongly. However, the fall of the Commune had proved the necessity of the political struggle, and this struggle was impossible without loosening international ties, for it could be carried on only within national frontiers.

In the last resort the demand for political abstinence, no matter how much it may have been exaggerated, arose out of a justifiable mistrust of the traps of bourgeois parliamentarism, a mistrust which was expressed in its sharpest form in Liebknecht's famous speech in 1869. In the same way the objection to the dictatorship of the General Council which developed in almost all countries after the fall of the Paris Commune arose in the last resort, apart from all exaggerations, from the more or less clear perception that a national working-class party must be guided first of all by the conditions of its existence within the nation of which it formed a part, that it could no more jump over these conditions than a man can jump over his own shadow and that, in other words, it was not possible to lead the movement from abroad. Although Marx had already pointed out in the statutes of the International that the political and social struggles of the

working-class were indissolubly connected, in practice he proceeded always from those social demands of the workers which
were common to all countries with a capitalist mode of production, and he touched on political questions only when they
resulted from such social demands—for instance, the demand for
the legal shortening of the working day. Political questions in
the actual and direct sense of the word—for instance, questions
relating to the constitution of the State, and therefore different
in every country—he preferred to leave until such time as the proletariat had been educated to greater clarity by the International.
For instance, he reproached Lassalle severely because the latter
adapted his agitation to one particular country.

It has been suggested that Marx would have maintained
this reserve much longer, but for the fact that the fall of the
Paris Commune and the agitation of Bakunin forced the political
question on him. That is easily possible and even probable,
but in accordance with his character Marx took up the struggle
immediately he was challenged, although he failed to recognize
that the problem with which he was faced could not be solved
within the framework of the statutes of the International, and
that the more the International attempted to centralize its forces
for the struggle against its external enemies, the more it would
suffer dissolution internally. The fact that the leading brain
of the General Council regarded the most highly developed working-class party, the most highly developed from his own point of
view, and at that in his own country, as a venal police tool offered
the most striking proof that the historic knell of the International
had sounded.

However, this was not the only proof. Wherever national
workers parties formed the International began to break up.
What violent reproaches Schweitzer had to suffer from Liebknecht on account of his alleged lukewarmness towards the
International ! But when Liebknecht found himself at the
head of the Eisenach fraction he had to listen to the same reproaches from Engels, and he answered them as Schweitzer had
answered his, namely by appealing to the German combination
laws : " I wouldn't dream of risking the existence of our organization on this question at the moment." If the unfortunate
Schweitzer had ever dared to use such insolent language—he
never did—the " King of the Tailors ", as he was called, who
insisted on having " his own party ", would have had to put
up with much more. The formation of the Eisenach fraction
had delivered the first blow at the " German-language section "
in Geneva, and the final blow at this oldest and strongest organi
zation of the International on the continent was given by the

formation of a Swiss workers party in 1871. At the end of the year Becker was compelled to discontinue the publication of *Der Vorbote*.

In 1872 Marx and Engels had not yet recognized the real causes of the situation, and they diminished their own services when they contended that the International had collapsed as the result of the machinations of one single demagogue, although in reality it could have retired from the arena in all honour after having fulfilled its share of a great historical task which had now grown beyond it. One must side with our present-day anarchists when they declare that nothing is more unmarxist than the idea that an unusually malicious individual, a " highly dangerous intriguer ", could have destroyed a proletarian organization like the International, rather than with those orthodox believers whose skin begins to creep with horror at the suggestion that Marx and Engels might not always have dotted their i's and crossed their t's to perfection. If Marx and Engels were alive to-day they would certainly have nothing but biting contempt for the suggestion that the merciless criticism which was their sharpest weapon should never be turned against themselves.

Their real greatness does not consist in the fact that they never made a mistake, but in the fact that they never attempted to persist in a mistake for one moment after they had recognized it as such. In 1874 Engels admitted that the International had outlived its time. " A general defeat of the working-class movement such as was suffered in the period from 1849 to 1864 will be necessary before a new international, an alliance of all proletarian parties in all countries, along the lines of the old one can come into being. At present the proletarian world is too big and too diffuse." He consoled himself with the fact that for ten years the International had dominated European history in the interests of the future and that it could look back with pride on its work.

In 1878 Marx wrote in an English publication attacking the contention that the International had been a failure and was now dead : " In reality the social-democratic workers parties in Germany, Switzerland, Denmark, Portugal, Italy, Belgium, Holland and North America, organized more or less within national frontiers, represent just as many international groups, no longer isolated sections sparsely distributed over various countries and held together by a General Council on the periphery, but rather the working-class itself in constant, active and direct connection, held together by the exchange of ideas, mutual assistance and joint aims. . . . Thus, far from dying out, the International has developed from one stage into another and higher one in which many of its original tendencies have already been fulfilled. During the course of this constant development it will experience many changes before the final chapter in its history can be written."

In these lines Marx once again demonstrated his prophetic vision. At a time when the national working-class parties were only just developing, and more than a decade before the new International was formed, he foresaw its historical character, but he granted even this second form no final permanence, certain of one thing only, that new life would spring continually from the ashes of the old until the spirit of the age had fulfilled itself.

8. The Hague Congress

The circular of the General Council issued on the 5th of March had announced the calling of the annual congress for the beginning of September, and in the meantime Marx and Engels had decided to propose that the seat of the General Council should be moved to New York.

Many disputes have taken place concerning the necessity and the utility of this proposal and the reasons which caused it to be made. It has been considered as a sort of first-class funeral for the International. Marx had sought to cloak the fact that the International was hopelessly lost. However, this idea is in opposition to the fact that both Marx and Engels continued to support the International with all possible energy and did their utmost to keep it alive even after the General Council had moved to New York. It has also been said that Marx had grown tired of his activities on behalf of the International and wished to devote himself undisturbed to his scientific work, and this idea has received a certain amount of support from a letter written by Engels to Liebknecht on the 27th of May 1872. He refers to a Belgian proposal to abolish the General Council altogether and adds : " As far as we are concerned we have no objection. Neither Marx nor myself will be members of it again in any case. As the situation is now we have no time for our work, and that must stop." However, this was no more than a passing remark made in a moment of annoyance. Even if Marx and Engels had refused to be re-elected to the General Council, that was no reason for moving it to New York, whilst Marx had repeatedly refused to neglect the International in favour of his scientific work until such time as it should be securely on the right lines.

It is therefore extremely unlikely that for this reason Marx had the idea of abandoning the International to its own devices during the most serious crisis of its whole existence.

We come probably nearer the truth in a letter he wrote to Kugelmann on the 29th of July : " The international congress (Hague, opens on the 2nd of September) will be a matter of life or death for the International and before I withdraw I want at least to protect it from the forces of dissolution." Part of Marx's plan to protect the International from " the forces of dissolution " was the moving of the General Council from London, where it was becoming more and more involved in dissensions, to New York. The Bakuninist tendencies were not represented at all in the General Council, or at the most they were so weakly represented that no danger threatened from them, but there was such confusion amongst its German, English and French members that it had been compelled to form a special sub-committee to deal with the constant disputes.

An estrangement had even taken place between Marx and those two members of the General Council who had been his most loyal and capable assistants for years, Eccarius and Jung, and in May 1872 a definite breach occurred between Marx and Eccarius. Eccarius was living in very straitened circumstances and gave notice to leave his position as General Secretary of the International, for he considered himself indispensable and wished to secure the doubling of his modest weekly salary of fifteen shillings. However, the Englishman John Hales was elected in his stead and Eccarius unjustly blamed Marx for this, although in fact Marx had always supported him against the English. On the other hand, Marx had often rebuked Eccarius for hawking information about the internal affairs of the International around the bourgeois press, and in particular information concerning the private conference of the International in London. Jung blamed Engels and the latter's autocratic manner for the estrangement between him and Marx and there may have been some truth in this, because since Marx had the opportunity of daily contact with Engels it is possible that without any bad intentions he no longer turned to Eccarius and Jung as much as he had done formerly, whilst " the General ", as Engels was nicknamed in the circle, cultivated, even according to the evidence of his best friends, an abrupt military tone, and when it was his turn to take the chair at the meetings of the General Council its members were usually prepared for squalls.

After the election of Hales as General Secretary a deadly enmity existed between him and Eccarius, whereby the latter enjoyed the support of a section of the English members. Marx received little support from the new General Secretary. On the contrary, when an English Federation was founded in accordance with the decisions of the London conference and held its first congress in Nottingham on the 21st and 22nd of July Hales proposed to the 21 delegates who were present that the Federation should establish touch with the other Federations not through the General Council, but direct, and that at the coming congress of the International the new Federation should support an alteration of the statutes of the International with a view to curtailing the authority of the General Council. All this was in accordance with the Bakuninist slogan of the " endangered autonomy of the Federations ". Hales withdrew the second proposal, but the first was adopted. The congress showed no inclination towards the Bakuninist programme, but it certainly did towards English radicalism ; for instance, it was in favour of the common ownership of the land, but not of all the means of production, which Hales also supported. Hales intrigued quite openly against the General Council, and in August it was compelled to remove him from his post.

The Blanquist tendency was dominant amongst the French members of the General Council, and as far as the two chief questions at issue, the question of political activity and the question of strict centralization, were concerned the Blanquists were perfectly reliable, but on account of their fundamental preference for revolutionary coups they threatened to become a still greater danger in the given situation with the European reaction only waiting for a pretext to let loose all its overwhelming power against the International. In fact, Marx's anxiety that the Blanquists might gain control of the General Council was probably the strongest motive for his proposal that the council should be moved from London to New York, where its international composition would be made possible and the safety of its archives guaranteed, a thing which was impossible anywhere on the continent.

Thanks to the strong representation of the Germans and the French amongst the 61 delegates at The Hague congress (which took place from the 2nd to the 7th of September 1872) Marx had a certain majority. His opponents have accused him of having manufactured this majority artificially, but this accusation is absolutely without foundation. Although the congress spent about half its time examining mandates, all of them were accepted with one exception. It is true, however, that in June Marx had written to America asking for mandates to be sent for French and German members. Some of the delegates represented sections in countries other than their own. Others used false names at the congress in order not to fall into the hands of the police, or for the same reason concealed the names of the sections they represented. This explains the fairly large discrepancies in the figures given by various reports on the congress concerning the representation of the various countries.

Strictly speaking, only eight delegates were present representing German organizations : Bernhard Becker (Brunswick), Cuno (Stuttgart), Dietzgen (Dresden) Kugelmann (Celle), Milke (Berlin), Rittinghausen (Munich), Scheu (Würtemberg) and Schumacher (Solingen). Marx, who was a representative of the General Council, also had one mandate each for New York, Leipzig and Mayence, whilst Engels had one mandate each from New York and Breslau. Hepner from Leipzig also had a mandate from New York, whilst Friedländer of Berlin had a mandate from Zürich. Two other delegates with German names, Walter and Swann, were in fact Frenchmen and their real names were Heddeghem and Dentraggues. Both of them were very doubtful characters, and at The Hague congress Heddeghem was already a Bonapartist spy. As far as the French delegates were Commune fugitives they appeared at the congress under their own names, Frankel and Longuet supporting Marx, whilst Ranvier, Vaillant and others were Blanquists, but the origin of their mandates was necessarily kept more or less in the dark. The General Council was represented by two Englishmen (Roach and Sexton), a Pole (Wroblevski), and three Frenchmen (Serraillier, Cournet and Dupont) and Marx himself. The Communist Workers Association in London was represented by Lessner. The British Federal Council sent four delegates, including Eccarius and Hales, who immediately began to flirt with the Bakuninists.

The Italian Bakuninists sent no representatives to the congress. At a conference held in Rimini in August they had broken off all relations with the General Council. The five Spanish delegates, with the exception of Lafargue, were Bakuninists, as also were the eight Belgian and the four Dutch representatives. The Jura Federation sent Guillaume and Schwitzguebel, whilst Geneva remained loyal to Becker. Four delegates came from America : Sorge, like Becker, was one of the most loyal supporters of Marx, Dereure, a former member of the Commune, was a Blanquist, and the third delegate was a Bakuninist, whilst the fourth mandate was the only one which was refused recognition by the congress. Denmark, Austria, Hungary and Australia were each represented by one delegate.

Stormy scenes took place even during the preliminary examination of the mandates, which lasted three days. Lafargue's

Spanish mandate was vigorously opposed, but finally recognized against a few abstentions. During the discussion on a mandate which one of the sections in Chicago had given to a member living in London, one of the representatives of the English Federal Council objected that the member was not a recognized leader of the workers, whereupon Marx replied that it was rather an honour than the contrary not to be an English workers' leader, for the majority of them had sold themselves to the liberals. The mandate was confirmed, but this observation created bad blood and it was zealously exploited against Marx by Hales and his friends after the congress. Marx invariably stood by his own actions and he neither regretted the observation nor did he withdraw it. After the mandates had been scrutinized a number of communications referring to Bakunin were handed over to a committee of five for preliminary sifting. As far as possible delegates were elected to this committee who had been least concerned with the dispute about the Alliance. The German Cuno was the chairman and its other members were the Frenchmen Lucain, Vichard and Walter-Heddeghem, and the Belgian Splingard.

The actual business of the congress began only on the fourth day with the reading of the report of the General Council. It was drawn up by Marx and read to the congress by him in German, by Sexton in English, by Longuet in French and by Abeele in Flemish. The report scourged all the acts of violence which had been committed against the International since the Bonapartist plebiscite, the bloody suppression of the Paris Commune, the villanies of Thiers and Favre, the infamies of the French chamber, and the high treason trials in Germany ; even the English government was taken to task on account of its terrorism against the Irish sections and on account of the inquiries it had caused to be made through its embassies concerning the branches of the association. The fierce campaign of the governments had been accompanied by an intense campaign of lies conducted with the full powers of the civilized world ; the International had been bombarded with slanders, sensational telegrams and the insolent falsification of public documents, such as the masterpiece of infernal slander the despatch which had described the great fire in Chicago as the work of the International. It was a wonder, declared the report, that the hurricane which had devastated the West Indies had not also been put down to the same account. As against this wild and reckless campaign the report of the General Council summed up the steady progress made by the International : its penetration into Holland, Denmark, Portugal, Ireland and Scotland, and its growth in the United States, Australia, New Zealand and Buenos Aires. The report was adopted with acclaim, and at the motion of a Belgian delegate the congress placed on record its admiration for and sympathy with all the victims of the proletarian struggle for emancipation.

The discussion on the General Council then began. Lafargue and Sorge justified its existence on the basis of the class struggle : the daily struggle of the working class against capitalism could not be conducted effectively without a central body. If no General Council existed it would be necessary to make one. The chief speaker for the opposition was Guillaume, who denied the necessity for a General Council, except as a central office for correspondence and statistics, and without any authority. The International was not the invention of a clever man in possession of an infallible political and social theory, but in the opinion of the Jura representatives it had grown out of the conditions of working-class existence and these conditions offered sufficient guarantee of the unity of working-class efforts.

The discussion ended on the fifth day of the congress behind closed doors, the discussion on the mandates had, by the way, also taken place behind closed doors. In a long speech Marx demanded not only that the previous powers of the General Council should be maintained, but even increased. The General Council should be given the right to suspend, under certain conditions, not only individual sections, but whole federations pending the decisions of the next congress. It had neither police nor soldiers at its disposal, but it could not permit its moral power to decay. Rather than degrade it to a letter-box it would be better to abolish the General Council altogether. Marx's viewpoint was carried with 36 votes against 6, 15 votes being withheld.

Engels then proposed that the General Council should be moved from London to New York. He pointed out that the removal of the council from London to Brussels had been considered on several occasions, but that Brussels had always refused, whilst the prevailing circumstances made it urgently necessary that London should be replaced by New York. The decision must be taken to move the General Council from London to New York for at least a year. The proposal caused general and for the most part unpleasant surprise. The French delegates protested against it with particular vigour, and they succeeded in securing a separate vote first on whether the seat of the General Council should be moved at all, and secondly whether it should be moved to New York. The motion that the seat of the General Council should be moved was carried with a small majority ;

26 against 23 votes with 9 abstentions, whilst 30 votes then decided on New York. Twelve members of the new General Council were then elected and given the right to co-opt seven other members.

The discussion on political action was opened in the same session. Vaillant brought in a resolution in the spirit of the decision of the London conference, declaring that the working-class must constitute itself its own political party independent of and hostile to all bourgeois political parties. Vaillant, and after him Longuet, appealed to the lessons of the Paris Commune, which had collapsed for want of a political programme. A German delegate who supported the resolution was far less convincing when he declared that owing to his abstention from the political struggle Schweitzer had become a spy, the same Schweitzer who three years previously at the Basle congress had been denounced by the German delegates as a spy precisely on account of his " parliamentarism ". Guillaume, on the other hand, pointed to the happenings in Switzerland, where at the elections the workers had concluded election alliances with Tom, Dick and Harry, sometimes with the radicals and sometimes with the reactionaries. The Jura sections wanted to have nothing to do with such trickery. They were also politicians, but nega-tive politicians. They wanted to destroy political power, not conquer it.

The discussion lasted until the next day, the sixth and last day of the congress, which began with a surprise. Ranvier, Vaillant and the other Blanquists had already left the congress on account of the decision to remove the General Council to New York, and in a leaflet which they issued shortly afterwards they declared : " Called upon to do its duty the International collapsed. It fled from the revolution over the Atlantic Ocean." Sorge took the chair in place of Ranvier. Vaillant's proposal was then adopted with 35 against 6 votes, 8 votes being withheld. A section of the delegates had already left for home, but most of them had left written declarations that they were in favour of the resolution.

The last hours of the last day of the congress were taken up with the report of the committee of five on Bakunin and the Alliance. It declared with 4 votes against 1 (that of the Belgian member) that it considered it as proved that a secret Alliance had existed with statutes directly contrary to the statutes of the International, but that there was not sufficient evidence to prove that the Alliance still existed. Secondly, it was proved by a draft of the statutes and by letters of Bakunin that he had attempted to form, and had perhaps succeeded in forming, a secret society within the International with statutes differing fundamentally from the statutes of the International both politically and socially. Thirdly, Bakunin had adopted fraudulent practices in order to obtain possession of the property of others, and in order to release himself from his just obligations either he or his agents had used intimidation. Upon these grounds the majority of the committee then demanded the expulsion of Bakunin, Guillaume and a number of their supporters from the International. Cuno, who gave the report on behalf of the committee, did not put forward any material evidence, but declared instead that the majority of the committee had reached the moral certainty that their conclusions were correct, and asked for a vote of confidence from the congress.

Called upon by the chairman to defend himself, Guillaume, who had already refused to appear before the Committee, declared that he would make no attempt to defend himself as he was unwilling to take part in a farce. The attack, he declared, was not directed against a number of individuals, but against the federalist tendencies as a whole. The representatives of those tendencies, as far as they were still present at the congress, had been prepared for this and had already drawn up an agreement of solidarity. This agreement was then read to the congress by a Dutch delegate. It was signed by five Belgian, four Spanish and two Jura delegates and by an American and a Dutch delegate. In order to avoid any split in the International the signatories declared themselves willing to maintain all administrative relations with the General Council, whilst rejecting any interference on its part in the internal affairs of the federations, providing such interference did not refer to violations of the general statutes of the International. In the meantime the signatories appealed to all federations and to all sections to prepare themselves for the next congress in order to carry the principle of free association (*autonomie fédérative*) to victory. The congress was not prepared to negotiate on the point, but expelled Bakunin immediately with 27 against 7 votes, 8 votes being withheld, and then Guillaume with 25 against 9 votes, 9 votes being withheld. The further expulsion proposals of the committee were rejected, but it was instructed to publish its material on the Alliance.

This concluding scene of The Hague congress was certainly unworthy of it. Naturally, the congress could not know that the decisions of the majority of the committee were invalid because one member was a police spy, and it would at least have been understandable if Bakunin had been expelled for political reasons, as a result of the moral conviction that he was an incorrigible mischief-maker and without being able to prove all his machinations in black and white, but that the congress attempted to rob him of his good name in questions of *meum et tuum* was inexcusable, and unfortunately Marx was responsible for this.

Marx had obtained the alleged decision of an alleged " revolutionary committee " threatening Liubavin with death should he insist on the repayment of the advance of 300 roubles paid to Bakunin by a Russian publisher through his good offices for the translation of the first volume of *Capital*. The actual text of this precious document has never become known, but when Liubavin, now himself a bitter enemy of Bakunin, sent it to Marx he wrote : " At the time it seemed to me that Bakunin's share in the despatch of the letter was undeniable, but to-day, on cooler consideration of the whole affair, I realize that the letter proves nothing against Bakunin, for it might have been written by Netchayeff without his knowledge." This was in fact the truth, but merely on the basis of this letter, whose addressee himself considered it not sufficiently incriminating as far as Bakunin was concerned, the latter was accused by The Hague congress of a contemptible piece of roguery.

Although Bakunin repeatedly recognized his obligation in connection with the advance and promised to pay it back in one way or the other, it would appear that his constant financial troubles never permitted him to do so. In the whole dismal affair nothing was heard from the only injured party, namely the publisher, who appears to have accepted his fate with philosophic resignation as one which is only too common in his profession. How many authors, including many of the most famous, have not at some time or the other found themselves in the position of having spent their advance and being unable to perform the promised work ? That is certainly far from praiseworthy, but for all that it is an exaggeration to demand the culprit's head on a charger.

9. Valedictory Twinges

Despite the efforts of Marx and Engels to keep it alive, the history of the First International closed with The Hague congress. They did their utmost to facilitate the task of the new General Council in New York, but it failed to secure a firm footing on American territory. Numerous dissensions between the various sections existed in America also and the movement lacked experience and connections, intellectual forces and material means. The life and soul of the new General Council was Sorge, who was well acquainted with American conditions and had opposed the removal of the council to New York. After first refusing he had then accepted his election as General Secretary, for he was much too conscientious and loyal to fail the International when his services were required.

It is always a disagreeable matter to use diplomatic methods in proletarian affairs. Marx and Engels had feared with good reason that their proposal to move the General Council from London to New York would meet with vigorous resistance from the German, French and English workers, and they had concealed their intentions as long as possible in order not to add to the already numerous points of contention. However, the fact that they were successful in surprising The Hague congress nevertheless had evil consequences. The resistance they had feared was not diminished thereby, but rather intensified and embittered.

The Germans offered, comparatively speaking, the least violent resistance. Liebknecht was against the moving of the General Council, and he always declared it to have been a mistake, but at the time he was in prison with Bebel in the Hubertusburg. His interest in the International had greatly diminished, and this was still more the case with regard to the majority of the Eisenach fraction, whilst the impression brought back from The Hague congress by the delegates from the fraction only increased the general lack of interest. Writing on the 8th of May 1873 to Sorge, Engels declared : " Although the Germans have their own squabbles with the Lassalleans they were very disappointed with The Hague congress, where they expected to find perfect harmony and fraternity, in contrast to their own wranglings, and they have become very disinterested." This is probably the rather unsatisfactory reason why the German members of the International did not offer any very energetic resistance to the moving of the General Council.

Much more serious was the secession of the Blanquists, upon whom Marx and Engels reckoned next to and with the Germans in the decisive questions at issue, and upon whom they reckoned in particular for support against the Proudhonists, the other French fraction, whose whole attitude made them tend towards the Bakuninists. The bitterness of the Blanquists was intensified by their realization that the decision to move the General Council to New York had been taken in order to prevent them obtaining control of it in support of their putsch tactics. However, they cut off their nose to spite their face, because as France was closed to their agitation they soon fell victim to the usual fate of emigrants after they had parted company with the International. Writing to Sorge on the 12th of September 1874 Engels declared : " The French emigrants are completely at sixes and sevens. They have quarrelled amongst themselves and with everyone else for purely personal reasons, mostly in connection with money, and we shall soon be completely rid of them. . . . The idle life during the war, the Commune and in exile has demoralized them frightfully, and only hard times can save a demoralized Frenchman." But that was very cold consolation.

The removal of the General Council to New York exercised the worst effect on the movement in England. On the 18th of September Hales moved a vote of censure in the British Federal Council against Marx on account of his statement concerning the venality of the English working-class leaders. The vote of censure was adopted, whilst an amendment to the effect that Marx had not believed the accusation himself but had made it merely to serve his own ends, was rejected, the voting being level. Hales also gave notice that he intended to table a resolution calling for the expulsion of Marx from the International, whilst another member gave notice for a resolution rejecting the decisions of The Hague congress. Hales then openly continued the relations with the Jura Federation which he had secretly established at The Hague. Writing in the name of the Federal Council on the 6th of November he declared that the hypocrisy of the old General Council had now been exposed. It had attempted to organize a secret society within the International on the pretext of destroying another secret society which it had invented to suit its aims. At the same time, however, he pointed out that the English were not in agreement with the Jura Federation politically. They were convinced of the usefulness of political action, but were naturally prepared to grant complete autonomy to all other federations as demanded by the differing conditions in the various countries.

Hales won zealous allies in Eccarius and Jung, particularly in Jung, who, after some hesitation, finally became one of the most violent opponents of Marx and Engels. Both Eccarius and Jung sinned deeply, first of all because they permitted their political judgment to be determined by personal considerations, jealousy and touchiness arising from the fact that Marx paid more attention to Engels than to them, or appeared to, and secondly by the abandonment of the honourable and influential position which they had won as old members of the General Council. Unfortunately the damage they did was intensified as a result of their former position. At a number of congresses they had become known to the whole world as the most zealous and reliable interpreters of the opinions which Marx held, and when they now appealed to the toleration of the Jura Federation for these same opinions against the intolerance of The Hague decisions the dictatorial hankerings of Marx and Engels seemed to be proved beyond all doubt.

In this case also it was cold consolation to observe that the two damaged themselves chiefly. They met with vigorous resistance in the English and in particular in the Irish sections, and even in the Federal Council itself, and they then carried out a sort of *coup d'état* in the English branch of the International by issuing an appeal to all sections and all members declaring that the British Federal Council was so divided against itself that further co-operation was impossible. They also demanded the calling of a congress to deal with the validity of The Hague decisions, which the appeal interpreted as meaning, not that political action was obligatory for all sections of the International —for that, declared the appeal, was the opinion of the majority also—but that the General Council should determine the policy to be pursued by each federation in its own particular country. The minority immediately replied to these machinations in a counter-appeal which seems to have been drawn up by Engels. This appeal condemned the proposed congress as illegal, but it took place nevertheless on the 26th of January 1873 because the majority of the sections decided in favour of it and they alone were represented at it.

Hales opened this congress by delivering violent attacks on the old General Council and on The Hague congress, and he was actively supported by Jung and Eccarius. The congress unanimously condemned The Hague decisions and refused to recognize the new General Council in New York. It also declared itself in favour of a new international congress whenever a majority of the federations should declare in favour of it. Thus the split in the British Federation was complete and both remnants proved themselves powerless to take any really effective part in the general elections of 1874 which overthrew the Gladstone Ministry. Their impotence was enhanced by the intervention of the trade unions, which put forward a number of candidates and succeeded for the first time in securing the election of two of them.

The sixth congress of the International which the General Council in New York called for the 8th of September in Geneva, drew up, so to speak, the death-certificate of the International. The Bakuninist counter-congress which took place in Geneva on the 1st of September was attended by two English delegates (Hales and Eccarius), five delegates each from Belgium, France and Spain, four delegates from Italy, one delegate from Holland

and six delegates from the Jura, whilst the Marxist congress consisted for the most part of Swiss, and most of those lived in Geneva. Not even the General Council was able to send a delegate and there were no English, French, Spaniards, Belgians or Italians, and only one German and one Austrian present. Becker boasted that he had produced thirteen of the not quite thirty delegates more or less by magic in order to increase the prestige of the congress by larger numbers and to ensure that the majority should be secure. Marx was naturally not to be had for such self-deception and he frankly admitted that the congress had been " a fiasco " and advised the General Council not to stress the formal organizational side of the International for the moment, but to retain control of the centre point in New York if possible in order that it should not fall into the hands of idiots and adventurers who might compromise the cause. Events themselves and the inevitable development and complexity of things would assure the resurrection of the International in an improved form.

It was the cleverest and most dignified decision which it was possible to take under the circumstances, but unfortunately its effects were tarnished by the final blow which Marx and Engels felt it necessary to deliver at Bakunin. The Hague congress had instructed the committee of five which had proposed the expulsion of Bakunin to publish the result of its inquiries, but the committee did not do so, but whether the real reason was that " the separation of its members over various countries " prevented it, or whether it felt that its authority was not strong enough on account of the fact that one of its members had declared Bakunin not guilty whilst another had in the meantime been exposed as a police spy, can no longer be settled. The protocol commission of The Hague congress, consisting of Dupont, Engels, Frankel, le Moussu, Marx and Serraillier, therefore took over the task and a few weeks before the Geneva congress it issued a memorandum entitled : *The Alliance of Socialist Democracy and the International Working-men's Association.* This memorandum was drawn up by Engels and Lafargue, whilst Marx's share in the work was no more than the editing of one or two of the concluding pages, though naturally he is no less responsible for the whole than its actual authors.

Any critical examination of the Alliance pamphlet, as it came to be called for the sake of brevity, with a view to determining the correctness or otherwise of its detailed charges would demand at least as much space as the original document. However, very little is lost by the fact that this is impossible for reasons of space. In such disputes hard blows and knocks are delivered by both sides, and the quality of the Bakuninist attacks on the Marxists was not such as to entitle them to complain all too bitterly when they themselves were attacked severely and occasionally unjustly.

It is quite another consideration which places this pamphlet below anything else Marx and Engels ever published. The positive side of the new knowledge released by negative criticism is that which gives their other polemical writings their own peculiar attraction and their lasting value, but the Alliance pamphlet shows nothing of this. It does not deal at all with the internal causes responsible for the decline of the International, but merely continues the line adopted in the " Confidential Communication " and in the circular of the General Council on the alleged disruption in the International : Bakunin and his secret Alliance had destroyed the International by their intrigues and machinations. The Alliance pamphlet is not a historical document, but a one-sided indictment whose tendencious character is apparent on every page of it. However, the German translator thought it necessary to go one better and, in the best traditions of the Attorney-General, he entitled his effort *A Complot against the International Working-men's Association*.

The decline of the International was caused by quite different matters than the existence of a secret Alliance within its ranks, but even so the Alliance pamphlet does not even offer proof of the very existence of such an Alliance. Even the committee of inquiry set up by The Hague congress had to content itself with possibilities and probabilities in this connection. No matter how strongly one may condemn a man in Bakunin's position for intoxicating himself with fantastic statutes and blood-and-thunder proclamations, one must, in the absence of any tangible evidence to the contrary, assume that it was his lively imagination which played the chief rôle in the whole affair. However, the Alliance pamphlet made up for the lack of evidence by filling its second section with revelations provided by the worthy Utin on the Netchayeff process and on Bakunin's Siberian exile, during which the latter was declared to have made his first efforts as a common blackmailer and footpad. No evidence at all was offered in support of these accusations, and for the rest the evidence was limited to putting down without any further examination everything Netchayeff had said and done to Bakunin's account.

The Siberian chapter in particular is sheer cheap sensationalism. The Governor of Siberia at the time when Bakunin was living there in banishment was said to be a relative of the latter, and thanks to this connection and to the other services which he had rendered to the Tsarist government, the banished

Bakunin had become a sort of " secret regent " and misused his power, in consideration for " moderate bribes ", to favour capitalist undertakings. This greed for money, however, had occasionally been curbed by Bakunin's " hatred of science ", as for instance when he prevented Siberian merchants from founding a University in their country, for which purpose they needed the permission of the Tsar.

Utin embroidered and embellished the story of Bakunin's attempt to borrow money from Katkoff with particular artistry. This was the same story with which Borkheim had tried to influence Marx and Engels years before without success. According to Borkheim Bakunin had written from Siberia to Katkoff in order to borrow a few thousand roubles for his flight. According to Utin, however, Bakunin had tried to borrow this money only after his safe arrival in London, his intention being to salve his troubled conscience by paying back the bribes he had received during the Siberian banishment from a manufacturer of spirits there. In the last resort, of course, that was a feeling of remorse, but to Utin's horror Bakunin could give expression to this, so-to-speak, human emotion only by borrowing from a man whom he knew to be " an informer and literary bushranger in the pay of the Russian government ". This was the dizzy height to which Utin's fantasy rose, but it was by no means exhausted thereby.

At the end of October 1873 he went to London to report " still more astonishing things " about Bakunin, and on the 25th of November Engels wrote to Sorge : " The fellow (Bakunin) has made good practical use of his precious Catechism. For years he and his Alliance have been living exclusively from blackmail, relying on the fact that nothing can be published without compromising people who are entitled to consideration. You have no idea what a despicable pack of scoundrels they are." Fortunately by the time Utin arrived in London the Alliance pamphlet had already seen the light of day for several weeks so that the " still more astonishing things " were kept locked up in his truth-loving bosom, and he then proceeded to throw himself penitently at the feet of the Little Father, as a result of which he increased his income from the spirits trade by war-profiteering.

It is the Russian section in which the Alliance pamphlet culminates which did most to destroy its political effects. Even those Russian revolutionaries whose relations to Bakunin were strained were repulsed by the pamphlet. Whilst Bakunin's influence on the Russian movement in the 'seventies remained unimpaired Marx lost much of the sympathy which he had won in Russia. The one success which the pamphlet achieved proved to be a blow in the air, for although it caused Bakunin to withdraw from the struggle it did not touch the movement which bore his name.

Bakunin answered the Alliance pamphlet first of all in a declaration sent to *Le Journal de Genève*. It revealed the deep bitterness which the attacks of the pamphlet had caused in him, and he demonstrated their baselessness by pointing out that two police spies had been members of The Hague committee which had drawn up the charges. In reality only one member had been a police spy. He then pointed out that he was already sixty years old and that heart disease was making it more and more difficult for him to take part in public life : " Let the younger ones go forward. As far as I am concerned I have no longer the strength, and perhaps no longer the necessary confidence, to continue rolling the stone of Sisyphus against the everywhere triumphant reaction. I am therefore withdrawing from the conflict, and from my worthy contemporaries I demand only one thing : forgetfulness. From now on I shall disturb no one ; let no one disturb me." Whilst he accused Marx of having turned the International into the instrument of his personal revenge, he nevertheless still gave him credit for having been one of the founders of " a great and fine association ".

In a letter of farewell which he addressed to the workers of the Jura Bakunin spoke more severely against Marx, but more objectively. He declared that the socialism of Marx no less than the diplomacy of Bismarck represented the centre of the reaction against which the workers must carry on a terrible struggle. In this letter also he explained his retirement from the struggle by declaring that his age and sickness would make his efforts more of a hindrance than a help to the workers, but declared its justification to lie in the fact that the two congress in Geneva had demonstrated the victory of his cause and the defeat of that of his enemies.

Naturally, the reasons of health advanced by Bakunin for his retirement were mocked at as excuses, but the few years which he still lived in bitter poverty and great suffering showed that his strength had really been broken. The confidential letters to his intimate friends show that he had " perhaps " lost confidence in the speedy victory of the revolution. He died on the 1st of July 1876 in Berne. He deserved a happier death and a better obituary than he received in numerous working-class circles, though not in all, for he fought bravely and suffered much for the cause of the working class.

With all his mistakes and weaknesses history will give him

a place of honour amongst the pioneers of the international proletariat, though that place may be contested so long as there are Philistines in the world, no matter whether they conceal their long ears under the night-cap of petty-bourgeois respectability or don the lion's skin of a Marx to cloak their trembling limbs.

CHAPTER FIFTEEN: THE LAST DECADE

1. Marx at Home

AT the close of the year 1853, after the last twitchings of the Communist League, Marx had withdrawn into his study, and he did the same towards the close of the year 1878 after the final twitchings of the International, but this time the withdrawal was for good.

The last decade of his life has been called " a slow death ", but this is greatly exaggerated. It is true that the struggles which took place after the fall of the Paris Commune dealt heavy blows at his health : in the autumn of 1873 he suffered much from his head and was seriously threatened with apoplexy, whilst the chronically depressed brain condition made him incapable of work and robbed him of all desire to write. However, after several weeks' treatment in Manchester at the hands of Dr. Gumpert, who was a friend of Engels, and in whom Marx had complete confidence, he recovered.

Acting on the advice of Dr. Gumpert he went to Karlsbad in 1874 and in the two following years. In 1877 he went to Bad Neuenahr for a change, but in 1878 the two attempts on the life of the German Kaiser and the fierce anti-socialist campaign which followed closed the continent to him. However, the three visits to Karlsbad had suited him " wonderfully ", and he had got over his old liver trouble almost completely. There remained still the chronic stomach disorders and nervous exhaustion, which caused him severe headaches and obstinate sleeplessness. However, these troubles disappeared more or less after a visit to the seaside or to a spa in the summer and returned again only in the following New Year.

A complete restoration of health would have been possible only if Marx had granted himself the peace and quiet which after the tremendous amount of work and suffering which had filled his adult life he would have been entitled to demand on the approach of his sixtieth birthday, but he did not dream of doing so and instead he flung himself with all his old zeal into the studies necessary for the completion of his scientific work, studies whose extent had greatly increased in the meantime.

" For a man who examined everything to discover its historical origin and the conditions of its development," Engels pointed out, " naturally every single question gave rise to a series of new questions. Ancient history, agronomics, Russian and American landowning relationships, geology, etc., were studied in particular in order to make the section of the third book on ground-rent more complete than any previous treatment. He read all the Germanic and Neo-Latin languages with ease and then learnt old Slav, Russian and Serbian." And all that was only half his day's work, for although Marx had withdrawn from active public life he nevertheless remained active in the European and American working-class movements. He was in correspondence with almost all working-class leaders in the various countries and whenever possible they came to him for advice on important matters. He became more and more the much-sought-after and always-willing adviser of the fighting proletariat.

Lafargue described the Marx of the 'seventies as charmingly as Liebknecht had described the Marx of the 'fifties. He declared that his father-in-law must have had a strong constitution in order to withstand such an unusual mode of life and such exhausting intellectual activities. " He was in fact very powerful. His height was above the average, his shoulders broad, his chest well developed and his limbs well proportioned, although the spine was a little long in comparison with the length of his legs, a tendency often to be found amongst the Jews." And not only amongst Jews. Goethe was similarly built and one of those people who are popularly termed " sitting giants " in Germany on account of the fact that the disproportionate length of their spines makes them appear much bigger when seated than they actually are.

In Lafargue's opinion Marx would have been an exceptionally powerful man had he gone in for gymnastics in his youth, but the only form of physical exercise he took regularly was walking. He could walk for hours, chatting all the time, or climb hills without the least sign of fatigue, but even this form of exercise was practised for the most part in his study and merely for the purpose of ordering his ideas. From the door to the window the carpet in his study showed a worn stretch like a footpath over a meadow.

Although he never went to bed until very late he was always up the next morning between eight and nine, drinking black coffee and reading the newspapers, and after that he would disappear into his study to remain there until midnight and still later, appearing only for his meals or, on fine evenings, for a walk across Hampstead Heath. During the afternoon he would perhaps lie down for an hour or two on the sofa. Work had become such a passion for him that he very often completely forgot his meals, and his stomach had to suffer for his tremendous mental activities. He was a poor eater and suffered from lack of appetite, and this he would counteract by eating highly-spiced foods, ham, smoked fish, caviar and pickles. A poor eater, and not a great drinker, although he was never an abstainer, and as a true son of the Rhineland he appreciated a good drop of wine. On the other hand, he was a passionate smoker and a demon for matches. He was accustomed to say jokingly that his *Capital* would not bring him in sufficient to pay for the cigars he had smoked whilst writing it. During the long years of poverty he undoubtedly had to put up with many inferior brands and, as a result, his passion for smoking certainly did his health no good and in fact his doctor prohibited smoking on a number of occasions.

He sought mental recreation and refreshment in literature and all his life it was a great consolation to him. He possessed widespread knowledge on this field without ever boasting of it. His works, with the one exception of his polemic against Vogt, show little trace of his wide reading, apart of course from the reading immediately necessary to his subject, but in the Vogt book he used numerous quotations from all the literatures of Europe for his artistic purpose. Just as his own scientific work mirrored a whole epoch, so his own literary favourites were those whose creations also mirrored their epoch : from Æschylus and Homer to Dante, Shakespeare, Cervantes and Goethe. According to Lafargue Marx read Æschylus in the original Greek text at least once a year. He was always a faithful lover of the ancient Greeks, and he would have scourged those contemptible souls out of the temple who would prevent the workers from appreciating the culture of the classic world.

He had a thorough knowledge of German literature reaching far back into the Middle Ages. Goethe and Heine were his favourites amongst the more modern German authors. The gushing enthusiasm of the German Philistine for the more or less misunderstood " idealism " of Schiller seems to have spoiled this poet for Marx from his early youth, and this " idealism " seemed to him little more than an attempt to cloak banal misery with high-flown phrases. After his final break with Germany he did not bother himself much about modern German literature and he does not mention even writers like Hebbel and Schopenhauer, who would really have been worthy of his attention, whilst Richard Wagner's manhandling of German mythology comes in for caustic criticism.

Amongst French literary men he thought highly of Diderot and considered his *Le Neveu de Rameau* to be a masterpiece from beginning to end. The French eighteenth-century enlightenment literature, which Engels once declared represented the highest achievement of French intellect both in form and in content (the latter being extremely high considering the contemporary state of scientific knowledge and the former never equalled since), also came in for appreciation, but the French romanticists were roundly rejected and in particular Chateaubriand, whose false depth, Byzantian exaggerations, twopence-coloured sentimentality—in short, his unparalleled hodge-podge of dishonesty—Marx always found objectionable. On the other hand, Balzac's *Comédie Humaine* filled him with enthusiasm as embracing a whole epoch in the mirror of art. In fact, it was his intention to write a study of Balzac after he had completed his own great work, but like so many other plans this one too came to nothing.

After Marx had become permanently domiciled in London English literature took first place, and the tremendous figure of Shakespeare dominated the field ; in fact, the whole family practised what amounted to a Shakespearian cult. Unfortunately Marx never at any time dealt with Shakespeare's attitude to the great questions of his day. Referring to Byron and Shelley, however, he declared that those who loved and understood these two poets must consider it fortunate that Byron died at the age of 36, for had he lived out his full span he would undoubtedly have become a reactionary bourgeois, whilst regretting on the other hand that Shelley died at the age of 29, for Shelley was a thorough revolutionary and would have remained in the van of socialism all his life. Marx thought highly of the English novels of the eighteenth century and in particular of Fielding's *Tom Jones*, which in its own way is also a mirror of its time, and he also recognized a number of Walter Scott's novels as being first class of their kind.

In his literary judgments he was completely free of all political and social prejudices, as his appreciation of Shakespeare and Walter Scott shows, but he never subscribed to the idea of " pure æstheticism ", of " art for art's sake ", which is so often coupled with political indifference or even servility. In this respect also his was a virile and independent intellect measurable by no stereotyped formula. At the same time he was by no means over-fastidious in his choice of reading matter and did not scorn to read productions which would have made scholarly æsthetes cross themselves with horror. Like Darwin and Bismarck, he was a great devourer of novels and he had a particular liking for adventurous and humorous tales. In his search for them he descended from Cervantes, Balzac and Fielding to Paul de Kock and Dumas the elder, the man with the Count of Monte Cristo on his conscience.

Marx also sought intellectual recreation on quite a different field, namely mathematics. Particularly in times of mental anguish and other sufferings he would seek consolation in mathematics, which exercised a soothing effect on him. Engels and Lafargue both contend that he made independent discoveries in this field, but this is beside the point here, and mathematicians who went through his manuscripts after his death are reported not to have endorsed this opinion.

With all his intellectual interests Marx was no Wagner who lived shut up in a museum and saw the world only from afar, nor a Faust in whose breast two souls had made their habitation. " Working for the world " was one of his favourite sayings, and he felt that whoever was fortunate enough to be able to devote himself to scientific research should place himself at the service of humanity. It was this intellectual attitude which kept the blood pulsing vigorously in his veins and the marrow fresh in his bones. In his family circle and amongst friends he was always a cheerful and witty companion whose deep-chested laughter came easily. Those who sought out the " Red Terrorist Doctor ", as he came to be called after the fall of the Paris Commune, found no gloomy fanatic and no dreamy arm-chair philosopher, but a man of the world thoroughly at home in all the topics of polite conversation.

The readers of his letters are struck with the easy way in which his fiery spirit glides almost unnoticeably from the tremendous tension of great bursts of anger into the deep but calm sea of philosophic speculation, and this seems to have struck his listeners also, for referring to his conversations with Marx Hyndman declares :

" Whilst speaking with fierce indignation of the policy of the Liberal Party, especially in regard to Ireland, the old warrior's small deep-sunk eyes lighted up, his heavy brows wrinkled, the broad, strong nose and face were obviously moved by passion, and he poured out a stream of vigorous denunciation, which displayed alike the heat of his temperament and the marvellous command he possessed over our language. The contrast between his manner and utterances when thus deeply stirred by anger and his attitude when giving his views on the economic events of the period was very marked. He turned from the rôle of prophet and vehement denunciator to that of the calm philosopher without any apparent effort, and I felt from the first that on this latter ground many a long year might pass before I ceased to be a student in the presence of a master." [1]

Marx continued to remain aloof from social intercourse, although he was by this time much better known than twenty years earlier, and in fact Hyndman had made his acquaintance through a conservative member of parliament. However, in the 'seventies Marx's house was the scene of much coming and going ; it was another " refuge of justice " for the fugitive communards, who were always certain of receiving advice and finding assistance there. The turbulent folk certainly brought much annoyance and many troubles in their train, and when the first flood had subsided Frau Marx, for all her hospitable spirit, could not suppress the sigh : " They gave us quite enough to do."

But there were exceptions. In 1872 Charles Longuet, who had been a member of the Council of the Commune and editor of its official newspaper, married Marx's daughter Jenny. He never became quite so closely connected with the family, either personally or politically, as Lafargue, but he was a capable man. " He cooks, shouts and argues as much as ever he did," wrote Frau Marx, " but to his credit I must say that he gives his King's College lectures regularly and to the satisfaction of his superiors." The happy marriage was clouded by the early death of the first-born, but then a " chubby, robust and fine youngster " made its appearance and waxed strong and healthy to the joy of the whole family and not least of its grandfather.

The Lafargues were also amongst the fugitives from the Commune and they lived in the neighbourhood. In the first years of their married life they had lost two children and under the impression of this misfortune Lafargue abandoned his practice, declaring that it was impossible to carry on without a certain amount of charlatanry and that he was not prepared to do so. " What a pity he has deserted old father Æsculapius ! " sighed Frau Marx. Lafargue then opened a photographic-lithographic atelier, but although fortunately his nature was sanguine and skies always blue to his eyes, and although he " worked like a Nigger " and was supported tirelessly and courageously by his wife, the business made very slow progress and he found it difficult to fight against competitive undertakings with more capital than he had.

The third daughter was also being courted by a French suitor at about this time. It was Lissagaray, who afterwards wrote the history of the Commune, in whose ranks he had fought.

[1] H. M. Hyndman, *The Record of an Adventurous Life.* Macmillan & Co., London, 1911.

Eleanor seems to have been favourably inclined towards him, but her father was doubtful about his reliability and in the end and after a certain amount of hesitation nothing came of the matter.

In the spring of 1875 the family again moved, this time to 41, Maitland Park Road, Haverstock Hill, in the same part of the town. Marx spent the last years of his life in this house, and it was there that he died.

2. The German Social Democracy

Thanks to the fact that it had developed along national lines from the very beginning, the German working-class movement escaped the crisis suffered by all other sections of the International when they began to develop into national working-class parties. On the 10th of January 1874, a few months before the fiasco of the Geneva congress, it celebrated its first great electoral victory at the Reichstag elections when it polled 350,000 votes and obtained nine seats, six of them falling to the share of the Eisenach fraction and three to the Lassalleans.

Searching light is cast on the causes which led to the decline of the First International by the fact that Marx and Engels, the leading brains of the General Council, were able only with difficulties to find a *modus vivendi* with that flourishing workers party which should have been most familiar to them on account of their own origin and which was nearer to their own theoretical opinions than any other party. Not even Marx and Engels could wander under palms with impunity, and the international vantage point which permitted them a general view of the whole at the same time prevented them from penetrating into the details characteristic of the individual countries. Even their most enthusiastic admirers in England and France have admitted that they never succeeded in mastering all the details of English and French life like natives, and once having parted company with Germany they never succeeded in re-establishing their former thorough and familiar touch with German conditions. This was true even of the German party questions proper, in which their judgment was clouded by their undiminished mistrust of Lassalle and everything Lassallean.

This was seen clearly when the newly-elected Reichstag met for the first time. Two of the six members of the Eisenach fraction, Liebknecht and Bebel, were still in prison and unable to take their seats, whilst the attitude of the remaining four, Geib, Most, Motteler and Vahlteich, caused great disappointment in the ranks of their own supporters. Bebel declares in his memoirs that bitter complaints were made to him from many sides that the four parliamentary representatives of the Eisenach fraction were letting themselves be outdone by the three Lassalleans, Hasenclever, Hasselmann and Reimer. Engels, on the other hand, was of quite a different opinion and wrote to Sorge : " The Lassalleans have been so discredited by their parliamentary representatives that the government has been compelled to take measures against them in order to create the impression that their movement is serious. For the rest, since the elections the Lassalleans have found themselves compelled to follow at the tail of our people. What a piece of good fortune that Hasenclever and Hasselmann were elected to the Reichstag ! They are discrediting themselves visibly. They must either go with our people or commit follies on their own, and both things will ruin them." It would be difficult to imagine a more thorough misunderstanding of the situation.

The parliamentary representatives of the two fractions got on very well together and did not waste much time bothering about whether this man or that had come off better than the other on the floor of the house. Both fractions had conducted the election campaign in such a fashion that it was impossible to accuse the Eisenach fraction of semi-socialism or the Lassalleans of flirting with the government ; both fractions polled approximately the same number of votes ; both fractions faced the same enemies in the house and put forward the same demands ; and as a result of their electoral successes both fractions were subjected to an equally violent campaign of persecution on the part of the government. Their only real differences were in organizational matters, but these differences were soon settled, thanks to the careerist zeal of the Public Prosecutor Tessendorff, who succeeded in obtaining judgments from the complaisant courts which destroyed both the loose form of organization adopted by the Eisenach fraction and the more centralized form adopted by the Lassalleans.

Thus the unification of the two fractions was automatically approaching when in October 1874 Tölcke brought the peace proposals of the Lassalleans to Liebknecht, who had in the meantime been released from prison. Liebknecht immediately jumped at them, perhaps somewhat arbitrarily, but with a zeal which was none the less praiseworthy because, it was regarded very unfavourably in London. Marx and Engels still regarded the Lassalleans as a dying sect which would have to surrender unconditionally sooner or later, and the idea of negotiating with them on a footing of equality seemed a frivolous offence against the interests of the German working class. And when in February 1875 the draft programme jointly drawn up by the two fractions was published Marx and Engels flew into a rage.

On the 5th of May after Engels had sent a detailed letter of protest to Bebel, Marx sent his so-called programmatic letter to the leader of the Eisenach fraction. In this letter he scourged Lassalle harder than ever. The latter had learned *The Communist Manifesto* by heart, but had falsified it clumsily in order to cloak his own alliance with the absolutist and feudalist enemy against the bourgeoisie, declaring all other classes to be one reactionary mass as against the working class. In truth, however, the slogan of the " reactionary mass " was not Lassalle's at all, but had been coined by Schweitzer after Lassalle's death and had met with the express approval of Engels. What Lassalle had really taken from *The Communist Manifesto* was what he called the iron law of wages, and for this he was rebuked by Marx as a supporter of the Malthusian theory of population, although he had condemned it as energetically as Marx and Engels had done.

Apart from this extremely disagreeable side of the programmatic letter it represented a highly instructive dissertation on the fundamental principles of scientific socialism, and it left not one stone upon the other as far as the coalition programme was concerned. However, as is known, the only result of this powerful letter was to cause the addressees to make a few minor and comparatively unimportant improvements in their draft. A few decades later Liebknecht declared that most of them, if not all, had been in agreement with Marx and that perhaps a majority might have been obtained at the unity congress for the latter's views, but a minority would have remained dissatisfied, and it had been necessary to avoid that because the aim of the congress was not to formulate scientific socialist principles, but to unite the two fractions.

A less edifying, but more practical explanation can be found for the way in which the programmatic letter was silently ignored in the fact that it went above the intellectual level of the members of the Eisenach fraction even more than it did above that of the Lassalleans. A few months previously Marx had complained that from time to time semi-scholarly Philistine fantasies were permitted to appear in the organ of the Eisenach fraction. The stuff came from schoolmasters, doctors and students, and Liebknecht must be taken to task for it. At the same time he feared that the realist ideas which had been laboriously instilled into the party and which had actually begun to take firm root, would now be overwhelmed by Lassallean sectarianism with its ideological legalist rubbish borrowed from the democrats and the French socialists.

Marx was quite wrong in this respect. In theoretical questions both fractions were more or less on the same level, and if there was any difference it favoured the Lassalleans. The draft of the unity programme met with no objection at all on the part of the Eisenach fraction whereas a workers congress held in West Germany and composed almost exclusively of Lassalleans subjected it to a criticism which was in many respects similar to that exercised by Marx a few weeks later. However, it is not necessary to attach any particular importance to this because the truth was that both fractions were still a long way from scientific socialism as founded by Marx and Engels. They had hardly a glimmering of the historical materialist method and the secret of the capitalist mode of production was still a secret for them. The clumsy fashion in which C. A. Schramm (the most prominent theoretician of the Eisenach fraction at the time) grappled with Marx's theory of value offered the most striking evidence of this.

In practice the unification of the two fractions turned out favourably, and therefore neither Marx nor Engels had anything to say against it, although they still thought perhaps that the Eisenach fraction had let itself be imposed upon by the Lassalleans. However, in his programmatic letter Marx had said himself : every practical step taken in the movement is worth a dozen programmes. In the upshot, however, the theoretical confusion increased rather than diminished in the new united party and Marx and Engels ascribed this to the unnatural amalgamation, and their dissatisfaction became more outspoken than ever.

The fact that the source of their annoyance was to be found chiefly amongst the members of the former Eisenach fraction rather than amongst the former Lassalleans should have given them pause, and Engels declared occasionally that the latter would soon be the clearest thinkers in the movement because their paper—which continued to exist for a year after the unification—published the least nonsense. The curse of paid agitators, the half-educated, weighed heavily on their own party, he declared. He was irritated in particular by Most, who " condensed the whole of *Capital* without understanding any of it " and vigorously supported Dühring's brand of socialism. Writing to Marx on the 24th of May 1876 Engels declared : " It is clear that in the minds of these people Dühring has made himself invulnerable as a result of his execrably vulgar attacks on you, for if we now ridicule his theoretical nonsense then that is nothing but our personal revenge on him." Liebknecht also did not get off scot-free : " Wilhelm is anxious to make up for the deficiency of our theories, to have an answer ready for every Philistine objection, to have a picture of the future society ready-made in his mind because the Philistines might question him about it, and at the same time to be as independent as possible in theoretical matters, an endeavour in which he has been more successful than he realizes owing to his complete lack of any theory." However, all that had nothing whatever to do with Lassalle or the Lassallean traditions.

It was the rapid growth of its practical successes which made the new party indifferent to theory, and even that is saying too much. They were not indifferent to theory as such, but rather to what, in their vigorous advance, they regarded as theoretical hair-splitting. Unappreciated inventors and mis-understood reformers, anti-vaccinationists, nature healers and similar cranks flocked to the standard of the new party because they hoped to find in the active ranks of the working class the recognition which had been denied them in the bourgeois world. Whoever showed good-will and offered some remedy for the sick body politic was sure of a welcome, particularly those who came from academic circles and whose presence promised to seal the alliance between the proletariat and science. A university professor who befriended or seemed to befriend socialism in one or the other of its manifold interpretations, had no need to fear any very strict criticism of his intellectual stock-in-trade.

Dühring in particular was secure against such criticism because he had many qualities, both personal and otherwise, which necessarily attracted the most active intellectual elements in the Berlin working-class movement. Without a doubt he possessed great gifts and great capacity, and his whole character and career won much sympathy for him amongst the workers. He was without financial resources and had gone blind in early years, but nevertheless he had fought his way through life as a University lecturer, had never made any concessions to the ruling classes and had always stoutly maintained his radicalism in the lecture hall, not hesitating to praise Marat, Babeuf and the heroes of the Commune. The disagreeable side of his character, the arrogance with which he claimed to master completely half a dozen fields of scientific investigation whilst in fact, owing to his physical disability, he was thoroughly at home on none of them, and the increasing megalomania with which he bludgeoned his predecessors out of existence, Fichte and Hegel on the philo-sophic field, and Marx and Lassalle on the economic field, remained in the background or was excused as the result of his intellectual isolation and the arduous struggles he had been compelled to fight.

Marx had paid no attention to the " execrably vulgar " attacks of Dühring and in fact their content was not of sufficient weight to cause him to take up the challenge. The growing enthusiasm of the Berlin socialists for Dühring made no impression on Marx for a long time, although with his claim to infallibility and his system of " final truths " Dühring displayed all the characteristics of the born sectarian. Even when Liebknecht, who was quite on the alert this time, sent in letters from workers and pointed out the danger of the party propaganda becoming superficial, Marx and Engels still refused to reply to Dühring on the ground that it was " too subaltern a task ", but when, in May 1876, Most wrote an insolent letter to Engels that seems to have been the last straw.

Engels then began to examine Dühring's " systematic truths ", and he set down his criticism in a number of articles which began to appear in the beginning of 1877 in the *Vorwärts*, which was now the central organ of the united party. These articles developed into one of the most important and successful literary presentations of scientific socialism, taking a place side by side with Marx's *Capital*, but the reception of the work by the party showed that danger was really at hand. For two pins the annual congress of the party which took place in May 1877 in Gotha would have held an inquisition for heresy on Engels similar to the one then being held by the orthodox university clique against Dühring. Most brought in a resolution against the publication of any further articles by Engels against Dühring in the central organ of the party, on the ground that they were " completely without interest or even objectionable to the great majority of the readers of the *Vorwärts* ", whilst Vahlteich, who was in all other respects a bitter enemy of Most, made common cause with him on this issue and declared that the tone adopted by Engels was in the worst of taste and liable to make the intellectual fare provided by the *Vorwärts* indigestible. Fortunately the worst was avoided by the adoption of a compromise proposal suggesting that for practical and agitational reasons the polemic should be continued in a scientific supplement and not in the main paper.

At the same time the congress decided to issue a fortnightly scientific organ from October on. This proposal was adopted at the suggestion of Karl Höchberg, who also promised financial support for the venture. Höchberg was one of those bourgeois adepts at socialism who were so numerous in Germany at the time. He was the son of a lottery promoter in Frankfort, still young and very well-to-do and at the same time extremely self-sacrificing and unselfish. Everyone who knew him gave him the highest possible personal character. However, the judgment on his literary and political abilities as they were expressed in his publications was less favourable. Höchberg was then seen to be a colourless and tiresome person who knew nothing about the history and theory of socialism and nothing whatever about the scientific opinions developed by Marx and Engels. He did not consider the proletarian class struggle as the lever for the emancipation of the workers, but thought to win the ruling classes, and in particular their educated members, for the cause of the workers along the lines of peaceful and legal development.

However, Marx and Engels knew very little about him when they refused to co-operate in *Die Zukunft*, as the new publication was called. An invitation to contribute had been extended to them only through a general circular together with numerous others. Engels declared that whilst the decisions of congress might be very useful in the practical daily agitation, their value as far as scientific achievement was concerned was nil, and certainly not sufficient to ensure that the publication would really be scientific, a consummation which could not be achieved by decree. A scientific socialist publication without a definite policy and a definite tendency was an impossibility, and in view of the great diversity and ambiguity of the tendencies at present flourishing in Germany there could be no guarantee that the particular policy adopted would prove suitable.

The first number of *Die Zukunft* showed how right they had been to adopt a reserved attitude towards it. The introductory article written by Höchberg proved to be a new collection of all the tendencies which they had fought as enervating and debilitating in the socialism of the 'forties. Thus they were spared any embarrassing disputes. When a member of the German party asked them whether they felt resentful on account of the debate at the Gotha congress, Marx replied : " To quote Heine, I harbour no resentment, nor does Engels. Neither of us cares a snap of the fingers for popularity. As a proof there is my constant opposition to all forms of personal cults. During the period of the International I never permitted the numerous manœuvres of recognition with which I was molested from various countries to be made public and I never answered them except perhaps with a rebuke." And he added : " But such happenings as those which took place at the last party congress —they are being thoroughly exploited by the enemies of the party abroad—have in any case taught us to be careful in our relations with members of the party in Germany." Still, this proved to be not as bad as it sounded, and Engels continued to publish his articles against Dühring in the scientific supplement of the *Vorwärts.*

However, Marx was seriously perturbed by the "rotten spirit" which began to show itself not so much amongst the masses as amongst the leaders, and writing to Sorge on the 19th of October he declared : " The compromise with the Lassalleans has led to compromises with the other pseudo-socialists, in Berlin (Most, for example) with Dühring and his 'admirers', and further with a whole host of immature students and priggish academicians, who want to give socialism 'a higher, idealist tendency', or, in other words, to replace the materialist basis of socialism (which needs a serious and objective study if one is to operate on it successfully) with a modern mythology whose Gods are Liberty, Equality and Fraternity. Herr Höchberg, who publishes *Die Zukunft,* is a representative of this tendency. He has 'bought himself in' to the party, so to speak. I am prepared to assume the 'noblest' intentions on his part, but I don't give a fig for 'intentions'. Anything more pitiful than his programme in *Die Zukunft* has seldom been presented to the world with more 'modest presumption'."

In truth, Marx and Engels would have had to disavow their whole past in order to reconcile themselves with this " tendency ".

3. Anarchism and the War in the Near East

The Gotha congress in 1877 also decided that the party should be represented at a world socialist congress which had been called to take place in Ghent in September of the same year and Liebknecht was elected as the party representative.

This congress had been initiated by the Belgians, who in the meantime had found a hair in the anarchist soup and were anxious to bring about a reunion of the two groups which had parted company at The Hague congress. The Bakuninist group had held its congress in 1873 in Geneva, in 1874 in Brussels and in 1876 in Berne, but with steadily diminishing numbers. It broke up in face of the practical necessities of the proletarian struggle for emancipation as it had developed out of them.

The real antagonisms were revealed at the very beginning of the quarrel, the Geneva dispute between the *fabrique* and the *gros métiers.* On the one hand a well-paid section of the workers with political rights opening up the parliamentary struggle for them, but also tempting them into various doubtful alliances with bourgeois parties, and on the other hand a badly paid section of the workers without political rights and dependent solely on their own strength. This practical antagonism was at the basis of the whole quarrel and not, as legend would have it, a theoretical struggle between reason and unreason.

The matter was far less simple, and it is still far from simple to-day, as the repeated resuscitation of anarchism demonstrates after it has been killed again and again. To understand anarchism need not mean to support it. In the same way it is not necessary to disavow parliamentary political action in order to recognize that with all its quite acceptable reforms it can lead the working-class movement to a point where it loses all its revolutionary energies. It was not at all by chance that amongst Bakunin's supporters were men who had rendered great services to the proletarian struggle for emancipation. Liebknecht was certainly never his friend, but at the time of the Basle congress he demanded political abstention with equal zeal. On the other hand, men like Jules Guesde in France, Carlo Cafiero in Italy, Cæsar de Paepe in Belgium and Paul Axelrod in Russia were zealous supporters of Bakunin at the time of The Hague congress and long afterwards. When later on they became just as zealous Marxists this was not because they had thrown their previous convictions overboard, but, as a number of them declared expressly, because they had continued their development on the basis of that which Bakunin had in common with Marx.

Both men wanted a proletarian mass movement, and their dispute concerned the line which this mass movement should take. In the meantime, however, the congresses of the Bakuninist International had demonstrated that the anarchist way was impassable.

It would lead too far here to show the rapid decline of anarchism on the basis of the various congresses. Its destruction proceeded merrily and thoroughly enough. The General Council and the annual subscription were abolished, the congresses were forbidden to adopt any decisions in matters of principle, and with great difficulty an attempt was repulsed to close the ranks of the International to brain workers. However, the constructive side of the matter was in a deplorable state and the drafting of a new programme and new tactics made little progress. The Geneva congress disputed in particular about the general strike as the only and infallible means of social revolution, but no agreement was reached, whilst the next congress in Brussels was no more able to agree on question of the public services, which represented the chief question at the congress and upon which de Paepe spoke in a manner which brought him in the not unjustifiable reproach that he had left the basis of anarchism altogether. It is clear how necessary was de Paepe's deviation when something tangible had to be said about such a question. After violent debates the question was postponed to the next congress for settlement, but the next congress also failed to solve it. The Italians declared that " the era of congresses " was over and done with, anyway, and they demanded " propaganda of deed ". Utilizing the famine in Italy they achieved the respectable performance of sixty putsches within two years, but the success for their cause was nil.

The fact that anarchism adopted a purely negative attitude to all those practical questions which touched intimately the immediate interests of the modern proletariat, even more than the hopeless confusion of its theoretical views, caused it to degenerate into a hopelessly hidebound sect. When a mass movement in favour of the legal limitation of the working day to ten hours developed amongst the workers in Switzerland the anarchists refused to have anything to do with it, and they adopted the same negative attitude towards a petition which the Flemish socialists organized to secure the legal prohibition of child-labour in the factories. Naturally, they also rejected any struggle for the general franchise or, where it already existed, for its utilization by the workers. Compared with this barren and hopeless policy the successes of the German socialist working-class movement shone all the more brilliantly, and everywhere the masses began to reject anarchist propaganda.

The calling of a world socialist congress for the following year in Ghent which was decided by the anarchist congress in Berne in 1876 was due to the recognition that anarchism had completely failed to win the masses. The congress took place from the 9th to the 15th of September in Ghent ; 42 delegates were present and the anarchists controlled only a nucleus of 11 delegates under the leadership of Guillaume and Kropotkin. Many of their former supporters, including the majority of the Belgian delegates and the Englishman Hales, went over to the socialist wing, which was led by Liebknecht, Greulich and Fränkel. A sharp collision took place between Liebknecht and Guillaume when the latter accused the German socialists of putting their programme in their pocket at the elections, but on the whole the proceedings of the congress were peaceable enough. The anarchists had lost their usual love for high-sounding phrases, and their speeches were pitched in a minor and conciliatory key which made it possible for their opponents to adopt a more accommodating attitude. However, nothing came of the proposed " solidarity pact ", for the opposing opinions were too dissimilar.

Marx had hardly expected any other result, and his attention was now directed towards another storm-centre from which he expected revolutionary happenings—the Russo-Turkish War. The first of two letters of advice which he sent to Liebknecht, the letter of the 4th of February 1878, began : " We are decidedly in favour of the Turks for two reasons : first of all because we have studied the Turkish peasant, i.e. the masses of the Turkish people, and found him to be undoubtedly one of the most capable and morally upright representatives of the European peasantry, and secondly because a Russian defeat would greatly accelerate the social transformation, whose elements are present everywhere in Russia, and thereby accelerate also the transformation in the whole of Europe." Three months earlier Marx had written to Sorge : " This crisis is a new turning-point in European history. Russia—and I have studied Russian conditions from the original sources, both unofficial and official (the latter are available only to very few people and I obtained them through the good offices of friends in Petersburg)—has long been on the threshold of a revolution and all the necessary elements are ready. The good Turks have hastened the explosion by years thanks to the drubbing they have given not only the Russian army and the Russian finances, but also the Russian dynasty (the Tsar, the heir apparent and six other Romanovs) in person. The foolish antics of the Russian students are only a symptom and valueless in themselves, but they are a symptom. All sections of Russian society are economically, morally and intellectually in a state of disintegration." These observations of Marx proved to be absolutely correct, but, as so often happened, in his revolutionary impatience and owing to the clarity with which he observed the way things were going, he underestimated the time factor.

The initial defeats of the Russians gave way to successes as a result, as Marx assumed, of secret support from Bismarck, of the treachery of England and Austria, and not least of the fault of the Turks themselves, who failed to overthrow the old Serail régime in Constantinople by a revolution, although that régime had been one of the best friends of the Tsar. A people which failed to act in a determinedly revolutionary fashion at a moment of extreme crisis was lost, declared Marx.

Thus the Russo-Turkish War ended not with a European revolution but with a diplomatic congress in the same place where and at the same time when the German socialist movement seemed to have been shattered with one terrible blow.

4. The Dawn of a New Day

Despite these reverses, however, the dawn of a new day began to show above the world horizon. The anti-socialist law with which Bismarck had hoped to shatter the German socialist movement actually opened up its heroic age and swept away all the confusion and dissensions which existed between it and the two veterans of socialism in London, although one more struggle took place first.

The German party gallantly stood the test of the anti-socialist crusade and the anti-socialist elections which took place in the summer of 1878 after the attempts on the life of the German Kaiser,[1] but in its preparations for the threatening blow it had not realized with what an accumulation of bitter hatred it would have to reckon. The Bill had hardly become law when the representatives of the government forgot all the promises of " impartial administration " with which they had soothed the misgivings of the Reichstag, and all the institutions of the party were suppressed, depriving hundreds of people of their livelihood. A few weeks later the so-called minor state of martial law was proclaimed over Berlin and the surrounding districts, although this was in obvious violation of the text of the Bill, and about sixty socialists were banished, losing not only their occupations but also their homes.

This alone caused understandable and hardly avoidable confusion in the socialist ranks. After the fall of the Paris Commune the General Council of the International had complained that owing to the necessity of providing assistance for the fugitives it had been prevented for months from carrying on its normal activities, but now the leadership of the German party was faced with a still more difficult task, for it was hampered at every step by police persecutions whilst a terrible economic crisis paralysed the country. It cannot be denied that the storm separated the wheat from the chaff : the bourgeois elements which had been drawn to the party in previous years frequently showed themselves to be unreliable ; some of the leaders also failed to stand the test, whilst others, including many capable and valuable men, lost courage under the heavy blows dealt by the reaction and feared to provoke the enemy to still more violent attacks by offering any energetic resistance.

All this naturally gave Marx and Engels very little satisfaction, and they certainly underestimated the difficulties of the

---

[1] On 11th May 1878 an unsuccessful attempt on the life of the German Kaiser Wilhelm I was made by Max Hödel, and a second unsuccessful attempt was made on 2nd June by Karl Nobiling.—Tr.

situation. But even the attitude of the social democratic Reichstag's fraction, which weathered the storm and reappeared in the Reichstag nine strong, gave them just cause for complaint. One of the members of the fraction, Max Kayser, thought it necessary to speak in favour of higher import duties on iron during the debate on the new import duties bill, and he even voted in favour of increased duties, a fact which made a very bad impression, for everyone knew that the aim of the new import duties was to obtain a few hundred more millions annually for the Reich's treasury, to protect the ground-rent of the landowners against American competition, and to assist large-scale industry to repair the damage it had inflicted on itself in the frenzy of the bubble years, and everyone knew that in the last resort the aim of the anti-socialist law was to break the resistance of the working-class to the threatening attacks on its standards of living.

When Bebel tried to defend Kayser's attitude by pointing out that he had made a particular study of the question, Engels answered abruptly : " If his studies were worth a snap of the fingers he would know that there are two iron foundries in Germany, the Dortmunder Union and the Königs und Laura Foundry, each of which is in a position to satisfy the whole of Germany's iron requirements, and that apart from these two there are a number of smaller works. And that therefore import duties on iron are idiotic and the only solution is the conquest of foreign markets, that is to say, the alternatives are absolute free trade or bankruptcy. He ought to know that the iron foundry capitalists themselves can want import duties on iron only if they have formed themselves into a ring, into a conspiracy, to impose monopoly prices on the home market and to get rid of their surplus products at dumping prices on the foreign market, something which they are already doing to a considerable extent. Kayser spoke in the interests of this ring, of this monopolist conspiracy, and when he voted for higher import duties on iron he voted in their interests too." When Karl Hirsch unceremoniously attacked Kayser's tactics in *Die Laterne*, the social-democratic Reichstag's fraction unfortunately adopted an attitude of injured dignity because Kayser had spoken with the permission of the fraction. This attitude was the last straw for Marx and Engels and the former declared : " Parliamentary cretinism has already eaten so thoroughly into their bones that they imagine themselves above criticism and condemn it indignantly as though it were lèse-majesté."

Karl Hirsch was a young journalist who had won his spurs as Liebknecht's representative on the *Volksstaat* during the years whilst Liebknecht was in prison. Afterwards he had lived in Paris, but on the passing of the German exceptional law he had been deported. He then did what the German party leadership should have done from the beginning : in the middle of December 1878 he began to issue *Die Laterne* from Breda in Belgium, a weekly in the style and format of Rochefort's *la Lanterne* so that it could be folded up and sent into Germany in ordinary letter envelopes and act as a rallying point for the socialist movement. The idea was good and Hirsch himself was thoroughly clear on questions of principle, but his style of writing, short, brilliant, pointed and epigrammatic, was little suited to the needs of working-class readers. In this respect *Die Freiheit*, a weekly which Most began to issue a few weeks later from London with the assistance of the Communist Workers Educational League, was more suitable, but unfortunately after a very fair beginning it lost itself in amateur revolutionism.

With the appearance of these two, so to speak, " wild " and independent papers, the question of an official party organ abroad became an urgent one for the German party leadership. Both Bebel and Liebknecht energetically supported the idea and finally they succeeded in overcoming the obstinate resistance of influential party circles which wished to maintain a policy of cautious reserve. It was no longer possible to come to any agreement with Most, but Hirsch abandoned *Die Laterne* and declared himself prepared to take over the editorship of the new party organ. Marx and Engels, who had complete confidence in him, were also prepared to contribute. The new publication was to appear weekly in Zürich, and three members of the party living there were instructed to make the necessary preparations for its appearance : the insurance agent Schramm, who had been expelled from Berlin, Karl Höchberg and Eduard Bernstein, whom Höchberg had won as his literary adviser.

They proved to be in no hurry to carry out their instructions and the reason for the delay became obvious when in July 1879 they issued *Das Jahrbuch für Sozialwissenschaft und Sozialpolitik* (Annual for Social Science and Social Politics) on their own account. This *Jahrbuch* was to appear semi-annually and the spirit in which it was edited was revealed in an article entitled "A Review of the Socialist Movement", which was signed with three stars. Its real authors were Höchberg and Schramm, whilst Bernstein contributed only a few lines to it.

The article was an incredibly tactless and ill-considered sermon on the sins of the party, its ill-mannered tone, its tendency to abuse its opponents, its flirting with the masses to the neglect of the educated classes, and in fact everything about a proletarian party which usually annoys a petty-bourgeois Philistine. The epitome of its practical wisdom was that the party should make use of the leisure forced on it by the anti-socialist law in order to repent and atone. Marx and Engels were highly indignant, and in a private letter with which they circularized the leaders of party they demanded categorically that if the latter found it necessary to tolerate the presence of people with such ideas in the party they should at least not be permitted to speak on behalf of the party. In reality Höchberg had not been given much authority by the party, but had taken it on himself, just as he did when he demanded that the trio in Zürich should have the right to control Hirsch's editorial activities and that Hirsch should abandon the style in which he edited *Die Laterne*. After this Hirsch and the two veterans in London refused to have anything further to do with the new organ.

Only remnants of the voluminous correspondence which was despatched on the point are still extant. These remnants indicate that Liebknecht and Bebel were far from agreeing with the attitude of the trio in Zürich, but it is difficult to see why they did not intervene energetically. Höchberg himself went to London, where he met Engels, but not Marx. His intellectual confusion made the worst possible impression on Engels, though neither he nor Marx ever doubted the fellow's good intentions. The mutual bitterness caused by the affair made it difficult to arrive at any agreement, and on the 19th of September 1879 Marx wrote to Sorge that if the new party weekly was edited in Höchberg's spirit they would be compelled to protest publicly against such " adulteration " of the party and its principles. " The gentlemen have been warned and they know us well enough to realize that the question must now be settled definitely one way or the other. If they insist on compromising themselves, so much the worse for them, but they will under no circumstances be permitted to compromise us."

Fortunately matters were not pushed to extremes. Vollmar took over the editorship of the Zürich *Sozialdemokrat* and conducted it " miserably enough ", in the opinion of Marx and Engels, but still not so badly that it became necessary to make any public protest. There were " constant disputes by letter with the people in Leipzig and the atmosphere was often heated ", but the trio in Zürich turned out to be harmless. Schramm kept completely in the background, Höchberg was often travelling, and under the influence of subsequent events Bernstein freed himself from the depression caused by the first onslaughts of the reaction, as also did many other members of the party who at first had been rather inclined to let things go as they pleased.

And finally, the fact that Marx and Engels subsequently showed greater appreciation of the enormous difficulties with which the party leaders had to contend also probably contributed to calming down the general anger and irritation. Writing to Sorge on the 5th of November 1880 Marx declared : " Those who enjoy the comparative peace and quiet of foreign countries have no right to make things harder, to the delight of the bourgeoisie, for those who are working under the most difficult circumstances and making great sacrifices in Germany." And a few weeks later peace was formally concluded between the contending parties.

On the 31st of December 1880 Vollmar resigned his editorial activity, and when the German party leaders then decided to appoint Karl Hirsch as his successor it was their intention to conciliate Marx and Engels. As Hirsch was living in London Bebel decided to go to London to negotiate with him personally and at the same time (as had been planned for a long time) to discuss the situation thoroughly with Marx and Engels. He took Bernstein with him in order to dissipate the prejudice which still existed against the latter in London, for in the meantime Bernstein had thoroughly rehabilitated himself. The journey to Canossa, as the visit to London was called in party circles, achieved its various aims, except that Karl Hirsch modified his original acceptance of the editorship by declaring that he wished to do the work in London. This was considered undesirable, and in the end Bernstein was appointed provisional editor. Finally his position became permanent, and he carried out his task with honour and to the satisfaction of everyone, including Marx and Engels. When the first elections took place under the anti-socialist law a year later Engels was jubilant and declared that no proletariat had ever fought more gallantly.

The movement in France also developed under a favourable star. After the wholesale massacres in May 1871 Thiers announced to the trembling bourgeoisie in Versailles that socialism in France was now dead for ever, ignoring the fact that he had soothed it with the same assurance once before, i.e. after the June slaughter of 1848, and proved himself a false prophet. Perhaps he thought that the still greater torrents of blood which had been shed in 1871 would prove more effective, for the losses of the Parisian proletariat as a result of the street fighting, the wholesale executions, the deportations, the galley sentences and the emigration were calculated at 100,000. After 1848 socialism had needed almost two decades in order to recover from the numbing blow it had received, but after 1871 it needed only half a decade to make its voice heard again. In 1876, when the courts martials were still performing their bloody work and defenders of the Commune were still falling under the volleys of the execution squads, the first workers congress took place in Paris.

True, for the moment it was no more than an indication, for the congress was under the patronage of the bourgeois republicans, who sought support from the workers against the monarchist landowners, and its decisions referred exclusively to harmless co-operative affairs such as were supported by Schulze-Delitzsch in Germany. However, it was quite clear that it would not stop at this. Mechanical large-scale industry, which had begun to develop gradually after the trade agreement with England in 1803, had developed much more rapidly from 1871 onwards. It was faced with big tasks : to make good the damage done over a wide area during the Franco-Prussian War, to accumulate the capital necessary for the rebuilding of militarism on a still greater scale, and finally to make good the deficiency caused by the loss of Alsace, the most highly industrialized French province, in 1870. Large-scale industry was quite capable of satisfying the demands placed upon it. All over the country factories sprang up and a strong industrial proletariat was created, whereas in the halcyon days of the old International an industrial proletariat had existed only in a few towns in North-Eastern France.

These conditions made possible the rapid success of Jules Guesde, who flung himself with fiery eloquence into the working-class movement which had begun again with the Paris congress of 1876. A recent convert from anarchism, Guesde did not distinguish himself by any very great theoretical clarity, as can be seen from the *Égalité* which he founded in 1877. Although the first volume of Marx's *Capital* had already been translated into French and published, he knew nothing about Marx, and his attention was first drawn to the latter's theories by Karl Hirsch, but he had thoroughly grasped the idea of the joint ownership of the land and of the means of production, and thanks to his brilliant eloquence and his great polemical ability he succeeded in rousing the French working-class on behalf of these demands as the last word in the proletarian class struggle, although they had always met with fierce opposition from the French delegates at all the congresses of the old International.

At the second workers congress which took place in Lyon in February 1878, and which was intended by its organizers to be no more than a repetition of the Paris congress, Guesde succeeded in rallying a minority of twenty delegates around his banner. Matters now became serious for the government and the bourgeoisie, and persecutions of the working-class movement again began, whilst by means of heavy fines and sentences of imprisonment imposed on its editors the *Égalité* was forced out of existence. However, Guesde and his supporters were not discouraged and they worked on unflaggingly until at the third workers congress, which took place in Marseilles in October 1879, they won over the majority of the delegates and immediately founded a Socialist Federation [1] which prepared to organize the political struggle. The *Égalité* came to life again and won a valuable contributor in Lafargue, who wrote almost all its theoretical articles, and a little later Malon, also a former Bakuninist, began to issue the *Revue Socialiste*, which Marx and Engels supported with occasional contributions.

In the spring of 1880 Guesde went to London in order to draw up an election programme for the young socialist party with the assistance of Marx, Engels and Lafargue. An agreement was reached on the so-called minimal programme, which, after a short introduction explaining the final communist aim of the movement, consisted in its economic section exclusively of demands which originated directly from the existing working-class movement. Agreement was certainly not obtained on every single point, and when Guesde insisted that the programme should contain a demand for the legal fixing of a minimum wage, Marx declared roundly that if the French proletariat was still childish enough to need such baits it was hardly worth while drawing up a programme at all.

However, things were not as bad as that, and on the whole Marx regarded the programme as a tremendous step towards freeing the French workers from confused phraseology and placing them on a basis of reality, and both from the opposition and the approval with which the programme met he assumed that the first real working-class movement was developing in France. In his opinion there had been nothing but sects in France up to that time, sects whose slogans were naturally manufactured by sectarians, whilst the great masses of the proletariat had remained aloof and followed in the wake of the radical or pseudo-radical bourgeoisie, fighting heroically for this bourgeoisie, only to be massacred and deported the next day by the very people they had helped to power. Marx was therefore completely in agreement with the return of his two sons-in-law to France immediately the amnesty, which had been wrung from the government for the communards, permitted them to do so. Lafargue returned to work together with Guesde, whilst Longuet took an influential position on *La Justice*, the organ of Clémenceau, who was at the head of the extreme left.

[1] *Fédération du parti des travailleurs socialistes en France.*

The situation in Russia was different, but even more fortunate from Marx's point of view. His *Capital* was more widely read and received greater recognition in Russia than anywhere else, particularly in the younger world of science and literature where Marx won many supporters and not a few personal friends. However, the two main tendencies of the Russian mass movement, as far as one can speak of such a thing at that time, the Party of the People's Will and the Party of Black Distribution still found his ideas completely foreign. Both parties were wholly Bakuninist in so far as they both aimed above all at winning the peasants. The chief question at issue for them was formulated by Marx and Engels as follows: Can the Russian peasant community, an already very degenerate form of primitive common ownership of the land, develop directly into a higher communist form of landownership, or must it first of all go through the same process of dissolution seen in the historical development of the Western European countries?

The "only possible answer to this question to-day" was given by Marx and Engels in a preface to a new translation of *The Communist Manifesto* by Vera Sassulitch [1] in the words: "If the Russian revolution gives the signal for a workers revolution in the West, so that both revolutions supplement each other, then the existing form of communal property in Russia can serve as the starting-point of a communist development." This point of view explains the passionate support Marx gave to the Party of the People's Will, whose terrorist policy had practically made the Tsar a prisoner of the revolution in Gatschina, whilst rather severely condemning the Party of Black Distribution because it rejected all forms of political and revolutionary action, and limited itself to propaganda, although men like Axelrod and Plechanov, who did so much to imbue the Russian working-class movement with the spirit of Marxism, were members of this latter party.

And finally the day began to dawn in England also. In June 1881 a little book entitled *England for All* appeared. It was written by Hyndman and represented the programme of the Democratic Federation, an association which had just been formed out of various English and Scottish radical societies, half-bourgeois, half-proletarian. The chapters on labour and capital consisted of literal extracts from Marx's *Capital* or of summaries of its ideas, but Hyndman mentioned neither the work itself nor its author and contented himself with remarking

---

[1] Engels quotes from this preface in his own preface to the German edition of 1890. The latter preface is given in Messrs. Martin Lawrence's edition of *The Communist Manifesto.*—Tr.

at the conclusion of his preface that he was indebted to the work of a great thinker and original writer for the ideas and much of the matter. This peculiar way of treating Marx's work was made still more irritating by the excuses with which Hyndman tried to justify himself to Marx : Marx's name was " so much detested ", the English didn't like to be taught by foreigners, and similar pretexts. Marx then broke off relations with Hyndman, whom he in any case held to be " a weak vessel ".

In the same year, however, Marx was greatly pleased by an article written about him by Belfort Bax and published in the December issue of one of the English monthlies.[1] It is true that he found most of the biographical information false and the description of his economic principles incorrect in many respects and confused, but he valued it as the first English publication of its kind which was filled with a real enthusiasm for the new ideas and which daringly set itself up against British Philistinism. The appearance of the article, which had been advertised in great letters on the walls and hoardings of the West End, created a great sensation.

In a letter written to Sorge, the man of iron, who was so indifferent to praise or blame, would seem to have experienced a mild attack of self-complacency, and nothing would have been more excusable, but in fact the letter was written at a moment of deep emotion as can be seen from its concluding sentences : " The most important thing for me was that I received my copy on the 30th of November so that the last days of my dear wife were made a little more cheerful. You know what a passionate interest she took in all such things." Frau Marx died on the 2nd of December 1881.

5. Twilight

Whilst the clouds gradually lifted from the social and political horizon everywhere—and that was always the chief thing for Marx—the dusk sank deeper and deeper on him and his house. When the continent was closed against him and he could no longer visit its health-giving spas his physical ailments grew worse again and rendered him more or less unfit for work. Since 1878 he had done nothing further to complete his main

---

[1] The article in question was published as one of a series entitled " Leaders of Modern Thought," in *Modern Thought*. No. XXIII, Karl Marx, by Ernest Belfort Bax.—Tr.

work and about the same time the gnawing anxiety for his wife's health began.

She had enjoyed the carefree days of her later life with the happy serenity of her harmonious and equable character. In a consolatory letter to the Sorges, who had lost two children in the years of adolescence, she wrote : " I know only too well how terrible it is and how long it lasts before one can again find one's equanimity after such a loss, but everyday life with its little pleasures and its great troubles, with all its petty worries and its minor torments, comes to our assistance and gradually the great suffering is numbed by the troubles and worries of the moment so that almost unnoticeably the violent anguish diminishes ; not that such wounds ever heal completely, and certainly not in a mother's heart, but gradually one recovers one's receptivity and even one's sensitiveness for new sufferings and new pleasures, and one lives on and on with a broken, but still hopeful heart until finally it is stilled for ever and eternal peace is there." Who deserved an easy death by the gentle loosening of earthly ties at the hands of Nature more than this gallant and patient woman ? But it was not to be her lot, and she once again had to bear great sufferings before the end came.

In the autumn of 1878 Marx informed Sorge that his wife was " very unwell ", and a year later he wrote : " My wife is still dangerously ill and I am not properly on my feet myself." Apparently after a long period of uncertainty it transpired that Frau Marx was suffering from incurable cancer, which must gradually and inevitably, and with much pain and suffering, bring about her death. What Marx himself suffered during this terrible illness can be measured only against the rôle his wife had played in his life. She herself bore her sufferings with greater stoicism than did her husband and her family. With heroic courage she suppressed all signs of pain in order always to show a serene face. In the summer of 1881, when the disease was already far progressed, she summoned up sufficient courage to make the journey to Paris to visit her married daughters. As the case was hopeless the doctors agreed to let her brave the dangers of the journey. In a letter to Madame Longuet on the 22nd of June 1881 Marx announced their visit : " Answer immediately for Mama will not leave until she knows what you would like her to bring you from London. You know she loves doing such things." The undertaking was carried out as satisfactorily for Frau Marx as was possible under the circumstances, but on their return Marx himself went down with a violent attack of pleurisy complicated with bronchitis and incipient pneumonia. It was a dangerous illness, but he got over it thanks chiefly to the self-sacrificing care and attention he received at the hands of his daughter Eleanor and from Lenchen Demuth. They were sad days and Eleanor wrote : " Mother lay in the big front room and the Moor lay in the little room next to it. The two who had grown so used to each other, whose lives had completely intertwined, could no longer be in the same room together. . . . The Moor got over his illness once again. I shall never forget the morning when he felt himself strong enough to get up and go into mother's room. It was as though they were young again together—she a loving girl and he an ardent youth starting out together through life, and not an old man shattered by ill-health and a dying old lady taking leave of each other for ever."

When Frau Marx died on the 2nd of December 1881 Marx was still so weak that the doctor forbade him to accompany his beloved wife on her last journey. " I submitted to his orders ", Marx wrote to his daughter Madame Longuet, " because a few days before she died your dear mother expressed the wish that there should be no ceremony at her funeral : ' We attach no importance to outward show '. It was a great consolation to me that her strength ebbed so rapidly. As the doctor prophesied, the disease took on the form of a general decline, as though it were caused by old age. Even in the final hours—no struggle with death, a slow sinking into sleep, and her eyes were bigger, more beautiful and brighter than ever."

Engels spoke at the grave of Jenny Marx. He spoke of her with the deepest respect and admiration as the loyal comrade of her husband and closed his speech with the words : " There is no need for me to speak of her personal virtues. Her friends know them and will never forget them or her. If there was ever a woman whose greatest happiness was to make others happy it was this woman."

6. The Last Year

Marx survived his wife little more than a year, but this period was really nothing but " a slow death ", and Engels' instinct was right when he declared on the day Frau Marx died, " The Moor has also died ".

As the two friends were again separated for the greater part of this short period their correspondence took on a last lease of life and in it the final year passes in melancholy grandeur, deeply moving on account of the painful details in which the relentless fate of all human kind dissolved this powerful spirit too.

All that still held him to life was a burning desire to devote his remaining strength to the great cause to which he had given his whole life. Writing to Sorge on the 15th of December 1881 he declared : " I have emerged from the last illness doubly crippled : morally through the death of my wife and physically as a result of the fact that it has left me with a congestion of the pleura and an increased sensitiveness of the bronchial tubes. I shall lose a certain amount of time altogether in attempts to restore my health." This time lasted until the day of his death, for all efforts to restore his health failed.

The doctors first of all sent him to Ventnor on the Isle of Wight and then to Algiers. He arrived in Algiers on the 20th of February 1882, but with a new attack of pleurisy brought on by the cold journey. New cause for misgivings was the fact that the winter and spring in Algiers was unusually cold, wet and disagreeable. He had no better luck in Monte Carlo, where he arrived on the 2nd of May with a new attack of pleurisy on account of the raw cold journey, and found persistently bad weather.

Only when he went to stay with the Longuets in Argenteuil at the beginning of June did his health improve a little. No doubt the agreeable comfort of family life did much to help him, and in addition he took the waters of the sulphur springs in the nearby spa of Enghien for his chronic bronchitis. Afterwards he stayed with his daughter Laura for six weeks in Vevey on the shores of Lake Geneva and this also helped considerably to improve his health so that when he returned to London in September he seemed quite strong again and often walked up to Hampstead Heath, which was about 300 feet higher than his home, without showing any signs of exhaustion.

He then intended to resume his work, for although the doctors had forbidden him to stay in London during the winter they had permitted him to stay on the south coast. When the November fogs threatened he went to Ventnor again, but he found mist and wet weather such as he had found in Algiers and Monte Carlo the winter before. He caught cold again, and instead of enjoying health-giving walks in the fresh air he was compelled to keep to his room and grow weaker. Any scientific work was impossible, although his interest in all scientific progress (even that which had no direct connection with his own field of work, such as the electrical experiments of Deprez at the Munich Electrical Exhibition) was still active. In general his letters reveal a discontented and depressed mood. When the inevitable growing pains began to manifest themselves in the young workers party of France he was dissatisfied with the way in which his sons-in-law represented his ideas : " Longuet as the last Proudhonist and Lafargue as the last Bakuninist. The devil take them." It was in this period that he used the phrase which has since so intrigued the Philistine world : that as far as he was concerned he was certainly not a Marxist.

On the 11th of January 1883 he suffered the last decisive blow with the death of his daughter Jenny, and the very next day he returned to London with a bad attack of bronchitis which was soon complicated by laryngitis and made it almost impossible for him to swallow. " He who had borne the greatest pains with stoic resignation now preferred to drink milk (which he hated all his life) rather than try to take any more solid nourishment." In February a tumour developed in one lung. The medicines he swallowed had no further effect on a body which had been overdosed with medicines for fifteen months. At the most they impaired his appetite and weakened his digestion. Almost noticeably he fell away from day to day, but the doctors had not given up hope, because the bronchitis had almost completely disappeared and it became easier for him to swallow. However, the end came unexpectedly. In the afternoon of the 14th of March 1883, whilst sitting in his easy chair, Karl Marx fell gently and without pain into his last sleep.

Despite great sorrow at this irreparable loss, Engels found that it contained a grain of consolation. " Medical skill might perhaps have made it possible for him to drag on another few years, living the life of a helpless invalid dying, not suddenly but by inches, to the greater glory of the medical profession. Our Marx could never have stood that. To live on with so much unfinished work before him and to suffer the tantalizing desire to finish it and to know that he would never be able to do so—that would have been a thousand times more bitter than the gentle death which took him. With Epicurus he was wont to say that death was no misfortune for him who died, but for those who survived. And to see this great genius lingering on as a physical wreck to the greater glory of medicine and the mockery of the Philistines whom he so often flayed in the prime of his life—no, a thousand times better as it is, a thousand times better that we carry him to the grave where his wife lies."

On the 17th of March, on a Saturday, Karl Marx was buried in the grave of his wife. His family tactfully dispensed with " all ceremony " such as would have closed his life with a painfully discordant note. No more than a few faithful friends were at the graveside. Engels with Lessner and Lochner, his old comrades from the days of the Communist League, Lafargue and Longuet from France and Liebknecht from Germany. Science was represented by two of its most prominent pioneers, the chemist Schorlemmer and the biologist Ray Lankester.

The farewell words which Engels addressed to his dead friend in English sum up so truthfully and straightforwardly and in such simple words what Karl Marx was to mankind and what he will always remain that it is fitting that they should close this book :

" On the afternoon of the 14th of March at a quarter to three the greatest living thinker ceased to think. Left alone for less than two minutes, when we entered we found him sleeping peacefully in his chair—but for ever.

" It is impossible to measure the loss which the fighting European and American proletariat and historical science has lost with the death of this man. Soon enough we shall feel the breach which has been broken by the death of this tremendous spirit.

" As Darwin discovered the law of evolution in organic nature, so Marx discovered the law of evolution in human history : the simple fact, previously hidden under ideological growths, that human beings must first of all eat, drink, shelter and clothe themselves before they can turn their attention to politics, science, art and religion ; that therefore the production of the immediate material means of life and consequently the given stage of economic development of a people or of a period forms the basis on which the State institutions, the legal principles, the art and even the religious ideas of the people in question have developed and out of which they must be explained, instead of exactly the contrary, as was previously attempted.

" But not only this, Marx discovered the special law of development of the present-day capitalist mode of production and of the bourgeois system of society which it has produced. With the discovery of surplus-value light was suddenly shed on the darkness in which all other economists, both bourgeois and socialist, had been groping.

" Two such discoveries would have been enough for any life. Fortunate indeed is he to whom it is given to make even one, but on every single field which Marx investigated (and there were many and on none of them were his investigations superficial) he made independent discoveries, even on the field of mathematics.

" That was the man of science, but that was by no means the whole man. For Marx science was a creative historic and revolutionary force. Great as was his pleasure at a new discovery on this or that field of theoretical science, a discovery perhaps whose practical consequences were not yet visible, it was still greater at a new discovery which immediately affected industrial development, historical development as a whole, in a revolutionary fashion. For instance he closely followed the development of the discoveries on the field of electrical science and towards the end the work of Marcel Deprez.

" For Marx was above all a revolutionary, and his great aim in life was to co-operate in this or that fashion in the overthrow of capitalist society and the State institutions which it has created, to co-operate in the emancipation of the modern proletariat, to whom he was the first to give a consciousness of its class position and its class needs, a knowledge of the conditions necessary for its emancipation. In this struggle he was in his element, and he fought with a passion and tenacity and with a success granted to few. The first *Rheinische Zeitung* in 1842, the *Vorwärts* in Paris in 1844, the *Deutsche Brüsseler Zeitung* in 1847, the *Neue Rheinische Zeitung* from 1848 to 1849, *The New York Tribune* from 1852 to 1861—and then a wealth of polemical writings, the organizational work in Paris, Brussels and London, and finally the great International Working-men's Association to crown it all. In truth, that alone would have been a life's work to be proud of if its author had done nothing else.

" And therefore Marx was the best-hated and most-slandered man of his age. Governments, both absolutist and republican, expelled him from their territories, whilst the bourgeois, both conservative and extreme-democratic, vied with each other in a campaign of vilification against him. He brushed it all to one side like cobwebs, ignored them and answered only when compelled to do so. And he died honoured, loved and mourned by millions of revolutionary workers from the Siberian mines over Europe and America to the coasts of California, and I make bold to say that although he had many opponents he had hardly a personal enemy.

" His name will live through the centuries and so also will his work." [1]

---

[1] This speech was delivered in English but published, apparently, only in a German translation in the *Sozialdemokrat* in Zürich. Engels' notes were also written in German. The above is a retranslation from the German.—Tr.

NOTES AS TO SOURCES

It is not in accordance either with the character or the aim of this book that it should be loaded with scholarly annotations. I shall therefore limit myself to giving the reader who would like more detailed information one or two indications as to the main highway and he will then be able to find his own way about in the by-ways.

In the tremendously increasing literature about Marx and Marxism there have been comparatively few biographical attempts. There were always short sketches of his life available, but as a rule they were full of errors and tended to grow more and more superficial as their matter was dragged from one book into the next. Engels was the first to create some sort of order here with the biographical sketch he published in Bracke's *Volkskalender* in 1878. Later on he wrote an article on Marx for the *Handwörterbuch fur Staatswissenschaften*, but although this article is generally reliable, it is not completely free of error.

Noteworthy amongst the other biographical contributions is Wilhelm Liebknecht's *Karl Marx zum Gedächtnis. Ein Lebensabriss und Erinnerungen* (*In Memory of Karl Marx. A Biographical Sketch and Memories.*), Nuremberg, 1896. This deals chiefly with the 'fifties and gives a fine picture of Marx, but it contains many inaccuracies. No less excellent, but in another fashion is a lecture delivered by Clara Zetkin and extended for print : *Karl Marx und sein Lebenswerk* (*Karl Marx and his Life's Work*), Elberfeld, 1913. Based on a thorough knowledge of the matters dealt with this publication is made still more valuable by an appendix which provides a guide for the reader, step by step, into the world of ideas which was opened up by Marx in his works.

One of the main sources for any biography of Marx up to 1850 is the four-volume edition known popularly as the *Nachlassausgabe* (Posthumous Edition), though it is now by no means the only publication from Marx's literary remains.[1] This edition has stood the test of a generation, and an appendix to a new edition issued in 1913 corrected one or two details. The first volume has been admirably supplemented by the work of Gustav Mayer on the *Rheinische Zeitung*, the *Deutsch-Französische Jahrbücher* and Friedrich Engels, and the fourth volume has been supplemented by five letters from Lassalle to Marx, which were discovered later on by Bernstein and published in *Die Neue Zeit*. In the introduction and the notes to this edition I collected a wealth of biographical material from written and printed sources so that the first chapters of this book represent to a certain degree only an extract of this material.

Another important biographical source for the two decades from 1850 to 1870 is the four-volume edition of the correspondence between Marx and Engels.[2] This monumental work was greeted with the necessary respect even by the enemy camp and numerous detailed reviews appeared in the German scientific press.

A third important biographical source for the years from 1870 to 1883 is the correspondence with Sorge.[3] The originals of these letters together

[1] *Aus dem literarischen Nachlass von Karl Marx*, see Bibliography.
[2] *Der Briefwechsel zwischen Friedrich Engels und Karl Marx, 1844 bis 1883*, see Bibliography.
[3] *Briefe und Auszüge aus Briefen von Joh. Phil. Becker, Jos. Dietzgen, Friedrich Engels, Karl Marx an F. A. Sorge und andere*, see Bibliography.

with all other handwritten material were presented by Sorge to the New York Public Library.

I shall mention further correspondence (with Kugelmann, Weydemeyer, Freiligrath, etc.) in cases where I have used it. I should like at this stage to express my lively thanks for the assistance which was rendered to me throughout the course of my work by Carl Grünberg's *Archiv für die Geschichte des Sozialismus und der Arbeiterbewegung*.[1] Despite the comparatively short time which has passed since the foundation of this publication it has developed, thanks to the splendid editorial guidance of its founder, into the centre of socialist research.

References : PE : Posthumous Edition. CME : Correspondence Marx-Engels. SC : Sorge Correspondence. GA : Grünberg's Archive.

EARLY YEARS : I was permitted to examine the process files from which I took the genealogical notes on Marx in the excellent library of Mauthner and Pappenheim in Vienna. Franz Mehring, *Splitter zur Biographie von Karl Marx* (*Fragments for a Biography of Karl Marx*), published in *Die Neue Zeit* (with details on the finishing examination). Franz Mehring, *Die von Westphalen* (*The Westphalens*), published in *Die Neue Zeit*.

A PUPIL OF HEGEL : Marx's letter to his parents was obtained in full from Eleanor Marx and published in *Die Neue Zeit*. Young Hegelian literature : Karl Friedrich Köppen, *Friedrich der Grosse und seine Widersacher* (*Frederick the Great and his Opponents*), Leipzig, 1840. Bruno Bauer, *Kritische Geschichte der Synoptiker* (*Critical History of the Synoptists*), Leipzig, 1841. Arnold Ruge, *Briefwechsel und Tagebuchblätter* (*Correspondence and Daily Memoranda*), Berlin, 1886. *Doktordissertation* (*The Doctoral Dissertation*), PE, I, 63. *Anekdota zur neuesten Philosophie und Publizistik* (*Anecdota on the Latest Philosophy and Publications*), Zürich, 1843. The *Rheinische Zeitung* from the 1st of January 1842 to the 31st of March 1843, complete file in the State Library in Berlin. Gustav Mayer in his *Die Anfänge des politischen Radikalismus im vormärzlichen Preussen* (*The Beginnings of Political Radicalism in pre-March Prussia*), published in *Die Zeitschrift für Politik*, Vol. VI, provides documentary material taken from the archives on the history of this newspaper together with valuable information on the sallies of the Young Hegelians into the political field. Important information on the internal crisis of the newspaper is given in eight letters which Marx wrote to Ruge and which were published by Bernstein in 1902 in his *Dokumente des Sozialismus* (*Documents of Socialism*). The most important articles written by Marx for the *Rheinische Zeitung* have since been collected PE, I, 71. *Ludwig Feuerbach, Briefwechsel und Nachlass* (*Ludwig Feuerbach, Correspondence and Literary Remains*), Heidelberg, 1874.

EXILE IN PARIS : The *Deutsch-Französische Jahrbücher*. The one and only double issue containing the first two numbers appeared in Paris in March 1844. The introductory *Briefwechsel* (*Correspondence*) and the two contributions each from Marx and Engels have been reprinted, PE, L, 360. Gustav Mayer in his *Untergang der Deutsch-Französischen Jahrbücher und der Pariser Vorwärts* (*The End of the Deutsch-Französische Jahrbücher and the Paris Vorwärts*), G.A., vol. III, provides much material from the archives on the history of this publication. Arnold Ruge, *Aus Früherer Zeit* (*From Earlier Days*), Berlin, 1866. Marx explains in a letter to Weydemeyer on the 5th of March 1852 how much he claims as his own intellectual achievement in the theory of the class struggle. See Franz Mehring, *Neue Beiträge zur Biographie von Marx und Engels* (*New Contributions to a Biography of Marx and*

---

[1] *Archive for the History of Socialism and the Working Class Movement* issued by Professor Dr. Carl Grünberg in Frankfort-on-Main and published by C. L. Hirschfeld in Leipzig.

Engels), *Die Neue Zeit.* See also Plechanov, *Ueber die Anfänge der Lehre von Klassenkampt* (*On the Beginnings of the Doctrine of the Class Struggle*), *Die Neue Zeit*, and Rothstein, *Verkünder des Klassenkampfes vor Marx* (*Preachers of the Class Struggle before Marx*), *Die Neue Zeit.* The Municipal Library in Vienna possesses a file of the *Vorwärts*, and the only article which Marx contributed to it has been reprinted in PE, II, 41.

FRIEDRICH ENGELS : Gustav Mayer has rediscovered, so to speak, the young Engels, *Ein Pseudonym von Friedrich Engels* (*A Pseudonym of Friedrich Engels*), GA, Vol. IV. The letters of Engels to a number of his youthful friends are of very great interest. They were published by Gustav Mayer in the September and October numbers of the *Neue Rundschau* in 1913. Engels and Marx, *Die Heilige Familie* (*The Holy Family*), PE, II, with a detailed commentary. Engels, *Die Lage der arbeitenden Klassen in England* (*The Condition of the Working Class in England*), Leipzig, 1845.

EXILE IN BRUSSELS : In his *Dokumente des Sozialismus* Bernstein has published long extracts from the polemic conducted by Marx and Engels against Max Stirner. Concerning their connections with " True Socialism " see PE, II. Wilhelm Weitling, *Garantien der Harmonie und Freiheit* (*Guarantees of Harmony and Freedom*), with a biographical introduction and notes by Franz Mehring, Berlin, 1908. Pierre Joseph Proudhon, *Correspondance*. Marx, *Das Elend der Philosophie* (*The Poverty of Philosophy*), Stuttgart, 1885. The *Deutsche Brüsseler Zeitung*, of which an almost complete file is in the party achives.[1] The most important contributions of Marx and Engels have been reprinted, PE, II. The comparatively sparse material extant on the Communist League is collected in Marx's *Enthüllungen über den Kommunistenprozess in Köln* (*Revelations on the Communist Trial in Cologne*), with an introduction by Engels and documents. Fourth edition with an introduction and notes by Franz Mehring, Berlin, 1914. Bertrand, *Die Sozialdemokratische Bewegung in Belgien vor 1848* (*The Social Democratic Movement in Belgium prior to 1848*), *Die Neue Zeit.* Rothstein, *Aus der Vorgeschichte der Internationalen* (*From the Early History of the International*), *Die Neue Zeit.* Wilhelm Wolff, *Gesammelte Schriften* (*Collected Writings*), issued by Franz Mehring, Berlin, 1909. Marx, *Lohnarbeit und Kapital* (*Wage-Labour and Capital*), with an introduction by Friedrich Engels, Berlin, 1891. Marx and Engels, *Das kommunistische Manifest* (*The Communist Manifesto*). The last edition issued under the direction of Friedrich Engels appeared in Berlin in 1890.

REVOLUTION AND COUNTER-REVOLUTION : The *Neue Rheinische Zeitung.* A number of leading articles reprinted in PE, II. Franz Mehring, *Freiligrath und Marx in ihrem Briefwechsel* (*Freiligrath and Marx in their Correspondence*), *Die Neue Zeit.* Lassalle and Marx, PE, IV, and CME, Vols. II and III.

EXILE IN LONDON : The *Revue der Neuen Rheinischen Zeitung.* Reprinted contribution, Marx, *Die Klassenkämpfe in Frankreich 1848 bis 1850* (*The Class Struggles in France*), with an introduction by Engels, Berlin, 1895. Other reprints, including a number of monthly reviews and book reviews, and Engels, *Die deutsche Reichsverfassungskampagne* (*The Campaign for the German Reich's Constitution*), PE, III. The Kinkel affair was cleared up for the first time by a number of articles based on material from the archives which appeared in 1914 in the *Preussische Jahrbücher*. Concerning life in exile in London see Franz Mehring, *Neue Beiträge* (*New Contributions*), taken from the correspondence Marx-Weydemeyer. Marx, *Der achtzehnte Brumaire des Louis Bonaparte* (*The Eighteenth Brumaire of Louis Bonaparte*), Stuttgart, 1914. Marx, *Enthüllungen über den Kommunistenprozess in Köln* (*Revelations concerning the Communist Trial in Cologne*).

[1] The archives of the German Social Democratic Party.—Tr.

MARX AND ENGELS : This chapter is based chiefly on CME, and it is unnecessary to quote detailed sources.

THE CRIMEAN WAR AND THE CRISIS : As this chapter was already in print when N. Riazanov published *Marx und Engels : Gesammelte Schriften 1852 bis 1862 (Collected Writings 1852 to 1862)*, Stuttgart, 1917, I was no longer able to use its material. However, the biographical value of the two big volumes which have already appeared is so slight that there is no need either to correct or supplement my own text. In general the impression is strengthened that Marx's work for *The New York Tribune* was by no means the lightest part of the burden he had to bear. The fact that Dana was not the actual owner of the paper, but only the slave-driver of the real owners Greeley and MacEkrath, will not lead all readers to Riazanov's conclusion that in the circumstances Dana treated Marx fairly. During the ten years in which he was working for the paper Marx never had the least idea that Dana was only his companion in misfortune. The writings and articles of Marx and Engels which Riazanov has collected are of very diverse value. In part they round off brilliantly and admirably the great scientific writings of their authors, and in part they are—particularly in the second volume—" merely newspaper correspondence ", and in the latter case their authors would certainly not be pleased with their resuscitation. Concerning Urquhart, Harney, Jones and the other personal acquaintances of Marx who are mentioned in this chapter, see CME, Gustav Mayer, *Zwei unbekannte Briefe von Marx and Lassalle (Two Unknown Letters of Marx to Lassalle)* from the year 1885, published in the *Frankfurter Zeitung* on the 10th of August 1913. Marx, *Zur Kritik der politischen Oekonomie (Critique of Political Economy)*, Berlin, 1859.

DYNASTIC CHANGES : Engels : *Po und Rhein ; Savoyen, Nizza und der Rhein (Po and Rhein ; Savoy, Nice and the Rhine)*, reissued by Bernstein, Stuttgart, 1915. Lassalle, *Der italienische Krieg und die Aufgabe Preussens (The Italian War and the Task of Prussia)*, Berlin, 1892. Vogt, *Mein Prozess gegen die Allgemeine Zeitung (My Action against the Allgemeine Zeitung)*, Geneva, 1859. Marx, *Herr Vogt.* Correspondence with Lassalle, Freiligrath and Weydemeyer and CME.

THE EARLY YEARS OF THE INTERNATIONAL : The early literature on the International (Testut, Villetard, etc.) is completely out of date, but useful occasionally if treated with the necessary caution. Rudolf Meyer, *Emanzipationskampf des vierten Standes (The Struggle for Emancipation of the Fourth Estate)*, Berlin, 1874. The first really scientific attempt to write a history of the great association was Jaeckh's *Die Internationale (The International)*, Leipzig, 1904. Originally written as a monograph on the fortieth anniversary of the foundation of the International, the small volume is still valuable to-day and obsolete in one respect only, though that is certainly a very important one, namely in its one-sided and harsh condemnation of all non-Marxist elements in the International, and in particular Bakunin. Jaeckh failed to see through the intrigues of Utin and the antics of Borkheim, and he relied too much on the Alliance pamphlet. Apart from Jaeckh's work, the six annual volumes of *Der Vorbote* issued by Joh. Philipp Becker in Geneva from 1866 to 1871 are still the best source of information on the International. Naturally, I have not wasted as much as a word in my text on the alleged treachery of Schweitzer. See Schweitzer, *Politische Aufsätze und Reden (Political Writings and Speeches)*, issued by Franz Mehring, Berlin, 1912, and Gustav Mayer, *J.B. von Schweitzer und die Sozialdemokratie (J. B. von Schweitzer and the Social Democracy)*, Jena, 1909. H. Laufenberg gives a good picture of Schweitzer's character and policy in his *Geschichte der Arbeiterbewegung in Hamburg, Altona und Umgegend (History of the Working-Class Movement in Hamburg, Altona and the Neighbourhood)*, Hamburg, 1911. Bebel, *Aus meinem Leben (From my Life)*, Vol. II, pp. 1 to 137, " The Period of Herr von Schweitzer ", merely repeats the old, long-since refuted accusations without making any attempt to come to grips with the refutation. Concerning the conference of the International in London, see M. Bach in *Die Neue Zeit* and " Briefe von Karl Marx to L. Kugelmann " (" Letters from Karl Marx to L. Kugelmann "), *Die Neue Zeit*.

DAS KAPITAL : The fragmentary material for a fourth volume which was to deal with the history of economic theories, has been collected by Karl Kautsky and published under the title, *Theorien über den Mehrwert* (*Theories on Surplus Value*), Stuttgart, 1904. All the popularizations of *Capital* are obsolete for one reason, if no other, namely that they refer exclusively to the first volume. Kautsky issued a "popular edition" of the first volume in Stuttgart, 1914. The tremendous literature which has been written around this classic economic work is more noteworthy for its volume than for its content, and this applies not only to the books written by opponents of Marx. The nearest approach to the original in breadth of knowledge, brilliance of style, logical trenchancy of argumentation and independence of thought is Rosa Luxemburg's *Die Akkumulation des Kapitals. Ein Beitrag zur ökonomischen Erklärung des Imperialismus* (*The Accumulation of Capital. A Contribution to an Economic Explanation of Imperialism*), Berlin, 1913, and at the same time it goes beyond the limits of the original and opens up new scientific knowledge. The way in which this book has been attacked, particularly by the so-called Austro-Marxists (Eckstein, Hilferding, etc.), represents one of the most brilliant achievements of hidebound Marxism.

THE INTERNATIONAL AT ITS ZENITH : For this and the following chapter attention must be given to the Bakuninist literature, apart from CME and *Der Vorbote*. Michel Bakounin, *Œuvres*, Vols. I–VI, Paris, 1907–13. James Guillaume, *L'Internationale. Documents et Souvenirs* (*The International. Documents and Memoirs*), Vols. I–IV, Paris, 1905–10. Max Netlau, *Bakunin und die Internationale in Italien bis zum Herbst 1872* (*Bakunin and the International in Italy up to the Autumn of 1872*), GA. The same, *Bakunin und die Internationale in Spanien 1868 bis 1873* (*Bakunin and the International in Spain from 1868 to 1873*), GA. The same, *Bakunin und die russische revolutionäre Bewegung von 1868 bis 1873* (*Bakunin and the Russian Revolutionary Movement from 1868 to 1873*), GA. Brupbacher, *Marx und Bakunin*, Munich, 1913. When I stress the importance of this literature in connection with the history of the International I do not mean that it contains nothing but wisdom and truth. On the contrary, it is much to be regretted that its authors have failed to treat Marx with the justice they rightly demand for Bakunin. However, it is as true in historical investigation as in all other matters that there are at least two sides to all questions and that in order to arrive at a reliable conclusion one must hear both sides. Good service is rendered in this respect by Steklov in his *Michael Bakunin*, Stuttgart, 1913. Steklov is a real Marxist, but just for this reason he demands that the German Social Democracy should at last do justice to Bakunin's memory. *The Confidential Communication* is printed in full in Marx's *Letters to Kugelmann*.

THE DECLINE OF THE INTERNATIONAL : *Der Bürgerkrieg in Frankreich* (*The Civil War in France*), with an introduction by Friedrich Engels, Berlin, 1891, containing the three Addresses of the International on the Franco-Prussian War and the Paris Commune. References of Marx to the Paris Commune in letters, see *Die Neue Zeit*. The fragmentary remnants of Marx's letters written during the Paris Commune to members of its Council, see *Die Neue Zeit*. *Mémoire présenté par la Fédération jurassienne de l'Association Internationale des Travailleurs à toutes les Fédérations de l'Internationale* (*Memorandum presented by the Jura Federations of the International Working-men's Association to all the Federations of the International*), Sonvillier, 1871. *Les prétendues scissions dans l'Internationale Circulaire privé du Conseil général de l'Association Internationale des Travailleur*

(*The Alleged Disruption in the International. Private circular of the General Council of the International Working-men's Association*), Geneva,1872. M. Bach,*Die Spaltung in der englischen Internationalen (The Split in the English International)*, see *Die Neue Zeit*. *L'Alliance de la démocratie socialiste et l'Association Internationale des Travailleurs (The Alliance of Socialist Democracy and the International Working-men's Association)*, London and Hamburg, 1873. The so-called Alliance Pamphlet.

THE LAST DECADE : Lafargue, *Persönliche Erinnerungen an Karl Marx (Personal Memories of Karl Marx)*, see *Die Neue Zeit*. Marx Programmatic letter. A similar letter from Engels to Bebel printed in *Aus meinem Leben*. Steklov, *The Bakuninistische Internationale nach dem Haager Kongress (The Bakuninist International after The Hague Congress)*, see *Die Neue Zeit*. Marx on the war in the Near East see SC, and the appendix to Liebknecht's *Zur orientalischen Frage (On the Oriental Question)*, Leipzig, 1878. Concerning the disputes during the first years of the anti-socialist law see SC, and Bebel, *Aus meinem Leben*. The last letter from Frau Marx, see SC. Concerning the last illness, death and burial of Marx, see Engels, SC, and in the *Sozialdemokrat*, Zürich, on the 22nd March 1883.

APPENDIX

THE preface to the first edition of Mehring's biography of Marx is dated March 1918. The work is therefore based on the material which had become available up to the beginning of 1918. Mehring's preparatory work, if one takes this expression in its wider sense, occupied, one may say, the whole of his life as a Marxist writer, or practically three decades since the beginning of the 'nineties. His *History of the German Social Democracy*, his editing and publishing of of the Posthumous Edition, his collaboration in the publication of the Marx-Engels Correspondence, and a wealth of minor writings on Marxist and related matters all belong to this period of preparatory work. One has only to consider what was known about the life and works of Marx and Engels before Mehring in order to realize that Mehring laid the basis and sketched the general outlines.

Mehring's biography of Marx comprises and concludes a whole epoch of Marxist research—if we adopt such a concise term for the tremendous theme represented by the lives and writings and the political and organizational activities of Marx and Engels in relation to the economic, political, literary and philosophic development of their day—an epoch in which Mehring was certainly not the only figure, but equally certainly the greatest one. In addition this comprehensive work was given a classic literary form.

The main part of the biography of Marx was written during the war years, whilst its author was active as one of the founders and pioneers of the Spartakist League, the predecessor of the Communist Party of Germany. This fact is important as an indication of the political standpoint adopted by Mehring in his work, and it can be seen in particular in his description of the attitude of Marx and Engels towards war and towards the practical forms in which they were faced with it, above all in the Franco-Prussian War of 1870-1. In the form of history Mehring had much to say concerning the Marxist attitude towards war and towards its various historical forms which could no longer have been said legally in a direct and critical fashion, and even within the limits of historical representation the military censorship compelled him to adopt many detours and circumlocutions in order to arrive at his aim.

Franz Mehring died in January 1919, and since then a new stage in Marxist research has begun whose centre is undoubtedly the Marx-Engels Institute in Moscow founded by D. Riazanov and directed by him for many years under the auspices of the Central Executive Committee of the Soviet Union. With the assistance of a large staff of collaborators great masses of new material have been collected, classified and edited. After 1918 many governmental, police and other archives were opened up, archives which had previously been completely closed to all investigations or which were open only to such investigators whose anti-Marxist attitude was beyond all doubt. The collected works of Marx and Engels being published by the Marx-Engels Institute are already far progressed and include a complete and authentic edition of the correspondence between Marx and Engels. In addition there are the textual publications and investigations of the Marx-Engels Archives, the publication of the literary remains of Lassalle and the correspondence between Lassalle and Bismarck by Gustav Mayer, the latter's work on the early writings of Engels, the publication of the " Confession " of Bakunin and other important material on Bakunin taken from the Russian archives, and the painstaking search through archives and libraries in the Rhineland, in London and in Paris, etc.

However, not only has the material itself tremendously increased, but the historical horizon of Marxist research has been tremendously widened as a result of the revolutionary upheavals whose starting-point was the Russian Revolution in November 1917, as a result of the first historical appearance of a State based on the proletarian dictatorship and destined to be more than the historical episode represented by the Paris Commune, and finally as a result of the fact that the basis of bourgeois society has been shaken and in part shattered. In the light of these tremendous historic events Marxist questions have often taken on quite a different signifiance and form than they had in the period when the capitalist system of society enjoyed comparative stabilization. " Theory " became practice, the " word " became " flesh ".

The present stage of Marxist research is still a long way from its end. The study of details will continue for many years still and any comprehensive work on the whole of the present stage of research will remain impossible for a very long time to come. Its basis will naturally be the complete publication of the collected works and correspondence of Marx and Engels. In the meantime, the work which concludes and sums up the period of Marxist research from 1890 to 1918—the Mehring biography of Marx—is indispensable.

The aim of this appendix is to make the reader acquainted as far as its brevity permits with the most important points which have been raised since by the texts of Marx and Engels, the new documents which have been published and the results of later research.

It would go far beyond the limits of this popular biography to quote all details and even then it would at the present stage be no more than patchwork and could not satisfy the stern demands of scientific accuracy and comprehensiveness, whilst at the same time it would disturb the classic unity of form which Mehring gave to his work.

Here and there Mehring's standpoint must be altered in important respects and in accordance with the general aim of his book this will be done objectively and not polemically and critically.

1. The Preparatory Work for Marx's Doctoral Dissertation

The collected works of Marx and Engels being published by the Marx-Engels Institute (hereinafter briefly referred to as CW) make Marx's preparatory work for his doctoral dissertation on " The Difference between the Democritean and Epicurean Natural Philosophy " available to the public for the first time. The preparatory work was begun in Berlin in the winter of 1839, and it shows still more clearly Marx's independence of Hegel even at that time. The work confirms what Engels declared in later years in answer to the question of A. Woden, a young follower of Plechanov, " Whether at any time Marx was a Hegelian in the actual sense of the word ? " Engels answered, " that precisely the dissertation on the difference between Democritus and Epicurus makes it possible to assert that right at the beginning of his literary activity Marx, completely mastering the Hegelian dialectical method and not yet compelled by the progress of his own work to transform that method into the materialist dialectical method, nevertheless showed complete independence of Hegel precisely on that field where Hegel was undoubtedly at his strongest, namely, on the field of the history of thought. Hegel gives no reconstruction of the immanent dialectic of the Epicurean system, but a number of careless extracts from this system, whilst Marx gave a reconstruction of the immanent dialectic of Epicureanism, but without in the least idealizing it, and exposing its sparse content as compared with the Aristotelian system. Engels then explained in detail the great difference between the attitude of Marx to Hegel and the attitude of Lassalle to Hegel, pointing out that Lassalle ' never emancipated himself from his relation as a pupil to Hegel '. . . . Engels also recalled that Marx had intended to occupy himself still further with the history of Greek philosophy, and that even shortly before the end Marx had spoken to him on the subject, whereby he did not conceal his preference for the materialist systems, and based himself chiefly on the dialectic of Plato and Aristotle, and—from the newer philosophy—Leibniz and Kant." (A. Woden, *On the Threshold of Legal Marxism, The Annals of Marxism.*)

Particularly interesting in this preparatory work is the severe criticism of the idea of individual immortality as represented by the antique " Philistine " Plutarch, the praise of the " really Roman epic poet ", materialist and enemy of the Gods, Lucretius, and further the proclamation of the coming attack by philosophy on the existing world :

" Just as there are junctions in philosophy which raise it to concretion in themselves, which embrace abstract principles in a totality, and thus interrupt the straight line of progress, so there are also moments in which philosophy, no longer comprehending, but like a practical person spinning intrigues with the world, leaves the pellucid orbit of Amenthes and throws itself on the bosom of the mundane siren. . . . but like Prometheus who stole fire from heaven and began to build houses and settle down on the earth, philosophy which has extended itself to the world turns against the world of phenomena. This is what the Hegelian philosophy is now doing " (CW, I, i, p. 172).

The suggestion is already present that philosophy which turns against the world of phenomena and takes up the struggle against it must change its own form. And Marx quickly comes to the conclusion that in order to fulfil itself philosophy must liquidate itself.

And finally, a fruitful seed for future materialist development is contained in the observations of Marx concerning the " philosophic historical writings ". In every philosophic system one must differentiate " the definitions themselves, the constant real crystallizations, from the proofs, the justification in conversations, and the representation of the philosophers, as far as they know themselves " (CE, I, i, p. 143).

Later on, as an historical materialist, Marx proceeds still further to the differentiation between what a certain historical epoch thinks about itself, its " ideology ", and what it really, materially is.

2. THE CRITIQUE OF THE HEGELIAN PHILOSOPHY OF LAW

This has been published for the first time in CE, I, pp. 403–63. Its editors assume that it was written from March to August 1843, that is to say, after the resignation of Marx from the editorship of the *Rheinische Zeitung*. In their introduction to the earlier works of Marx and Engels (Karl Marx, *Historical Materialism, etc.*, Alfred Kröner, Leipzig, 1932.) S. Landshut and I. P. Mayer seek to prove that the work must be given an earlier date and that it was practically finished in March 1842 when Marx offered it to Ruge for publication in his *Anekdota Philosophica*.

The great significance of this work, which was primarily intended by Marx as an attempt to get straight with himself on the issue, consists in three things. First of all in the discovery of the inverted " mystical " process of Hegelian idealistic dialectic, secondly in the discovery that not the State, as Hegel contends, but " bourgeois society " is the source of historical development, and thirdly in the contention that the bourgeois republic is itself an unsolved contradiction which not only fails to realize the real community of humanity but intensifies its opposite to the extreme, and that the basis of the bourgeois State in all its forms is private property.

First of all concerning the " logical pantheistic mysticism " of Hegel :

" Reality (with Hegel) becomes a phenomenon, but the idea has no other content apart from this phenomenon. It has also no other purpose but the logical one ' of being the eternal real spirit in itself '. This paragraph contains the whole mystery of the Hegelian philosophy of law and of the Hegelian philosophy in general " (p. 408).

" It is important that everywhere Hegel makes the idea the subject, and the actual real subject, for instance, " political opinions ", the predicate. Development, however, proceeds always on the side of the predicate " (p. 416).

" The only aim (of Hegel) is to find ' the idea ' in itself, the ' logical idea ' in each element, whether it is the State, or nature, whilst real subjects, in this case the ' political constitution ', become merely their names, so that only the appearance of a real recognition is present. They are and remain unconceived because they are not conditions conceived in their specific essence " (p. 412).

" He (Hegel) does not develop his thought from the thing, but the thing according to a completed thought at one with itself in the abstract sphere of logic. The aim is not to develop the definite idea of the political constitution, but to arrange it as a link in its own history (as an idea), an obvious mystification " (p. 415).

" Just because Hegel proceeds from the predicates of the general definition instead of from the real Ens (ὑποκεί·μενον, subject) and nevertheless a basis for these definitions must exist, the mystic idea becomes this basis. This is Hegel's dualism ; he does not regard the general as the real essence of the real-finite, i.e. the existing, definite, or the real Ens (being) as the real subject of infinity " (pp. 426–7).

Thus Marx critically dissolves the mysticism of the Hegelian idealist dialectic, lays bare its process in all its details, and demands a dialectic based on reality, that is to say, a materialist dialectic. This represents a tremendous and fundamental advance not only on Hegelian idealism, but on all idealism, whilst still retaining the " rational ", that is to say, material nucleus of the Hegelian dialectic. Thus an advance beyond Feuerbach also.

The State and bourgeois society : " What is therefore the power of the proletarian State over private property ? The special power of private property itself, its essence brought into existence. What remains to the political State in contradiction to this essence ? The illusion that it determines where it is itself determined " (p. 519).

" Private property is the general category, the general State bond " (p. 530).

The contradiction of the representative constitution, of formal democracy : " The representative constitution (compared with the corporative) represents a certain progress because it is the frank, unfalsified and logical expression of modern State conditions. It is the unhidden contradiction " (p. 492).

The contradiction as it is expressed in the deputy : " They are formerly deputized, but immediately, they are really so they are no longer deputies. They are supposed to be deputies, but they are not " (p. 542).

In the beginning Marx was able to give the solution of the contradiction only in general outlines : " The political republic is democracy within the abstract State form. The abstract State form of democracy is therefore the republic. However, here it ceases to be the merely political constitution (p. 436).

" Hegel proceeds generally from the separation of the State and ' bourgeois society ', from the ' particular interests ' and from ' being in itself ', and the bureaucracy is certainly based on this separation " (p. 454).

" The liquidation of the bureaucracy can only be that the general interest really becomes the particular interest and not merely, as with Hegel, in the idea, in the abstraction, and this is possible only if the particular interest becomes the general interest " (pp. 457–8).

" Governmental power is the most difficult to develop. It belongs to the whole people to a far greater degree than the legislative power " (p. 464).

It is really astonishing how far Marx has already obtained clarity on the essence of the bourgeois State in its most highly developed form, the democratic republic, through his thoroughgoing criticism of the reality of the bourgeois State and of the most highly developed philosophy of law of his own day, the Hegelian, and how he already begins to draw the general outlines of another and further form of State, a State which for the moment, however, he refers to as the " true " State. In this definition we can still sense the restraining influence of Feuerbach, but Marx was soon to throw it off.

The most important conclusion offered by these early writings of Marx is that he was never a democrat in the sense of bourgeois and formal democracy.

3. FRIEDRICH ENGELS

Since the publication of Mehring's biography of Marx a great amount of new material has been published on the development and activity of Engels. In 1920 the first volume of a biography by Gustav Mayer appeared together with a supplementary volume, *Schriften der Frühzeit* (*Earlier Writings*). In 1930 the second volume of the CW appeared containing the works of Engels up to the beginning of 1844, together with letters and comments, a volume amounting to almost 700 pages. The volumes of the CW up to 1848 also contain new and important Engels material. Engels' *Dialectics in Nature* has been published in full in Volume II of the Marx-Engels Archive. A number of other hitherto unpublished minor works of Engels are contained in the *Annals of Marxism*. In this way the information concerning his career and activity has been greatly enriched, and the more information we obtain about him the more he emerges from the comparative obscurity in which his own great modesty placed him.

4. THE FIRST ECONOMIC STUDIES AND WORKS OF KARL MARX

Marx began his economic studies in Paris in 1843 on the basis of the works of the great English and French writers. His starting-point was Engels' " Outline of a Critique of Political Economy " which appeared in the *Deutsch-Französische Jahrbücher*. The still extant note-books abstract from Adam Smith, Ricardo, James S. Mill, McCulloch, I. B. Say, Friedrich List and others. Boisguillebert was the first of the old French economists he read. Marx intended to issue the results of his economic studies in a special brochure to be followed by a number of further independent brochures on the critique of law, morality, politics, etc., then a special work on the connection of the whole and the relations of the individual parts, and finally a critique of the speculative study of the material. These economic-philosophic manuscripts have now been published in Vol. III of the CW, pp. 29 to 172, together with a review of the most important of the note-books, *ibid.*, pp. 437–83.

The terminology of these works is still strongly under the influence of Ludwig Feuerbach. In the sketch for his introduction to the drafts for a critique of political economy Marx points out that the only preliminary works were W. Weitling, M. Hess in the *Deutsch-Französische Jahrbücher* and F. Engels' " Outline of a Critique of Political Economy ". " Positive criticism in general, including therefore also the German positive criticism of political economy " must thank " the discoveries of Feuerbach " in his *Philosophy of the Future* and his *Theses for a Reform of Philosophy* for its " real basis ". " Positive humanist

and naturalist criticism " dated first from Feuerbach. The following
points will indicate the stage of Marx's economic criticism at the
time :

The law of wages put forward by Adam Smith is accepted as
correct. "According to Smith the usual wage is the lowest com-
patible with simple *humanité*, namely, an animal existence " (p. 39).
Overproduction is the result of a state of social affairs which is the
most favourable for the worker, namely, increasing and extending
riches (p. 43). The situation of the working class is characterized as
follows : " Therefore in a declining situation of society we find progressive misery for the workers, in a progressive situation complicated
misery for the workers, and in the completed situation stationary
misery." Errors of the " Reformers *en détail*, who want to raise wages,
or who, like Proudhon, want to establish ' equality of wages ' "
(p. 46). From the German economist Schultz Marx borrows the
conception of the " relative impoverishment of the worker " in view
of the increasing wealth of society and the stationary income of the
worker. Capital is defined on one occasion as " stored-up labour "
(according to Adam Smith) and then as " the governing power over
labour and its products ". There is no analysis of capital profits.
Under the rule of private property the accumulation of capital results
in its concentration in the hands of a few as the natural destiny of
capital encouraged by competition (p. 57). The categories of fixed
and circulating capital are borrowed from Adam Smith. Constant
and variable capitals have not yet made their appearance. He also
takes over the ground-rent theory of Adam Smith, but observes
critically : " Thus clearly proving the inversion of conceptions in
political economy which turns the fruitfulness of the earth into an
attribute of the landowner " (p. 62). Ground-rent is established in
a struggle between tenant and landowner. " Everywhere in political
economy we find the hostile play of interests, a struggle, war, recognized
as the basis of social organization." The small-scale working landowner stands in the same relation to the large-scale landowner as
does the artisan who owns his own tools to the " factory owner "
(p. 74). And finally society falls into two classes, the property owners
and the propertyless workers (p. 81). (Bourgeois) political economy
proceeds from the factor of private property ; it sums up the material
process of private property in general abstract forms, in laws, but it
does not understand these laws, i.e. it does not show how they proceed
from the essence of private property. With this Marx arrives at
his historical critical, i.e. his revolutionary standpoint towards the
question. An explanation must be found not from any " invented
original state ", but from " the existing political and economic
factors ". In what does this consist ? " Labour produces not only
commodities, it produces itself and the worker as a commodity, and
in the same relation in which it produces commodities in general "
(pp. 82-3). The object which labour produces presents itself as
" an alien entity ", as a power independent of the producer. Alienation and externalization of labour. " All these consequences lie in
the condition that the worker adopts an attitude to the product of his

labour as an alien entity.   For according to this condition it is clear :
the more the worker expends his labour the more powerful becomes
the alien objective world which he creates outside himself, and the
poorer he and his inner-world become and the less he can call his
own.   It is just the same in religion, the more man places in God the
less he retains in himself . . ." (p. 83).

The "alienation of labour" expresses itself in the following
fundamental phenomena :

(a) Labour is "external" to the worker, that is to say, it does not
belong to his being ; he feels unhappy in it, he develops no free
physical and intellectual energy, but "mortifies" his flesh and ruins
his spirit.   The worker therefore "feels his individuality only outside
labour and in labour outside himself" ;

(b) His labour belongs not to him, but to another ; and

(c) Because externalized labour alienates the human being, (1)
from nature, and (2) from himself, from his own active functions, from
his active life, it also alienates him from the species.

Alienated labour produces "the dominance of those who do not
produce over production and its product" (p. 91).   Private property,
apparently the reason and basis for alienated labour, is in reality one
of its consequences (pp. 91–2).   All political economic categories can
be developed from the conception of alienated labour and private
property.

The conception of "alienation", "externalization", comes
directly from Feuerbach and further back from Hegel, but it would
be wrong not to observe, as most bourgeois critics of the early economic
works of Marx fail to do, that here Marx grasps one of the fundamental
facts of the bourgeois economic order from a revolutionary standpoint :
the separation of the worker from the tools of production.   Although
the terminology is still that of Hegel and Feuerbach, the analysis is
revolutionary and materialist, and grasps the basic relation of capital
from the standpoint of the working-class and socialism, thus going far
beyond both Hegel and Feuerbach.   The essential factor of Marxist
analysis at this stage is not the formal shell of Feuerbachianism, but
the material content which is seen to be already far in advance of
Feuerbach.

Marx still distinguishes between "primitive communism", that
is to say a general levelling, the abstract negation of the world of
civilization and culture (with this expression he means primitive
artisan communism with its idea of asceticism, the overthrow of the
previous cultural world, etc.), and the higher stage which is communism, "the positive liquidation of private property, as human self-
alienation, and thus the real appropriation of the attributes of humanity
by and for humanity ; thus as a completely conscious return, on the
basis of the whole wealth of previous development, of the human being
as a social, that is to say, as a real human being" (p. 114).   Communism on the basis of the technical and cultural achievements of
capitalism !   At this stage Marx still calls this sort of communism
"completed naturalism" and "humanism".

"Communism", he declares further, "is the position of the negation of the negation and therefore the real factor necessary for the next stage of historical development of human emancipation and self-recovery. Communism is the necessary form and the energizing principle of the immediate future, but communism is not as such the aim of human development—the form of human society " (p. 126).

The further and definitive development of this idea is to be found in Marx's marginal notes to the Gotha Programme sketching the various stages of the development of socialism and communism. Later on Marx abandoned the idea of " the aim of human development " altogether, whilst in his *Anti-Dühring* Engels (in agreement with Marx) develops the idea that a rising branch of human development necessarily supposed a declining branch and finally the historical end of humanity.

Here we can also find the nucleus of the fundamental idea of historical materialism that the social consciousness of man is determined by his social being : " In his generic consciousness man confirms his real social life and merely repeats his real existence in thought" (p. 117). The term " generic consciousness " is still Feuerbach, but the content is fundamentally in advance of Feuerbach.

Following on his analysis of " alienated labour " Marx again gives a criticism of Hegelian idealist dialectics on the basis of Hegel's *Phenomenonology* (1807). The genius of Hegel : (1) that he grasps the self-creation of humanity as a process, and (2) analyses human labour. However, Hegel takes only " abstract intellectual labour " as labour. He sees only the positive side of labour and not its negative side. The human being is regarded as an immaterial spiritual entity. The world of the spirit is recognized and liquidated as the self-alienation of the human being, but at the same time presented as the real existence of the latter. " Here is the root of the false positivism of Hegel, or his merely apparent criticism " (p. 163).

5. Marx as the Organizer of the International

The organizational activities of Marx and Engels which culminated in the entry of their organizations into the Communist League and the adoption of scientific communism by the league were first revealed by D. Riazanov, who was assisted by the analogy between the Russian circles in the 'eighties and 'nineties which finally led to the formation of the Social Democratic Party of Russia as a centralized party, and the corresponding stage in the communist movement in the 'forties. Marx and Engels organized the " Workers' Educational League " in Brussels. From Brussels they established connections with communist circles in Germany, London, Paris and Switzerland. " Correspondence Committees " were formed and directed by them and their supporters in Brussels, Paris and London. Marx wrote to Proudhon to secure his assistance for the " Correspondence Committee " in Paris. In 1846 the Central Correspondence Bureau in Brussels was led by Marx, a bureau in Paris by Engels, and another one in London by Bauer, Schapper and Moll. On the 20th of January 1847 Moll came to Brussels as the delegate of the London Correspondence Committee in order to report on the situation in the London society.

This visit led to a decision to hold an international congress in London. The Communist League was founded at this congress. Wilhelm Wolff was present as the representative of the Brussels organization. Draft statutes were adopted to be discussed by the individual branches until the next congress. The organizational unit was the "commune" or branch. The "communes" were organized in districts. The "central district" elected the Central Committee. The first communist journal was issued as the official organ of the league. (Only one number appeared.) The second congress took place in November 1847. This time Marx was present. Detailed discussions on the programme took place and Marx was instructed to draw up the Manifesto of the Communist Party. The Manifesto was published in the second half of February 1848. It is worth noting that in its first two editions *The Communist Manifesto* was entitled *The Manifesto of the Communist Party*.

From these details it is clear that Marx and Engels did not act as isolated authors drawing up a manifesto and making it the programme of the first international communist party, but as leaders of an international communist movement organized by them. Although this movement was numerically very weak, nevertheless it represented the concentration of all the most progressive elements in the working-class movement of the day, and it was the real starting-point of the socialist and communist working-class movement of the nineteenth and twentieth centuries. The organization took account of the need for illegality, but it was no longer a "conspiratorial organization" in the old sense, but an internationally organized revolutionary party whose main aim for the moment was the dissemination of consistent communist propaganda on the basis of scientific communism or socialism as developed by Marx and Engels.

6. The *German Ideology*

The *German Ideology, a Criticism of the Latest German Philosophy and its Representatives Feuerbach, B. Bauer, and Stirner and of German Socialism and its Various Prophets* has now been published in full in Vol. V. of the CW.

The first section *Feuerbach* contains a description of the main factors of historical materialism as developed by Marx and Engels, and a summary criticism of Feuerbach. The development of humanity begins with the production of the means of life by humanity. A certain "mode of life" is characterized by what is produced and how it is produced. The stages of the "division of labour" determine the various historical forms of property, i.e. the prevailing stage of the division of labour determines also the relations of the individuals to each other with regard to the material, the instruments and the product of labour (p. 11). Main stages of property : (1) "Tribal property" (i.e. primitive communism), the beginnings of slavery ; (2) "Ancient communal and State property (Slavery still existing). Later on personal and then real property developed ; (3) "Feudal or corporative property " ; (4) Bourgeois property. "Consciousness can never be anything but conscious being, and the being of humanity is its real living process " (p. 15). With the representation of reality " independent philosophy " loses the medium of its existence. At the utmost its place can be taken by a summary of the most general results which can be abstracted from the contemplation of the historical development of humanity (p. 16). " The production of life, both one's own in labour and new life in procreation, thus appears as a double relation, on the one hand as a natural relation, and on the other hand as a social relation—social in the sense that thereby the co-operation of several individuals is understood irrespective of the conditions, the fashion and the aim of such co-operation " (p. 19). This passage is very important because it shows irrefutably that the formula later used by Engels summing up the production and re-production of human life as the basic factors of social development, was not a fortuitous improvization of his own, as some critics of Marxism contend, but one already used by Marx and Engels together as early as 1845–86. Language is as old as consciousness ; it is a social product. The first division of labour is in the sexual act, and later as the result of the diversity of physical characteristics, etc. The State develops from the contradiction between particular and general interests. All the struggles within the State are the illusory forms in which the real struggles between the classes are conducted (p. 23). Every class aiming at domination must first conquer political power. " Bourgeois society " is the real basis and stage of all history. The later expression " ideological superstructure " is here represented by the expression " idealist superstructure ", which raises itself on the economic basis of society (p. 26). Feuerbach wishes to turn the term communist as referring to the supporters of a particular political party into a mere category (p. 31). Feuerbach goes as far as a theoretician can go at all without ceasing to be a theoretician and philosopher. Feuerbach limits himself to the mere contemplation of the physical world. He remains stationary at the abstraction " the human being ". He appreciates the human being as a physical object, but not as a " physical activity ". He gives no criticism of the existing conditions of life. He falls back into idealism " where the communist materialist sees the necessity and at the same time the conditions for a trans-formation both of industry and the social organism. As far as Feuer-bach is a materialist history has no say with him, and in so far as he examines history he is no materialist " (p. 34). Within the ruling class a division of labour takes place between its " active conceptive ideologists " and the remaining mass, which represents in reality the " active members of this class ". The " State " is " nothing more than the form of organization which the bourgeoisie necessarily adopts to guarantee its property and its interests both from within and without. The State is independent to-day only in countries where the estates have not yet completely developed into classes, in countries where the estates, which have been abolished in the more progressive countries, still play a rôle, countries therefore in which no section of society has yet succeeded in gaining the upper hand. This is the case particularly in Germany " (p. 52).

A stage is reached in the development of the productive forces when means of production and means of transport are produced which under the given circumstances can cause only damage, "forces of destruction". The class which bears all the burdens of society, which is forced into an antagonism to all other classes, which represents the majority of all the members of society and in whose ranks the consciousness of the necessity of a fundamental revolution, the communist consciousness, arises, is the active factor of the necessary revolution. It carries on a revolutionary struggle against the previous ruling classes. The communist revolution "liquidates the dominance of all classes and the classes themselves". The revolution is necessary not only because the ruling class can be overthrown only in this way, but also because only in this way can the rising class "rid itself entirely of all the accumulated evils of the past and become capable of founding a new society" (p 59).

"In our opinion therefore all previous collisions in history have their origin in the contradiction between the productive forces and the mode of society. . . . It is, by the way, not at all necessary that in order to lead to collisions in a particular country this contradiction must necessarily be intensified to breaking point in that particular country. Competition with more highly industrialized countries brought about by an extension of international relations is quite enough to produce a similar contradiction in countries whose industries are less developed (for instance, the latent proletariat in Germany brought to light by the competition of English industry)" (p. 63). This passage indicates that even at that time Marx and Engels were well aware of the possibility that the communist revolution might not necessarily break out first in the most highly industrialized countries.

The criticism of Max Stirner takes up the greater part of the *German Ideology* (pp. 97–428). Mehring observes : "It is a still more discursive super-polemic than even *The Holy Family* in its most arid chapters, and the oases in the desert are still more rare, although they are by no means entirely absent" (see this volume, Chapter V, No. 1, the *German Ideology*).

It is certainly difficult for the workers of our day to follow the detailed polemic of Marx and Engels against Max Stirner, but nevertheless it is absolutely necessary to point out that it is not a question of any philosophical chimeras of no importance to the reader of to-day, but a fundamental discussion between communism and anarchism. Stirner is one of the chief sources of anarchism. It would be a very valuable work to extract everything from this discussion which is of fundamental importance for the relation of socialism and communism to anarchism. The discussion contains in fact all the essential factors for such a critique. The work proves in detail that Stirner's "association of free men" is nothing but "an idealist reflection of present-day society" (p. 188). The petty-bourgeoisie, its needs and its ideals, are revealed as the basis of Stirner's criticism. Stirner propagates "the revolt" as against the communist revolution.

"The whole philosophy of revolt", observe Marx and Engels, "which has just been presented to us in poor antitheses and faded flowers of eloquence is in the last resort nothing but bombastic apologia for parvenuism. Every upstart has something particular in mind when he undertakes his 'egoist action', something above which he wishes to raise himself irrespective of the general conditions. He seeks to overcome the existing something only in so far as it is a hindrance, and for the rest he seeks to appropriate it. The weaver who has 'risen' to become a factory owner has got rid of his weaving loom, has left it. Otherwise the world continues its daily round as usual, and our 'flourishing' upstart now turns to the others with the hypo-critical moral demand that they should also become parvenus like him. Thus the whole belligerent rodomontade of Stirner resolves itself into nothing but moral conclusions from Gellert's fables and speculative interpretations of bourgeois misery" (pp. 360–1).

The following is an important passage from the criticism of "True Socialism":

"True socialism is the completest social literary movement; it developed without any real party interests, and after the formation of the Communist Party it wished to continue its existence despite the latter. It is clear that since the development of a real Communist Party in Germany the True Socialists will be limited more and more to the petty-bourgeoisie as their public and to impotent degenerate scribblers as representatives of this public."

It was necessary to dissociate the Communist Party, as the or-ganized movement of the proletarian advance-guard, from the amor-phous movement of the petty-bourgeoisie and of those writers whose ideology was petty-bourgeois.

7. MARX AND THE COLOGNE "WORKERS ASSOCIATION", 1848–9

Marx and Engels entered the revolutionary movement in 1848–9, forming the left wing of the democratic movement, which they strove to force forward as far as they possibly could. The chief democratic mass in 1848–9 consisted of the revolutionary petty-bourgeoisie, the artisans and shop-keepers in the towns, and the small-scale and middle-scale peasants in the country. This petty-bourgeoisie repre-sented the main contingent of the revolutionary movement in Germany. The working-class movement, numerically still very weak, operated up to a certain point as the ally, as the left wing of this petty-bourgeois movement. The tactical line adopted by Marx and Engels was an alliance between the working-class movement and the revolutionary petty-bourgeoisie so long as the latter was still progressive and did not hamper the working-class movement, the general aim being to urge forward the revolutionary petty-bourgeoisie up to that point where it would seize power, to persuade it to take energetic revolutionary measures against the Junkers and the bourgeoisie, and then to organize the working class as an independent revolutionary power against the petty-bourgeoisie with a view to taking power from the hands of the latter at a suitable moment. The example before their eyes was the Great French Revolution with its Jacobin dictatorship, the dictatorship of the urban petty-bourgeoisie, the workers and the peasants.

However, revolutionary development in Germany took a different course. The bourgeoisie concluded a compromise with the Junkers and the Crown, whilst the petty-bourgeoisie, after short onsets which did not give it power on any wide scale, retreated, for the most part miserably.

The activity of Marx and Engels at the head of the democratic movement in the Rhineland is well known and has been described often enough. However, it was Mehring who first made known the rôle which Marx and Engels played in the working-class movement in Cologne and in the Rhineland.

On the 13th of April 1848 a doctor named Gottschalk founded the Cologne Workers Association, and it grew rapidly. On the 8th of May Gottschalk gave its membership as 5,000. The association was represented in the " District Committee of Rhenish Democratic Associations ", and from the beginning Marx exercised influence on it through Moll and Schapper. In the beginning, however, the " Marx tendency " was in the minority. The majority under the leadership of Gottschalk wanted to hear nothing of an alliance with the petty-bourgeois democrats, and it decided to boycott the elections to the Prussian and German National Assembly. On the 3rd of July Gottschalk and his assistant Anneke were arrested. The Marx group then obtained a majority in the association, and Joseph Moll was elected President on the 6th of July and worked hand in hand with Marx and Engels. The struggles intensified, and on the 25th of September Karl Schapper (also a communist) and the young lawyer Becker were also arrested. An attempt was also made to arrest Moll, who had to go into hiding. Nothjung and Röser, who were the successors of Moll, felt themselves too weak for the job and therefore Marx himself took it over on the 16th of October, and on the 22nd of October he was confirmed in his position by a general meeting of the association in Gürzenich. He succeeded in persuading it to take part in the elections after all, and new statutes were introduced and confirmed on the 25th of February. On the 28th of February 1849 Schapper again took over the leadership. On the 15th of April 1849 Marx, W. Wolff, Schapper and Anneke resigned from the District Committee of Rhenish Democratic Associations and at the same time the Workers Association withdrew also. Marx had decided that the time was ripe for the independent organization of the workers. On the 6th of May a congress of workers associations in the Rhineland and Westphalia took place. Its agenda was : (1) Organization of the Rhenish-Westphalian workers associations ; (2) Election of delegates for the congress of all workers associations (June, in Leipzig) ; and (3) Resolutions for this congress. On the 16th of May 1849 Marx received the order expelling him from Cologne.

8. The First International

D. Riazanov has collected much new material on the history of the foundation of the First International (Marx-Engels Archive, Vol. I). We shall confine ourselves here to enumerating the most important events which led up to it.

February 21st, 1862.—Appeal of a committee to the workers of Paris to send delegates to visit the London World Exhibition. 200,000 workers take part in the elections and 200 delegates are elected. The first group leaves on the 19th of July and the last on the 15th of October 1862.

At the suggestion of the editor of *The Working Man* a reception committee for the French workers is formed in London in July. On the 5th of August a meeting takes place in the Freemasons' Hall, but as it is of a bourgeois character the London trades council does not take part in it. A number of French delegates, including the building worker Tolain, establish connections with the London trade unions.

The French commission splits; the non-Bonapartist elements (Tolain, etc.) withdraw from the commission and act independently.

Lively agitation on behalf of the Polish insurrection in France and England. French workers invited to come to London.

July 2nd, 1863.—Meeting in St. James's Hall. Representatives of the London trade unions and of the French workers (Tolain, etc.) present. Discussions after the meeting between English and French participants and delegates.

July 23rd.—Meeting in the " Bell Inn ", Old Bailey, called by the London trades council with the French delegates. Decision to elect committee (5 members) to issue appeal to the French workers. Address read at second meeting in " Bell Inn " on the 10th November and adopted. Address printed in *The Beehive* on the 5th of December 1863. Eight months pass before the answer of the French workers arrives. Answer read and discussed in a public meeting in St. Martin's Hall, London, on the 28th of September 1864. Marx present on the platform, but takes no active part in the meeting. Eccarius proposed by him as speaker. A provisional committee elected, including Eccarius and Marx for the Germans, to deal with the addresses. Decision taken to form an " International Association " on the basis of the English and French Addresses, in the sense of an international organization for information and discussion. Sub-committee appointed, including Marx, to work out the " Rules and Regulations " of the new association. The rest is already known.

An examination of the Austrian police archives which became possible after November 1918 reveals the fact that Georg Eccarius, who was for many years a member of the General Council of the International Working-men's Association and with whom Marx quarrelled later on, supplied the Austrian secret service with reports concerning the proceedings of the General Council (Brügel, in *Der Kampf*, Vol. XVIII, Vienna).

9. MARX-ENGELS AND LASSALLE-SCHWEITZER

Mehring's attitude towards Lassalle-Schweitzer and their policy is no longer tenable to-day. Important facts which became known only after the death of Mehring, and new questions raised by the subsequent development of the working-class movement, compel the abandonment of Mehring's attitude towards the Lassallean movement. The whole question has been dealt with in detail in L. Pollnau's introduction to Vol. V. of the Collected Works of Franz Mehring,

Zur Deutschen Geschichte. We shall confine ourselves here to enumerating briefly the new facts and the new fundamental considerations which make it necessary to revise Mehring's opinion of the Lassallean movement.

The first fact is the correspondence between Bismarck and Lassalle which was accidentally discovered in 1928 in the Cabinet of the Prussian Prime Minister Otto Braun amongst an assortment of nondescript and forgotten papers. The letters were given by Otto Braun to G. Mayer for publication : G. Mayer, *Bismarck und Lassalle, ihr Briefwechsel und ihre Gespräche (Bismarck and Lassalle, their Correspondence and Discussions)*, Berlin, 1928. This correspondence begins as early as the 11th of May 1863 with a short letter from Bismarck to Lassalle inviting the latter to meet him for a discussion " on the labour question ", i.e. before the founding of Lassalle's Workers Association. The following passage taken from a letter written by Lassalle on the 8th of June 1863 shows his attitude towards Bismarck and the Prussian Crown :

" However, you will realize clearly from this miniature (the statutes of the *Allgemeiner Deutscher Arbeiterverein*) how true it is that the labouring classes incline instinctively to a dictatorship once they can be convinced with justification that the dictatorship is being exercised in their interests, and how much they would be inclined, as I suggested to you recently, despite their republican leanings—or rather just because of them—to accept the Crown as the natural instrument of a social dictatorship rather than the egoism of the bourgeois class, if the Crown on its part could make up its mind to take the—truly very improbable—step of adopting a really revolutionary and national policy, and turn itself from a monarchy of the privileged classes into a social and revolutionary people's monarchy."

The second fact is a document found amongst the literary remains of Hermann Wagener, also published by G. Mayer : a receipt for a loan of 2,500 thaler from Bismarck signed by von Hofstetten, a close friend and confidant of B. Schweitzer and one of the editors of *Der Sozialdemokrat*. See G. Mayer, *Der Deutsche Allgemeine Arbeiterverein und die Krisis 1866 (The Deutsche Allgemeine Arbeiterverein and the Crisis of 1866)*, published in the *Archiv für Sozialwissenschaft und Sozialpolitik (Archive for Social Science and Social Policy*, Vol. 57 (1927), p. 167 and the following pages.

These documents prove that Lassalle and Schweitzer pursued a policy which made them dependent on the feudal-absolutist reaction of Bismarck and the Prussian Crown to an impossible and intolerable extent for the working class. The policy which Marx and Engels pursued was : (1) the complete independence of the working-class movement ; (2) co-operation with the revolutionary elements amongst the petty-bourgeoisie and the peasantry against the main enemy, the feudal reaction ; and (3) to urge on the bourgeoisie whenever it came into conflict with the Junkers and the Crown. This policy was the only one in accordance with the interests and the principles of a revolutionary working-class party. Marx and Engels immediately rejected the hypothesis of the Lassallean movement as an opportunist relapse into " Realpolitik " from the principles and clarity already reached by the communist movement in 1848–9. In the conflict Marx-Engels *v.* Lassalle-Schweitzer, the former were completely right.

10. MARX AND BAKUNIN

Mehring's attitude to the conflict between Marx and Bakunin in the First International is also untenable to-day, and in this case also it is the revelation of new facts and the development of new questions of working-class policy which make it necessary to revise his attitude. The following circumstances will serve to explain his errors in this question. First of all the fact that the social-democratic attacks on Bakunin and on the anarchist ideas he propagated were often (but not always and above all not as far as Marx and Engels were concerned) dictated by opportunist considerations coupled with considerations of Philistine morality. Secondly, the fact that from 1890 to 1914 anarchism in Germany never represented any serious danger to the social-democratic movement. Thus Mehring overlooked the fact that the situation was fundamentally different in the days of the First International, and further that during certain periods of the revolutionary struggle anarchism raises its head almost unavoidably, and that when it appears it necessarily plays under certain circumstances a counter-revolutionary rôle. (For instance the rôle of Machnow in Ukrainia.) [1]

The new facts concerning Bakunin were obtained from the Russian Imperial Archives when they were opened after the November Revolution. The most important document concerning Bakunin which has come to light is the so-called " Confession " which Bakunin wrote to the Tsar at the suggestion of Count Orlov after he had been delivered into the hands of the Tsarist police by the Austrian government. This document was completed by Bakunin on the 15th of September 1851 and soon afterwards handed to the Tsar, who gave it to the heir to the throne to read, after which it was filed in the archives of " Department III ", the notorious Ochrana. The document was discovered in 1919 in the Central Archives in Leningrad and published soon afterwards. A letter written by Bakunin to the Tsar on the 14th of February 1857 was also discovered and published.

The aim of both documents was to obtain a mitigation of punishment. In the " Confession " Bakunin gives a description of his revolutionary career from the standpoint of " a penitent sinner ", which is the literal expression he uses when signing it. The letter of the 14th of February 1857 is even worse than the " Confession " and contains passages like the following : " With what name shall I call my past life ? Beginning with chimerical and fruitless endeavours, it ended with crimes. . . . I curse my errors and my aberrations and my crimes. . . ." Politically considered the " Confession " and the letter of the 14th of February represent a speculation on the pan-Slav reactionary inclinations of Tsarism. Bakunin also did not hesitate to speculate on the reactionary antipathies of Tsarism to the democratic and revolutionary movement in Western Europe.

[1] And during the recent revolutionary struggles in Spain.

On the basis of the material which is now available concerning Bakunin the only objection which one can make to the attitude of Marx and Engels towards him is that they did not subject his rôle to a critical examination still earlier.

Any discussion of " the moral qualities " of the methods used in the fractional struggles between Marx and Bakunin and their followers can be of only very subordinate interest to-day. Marx and Engels were not " innocent lambs ", but Bakunin and his friends were also not, and they waged the fractional struggle by no means in strict accordance with the categorical imperative. In any case, all this is of very subsidiary importance. In the struggle between Bakunin and his followers on the one hand and Marx and Engels and their followers on the other, fundamental principles and history were on the side of Marx and Marxism and therefore, we may assume, " moral " justification also.

BIBLIOGRAPHY

THIS bibliography is in five parts :
    I.   The Collected Works ;
    II. Collections and Anthologies ;
   III. *Capital* ;
   IV. Books, Articles, Speeches, etc., as far as they have already been
        identified and printed ; and
    V. Letters.
It makes no claim to be definitive. It will not be possible to issue a
complete bibliography until all the collected works have been issued and
until the research work to disinter Marx's numerous contributions to newspapers and other periodicals and encyclopædias has been concluded.

I. THE COLLECTED WORKS

1. *Karl Marx/Friedrich Engels. Historisch-kritische Gesamtausgabe.* Works,
   Essays, Letters. Issued by D. Riazanov (since 1931 by V. Adoratzki)
   on behalf of the Marx-Engels Institute in Moscow.
       This edition complies completely with all scientific demands. Each
   volume contains a detailed index and voluminous critical annotations
   and notes. The edition is divided into three parts : the first contains
   all the writings of Marx and Engels (with the exception of *Capital*) in
   chronological order ; the second contains *Capital* together with all
   the previously unpublished preparatory work ; and the third contains
   the correspondence. Almost every volume contains previously unpublished material or material never before published in full. Hereinafter
   referred to as CW.

II. COLLECTIONS AND ANTHOLOGIES

2. *Gesammelte Aufsätze von Karl Marx.* Edited and published by Hermann
   Becker, Cologne, 1851. Only one volume appeared.
3. *Aus dem literarischen Nachlass von Karl Marx, Friedrich Engels und Ferdinand
   Lassalle.* Collected by Franz Mehring and published in 4 vols. by
   Dietz, Stuttgart, 1902.
       The fourth edition was published in 1923. It contains many of
   the works written up to 1850, occasionally abridged. This is the
   famous " Posthumous Edition ". Hereinafter referred to as PE.
4. *Gesammelte Schriften von Karl Marx und Friedrich Engels, 1852–62.* Edited by
   D. Riazanov and published in 2 volumes by Dietz, Stuttgart, 1917.
       This publication contains chiefly articles taken from *The New York
   Tribune*, *The People's Paper* and the *Neue Oderzeitung*. Hereinafter
   referred to as R.
5. *Geschichtliche Tat.* Extracts from the works and letters of Karl Marx
   chosen by Franz Diederich, *Vorwärts*, Berlin, 1918.
       A third edition was issued under the title, *Marx Brevier* by Dietz,
   Berlin, in 1926. The book is a collection of extracts grouped under
   the headings : " Revolutionary Theory ", " The Era of Capitalist
   Production ", " Surplus Labour and the Working Day ", " Socialism
   and the Working-Class Movement ", " The Historical Conception ",
   and " Aphorisms on Science ".
6. *Karl Marx und Friedrich Engels über die Diktatur des Proletariats.* With observations on the tactical attitude of the communists. Compiled and

provided with an epilogue by Ernst Drahn, *Der Rote Hahn*, Vols. 51–2, Aktion, Berlin-Wilmersdorf, 1920.

7. *Selected Essays*. Translated by H. J. Stenning. Leonard Parsons, London, 1926. Allen & Unwin, London, 1929.
   With deletions.

8. *Karl Marx und die Gewerkschaften*. Essays and documents. With a preface by Friedrich Hertneck. Weltgeistbücher 278–9, Berlin-Charlottenburg, 1928.

9. *Über historischen Materialismus*. Elementarbücher des Kommunismus. Vols. 13–14. Edited by Hermann Duncker. Internationaler Arbeiterverlag, Berlin, 1930.
   A collection of the most important passages in the works of Marx and Engels on historical materialism.

10. *Der deutsche Sozialismus von Ludwig Gall bis Karl Marx*. Issued by Fritz Brügel and Benedikt Kautsky. Hess & Co., Vienna-Leipzig, 1931.
    Contains of Marx's work : *The Communist Manifesto* and quotations (brief for the most part) from *The Poverty of Philosophy*, *A Critique of Political Economy*, *The Inaugural Address* and *Capital*.

11. *Karl Marx, Der historische Materialismus*. Issued by S. Landshut and J. P. Mayer in 2 vols. Kröner, Leipzig, 1932.
    Contains the economic and philosophical MSS. (incomplete) of 1844, and a reprint (complete with the exception of one short passage) of the *German Ideology*. Hereinafter referred to as K.

III.   " CAPITAL "

12. *Das Kapital. Kritik der politischen Ökonomie. Vol. 1. The Process of Capitalist Production*. Meissner, Hamburg, 1867.

12*a*. Ditto. 2nd Edition. With alterations and additions by Karl Marx. Meissner, Hamburg, 1872–3.

12*b*. Le Capital. Translated by J. Roy, Paris, 1875. With alterations by Karl Marx.

12*c*. 3rd German Edition. Meissner, Hamburg, 1883. Edited by Friedrich Engels with corrections and notes from Marx's MSS., and from the French translation.

12*d*. Capital. A Critical Analysis of Capitalist Production. Translated from the 3rd German Edition by Samuel Moore and Edward Aveling, and edited by Friedrich Engels. 2 vols. Swan Sonnenschein & Co., London, 1887.

12*e*. 4th German Edition. Meissner, Hamburg, 1890. Edited by Friedrich Engels with the use of the English translation of 1887.

12*f*. The First Nine Chapters of Capital. Translated from the 3rd German Edition. Swan Sonnenschein & Co., London, 1897.

12*g*. The Theory of Value Complete, forming the first nine chapters of Capital. The Bellamy Library, 1890.

12*h*. Capital. Vol. 1. Translated from the 2nd German Edition by Ernst Untermann. Charles H. Kerr & Co., Chicago, 1906.

12*i*. Capital. Vol. 1. Translated from the 4th German Edition by Eden and Cedar Paul. Allen & Unwin Ltd., London, 1928.

12*j*. Ditto. Same translation. With an introduction by G. D. H. Cole. J. M. Dent & Sons, London and Toronto, E. P. Dutton & Co., New York, 1930.

12*k*. Ditto. Ditto. A reissue in 2 vols. Dent, London, 1933. Everyman ed.

13. *Das Kapital. Kritik der politischen Ökonomie. Vol. 2. The Process of Capitalist Circulation*. Meissner, Hamburg, 1885. Issued by Friedrich Engels after the death of the author.

13*a*. Capital. A Critique of Political Economy. Vol. 2. The Process of the Circulation of Capital. Edited by F. Engels. Translated from the 2nd German Edition by Ernst Untermann. Charles H. Kerr & Co., Chicago, Swan Sonnenschein & Co., London, 1907.

14. *Das Kapital. Kritik der politischen Ökonomie.* Vol. 3 (in two parts). The Complete Process of Capitalist Production. Meissner, Hamburg, 1894. Issued by Friedrich Engels after the death of the author.

14*a*. Capital. A Critique of Political Economy. Vol. 3. Translated from the 1st German Edition by Ernst Untermann. Charles H. Kerr & Co., Chicago, 1909.

15. *Theorien über den Mehrwert.* Issued from Marx's MSS., by Karl Kautsky. 4 Vols. Dietz, Stuttgart, 1905–10. *Vol. 1. The Theory of Surplus-Value up to Adam Smith ; Vol. 2.* (in two parts) *David Ricardo ; Vol. 3. From Ricardo to Vulgar Political Economy.* Contains the results of Marx's studies of the history of the theory of value which were to have formed the fourth volume of *Capital.*

16. *Das Kapital. Kritik der politischen Ökonomie.* 3 vols. in 4. Popular Edition issued by Karl and Benedikt Kautsky. Dietz, Berlin, 1914–29.

17. *Das Kapital. Kritik der politischen Ökonomie.* Popular Edition edited by Julian Borchardt. Lichtstrahlen, Berlin-Lichterfelde, 1919.

17*a*. The People's Marx. Abridged Popular Edition of Capital. Edited by Julian Borchardt. Translated by Stephen L. Trask. International Bookshops, London (printed in Potsdam), 1921.

18. *Das Kapital. Kritik der politischen Ökonomie.* Popular edition issued by the Marx-Engels-Lenin Institute, Moscow. Vol. 1. With a preface by V. Adoratzki and a reprint of *Karl Marx*, by V. I. Lenin. Verlag für Literatur und Politik, Vienna-Berlin, 1932.

With an appendix containing F. Engels' review of *Capital* in the *Demokratisches Wochenblatt*, letters of Marx and Engels on *Capital*, and the first publication in German of Marx's marginal notes to Adolf Wagner's *Lehrbuch der politischen Ökonomie.*

IV. Books, etc., with the Exception of " Capital "

19. *Differenz der demokritischen und epikureischen Naturphilosophie.* The Doctoral Dissertation. First published in PE, I. With preparatory work and appendix, CW, I, 1.

20. *Articles in the " Rheinische Zeitung ".* Cologne, 1842–3. On the proceedings of the Rhenish Diet ; the philosophical manifesto of the historical legal school ; the situation of the Moselle vintners ; the debates on the wood-pilfering law, etc. In part in PE, I. In full in CW, I, 1.

21. *Bemerkungen über die neueste preussische Zensurinstruktion—Luther als Schiedsrichter zwischen Strauss und Feuerbach.* Contained in the *Anekdota zur neuesten Philosophie und Publizistik* issued by Arnold Ruge, Zürich and Winterthur, 1843. Reprinted in PE, I, and CW, I, 1.

22. *Kritik des hegelschen Staatsrechts, d.i. Hegels Rechtsphilosophie.* (1841 ?) First published in CW, I, 1, and K, I.

23. *Zur Kritik der hegelschen Rechtsphilosophie Einleitung.—Zur Judenfrage.* First published in the *Deutsch-Französische Jahrbücher*, issued by Arnold Ruge and Karl Marx, Paris, 1843. Reprinted in PE, I, CW, I, 1, and K, I.

23*a*. Ditto. Translated by Edward Fitzgerald and published by Martin Lawrence Ltd., under the title " The Jewish Question ", London, 1935.

24. *Article in the " Vorwärts "*, Paris, 1844.
    In part in PE, II. In full in CW, I, 1.
25. *Ökonomisch-philosophische Manuskripte, 1844.*
    On alienated labour, wages, money, etc., and with a critique of Hegelian philosophy. CW, III, also K, I, but without the " First Manuscript ".
26. *Die Heilige Familie oder Kritik der kritischen Kritik, gegen Bruno Bauer und Konsorten.* By Friedrich Engels and Karl Marx, Frankfort-on-Main, 1845.
    Reprinted in PE, II, and CW, III.
27. *Articles in the " Westphälisches Dampfboot " and in the " Gesellschaftsspiegel."* 1845–7.
    Reprinted in CW, III, and IV.
28. *Die Deutsche Ideologie. Kritik der neuesten deutschen Philosophie in ihren Repräsentanten, Feuerbach, B. Bauer and Stirner, und des deutschen Sozialismus in seinen verschiedenen Propheten.* By Karl Marx and Friedrich Engels. 1845–6.
    First published in full in CW, V (also a popular edition by the Verlag fur Literatur und Politik, Vienna-Berlin, 1932). Complete print in K, II, with the exception of one short passage.
28a. An English translation is in preparation and will be published by Martin Lawrence Ltd., in 1936.
29. *Circular against the " Volkstribun ",* edited by H. Kriege. By Marx and Engels (and others), 1846.
    Reprinted in CW, VI.
30. *Misère de la Philosophie. Réponse à la Philosophie de la misère de M. Proudhon.* By Karl Marx, Paris, 1847.
30a. Ditto. Translated into German by E. Bernstein and K. Kautsky. With a preface and notes by Friedrich Engels, 1885.
30b. The Poverty of Philosophy. With a preface by F. Engels. Translated by Harry Quelch. The Twentieth Century Press, London, 1900.
·31. *Articles in the " Deutsche Brüsseler Zeitung ", in the " Triersche Zeitung ", and in the " Réforme ".* 1847–8.
    Contains the speech on Poland and the articles against Grün and Heinzen. Reprinted in part in PE, II, and in full in CW, VI.
32. *Speech of Dr. Marx on Protection, Free Trade and the Working Classes.* Published in *The Northern Star* in 1847.
32a. Discours sur la question du libre échange. Brussels, 1848.
32b. Free Trade. A speech delivered before the Democratic Club, Brussels, in 1848. With an extract from " La misère de la philosophie ". Translated by Florence Wischnewetzky. With a preface by Friedrich Engels. Lee & Shepard, Boston (Mass.), 1888.
32c. Zwei Reden über die Freihandels- und Schutzzollfrage. Translated from the French with a preface and notes by J. Weydemeyer. Hamm, 1848.
    32. 32a, and 32c, reprinted in CW, VI.
33. *Manifest der Kommunistischen Partei.* By Karl Marx and Friedrich Engels. London, February 1848.
33a. Ditto. New Edition with preface by the authors. Leipzig, 1872.
33b. Ditto. 3rd Edition with preface by Friedrich Engels. Hottingen-Zürich, 1883.
33c. Ditto. 4th Edition with new preface by Friedrich Engels. London, 1890.
33d. The Manifesto of the Communist Party. English translation by Helen Macfarlane, published in *The Red Republican*, London, 1850.

33*e*. Ditto. Russian translation with a new preface by Karl Marx. Geneva, 1882.

33*f*. The Manifesto of the Communists. By Karl Marx and Friedrich Engels. International Publishing Co., London, 1886.

33*g*. Manifesto of the Communist Party. By Karl Marx and Friedrich Engels. Authorized English translation by Samuel Moore. Edited and annotated by Friedrich Engels. William Reeves, 185, Fleet Street, London, 1888.

33*h*. Ditto. Charles H. Kerr & Co., Chicago, 1919.

33*i*. The Communist Manifesto. By Karl Marx and Friedrich Engels. Translated by Lily G. Aitken and Frank Budgen. The Socialist Labour Press, Glasgow, 1919.

33*j*. The Communist Manifesto of Karl Marx and Friedrich Engels. With an introduction and explanatory notes by D. Riazanov. Translated by Eden and Cedar Paul. Martin Lawrence Ltd., London, 1930.

33*k*. Reprint of 33*g*, with all the most important prefaces. Martin Lawrence Ltd., London, 1933.

34. *Lohnarbeit und Kapital*. A series of articles published in the *Neue Rheinische Zeitung* in 1849 based on lectures delivered by Karl Marx to the German Workers Association in Brussels.

34*a*. Reprinted together with a MS. on wages from the year 1847 in CW, VI.

34*b*. Reprinted together with an introduction by Friedrich Engels and with additions and alterations. Berlin, 1891.

34*c*. Wage-Labour and Capital. Translated by J. L. Joynes. The Modern Press, London, 1885.

34*d*. Ditto. With an introduction by Friedrich Engels. The Socialist Labour Press, Edinburgh, 1908.

34*e*. Ditto. Translated by Florence Baldwin, C.P.G.B. London, 1925.

34*f*. Ditto. Martin Lawrence Ltd., London, 1933.

35. *Articles in the " Neue Rheinische Zeitung "*. Cologne, 1848–9.
Reprinted in part in PE, III, and in full by Dietz, Berlin, 1928.

36. *Articles in the " Neue Rheinische Zeitung. Politisch-Ökonomische Revue "*. London, Hamburg and New York, 1850. Including :

36*a*. *Die Klassenkämpfe in Frankreich 1848–50*. Reprinted under this title with an introduction by Friedrich Engels, Berlin. 1895.

36*b*. The Class Struggles in France, 1848–50. With an introduction by Friedrich Engels. Translated by Henry Kuhn. New York, Labor News Co., New York, 1924.

36*c*. Ditto. With an introduction by Friedrich Engels. New translation. Martin Lawrence Ltd., London, 1934.

37. *Der achtzehnte Brumaire des Louis Bonaparte*. Published in the second number of J. Weydemeyer's *Die Revolution*, New York, 1852.

37*a*. Ditto. With a preface by Karl Marx. Hamburg, 1869.

37*b*. Ditto. With prefaces by Friedrich Engels and D. Riazanov. Verlag für Literatur und Politik, Vienna-Berlin, 1927.

37*c*. The Eighteenth Brumaire of Louis Bonaparte. Translated by Daniel de Leon. Published in *The People* and afterwards in book form by The International Publishing Co., New York, 1898.

37*d*. Ditto. Translated by Eden and Cedar Paul. Allen & Unwin, London, 1926.

37*e*. Ditto. New translation with explanatory notes. Martin Lawrence Ltd., London, 1935.

38. (*Materialien, Erklärungen und Schriften zum Kölner Kommunistenprozess 1851–2*) *Enthüllungen über den Kommunistenprozess zu Köln*. Basle and Boston, 1853.

38*a*. Ditto. With an historical introduction by Friedrich Engels on the Communist League, and supplementary material and documents. With an epilogue written by Karl Marx in 1875. Hottingen-Zürich, 1885.

38*b*. Ditto. With an introduction and notes by Franz Mehring. Singer, Berlin, 1914.

39. *Articles in " The New York Tribune " (1851–62) and in " Notes to the People ".* Not yet all identified and reprinted. Reprinted in part in R. Reprinted separately :

39*a*. *Revolution and Counter-Revolution in Germany in 1848.* Edited by E. M. Aveling. Swan Sonnenschein & Co., London, 1896.
The articles published under this title are now known to have been chiefly the work of Engels.

39*b*. Revolution und Konterrevolution in Deutschland. Translated into German by Karl Kautsky and published together with an appendix on the Cologne Communist Trial. Stuttgart, 1896.

39*c*. Reprint of 39*a*, by Allen & Unwin Ltd.,London, 1920, and by the Socialist Labour Press, Glasgow, 1920.

39*d*. Revolution and Counter-Revolution in Germany. By Friedrich Engels, revised by Karl Marx. With three appendices : The history of the Communist League ; The demands of the Communist Party in Germany ; and The first address of the Central Committee of the Communist League to its members in Germany. Martin Lawrence Ltd., London, 1933.

39*e*. *The Eastern Question.* A reprint of letters written 1853–6 dealing with the events of the Crimean War by Karl Marx. Edited by E. M. Aveling and E. Aveling. Swan Sonnenschein & Co., London, 1897.

39*f*. *Palmerston and Russia.* Political Fly-sheets, No. 1. E. Tucker, London, 1853. 2nd Edition under the title : *Palmerston and Poland.* 1854.

39*g*. *Palmerston, What has He Done ?* Political Fly-sheets, No. 2. E. Tucker, London, 1854.

40. *Articles in " The People's Paper ",* London, 1853–8.
Including the speech of Marx on the 1848 Revolution at the fourth anniversary of the founding of the paper. Not yet all identified and reprinted.

41. *Der Ritter vom edelmüthigen Bewusstsein.* London and New York, 1853. Polemic against August Willich.

42. *Articles in the " Neue Oder-Zeitung ",* Breslau, 1855.
Reprinted in part in R, II, and in *Die Neue Zeit.*

43. *Articles for " The Free Press ", " The Diplomatic Review ",* etc., 1856–8.
Reprinted separately :

43*a*. *Secret Diplomatic History of the Eighteenth Century.* By Karl Marx. Edited by his daughter E. M. Aveling. Swan Sonnenschein & Co., Ltd., London, 1899.

43*b*. *The Story of the Life of Lord Palmerston.* By Karl Marx. Edited by his daughter E. M. Aveling. Swan Sonnenschein & Co., Ltd., London, 1899.

44. *Articles for " The New American Cyclopædia ",* issued by George Ripley and Charles Dana. New York, 1860.
Including articles on Jean Baptiste Bernadotte, Simon Bolivar and Blücher.

45. *Zur Kritik der politischen Ökonomie.* First (and only) volume. Franz Dunker, Berlin, 1859.

45*a*. Ditto. Issued by Karl Kautsky together with the " General Introduction " from the Marx papers. Dietz, Stuttgart, 1907.

45b. A Contribution to the Critique of Political Economy. Translated by I. N. Stone. With an appendix containing Marx's introduction to the Critique recently published from among his posthumous papers. International Library Publishing Co., New York, and Kegan Paul & Co., London, 1909. And Charles H. Kerr & Co., Chicago.

46. *Articles in " Das Volk ",* 1859.

47. *Herr Vogt.* London, 1860.

47a. Ditto. Together with an appendix by Friedrich Engels and an introduction by Rudolf Franz. Leipzig, 1927.

48. *Articles for " Die Presse ",* Vienna, 1861–2.
   Including articles on the civil war in North America.

49. *Articles in " The Beehive ",* London, 1864–70.
   Including the Addresses drafted by Karl Marx on behalf of the English workers to Presidents Lincoln and Johnson.

49a. Lincoln, Labor and Slavery by Hermann Schlüter, New York, 1913. Containing the addresses.

50. *Address and Provisional Rules of the International Working-men's Association,* established September 28th, 1864, at a public meeting held at St. Martin's Hall, Long Acre, London, London, 1864.

50a. Manifest an die arbeitende Klasse Europas. First German translation in *Der Vorbote,* Geneva, 1866.

50b. Address and Provisional Rules of the International Working-men's Association, September 28th, 1864. Reprinted from the original. The Labour and Socialist International. London, 1924.

50c. Die Inauguraladresse der Internationalen Arbeiter-Association. Translated by Luise Kautsky. With an introduction and notes by Karl Kautsky. Dietz, Berlin, 1928.

50d. Reprint of 50, as an appendix to *The History of the First International.* Martin Lawrence Ltd., London, 1929.

51. *Article against Proudhon* in the *Sozial-Demokrat* in 1865.
   Reprinted in the German edition of *The Poverty of Philosophy.* Stuttgart, 1892, and later.

52. *Declarations against J. B. von Schweitzer* in the *Düsseldorfer Zeitung* (March 1865), in the Berlin *Reform* (April 1865) and in the *Sozial-Demokrat* (1865).

53. *Value, Price and Profit.* An Address delivered by Karl Marx to the General Council of the International in 1865.

53a. Ditto. Addressed to working-men. Edited by E. M. Aveling. Swan Sonnenschein & Co., London, 1898.

53b. Ditto. Socialist Labour Press, Edinburgh, 1908.

53c. Ditto. Allen & Unwin Ltd., London, 1931.
   There are also American editions by Charles H. Kerr & Co., and by International Publishers, New York.

53d. Lohn, Preis und Profit. Translated by Eduard Bernstein. Frankfort-on-Main, 1910.
   And many subsequent editions and translations.

54. *Manifestos, Programmes and Declarations of the General Council of the International.* 1867–73.
   Including the Inaugural Address, the Addresses to Presidents Lincoln and Johnson, the Address on the Belgian massacres, les prétendues scissions, l'Alliance de la démocratie socialiste, etc., the Addresses on the civil war in France, etc. Variously reprinted.

55. *Co-operation with J. G. Eccarius : " A Working-man's Refutation of J. S. Mill ".*
   A series of articles published in *The Commonwealth.*

55a. The Hours of Labour. By J. G. Eccarius. London, etc.

56. *Addresses of the General Council of the International " On the War " and " The Civil War in France ".* London, 1871.

56a. Der Bürgerkrieg in Frankreich. Printed in *Der Vorbote*, Geneva, and in the *Volksstaat*, Leipzig, 1871.

56b. Ditto. With an introduction by Friedrich Engels, Dietz, Berlin, 1932.

56c. The Civil War in France. Preceded by the two Manifestos of the General Council of the International on the Franco-Prussian War. With a historical introduction by R. W. Postgate. The Labour Publishing Co., London, and Allen & Unwin Ltd., London, 1921.

56d. Ditto. With an introduction by Friedrich Engels and a speech by Lenin on the Paris Commune. Martin Lawrence Ltd., London, 1933.

57. *l'Alliance de la démocratie socialiste et l'Association internationale des travailleurs.* Rapports et documents, etc. London and Hamburg, 1873.
      The so-called " Alliance Pamphlet ", being the report drawn up at the instructions of The Hague congress of the International on the activities of Bakunin and his Alliance.

58. (*Randglossen zum Gothaer Parteiprogramm*) *Zur Kritik des sozialdemokratischen Parteiprogramms.* 1875.
      Published by Friedrich Engels from the posthumous papers of Marx (1891).

58a. Kritiken der sozialdemokratischen Programmentwürfe von 1875 und 1891. By Marx and Engels. With the programmes of the Social Democratic Party of Germany from 1863 to 1925 and other material. Edited by Hermann Duncker. Internationaler Arbeiterverlag, Berlin, 1930.

58b. The Socialist Programme. Translated from *Zur Kritik des sozialdemokratischen programms von Gotha* by Eden and Cedar Paul. The Socialist Labour Press, Glasgow, 1919.

58c. Critique of the Gotha Programme. Containing also Engels' letters to Bebel, Bracke and Kautsky, Engels' introduction, the notes made by Lenin on a copy of the book, and some extracts from Lenin's *State and Revolution.* Martin Lawrence Ltd., London, 1933.

59. Co-operation with Friedrich Engels : *Herrn Eugen Dühring's Umwälzung der Wissenschaft.* First published in the *Vorwärts* and the *Volksstaat*. 1877–8. First published in book form by the Leipziger Genossenschaftsdruckerei 1878. Marx co-operated in the writing of the whole book and Part II, Chapter X, " From the Critical History ", is completely his.

59a. Herr Eugen Dühring's Revolution in Science. By Friedrich Engels. Translated by Emile Burns. Martin Lawrence Ltd., London, 1935.

59b. Marx and Engels on Religion. A compilation. Martin Lawrence, London, 1935.

60. *A Worker's Inquiry.* By Karl Marx. Translation of an article in the *Revue Socialiste* of the 5th of November 1880. C.P.G.B., London, 1933.

V. CORRESPONDENCE

61. *Karl Marx/Friedrich Engels. Briefwechsel.* C.W., issued by D. Riazanov and V. Adoratzki. Marx-Engels Verlag, Berlin, 1929–31.
      Complete edition.

61a. Der Briefwechsel zwischen Fr. Engels und Karl Marx, 1844–83. Issued by Bebel and Bernstein in 4 vols. Dietz, Stuttgart, 1913. With abridgements and deletions.

61b. Marx/Engels : Selected Correspondence 1864–95. A selection with commentary and notes. Translated and edited by Dona Torr. With a preface by V. Adoratzki of the Marx-Engels Institute. Martin Lawrence Ltd., London, 1934.

62. *Briefe und Auszüge aus Briefen von J. P. Becker, J. Dietzgen, Fr. Engels, Karl Marx u.a. an F. A. Sorge u. andere.* Issued by F. A. Sorge. Dietz, Stuttgart, 1921.

63. *Karl Marx : Briefe an Kugelmann* (Aus den Jahren 1862–74). With an introduction by Lenin. Viva, Berlin, 1927.

63a. Letters to Kugelmann. With Lenin's introduction to the Russian edition and an historical preface by the Marx-Engels Institute. Martin Lawrence Ltd., 1934.

64. *Die Briefe von K. Marx und Fr. Engels an Danielson.* (Nikolai-on). With an introduction by Gustav Mayer. Liebing, Leipzig, 1929.

65. *Briefwechsel zwischen K. Marx und Bruno Bauer, Arnold Ruge u.a., ferner zwischen Marx und seinem Vater.* CW, I, 1.

66. *Briefe von Marx· an Weydemeyer und Frau.* Waffenkammer des Sozialismus, Frankfort-on-Main, 1907.

67. *Freiligrath und Marx in ihrem Briefwechsel.* Published by Franz Mehring in the *Neue Zeit*, 1912.

68. *Drei Briefe von Karl Marx an Heinrich Heine.* Published by Gustav Mayer in Grünberg's Archive, IX, 1921.

69. *Briefwechsel zwischen Lassalle und Marx.* Published by Gustav Mayer, Stuttgart, 1922.

70. *Briefwechsel zwischen Vera Zasulic und Karl Marx.* Marx-Engels Archive, issued by D. Riazanov on behalf of the Marx–Engels Institute. Frankfort-on-Main, 1926.

Further Marx material in English can be found in the files of *The Labour Monthly*, London :

Karl Marx and the Proletarian Dictatorship (Section 5 of Max Beer's Inquiry into Dictatorship), Vol. III, No. 2, August 1922.

Address to the Communist League (1850) by Karl Marx, Vol. III, No. 3, September 1922.

Selections from the Literary Remains of Karl Marx. (Edited by Max Beer.) Vol. V, Nos., 1 to 3. July, August and September 1923.

Karl Marx on Robert Applegarth. (Extracts from the Correspondence selected by Max Beer.) Vol. VI, No. 8, August 1924.

India under British Rule. Two articles by Karl Marx reprinted from *The New York Tribune*, Vol. VII, No. 12, December 1925.

The Revolution in China and in Europe. By Karl Marx. Reprinted from *The New York Tribune*. Vol. VIII, No. 3, March 1926.

The Chartist Movement. By Karl Marx. Reprinted from *The New York Tribune*, Vol. XI, No. 12, December 1929.

Marx and the Labour Parliament of 1854. Letter to *The People's Paper*, March 18th, 1854. By Reg. Groves. Vol. XII, No. 3, March 1930.

Marx on Kautsky. Letter to his daughter Jenny, Vol. XIII, No. 7, July 1931.

Marx and Engels on Ireland. Edited by T. A. Jackson. Vol. XIV, Nos. 10, 11 and 12. October, November and December 1932. Vol. XV, No. 1, January 1933.

Ideology in General. (Extracts from *Die Deutsche Ideologie* by Karl Marx and Friedrich Engels 1845–6). Vol. XV, No. 3, March 1933.

Marx and Engels on India. Vol. XV, Nos. 6, 7 and 8. June, July and August 1933.

Marx and Engels on the British Working-Class Movement, Vol. XV, Nos. 9, 10 and 11. September, October and November 1933. Vol. XVI, Nos. 2, 3, 4, 5, 6 and 10. February, March, April, May, June and October 1934.

INDEX

ANN ARBOR PAPERBACKS FOR THE STUDY OF COMMUNISM AND MARXISM

For a complete list of Ann Arbor Paperback titles write:
THE UNIVERSITY OF MICHIGAN PRESS / ANN ARBOR